VIENNA TO SALZBURG

1ST EDITION

Where to Stay and Eat
for All Budgets

Must-See Sights
and Local Secrets

Ratings You Can Trust

Fodor's Travel Publications   New York, Toronto, London, Sydney, Auckland

www.fodors.com

FODOR'S VIENNA TO SALZBURG

Editor: Robert I. C. Fisher

Editorial Production: Jacinta O'Halloran
Editorial Contributors: Bonnie Dodson, Gary Dodson, Diane Naar-Elphee, Horst Ernst Reisenböck
Maps: David Lindroth, *cartographer;* Rebecca Baer and Bob Blake, *map editors*
Design: Fabrizio La Rocca, *creative director;* Guido Caroti, *art director;* Moon Sun Kim, *cover designer;* Melanie Marin, *senior picture editor*
Production/Manufacturing: Angela L. McLean
Cover Photo (Mozart Boys' Choir): Wiesenhofer/Austrian Views

First Edition

ISBN 1–4000–1475–1

SPECIAL SALES

This book is available for special discounts for bulk purchases for sales promotions or premiums. Special editions, including personalized covers, excerpts of existing books, and corporate imprints, can be created in large quantities for special needs. For more information, write to Special Markets/Premium Sales, 1745 Broadway, MD 6-2, New York, New York 10019, or e-mail specialmarkets@randomhouse.com.

AN IMPORTANT TIP & AN INVITATION

Although all prices, opening times, and other details in this book are based on information supplied to us at press time, changes occur all the time in the travel world, and Fodor's cannot accept responsibility for facts that become outdated or for inadvertent errors or omissions. So **always confirm information when it matters,** especially if you're making a detour to visit a specific place. Your experiences—positive and negative—matter to us. If we have missed or misstated something, **please write to us.** We follow up on all suggestions. Contact the Vienna editor at editors@fodors.com or c/o Fodor's at 1745 Broadway, New York, New York 10019.

PRINTED IN THE UNITED STATES OF AMERICA

10 9 8 7 6 5 4 3 2 1

DESTINATION: VIENNA TO SALZBURG

When it comes to Austria, we are all culturally connected—after all, this is the country that gave us not only Beethoven, Schubert, and Brahms, but *The Sound of Music,* the "Blue Danube" waltz, psychoanalysis, the Vienna Boys' Choir, *The Merry Widow,* apple strudel, the Vienna New Year's Day concert, and Der Schwartzenegger. And these six degrees of separation will grow even closer in 2006 when Vienna and Salzburg co-host a year-long celebration to honor the 250th birthday of Mozart, Austria's most famous home boy. Just in time for the festivities, *Fodor's Vienna to Salzburg* is here to be your Master of Ceremonies. So get ready to "ooh" at the white-gloved, waltzing whirl of once-Imperial Vienna. Prepare to "ahh" at Salzburg's champagne Gemütlichkeit. Plan to savor the Danube Valley's never-never land of castles, turrets, and clouds of whipped cream. And don't be too suprised by the "new" Austria: As you'll discover, hip new museums and hot new restaurants are springing up across the country as fast as edelweiss.

Tim Jarrell, Publisher

CONTENTS

ABOUT THIS BOOK

Once you've learned to find your way around the pages of *Fodor's Vienna to Salzburg,* you'll be in great shape to find your way around your destination.

SELECTION

Our goal is to cover the best properties, sights, and activities in their category, as well as the most interesting communities to visit. We make a point of including local food-lovers' hot spots as well as neighborhood options, and we avoid all that's touristy unless it's really worth your time. It goes without saying that no property mentioned in the book has paid to be included.

RATINGS

Orange stars ★ denote sights and properties that our editors and writers consider Fodor's Choice, the very best in the area covered by the entire book. These, the best of the best, are listed in the Fodor's Choice section in the front of the book. Black stars ★ highlight the sights and properties we deem Highly Recommended, the don't-miss sights within any region. Use the index to find complete descriptions. In cities, sights pinpointed with numbered map bullets ❶ in the margins tend to be more important than those without bullets.

SPECIAL SPOTS

Pleasures & Pastimes focuses on types of experiences that reveal the spirit of the destination. Watch for Off the Beaten Path sights. If the munchies hit while you're exploring, look for Need a Break? suggestions.

TIME IT RIGHT

Check On the Calendar up front and chapters' Timing sections for weather and crowd overviews and best days and times to visit.

SEE IT ALL

Use Fodor's exclusive Great Itineraries as a model for your trip. In cities, Good Walks guide you to important sights in each neighborhood; ☛ indicates the starting points of walks and itineraries in the text and on the map.

BUDGET WELL

Hotel and restaurant price categories from ¢ to $$$$ are defined in the opening pages of each chapter—expect to find a balanced selection for every budget. For attractions, we always give standard adult admission fees; reductions are usually available for children, students, and senior citizens. AE, D, DC, MC, V following restaurant and hotel listings indicate whether American Express, Diners Club, MasterCard, or Visa are accepted.

BASIC INFO

Smart Travel Tips lists travel essentials for the entire area covered by the book; city- and region-specific basics end each chapter. To find the best way to get around, see individual modes of travel (car, bus, train, etc.).

ON THE MAPS

Maps throughout the book show you what's where and help you find your way around. Black and orange numbered bullets ❶ ① in the text correlate to bullets on maps.

BACKGROUND	In general, we give background information within the chapters in the course of explaining sights as well as in Close-Up boxes and in Understanding Vienna to Salzburg at the end of the book. To get in the mood, review the suggestions in Books & Movies.
FIND IT FAST	Within *Fodor's Vienna to Salzburg*, chapters are arranged in a roughly east-to-west direction starting with Vienna and ending in Salzburg. In the "to" chapter—"The Danube Valley to Salzkammergut"—the text is divided into two regions, within which towns are covered in logical geographical order. Heads at the top of each page help you find what you need within a chapter.
DON'T FORGET	Restaurants are open for lunch and dinner daily unless we state otherwise; we mention reservations only when they're essential or not accepted—it's always best to book ahead. If not noted otherwise, hotels have private baths, phone, TVs, and air-conditioning and operate on the European Plan (a.k.a. EP, meaning without meals), unless otherwise indicated (all-inclusive, with meals and beverages included; BP, breakfast plan with full breakfast; FAP, full American plan with all meals; MAP, modified American plan with breakfast and dinner). We list facilities but not if you'll be charged extra to use them, so inquire when booking.

SYMBOLS

Many Listings

- ★ Fodor's Choice
- ★ Highly recommended
- ⊠ Physical address
- ✛ Directions
- ✑ Mailing address
- ☎ Telephone
- 🖷 Fax
- ⊕ On the Web
- ✉ E-mail
- 🎫 Admission fee
- ☺ Open/closed times
- ► Start of walk/itinerary
- Ⓜ Metro stations
- ▤ Credit cards

Outdoors

- ⛳ Golf
- ⛺ Camping

Hotels & Restaurants

- 🏨 Hotel
- ⇩ Number of rooms
- ♿ Facilities
- ❙◎❙ Meal plans
- ✕ Restaurant
- ✑ Reservations
- 🏛 Dress code
- ↘ Smoking
- 🔮 BYOB
- ✕🏨 Hotel with restaurant that warrants a visit

Other

- ☽ Family-friendly
- 🛈 Contact information
- ⇨ See also
- ⊠ Branch address
- ☞ Take note

A trip takes you out of yourself. Concerns of life at home completely disappear, driven away by more immediate thoughts—about, say, what marvels will beguile the next day, or where you'll have dinner. That's where Fodor's comes in. We make sure that you know all your options, so that you don't miss something that's around the next bend just because you didn't know it was there. Because the best memories of your trip might well have nothing to do with what you came to Vienna and Salzburg to see, we guide you to sights large and small all over the region. You might set out to savor the sublime paintings by Pieter Brueghel in Vienna's Kunsthistoriches Museum but back at home you find yourself unable to forget experiencing high noon at the city's Clock Museum, when more than 3,000 cuckoo-clocks, wall-pieces, and watches peal forth with full cacophony. With Fodor's at your side, such serendipitous discoveries are never far away.

Our success in showing you the most fascinating corners of Vienna, the Danube Valley, the Salzkammergut, and Salzburg is a credit to our extraordinary writers. Although there's no substitute for travel advice from a good friend who knows your style, our contributors are the next best thing—the kind of people you would poll for travel advice if you knew them.

Just when **Bonnie Dodson** thinks she's seen everything Austria has to offer, she makes another discovery. That's one of the happy end results of her work on several editions of this book (for this edition, she updated the Exploring and Where to Stay chapters of Vienna, as well as the Danube Valley chapter and our Smart Travel Tips chapter). A native of Minneapolis with a graduate degree in writing, Bonnie moved to Vienna eight years ago with her husband and still gets a thrill every time she walks around the cobblestone streets of the historic First District. Like a true Viennese, she believes that coffee-drinking

is a life's work. Updating our section on Vienna's cafés, she rarely could resist stopping into her favorite coffeehouses for a *Mazagran*—a melange with a dollop of whipped cream—and, of course, for the latest city news and gossip. Doing research for this edition also involved lots of driving, making the best of snowy mountain roads, and lots of good eating. Bonnie's husband, **Gary Dodson,** has worked around the globe and speaks five languages. His passions are travel, wine, movies, and Mozart, and he enjoys partaking of all four in Austria.

Diane Naar-Elphee adores her "adopted" Vienna, having lived in the imperial city since she left her native Yorkshire in the early 1970s. As a guide-lecturer, she has shared her passion with many travelers (including Mary Tyler Moore and Dick Cavett) on her private, bespoke tours through historic Vienna. Nowadays, Diane has broadened her horizons—sheparding travelers through the Balkans, for instance—and now finds as much pleasure extolling the beauty of Alt Wien on paper rather than over the microphone. "Vienna is a village—*everyone* is familiar," she laughs. "That particular feeling of intimacy is what makes it so special." So much so that she's been able to rub shoulders with José Carreras, Dame Joan Sutherland, and, only very recently, Thomas Quasthoff, since she considers the fabled Vienna State Opera house her home-away-from-home. But then there's always that cozy coffeehouse waiting just around the corner, and if you look long enough, you'll probably find Diane there, editing or updating one of the many guide books her husband Walter has written. For this edition, she has written our Where to Eat, Nightlife & the Arts, and Shopping chapters.

"To the age, its art; to art, its freedom" was the motto of the famous Vienna Secession group, and **George Sullivan** firmly believes in this maxim, as any reader of our magisterial Vienna Exploring texts (*in* Chapter 1) can vouch. The history, art, and architecture of European cities have been his favorite subjects since he spent a college summer in London many years ago. A native of Virginia, he gets to Europe as often as he can (he's also written about Florence for Fodor's) and is currently working on an architectural guide to Rome. Austria—the country that gave us *Silent Night, Holy Night*—is never too far from his thoughts: in addition to his writing assignments, he helps run his family's Christmas tree farm.

At the height of 6 feet 5½ inches, Horst Erwin Reischenböck is considered by some to be a significant landmark himself in his home base of Salzburg (the city's steeples and castellated peaks offering a lot of competition). His family has been living there since the 19th century and, like all children growing up in Mozart's home town, he was already humming "Exultate, Jubilate" barely out of the nursery. A music critic for various newspapers for three decades and author of two books in German (their English titles are *The Mozarts in Salzburg* and *1,200 Years of Music in Salzburg*), Horst can't begin to count the number of Mozart concerts he's attended but can only agree with Robert Schumann's famous observation—"Does

it not seems that Mozart's works become fresher and fresher the oftener we hear them?" Today, Horst is known as one of the best personal guides for English-speaking visitors to Salzburg and the Salzkammergut. For this edition, he wrote and updated our chapter on Salzburg.

Robert I.C. Fisher—editor of *Fodor's Vienna to Salzburg,* art history buff, and Mozart-worshipper—toasts the Austria team with a hearty *"Prosit"* (cheers). Robert comes to Austria via the legends of Hollywood—such films as Disney's *Miracle of the White Stallions* (the famed Lipizzaners) and *Almost Angels* (on the Vienna Boys Choir), and, of course, *The Sound of Music.* In fact, growing up around the corner from the Greenwich Village atelier-theater of the Bil Baird Marionettes, he remembers sitting in on the first rehearsals of the movie's "Lonely Goatherd" number. Today, he urges readers to discover the perfect antidote for the high sugar content of the Rodgers and Hammerstein musical: the inspiring book, written by Baroness von Trapp (the real Maria) that served as the basis for the film. The *Story of the Trapp Family Singers,* first published in the 1950s, is filled with great good nature and wit, and for travelers there could be no better introduction to the endearing qualities of the Austrian people.

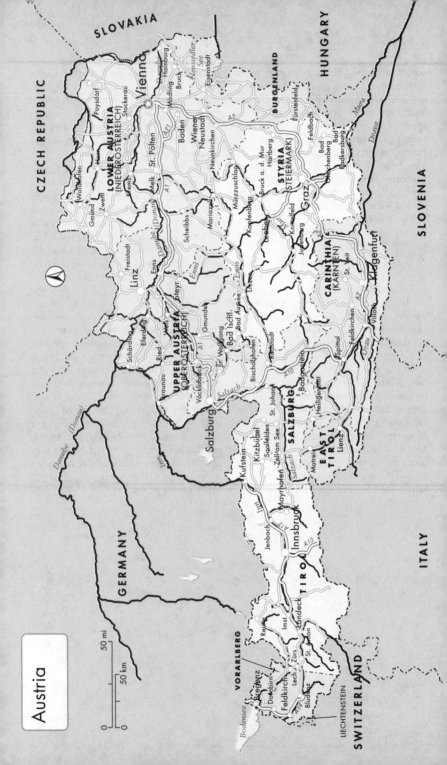

WHAT'S WHERE

Vienna

Think of Vienna and you think of operettas and psychoanalysis, Apfel-strudel and marble staircases, Strauss waltzes and Schubert melodies. Baroque and imperial, it goes without saying that the city has an Old World charm—a fact that the natives are both ready to acknowledge and yet hate being reminded of. Today, Vienna is a white-gloved yet modern metropolis, a place where Andrew Lloyd Webber's *Phantom of the Opera* plays in the same theater that premiered Mozart's *Magic Flute*. A walk through the city's neighborhoods—many dotted with master-pieces of Gothic, Baroque, and Secessionist architecture—offers a fascinating journey thick with history and peopled by the spirits of Empress Maria Theresa, Haydn, Beethoven, Metternich, Mozart, and Klimt.

Most visitors start along the **Ringstrasse,** the grand boulevard that surrounds the inner city, whose broad sweep grandly evokes the imperial era of Strauss, Metternich, and emperor Franz Josef during the cultural heyday of the Austro-Hungarian empire. Here you'll find great art treasures in great museums and magnificent spectacles at Austria's finest opera house.

Even within the shadow of the city's spiritual heart—the great **Stephans-dom** cathedral (which leads off the massive roll call of dazzling Gothic and Baroque churches in the city), Vienna comes alive during the "Merry Season"—the first two months of the year—when raised trumpets and opera capes adorn its great Fasching balls; then more than ever, Vienna moves in three-quarter time. **Café Hawelka** and the city's other famous coffeehouses—of which Vienna is said to have more than Switzerland has banks—are havens in which to share gossip, read, and conduct a little business, but most of all to engage in the age old coffee drinking ritual that every dutiful Viennese observes daily.

Pomp, circumstance, and no small amount of innovation hold sway in Vienna's 90 museums and its hundreds of houses of worship and other landmarks. The city's vast holdings range from the Brueghels, Rembrandts, Vermeers, and other treasures in the **Kunsthistorisches Museum** to the magnificent **National Library,** where rare manuscripts are as lovingly showcased as the rooms' splendid frescoes.

Travelers in search of Imperial Vienna will find no dearth of Habsburgian opulence throughout the city: there's **Schönbrunn Palace,** in whose Grand Salon the Congress of Vienna celebrated the defeat of Napoléon; there's the Imperial Palace known as the **Hofburg,** where the Lipizzaner horses of **Spanish Riding School** fame still prance to a measured cadence, just as they did when pulling emperor Franz Josef's royal carriage; and then there's the **Karlskirche.** This Baroquely ornate church looks, especially when illuminated at night, like a magical vision, although, to the architectural purists who first denounced its Trajan columns, it seemed a bad dream. This uncharacteristic, over-the-top embellishment nevertheless set the stage for the emergence of the city's visionary art and artists, among whom the most famous is Gustav Klimt. This Jugendstil artist was among the first to shock turn-of-the-century Vienna with his luxuriously nontraditional paintings, such as *The Kiss*—housed in truly regal splendor in the **Belvedere Palace** museum—and his artistic bravado was soon emulated by legions of other painters and architects.

In our own age, that honor has been bestowed on Friedensreich Hundertwasser, whose **Hundertwasserhaus** has, until recently, been the city's most outrageous, anti-traditional structure. Today, the modernist laurels have been bestowed instead on the gigantic new **MuseumsQuartier** complex, home to several fabled modern art collections, and itself a Baroque landmark now fitted out with strikingly contemporary architectural additions.

There are also some magical neighborhoods—called "Grätzl"—in Vienna. About the oldest and quaintest remains the sector around the intersection of the Fleischmarkt (Meat Market) street and the cobblestoned Griechengasse. Here, you'll find Vienna's only surviving 14th-century watchtower, houses bearing statues of the Virgin Mary, and that postcard-perfect, ivy-covered tavern, the **Greiechenbeisl,** which has been in business for some 500 years and once the favored watering hole for the likes of Schubert, Mark Twain, Wagner, and Johann Strauss. Another winner of a neighborhood is the "Biedermeier" district known as the **Spittelberg Quarter,** located behind the MuseumsQuartier complex. Spittelberg's art ateliers, trendy shops, Baroque town houses, and hip cafés all combine to create a kind of nouvelle gemütlichkeit charm.

Thanks to the great musicians and composers who, at times, made Vienna their own, travelers are quite likely to approach the city with a song in their heart. The Vienna of the past has inspired some of the world's most beautiful music, from Beethoven's *Pastoral Symphony* to Johann Strauss the Younger's "Blue Danube Waltz." As a traveler soon discovers, these and other ineffable strains are heard nonstop in the Vienna of the present as well.

In fact, monuments commemorating many of the musical geniuses who have lived here are to be found throughout the city in various forms. Check out the bust of Mozart in the **Figarohaus,** one of the composer's many residences in the city, where he wrote some of his most famous works and which are holding celebrations in honor of his 250th birthday in 2006; pay your respects at the **Pasqualatihaus,** which was Beethoven's address when he composed *Fidelio*, his only opera; and tip your hat to the merrily gilded statue of Johann Strauss II in the Stadtpark.

Chances are that somewhere nearby an orchestra or an opera company or a church organist will be performing the works of these great men; the city is, after all, home to two of the world's greatest symphony orchestras (the Vienna Philharmonic and the Vienna Symphony) and is graced with a top opera house (the Staatsoper) as well as a world-renowned concert hall (the Musikverein). Head for the Theater an der Wien to hear beloved operettas (*Die Fledermaus* and *The Merry Widow* both premiered here) or to the Volksoper. Amble into the Gothic interior of the Augustinerkirche any Sunday morning and you may have the pleasure of hearing its mighty organ accompany a high mass oratorio by Mozart or Haydn.

Unfortunately, a seat at the Philharmonic's famous New Year's Eve concert is harder to come by, much. Equally prized is a ticket to the annual Opernball at the Staatsoper; if you do manage to snag one, and if you are one of those romantic souls for whom the mere mention of Vienna conjures up images of hand kissing, deep bows, and white-tied men twirling white-gloved women across the floor, you may think you've died and ascended into heaven—to the accompaniment of a waltz, of course.

The Danube Valley

To get to the heart of the Danube Valley—one of Austria's most fabled beauty spots—travelers simply head about 80 km (50 mi) northwest of Vienna to the Wachau section of the river, the "crown jewel of the Austrian landscape." Here, via car, bike, and boat, you can view the famously blue Danube, whose banks are dotted with medieval abbeys, fanciful Baroque monasteries, verdant vineyards, and compact riverside villages. Though the river's hue is now somewhat less than pristine, this is still one of Europe's most important waterways, and to traverse its scenic length is to immerse yourself with a heady dose of history and culture, and, of course, to enjoy some pleasant scenery while doing so.

Hereabouts, legends and myths stoke the imagination. In enchantingly picturesque **Dürnstein,** Richard the Lion-Hearted spent a spell locked in a dungeon. Not far away, the Nibelungs—immortalized by Wagner—caroused at the top of their lungs in battlemented forts. The Danube is liquid history, and you can enjoy drifting eight hours downriver in a steamer or—even better—traveling 18 hours upriver against the current.

Along the way you discover the storybook Gothic market town of **Steyr,** where Anton Bruckner composed his Sixth Symphony. For 10 years he was the organist at the neighboring Abbey of St. Florian, where he is buried; his organ still fills the high-ceiling church with its rich, sorrowful notes. **Krems,** founded just over 1,000 years ago, is another delightful spot, where wine is the main business of the day. For nonpareil splendor, head to nearby **Melk Abbey,** best appreciated in the late afternoon when the setting sun lights the twin towers cradling its Baroque dome. Inside, its magnificent library was the real-life setting of Umberto Eco's novel *The Name of the Rose.*

Salzkammergut (The Lake District)

The Salzkammergut, the country's "salt shaker" if you will, stretches across three states—from Salzburg through Styria to Upper Austria. The German word *Salz* is frequently encountered here; indeed, the entire economy has been based on salt mining for millennia. Think of *The Sound of Music,* filmed here on the home turf of the musically inclined von Trapp family, and you will easily envision the region's scenic pleasures.

The clear blue Wolfgangsee, with the popular vacation village of **St. Wolfgang** on its shores, is the choice of many travelers, while **Gmunden,** along the Traunsee, is famed for its tree-lined promenade along the lake, where composers Franz Schubert, Johannes Brahms, Béla Bartók, and Erich Wolfgang Korngold used to stroll. Mozart-lovers will make a bee-line for the pastel-hue village of **St. Gilgen**, birthplace of his mother. For a heaping spoonful of sugar, everyone repairs to **Bad Ischl**, famed for its pastries. This charming turn-of-the-20th-century resort was where Emperor Franz Josef kept a villa (his birthday is still celebrated on August 18) and where Franz Lehár wrote *The Merry Widow*.

Salzburg

Depending on who is describing this elegant city filled with gilded salons, palatial mansions, and Italianate churches, Salzburg is alternately known as the "Golden City of the High Baroque," the "Austrian Rome," or, thanks to its position astride the River Salzach, the "Florence of the North."

What you choose to call this beloved city will depend on what brings you here. It may well be music, of course, as Mozart was born here in 1756 on the third floor of a house now cherished as **Mozarts Geburtshaus.** His operas and symphonies ripple through the city constantly, most particularly during its acclaimed, celebrity-packed, summer music festival, most fervently during the year-long celebration the city is hosting to honor the 2006 Mozart Year. Art lovers, on the other hand, will pounce on the city's heritage of Baroque churches, cloistered abbeys, and Rococo palaces, such as **Schloss Leopoldskron,** and, inevitably, climb the hill to **Hohensalzburg,** the brooding medieval fortress towering over the city, whose lavish state rooms are belied by its grim exterior.

Many come here to follow in the footsteps of the von Trapp family, or, at least, their Hollywood counterparts, as many of the city's most celebrated sights, such as the **Mirabell Gardens,** were used as ageless backdrops for that beloved Oscar-winner, *The Sound of Music*. Those in search of drama—as if the setting here amid Alpine peaks and glacial lakes doesn't provide enough—will want to attend the annual performances of *Jedermann* (*Everyman*) on the cathedral square, or take in a show at the famed **Marionettentheater.**

Of course, you need not come to Salzburg with a goal any more ambitious than relaxing over a meal of Neue Küche cuisine, which is a little lighter than traditional Austrian fare, at nearby Hotel Schloss Fuschl (while trying not to peek at the opera diva across the room). Music may top the bill for some, but everyone will enjoy the stupendous panoply of churches and museums, old-fashioned cafés, narrow medieval streets, and glorious fountains. Indeed, the playful water gardens of **Hellbrunn Castle** remind us that not all archbishops were stern and unpleasant.

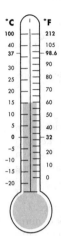

Austria has two main tourist seasons. The weather usually turns glorious around Easter to mark the start of the summer season and holds until about mid-October, sometimes later. Because much of the country remains "undiscovered," you will usually find crowds only in the major cities and resorts. May and early June, September, and October are the most pleasant months for travel; there is less demand for restaurant tables, and hotel prices tend to be lower. A foreign invasion takes place between Christmas and New Year's Day, and over the long Easter weekend, and hotel rooms in Vienna are then at a premium.

Climate

Austria has four distinct seasons, all fairly mild. But because of altitudes and the Alpine divide, temperatures and dampness vary considerably from one part of the country to another; for example, northern Austria's winter is often overcast and dreary, while the southern half of the country basks in sunshine. The eastern part of the country, especially Vienna and the areas near the Czech border, can become bitterly cold in winter. The *Föhn* is a wind that makes the country as a whole go haywire. It comes from the south, is warm, and announces itself by very clear air, blue skies, and long wisps of cloud. Whatever the reason, the Alpine people (all the way to Vienna) begin acting up; some become obnoxiously aggressive, others depressive, many people have headaches, and (allegedly) accident rates rise. The Föhn breaks with clouds and rain. The following are average monthly maximum and minimum temperatures for three cities in Austria.

🗓 Forecasts **Weather Channel Connection** ☎ 900/932–8437 95¢ a minute from a Touch-Tone phone ⊕ www.weather.com.

VIENNA

Jan.	34F	1C	May	66F	19C	Sept.	68F	20C
	25	– 4		50	10		52	11
Feb.	37F	3C	June	73F	23C	Oct.	57F	14C
	27	– 3		57	14		45	7
Mar.	46F	8C	July	77F	25C	Nov.	45F	7C
	34	1		59	15		37	3
Apr.	59F	15C	Aug.	75F	24C	Dec.	37F	3C
	43	6		59	15		30	– 1

SALZBURG

Jan.	36F	2C	May	66F	19C	Sept.	68F	20C
	21	– 6		46	8		50	10
Feb.	39F	4C	June	72F	22C	Oct.	57F	14C
	23	– 5		52	11		41	5
Mar.	48F	9C	July	75F	24C	Nov.	46F	8C
	30	– 1		55	13		32	0
Apr.	57F	14C	Aug.	73F	23C	Dec.	37F	3C
	39	4		55	13		25	– 4

Hundreds of festivals and events are held annually in Austria. Here are some of the better known and better attended in and around Vienna and Salzburg. If you plan to visit during one of them, book well in advance.

WINTER

December

The world-famous Christkindlmärts set up shop in various locales in major cities in Austria. In Vienna the biggest Christmas Market goes up in late November in the plaza in front of the city's Rathaus town hall; there are smaller ones in the Spittelberg Quarter and on the Freyung square, as well on the main square in Salzburg. Christmas Eve midnight mass at St. Stephan's Cathedral in Vienna is an impressive, if crowded, event; get an entrance pass at the cathedral in advance. The Christmas Eve service in the tiny memorial chapel at Oberndorf, north of Salzburg, features the singing of *Silent Night,* which Franz Gruber wrote when he was an organist here in the early 19th century. The New Year opens in Vienna with the world-famous concert by the Wiener Philharmoniker Orchestra; write a year—or more—in advance (✉ Wiener Philharmoniker, Musikverein, Bösendorferstrasse 12, A–1010 Vienna ☎ 01/505–6525 ⊕ www.musikverein.at). Those who can't get into the Philharmonic concert can try for one of the performances of the Johann Strauss operetta *Die Fledermaus* or another light delight in the Volksoper (✉ Währinger Strasse 78, A–1090 Vienna ☎ 01/513–1513 ⊕ www.volksoper.at) or at the intimate Kammeroper (✉ Fleischmarkt 24, A–1010 Vienna ☎ 01/513–1513). The New Year is marked by an array of balls, such as the Kaiserball, held in the elegant rooms of the Hofburg (✉ WKV, Hofburg, Heldenplatz, A–1014 Vienna ☎ 01/587–3666–14).

January

On January 6, children disguised as the Magi walk the streets, especially out in the country, knock at doors, sing a song, and recite poems about coming from afar, and ask for a small donation. They then chalk a "C&M&B" and the year on entrance door frames to bless the house for a year. Also special at this time is the ancient pre-Christian custom of the *Perchtenlauf,* masked figures that go on a rampage, mostly found in Salzburg Province, in Bad Gastein, for example.

Week of Jan. 27

Mozart's Birthday is always celebrated in Salzburg with the Mozart Week, a festival organized by the city's Mozarteum (✉ Mozarteum, Schwarzstrasse 26, A–5020 Salzburg ☎ 0622/872996 ⊕ www. mozart2006.net), featuring operas, recitals, and theme concerts. In 2006, however, the great composer will see a year-long, 24/7 celebration throughout Austria to honor his 250th birthday. The initial champagne corks will be popped in Salzburg, but Vienna and the entire country will soon follow with a full slate of special concerts, galas, and exhibitions. See the various Close-Up boxes on Mozart in Chapters 1 and 7 for more details.

Feb.	Fasching (or Fasnacht, as its called in the western part of the country), the carnival period before Lent, can become very wild with huge processions of disguised figures, occasional unwilling participation by spectators, who may even suffer (light) blows. The entire country starts going to dances—and the ball season begins. In Vienna, which is comparatively quiet at this time, the ball season opens on the Thursday before Fasching and lasts through Shrove Tuesday (Mardi Gras). The biggest gala is the Opernball (Opera Ball), held at the Staatsoper (☎ 01/514-44-2606 ⊕ www.staatsoper.at). For more information on these balls, see the Close-Up box, "Get the Ball Rolling" in Chapter 4.
SPRING	
Late Mar.–early Apr.	Easter Festival, Salzburg's "other" major music festival, offers opera and concerts of the highest quality, with ticket prices to match (⊠ Hofstallgasse 1, A–5020 Salzburg ☎ 0662/8045–361).
Mid-May–mid-June	The Wiener Festwochen takes place in Vienna—a festival of theater, music, films, and exhibitions (⊠ Lehargasse 11, A–1060 Vienna ☎ 0222/582-2222 ⊕ www.festwochen.at).
SUMMER	
June 2	The religious holiday Corpus Christi is celebrated throughout Austria with colorful processions and parades. In the Lungau region of Land Salzburg, villagers dress up in local costumes. Equally colorful are the processions of gaily decorated boats and barges on the Traun and Hallstätter lakes.
June 21	Midsummer Night is ablaze with bonfires throughout the country, with the liveliest celebrations taking place in the Wachau region along the Danube in Lower Austria.
July and Aug.	Musical Summer/KlangBogen in Vienna has nightly recitals in one of the city's many palaces or orchestral concerts in the courtyard of the city hall (⊠ KlangBogen Wien, Stadiongasse 29, A–1010 Vienna ☎ 01/4000–8410 🖷 01/4000–99–8410).
Last week July and Aug.	The Salzburger Festspiele brings together the world's greatest musical artists for a citywide celebration, with many events and performances revolving around the town's most famous native son, Mozart. Write several months in advance, especially for the festival events scheduled for the Mozart Year of 2006, when the city (and the world) will go Mozart-mad celebrating the composer's 250th birthday. (⊠ Salzburger Festspiele, Postfach 140, A–5010 Salzburg ☎ 0662/8045–322 ⊕ www.salzburgfestival.at). For complete information, see Chapter 7.
FALL	
Sept. 1	This date marks the start of the theater and music season in Vienna.

Celebrating the Mozart Year

Somewhere, at almost any hour, an orchestra will be playing his music; somewhere, shoulders will be swaying, fingers tapping. It may be at a gala evening concert, an outdoor festival, or an Easter Mass. But chances are the music of Johannes Chrysostomus Theophilus Wolfgang Amadeus Mozart will be traveling through the air when you visit Austria, and at no time more than during the 2006 celebrations honoring the 250th birthday year of Austria's most famous home boy. The most purely inspired of any composer crammed a prodigious amount of composing into his short 35-year life (January 27, 1756–December 5, 1791). Today—thanks to Tom Hulce's characterization in the film *Amadeus*—this youthful genius wears the crown of the rock star of the 18th century. Everywhere you go in Austria you can wind up suddenly tripping over a concert, a recital, an orchestra rehearsing, or a soprano going through her scales, all to the immortal tunes of "Wolfie." Clearly, it's music in general—and Mozart in particular—that seems to be the spiritual fuel of Austria. But most of the 2006 birthday festivities will center around the two main focal points of Mozart's life: Salzburg, his hometown, and Vienna, where he spent the last ten (and most productive) years of his life. Both cities will be mounting 24/7 year-long parties featuring hundreds of special events, including museum exhibitions, gala concerts, and open-air spectaculars. To read all about these, check out the Close-Up boxes on Mozart in Chapters 1, 4, and 7.

Amadeus: Marvel & Mystery

But how exactly do you explain away the genius that is the world's most beloved composer? Antonin Dvorak, the great composer, may have said it best: "Mozart is sunshine." Listen to Mozart's Rococo orchestrations, his rose-strewn melodies, and insouciant harmonies, and many listeners seem to experience the same giddiness as happiness. Scientists have found Mozart's music can be so seductive it can cause the heart to pound, brings color to the cheek, and provides the expansive feeling of being thrilllingly alive. Yet, somehow, Mozart must have sensed how hard it is to recognize happiness, which is often something vaguely desired, its presence frequently not detected until gone. It is this melancholic undertow that makes Mozart modern. So modern, in fact, that he is now the most popular classical composer, having banished the great Beethoven to second place. Shortly after Peter Schaffer's *Amadeus* won the 1984 Oscar for Best Film—with its portrayal of Mozart as a giggling, foul-mouthed genius—*Don Giovanni* began to rack up more performances than *La Boheme*, Frank Sinatra named Mozart his favorite composer, and Mostly Mozart festivals continued to famously pay him homage. But take a look behind the glare of the spotlights and you'll discover that this blonde, slightly built tuning-fork of a fellow was a quicksilver enigma.

An 18th-century version of Michael Jackson, Mozart was doomed to live as an "eternal child," thanks to the education—nay, exploitation—he suffered at the hands of his father, Leopold. Already a skilled pianist at age three, the musical prodigy was dragged across Europe to perform for empresses and kings. In a life that lasted a mere 35 years, he spent ten on the road— a burden which contributed to making him the first truly European composer. Back home in Salzburg, the wunderkind grew up and, like many a fading Hollywood child star, became less of a wunder as time went by. Prince-Archbishop Hieronymus von Colloredo enjoyed dissing his resident composer by commanding him to produce "table music" in the same, disdainful tone in which he gave his chefs dinner orders. Being literally forced to sit with those cooks, Mozart finally rebelled. In March 1781, he set out to conquer Vienna, a dire necessity as he was soon to marry Constanze Weber. Hated by Mozart's father, Constanze is adored today, since we now know she was Mozart's greatest ally. Highly repressed by stuffy Salzburg, Mozart came to like his humor glandular (he titled one cantata "Kiss My XXX") and his women globular, a bill Constanze adequately filled. She no doubt heartily enjoyed the fruits of his first operatic triumph, the naughty *Abduction from the Seraglio* (1782): the gilt-trimmed frock coats, the lavishly gemütlich apartment, and the high-stepping horse and carriage. Was this a spendthrift lifestyle—or was Mozart simply savvy enough to want to one-up the purse-proud Viennese? His next opera, *The Marriage of Figaro* (1786), to no one's surprise, bombed; Always eager to thumb his nose at authority (paging Dr. Freud), Mozart had adapted a Beaumarchais play so inflammatory, in its depiction of aristos as pawns of their own servants, it soon helped ignite the French Revolution. In revenge, wealthy Viennese gave a cold shoulder to his magisterial *Don Giovanni* (1787). As he neared the backstretch, Mozart was relegated to composing, for a lowly vaudeville house, the now immortal *Magic Flute* (1790), and to ghosting a *Requiem* for a wealthy count (see "Was Amadeus Murdered?" in Chapter 1). Sadly, his star only began to soar after a tragic, early death. But, in company with fellow starblazers Vincent van Gogh and Marilyn Monroe, we assume he must be enjoying the last laugh.

In Wolfgang's Footsteps
Well, it's time to step up to the Mozart Magical Mystery Tour. How can you connect-the-dots and map out your own Mozart pilgrimage? Here a game-plan for some of the main places to head for. Let's start in Vienna—if only to snub Salzburg, the composer's birthplace, which did so much to cold-shoulder him—and begin at the city's very heart, the Stephandom. It was at this great cathedral that Mozart was married to his beloved Constanze (1782) and where his funeral procession departed, leaving from the Crucifixion Chapel crypt on the cathedral's outer north side. Just a block away is Domgasse 5, the Figarohaus (where he wrote *The Marriage of Figaro*), his most famous Vienna residence and museum. Walk south a block or south to Singerstrasse 7 and the Deutschritterordenshaus, the palace where Mozart's patron, Archbishop Colloredo, "fired" Wolfie. As he was

literally booted out of the door here, let's pick ourselves up and dust ourselves off and head two blocks further south to see the site of Mozart's last Vienna abode, at Rauhensteingasse 8 (sadly now replaced by the modern Steffl store). Head down the street to Himmelpfortgasse to find Café Frauenhuber, a 19th-century jewel that occupies a building where Mozart once lived and often peformed in, as the Ignaz Jahn concert "rooms" were once here, the legendary site of the first performance of Mozart's *Requiem*. Head three blocks south to Seilerstätte 30 to take in the Haus der Musik museum and their multimedia galleries devoted to Mozart. The Staatsoper is two blocks away so this may be the time to see if you can snare those tickets for *Così fan tutte*. Just to the north of the opera house is Albertinaplatz, site of Café Mozart, 20th-century but with some memorabilia. Then promenade up Augustinerstrasse to the great Hofburg palace; here in the spectacular Court Library, Mozart often performed at Baron Gottfried van Swieten's Sunday concerts. Today, his music is still performed in the palace's massive Redoutensaal and its famous Hofburgkapelle, home to the Vienna Boys' Choir. Head across Michaelerplatz—the Burg Theater, which saw many Mozart premieres, once stood on this square—and up Herrengasse to the center of poshest, most palatial Vienna, the Freyung square. Here, at No. 3, the Palais Harrach, and, at No. 4, the fabulous Palais Daum-Kinsky, the Mozart kiddies once entertained *le tout Vienna*. To have dinner in an inn Mozart might still recognize, head east about 15 blocks to the magical and medieval Fleischmarkt district to savor Vienna's oldest inn, the Griechenbeisl (at Fleischmarkt 11)—ask the waiter to point out Mozart's signature on the wall. Then perhaps cap the night off with a train ride out to spectacular Schönbrunn Palace, in the Hietzing district, for a Mozart concert in its Orangerie. You could go out to the Landstrasse district to see the St. Marxer Friedhof cemetery, where Mozart was laid to rest in a common, unmarked grave—but don't (after all, even Constanze didn't bother). Wolfie was a true child of the Enlightenment and only wanted to be remembered for his soul—his music (not by the cemetery's truncated Mozartgrab column memorial).

Mozart's hometown, Salzburg—one of the most regal and elegant cities in Europe—sits some 200 miles west of Vienna. These two bookends are connected by Austria's incomparably scenic Danube Valley. Here, too, Mozart, often traveled, most notably to the splendorous Benedictine abbey at Melk, where he once played the organ, and to the city of Linz. Beyond, lies the gateway to Salzburg, the beauteous Salzkammergut region. Here, Mozartians visit St. Gilgen, hometown of the composer's mother. To conclude this Mozart Magical Mystery Tour, jump to the Altstadt tour found in our chapter on Salzburg—and don't forget to take some Mozart CD's for your Walkman. And for two great Mozart reads, pack H. C. Robbins Landon's *1791: Mozart's Last Year* and William Stafford's *Mozart Myths*.

FODOR'S CHOICE

The sights, restaurants, hotels, and other travel experiences on these pages are our editors' top picks—our Fodor's Choices. They're the best of their type in the area covered by the book—not to be missed and always worth your time. In the destination chapters that follow, you will find all the details.

LODGING

$$$$ **Imperial, Vienna.** A symphony of potted-palm luxe, this great Ringstrasse landmark has exemplified the grandeur of imperial Vienna ever since Emperor Franz Josef opened its doors in 1873. Adjacent to the famed Musikverein concert hall and two blocks from the Staatsoper, the emphasis here is on Old Vienna splendor, as seen in its famous grand marble staircase, its Marmorsaal, or Marble Hall, or tis whipped-cream rococo suites but who can resist the top-floor rooms done in an enchanting Biedermeier style?

$$$$ **Le Méridien, Vienna.** Occupying three former 19th-century Ringstrasse palaces, this luxe outpost is now as sleek as a *Wallpaper* magazine layout: Mies van der Rohe–style sofas and ottomans, acres of nouvelle fluorescent light panels, Shambala (the luxe restaurant of Michel Rostang, the Parisian chef-guru), roomy showers, and arguably the best buffet breakfast in the country. *Ach,* the good life!

$$$$ **Palais Coburg, Vienna.** An eye-knocking marriage of 19th-century luxe and 21st-century comfort, this grand 19th-century palace retains the hyperopulent pink-and-yellow marble ballroom where Johann Strauss once conducted his orchestra but is now ashimmer with modern white stone and plate glass. Many guest rooms—two-storied showpieces, the best done in a gilded-yellow 19th-century Biedermeier or Empire style—have fully equipped kitchenettes (and complimentary champagne), but who know why? One of the best chefs in Austria presides over the hotel restaurant.

$$$$ **Palais Schwarzenberg, Vienna.** It's hard to believe you're in the heart of the city at this secluded hotel, set in its own vast, formal park. Built in the early 1700s, the palace is still privately owned by the Princes Schwarzenberg and retains a sense of history while offering luxuriously appointed rooms. Guests are made to feel at home, whether strolling through the gardens or sipping a drink in front of a roaring fire in the drawing room on cold winter nights.

$$$$ **Sacher, Vienna.** Still exuding the monarchical magic of yore, this great landmark—once redoubt of Eduard Sacher, chef to Prince Metternich—has dropped the chilly monocle treatment with its newest refurbishment. The lily is now truly gilded: sparkling chandeliers, gilt-framed portraits, the red-and-crystal Café and its inimitable Sachertortes, entice off-duty celebrities (if no archduchesses).

$$$$ **Sacher Salzburg, Salzburg.** From its vantage point along the banks of the Salzach with a staggering view of the Old City and looming fortress, this grande dame of Salzburg hotels has gone out of its way to provide beauty and comfort in each of the exquisitely decorated rooms. The danger is that you won't want to leave the hotel to explore the sights.

$$$ **König von Ungarn, Vienna.** In the shadow of St. Stephan's Cathedral, once favored retreat of Empress "Sisi" (her Hungarian friends used to live here), and joined to the Figarohaus—Mozart's most famous lodging in Vienna—this hotel would undoubtedly please Wolfie today, thanks to its glowing "Mozartstuberl" restaurant, beautifully aglow in "Schönbrunn yellow."

$$–$$$ **Römischer Kaiser, Vienna.** Pretty, *ja*? A pastel pink confection of a hotel (with whipped-cream white stone trim), housed in a late-17th-century former town palace, the Roman Emperor's guest-book is littered with names like Liszt, Wagner, and Grieg. They could walk in today and find little changed, as the style here remains staidly, wonderfully "Viennese."

$–$$ **Pension Nossek, Vienna.** A family-run establishment on the upper floors of a 19th-century office and apartment building, the Nossek offers front rooms offering a magnificent view of the Graben and nookies and crannies that are still spirit-warm with the ghosts of the past: Mozart worked on *The Abduction from the Seraglio* here.

$ **Pension Suzanne, Vienna.** Step inside here and you'll be enveloped in Viennese warmth and coziness, with guest rooms charmingly and comfortably furnished in 19th-century Biedermeier style. Another plus: the Vienna State Opera house is a stone's throw away.

RESTAURANTS

$$$$ **Steirereck, Vienna.** A true culinary temple, Austria's most raved-about restaurant is now housed in a Jugendstil-vintage Milkhaus-pavilion. The menu is nouvelle Styrian and just one bite of the warm artichoke "cocktail" with caviar promises a meal with great flair.

$$$–$$$$ **Ruben's Palais, Vienna.** Once you've feasted your eyes on the Prince of Liechtenstein's fabled Old Master paintings, head to his garden palace's restaurant for a true feast for the tastebuds.

$$–$$$$ **Stiftskeller St. Peter, Salzburg.** Europe's oldest Gasthaus—Mephistopheles supposedly met Faust here—this abbey landmark offers everything from candlelit Mozart dinners to fingerlickingly good schnitzels.

$$–$$$$ **Villa Schratt, Bad Ischl.** Fabled retreat of the actress Katharina Schratt—Franz Josef's beloved amour—this enchanting villa now

attracts discerning diners, not European royalty. Who can resist the emperor's favorite, warm-from-the-oven Guglhupf cake?

$$$-$$$ **Zum Eulenspiegel, Salzburg.** This little cottage looks as if it's straight out of a fairy tale, and happily the food matches the unique setting. Nooks, crannies, odd staircases: Forget kitsch, this is genuine Old World authentic.

$$$-$$$ **Griechenbeisl, Vienna.** Head to the Zitherstu[u]berl room to tap your toes to the zither at this time-stained tavern, once graced by the likes of Beethoven, Schubert, and Gina Lollabrigida, and set on the most charming square.

$$$-$$$$ **Palmenhaus, Vienna.** Vienna has rarely looked better than from a table at this soaring Jugendstil-style glass-and-marble conservatory, created in 1904 to harbor the Emperor Franz Josef's orchids. Today, the crowd is orchidaceous, the food is fun, and the twenty-foot-high palm trees impress.

$-$$ **Zum Finsteren Stern, Vienna.** Paging all Mozart maniacs! This is the old Gothic cellar of the one and only Palais Collalto, where the six-year-old Amadeus first "played the palace." Not much has changed in the *Keller* since 1762—and even Wolfie would love the rabbit with sweet and sour lentils or the lamb steak with polenta tomato, zucchini cakes, and red-wine shallot sauce. On summer eves, head for the outdoor tables under an old bluebell tree.

$ **Café Central, Vienna.** Nothing embodies the spirit of Viennese cafe[ac] society than this grand, plush coffeehouse. Trotsky supposedly plotted the Russian Revolution here under portraits of the Austrian imperial family.

QUINTESSENTIAL AUSTRIA

New Year's Day concert in Vienna's Musikverein. You've seen it on television, but now you're *here* in the Golden Hall—its gilt bare-breasted ladies supporting the balconies, the walls festooned with floral displays—sharing in the excitement of a Vienna Philharmonic concert seen and heard by millions around the world.

Waltzing around the clock at a Fasching ball. Whether you go to the Opera Ball or the Zuckerbäckerball (sponsored by pastry cooks), remember that gala etiquette states a gentleman can kiss only a lady's hand.

Taking a boat through the Wachau on the Danube. The vineyards are glowing in all fall colors or the apricot and cherry trees are in bloom. Spring or fall or warm breezy summer, this is heaven on earth. The setting sun always makes the villages radiate, and the great Baroque monastery of Melk seems like poured gold.

A summer evening. The hills of the Southern Wine Road (südliche Weinstrasse) are dotted with little family-run Heurige, where the wine is excellent, the food simple and good, the people hospitable. Often, the house's garden serves as a guest garden (*Gastgarten*); you can stay as long as the place stays open, meet other people, and make friends.

The Lipizzaner stallions at the Spanish Riding School. Where else can you see horses dance to a Mozart minuet? For sheer elegance, the combination of the chestnut-color riding habits of the trainers and the pure white of the horses' coats can't be beat.

A hike up a mountain. Pack a bag with water, bread, cheese, cold cuts, and fresh fruit, and spend a day roaming the mountains, crossing icy streams, traversing cool forests, meeting cows and sheep—maybe the odd deer or fox, or kindred walker, or farmer. What's good for the body is good for the soul!

Vienna from the Leopoldsberg. The metropolis sprawls on a plain embraced on the one side by hills, traversed on the other by the flows and canals of the Danube, its barges like toys. Every detail of the city is visible on a clear day, the great Ferris wheel of the Prater, St. Stephen's Cathedral, the refinery of Schwechat. You can see way into the distance almost all the way to Bratislava.

Salzburg from the Kapuzinerberg after the first snow. A blanket of white softens the somber gray of the city and brings buildings and squares to life; you'll see features you've overlooked before, with the solid Festung watching patiently over the Christmas-card scene.

The Wachau when its apricot trees are in blossom. In spring the narrow Danube Valley becomes a riot of fruit trees in delicate pastel blossom sweeping up hillsides from the very riverbanks.

Steyr, Upper Austria. Wonderfully colorful decorative facades address the main square, brooded over by the castle above. Tiny, half-concealed stairways lead upward to the castle area, while other stone steps take you down the opposite side to the riverbank. The setting is an ensemble worthy of Hollywood; in this case, it's all charmingly real.

CHURCHES & ABBEYS

Melk, Lower Austria. Probably the most impressive of Europe's abbeys, Melk perches like a magnificent yellow-frosted wedding cake overlooking the Danube, its ornate library holding rows of priceless treasures. If you can visit only one abbey in all of Europe, Melk should be among the top contenders.

St. Florian, Upper Austria. This abbey, where composer Anton Bruckner was organist, is impressive for its sheer size alone. Add to the symmetrical structure the glorious church and the representational rooms, and you have one of Austria's religious highlights.

St. Stephan's Cathedral, Vienna. The country's Catholic life centers on St. Stephen's, rebuilt after burning during the last days of World War II. It is one of Europe's finest Gothic structures, with two different towers, one of which can be climbed on foot; the other has an elevator and holds the *Pummerin,* Austria's largest bell. Like the exterior, the interior of the cathedral is a masterpiece, especially of stone carving.

PARKS & GARDENS

Mirabell Gardens, Salzburg. For an idyllic view, look up through the formal garden to the castle (Festung) dominating the city, but don't miss the droll Baroque side garden with its amusing stone dwarfs.

Schönbrunn, Vienna. Was the palace an excuse for the gardens, or vice versa? The manicured trees, the symmetrical walkways, the discoveries at various intersections—all add to the pleasure of exploration here. Climb to the Gloriette, which is now a moderately good café, for a sweeping perspective of the gardens and the city beyond.

SMART TRAVEL TIPS

Half the fun of traveling is looking forward to your trip—but when you look forward, don't just daydream. There are plans to be made, things to learn about, serious work to be done. The following chapter will give you helpful pointers on many of the questions that arise when planning your trip and also when you are on the road. Finding out about your destination before you leave home means you won't squander time organizing everyday minutiae once you've arrived. You'll be more streetwise when you hit the ground as well, better prepared to explore the aspects of Austria that drew you here in the first place. The organizations in this section can provide information to supplement this guide; contact them for up-to-the-minute details. Many trips begin by first contacting the Austrian tourist bureau: consult the Austrian National Tourist Offices listed under Visitor Information, below. Happy landings!

ADDRESSES

Willkommen in Österreich—-welcome to Austria! Now that you are about to hit the ground running, here's a quick rundown on the basic geographical terms you'll want to be familiar with. The word for city is Stadt—prominently used when referring to Vienna's big First District, the Inner Stadt, or the historic center of Salzburg, the Alt Stadt (or Old City). The most frequently used term is Strasse, or street, and it is sometimes merged with the actual name of the street, as in Mahlerstasse 9 (note that the number of the street address comes after the name), or not, as in Ottakringer-Strasse. Next up is the word for square, or plaza: Platz, as in Mozartplatz or Südtirolerplatz. Many cities and towns have their marketplace squares, and this word translates into Markt, as in Neumarkt. Other words to know are Brückenpfeiler for pier, and Bastei, which means bastion. Another term is Weg, which means way or path, as in the street name of Rennweg. The word for castle is Burg, while Schloss usually means palace. If lost, try the following German phrase: Entschuldigen Sie, können

Sie mir sagen wo ist der Rennweg or *wo ist die Kärntnerstrasse*—"Please, can you show me where is Rennweg or Kärnter Street." Or you can use the simpler *Kennen Sie den Rennweg?* which means "Do you know Rennweg?" Every Austrian will know you mean you need directions to this street.

AIR TRAVEL

CARRIERS & CONSOLIDATORS

When flying internationally, you must usually choose between a domestic carrier, the national flag carrier of the country you are visiting, and a foreign carrier from a third country. You may, for example, choose to fly **Austrian Airlines** to Austria. National flag carriers have the greatest number of nonstops. Domestic carriers may have better connections to your home town and serve a greater number of gateway cities. Third-party carriers may have a price advantage.

Austrian Airlines is the only air carrier that flies nonstop to Vienna from various points in the United States. There are no longer any American or Canadian carriers that fly directly to Vienna. Many major American carriers—such as American, Northwest, and United—instead fly passengers to major European hubs, such as London, Amsterdam, or Frankfurt, for transfers to flights with other airlines. Austrian Airlines is currently in partnership with United Airlines. Austrian Airlines also has many routes connecting Vienna with every major European destination.

Travelers from North America should note that many international carriers do service Vienna after stopovers at major European airports. For instance, Lufthansa flies from the U.S. to Frankfurt, Düsseldorf, and Munich, then can offer you connections to Vienna. British Airways (which has 15 gateways from the U.S. alone) offers many direct flights to Vienna from London's Heathrow and Gatwick airports. Note, too, that the western sector of Austria—including Innsbruck, the Tirol, and Vorarlberg—are actually closer by air to Munich than Vienna, so you might consider the option of using an international carrier to Munich, then traveling by train or con-

necting by air to Innsbruck or even Salzburg. Also, Ryanair flies from London Stansted to major destinations in Austria—except Vienna—for rock bottom prices, if you book early.

Within Austria, Austrian Airlines and its subsidiary, **Austrian Arrows,** offer service from Vienna to Linz and Innsbruck; they also provide routes to and from points outside Austria. In addition, **Welcome** is now providing some air links between Innsbruck, Graz, and other European cities. Winter schedules on all domestic lines depend on snow conditions.

Other than the main carriers, consolidators are another good source. They buy tickets for scheduled international flights at reduced rates from the airlines, then sell them at prices that beat the best fare available directly from the airlines, usually without restrictions. Sometimes you can even get your money back if you need to return the ticket. Carefully read the fine print detailing penalties for changes and cancellations, and **confirm your consolidator reservation with the airline.**

Major Airlines Austrian Airlines ☎ 800/843-0002. **British Airways** ☎ 800/247-9297, 020/8897-4000 London, 0345/222-111 outside London. **Lufthansa** ☎ 800/645-3880.

From the U.K. Austrian Airlines ☎ 020/7434-7300. **Ryanair** ⊕ www.ryanair.com. **British Airways** ☎ 020/8897-4000, 0345/222-111 outside London.

Within Austria Austrian Airlines ✉ Main Austrian office Kärntner Ring 18, A-1010 Vienna ☎ 05/1789 from all over Austria. **Welcome** ☎ 0512/295-296 in Innsbruck ⊕ www.welcomeair.at.

Consolidators Cheap Tickets ☎ 800/377-1000. **Discount Airline Ticket Service** ☎ 800/576-1600. **Unitravel** ☎ 800/325-2222. **Up & Away Travel** ☎ 212/889-2345 ⊕ www.upandaway.com. **World Travel Network** ☎ 800/409-6753.

CHECK-IN & BOARDING

Assuming that not everyone with a ticket will show up, airlines routinely overbook planes. When everyone does, airlines ask for volunteers to give up their seats. In return, these volunteers usually get a certificate for a free flight and are rebooked on the next flight out. If there are not enough volunteers, the airline must choose who will be denied boarding. The first to get bumped are passengers who checked in late and those flying on discounted tickets, so **get to the gate and check in as early as possible,** especially during peak periods. Although the trend on international flights is to drop reconfirmation requirements, many airlines still ask you to reconfirm each leg of your international itinerary. Failure to do so may result in your reservation's being canceled. Always **bring a government-issued photo ID to the airport.** You will be asked to show it before you are allowed to check in.

FLYING TIMES

Flying time is 8 hours to Vienna from New York, 9 hours from Washington, D.C., and 90 minutes from London.

AIRPORTS

The major airport is Vienna's **Schwechat Airport,** about 12 mi southeast of the city. Just south of Graz, in Thalerhof, is the **Graz Airport. Salzburg Airport** is Austria's second largest airport, about 2½ mi west of the center.

🛫 Airport Information **Graz Airport** ☎ 0316/2902-0. **Schwechat Airport (Vienna)** ☎ 01/7007-0. **Salzburg Airport** ☎ 0662/8580.

AIRPORT TRANSFERS

The fastest way into Vienna from Schwechat Airport is the sleek, double-decker **City Train.** The journey from the airport to Wien–Mitte (the center of the city) takes 16 minutes and operates daily every 30 minutes between 5:30 AM and midnight. The cost is €8 one-way and €15 round-trip.

The cheapest way to get to Vienna from the airport is the **S7 train,** called the *Schnellbahn,* which shuttles twice an hour between the airport basement and the Landstrasse/Wien–Mitte (city center) and Wien–Nord (north Vienna) stations; the fare is €3 and it takes about 35 minutes (19 minutes longer than the City Train). Your ticket is also good for an immediate transfer to your destination within the city on the streetcar, bus, or U-Bahn. Another cheap option is the **bus,** which has two separate lines. One line goes to the City Air Terminal at the Hilton Hotel (near the city's 1st District)

every 20 minutes between 6:30 AM and 11 PM, and every 30 minutes after that; travel time is 20 minutes. The other line goes to the South and West train stations (Südbahnhof and Westbahnhof) in 20 and 35 minutes, respectively. Departure times are every 30 minutes from 8:10 AM to 7:10 PM, hourly thereafter, and not at all 12:10–3:30 AM. Fare is €5.80 one-way, €10.90 round-trip. Prices may be higher in 2005 and beyond. Another possibility is via taxi with **C+K Airport Service** (☎ 01/44444 🖷 01/689–6969), charging a set price of €25 (don't forget to tip). This service will also meet your plane at no extra charge if you let them know your flight information in advance.

If you land in **Salzburg,** the bus line No. 77 shuttles every 15 minutes from the airport to the train station, otherwise take a taxi. If you land in **Munich,** the cheapest way of getting to town is the S8 train, which takes about 45 minutes to the main train station (Hauptbahnhof) with stops along the way and connecting rides.

BIKE TRAVEL

Biking is a popular sport in Austria. In central Vienna, special bike lanes make transportation fast, easy, and safe. Throughout Austria there are several cycling trails, including the well-known Passau (Germany) to Vienna route, which follows the Danube across the country, passing through the spectacular Danube Valley. There are other cycling trails in the Alps and around lakes in Carinthia and the Salzkammergut (*see* Sports & the Outdoors, *below*). Mountain biking is increasingly popular, with "mountain bike hotels" welcoming enthusiasts, along with rigorous guided tours.

🚲 **Mountain Bike Hotels** ✉ Margaretenstrasse 1, A-1010 Vienna ☎ 0810/101818 🖷 0810/101819 ⊕ www.austria.info.

BIKES IN FLIGHT

Most airlines accommodate bikes as luggage, provided they are dismantled and boxed. For bike boxes, often free at bike shops, you'll pay about $5 from airlines (at least $100 for bike bags). International travelers can sometimes substitute a bike for a piece of checked luggage at no charge; otherwise, the cost is about $100. Domestic and Canadian airlines charge $25–$50.

BOAT & FERRY TRAVEL

For leisurely travel between Vienna and Linz or eastward across the border into Slovakia or Hungary, consider taking a Danube boat. More than 300 km (187 mi) of Austria's most beautiful scenery awaits you as you glide past castles and ruins, medieval monasteries and abbeys, and lush vineyards. One of the lovelier sections, particularly in spring, is the *Wachau* (Danube Valley) west of Vienna. **Blue Danube Schifffahrt** offers a diverse selection of pleasant cruises, including trips to Melk Abbey and Dürnstein in the Wachau, a grand tour of Vienna's architectural sights from the river, and a dinner cruise, featuring Johann Strauss waltzes as background music. **Brandner Schifffart** offers the same kind of cruises between Krems and Melk, in the heart of the Danube Valley.

Most of the immaculate white-painted craft carry about 1,000 passengers each on their three decks. As soon as you get on board, give the steward a good tip for a deck chair and ask him to place it where you will get the best views. Be sure to book cabins in advance. Day trips are also possible on the Danube. You can use boats to move from one riverside community to the next, and along some sections, notably the Wachau, the only way to cross the river is to use the little shuttles (in the Wachau, these are special motorless boats that use the current to cross).

For the cruises up and down the Danube, the Blue Danube Steamship Company/DDSG departs and arrives at Praterlände near Vienna's Mexikoplatz. The Praterlände stop is a two-block taxi ride or hike from the Vorgartenstrasse subway station on the U1 route of Vienna's U-Bahn. There is no pier number, but you board at Handelskai 265. Boat trips from Vienna to the Wachau are on Sunday only from May to September. The price is €19 one-way and €25 round-trip. There are other daily cruises within the Wachau, such as from

Melk to Krems. Other cruises, to Budapest for instance, operate from April to early November. The Web site has dozens of options and timetables in English. For more information, see the "And the Danube Waltzes On" Close-Up box in Chapter 6.

Boat & Ferry Information Contact your travel agent or, in Austria, the **Blue Danube Schifffahrt:** ✉ Friedrichstrasse 7, A-1043 Vienna ☎ 01/588-800 🖷 01/588-8044-0 ⊕ www.ddsg-blue-danube.at For cruises from Krems to Melk, contact **Brandner Schifffahrt** ✉ Ufer 50, A-3313 Wallsee ☎ 07433/2590-21 ⊕ www.brandner.at.

BUS TRAVEL IN AUSTRIA

BUS TRAVEL TO & FROM VIENNA

International long-distance bus service (Bratislava, Brno) and most postal and railroad buses arrive at the Wien–Mitte central bus station, across from the Hilton Hotel on the Stadtpark.

Bus Information Wien-Mitte ✉ Landstrasser Hauptstrasse 1b ☎ 01/711-01.

BUS LINES

Austria features extensive national networks of buses run by post offices and railroads. Where Austrian trains don't go, buses do, and you'll find the railroad and post-office buses (bright yellow for easy recognition) in even remote regions carrying passengers as well as mail. You can get tickets on the bus, and in the off-season there is no problem getting a seat, but on routes to favored ski areas during holiday periods reservations are essential. Bookings can be handled at the ticket office (there's one in most towns with bus service) or by travel agents. In most communities, bus routes begin and end at or near the railroad station, making transfers easy. Increasingly, coordination of bus service with railroads means that many of the discounts and special tickets available for trains apply to buses as well. There are private bus companies in Austria, too. Buses in Austria run like clockwork, typically departing and arriving on time. Smoking is generally allowed.

Private Bus Lines Columbus ☎ 01/53411-0. **Blaguss Reisen** ☎ 01/50180-150. **Post und Bahn** ☎ 01/71101. **Dr. Richard** ☎ 01/33100-0.

BUSINESS HOURS

BANKS & OFFICES

In most cities, banks are open weekdays 8–3, Thursday until 5:30 PM. Lunch hour is from 12:30 to 1:30. All banks are closed on Saturday, but you can change money at various locations (such as American Express offices on Saturday morning and major railroad stations around the clock), and changing machines are also found here and there in the larger cities.

GAS STATIONS

Gas stations on the major autobahns are open 24 hours a day, but in smaller towns and villages you can expect them to close early in the evening and on Sunday. You can usually count on at least one station to stay open on Sunday and holidays in most medium-size towns, and buying gas in larger cities is never a problem.

MUSEUMS & SIGHTS

Museum hours vary from city to city and museum to museum; if museums are closed one day, it is usually Monday. Few Austrian museums are open at night. In summer, the Salzburg Zoo at Hellbrunn has nighttime hours for viewing the nocturnal animals.

PHARMACIES

Pharmacies (called *Apotheken* in German) are usually open from 9 to 6, with a mid-day break between noon and 2. In each area of the city one pharmacy stays open 24 hours; if a pharmacy is closed, a sign on the door will tell you the address of the nearest one that is open. Call 01/1550 for names and addresses (in German) of the pharmacies open that night. You may find over-the-counter remedies for headaches and colds much less effective than those sold in the U.S. Austrians are firm believers in natural remedies, such as herbal teas.

SHOPS

In general, you'll find shops open weekdays from 8:30 or 9 until 6, with a lunchtime closing from noon to 1 or 1:30. In smaller villages, the midday break may run until 3. Many food stores, bakeries, and small grocery shops open at 7 or 7:30 and, aside from the noontime break, stay open until 7 or 7:30 PM. Shops in large city centers forego the noon break. On Saturday most shops stay open until 5 or 6 PM, though a few follow the old rules and close by 1 PM. Food stores stay open until 5 on Saturday. Barbers and hairdressers traditionally take Monday off, but there are exceptions. It is fashionable these days for hairdressers to work evenings and nights on certain "good-for-haircutting" moon days! Also in the country, many shops close on Wednesday afternoon, and in parts of Burgenland they may also close on Thursday afternoon.

CAMERAS & PHOTOGRAPHY

📷 Photo Help **Kodak Information Center** ☎ 800/242–2424. *Kodak Guide to Shooting Great Travel Pictures* ☎ 800/533–6478 🖃 $18 plus $5.50 shipping available in bookstores or from Fodor's Travel Publications.

EQUIPMENT PRECAUTIONS

Always **keep your film and tape out of the sun.** Carry an extra supply of batteries, and **be prepared to turn on your camera or camcorder** to prove to security personnel that the device is real. Always **ask for hand inspection of film,** which becomes clouded after repeated exposure to airport X-ray machines, and **keep videotapes away from metal detectors.**

FILM & DEVELOPING

All kinds of film are available for purchase in Austria, with the best prices at grocery and drug stores. Developing is very expensive, especially for one-hour service.

VIDEOS

Austrian video tapes use the PAL system, which is not compatible with NTSC players in the U.S. The same goes for DVDs.

CAR RENTAL

Rates in Vienna begin at €44 a day and €132 a weekend for an economy car with manual transmission and unlimited mileage. This includes a 21% tax on car rentals. Rates are more expensive in winter months, when a surcharge for winter tires is added. Renting a car may be cheaper in Germany, but make sure the rental agency knows you are driving into Austria and that the car is equipped with an autobahn sticker (*see* Car Travel, *below*) for Austria.

When renting an RV be sure to compare prices and reserve early. It's cheaper to arrange your rental car from the U.S., but **be sure to get a confirmation of your quoted rate in writing.**

Before you pick up a car in one city and leave it in another, **ask about drop-off charges or one-way service fees,** which can be substantial. Note, too, that some rental agencies charge extra if you return the car before the time specified in your contract.

🚗 Major Agencies **Alamo** ☎ 800/522-9696 ⊕ www.alamo.com. **Avis** ☎ 800/331-1084, 800/879-2847 in Canada, 0870/606-0100 in U.K., 02/9353-9000 in Australia, 09/526-2847 in New Zealand ⊕ www.avis.com. **Budget** ☎ 800/527-0700, 0870/156-5656 in U.K. ⊕ www.budget.com. **Dollar** ☎ 800/800-6000, 0124/622-0111 in U.K., where it's affiliated with Sixt, 02/9223-1444 in Australia ⊕ www.dollar.com. **Hertz** ☎ 800/654-3001, 800/263-0600 in Canada, 020/8897-2072 in U.K., 02/9669-2444 in Australia, 09/256-8690 in New Zealand ⊕ www.hertz.com. **National Car Rental** ☎ 800/227-7368, 020/8680-4800 in U.K. ⊕ www.nationalcar.com.

🚗 Local Agencies **Denzel Drive** ⊠ Erdberg Center/U-Bahn (U3), A-1110 Vienna ☎ 01/740-50. **Autoverleih Buchbinder** ⊠ Schlachthausgasse 38, A-1030 Vienna ☎ 01/717-50-0 🖷 01/717-5022 with offices throughout Austria.

CUTTING COSTS

To get the best deal, **book through a travel agent who will shop around.** Also **ask your travel agent about a company's customer-service record.** How has the company responded to delayed plane arrivals and vehicle mishaps? Are there often lines at the rental counter? If you're traveling during a holiday period, does a confirmed reservation guarantee you a car? Make sure to fill up the tank before returning the car, and **get a confirmation in writing that it is full before leaving the dealership** to avoid being mistakenly billed for gas.

Do **look into wholesalers,** companies that do not own fleets but rent in bulk from those that do at often better rates than traditional car-rental operations. Prices are best during off-peak periods. Payment must be made before you leave home.

🚗 Wholesalers **Auto Europe** ☎ 207/842-2000 or 800/223-5555 🖷 800-235-6321 ⊕ www.autoeurope.com. **Europe by Car** ☎ 212/581-3040 or 800/223-1516 🖷 212/246-1458 ⊕ www.europebycar.com. **DER Travel Services** ⊠ 9501 W. Devon Ave., Rosemont, IL 60018 ☎ 800/782-2424 🖷 800/282-7474 for information, 800/860-9944 for brochures ⊕ www.dertravel.com. **Kemwel Holiday Autos** ☎ 800/678-0678 🖷 914/825-3160 ⊕ www.kemwel.com.

INSURANCE

When driving a rented car you are generally responsible for any damage to or loss of the vehicle. Before you rent, see what coverage your personal auto-insurance policy and credit cards already provide. Collision policies that car-rental companies sell for European rentals usually do not include stolen-vehicle coverage. Before you buy it, check your existing policies—you may already be covered.

REQUIREMENTS & RESTRICTIONS

In Austria your own driver's license is acceptable. An International Driver's Permit is a good idea; it's available from the American or Canadian automobile association, and, in the United Kingdom, from the Automobile Association or Royal Automobile Club. These international permits are universally recognized, and having one in your wallet may save you a problem with the local authorities. There is no age limit to renting a car at most agencies in Austria. However, you must have had a valid driver's license for one year. For some of the more expensive car models, drivers must be at least 25 years of age. There is no extra charge to drive over the border into Italy, Switzerland, or Germany, but there are some restrictions and possible additional charges for taking a rental car into Slovakia, Slovenia, Hungary, the Czech Republic, or Poland.

CAR TRAVEL IN AUSTRIA

Vienna is 300 km (187 mi) east of Salzburg, 200 km (125 mi) north of Graz. Main routes leading into the city are the A1 Westautobahn from Germany, Salzburg, and Linz and the A2 Südautobahn from Graz and points south. Also *see* Vienna by Car section, *below.*

AUTO CLUBS

Austria has two automobile clubs, ÖAMTC and ARBÖ, both of which operate motorist service patrols. You'll find emergency (orange-color) phones along all the highways. If you break down along the autobahn, a small arrow on the guardrail will direct you to the nearest phone. Otherwise, if you have problems, call **ARBÖ** (☎ 123) or **ÖAMTC** (☎ 120) from anywhere in the country. No area or other code is needed for either number. Both clubs charge nonmembers for emergency service. Remember to get proper coverage from your home club.

🖪 In Austria **Austrian Automobile Club/ÖAMTC** ✉ Schubertring 1–3, A-1010 Vienna ☎ 01/71199 ⊕ www.oemtc.at.

🖪 In Australia **Australian Automobile Association** ☎ 06/247-7311.

🖪 In Canada **Canadian Automobile Association** CAA ☎ 613/247-0117.

🖪 In New Zealand **New Zealand Automobile Association** ☎ 09/377-4660.

🖪 In the U.K. **Automobile Association AA** ☎ 0990/500-600. **Royal Automobile Club RAC** ☎ 0990/722-722 for membership, 0345/121-345 for insurance.

🖪 In the U.S. **American Automobile Association** ☎ 800/564-6222.

FROM THE U.K.

The best way to reach Austria by car from England is to take North Sea/Cross Channel ferries to Oostende or Zeebrugge in Belgium or Dunkirk in northern France. An alternative is the Channel Tunnel; motoring clubs can give you the best routing to tie into the continental motorway network. Then take the toll-free Belgian motorway (E5) to Aachen, and head via Stuttgart to Innsbruck and the Tirol (A61, A67, A5, E11, A7), or east by way of Nürnberg and Munich, crossing into Austria at Walserberg and then on to Salzburg and Vienna. Total distance to Innsbruck from London is about 1,100 km (650 mi); to Vienna, about 1,600 km (1,000 mi). The most direct way to Vienna is virtually all on the autobahn via Nürnberg, Regensburg, and Passau, entering

Austria at Schärding. In summer, border delays are much shorter at Schärding than at Salzburg. The trip to Innsbruck via this route will take 2–3 days.

If this seems like too much driving, in summer you can **put the car on a train** in s'Hertogenbosch in central southern Netherlands on Thursday, or in Schaerbeek (Brussels) on Friday, for an overnight trip, arriving in Salzburg early the following morning and in Villach three hours later.

🖪 Agencies **DER Travel Service** ✉ 18 Conduit St., London W1R 9TD ☎ 020/7290-0111 🗗 020/7629-7442 has details on fares and schedules.

EMERGENCY SERVICES

See Auto Clubs, *above.*

GASOLINE

Gasoline and diesel are readily available, but on Sunday stations in the more out-of-the-way areas may be closed. Stations carry only unleaded (*bleifrei*) gas, both regular and premium (super), and diesel. If you're in the mountains in winter with a diesel, and there is a cold snap (with temperatures threatening to drop below −4°F [−20°C]), add a few liters of gasoline to your diesel, about 1:4 parts, to prevent it from freezing. Gasoline prices are the same throughout the country, slightly lower at discount and self-service stations. Expect to pay about €0.98 per liter for regular, €1 for premium, and €0.87 for diesel. If you are driving to Italy, fill up before crossing the border because gas in Italy is even more expensive. Oil in Austria is expensive, retailing at €9 upward per liter. If need be, purchase oil, windshield-wipers, and other paraphernalia at big hardware stores.

ROAD CONDITIONS

Roads in Austria are excellent and well-maintained—perhaps a bit too well-maintained judging by the frequently encountered construction zones on the autobahns.

ROAD MAPS

A set of eight excellent, detailed road maps is available from the Austrian Automobile Club/ÖAMTC (*see above*), at most service stations, and at many bookstores. The maps supplied without charge by the Austrian National Tourist Office are adequate for most needs, but if you will be covering much territory, the better ÖAMTC maps are a worthwhile investment.

RULES OF THE ROAD

Tourists from EU countries may bring their cars to Austria with no documentation other than the normal registration papers and their regular driver's license. A Green Card, the international certificate of insurance, is recommended for EU drivers and compulsory for others. All cars must carry a first-aid kit (including rubber gloves) and a red warning triangle to use in case of accident or breakdown. These are available at gas stations along the road, or at any automotive supply store or large hardware store.

The minimum driving age in Austria is 18, and children under 12 must ride in the back seat; smaller children require a restraining seat. Note that all passengers must use seat belts.

Drive on the right side of the street in Austria. Vehicles coming from the right have the right of way, except that at unregulated intersections streetcars coming from either direction have the right of way. No turns are allowed on red. In residential areas, the right of way can be switched around; the rule is, be careful at any intersection.

Drinking and driving: the maximum blood-alcohol content allowed is 0.5 parts per thousand, which in real terms means very little to drink. Remember when driving in Europe that the police can stop you anywhere at any time for no particular reason.

Unless otherwise marked, the speed limit on autobahns is 130 kph (80 mph), although this is not always strictly enforced. But if you're pulled over for speeding, fines are payable on the spot, and can be heavy. On other highways and roads, the limit is 100 kph (62 mph), 80 kph (49 mph) for RVs or cars pulling a trailer weighing more than 750 kilos (about 1,650 lbs). In built-up areas, a 50 kph (31 mph) limit applies and is likely to be taken seriously. In some towns, special 30 kph

(20 mph) limits apply. More and more towns have radar cameras to catch speeders. Remember that insurance does not necessarily pay if it can be proved you were going above the limit when involved in an accident.

Sometimes the signs at exits and entrances on the autobahns are not clear—a reason why Austria has a special problem, called the "*Geisterfahrer*," which means a driver going the wrong way in traffic. Efforts are being made to correct this problem with clearer signage.

If you're going to travel Austria's highways, make absolutely sure your car is equipped with the *Autobahnvignette*, as it is called, a little trapezoidal sticker with a highway icon and the Austrian eagle, or with a calendar marked with an M or a W. This sticker allows use of the autobahn. It costs €72.60 for a year and is available at gas stations, tobacconists, and automobile-club outlets in neighboring countries or near the border. You can also purchase a two-month Vignette for €21.80, or a 10-day one for €7.60. Prices are for vehicles up to 3.5 tons and RVs. For motorcycles it is €29.00 for one year, €10.90 for two months, and €4.30 for 10 days. Not having a Vignette (which is generally called the *Pickerl*) can lead to extremely high fines if you're caught. Get your Pickerl before driving to Austria.

Besides the Pickerl, if you are planning to drive around a lot, budget in a great deal of toll money: for example, the tunnels on the A10 autobahn cost €9.50, the Grossglockner Pass road will cost €26 per car, or €13 after 6 PM, while passing through the Arlberg Tunnel costs €8.50. Driving up some especially beautiful valleys, such as the Kaunertal in Tirol, or up to the Tauplitzalm in Styria, also costs money—€5.50 per person and €19 per car for the Kaunertal, and €2.55 per person and €9.45 per car for the Tauplitzalm.

The Austrian highway network is excellent, and roads are well maintained and well marked. Secondary roads may be narrow and winding. Remember that in winter you will need snow tires and often chains, even on well-traveled roads. It's wise to check with the automobile clubs for weather conditions, since mountain roads are often blocked, and ice and fog are hazards.

CHILDREN IN AUSTRIA
Be sure to plan ahead and **involve your youngsters** as you outline your trip. When packing, include things to keep them busy en route. On sightseeing days try to schedule activities of special interest to your children. If you are renting a car, don't forget to **arrange for a car seat** when you reserve. Austria is filled with wonders and delights for children, ranging from the performing Lipizzaner horses at the Spanish Riding School in Vienna to the Salzburg Marionettentheater and the rural delights of farm vacations.

🚸 **Babysitting** In Vienna, the central babysitting services are **Dienstleistungzentrum** ✉ Neubaugasse 66, A-1070 ☎ 01/523-4601 and **Wiener Hilfwerk** ✉ Schottenfeldgasse 29, A-1070 ☎ 01/512-3661-29. It's best to have your hotel call to make the arrangements, unless you speak German.

DINING
The best restaurants in Vienna do not welcome small children; fine dining is considered an adult pastime. With kids, **you're best off taking them to more casual restaurants and cafés.** *Heurige* are perfect for family dining, and they usually open by 4 PM. To accommodate flexible meal times, look for signs that say *Durchgehend warme Küche,* which means warm meals are available all afternoon. Cafés offer light meals all day, and you can always get a sausage from a *Würstelstand.* Several chain restaurants have high chairs (*Hochstühle*), and a few serve children's portions (*Für den kleinen Hunger*), usually *Wienerschnitzel,* a thin slice of veal, breaded and fried.

LODGING
Most hotels in Austria allow children under a certain age to stay in their parents' room at no extra charge, but others charge for them as extra adults; be sure to **find out the cutoff age for children's discounts.**

SIGHTS & ATTRACTIONS
Places that are especially appealing to children are indicated by a rubber duckie icon—🦆—in the margin.

SUPPLIES & EQUIPMENT
Supermarkets and drug stores (look for *DM Drogerie* and *Bipa*) carry *Windeln* (diapers), universally referred to as Pampers. Remember that weight is given in kilos (2.2 pounds equals 1 kilo). Baby formula is available in grocery stores, drug stores, or pharmacies. There are two brands of formula: Milupa and Nestlé, for infants and children up to three years old. Austrian formulas come in powder form and can be mixed with tap water.

COMPUTERS ON THE ROAD
If you use a major Internet provider, getting online in Vienna and Salzburg shouldn't be difficult. Call your Internet provider to get the local access number in Austria. Many hotels have business services with Internet access and even in-room modem lines. You may, however, need an adapter for your computer for the European-style plugs. As always, if you're traveling with a laptop, carry a spare battery and adapter. Never plug your computer into any socket before asking about surge protection. IBM sells a pen-size modem tester that plugs into a telephone jack to check whether the line is safe to use.

🖥 **Access Numbers in Austria AOL** ☎ 01/585-8483. For **Compuserve** ☎ 0049/1805-7040-70 or 0190/7500-75, you must call Germany.

CUSTOMS & DUTIES
When shopping, **keep receipts** for all purchases. Upon reentering the country, **be ready to show customs officials what you've bought.** If you feel a duty is incorrect or object to the way your clearance was handled, note the inspector's badge number and ask to see a supervisor. If the problem isn't resolved, write to the appropriate authorities, beginning with the port director at your point of entry.

IN AUSTRIA
Travelers over 17 who are residents of European countries—regardless of citizenship—may bring in, duty free, 200 cigarettes or 50 cigars or 250 grams of tobacco, 2 liters of wine and 2 liters of 22% spirits or 1 liter of over 22% spirits, and 50 milliliters of perfume. These limits may be liberalized or eliminated under terms of

the European Union agreement. Travelers from all other countries (such as those coming directly from the United States or Canada) may bring in twice these amounts. All visitors may bring gifts or other purchases valued at up to €175 (about $210), although in practice you'll seldom be asked.

IN AUSTRALIA
Australian residents who are 18 or older may bring home $A400 worth of souvenirs and gifts (including jewelry), 250 cigarettes or 250 grams of tobacco, and 1,125 ml of alcohol (including wine, beer, and spirits). Residents under 18 may bring back $A200 worth of goods. Prohibited items include meat products. Seeds, plants, and fruits need to be declared upon arrival.

🛈 **Australian Customs Service** Regional Director, Box 8, Sydney, NSW 2001 ☎ 02/9213-2000 or 1300/363263, 1800/020504 quarantine-inquiry line 📠 02/9213-4043 ⊕ www.customs.gov.au.

IN CANADA
Canadian residents who have been out of Canada for at least 7 days may bring home C$500 worth of goods duty free.
If you've been away less than 7 days but more than 48 hours, the duty-free allowance drops to C$200; if your trip lasts 24–48 hours, the allowance is C$50. You may not pool allowances with family members. Goods claimed under the C$500 exemption may follow you by mail; those claimed under the lesser exemptions must accompany you. Alcohol and tobacco products may be included in the 7-day and 48-hour exemptions but not in the 24-hour exemption. If you meet the age requirements of the province or territory through which you reenter Canada, you may bring in, duty free, 1.14 liters (40 imperial ounces) of wine or liquor *or* 24 12-ounce cans or bottles of beer or ale. If you are 16 or older you may bring in, duty free, 200 cigarettes and 50 cigars. Check ahead of time with Revenue Canada or the Department of Agriculture for policies regarding meat products, seeds, plants, and fruits.

You may send an unlimited number of gifts worth up to C$60 each duty-free to Canada. Label the package UNSOLICITED

GIFT—VALUE UNDER $60. Alcohol and to-bacco are excluded.

🛈 **Revenue Canada** ✉ 2265 St. Laurent Blvd. S, Ottawa, Ontario K1G 4K3 ☎ 613/993-0534, 800/461-9999 in Canada ⊕ www.ccra-adrc.gc.ca.

IN NEW ZEALAND
Homeward-bound residents 17 or older may bring back $700 worth of souvenirs and gifts. Your duty-free allowance also includes 4.5 liters of wine or beer; one 1,125-ml bottle of spirits; and either 200 cigarettes, 250 grams of tobacco, 50 cigars, or a combination of the three up to 250 grams. Prohibited items include meat products, seeds, plants, and fruits.

🛈 **New Zealand Customs** Head office ✉ The Customhouse, 17-21 Whitmore St., Box 2218, Wellington ☎ 09/300-5399 or 0800/428-786 ⊕ www.customs.govt.nz.

IN THE U.K.
If you are a U.K. resident and your journey was wholly within the European Union (EU), you won't have to pass through customs when you return to the United Kingdom. If you plan to bring back large quantities of alcohol or tobacco, check EU limits beforehand. In most cases, if you bring back more than 200 cigars, 800 cigarettes, 10 liters of spirits, and/or 90 liters of wine, you have to declare the goods upon return.

🛈 **HM Customs and Excise** ✉ Portcullis House, 21 Cowbridge Rd. E, Cardiff CF11 9SS ☎ 029/2038-6423 or 0845/010-9000 ⊕ www.hmce.gov.uk.

IN THE U.S.
U.S. residents who have been out of the country for at least 48 hours may bring home, for personal use, $400 worth of foreign goods duty-free, as long as they haven't used the $400 allowance or any part of it in the past 30 days. This exemption may include 1 liter of alcohol (for travelers 21 and older), 200 cigarettes, and 100 non-Cuban cigars. Family members from the same household who are traveling together may pool their $400 personal exemptions. For fewer than 48 hours, the duty-free allowance drops to $200, which may include 50 cigarettes, 10 non-Cuban cigars, and 150 milliliters of alcohol (or perfume containing alcohol). The $200 al-

lowance cannot be combined with other individuals' exemptions, and if you exceed it, the full value of all the goods will be taxed. Antiques, which the U.S. Customs Service defines as objects more than 100 years old, enter duty-free, as do original works of art done entirely by hand, including paintings, drawings, and sculptures.

You may also send packages home duty free: up to $200 worth of goods for personal use, with a limit of one parcel per addressee per day (except alcohol or tobacco products or perfume worth more than $5); label the package PERSONAL USE and attach a list of its contents and their retail value. Do not label the package UNSOLICITED GIFT or your duty-free exemption will drop to $100. Mailed items do not affect your duty-free allowance on your return.

🚩 **U.S. Customs Service** ✉ 1300 Pennsylvania Ave. NW, Washington, DC 20229 ☏ 202/354-1000 inquiries ⊕ www.customs.gov ✉ Complaints c/o ✉ Office of Regulations and Rulings ✉ Registration of equipment c/o ✉ Resource Management ☏ 202/927-0540.

DINING

Austria has the largest number of organic farms in Europe, as well as the most stringent food quality standards. (Finland comes in second, followed by Italy and Sweden, though they all fall far behind Austria; France, Spain, and the U.K. are at the bottom of the list.) An increasing number of restaurants use food and produce from local farmers, ensuring the freshest ingredients for their guests.

When dining out, you'll get the best value at simpler restaurants. Most post menus with prices outside. If you begin with the *Würstelstand* (sausage vendor) on the street, the next category would be the *Imbiss-Stube,* for simple, quick snacks. Many meat stores serve soups and a daily special at noon; a blackboard menu will be posted outside. A number of cafés also offer lunch, but watch the prices; some can turn out to be more expensive than restaurants. *Gasthäuser* are simple restaurants or country inns. Austrian hotels have some of the best restaurants in the country, often with outstanding chefs. In the past few years the restaurants along the autobahns

have developed into very good places to eat (besides being, in many cases, architecturally interesting). Some Austrian chain restaurants offer excellent value for the money, such as Wienerwald, which specializes in chicken dishes, and Nordsee, which has a wide selection of fish.

In all restaurants, be aware that the basket of bread put on your table isn't free. Most of the older-style Viennese restaurants charge €0.70–€1.25 for each roll that is eaten, but more and more establishments are beginning to charge a per-person cover charge—anywhere from €1.5 to €4—which includes all the bread you want, plus usually an herb spread and butter. Tap water (*Leitungswasser*) in Austria comes straight from the Alps and is among the purest in the world. Be aware, however, that a few restaurants in touristy areas are beginning to charge for tap water.

For a discussion of the delights of Austrian cuisine, *see* "Schnitzels, Strudels & Sachertortes" *in* Pleasures and Pastimes near the front of this book, along with the introduction to our Where to Eat chapter.

MEALTIMES

Besides the normal three meals—*Frühstück* (breakfast), *Mittagessen* (lunch), and *Abendessen* (dinner)—Austrians sometimes throw in a few snacks in between, or forego one meal for a snack. The day begins with a very early continental breakfast of rolls and coffee. *Gabelfrühstück* is a slightly more substantial breakfast with eggs or cold meat. A main meal is usually served between noon and 2, and an afternoon *Jause* (coffee with cake) is taken at teatime. Unless dining out, a light supper ends the day, usually between 6 and 9, but tending toward the later hour. Many restaurant kitchens close in the afternoon, but some post a notice saying DURCHGEHEND WARME KÜCHE, meaning that hot food is available even between regular mealtimes. In Vienna some restaurants go on serving until 1 and 2 AM, a tiny number also through the night. The rest of Austria is more conservative. Unless otherwise noted, the restaurants listed in this guide are open daily for lunch and dinner.

RESERVATIONS & DRESS

Reservations are always a good idea: we mention them only when they're essential or not accepted. Book as far ahead as you can, and reconfirm as soon as you arrive. We mention dress only when men are required to wear a jacket or a jacket and tie.

ELECTRICITY

To use your U.S.-purchased electric-powered equipment, **bring a converter and adapter.** The electrical current in Austria is 220 volts, 50 cycles alternating current (AC); wall outlets take continental-type plugs, with two round prongs. If your appliances are dual-voltage, you'll need only an adapter. Don't use 110-volt outlets marked FOR SHAVERS ONLY for high-wattage appliances such as blow-dryers. Most laptops operate equally well on 110 and 220 volts and so require only an adapter.

EMBASSIES

🚩 Australia **Embassy of Australia** ⊠ Mattiellistrasse 2-3, 4th District, Vienna ☎ 01/50674.
🚩 Canada **Embassy of Canada** ⊠ Laurenzerberg 2, on the 3rd floor of Hauptpost building complex, 1st District, Vienna ☎ 01/53138-3000.
🚩 New Zealand **Mission of New Zealand** ⊠ Mattiellistrasse 2-4, 4th District, Vienna ☎ 505-3021.
🚩 United Kingdom **Embassy of United Kingdom** ⊠ Jauresgasse 12, 3rd District, Vienna ☎ 01/71613-0.
🚩 United States **Embassy of the United States** ⊠ Boltzmanngasse 16, A-1090, 9th District, Vienna ☎ 31339-0. **Consulate of the U.S./Passport Division** ⊠ Gartenbaupromenade 2-4, A-1010, 1st District, Vienna ☎ 31339-0.

EMERGENCIES

On the street, some German phrases that may be needed in an emergency are: *Zur Hilfe!* (Help!), *Notfall* (emergency), *Rettungswagen* (ambulance), *Feuerwehr* (fire department), *Polizei* (police), *Arzt* (doctor), and *Krankenhaus* (hospital).
🚩 **Ambulance** ☎ 144. **Fire** ☎ 122. **Police** ☎ 133.

ENGLISH- & GERMAN-LANGUAGE MEDIA

The *International Herald Tribune, The Wall Street Journal,* and *USA Today* are readily available in most larger cities in Austria. For local Austria-specific information in English, the choice is more limited. For a vast selection of American magazines, go to the bookstore *Morawa* (⊠ Wollzeile 11, Vienna). There is no longer an exclusive English-language radio station in Austria. You can hear short English news broadcasts at 103.8 Mhz from early morning until 6 PM.

BOOKS

In Vienna and Salzburg it's fairly easy to find English-language bookstores. Bookstores in smaller towns sometimes have an English section or rack.
🚩 Local Resources **British Bookstore** ⊠ Weihburggasse 24-26, 1st District, Vienna ☎ 01/512-1945-0 ⊠ Mariahilferstrasse 4, 7th District, Vienna ☎ 01/522-6730. **Shakespeare & Co.** ⊠ Sterngasse 2, 1st District, Vienna ☎ 01/535-5053.

AUSTRIAN NEWSPAPERS & MAGAZINES

The most balanced coverage of any German newspaper, with the most sophisticated cultural coverage, is *Der Falter* (www.falter.at), which comes out on Wednesday. Even though the listings are in German, it's easy to understand. The most widely read Austrian German-language newspaper is the *Kronen Zeitung,* with a culture section on Friday. Like many of the other German newspapers, this is conservative in slant and offers what many will consider a reactionary political menu (along with a bevy of tabloid and sensationalistic photos). There is a daily newspaper in English for the international community here, *Austria Today* (www.austria-today.at). Popular magazines are readily available at Tabak shops and newspaper stands and include the international weekly editions of *Time* and *Newsweek,* European editions of the fashion magazines *Marie-Claire,* and *Elle* (in German), and *Cosmopolitan,* also in German. Also look for a good magazine about dining in Austria called *A La Carte,* but it's only in German.

RADIO & TELEVISION

For news and weather broadcasts in English on the hour from early morning until 6 PM, go to the eclectic rock music station

U4 at 103.8 Mhz. For classical music interrupted with a lot of German poetry readings, tune into *Radio Stephansdom* at 107.4 Mhz. *RTL* and *Radio Wien* offer American and British soft rock music at 92.9 Mhz and 89.9 Mhz, respectively. British and American pop can be found at *Energy,* 104.2 Mhz, and *Neue Antenne,* 102.5 Mhz. There are two non-cable television stations in Austria, the state-owned ORF 1 and ORF 2. Service is entirely in German, and American and English movies are dubbed in German. ORF 1 leans more toward sports events and children's shows, while ORF 2 schedules documentaries and Austrian and American TV series and films. A private television station, ATV (Austrian TV) was granted a license in 2002 but has yet to start broadcasting.

ETIQUETTE & BEHAVIOR

The most common form of greeting in Austria is *Grüss Gott,* which literally means "God greets you." When it comes to table manners, there are some surprising differences from American usage: Austrians eat hamburgers, french fries, and pizza with a knife and fork—and even sometimes ribs. Toothpicks are sometimes found on restaurant tables, and it is normal to see people clean their teeth after a meal, discreetly covering their mouth with their free hand. Austria is a dog-loving society and you will often find dogs accompanying their masters to restaurants—some even sharing the banquette with them. Dogs are almost always beautifully behaved and accustomed to going out.

Cigarette smoking is going strong in Austria, especially among the younger population. Though Ireland passed a no-smoking law in restaurants and pubs, and Italy bans smoking in many restaurants and bars, it is doubtful this will happen in Austria any time soon. The tobacco industry is subsidized by the government and very little advertising is done to discourage smoking.

If you're invited to an Austrian's home for dinner, do not arrive with only your appetite. It's proper to bring flowers to your hostess, but never red roses (which are reserved for lovers). Note that if you bring wine, it's considered a gift and is not served. Other little hostess gifts are considered appropriate, such as honey or chocolates.

Austrians are comfortable with nudity, and public and hotel saunas are used by both sexes; in such facilities, people are seldom clothed (though this is an option).

GAY & LESBIAN TRAVEL

Austria is a gay-tolerant country in general. In Vienna, the twice-monthly free magazine *Xtra!* runs a calendar of daily events and addresses. Also look for the *Vienna Gay Guide,* a map showing locations of gay-friendly bars, restaurants, hotels, and saunas. Tours of historical gay Vienna are offered by the tourist office. Check ⊕ www.info-wien.at. For additional information, check the Web site ⊕ www.gayguide.at.

⚑ Gay- & Lesbian-Friendly Travel Agencies **Different Roads Travel** ✉ 8383 Wilshire Blvd., Suite 902, Beverly Hills, CA 90211 ☎ 323/651-5557 or 800/429-8747 ᐧ 323/651-3678 ✆ leigh@west.tzell.com. **Kennedy Travel** ✉ 314 Jericho Turnpike, Floral Park, NY 11001 ☎ 516/352-4888 or 800/237-7433 ᐧ 516/354-8849 ✆ main@kennedytravel.com ⊕ www.kennedytravel.com. **Now, Voyager** ✉ 4406 18th St., San Francisco, CA 94114 ☎ 415/626-1169 or 800/255-6951 ᐧ 415/626-8626. **Skylink Travel and Tour** ✉ 1006 Mendocino Ave., Santa Rosa, CA 95401 ☎ 707/546-9888 or 800/225-5759 ᐧ 707/546-9891 ✆ skylinktvl@aol.com, serving lesbian travelers.

⚑ Local Resources **Homosexuelle Initiative (HOSI)** ✉ Novaragasse 40, A-1020 Vienna ☎ 01/216-6604 ⊕ www.hosi.at ✉ Müllner Haupstrasse 11, A-5020 Salzburg ☎ 0662/435927 ᐧ 0662/435927-27. **Referat für gleichgeschlechtliche Lebensweisen** ✉ Rechbauerstrasse 12, A-8010 Graz ☎ 0316/873-5111.

HEALTH
MEDICAL PLANS

No one plans to get sick while traveling, but it happens, so **consider signing up with a medical-assistance company.** Members get doctor referrals, emergency evacuation or repatriation, 24-hour telephone hotlines for medical consultation, cash for emergencies, and other personal and legal assistance. Coverage varies by plan, so **review the benefits of each carefully.** English-speaking doctors are readily available, and health care in Austria is usually excellent.

OVER-THE-COUNTER REMEDIES
You must buy over-the-counter remedies in an *Apotheke,* and most personnel speak enough English to understand what you need. Pain relievers are much milder than those available in the U.S.

SHOTS & MEDICATIONS
No special shots are required before visiting Austria, but if you will be cycling or hiking through the eastern or southeastern parts of the country, get inoculated against encephalitis; it can be carried by ticks.

HOLIDAYS
All banks and shops are closed on national holidays: New Year's Day; Jan. 6, Epiphany; Easter Sunday and Monday; May 1, May Day; Ascension Day; Pentecost Sunday and Monday; Corpus Christi; Aug. 15, Assumption; Oct. 26, National Holiday; Nov. 1, All Saints' Day; Dec. 8, Immaculate Conception; Dec. 25–26, Christmas. Museums are open on most holidays but closed on Good Friday, on Dec. 24 and 25, and New Year's Day. Banks and offices are closed on Dec. 8, but most shops are open.

LANGUAGE
German is the official national language in Austria. In larger cities and in most resort areas you will usually have no problem finding people who speak English; hotel staffs in particular speak it reasonably well, and many young Austrians speak it at least passably. However, travelers do report that they often find themselves in stores, restaurants, and railway and bus stations where it's hard to find someone who speaks English—so it's best to have some native phrases up your sleeve (*see* Chapter 8). Note that all public announcements on trams, subways, and buses are in German. Train announcements are usually given in English as well, but if you have any questions, try to get answers before boarding.

LANGUAGES FOR TRAVELERS
A phrase book and language-tape set can help get you started.

📕 Phrase Book & Language-Tape Set *Fodor's German for Travelers* ☎ 800/733-3000 in U.S., 800/668-4247 in Canada ✉ $7 for phrasebook, $16.95 for audio set.

LODGING
You can live like a king in a real castle in Austria or get by on a modest budget. Starting at the lower end, you can find a room in a private house or on a farm, or dormitory space in a youth hostel. Next up the line come the simpler pensions, many of them identified as a *Frühstück-spension* (bed-and-breakfast). Then come the Gasthäuser, the simpler country inns. The fancier pensions in the cities can often cost as much as hotels; the difference lies in the services they offer. Most pensions, for example, do not staff the front desk around the clock. Among the hotels, you can find accommodations ranging from the most modest, with a shower and toilet down the hall, to the most elegant, with every possible amenity.

The lodgings we list are the cream of the crop in each price category. We always list the facilities that are available—but we don't specify whether they cost extra: when pricing accommodations, always ask what's included and what costs extra (two items that occasionally fall into the latter category are parking and breakfast). Properties marked ✕🏨 are lodging establishments whose restaurants warrant a special trip.

Assume that hotels operate on the European Plan (EP, with no meal provided) unless we note that they use the Breakfast Plan (BP), Modified American Plan (MAP, with breakfast and dinner daily, known as demi-pension (*halb pension*), or Full American Plan (FAP, or *voll pension,* with three meals a day). Higher prices (inquire when booking) prevail for any meal plans. Increasingly, more and more hotels in the lower to middle price range are including breakfast with the basic room charge, but check when booking. Room rates for hotels in the rural countryside can often include breakfast and one other meal (in rare cases, all three meals are included). Happily, many of these lodgings will also offer a breakfast buffet–only rate if requested.

Faxing is the easiest way to contact the hotel (the staff is probably more likely to read English than to understand it over the phone long-distance), though calling also works, but using e-mail messages is increasingly popular. In your fax (or over the phone), specify the exact dates you want to stay at the hotel (when you will arrive and when you will check out); the size of the room you want and how many people will be sleeping there; what kind of bed you want (single or double, twin beds or double, etc.); and whether you want a bathroom with a shower or bathtub (or both). You might also ask if a deposit (or your credit card number) is required and, if so, what happens if you cancel. Request that the hotel fax you back so that you have a written confirmation of your reservation in hand when you arrive at the hotel.

Here is a list of German words that can come in handy when booking a room: air-conditioning (*Klimaanlage*); private bath (*privat Bad*); bathtub (*Badewanne*); shower (*Dusche*); double bed (*Doppelbett*); twin beds (*Einzelbetten*).

RESERVING A ROOM IN VIENNA

If you need a room upon arrival and have not made previous reservations, go to Information-Zimmernachweis, operated by the Verkehrsbüro in the Westbahnhof and in the Südbahnhof. At the airport, the information and room-reservation office in the arrivals hall is open daily 8:30 AM–9 PM. If you're driving into Vienna, get information or book rooms through the Vienna Tourist Board's hotel assistance hotline. It's open daily from 9–7.

⚐ Information-Zimmernachweis ☎ 01/892-3392 in Westbahnhof, 930-0031-05-0 in Südbahnhof. **Vienna Tourist Board's hotel assistance hotline** ☎ 01/24555 🖷 01/24-555-666 ⊕ www.info.wien.at.

APARTMENT & CHALET RENTALS

If you want a home base that's roomy enough for a family and comes with cooking facilities, **consider a furnished rental.**

These can save you money, especially if you're traveling with a large group of people. Home-exchange directories list rentals (often second homes owned by prospective house swappers), and some services search for a house or apartment for you (even a castle, if that's your fancy) and handle the paperwork. Some send an illustrated catalog; others send photographs only of specific properties, sometimes at a charge. Up-front registration fees may apply.

⚐ International Agents Drawbridge to Europe ✉ 5456 Adams Rd., Talent, OR 97540 ☎ 541/512-8927 or 888/268-1148 🖷 541/512-0978 ✍ requests@drawbridgetoeurope.com ⊕ www.drawbridgetoeurope.com. **Hometours International** ⌂ Box 11503, Knoxville, TN 37939 ☎ 865/690-8484 or 800/367-4668 ✍ hometours@aol.com ⊕ http:thor.he.net/~hometour. **Interhome** ✉ 1990 N.E. 163rd St., Suite 110, North Miami Beach, FL 33162 ☎ 305/940-2299 or 800/882-6864 🖷 305/940-2911 ⊕ www.interhome.com. **Villas International** ✉ 4340 Redwood Hwy., Suite D309, San Rafael, CA 94903 ☎ 415/499-9490 or 800/221-2260 🖷 415/499-9491 ⊕ www.villasintl.com.

CASTLES

⚐ Schlosshotels und Herrenhäuser in Österreich ✉ Moosstrasse. 60, A-5020 Salzburg ☎ 0662/8306-8141 🖷 0662/8306-8161 ⊕ www.schlosshotels.co.at.

HOME EXCHANGES

If you would like to exchange your home for someone else's, **join a home-exchange organization,** which will send you its updated listings of available exchanges for a year and will include your own listing in at least one of them. It's up to you to make specific arrangements.

⚐ Exchange Clubs HomeLink International ⌂ Box 650, Key West, FL 33041 ☎ 305/294-7766 or 800/638-3841 🖷 305/294-1448 ✍ usa@homelink.org ⊕ www.homelink.org 🖃 $98 per year. **Intervac U.S.** ⌂ Box 590504, San Francisco, CA 94159 ☎ 800/756-4663 🖷 415/435-7440 ⊕ www.intervac.com 🖃 $89 per year includes two catalogues.

HOSTELS

No matter what your age, you can **save on lodging costs by staying at hostels.** In some 5,000 locations in more than 70 countries around the world, Hostelling

International (HI), the umbrella group for a number of national youth-hostel associations, offers single-sex, dorm-style beds and, at many hostels, rooms for couples and family accommodations. Membership in any HI national hostel association, open to travelers of all ages, allows you to stay in HI-affiliated hostels at member rates; one-year membership is about $25 for adults (C$35 for a two-year minimum membership in Canada, £13 in the U.K., A$52 in Australia, and NZ$40 in New Zealand); hostels run about $10–$30 per night. Members have priority if the hostel is full; they're also eligible for discounts around the world, even on rail and bus travel in some countries.

Austria has more than 100 government-sponsored youth hostels, for which you need an International Youth Hostel Federation membership card. Inexpensively priced, these hostels are run by the Österreichischer Jugendherbergsverband and are popular with the back-pack crowd, so be sure to reserve in advance.

☐ In Austria Österreichischer Jugendherbergsverband ⊠ Schottenring 28, A-1010 Vienna ☎ 01/533-53-53 🖷 01/535-0861.

☐ Organizations Hostelling International–American Youth Hostels ⊠ 733 15th St. NW, Suite 840, Washington, DC 20005 ☎ 202/783-6161 🖷 202/783-6171. Hostelling International–Canada ⊠ 400-205 Catherine St., Ottawa, Ontario K2P 1C3 ☎ 613/237-7884 or 800/663-5777 🖷 613/237-7868. Youth Hostel Association of England and Wales ⊠ Trevelyan House, Dimple Rd., Matlock, Derbyshire DE4 3YH, U.K. ☎ 0870/870-8808 🖷 0169/592-702 ⊕ www.yha.org.uk.

HOTELS

See the hotel reviews in Chapters 3, 6, and 7.

MAIL & SHIPPING

Post offices are scattered throughout every district in Vienna and are recognizable by a square yellow sign that says "Post." They are usually open weekdays 9–noon and 2–6, Saturday 8–10 AM. The **main post office** (⊠ Fleischmarkt 19, A-1010 Vienna), near Schwedenplatz, is open 24 hours daily. For overnight services, Federal Express, DHL, and UPS service Vienna

and Austria; check with your hotel concierge for the nearest address and telephone number.

POSTAL RATES

All mail goes by air, so there's no supplement on letters or postcards. Within Europe, a letter or postcard of up to 20 grams (about ¾ ounce) costs €0.55. To the United States or Canada, a letter of up to 20 grams takes €1.25 for airmail. If in doubt, mail your letters from a post office and have the weight checked. The Austrian post office also adheres strictly to a size standard; if your letter or card is outside the norm, you'll have to pay a surcharge. Postcards via airmail to the United States or Canada need €1.25. Always place an airmail sticker on your letters or cards. Shipping packages from Austria to destinations outside the country is extremely expensive.

RECEIVING MAIL

When you don't know where you'll be staying, **American Express** (⊠ Kärntnerstrasse 21–23, A-1015 Vienna ☎ 01/515-4077–0 ⊠ Mozartplatz 5, A-5020 Salzburg ☎ 0662/8080–0 ⊠ Bürgerstrasse 14, A-4021 Linz ☎ 0732/669013) mail service is a great convenience, with no charge to anyone either holding an American Express credit card or carrying American Express traveler's checks. Pick up your mail at the local offices. You can also have mail held at any **Austrian post office** (⊠ Fleischmarkt 19, A-1010 Vienna ☎ 01/515–09–0); letters should be marked *Poste Restante* or *Postlagernd*. You will be asked for identification when you collect mail. In Vienna, if not addressed to a specific district post office, this service is handled through the main post office.

MONEY MATTERS

Prices throughout this guide are given for adults. Substantially reduced fees are almost always available for children, students, and senior citizens. For information on taxes, *see* Taxes, *below*.

ATMS

Called *Bankomats* and fairly common throughout Austria, **ATMs are one of the**

easiest ways to get euros. Although ATM transaction fees may be higher abroad than at home, banks usually offer excellent, wholesale exchange rates through ATMs. Cirrus and Plus locations are easily found throughout large city centers, and even in small towns. If you have any trouble finding one, ask your hotel concierge. Note, too, that you may have better luck with ATMs if you're using a credit card or debit card that is also a Visa or MasterCard rather than just your bank card.

To get cash at ATMs in Austria, **your personal identification number (PIN) must be four digits long.** Note, too, that you may be charged by your bank for using ATMs overseas; inquire at your bank about charges.

🔢 **ATM Locations** Cirrus ☎ 800/424–7787. **Plus** ☎ 800/843-7587.

COSTS

A cup of coffee in a café will cost about €3–€4; a half-liter of draft beer, €3–€4; a glass of wine, €4–€8; a Coca-Cola, €3; an open-face sandwich, €3.50; a mid-range theater ticket €20; a concert ticket €30–€50; an opera ticket €40 upward; a 1-mi taxi ride, €4. Outside the hotels, laundering a shirt costs about €4; dry cleaning a suit costs around €12–€18; a dress, €9–€12. A shampoo and set for a woman will cost around €25–€35, a manicure about €12–€15; a man's haircut about €25–€35.

CREDIT & DEBIT CARDS

Both credit and debit cards will get you cash advances at ATMs worldwide if your card is properly programmed with your personal identification number (PIN). Both offer excellent, wholesale exchange rates. And both protect you against unauthorized use if the card is lost or stolen. Your liability is limited to $50 as long as you report the card missing. Be aware that several U.S. credit card companies are now adding a 2%–3% conversion surcharge on all charges made in Europe. This can really add up on big purchases and hotel charges. Check with your credit card company, so you'll know in advance.

Throughout this guide, the following abbreviations are used: **AE,** American Express; **DC,** Diners Club; **MC,** MasterCard; and **V,** Visa.

🔢 Reporting Lost Cards American Express ☎ 336/939–1111 or 336/668–5309 call collect. **Diners Club** ☎ 303/799-1504 call collect. **MasterCard** ☎ 0800/90–1387. **Visa** ☎ 0800/90–1179, 410/581-9994 collect.

CURRENCY

As it is a member of the European Union (EU), Austria's unit of currency is the euro. Under the euro system there are eight coins: 1 and 2 euros, plus 1, 2, 5, 10, 20, and 50 euro cent, or cents of the euro. All coins have one side that has the value of the euro on it and the other side with each country's own unique national symbol. There are seven banknotes: 5, 10, 20, 50, 100, 200, and 500 euros. Banknotes are the same for all EU countries. Please note that at this writing (fall 2004), the euro was stronger than the dollar, but fluctuating considerably. At this writing the exchange rate was about €1.20 to the U.S. dollar, €0.67 to the British pound, €1.65 to the Canadian dollar, €1.70 to the Australian dollar, €1.94 to the New Zealand dollar. These rates can and will vary.

CURRENCY EXCHANGE

Generally, exchange rates are far less favorable outside of Austria, and there is no need to exchange money prior to your arrival. ATMs are throughout city centers. Although fees charged for ATM transactions may be higher abroad than at home, Cirrus and Plus exchange rates are excellent, because they are based on wholesale rates offered only by major banks. Otherwise, the most favorable rates are through a bank. You won't do as well at exchange booths in airports or rail and bus stations, in hotels, in restaurants, or in stores, although you may find their hours more convenient than at a bank. Now that the euro has become accepted as a standard of exchange, many currency conversions have been radically simplified.

🔢 Exchange Services Chase *Currency To Go* ☎ 800/935–9935, 935–9935 in NY, NJ, and CT. International Currency Express ☎ 888/278-6628 for orders.

TRAVELER'S CHECKS

Do you need traveler's checks? It depends on where you're headed. If you're going to rural areas and small towns, go with cash; traveler's checks are best used in cities (although you can always rely on the corner ATM machine to supply ready euros). Lost or stolen checks can usually be replaced within 24 hours. To ensure a speedy refund, buy your own traveler's checks—don't let someone else pay for them; irregularities like this can cause delays. The person who bought the checks should make the call to request a refund.

PACKING

PACKING LIST

Dressing in Austria ranges from conservative to casual, and is somewhat dependent on age. Middle-age and older people tend to dress conventionally. Jeans and tennis shoes on women are as rare as loud sport shirts are on men. Young people tend to be very trendy, and the trend is basically U.S., with kids in baseball caps, baggy trousers, loud shirts with all kinds of things written on them in (sometimes poor) English. In the country or more rural areas of, say, Styria or Burgenland, things are a little less loud. Jeans are ubiquitous in Austria as elsewhere, but are considered inappropriate at concerts (other than pop) or formal restaurants. For concerts and opera, women may want a skirt or dress, and men a jacket; even in summer, gala performances at small festivals tend to be dressy. And since an evening outside at a Heuriger (wine garden) may be on your agenda, be sure to take a sweater or light wrap. Unless you're staying in an expensive hotel or will be in one place for more than a day or two, take hand-washables; laundry service gets complicated. Austria is a walking country, in cities and mountains alike. If intending to hike in the mountains, bring boots that rise above the ankle and have sturdy soles. For lots of city walking a good pair of sports shoes is needed.

Mountainous areas are bright, so bring sunscreen lotion, even in winter. Consider packing a small folding umbrella for the odd deluge, or a waterproof windbreaker of sorts. Sunglasses are a must as well, and if you intend to go high up in the mountains, make sure your sunglasses are good and prevent lateral rays. Mosquitoes can become quite a bother in summer around the lakes and along the rivers, especially the Danube and the swampy regions created by its old arms. Bring some good insect repellent.

In your carry-on luggage, **pack an extra pair of eyeglasses or contact lenses and enough of any medication you take** to last a few days longer than the entire trip. You may also ask your doctor to write a spare prescription using the drug's generic name, since brand names may vary from country to country. In luggage to be checked, **never pack prescription drugs or valuables.** To avoid customs delays, carry medications in their original packaging. And don't forget to carry with you the addresses of offices that handle refunds of lost traveler's checks.

PASSPORTS & VISAS

When traveling internationally, **carry your passport even if you don't need one** (it's always the best form of ID) and **make two photocopies of the data page** (one for someone at home and another for you, carried separately from your passport). If you lose your passport, promptly call the nearest embassy or consulate and the local police.

ENTERING AUSTRIA

U.S., Australian, Canadian, New Zealand, and U.K. citizens need only a valid passport to enter Austria for stays of up to three months.

PASSPORT OFFICES

The best time to apply for a passport or to renew is in fall and winter. Before any trip, check your passport's expiration date, and, if necessary, renew it as soon as possible. (Some countries won't allow you to enter on a passport that's due to expire in six months or less.)

🛂 Australian Citizens Australian Passport Office ☎ 131–232 ⊕ www.passports.gov.au.
🛂 Canadian Citizens Passport Office to mail in applications ✉ Department of Foreign Affairs and International Trade, Ottawa, Ontario K1A 0G3 ☎ 800/567–6868 toll-free in Canada or 819/994–3500 ⊕ www.dfait-maeci.gc.ca/passport.

New Zealand Citizens **New Zealand Passport Office** ☎ 0800/22-5050 or 04/474-8100 ⊕ www.passports.govt.nz.

U.K. Citizens **London Passport Office** ☎ 0990/210-410 ⊕ www.passport.gov.uk for fees and documentation requirements and to request an emergency passport.

U.S. Citizens **National Passport Information Center** ☎ 900/225-5674 ⊠ 35¢ per minute for automated service or $1.05 per minute for operator service ⊕ www.travel.state.gov.

SENIOR-CITIZEN TRAVEL

To qualify for age-related discounts, **mention your senior-citizen status up front** when booking hotel reservations (not when checking out) and before you're seated in restaurants (not when paying the bill). When renting a car, ask about promotional car-rental discounts, which can be cheaper than senior-citizen rates. Austria has so many senior citizens that facilities almost everywhere cater to the needs of older travelers, with discounts for rail travel and museum entry. Check with the Austrian National Tourist Office to find what form of identification is required, but generally if you're 65 or over (women 60), once you're in Austria the railroads will issue you a *Seniorenpass* (you'll need a passport photo and passport or other proof of age) entitling you to the senior-citizen discounts regardless of nationality.

Educational Programs **Elderhostel** ⊠ 75 Federal St., 3rd fl., Boston, MA 02110 ☎ 877/426-8056 ⊟ 877/426-2166 ⊕ www.elderhostel.org. **Interhostel** ⊠ University of New Hampshire, 6 Garrison Ave., Durham, NH 03824 ☎ 603/862-1147 or 800/733-9753 ⊟ 603/862-1113 ⊕ www.learn.unh.edu.

STUDENTS IN AUSTRIA

To save money, **look into deals available through student-oriented travel agencies.** To qualify you'll need a bona fide student ID card. Members of international student groups are also eligible. Information on student tickets, fares, and lodgings is available from Jugend Info Wien (Youth Information Center) in Vienna.

Local Resources **Jugend Info Wien** ⊠ Babenbergerstrasse 1, Vienna ☎ 01/1799 ⊟ 01/585-2499 🕐 Mon.-Sat., noon-7 PM.

IDs & Services **STA Travel** ⊠ CIEE, 205 E. 42nd St., 14th fl., New York, NY 10017 ☎ 212/822-2700 or 888/268-6245 ⊟ 212/822-2699 ✉ info@councilexchanges.org ⊕ www.councilexchanges.org for mail orders only, in the U.S. **Travel Cuts** ⊠ 187 College St., Toronto, Ontario M5T 1P7, Canada ☎ 416/979-2406 or 888/838-2887 ⊟ 416/979-8167 ⊕ www.travelcuts.com.

Student Tours **AESU Travel** ⊠ 2 Hamill Rd., Suite 248, Baltimore, MD 21210-1807 ☎ 410/323-4416 or 800/638-7640 ⊟ 410/323-4498. **Contiki Holidays** ⊠ 300 Plaza Alicante, Suite 900, Garden Grove, CA 92840 ☎ 714/740-0808 or 800/266-8454 ⊟ 714/740-2034.

TAXES
VALUE-ADDED TAX

The Value Added Tax (V.A.T.) in Austria is 20% generally but only 10% on food and clothing. If you are planning to take your purchases with you when you leave Austria (export them), you can get a refund. The shop will give you a form or a receipt, which must be presented at the border, where the wares are inspected. The Austrian government will send you your refund, minus a processing fee.

Wine and spirits are heavily taxed—nearly half of the sale price goes to taxes. For every contract signed in Austria (for example, car-rental agreements), you pay an extra 1% tax to the government, so tax on a rental car is 21%.

Global Refund is a V.A.T. refund service that makes getting your money back hassle-free. The service is available Europe-wide at 130,000 affiliated stores. In participating stores, **ask for the Global Refund form** (called a Shopping Cheque). Have it stamped like any customs form by customs officials when you leave the European Union. Then take the form to one of the more than 700 Global Refund counters—at every major airport and border crossing—and your money will be refunded on the spot in the form of cash, check, or a refund to your credit-card account (minus a small percentage for processing).

Global Refund (⊠ 707 Summer St., Stamford, CT 06901 ☎ 800/566-9828 ⊟ 203/674-8709 ✉ taxfree@us.globalrefund.com ⊕ www.globalrefund.com).

TELEPHONES
AREA & COUNTRY CODES

The country code for Austria is 43. When dialing an Austrian number from abroad, drop the initial 0 from the local Austrian area code. For instance, the full number to dial for the Hotel Palais Schwarzenberg in Vienna from America is 011 (international dial code)–43 (Austria's country code)–1 (Vienna's full city code is 01, but drop the "0")—798–4515 (the hotel number). All numbers given in this guide include the city or town area code; if you are calling within that city or town, dial the local number only.

DIRECTORY & OPERATOR INFORMATION

For information in EU and neighboring countries, dial 118877; for information outside Europe, dial 0900/118877. Most operators speak English; if yours doesn't, you'll be passed along to one who does.

INTERNATIONAL CALLS

You can dial direct to almost any point on the globe from Austria. However, it costs more to telephone from Austria than it does to telephone to Austria. Calls from post offices are always the least expensive and you can get helpful assistance in placing a long-distance call; in large cities, these centers at main post offices are open around the clock. To use a post office phone, you first go to the counter to be directed to a certain telephone cabin; after your call, you return to the counter and pay your bill.

To make a collect call—you can't do this from pay phones—dial the operator and ask for an *R-Gespräch* (pronounced air-ga-*shprayk*). Most operators speak English; if yours doesn't, you'll be passed to one who does.

The international access code for the United States and Canada is 001, followed by the area code and number. For Great Britain, first dial 0044, then the city code without the usual "0" (171 or 181 for London), and the number. Other country and many city codes are given in the front of telephone books (in Vienna, in the A-H book).

LOCAL CALLS

When making a local call in Vienna, **dial the number without the city prefix.** A local call costs €0.20 for the first minute, and €0.20 for every three minutes thereafter.

LONG-DISTANCE CALLS

When placing a long-distance call to a destination within Austria, you'll need to know the local area codes, which can be found by consulting the telephone numbers that are listed in this guide's regional chapters (for instance, 0662 for Salzburg and 02711 for Dürnstein in the Danube Valley). When dialing from outside Austria, the 0 should be left out. Note that calls within Austria are one-third cheaper between 6 PM and 8 AM on weekdays and from 1 PM on Saturday to 8 AM on Monday.

LONG-DISTANCE SERVICES

AT&T and MCI access codes make calling long distance relatively convenient, but you may find the local access number blocked in many hotel rooms. First ask the hotel operator to connect you. If the hotel operator balks, ask for an international operator, or dial the international operator yourself. One way to improve your odds of getting connected to your long-distance carrier is to travel with more than one company's calling card (a hotel may block Sprint, for example, but not MCI). If all else fails, call from a pay phone.

🖪 Access Codes **AT&T Direct** ☎ 01/0800-200-288, 800/435-0812 for other areas. **MCI WorldPhone** ☎ 0800-200-235, 800/444-4141 for other areas.

PHONE CARDS

If you plan to make calls from pay phones, a *Telephon Wertkarte* is a convenience. You can buy this electronic phone card at any post office for €6.90 or €3.60, which allows you to use the card at any SOS, or credit-card phone booth. You simply insert the card and dial; the cost of the call is automatically deducted from the card, and a digital window on the phone tells you how many units you have left (these are not minutes). A few public phones in the cities also take American Express, Diners Club, MasterCard, and Visa credit cards.

PUBLIC & CELL PHONES

Cell phones (called "Handys") are extremely popular in Austria for everyone over the age of 5. As a result, coin-operated pay telephones are dwindling in number, and if you're lucky enough to find one, it may be out-of-order or available only for emergency calls. But if you find one that works, a local call costs €0.20 for the first scant minute. Quickly add another €0.10 before you are cut off. If there is no response, your coin will be returned into the bin to the lower left. Most pay phones have instructions in English. When dialing an Austrian "Handy" phone from abroad (generally 0676, 0699, or 0664), dial 00–43, then the number without the 0. Faxes can be sent from post offices and received as well, but neither service is very cheap.

TIME

The time difference between New York and Austria is 6 hours (so when it's 1 PM in New York, it's 7 PM in Vienna). The time difference between London and Vienna is 1 hour; between Sydney and Vienna, 14 hours; and between Auckland and Vienna, 13 hours.

TIPPING

Although virtually all hotels and restaurants include service charges in their rates, tipping is still customary, but at a level lower than in the United States. Tip the hotel doorman €1 per bag, and the porter who brings your bags to the room another €1 per bag. In very small country inns such tips are not expected but are appreciated. In family-run establishments, tips are generally not given to immediate family members, only to employees. Tip the hotel concierge only for special services or in response to special requests. Room service gets €1 for snacks or ice, €2 for full meals. Maids normally get no tip unless your stay is a week or more or service has been special.

In restaurants, tip about 5%–7%. You can tip a little more if you've received exceptional service. Big tips are not usual in Austrian restaurants, since 10% has already been included in the prices. Checkroom attendants get €1–€2, depending on the locale. Washroom attendants get about €0.50. Wandering musicians and the piano player get €2, €5 if they've filled a number of requests.

Round up taxi fares to the next €0.50; a minimum €0.50 tip is customary. If the driver offers (or you ask for) special assistance, such as carrying your bags beyond the curb, an added tip of €0.50–€1 is in order.

TOURS & PACKAGES

VISITING AUSTRIA

Buying a prepackaged tour or independent vacation can make your trip to Austria less expensive and more hassle-free. Because everything is prearranged, you'll spend less time planning. Operators that handle several hundred thousand travelers per year can use their purchasing power to give you a good price. Their high volume may also indicate financial stability. But some small companies provide more personalized service; because they tend to specialize, they may also be more knowledgeable about a given area.

BOOKING WITH AN AGENT

Travel agents are excellent resources. But it's a good idea to collect brochures from several agencies as some agents' suggestions may be influenced by relationships with tour and package firms that reward them for volume sales. If you have a special interest, **find an agent with expertise in that area**; ASTA (*see* Travel Agencies, *below*) has a database of specialists worldwide.

Make sure your travel agent knows the accommodations and other services of the place they're recommending. Ask about the hotel's location, room size, beds, and whether it has a pool, room service, or programs for children, if you care about these. Has your agent been there in person or sent others whom you can contact?

Do some homework on your own, too: local tourism boards can provide information about lesser-known and small-niche operators, some of which may sell only direct.

BUYER BEWARE

Every year consumers are stranded or lose their money when tour operators—even large ones with excellent reputations—go out of business. So **check out the operator.** Ask several travel agents about its reputation, and try to **book with a company that has a consumer-protection program.** (Look for information in the company's brochure.)

In the United States, members of the National Tour Association and the United States Tour Operators Association are required to set aside funds to cover your payments and travel arrangements in the event that the company defaults. It's also a good idea to choose a company that participates in the American Society of Travel Agents' Tour Operator Program (TOP); ASTA will act as mediator in any disputes between you and your tour operator.

Tour-Operator Recommendations American Society of Travel Agents (*see* Travel Agencies, *below*). **National Tour Association** (NTA) ⊠ 546 E. Main St., Lexington, KY 40508 ☎ 606/226-4444 or 800/682-8886 ⊕ www.ntaonline.com. **United States Tour Operators Association** (USTOA) ⊠ 342 Madison Ave., Suite 1522, New York, NY 10173 ☎ 212/599-6599 or 800/468-7862 ⊕ 212/599-6744 ✉ ustoa@aol.com ⊕ www.ustoa.com.

COSTS

The more your package or tour includes, the better you can predict the ultimate cost of your vacation. Make sure you know exactly what is covered, and **beware of hidden costs.** Are taxes, tips, and service charges included? Transfers and baggage handling? Entertainment and excursions? These can add up. Prices for packages and tours are usually quoted per person, based on two sharing a room. If traveling solo, you may be required to pay the full double-occupancy rate. Some operators eliminate this surcharge if you agree to be matched with a roommate of the same sex, even if one is not found by departure time.

GROUP TOURS

Among companies that sell tours to Austria, the following are nationally known, have a proven reputation, and offer plenty of options.

Super-Deluxe Abercrombie & Kent ⊠ 1520 Kensington Rd., Oak Brook, IL 60521-2141 ☎ 630/954-2944 or 800/323-7308 ⊕ 630/954-3324. **Trav-**

coa ⊠ Box 2630, 2350 S.E. Bristol St., Newport Beach, CA 92660 ☎ 714/476-2800 or 800/992-2003 ⊕ 714/476-2538.

Deluxe Globus ⊠ 5301 S. Federal Circle, Littleton, CO 80123-2980 ☎ 303/797-2800 or 800/221-0090 ⊕ 303/347-2080. **Maupintour** ⊠ 1515 St. Andrews Dr., Lawrence, KS 66047 ☎ 785/843-1211 or 800/255-4266 ⊕ 785/843-8351. **Tauck Tours** ⊠ Box 5027, 276 Post Rd. W, Westport, CT 06881-5027 ☎ 203/226-6911 or 800/468-2825 ⊕ 203/221-6866.

First-Class Brendan Tours ⊠ 15137 Califa St., Van Nuys, CA 91411 ☎ 818/785-9696 or 800/421-8446 ⊕ 818/902-9876. **Caravan Tours** ⊠ 401 N. Michigan Ave., Chicago, IL 60611 ☎ 312/321-9800 or 800/227-2826 ⊕ 312/321-9845. **Collette Tours** ⊠ 162 Middle St., Pawtucket, RI 02860 ☎ 401/728-3805 or 800/340-5158 ⊕ 401/728-4745. **DER Travel Services** ⊠ 9501 W. Devon Ave., Rosemont, IL 60018 ☎ 800/937-1235 ⊕ 847/692-4141, 800/282-7474, 800/860-9944 for brochures. **Gadabout Tours** ⊠ 700 E. Tahquitz Canyon Way, Palm Springs, CA 92262-6767 ☎ 619/325-5556 or 800/952-5068. **Trafalgar Tours** ⊠ 11 E. 26th St., New York, NY 10010 ☎ 212/689-8977 or 800/854-0103 ⊕ 800/457-6644.

Budget Cosmos (*see* Globus, *above*). **Trafalgar Tours** (*see above*).

THEME TRIPS

Barge/River Cruises Abercrombie & Kent (*see* Group Tours, *above*). **KD River Cruises of Europe** ⊠ 2500 Westchester Ave., Purchase, NY 10577 ☎ 914/696-3600 or 800/346-6525 ⊕ 914/696-0833 ⊕ www.abercrombiekent.com. **Annemarie Victory Organization** ⊠ 136 E. 64th St., New York, NY 10021 ☎ 212/486-0353 ⊕ 212/751-3149 ⊕ www.annemarievictory.com offers luxury cruises on the River Cloud liner up and down the Danube. **Smolka Tours** ⊠ 82 Riveredge Rd., Tinton Falls, NJ 07724 ☎ 732/576-8813 or 800/722-0057 ⊕ www.smolkatours.com/ offers a Beautiful Blue Danube Cruise.

Bicycling Backroads ⊠ 801 Cedar St., Berkeley, CA 94710-1800 ☎ 510/527-1555 or 800/462-2848 ⊕ 510/527-1444. **Butterfield & Robinson** ⊠ 70 Bond St., Toronto, Ontario, Canada M5B 1X3 ☎ 416/864-1354 or 800/678-1147 ⊕ 416/864-0541 ⊕ www.butterfield.com. **Euro-Bike Tours** ✉ Box 990, De Kalb, IL 60115 ☎ 800/321-6060 ⊕ 815/758-8851. **VBT (Vermont Biking Tours)** ⊠ 614 Monkton Rd., Bristol, VT 05443 ☎ 800/245-3868 ⊕ www.vbt.com offers a spectacular Salzburg Sojourn tour.

🎄 Christmas/New Year's **Annemarie Victory Organization** ✉ 136 E. 64th St., New York, NY 10021 ☎ 212/486-0353 ☎ 212/751-3149 ⊕ www.annemarievictory.com is known for its spectacular "New Year's Eve Ball in Vienna" excursion. This highly respected organization has been selling out this tour—which includes deluxe rooms at the Bristol, the Imperial Palace Ball, and a Konzerthaus New Year's Day concert—for 10 years running. In the 1990's, Annemarie Victory premiered a "Christmas in Salzburg" trip, with rooms at the Goldener Hirsch and a side trip to the Silent Night Chapel in Oberndorf. **Smolka Tours** (*see* Barge/River Cruises, *above*) has also conducted festive holiday-season tours that included concerts, gala balls, and the famous Christmas Markets of Vienna and Salzburg.

🥾 Hiking/Walking **Alpine Adventure Trails Tours** ✉ 322 Pio Nono Ave., Macon, GA 31204 ☎ 912/478-4007. **Mountain Travel-Sobek** ✉ 6420 Fairmount Ave., El Cerrito, CA 94530 ☎ 510/527-8100 or 800/227-2384 ☎ 510/525-7710.

🧗 Mountain Climbing **Mountain Travel-Sobek** (*see* Hiking/Walking, *above*).

🎵 Music **Dailey-Thorp Travel** ✉ 330 W. 58th St., #610, New York, NY 10019-1817 ☎ 212/307-1555 or 800/998-4677 ☎ 212/974-1420 ⊕ www.daileythorp.com. **Smolka Tours** (*see* Barge/River Cruises, *above*).

TRAIN TRAVEL

ARRIVING IN VIENNA

Trains from Germany, Switzerland, and western Austria arrive at the Westbahnhof (West Station), on Europaplatz, where Mariahilferstrasse crosses the Gürtel. If you're coming from Italy or Hungary, you'll generally arrive at the Südbahnhof (South Station). There are two current stations for trains to and from Prague and Warsaw: Wien Nord (North Station) and Franz-Josef Bahnhof. Central train information will have details about schedule information for train departures all over Austria. However, it's hard to find somebody who can speak English, so it's best to ask your hotel for help in calling.

🚆 Train Information **Central train information** ☎ 05/1717. **Westbahnhof** ✉ Westbahnhof, 15th District/Fünfhaus. **Franz-Josef Bahnhof** ✉ Julius-Tandler-Platz, 9th District/Alsergrund. **Südbahnhof** ✉ Wiedner Gürtel 1, 4th District/Wieden. **Wien Nord** ✉ Praterstern, 2nd District/Leopoldstadt.

TRAINS IN AUSTRIA

Austrian train service is excellent: it's fast and, for Western Europe, relatively inexpensive, particularly if you take advantage of the discount fares. Trains on the mountainous routes are slow, but no slower than driving, and the scenery is gorgeous! Many of the remote rail routes will give you a look at traditional Austria, complete with Alpine cabins tacked onto mountainsides and a backdrop of snow-capped peaks.

Austrian Federal Railways trains are identifiable by the letters that precede the train number on the timetables and posters. The IC (InterCity) or EC (EuroCity) trains are fastest, and a supplement of about €5 is included in the price of the ticket. EN trains have sleeping facilities. **Allow yourself plenty of time to purchase your ticket before boarding the train. If you purchase your ticket on board the train, you must pay a surcharge, which is around €7** or more, depending on how far you're going. All tickets are valid without supplement on D (express), E (*Eilzug;* semi-fast), and local trains. You can reserve a seat for €3.40 up until a few hours before departure. Be sure to do this on the main-line trains (Vienna–Innsbruck, Salzburg–Klagenfurt, Vienna–Graz, for example) at peak holiday times. The EC trains usually have a dining car with fairly good food. The trains originating in Budapest have good Hungarian cooking. Otherwise there is usually a fellow with a cart serving snacks and hot and cold drinks. Most trains are equipped with a card telephone in or near the restaurant car.

Make certain that you inquire about possible supplements payable onboard trains traveling to destinations outside Austria **when you are purchasing your ticket.** Austrians are not generally forthcoming with information, and you might be required to pay a supplement in cash to the conductor while you are on the train. For information, call 05/1717 from anywhere in Austria. Unless you speak German fairly well, it's a good idea to have your hotel call for you.

CLASSES

The difference between first and second class on Austrian trains is mainly a matter of space. First- and second-class sleepers, and couchettes (six to a compartment), are available on international runs, as well as on long trips within Austria. If you're driving and would rather watch the scenery than the traffic, you can put your car on a train in Vienna and accompany it to Salzburg, Innsbruck, Feldkirch, or Villach. You relax in a compartment or sleeper for the trip, and the car is unloaded when you arrive.

DISCOUNT PASSES

To save money, **look into rail passes.** But be aware that if you don't plan to cover many miles you may come out ahead by buying individual tickets.

Austria is one of 17 countries in which you can **use Eurailpasses,** which provide unlimited first-class rail travel, in all of the participating countries, for the duration of the pass. If you plan to rack up the miles, get a standard pass. These are available for 15 days ($588), 21 days ($762), one month ($946), two months ($1,338), and three months ($1,654).

In addition to standard Eurailpasses, **ask about special rail-pass plans.** Among these are the Eurail Youthpass (for those under age 26), the Eurail Saverpass (which gives a discount for two or more people traveling together), a Eurail Flexipass (which allows a certain number of travel days within a set period), the Euraildrive Pass, and the Europass Drive (which combines travel by train and rental car). Whichever pass you choose, remember that you must **purchase your pass before you leave** for Europe.

Many travelers assume that rail passes guarantee them seats on the trains they wish to ride. Not so. You need to **book seats ahead even if you are using a rail pass**; seat reservations are required on some European trains, particularly high-speed trains, and are a good idea on trains that may be crowded—particularly in summer on popular routes. You will also need a reservation if you purchase sleeping accommodations.

Another option that gives you discount travel through various countries is the European East Pass, offered by Rail Europe, good for travel within Austria, the Czech Republic, Hungary, Poland, and Slovakia: cost is $226 (first class) or $160 (second class) for any 5 days unlimited travel within a one-month period.

The ÖBB, the Austrian Austrian Federal Train Service has a Web site, but it is not particularly user-friendly. As it is often impossible to get through to them on the phone, it is best to get to the train station early for questions. The ÖBB offers a large number of discounts for various travel constellations. If you are traveling with a group of people, even small, there are percentages taken off for each member. Families can also get discounts. School children and students also get good deals. The Vorteilscard is valid for a year and costs about €100, allowing 45% fare reduction on all rail travel. If you are planning lots of travel in Austria, it could be a good deal. Ask for other special deals, and check travel agencies. Children between 6 and 15 travel at half price, under 6 years of age for free.

You can buy an Austrian Rail Pass in the United States for travel within Austria for 15 days ($158 first class, $107 second class). It's available for purchase in Austria also, but only at travel agencies, such as SNS Tours.

For €26.90 and a passport photo, women over 60 and men over 65 can obtain a Seniorenpass, which carries a 45% discount on rail tickets. The pass also has a host of other benefits, including reduced-price entry into museums. Most rail stations can give you information.

Travelers under 26 should inquire about discount fares under the Billet International Jeune (BIJ). The special one-trip tickets are sold by Eurotrain International, travel agents, and youth-travel specialists, and at rail stations.

🚈 Information & Passes **CIT Tours Corp** ✉ 15 W. 44th St., 10th fl., New York, NY 10036 ☎ 212/730–2400, 800/248–7245 in U.S., 800/387–0711, 800/361–7799 in Canada ⊕ www.cit-tours.com. **DER Travel Services** ✉ 9501 W. Devon Ave., Rosemont, IL

60018 ☎ 800/782-2424 ☐ 800/282-7474 for information ⊕ www.dertravel.com. **ÖBB (Österreichische Bundesbahnen)** ⊕ www.oebb.at. **Rail Europe** ✉ 500 Mamaroneck Ave., Harrison, NY 10528 ☎ 914/682-5172 or 800/438-7245 ☐ 800/432-1329 ⊕ www.raileurope.com ✉ 2087 Dundas E, Suite 106, Mississauga, Ontario L4X 1M2 ☎ 800/361-7245 ☐ 905/602-4198. **SNS Tours** ⊕ snstours.com/ausrail.htm.

FARES & SCHEDULES

For train schedules from the Austrian rail service, the ÖBB, ask at your hotel, stop in at the train station and look for large posters labeled ABFAHRT (departures) and ANKUNFT (arrivals), or log on to their Web site. In the Abfahrt listing you'll find the departure time in the main left-hand block of the listing and, under the train name, details of where it stops en route and the time of each arrival. There is also information about connecting trains and buses, with departure details. Workdays are symbolized by two crossed hammers, which means that the same schedule might not apply on weekends or holidays. A little rocking horse means that a special playpen has been set up for children in the train. Women traveling alone may book special compartments on night trains or long-distance rides (ask for a *Damenabteilung*).

🚊 **ÖBB (Österreichische Bundesbahnen)** ⊕ www. oebb.at.

FROM THE U.K.

There's a choice of rail routes to Austria, but check services first; long-distance passenger service across the Continent is undergoing considerable reduction. There is daily service from London to Vienna via the *Austria Nachtexpress*. Check other services such as the *Orient Express*. If you don't mind changing trains, you can travel via Paris, where you change stations to board the overnight *Arlberg Express* via Innsbruck and Salzburg to Vienna. First- and second-class sleepers and second-class couchettes are available as far as Innsbruck.

When you have the time, a strikingly scenic route to Austria is via Cologne and Munich; after an overnight stop in Cologne you take the *EuroCity Express Johann Strauss* to Vienna.

🚊 **Information & Reservations** Contact **Eurotrain** ✉ 52 Grosvenor Gardens, London SW1W OAG ☎ 020/7730-3402, which offers excellent deals for those under 26, or **British Rail Travel Centers** ☎ 020/7834-2345. For additional information, call **DER Travel Service** ☎ 020/7408-0111 or the **Austrian National Tourist Office** (*see* Visitor Information, *below*).

TRAVEL AGENCIES

IN AUSTRIA

American Express, Kuoni Cosmos, Carlson/Wagons-Lit and Österreichisches Verkehrsbüro serve as general travel agencies. American Express, Kuoni Cosmos, and Vienna Ticket Service/Cityrama are agencies that offer tickets to various sights and events in Vienna.

🚊 **Austrian Agent Referrals American Express** ✉ Kärntnerstrasse 21-23, 1st District ☎ 01/515-4077-0 ☐ 01/515-40-777. **Carlson/Wagons-Lit** ✉ Millennium Tower 94/Handelskai, 20th District ☎ 01/240600 ☐ 01/24060-65. **Kuoni Cosmos** ✉ Kärntner Ring 15, 1st District ☎ 01/515-33-0 ☐ 01/513-4147.**Österreichisches Verkehrsbüro** ✉ Opernring 3-5, 1st District ☎ 01/588-628 ☐ 01/588-000-130. **Vienna Ticket Service/Cityrama** ✉ Börsegasse 1, 1st District ☎ 01/534130 ☐ 01/534-1328.

AT HOME

A good travel agent puts your needs first. Look for an agency that has been in business at least five years, emphasizes customer service, and has someone on staff who specializes in your destination. In addition, **make sure the agency belongs to a professional trade organization.** The American Society of Travel Agents (ASTA), with more than 24,000 members in some 140 countries, is the largest and most influential in the field. Operating under the motto "Integrity in Travel," it maintains and enforces a strict code of ethics and will step in to help mediate any agent-client disputes if necessary. ASTA also maintains a Web site that includes a directory of agents. (If a travel agency is also acting as your tour operator, *see* Buyer Beware *in* Tours & Packages, *above*.)

🚊 **Local Agent Referrals American Society of Travel Agents** (ASTA) ☎ 800/965-2782 24-hr hotline ☐ 703/739-3268 ⊕ www.astanet.com. **Associ-**

ation of British Travel Agents ✉ 68–71 Newman St., London W1P 4AH ☎ 020/7637–2444 🖷 020/7637–0713 ✑ information@abta.co.uk ⊕ www.abtanet.com. **Association of Canadian Travel Agents** ✉ 1729 Bank St., Suite 201, Ottawa, Ontario K1V 7Z5 ☎ 613/521–0474 🖷 613/521–0805 ✑ acta.ntl@sympatico.ca ⊕ www.acta.ca. **Australian Federation of Travel Agents** ✉ Level 3, 309 Pitt St., Sydney 2000 ☎ 02/9264–3299 🖷 02/9264–1085 ⊕ www.afta.com.au. **Travel Agents' Association of New Zealand** ✑ Box 1888, Wellington 6001 ☎ 04/499–0104 🖷 04/499–0827 ✑ taanz@tiasnet.co.nz.

VIENNA BY CAR

On highways from points south or west or from Vienna's airport, ZENTRUM signs clearly mark the route to the center of Vienna. From there, however, finding your way to your hotel can be no mean trick, for traffic planners have installed a devious scheme prohibiting through traffic in the city core (the 1st District), scooting cars out again via a network of exasperating one-way streets. In the city itself a car is a burden, though very useful for trips outside town.

Traffic congestion within Vienna has gotten out of hand, and driving to in-town destinations generally takes longer than public transportation. City planners' solutions have been to make driving as difficult as possible, with one-way streets and other tricks, and a car in town is far more of a burden than a pleasure. Drivers not familiar with the city literally need a navigator.

The entire 1st and 6th through 9th districts of Vienna are limited-parking zones and require that a *Parkschein,* a paid-parking chit available at most newsstands and tobacconists, be displayed on the dash during the day. Parkscheine cost €0.40 for 30 minutes, €0.80 for 1 hour, and €1.20 for 90 minutes. You can park 10 minutes free of charge, but you must get a violet "gratis" sticker to put in your windshield. You can also park free in the 1st District on weekends, but not overnight. Overnight street parking in the 1st and 6th through 9th districts is restricted to residents with special permits; all other cars are subject to expensive ticketing or even towing, so in these districts be sure you have off-street garage parking.

VIENNA GUIDED TOURS

BUS TOURS

When you're pressed for time, a good way to see the highlights of Vienna is via a sightseeing bus tour, which gives you a once-over-lightly of the heart of the city and allows a closer look at Schönbrunn and Belvedere palaces. You can cover almost the same territory on your own by taking either Streetcar 1 or 2 around the Ring and then walking through the heart of the city. For tours, there are a couple of reputable firms: Vienna Sightseeing Tours and Cityrama Sightseeing. Both run daily "get acquainted" tours lasting about three hours (€34), including visits to the Schönbrunn and Belvedere palace grounds. The entrance fee and guided tour of Schönbrunn is included in the price, but not a guided tour of Belvedere, just the grounds. Both firms offer a number of other tours as well (your hotel will have detailed programs) and provide hotel pickup for most tours. These tour operators offer short trips outside the city. Check their offerings and compare packages and prices to be sure you get what you want. Your hotel will have brochures.

🔳 **Fees & Schedules Cityrama Sightseeing** ✉ Börsegasse 1 ☎ 01/534–130 🖷 01/534–13–28 ⊕ www.cityrama.at. **Vienna Sightseeing Tours** ✉ Graf Starhemberggasse 25 ☎ 01/712–4683–0 🖷 01/714–1141 ⊕ www.viennasightseeingtours.com.

STREETCAR TOURS

From early May to early October, a 1929 vintage streetcar leaves each Saturday at 11:30 AM and 1:30 PM and Sunday and holidays at 9:30, 11:30 AM, and 1:30 PM from the Otto Wagner Pavilion at Karlsplatz for a guided tour. For €15 (€13.50 if you have the Vienna-Card), you'll go around the Ring, out past the big Ferris wheel in the Prater and past Schönbrunn and Belvedere palaces in the course of the two-hour trip. Prices may go up in 2005, and departure times may change; be sure to check ahead. The old-timer trips are popular, so make your reservation early by phone or e-mail. You must buy your ticket on the streetcar.

🔳 **Fees & Schedules Transport-information office** ☎ 01/790–9100 ✑ oldtimer@wienerlinien.at.

WALKING TOURS

Guided walking tours (in English) are a great way to see the city highlights. The city tourist office offers around 40 tour topics, ranging from "Unknown Underground Vienna" to "Hollywood in Vienna," "For Lovers of Music and Opera," "Old World Vienna–Off the Beaten Track," "Jewish Families and Their Past in Vienna," and many more. Vienna Walks and Talks offers informative walks through the old Jewish Quarter and a *Third Man* tour from the classic film starring Orson Welles, among other subjects. Tours take about 1½ hours, are held in any weather provided at least three people turn up, and cost €11, plus any entry fees. No reservations are needed for the city sponsored tours. Get a full list of the guided-tour possibilities at the city information office. Ask for the monthly brochure "Walks in Vienna," which details the tours, days, times, and starting points. You can also arrange to have your own privately guided tour for €120 for a half day.

If you can, try to get a copy of "Vienna Downtown Walking Tours" by Henriette Mandl from a bookshop. The six tours take you through the highlights of central Vienna with excellent commentary and some entertaining anecdotes that most of your Viennese acquaintances won't know. The booklet "Vienna from A–Z" (in English, €3.60; available at bookshops and city information offices) explains the numbered plaques attached to all major buildings.

7 **City information office** ✉ Am Albertinaplatz 1. **Vienna Guide Service** ✉ Werdertorgasse 9/2 ☎ 01/774-8901 ⊕ www.wienguide.at. **Vienna Walks and Talks** ✉ Werdertorgasse 9/2, 1st District ☎ 01/774-8901 📠 01/774-8933 ⊕ www.viennawalks.tix.at.

VIENNA TAXIS

Unlike urban centers like New York City, you can't just flag a cab down in the street in Vienna. Look for a taxi stand (the German word is also "taxi"). Taxi fares are reasonable. The initial charge is €2 for as many as four people daytime, and about 5% more from 11 PM until 6 AM. Radio cabs ordered by phone have an initial charge of €4. They also may charge for each piece of luggage that must go into the trunk, and a charge is added for waiting beyond a reasonable limit. It's customary to round up the fare to cover the tip. Service is usually prompt, but when you hit rush hour, the weather is bad, or you need to keep to an exact schedule, call ahead and order a taxi for a specific time. If your destination is the airport, ask for a reduced-rate taxi. For the cheapest taxi to the airport, *see* Airport Transfers, *above*. There are several companies that offer chauffeured limousines, which are listed below.

Vienna is divided into 23 numbered districts; for a complete rundown on the various districts, or *Bezirke* Taxi drivers may need to know which district you seek, as well as the street address. The district number is coded into the postal code with the second and third digits; thus A-1010 (the "01") is the 1st District, A-1030 is the 3rd, A-1110 is the 11th, and so on. Some sources and maps still give the district numbers, either in Roman or Arabic numerals, as Vienna X or Vienna 10.

7 Taxi Companies **Göth** ☎ 01/713-7196. **Mazur** ☎ 01/604-2530. **Peter Urban** ☎ 01/713-5255.

VIENNA TRANSPORTATION: BUSES, TRAMS & U-BAHNS

When it comes to seeing the main historic sights, Vienna is a city to tackle on foot. With the exception of the Schönbrunn and Belvedere palaces and the Prater amusement park, most sights are concentrated in the center, the 1st District (A-1010), much of which is a pedestrian zone anyway. However, Vienna does have an impressive public transport system, comprising its subway, called the U-Bahn, as well as extensive tram and bus routes, that can make touring the inner city a little easier if you don't have bionic feet. Each sight write-up in our Exploring Vienna chapter, as well as each listing for a restaurant, hotel, and nightlife spot, lists the nearest public transportation stop. Vienna's public transportation system, run by the VOR, or Vorverkaufsstellen der Wiener Linen, is fast, clean, safe, and easy to use. Get public transport maps at a tourist office or at the transport-information offices (*Wiener Verkehrsbetriebe*), underground at

Vienna
Subways

Karlsplatz, Stephansplatz, and Praterstern. You can transfer on the same ticket between subway, streetcar, bus, and long stretches of the fast suburban railway, *Schnellbahn* (*S-Bahn*).

U-BAHNS

Five subway (*U-Bahn*) lines, whose stations are prominently marked with blue U signs, crisscross the city. Karlsplatz and Stephansplatz are the main transfer points between lines. The last subway (U4) runs at about 12:30 AM. Track the main lines of the U-Bahn system by their color-codes on the subway maps: U1 is red; U2, purple; U3, orange; U4, green; and U6, brown. Note that you have to open the subway door when the train stops, either by pushing a lighted button or pulling the door handle aside.

The main city center subway stops in the 1st District are Stephansplatz, Karlsplatz,

Herrengasse, Schottenring and Schwedenplatz. Stephansplatz is the the very heart of the city, at St. Stephan's cathedral, with exits to the Graben and Kärntnerstrasse. You can reach the famous amusement park of the Prater from Stephansplatz by taking the U1 to Praterstern. Near the southern edge of the Ringstrasse, the major Karlsplatz stop is right next to the Staatsoper, the pedestrian Kärntnerstrasse, and the Ringstrasse, with an easy connection to Belvedere Palace via the D Tram. You can also take the U4 from Karlsplatz to Schönbrunn Palace (Schönbrunn stop). Herrengasse is also directly in the city center, close to the Hofburg and Graben. Schottenring is on the Ringstrasse, offering quick tram connections or a short walk on foot to the Graben. Schwedenplatz is ideally situated for a 10-minute walk to St. Stephan's through some of Vienna's oldest streets, or you can hop on a tram and be on the Ringstrasse in five minutes. You can also take the U1 from Schwedenplatz to the Prater, getting off at Praterstern. Karlsplatz is serviced by the train lines U4, U2, U1), while U3 goes to Herrengasse and U2 to Schottentor. In addition, there are also handy U-Bahn stops that can stop along the rim of the city core, such as MuseumsQuartier, Stadtpark, Volkstheater, and Rathaus.

TRAMS & BUSES

The first trams, or streetcars (*Strassenbahnen*), run from about 5:15 AM. From then on, service (barring gridlock on the streets) is regular and reliable, and most lines operate until about midnight. The most famous tram lines are No. 1, which travels the great Ringstrasse avenue clockwise, and No. 2, which travels its counter-clockwise; each offers a cheap way to sightsee the glories of Vienna's 19th-century Ringstrasse monuments. Where streetcars don't run, buses—the word in German is *Autobus*—do; route maps and schedules are posted at each bus or subway stop. You can hop around the 1st District by using the Bus lines 1A, 2A, and 3A and these also prove to be useful crosstown buses if you don't want to walk 10 minutes from one U-Bahn stop to another. Should you miss the last streetcar tram or bus, special night buses with an N designation operate at half-hour intervals over several key routes; the starting (and transfer) points are the Opera House and Schwedenplatz. The night-owl buses now accept all normal tickets. There is no additional fare.

TICKETS

Tickets for public transportation are valid for all public transportation—buses, trams, and the subway. Buy single tickets for €2 from dispensers on the streetcar tram or from your bus driver; you'll need exact change for the former. Note that it's €0.50 cheaper to buy your ticket in advance from a ticket machine located at subway stations, and also good for buses and trams. The ticket machines at subway stations (*VOR-Fahrkarten*) give change and dispense 24-hour, 72-hour, and eight-day tickets, as well as single tickets sepa-

rately and in blocks of two and five. Tickets are sold singly or as strip tickets, *Streifenkarten*. At *Tabak-Trafik* (cigarette shops/newsstands) or the underground *Wiener Verkehrsbetriebe* offices you can get a block of five tickets for €7.50, each ticket good for one uninterrupted trip in more or less the same general direction with unlimited transfers. Or you can get a three-day ticket for €12, good on all lines for 72 hours from the time you validate the ticket; there's also a 24-hour ticket for €5. If you're staying longer, get an eight-day ticket (€24), which can be used on eight separate days or by any number of persons (up to eight) at any one time. Prices may go up in 2005. Children under six travel free on Vienna's public transport system; children under 15 travel free on Sunday, public holidays, and during Vienna school holidays. If you don't speak German, opt to purchase your transport tickets from a person at a Tabak or main U-Bahn station.

As with most transport systems within European cities, it is essential to "validate," or punch, your ticket when you start your trip. You'll find the validations machines on all buses, trams, and at the entrance of each U-Bahn station—look for the blue box and slide your ticket into the machine until you hear a "punch." Public transportation is on the honor system, but if you're caught without a punched ticket, the fine is €62, payable within three days, or €127 afterward. Tabak-Trafik Almassy is open every day from 8 AM to 7 PM and has tickets as well as film and other items.

FIAKERS

A *Fiaker*, or horse cab, will trot you around to whatever destination you specify, but this is an expensive way to see the city. A short tour of the inner city takes about 20 minutes and costs €40; a longer one including the Old Town and part of the Ringstrasse lasts about 40 minutes and costs €65, and an hour-long tour of the inner city and the whole Ringstrasse costs €95. The carriages accommodate four (five if someone sits next to the coachman). Starting points are Heldenplatz in front of the Hofburg, Stephansplatz beside the cathedral, and across from the Albertina, all in the 1st District. For longer trips, or any variation of the regular route, agree on the price first.

Tabak-Trafik Almassy ⊠ Stephansplatz 4, to the right behind cathedral ☎ 01/512–5909. **VOR, or Vorverkaufsstellen der Wiener Linen** ☎ 7909/105 ⊕ www.wienerlinien.at.

VISITOR INFORMATION

VIENNA

The main center for information (walk-ins only) is the Vienna City Tourist Office, open daily 9–9 PM and centrally located between the Hofburg and Kärntnerstrasse.

Ask at tourist offices or your hotel about a Vienna-Card; costing €15.25, the card combines 72 hours' use of public transportation and discounts at certain museums and shops.

If you've lost something valuable, check with the police at the Fundangelegenheiten (Lost and Found). If your loss occurred on a train in Austria, call the central number and ask for Reisegepäck. Losses on the subway system or streetcars can be checked by calling the Fundstelle U-Bahn.

Tourist Information Fundstelle U-Bahn ☎ 01/7909–43500. **Reisegepäck (Central Train Information)** ☎ 05/1717. **Vienna City Tourist Office** ⊠ Am Albertinaplatz 1, 1st District ☎ 01/24555 🖷 01/216–84–92 or 01/24555–666.

Austrian National Tourist Office In the U.S. ⊠ 500 5th Ave., 20th fl., New York, NY 10110 ☎ 212/944–6880 🖷 212/730–4568 ✉ Box 1142, New York, NY 10108. **In Canada** ⊠ 2 Bloor St. E, Suite 3330, Toronto, Ontario M4W 1A8 ☎ 416/967–3381 🖷 416/967–4101 ✉ 1010 Sherbrooke St. W, Suite 1410, Montréal, Québec H3A 2R7 ☎ 514/849–3709 🖷 514/849–9577 ✉ 200 Granville St., Suite 1380, Granville Sq., Vancouver, BC V6C 1S4 ☎ 604/683–5808 or 604/683–8695 🖷 604/662–8528. **In the U.K.** ⊠ 30 St. George St., London W1R 0AL ☎ 020/7629–0461. **Web site** ⊕ www.anto.com.

U.S. Government Advisories U.S. Department of State ⊠ Overseas Citizens Services Office, Room 4811 N.S., 2201 C St. NW, Washington, DC 20520 ☎ 202/647–5225 interactive hotline or 888/407–4747 ⊕ www.travel.state.gov; enclose a business-size SASE.

WEB SITES

Do check out the World Wide Web when you're planning. You'll find everything from up-to-date weather forecasts to virtual tours of famous cities. Fodor's Web site, ⊕ www.fodors.com is a great place to start your online travels—just search for the Vienna miniguide, then search for "Links." For basic information: **Vienna** (⊕ info.wien.at); **Salzburg** (⊕ www.salzburginfo.or.at). For **train information** (⊕ www.oebb.at).

For Vienna, here are some top Web sites: **Viennahype** (⊕ www.viennahype.at)—the Vienna Tourist Board's official Web site; **Vienna.info** (⊕ www.vienna.info)—an alternative site run by the Vienna Tourist Board; **Wien Online** (⊕ www.magwien.gv.at)—the city's official Web site; **Vienna Scene** (⊕ www.austria-tourism.com)—the Vienna Tourist Board Web site for Austria; **Wienerzeitung** (⊕ www.wienerzeitung.at)—the city's leading newspaper Web site; **Die Falter** (⊕ www.falter.at)—the city's most sophisticated newspaper and best cultural listings; **Time Out Vienna** (⊕ www.timeout.com/vienna/index.html); **Vienna tickets** (⊕ www.viennaticket.at/english); **MuseumsQuartier** (⊕ www.mqw.at) for the scoop on the big new museum district; and the **Austrian Travel Network** (⊕ www.tiscover.com). For Web sites about the Danube Valley, the Salzkammergut, and Salzburg, *see* Visitor Information in the A to Z sections of Chapters 6 and 7.

VIENNA

1

By George
Sullivan

Updated by
Bonnie Dodson

PROPER CITIZENS OF VIENNA, it has been said, waltz only from the waist down, holding their upper bodies ramrod straight while whirling around the crowded dance floor. The movement resulting from this correct posture is breathtaking in its sweep and splendor, and its elegant coupling of free-wheeling exuberance and rigid formality—of license and constraint—is quintessentially Viennese. The town palaces all over the inner city—built mostly during the 18th century—present in stone and stucco a similar artful synthesis. They make Vienna a Baroque city that is, at its best, an architectural waltz.

Those who tour Vienna today might feel they're keeping step in three-quarter time. As they explore churches filled with statues of gilded saints and cheeky cherubs, wander through treasure-packed museums, or take in the delights of a mecca of mocha (the ubiquitous cafés), they may feel destined to enjoy repeated helpings of the beloved *Schlagobers,* the rich, delicious whipped cream that garnishes the most famous Viennese pastry of all, the Sachertorte. The ambience of the city is predominantly ornate: White horses dance to elegant music; snow frosts the opulent draperies of Empress Maria Theresa's monument, set in the formal patterns of "her" lovely square; a gilded Johann Strauss perpetually plays amidst a grove of trees; town houses present a dignified face to the outside world while enclosing lavishly decorated interior courtyards; dark Greek legends are declawed by the voluptuous music of Richard Strauss; Klimt's paintings glitter with geometric impasto; a mechanical clock intones the hour with a stately pavane. All these will create in the visitor the sensation of a metropolis that likes to be visited and admired—and which indeed is well worth visiting and admiring.

For centuries, this has been the case. One of the great capitals of Europe, Vienna was for centuries the main stamping grounds of the Habsburg rulers of the Austro-Hungarian Empire. The empire is long gone, but many reminders of the city's imperial heyday remain, carefully preserved by the tradition-loving Viennese. When it comes to the arts, the glories of the past are particularly evergreen, thanks to the cultural legacy created by the many artistic geniuses nourished here.

From the late 18th century on, Vienna's culture—particularly its musical forte—was famous throughout Europe. Haydn, Mozart, Beethoven, Schubert, Brahms, Strauss, Mahler, and Bruckner all lived in the city, composing glorious music still played in concert halls all over the world. And at the tail end of the 19th century the city's artists and architects— Gustav Klimt, Egon Schiele, Oskar Kokoschka, Josef Hoffmann, Otto Wagner, and Adolf Loos among them—brought about an unprecedented artistic revolution, a revolution that swept away the past and set the stage for the radically experimental art of the 20th century. "Form follows function," the artists of the late-19th-century Jugendstil proclaimed. Their echo is still heard in the city's contemporary arts and crafts galleries—even in the glinting, Space Needle–like object that hovers over the north end of Vienna—actually the city's waste incinerator, designed by the late, great artist Friedensreich Hundertwasser.

At the close of World War I the Austro-Hungarian Empire was dismembered, and Vienna lost its cherished status as the seat of imperial

Magnificent, magnetic, and magical, Vienna beguiles one and all with its Old World charm and courtly grace. It is a place where headwaiters still bow as though addressing a Habsburg prince, and Lipizzaner stallions dance their intricate minuets to the strains of Mozart. Here is a city that waltzes and works in measured three-quarter time. Like a well-bred grande dame, Vienna doesn't rush about, and neither should you. Saunter through its stately streets—and rub elbows with the spirits of Beethoven and Strauss, Metternich and Freud—and marvel at its Baroque palaces. Then dream an afternoon away at a cozy *Kaffeehaus.*

In a city with as many richly stocked museums and marvels as Vienna, visitors risk seeing half of everything and all of nothing. One could easily spend two solid weeks exploring the many layers of the city, but if time is limited you'll need to plan carefully. The following suggested itineraries can help ensure an exciting and efficiently mapped-out visit. See this chapter for complete information about individual sights and detailed neighborhood walking tours.

If you have
1 day

Touring Vienna in a single day is a proposition as strenuous as it is unlikely, but those with more ambition than time should first get a quick view of the lay of the city by taking a streetcar ride around the Ringstrasse, the wide boulevard that encloses the city's heart. While you're at your most energetic, hop off at the **Kunsthistoriches Museum** ⑤⑨, one of the great art museums of the world. If art isn't your thing, then spend an hour or two exploring the city center, starting at Vienna's cathedral, the **Stephansdom** ①, followed by window shopping along the Graben and Kärntnerstrasse, the two main pedestrian shopping streets in the center. Around noon head for the **MuseumsQuartier** ⑥⓪, the huge, one of a kind, modern art complex in the city center, for lunch in one of several trendy restaurants. If you're up to seeing more art, there's plenty here to choose from. If you want a change of pace, zip over to **Schönbrunn Palace** ⑨⓪ to spend the afternoon touring the magnificent royal residence and strolling through the woods and gardens. Late in the afternoon visit a Viennese institution, the *Kaffeehaus,* for a *Melange* and chocolate torte, *mit Schlag, naturlich.* Demel and Café Central best exemplify this happy tradition. If the weather is fine, there is no more relaxing way to spend the evening than at a *Heuriger.* It's magical to sit in the vineyards on the outskirts of the city, sipping wine under the stars. If beer is more to your liking, go to the **Prater,** Vienna's famous amusement park, where the outdoor beer hall, Schweizerhaus, serves up huge, frosty mugs of fresh Czech Budweiser to go along with roast chicken or *Stelze.* Afterward, take the kids on some rides, or go for a romantic spin in the oldest Ferris wheel in Europe, the *Riesenrad,* for a glorious, slow-paced, bird's-eye view of Vienna. If you're in the mood for culture and the opera is in season, spend an elegant evening at the **Staatsoper,** or the less expensive **Volksoper.** Then, if you're not too tired, go for a late night walk through the Hofburg Palace complex, straight through the Imperial Gates from the Ring to the **Kohlmarkt** ㉟, perhaps stopping for a nightcap at one of the outdoor cafés on the **Graben** ㉝ before turning in.

If you have 3 days

Given three days, Day 1 can be a little less hectic, and in any case you'll want more time for the city center. Rather than going on the do-it-yourself streetcar ride around the Ringstrasse, take an organized sightseeing tour, which will describe the highlights. Plan to spend a full afternoon at **Schönbrunn Palace** (83). Reserve the second day for art, tackling the exciting **Kunsthistoriches Museum** (59) before lunch, and after you're refreshed, the dazzling **MuseumsQuartier** (60), which comprises several major modern art collections—the Leopold Museum; the Museum moderner Kunst Stiftung Ludwig (MUMOK); the temporary shows at the Kunsthalle; plus the children's ZOOM Kinder Museum; and the Architekturzentrum (Architecture Center). If your tastes tend to the grand and royal, visit instead the magnificent collection of Old Master drawings at the **Albertina Museum** (76) or Prince Liechtenstein's private art collection at the **Liechtenstein Museum** (70). For a contrasting step into modern art in the afternoon—don't miss Klimt's legendary *The Kiss* at **Belvedere Palace** (87). Do as the Viennese do, and fill in any gaps with stops at cafés, reserving evenings for relaxing over music or wine. On the third day, head for the world-famous **Spanische Reitschule** ㉞ and watch the Lipizzaners prance through morning training. While you're in the neighborhood, view the sparkling court jewels in the Imperial Treasury, the **Schatzkammer** ㊽, and the glitzy **Silberkammer** ㊹, the museum of court silver and tableware, and take in one of Vienna's most spectacular Baroque settings, the glorious Grand Hall of the **Hofbibliothek** ㊶. For a total contrast, head out to the Prater amusement park in late afternoon for a ride on the giant Ferris wheel and end the day in a wine restaurant on the outskirts, perhaps in Sievering or Nussdorf.

If you have 7 days

Spend your first three days as outlined in the itinerary above. Then begin your fourth day getting better acquainted with the 1st District—the heart of the city. Treasures here range from Roman ruins to the residences of Mozart and Beethoven, the **Figarohaus** (72) and the **Pasqualatihaus** ㉕; then, slightly afield, the **Freud Haus** (69) (in the 9th District) or the oddball **Hundertwasserhaus** (in the 3rd). Put it all in contemporary perspective with a backstage tour of the magnificent **Staatsoper** (77), the State Opera. For a country break on the fifth day, take a tour of the Danube Valley, particularly the glorious **Wachau district** (*see* Chapter 6), where vineyards sweep down to the river's edge. On the sixth day, fill in some of the blanks with a stroll around Vienna's **Naschmarkt** (81) food-market district, taking in the nearby **Secession Building** (80) with Gustav Klimt's famous Beethoven Frieze. Don't overlook the superb Jugendstil buildings on the north side of the market. If you're still game for museums, head for any one of the less usual offerings, such as the Jewish Museum, the Haus der Musik, or the Ephesus Museum, in the **Hofburg,** or visit the city's historical museum, **Wien Museum Karlsplatz** (85); by now, you'll have acquired a good concept of the city and its background, so the exhibits will make more sense. Cap the day by visiting the **Kaisergruft** (75) in the Kapuzinerkirche to view the tombs of the Habsburgs responsible for so much of Vienna.

---

power. Its influence was much reduced, and its population began to decline (unlike what happened in Europe's other great cities), falling from around 2 million to the current 1.8 million. Today, however, the city's future looks brighter, for with the collapse of the Iron Curtain, Vienna regained its traditional status as one of the main hubs of Central Europe.

For many first-time visitors, the city's one major disappointment concerns the not-so-blue Danube River (if you want to see it in a Johann Strauss shade, you will have to select a brilliant summer day and travel well up- or downstream from Vienna). The inner city, it turns out, lies not on the river's main course but on one of its narrow offshoots, known as the Danube Canal. As a result, the sweeping river views expected by most newcomers fail to materialize. For this the Romans are to blame, for when Vienna was founded as a Roman military encampment around AD 100, the walled garrison was built not on the Danube's main stream but rather on the largest of the river's eastern branches, where it could be bordered by water on three sides. The wide, present-day Danube did not take shape until the late 19th century, when, to prevent flooding, its various branches were rerouted and merged.

The Romans maintained their camp for some 300 years (the emperor Marcus Aurelius is thought to have died in Vindobona, as it was called, in 180) not abandoning the site until around 400. The settlement survived the Roman withdrawal, however, and by the 13th century development was sufficient to require new city walls to the south. According to legend, the walls were financed by the English: in 1192 the local duke kidnapped King Richard I (the Lion-Hearted), en route home from the Third Crusade, and held him prisoner in Dürnstein, upriver, for several months, then turning him over for two years to the Austrian king, until he was expensively ransomed by his mother, Eleanor of Aquitaine.

Vienna's third set of walls dates from 1544, when the existing walls were improved and extended. The new fortifications were built by the Habsburg dynasty, which ruled the Austro-Hungarian Empire for an astonishing 640 years, beginning with Rudolf I in 1273 and ending with Karl I in 1918. These walls stood until 1857, when Emperor Franz Josef decreed that they finally be demolished and replaced by the series of boulevards that make up the famous tree-lined Ringstrasse.

During medieval times the city's growth was relatively slow, and its heyday as a European capital did not begin until 1683, after a huge force of invading Turks laid siege to the city for a two-month period before being routed by an army of Habsburg allies. Among the supplies that the fleeing Turks left behind were sacks filled with coffee beans, and it was these beans, so the story goes, that gave a local entrepreneur the idea of opening the first public coffeehouse; they remain a Viennese institution to this day.

The passing of the Turkish threat encouraged a Viennese building boom, with the Baroque style becoming the architectural choice of the day. Flamboyant, triumphant, joyous, and extravagantly ostentatious, the new art form—imported from Italy—transformed the city into a vast theater over the course of the 17th and 18th centuries. Life became a dream—the gorgeous dream of the Baroque, with its gilt madonnas and cherubs; its soaring, twisted columns; its painted heavens on the ceilings; its graceful domes. In the early 19th century a reaction began to set in—with middle-class industriousness and sober family values leading the way to a new epoch, characterized by the Biedermeier style. Then followed the Strauss era—that lighthearted period that conjures up imperial balls, "Wine, Women, and Song," heel clicking, and hand kissing. Today's visitors will find that the last era has made the grandest impact on the city, style-wise. In the 1870s Vienna reached the zenith of its imperial prosperity. This was marked by such gigantic undertakings as the cutting of a new channel for the Danube, the building of the Great Exhibition of 1873—when the Big Wheel arose in the Prater—and, most spectacularly, the erection of a series of magnificent buildings built around the great new Ringstrasse boulevard: the Staatsoper opera house, the Kunsthistorisches national art gallery, the Naturhistorisches museum, the "new wing" of the Hofburg palace, the House of Parliament, the Rathaus, the University, and the Votiv Kirche. These mammoth structures all comprised essays in the new "Ringstrasse" style of architecture. As with England's Victorian buildings, these paid highly correct (some say lifeless) homage to the Gothic, Italian Renaissance, and Baroque styles of former centuries. Some will be impressed by these buildings' sheer bravado and exuberance. Others will find their plethora of "Rococo" cherubs, "Gothic" spires, and "Baroque" columns will remind them of nothing more than the icing of a wedding cake wilting in the hot sunshine. But surely the first thing we can demand of an art, an architectural style, is that it mirrors the spirit of contemporary life—in this case, the *kaiserlich und königlich* (imperial and royal) era of Emperor Franz Josef. The Ringstrasse esthetic does this perfectly. So much so that it gives Vienna the cohesive architectural character that sets the city so memorably apart from its great rivals—London, Paris, and Rome.

EXPLORING VIENNA

Most of Vienna lies roughly within an arc of a circle with the straight line of the Danube Canal as its chord. Its heart, the **Innere Stadt** ("Inner City"), or 1st District, is bounded by the Ringstrasse (Ring), which forms almost a circle, with a narrow arc cut off by the Danube Canal, diverted from the mother river just outside the city limits and flowing through the northern sector of the city to rejoin the parent stream beyond the city line. To the Viennese, the most prestigious address of Vienna's 23 *Bezirke,* or districts, is this fabled 1st District, also known as the Innere Stadt, which contains the vast majority of sightseeing attractions. Of course, what is now the 1st District used to encompass the entire city of Vienna. In 1857 Emperor Franz Josef decided to demolish the original ancient wall surrounding the city to create the more cosmopolitan Ringstrasse, the multilane avenue that still encircles the expansive heart of Vienna. At that time, several small villages bordering the inner city were given district numbers and incorporated into Vienna. Today the former villages go by their official district number, but they are still known by their old village or neighborhood name (Grätzl), too. In conversation, the Viennese most often say the number of the district they are referring to, though sometimes they use the neighborhood name instead.

The circular 1st District is bordered on its northeastern section by the Danube Canal and 2nd District, and clockwise from there along the Ringstrasse by the 3rd, 4th, 6th, 7th, 8th, and 9th districts. Across the

1

Café Society

It used to be said that there were more cafés and coffeehouses in Vienna than there were banks in Switzerland. Whether or not this can still be claimed, the true flavor of Vienna can't be savored without visiting some of its great café landmarks. Every afternoon at 4, the coffee-and-pastry ritual of *Kaffeejause* takes place from one end of the city to the other. Regulars take their *Stammtisch* (usual table), where they sit until they go home for dinner. And why not? They come to gossip, read the papers, negotiate business, play cards, meet a spouse (or someone else's), or—who knows?—perhaps just have a cup of coffee. Whatever the reason, the Viennese use cafés and coffeehouses as club, pub, bistro, and even a home away from home. (Old-timers recall the old joke: "Pardon me, would you mind watching my seat for a while so I can go out for a cup of coffee?")

In fact, to savor the atmosphere of the coffeehouse, you must allow time. There is no need to worry about outstaying one's welcome, even over a single small cup of coffee—so set aside a morning or afternoon, and take along this book. For historical overtones, head for the Café Central—Lev Bronstein, otherwise known as Leon Trotsky, at one time enjoyed playing chess here. For Old World charm, check out the opulent Café Landtmann, which was Freud's favorite meeting place, or the elegant Café Sacher (famous for its Sachertorte); for the smoky art scene, go to the Café Hawelka. Wherever you end up, never ask for a plain cup of coffee; at the very least, order a Melange *mit Schlag* (with whipped cream) from the *Herr Ober,* or any of many other delightful variations. Several of Vienna's coffeehouses are written up in this chapter—for a more extensive list, see Chapter 2.

Jugendstil Jewels

From 1897 to 1907, the Vienna Secession movement gave rise to one of the most spectacular manifestations of the pan-European style known as Art Nouveau. Viennese took to calling the look *Jugendstil,* or the "young style." In such dazzling edifices as Otto Wagner's Wienzeile majolica-adorned mansion and Adolf Loos's Looshaus, Jugendstil architects rebelled against the prevailing 19th-century historicism that had created so many imitation Renaissance town houses and faux Grecian temples. Josef Maria Olbrich, Josef Hoffman, and Otto Schönthal took William Morris's Arts and Crafts movement, added dashes of Charles Rennie Mackintosh and flat-surface Germanic geometry, and came up with a luxurious style that shocked turn-of-the-century Viennese traditionalists (and infuriated Emperor Franz Josef). Many artists united to form the Vienna Secession—whose most famous member was painter Gustav Klimt—and the Wiener Werkstätte, which transformed the objects of daily life with a sleek modern look. Today, Jugendstil buildings are among the most fascinating structures in Vienna. The shrine of the movement is the world-famous Secession Building—the work of Josef Maria Olbrich—the cynosure of all eyes on the Friedrichstrasse.

Museums & Marvels

You could spend months perusing the contents of Vienna's 90 museums. Subjects range, alphabetically, from art to wine, and in between are found marvels such as carriages and clocks, memorial dedicatees such as Mozart and martyrs, and oddities such as bricks and burials. If your time is short, the one museum not to be overlooked is the Kunsthistorisches Museum, Vienna's most famous art museum and one of the great museums of the world, with masterworks by Titian, Rembrandt, Vermeer, and Velásquez, and an outstanding collection of Brueghels.

Given a little more time, the Schatzkammer, or Imperial Treasury, is well worth a visit, for its opulent bounty of crown jewels, regal attire, and other trappings of court life. The Silberkammer, a museum of court silver and tableware, is fascinating for its "behind-the-scenes" views of state banquets and other elegant representational affairs. The best-known museums tend to crowd up in late-morning and mid-afternoon hours; you can beat the mobs by going earlier or around the noon hour, at least to the larger museums that are open without a noontime break.

Danube Canal from the 1st District, the 2nd District—**Leopoldstadt**—is home to the venerable Prater amusement park, with its famous *Riesenrad* (Ferris wheel), as well as a huge park used for horseback riding and jogging. Along the southeastern edge of the 1st District is the 3rd District—**Landstrasse**—containing a number of embassies and the famed Belvedere Palace. The southern tip, the 4th District—**Wieden**—is fast becoming Vienna's hippest area, with trendy restaurants, art galleries, and shops opening up every week, plus Vienna's biggest outdoor market, the Naschmarkt, which is lined with dazzling Jugendstil buildings.

The southwestern 6th District—**Mariahilf**—includes the biggest shopping street, Mariahilferstrasse, with small, old-fashioned shops competing with smart restaurants, movie theaters, bookstores, and department stores. Directly west of the 1st District is the 7th District—**Neubau.** Besides the celebrated Kunsthistorisches Museum and headline-making MuseumsQuartier, the 7th District also houses the charming Spittelberg quarter, its cobblestone streets lined with beautifully preserved 18th-century houses. Moving up the western side you come to the 8th District—**Josefstadt**—which is known for its theaters, good restaurants, and antiques shops. And completing the circle surrounding the Innere Stadt on its northwest side is the 9th District—**Alsergrund**—once Sigmund Freud's neighborhood and today a nice residential area with lots of outdoor restaurants, curio shops, and lovely early-20th-century apartment buildings.

The other districts—the 5th, and the 10th through the 23rd—form a concentric second circle around the 2nd through 9th districts. These are mainly residential suburbs and only a few hold sights of interest for tourists. The 11th District—**Simmering**—contains one of Vienna's architectural wonders, Gasometer, a former gas works that has been remodeled into a housing and shopping complex. The 13th District—**Hietzing**—whose centerpiece is the fabulous Schönbrunn Palace, is also a coveted residential area, including the neighborhood Hütteldorf. The 19th District—**Döbling**—is Vienna's poshest residential neighborhood and also bears the nickname the "Noble District" because of all the embassy residences on its chestnut-tree–lined streets. The 19th District also incorporates several other neighborhoods within its borders, in particular, the wine villages of Grinzing, Sievering, Nussdorf, and Neustift am Walde. The 22nd District—**Donaustadt**—now headlines Donau City, a modern business and shopping complex that has grown around the United Nations center. The 22nd also has several grassy spots for bathing and sailboat watching along the Alte Donau (old Danube).

It may be helpful to know the neighborhood names of other residential districts. These are: the 5th/**Margareten**; 10th/**Favoriten**; 12th/**Meidling**; 14th/**Penzing**; 15th/**Fünfhaus**; 16th/**Ottakring**; 17th/**Hernals**; 18th/**Währing**; 20th/**Brigittenau**; 21st/**Floridsdorf**; and 23rd/**Liesing.** For neighborhood site listings below, information will be given for both the district and neighborhood name, *except* the 1st District, which will not include a neighborhood name.

For hard-core sightseers who wish to supplement the key attractions that follow, the tourist office has a booklet, "Vienna from A–Z" (€3.60), that gives short descriptions of some 250 sights around the city, all numbered and keyed to a fold-out map at the back, as well as to numbered wall plaques on the buildings themselves. Note that the nearest U-Bahn (subway) stop to most city attractions described below is included at the end of the service information (also listed in this chapter's subway system map). The more important churches have coin-operated (€1–€2) tape machines that give an excellent commentary in English on the structure's history and architecture. You are going to be surprised at how many euro coins you can get through!

Vienna is a city to explore and discover on foot. The description of the city on the following pages is divided into eight areas: seven that explore the architectural riches of central Vienna and an eighth that describes Schönbrunn Palace and its gardens. Above all, *look up* as you tour Vienna: some of the most fascinating architectural and ornamental bits are on upper stories or atop the city's buildings.

THE INNER CITY: HISTORIC HEART OF VIENNA

A good way to break the ice on your introduction to Vienna is to get a general picture of its layout as presented to the cruising bird or airplane pilot. There are several beautiful vantage points from which you can look down and over the city—including the terrace of the Upper Belvedere Palace or atop the Prater's famous Riesenrad Ferris wheel—but the city's preeminent lookout point, offering fine views in all directions, is Vienna's mother cathedral, the Stephansdom, reached by toiling up the 345 steps of "der Alte Steffl" (Old Stephen, its south tower) to the observation platform. The young and agile will make it up in 8 to 10 minutes; the slower-paced will make it in closer to 20. An elevator, and no exertion, will present you with much the same view from the terrace. From atop, you can see that St. Stephan's is the veritable hub of the city's wheel.

If you gaze to the horizon, you'll take in a three-nation view of Austria, Hungary, and the Czech Republic. But directly below your feet, you'll

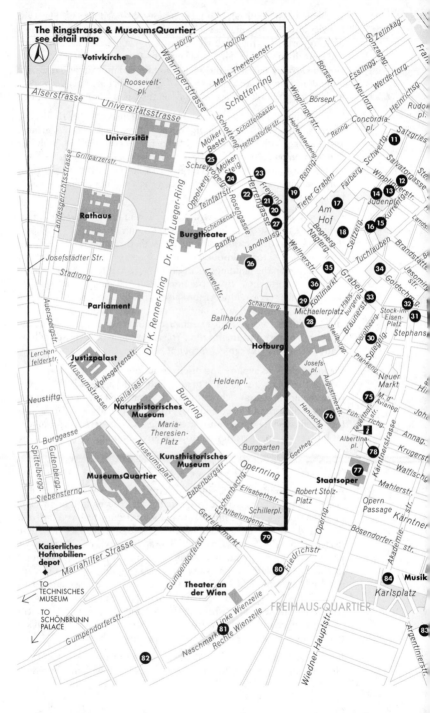

The Ringstrasse & MuseumsQuartier:
see detail map

Votivkirche

Roosevelt-
pl.

Alserstrasse

Universitätsstrasse

Universität

Grillparzerstr.

Rathaus

Josefstädter Str.

Stadiong.

Parliament

Justizpalast

Naturhistorisches
Museum

Maria-
Theresien-
Platz

Kunsthistorisches
Museum

MuseumsQuartier

Kaiserliches
Hofmobilien-
depot

Mariahilfer Strasse

TO
TECHNISCHES
MUSEUM

TO
SCHÖNBRUNN
PALACE

Gumpendorferstr.

Theater an
der Wien

Burgtheater

Hofburg

Heldenpl.

Ballhaus-
pl.

Burggarten

Opernring

Staatsoper

Robert Stolz-
Platz

Opern
Passage

FREIHAUS-QUARTIER

Naschmarkt

Musik

Karlsplatz

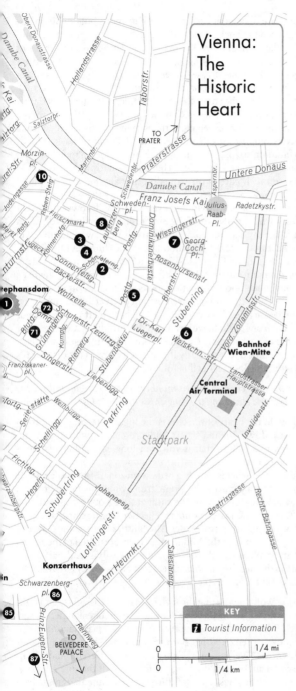

Vienna: The Historic Heart

TO PRATER

TO BELVEDERE PALACE

Konzerthaus

Stadtpark

Bahnhof Wien-Mitte

Central Air Terminal

ephansdom

Danube Canal

Franz Josefs Kai

Untere Donaus

Radetzkystr.

Julius-Raab-Pl.

Georg-Coch-Pl.

Dr. Karl Lueger-pl.

Schwarzenberg-pl.

Morzin-pl.

KEY

🛈 Tourist Information

0 ——— 1/4 mi

0 ——— 1/4 km

see that, for more than eight centuries, the enormous bulk of Stephans-dom has remained the nucleus around which the city has grown. Spreading out from the cathedral are Vienna's most densely packed miles of art and architecture, leading hotels, and best shops. The city center's main artery is the Kärntnerstrasse–Rotenturmstrasse, which runs straight through from the Opernring past the opera house to the Danube Canal. Half way down, where the street changes its name, is St. Stephan's Cathedral, whose *macédoine* of styles—Romanesque, Gothic, 19th-century—requires a little mental housekeeping. Perhaps its most authentically Vienna part is its never-completed northern tower, the "Adlerturn." Lack of funds held up its building so long that the church authorities clapped on to it a sort of tea-caddy lid in green patina. This truncated tower has become—since 1506—so much part of the cathedral that anyone who proposed completing it would be accused of sacrilege. That's the way it is in Vienna: Custom and usage will sanctify even a half-built tower to the extent that after a while no one would dare to finish it. Happily, this dilemma never marred the myriad museums and marvels that await discovery in the cathedral's immediate neighborhood. Historic churches like the Dominikanerkirche and the Ruprechtskirche, top museums like the MAK (heaven for lovers of Austrian Jugendstil design), and some of Vienna's most charming, once-upon-a-timefied nooks—Schönlaterngasse (Beautiful Lantern Street); the Heiligenkreuzerhof courtyard; and time-traveling Griechengasse (the "Greeks' Street")—all beckon. If you wish, your bird's-eye view from "Old Steve" can be left until the last day of your visit, when the city's landmarks will be more familiar. First day or last, the vistas are memorable, especially if you catch them as the cathedral's famous *Pummerin* (Boomer) bell is tolling.

Numbers in the text correspond to numbers in the margin and on the Vienna: The Historic Heart and the Ringstrasse & MuseumsQuartier maps.

a good
walk

Stephansplatz, in the heart of the city, is the logical starting point from which to track down Vienna's past and present, as well as any acquaintance (natives believe that if you wait long enough at this intersection of eight streets you'll run into anyone you're searching for). Although it's now in what is mainly a pedestrian zone, **Stephansdom ❶ ▶**, the mighty cathedral, marks the point from which distances to and from Vienna are measured. Visit the cathedral (it's quite impossible to view all its treasures, so just soak up its reflective Gothic spirit) and consider climbing its 345-step tower, der Alte Steffl, or descending into its Habsburg crypt. Vienna of the Middle Ages is encapsulated in the streets in back of St. Stephan's Cathedral. You could easily spend half a day or more just prowling the narrow streets and passageways—Wollzeile, Bäckerstrasse, Blutgasse—typical remnants of an early era.

Wander up the Wollzeile, cutting through the narrow Essiggasse and right into the Bäckerstrasse, to the **Universitätskirche ❷** or Jesuitenkirche, a lovely Jesuit church. Note the contrasting Academy of Science diagonally opposite (Beethoven premiered his *Battle* Symphony—today more commonly known as "Wellington's Victory"—in its Ceremonial Hall). Follow the Sonnenfelsgasse, ducking through one of the tiny alleys on the right to reach the Bäckerstrasse; turn right at Gutenbergplatz into the Köllnerhofgasse, right again into tiny Grashofgasse, and go through the gate into the surprising **Heiligenkreuzerhof** ❸, a peaceful oasis (unless a handicrafts market is taking place). Through the square, enter the **Schönlaterngasse** ❹ (Street of the Beautiful Lantern) to admire the house fronts—film companies at times block this street to take shots of the picturesque atmosphere—on your way to the **Dominikanerkirche** ❺, the Dominican church with its marvelous Baroque interior. Head east two blocks to that repository of Jugendstil treasures, the **Museum für Angewandte Kunst** ❻, then head north along the Stubenring to enjoy the architectural contrast of the **Postsparkasse** ❼ and former War Ministry, facing each other. Still on Postgasse retrace your steps into the picturesque square of Fleischmarkt to savor the historic inn, **Griechenbeisl** ❽. Nearby Hoher Markt, reached by taking Rotenturmstrasse west to Lichtensteg or Bauernmarkt, was part of the early Roman encampment; witness the Roman ruins under **Hoher Markt** ❾. The extension of Fleischmarkt ends in a set of stairs leading up past the eccentric Kornhäusal Tower. Up the stairs to the right on Ruprechtsplatz is the **Ruprechtskirche** ❿, St. Rupert's Church, allegedly the city's oldest. Take Sterngasse down the steps, turn left into Marc -Aurel-Strasse and right into Salvatorgasse to discover the lacework church of **Maria am Gestade** ⓫, which once sat above a small river, now underground.

TIMING If you're pressed for time and happy with facades rather than what's behind them, this route could take half a day, but if you love to look inside and stop to ponder and explore the myriad narrow alleys, figure at least a day for this walk. During services, wandering around the churches will be limited, but otherwise, you can tackle this walk any time, at your convenience.

HOW TO Stephansdom is considered the heart of Vienna, and is conveniently ac-
GET THERE cessible by the U1 and U3 subway, or on foot from the Ringstrasse boulevard using Trams 1, 2, and D. Buses 1A, 2A, and 3A travel right through the center of the city. For sights around the Fleishmarkt and Hoher Markt, it's easiest to go from Schwedenplatz, which can be reached by the U1 or U4, as well as Trams 1 and 2.

What to See

❺ **Dominikanerkirche** (Dominican Church). The Postgasse, to the east of Schönlaterngasse, introduces an unexpected visitor from Rome: the Dominikanerkirche. Built in the 1630s, some 50 years before the Viennese Baroque building boom, its facade is modeled after any number of Roman churches of the 16th century. The interior illustrates why the Baroque style came to be considered the height of bad taste during the 19th century and still has many detractors today. "Sculpt until you drop" seems to have been the motto here, and the viewer's eye is given no respite. This sort of Roman architectural orgy never really gained a foothold in Vienna, and when the great Viennese architects did pull out all the decorative stops—Hildebrandt's interior at the Belvedere Palace, for instance—they did it in a very different style and with far greater success. ✉ *Postgasse 4, 1st District* ☎ *01/512–7460–0* Ⓤ *U3 Stubentor/Dr.-Karl-Lueger-Platz.*

❽ Griechenbeisl (The "Greeks' Tavern"). If you want to find a Vienna nook-
Fodor'sChoice erie where time seems to be holding its breath, head to the intersection
★ of the Fleischmarkt (Meat Market) street and the picturesque, hilly, cobblestoned, and tiny Griechengasse. Part of the city's oldest core, this street
has a medieval feel that is quite genuine, thanks to Vienna's only surviving 14th-century watchtower, houses bearing statues of the Virgin
Mary, and the enchanting scene that greets you at the intersecting streets:
an ivy-covered tavern, the Greiechenbeisl, which has been in business
for some 500 years, "*zeit* 1447." Half a millennium ago, this quarter
was settled by Greek and Levante traders (there are still many Near Eastern rug dealers here) and many of them made this tavern their "local."
The wooden carving on the facade of the current restaurant commemorates Max Augustin—best known today from the song "Ach du lieber
Augustin"—an itinerant musician who sang here during the plague of
1679. A favored Viennese figure, he managed to fall into a pit filled with
plague victims but survived intact, presumably because he was so pick-
led in alcohol. In fact, this tavern introduced one of the great Pilsner
brews of the 19th century and everyone—from Schubert to Mark Twain,
Wagner to Johann Strauss—came here to partake. Be sure to dine here
to savor its low vaulted rooms, adorned with engravings, mounted
antlers, and bric-a-brac; the Mark Twain Zimmer has the ceiling covered with autographs of the rich and famous dating back two centuries.
Adjacent to the tavern is a Greek Orthodox Church partly designed by
the most fashionable Neoclassical designer in Vienna, Theophil Hansen.
The immediate neighborhood, dotted with cobbled lanes, is one of Vienna's most time-stained areas and a delight to explore. ⊠ *Fleishmarkt
11, 1st District* ⊕ *www.griechenbeisl.at/* Ⓤ *U1 or U4/Schwedenplatz.*

★ ❸ **Heiligenkreuzerhof.** Tiny side streets and alleys run off Sonnenfelsgasse,
parallel to Bäckerstrasse. Along the pretty Schönlaterngasse, you'll find
a coverage passage to Heiligenkreuzerhof (Holy Cross Court), one of
the city's most peaceful backwaters. Back when, the famous Stift Heili-
genkreuz abbey outside Vienna was owner of some of Austria's biggest
vineyards and was rich enough to own vast stretches of Vienna real estate. It, in fact, still owns this complex of buildings, which dates from
the 17th century but got an 18th-century face-lift; its most noted com-
ponent is the Chapel of St. Bernard. Appropriately, the restraint of the
architecture—with only here and there a small outburst of Baroque spirit—
gives the courtyard the distinct feeling of a retreat. The square is a favorite site for seasonal markets at Easter and Christmas and for occasional
outdoor art shows. ⊠ *1st District* Ⓤ *U1 or U3/Stephansplatz.*

❾ **Hoher Markt.** This square was badly damaged during World War II,
but the famous Anker Clock at the east end survived the artillery fire.
The huge mechanical timepiece took six years (1911–17) to build and
still attracts crowds at noon when the full panoply of mechanical figures representing Austrian historical personages parades by, including Emperor Marcus Aurelius, Charlemagne, and Maria Theresa. The
figures are identified on a plaque to the bottom left of the clock. The
graceless buildings erected around the square since 1945 are not aging
well and do little to show off the square's lovely Baroque centerpiece,

THE SOUND—AND SIGHTS—OF MUSIC

WHAT CLOSER ASSOCIATION to Vienna is there than music? Boasting one of the world's greatest concert venues (Musikverein), two of the world's greatest symphony orchestras (Vienna Philharmonic and Vienna Symphony), and one of the top opera houses (Staatsoper), it's no wonder that music and the related politics are subjects of daily conversation. During July and August—just in time for tourists—the city hosts the Vienna Summer of Music, with numerous special events and concerts. And around nearly every bend, there are musical landmarks, ranging from theaters that premiered Mozart operas and The Merry Widow to residences of some of the world's greatest composers. You'll find the apartment where Mozart wrote his last three symphonies, the house where Schubert was born, and, just a tram ride away, the path that inspired Beethoven's Pastoral Symphony, to name just a few.

Of course, there is also music to delight as well as inspire. The statue of Johann Strauss II in the Stadtpark tells all. To see him, violin tucked under his chin, is to imagine those infectious waltzes, "Wine, Women, and Song," "Voices of Spring," and best of all, the "Emperor." But quite possibly you will not need to imagine them. Chances are, somewhere in the environs, an orchestra will be playing them. Head for the Theater an der Wien to hear great operetta (Die Fledermaus and The Merry Widow both premiered here) or to the Volksoper. Although the traditional classics are the main fare for the conservative, traditional Viennese, acceptance of modern music is growing, as are the audiences for pop and jazz.

Musicians' residences abound, and many are open as museums. The most famous are Mozart's Figarohaus and Beethoven's Pasqualatihaus, which are discussed in the Exploring sections below. Vienna has many other music landmarks scattered over the city—here's a sample:

Schubert—a native of the city, unlike most of Vienna's other famous composers—was born at **Nussdorferstrasse 54** (☎ 01/317–3601 Ⓤ U2/Schottenring; Streetcar 37 or 38 to Canisiusgasse), in the 9th District, and died in the **4th District** (☎ 01/581–6730 Ⓤ U4/Kettenbrückengasse) at Kettenbrückengasse 6.

Joseph Haydn's house (☎ 01/596–1307 Ⓤ U4/Pilgramgasse or U3/Zieglergasse), which includes a Brahms memorial room, is at Haydngasse 19 in the 6th District.

Beethoven's Heiligenstadt residence (☎ 01/370–5408 Ⓤ U4/Heiligenstadt; Bus 38A to Armbrustergasse or Tram 37 to Geweygasse), where at age 32 he wrote the "Heiligenstadt Testament," an anguished cry of pain and protest against his ever-increasing deafness, is at Probusgasse 6 in the 19th District.

All the above houses contain commemorative museums. Admission is €2. All are open Tuesday–Sunday 9–12:15 and 1–4:30. The home of the most popular composer of all, waltz king Johann Strauss the Younger, can be visited at **Praterstrasse 54** (☎ 01/214–0121 Ⓤ U4/Nestroyplatz), in the 2nd District; he lived here when he composed "The Blue Danube Waltz" in 1867. This piano and composing desk are on view in a green velvet salon.

the St. Joseph Fountain (portraying the marriage of Joseph and Mary), designed in 1729 by Joseph Emanuel Fischer von Erlach, son of the great Johann Bernhard Fischer von Erlach. The Hoher Markt does harbor one wholly unexpected attraction, however: underground Roman ruins (where, reputedly, Marcus Aurelius died). ⊠ *1st District* Ⓤ *U1 or U4/Schwedenplatz.*

off the
beaten
path

HUNDERTWASSERHAUS – To see one of Vienna's most amazing buildings, travel eastward from Schwendenplatz or Julius-Raab-Platz along Radetzkystrasse to the junction of Kegelgasse and Löwengasse. Here you'll find the Hundertwasserhaus, a 50-apartment public-housing complex designed by the late Austrian avant-garde artist Friedensreich Hundertwasser. The structure looks as though it was decorated by a crew of mischievous circus clowns wielding giant crayons. The building caused a sensation when it was erected in 1985 and still draws crowds of sightseers. ⊠ *Löwengasse and Kegelgasse, 3rd District/Landstrasse* Ⓤ *U1 or U4/Schwedenplatz, then Tram N to Hetzgasse.*

KUNSTHAUS WIEN – Near the Hundertwasserhaus you'll find another Hundertwasser project, an art museum, which mounts outstanding international exhibits in addition to showings of the colorful Hundertwasser works. Like the apartment complex nearby, the building itself is pure Hundertwasser, with irregular floors, windows with trees growing out of them, and sudden architectural surprises, a wholly appropriate setting for modern art. ⊠ *Untere Weissgerberstrasse 13, 3rd District/Landstrasse* ☎ *01/712–0491–0* ⊕ *www.kunsthauswien.com* 🖃 *€9* ⊙ *Daily 10–7* Ⓤ *U1 or U4/ Schwedenplatz, then Tram N or O to Radetzkyplatz.*

⓫ **Maria am Gestade** (St. Mary on the Banks). The middle-Gothic, seven-sided tower of Maria am Gestade, crowned by a delicate cupola, is a sheer joy to the eye and dispels the idea that Gothic must necessarily be austere. Built around 1400 (but much restored in the 17th and 19th centuries), the church incorporated part of the Roman city walls into its foundation; the north wall, as a result, takes a slight but noticeable dogleg to the right halfway down the nave. Like St. Stephan's, Maria am Gestade is rough-hewn Gothic, with a simple but forceful facade. The church is especially beloved, however, because of its unusual details— the pinnacled and saint-bedecked gable that tops the front facade, the stone canopy that hovers protectively over the front door, and (most appealing of all) the intricate openwork lantern atop the south-side bell tower. Appropriately enough in a city famous for its pastry, the lantern lends its tower an engaging suggestion of a sugar caster, while some see an allusion to hands intertwined in prayer. ⊠ *Passauer Platz/Salvatorgasse, 1st District* Ⓤ *U1 or U3/Stephansplatz.*

★ ❻ **Museum für Angewandte Kunst (MAK)** (Museum of Applied Arts). Otto Wagner, Felician von Myrbach, Koloman Moser, Josef Hoffmann, and Alfred Roller are just a few of the great Austrian names whose design are showcased here in this major museum devoted to the decorative and applied arts of the nation. As London's Victoria and Albert Museum (whose creation inspired Emperor Franz Josef to create this "Imperial and Royal Austrian Museum of Art and Industry" in 1852), this is a glamorous "attic" stuffed with a vast collection of furniture, porcelain, art objects, and priceless Oriental carpets, in this instance, all from Austrian artists, architects, and craftspeople; the Jugendstil display devoted to Josef Hoffman and his followers at the Wiener Werkstätte is particularly fine. Elsewhere the collection encompasses everything from Art Nouveau dresses to Secession theatrical designs. The museum also presents a number of changing exhibitions of contemporary works and houses an excellent restaurant, MAK Café (closed Monday). Also check out the museum shop for contemporary furniture and other objects (including great bar accessories) designed by young local artists. ⊠ *Stuben-ring 5, 1st District* ☎ *01/711–36–0* ⊕ *www.mak.at* ☞ *€7.90, Sat. free* ☉ *Tues. 10 AM–midnight, Wed.–Sun. 10–6* Ⓤ *U3/Stubentor.*

❼ Postsparkasse (Post Office Savings Bank). The Post Office Savings Bank is one of modern architecture's greatest curiosities. It was designed in 1904 by Otto Wagner, whom many consider the father of 20th-century architecture. In his famous manifesto *Modern Architecture,* Wagner condemned 19th-century revivalist architecture and pleaded for a modern style that honestly expressed modern building methods. Accordingly the exterior walls of the Post Office Savings Bank are mostly flat and undecorated; visual interest is supplied merely by varying the pattern of the bolts used to hold the marble slabs in place on the wall surface during construction. Later architects were to embrace Wagner's beliefs wholeheartedly, although they used different, truly modern building materials: glass and concrete rather than marble. The Post Office Savings Bank was indeed a bold leap into the future, but unfortunately the future took a different path and today the whole appears a bit dated. Go inside for a look at the restored and functioning Kassa-Saal, or central cashier's hall, to see how Wagner carried his concepts over to interior design. ⊠ *Georg-Coch-Platz 2, 1st District* ☎ *01/51400* ☉ *Lobby weekdays 8–3* Ⓤ *U1 or U4/Schwedenplatz, then Tram 1 or 2/Julius-Raab-Platz.*

❿ Ruprechtskirche (St. Ruprecht's Church). Ruprechtsplatz, another of Vienna's time-warp backwaters, lies to the north of the Kornhäusel Tower. The church in the middle, Ruprechtskirche, is the city's oldest. According to legend it was founded in 740; the oldest part of the present structure (the lower half of the tower) dates from the 11th century. Set on the ancient ramparts overlooking the Danube Canal, it is serene and unpretentious. It is usually closed, but sometimes opens for local art shows and summer evening classical concerts. ⊠ *Ruprechtsplatz, 1st District,* Ⓤ *U1 or U4/Schwedenplatz.*

❹ Schönlaterngasse (Street of the Beautiful Lantern). Once part of Vienna's medieval Latin Quarter, Schönlaterngasse is the main artery of a historic neighborhood that has reblossomed in recent years. Thanks in part to government Kulturschillings—or renovation loans—the quarter has been revamped. Streets are lined with beautiful Baroque town houses (often with colorfully painted facades), now distinctive showcases for art galleries, chic shops, and coffeehouses. At No. 5 you'll find a cov-

FodorśChoice ★

UP, UP, AND AWAY

VIENNA'S MOST FAMOUS PARK, *the Prater, can be found by heading out northeast from the city center, across the Danube Canal (Donaukanal) along Praterstrasse. In 1766, to the dismay of the aristocracy, Emperor Joseph II decreed that this vast expanse of imperial parklands would henceforth be open to the public. Set between the Danube Canal and the Danube proper, the Prater is a public park to this day, notable for its long promenade (the Hauptallee, more than 4½ km, or 3 mi, in length), its sports facilities (a golf course, a stadium, a racetrack, and a swimming pool, for starters), a planetarium, and the Wurstelprater funfair, whose rides—including a lovely Lilliputian Railroad—are priced individually (open for business March–April, daily 10 AM–10 PM; May–September, daily 9 AM–midnight; Oct., daily 10–10; November–February, daily 10–8 PM). If you look carefully,*

discover the handful of charming rides dating from the 1920s and '30s. Towering over all is the landmark 200-foot Ferris wheel, the Riesenrad—star of the 1949 film The Third Man *and built in 1897 for Vienna's Universal Exposition. The wheel's progress is slow and stately (a revolution takes 20 minutes), the views from its cars magnificent (admission, €7.50). In 2002, it was spruced up with razzle-dazzle nighttime lighting and a café. But try to eat instead at the famous* Schweizerhaus *(⊠ Strasse des 1. Mai 116 ☎ 01/728–0152 ۞ closed Nov.–mid-Mar.), which has been serving frosty mugs of beer, roast chicken, and Stelze (a huge hunk of crispy roast pork on the bone) for more than 100 years. Its informal setting with wood-plank tables indoors or in the garden in summer adds to the fun. The U1 subway has a Praterstern stop.*

---

ered passage that leads to the historic **Heiligenkreuzerhof** courtyard. The most famous house of the quarter is the **Basiliskenhaus** (House of the Basilik; ⊠ Schönlaterngasse 7, 1st District). According to legend, it was first built for a baker; on June 26, 1212, a foul-smelling basilisk (half-rooster, half-toad, with a glance that could kill) took up residence in the courtyard and well, poisoning the water. An enterprising apprentice dealt with the problem by climbing down the well armed with a mirror; when the basilisk saw its own reflection, it turned to stone. The petrified creature can still be seen in a niche on the building's facade. Today modern science accounts for the contamination with a more prosaic explanation: natural-gas seepage. Be sure to take a look in the house's miniature courtyard for a trip back to medieval Vienna (the house itself is private). Next door, at the magnificently medieval No. 7a, the composer Robert Schumann resided 1838–39. The picturesque street is named for the ornate wrought-iron wall lantern at Schönlaterngasse 6. One more door over, note the Baroque courtyard at Schönlaterngasse 8—one of the city's prettiest. For a time-out, head to the end of the street to find Sonnenfelsgasse, where there are a number of cafés to tempt you.

★ ❶ **Stephansdom** (St. Stephan's Cathedral). Vienna's soaring centerpiece, this beloved cathedral enshrines the heart of the city—although it is curious to note that when first built in 1144–47 it actually stood outside the city walls. Vienna can thank a period of hard times for the Mother Church for the cathedral's distinctive silhouette. Originally the structure was to have had matching 445-feet-high spires, a standard design of the era, but funds ran out, and the north tower to this day remains a happy reminder of what gloriously is not. The lack of symmetry creates an imbalance that makes the cathedral instantly identifiable from its profile alone. The cathedral, like the Staatsoper and some other major buildings, was very heavily damaged in World War II. Since then it has risen from the fires of destruction like a phoenix, and like the phoenix, it is a symbol of regeneration.

It is difficult now, sitting quietly in the shadowed peace, to tell what was original and what parts of the walls and vaults were reconstructed. No matter: its history-rich atmosphere is dear to all Viennese. That noted, St. Stephan's has a fierce presence that is blatantly un-Viennese. It is a stylistic jumble ranging from 13th-century Romanesque to 15th-century Gothic. Like the exterior, St. Stephan's interior lacks the soaring unity of Europe's greatest Gothic cathedrals, with much of its decoration dating from the later Baroque era. However, it all began back in 1147, when Duke Heinrich Jasomirgott built the first structure, which, destroyed by fire, was replaced by a Romanesque building during the reign of King Ottocar of Bohemia. The Great West Front thus dates from the late 13th century, with the soaring Risentor (Giant Doorway) flanked by two small towers (Heidentürme). There are many attractive details in the carving here, Samson wrenching open the lion's jaws, a griffin, and all sorts of mythical beasts.

The wealth of decorative sculpture in St. Stephan's can be intimidating to the nonspecialist, so if you wish to explore the cathedral in detail, you may want to buy the admirably complete English-language description sold in the small room marked Dom Shop. One particularly masterly work, however, should be seen by everyone: the stone pulpit attached to the second freestanding pier on the left of the central nave, carved by Anton Pilgram around 1510. The delicacy of its decoration would in itself set the pulpit apart, but even more intriguing are its five sculpted figures. Carved around the outside of the pulpit proper are the four Latin Fathers of the Church (from left to right: St. Augustine, St. Gregory, St. Jerome, and St. Ambrose), and each is given an individual personality so sharply etched as to suggest satire, perhaps of living models. There is no satire suggested by the fifth figure, however; below the pulpit's stairs Pilgram sculpted a fine self-portrait, showing himself peering out a half-open window. Note the toads, lizards, and other creatures climbing the spiral rail alongside the steps up to the pulpit. As you walk among the statues and aisles, remember that many notable events occurred here, including Mozart's marriage in 1782 and his funeral in December 1791. The funeral service was conducted to the left of the main entrance in a small chapel beneath the Heidenturm, to the left of the cathedral's main doorway. The funeral bier on which his casket was placed is in the Crucifix Chapel, which marks the entrance to the crypt and can be reached from outside the church. His body rested on a spot not far from the famous open-air pulpit—near the apse, at the other end of the cathedral—named after the monk Capistranus who, in 1450, preached from it to rouse the people to fight the invading Turks. Continuing around the cathedral exterior at the apse, you'll find a centuries-old sculpted torso of the Man of Sorrows, known irreverently as Our Lord of the Toothache, because of its agonized expression. Inside, nearly every corner has something to savor: the Marienchor (Virgin's Choir) has the Tomb of Rudolph IV; the Wiern Neustadt altar is a wood-carved masterpiece; the gilded pulpit carved by Anton Pilgram between 1510 and 1550 with the heads of the Fathers of the Church; and the Catacombs, where the internal organs of the Habsburgs rest.

St. Stephan's was devastated by fire in the last days of World War II, and the extent of the damage may be seen by leaving the cathedral through the south portal, where a set of prereconstruction photographs commemorates the disaster. Restoration was protracted and difficult, but today the cathedral once again dominates the center of the city. Note the "05" carved into the stone to the right of the outer massive front door. The "0" stands for Österreich, or Austria, and the "5" is for the fifth letter of the alphabet. This translates into OE, the abbreviation for Österreich, and was a covert sign of resistance to the Nazi annexation of Austria. The bird's-eye views from the cathedral's beloved **Alter Steffl** tower will be a highlight for some. The tower is 450 feet high and was built between 1359 and 1433. The climb or elevator ride up is rewarded with vistas that extend to the rising slopes of the Wienerwald. ⊠ *Stephansplatz, 1st District* ☎ *01/515–5237–67* 🖾 *Guided tour, €4; catacombs, €4; elevator to Pummerin bell, €4* ☉ *Daily 6 AM–10 PM. Guided tours in English daily Apr.–Oct. at 3:45; catacombs tour (minimum 5 people) Mon.–Sat. every half hr 10–11:30 and 1:30–4:30, Sun. every half hr 1:30–4:30; North Tower elevator to Pummerin bell, Apr.–Oct., daily 8:30–5:30; July and Aug., daily 8:30–6; Nov.–Mar., daily 8:30–5* Ⓤ *U1 or U3/Stephansplatz.*

need a break? If you're in the mood for ice cream, head for **Zanoni & Zanoni** (⊠ Am Lugeck 7, 1st District ☎ 01/512–7979) near St. Stephan's, between Rotenturmstrasse and Bäckerstrasse, and open 365 days a year. Here you'll have trouble choosing from among 25 or more flavors of smooth, Italian-style gelato, including mango, caramel, and chocolate chip. There are also tables if you want to rest your feet and enjoy a sundae.

❷ Universitätskirche (Jesuit Church). The east end of Bäckerstrasse is punctuated by Dr.-Ignaz-Seipel-Platz, named for the theology professor who was chancellor of Austria in the 1920s. On the north side is the Universitätskirche, or Jesuitenkirche, built around 1630. Its flamboyant Baroque interior contains a fine trompe-l'oeil ceiling fresco by that master of visual trickery Andrea Pozzo, who was imported from Rome in 1702 for the job. You may hear a Mozart or Haydn mass sung here in Latin on Sunday. ⊠ *Dr.-Ignaz-Seipel-Platz, 1st District* ☎ *01/512–5232–0* Ⓤ *U3 Stubentor/Dr.-Karl-Lueger-Platz.*

BITTERSWEET VIENNA:
BAROQUE GEMS & COZY CAFÉS

As the city developed and expanded, the core quickly outgrew its early confines. New urban centers sprang up, to be ornamented by government buildings and elegant town residences. Since Vienna was the beating heart of a vast empire, nothing was spared to make the edifices as exuberant as possible, with utility often a secondary consideration. The best architects of the day were commissioned to create impressions as well as buildings, and they did their jobs well. That so much has survived is a testimony to the solidity of the designs and of the structures on which the ornamentation has been overlaid.

Those not fortunate enough to afford town palaces were relegated to housing that was often less than elegant and confining. Rather than suffer the discomfitures of a disruptive household environment, the city's literati and its philosophers and artists took refuge in cafés, which in effect became their combined salons and offices. To this day, cafés remain an important element of Viennese life. Many residents still have their *Stammtisch,* or regular table, at which they appear daily. Talk still prevails—but, increasingly, so do handy cell phones and laptops.

a good
walk

Start in the Wipplingerstrasse at the upper (west) end of Hoher Markt to find touches of both the imperial and the municipal Vienna. On the east side is the **Altes Rathaus** ⓬ ▶, which served as the city hall until 1885; on the west is the **Bohemian Court Chancery** ⓭, once diplomatic headquarters for Bohemia's representation to the Habsburg court. Turn south into the short Fütterergasse to reach Judenplatz, in the Middle Ages the center of Judaism in Vienna, and today site of the **Judenplatz Museum** ⓮, landmarked by a memorial created by Rachel Whitehead, one of contemporary art's most important sculptors. A clock-watcher's delight is down at the end of Kurrentgasse in the form of the **Uhrenmuseum** ⓯ (Clock Museum); around the corner through the Parisgasse to Schulhof, a children's delight is the **Puppen und Spielzeugmuseum** (Doll and Toy Museum) ⓰. Follow Schulhof into the huge **Am Hof** ⓱ square, boasting the **Kirche Am Hof** ⓲ and what must be the world's most elegant fire station. The square hosts an antiques and collectibles market on Thursday and Friday most of the year, plus other ad hoc events. Take the minuscule Irisgasse from Am Hof into the Naglergasse, noting the mosaic Jugendstil facade on the pharmacy in the Bognergasse, to your left. Around a bend in the narrow Naglergasse is the **Freyung** ⓳, an irregular square bounded on the south side by two wonderfully stylish palaces, including **Palais Ferstel** ⓴, now a shopping arcade, and the elegantly restored **Palais Harrach** ㉑ next door, now an outpost of the Kunsthistoriches Museum. Opposite, the privately run **Kunstforum** art museum mounts varied and outstanding exhibitions. The famous **Palais Daun-Kinsky** ㉒ at the beginning of Herrengasse is still partly a private residence. The north side of the Freyung is watched over by the **Schottenkirche** ㉓, a Scottish church that was, in fact, established by Irish monks; the complex also houses a small but worthwhile museum of the order's treasures. Follow Teinfaltstrasse from opposite the Schottenkirche, turning right into Schreyvogelgasse; at No. 8 is the famed **"Third Man" Portal** ㉔. Climb the ramp on your right past the so-called Dreimäderl-haus at Schreyvogelgasse 10—note the ornate facade of this pre-Bie-dermeier patrician house—to reach Molker Bastei, where Beethoven lived in the **Pasqualatihaus** ㉕, now housing a museum commemorating the composer. Follow the ring south to Löwelstrasse, turning left into Bankgasse; then turn right into Abraham-a-Sancta Clara-Gasse (the tiny street that runs off the Bankgasse) to Minoritenplatz and the **Minoritenkirche** ㉖, the Minorite Church, with its strangely hatless tower. Inside is a kitschy mosaic of the *Last Supper*. Landhausgasse will bring you to Herrengasse, and diagonally across the street, in the back corner of the Palais Ferstel, is the **Café Central** ㉗, one of Vienna's hangouts for the famous. As you go south up Herrengasse, on the left is the odd Hochhaus, a 20th-century building once renowned as Vienna's skyscraper. Opposite are elegant Baroque former town palaces, now used as museum and administration buildings by the province of Lower Austria.

TIMING   The actual distances in this walk are relatively short, and you could cover the route in 1½ hours or so. But if you take time to linger in the museums and sample a coffee with whipped cream in the Café Central, you'll develop a much better understanding of the contrasts between old and newer in the city. You could easily spend a day following this walk, if you were to take in all of the museums; note that these, like many of Vienna's museums, are closed Monday.

HOW TO GET THERE   Am Hof, that great Baroque square that was once a medieval marketplace, is the center from which all the Baroque gem sights can be easily reached. Take either Tram 1 or 2 to Schottentor on the Ring, then Bus 1A to Am Hof. Another option is the U3 to Herrengasse, which is just steps away. The "Third Man" portal and Pasqualatihaus can be reached on foot from Schottentor.

What to See

⓬ **Altes Rathaus** (Old City Hall). Opposite the elegantly imposing Bohemian Chancery stands the Altes Rathaus, dating from the 14th century but displaying 18th-century Baroque motifs on its facade. The interior passageways and courtyards, which are open during the day, house a Gothic chapel (open at odd hours); display cases exhibiting maps and photos illustrating the city's history; and one of the ladies Vienna is very partial to the sculpted nude at the heart of the Baroque-era **Andromeda Fountain,** sculpted by Georg Raphael Donner in 1741. The bronze nymph valiantly struggles away from the oncoming winged beast, who—delightfully—sprouts water from his mouth. ⊠ *Wipplingerstrasse/Salvatorgasse 7, 1st District* Ⓤ *U1 or U4/Schwedenplatz.*

⓱ **Am Hof.** Am Hof is one of the city's oldest squares. In the Middle Ages the ruling Babenberg family built their castle on the site of No. 2; hence the name of the square, which means simply "at court." The grand residence hosted such luminaries as Barbarossa and Walter von der Vogelweide, the famous Minnesinger who stars in Wagner's *Tannhäuser*. The Baroque **Column of Our Lady** in the center dates from 1667, marking the Catholic victory over the Swedish Protestants in the Thirty Years' War

(1618–48). The onetime **Civic Armory** at the northwest corner has been used as a fire station since 1685 (the high-spirited facade, with its Habsburg eagle, was "Baroqued" in 1731) and today houses the headquarters of Vienna's fire department. The complex includes a firefighting museum (open only on Sunday mornings). Presiding over the east side of the square is the noted Kirche Am Hof. In Bognergasse to the right of the Kirche Am Hof, around the corner from the imposing Bank Austria headquarters building, at No. 9, is the **Engel Apotheke** (pharmacy) with a Jugendstil mosaic depicting winged women collecting the elixir of life in outstretched chalices. At the turn of the 20th century the inner city was dotted with storefronts decorated in a similar manner; today this is the sole survivor. Around the bend from the Naglergasse is the picturesque Freyung square. At No. 13 is the fairly stolid 17th century **Palais Collalto,** famous as the setting for Mozart's first public engagement at the ripe age of six. This was but the first showing of the child prodigy in Vienna, for his father had him perform for three Viennese princes, four dukes, and five counts in the space of a few weeks. Having newly arrived from Salzburg, the child set Vienna on its ear and he was showered with money and gifts, including some opulent children's clothes from the Empress Maria Theresa. Next door is the Jesuit church where Leopold Mozart directed his son's *Father Dominicus Mass,* K. 66, in August 1773. Some years later, Mozart's first child, Raimund Leopold, was baptized here. Sadly, the child died two months later. ✉ *1st District* Ⓤ *U3/Herrengasse.*

⑬ Bohemian Court Chancery. One of the architectural jewels of the Inner City can be found at Wipplingerstrasse 7, the former Bohemian Court Chancery, built between 1708 and 1714 by Johann Bernhard Fischer von Erlach. Fischer von Erlach and his contemporary Johann Lukas von Hildebrandt were the reigning architectural geniuses of Baroque-era Vienna; they designed their churches and palaces during the building boom that followed the defeat of the Turks in 1683. Both had studied architecture in Rome, and both were deeply impressed by the work of the great Italian architect Francesco Borromini, who brought to his designs a wealth and freedom of invention that were looked upon with horror by most contemporary Romans. But for Fischer von Erlach and Hildebrandt, Borromini's ideas were a source of triumphant architectural inspiration, and when they returned to Vienna they produced them many of the city's most beautiful buildings. Alas, narrow Wipplingerstrasse allows little more than a oblique view of this florid facade. The back side of the building, on Judenplatz, is less elaborate but gives a better idea of the design concept. The building first served as diplomatic and representational offices of Bohemia (now a part of the Czech Republic) to the Vienna-based monarchy and, today, still houses government offices. ✉ *Wipplingerstrasse 7, 1st District* Ⓤ *U1 or U4/Schwedenplatz.*

★ ㉗ Café Central. Part of the **Palais Ferstel** complex, the Café Central is one of Vienna's more famous cafés. It's also one of its largest: people sipping coffee and reading books are dwarfed by gigantic neo-Romanesque columns and white-tile, cavernous corners that would not be out of place in a railway station. In its prime (before World War I), the café was "home" to some of the most famous literary figures of the day, who dined, socialized, worked, and even received mail here. The denizens of the Central favored political argument; indeed, their heated discussions became so well known that in October 1917, when Austria's foreign secretary was informed of the outbreak of the Russian Revolution, he dismissed the report with a facetious reference to a well-known local Marxist, the chess-loving (and presumably harmless) "Herr Bronstein from the Café Central." The remark was to become famous all over Austria, for Herr Bronstein had disappeared and was about to resurface in Russia bearing a new name: Leon Trotsky. Today, things are a good deal more yuppified and shiny (thanks to a big renovation some years ago): The coffee now comes with a little chocolate biscuit and is overpriced and the man tickling the piano keys is more likely to play Sinatra than Strauss. But no matter how crowded the café may become, you can linger as long as you like over a single cup of coffee and a newspaper from the huge international selection provided. Across the street at Herrengasse 17 is the **Café Central Konditorei,** an excellent pastry and confectionery shop associated with the café. ⊠ *Herrengasse 17, 1st District* ☎ *01/535–9905* ⊕ *www.palaisevents.at/* ⊟ *AE, DC, MC, V* Ⓤ *U3/Herrengasse.*

⑲ The Freyung. Naglergasse, at its curved end, flows into Heidenschuss, which in turn leads down a slight incline from Am Hof to one of Vienna's most prominent squares, the Freyung, meaning "freeing." The square was so named because for many centuries the monks at the adjacent Schottenhof had the privilege of offering sanctuary for three days. In the center of the square stands the allegorical **Austria Fountain** (1845), notable because its Bavarian designer, one Ludwig Schwanthaler, had the statues cast in Munich and then supposedly filled them with cigars to be smuggled into Vienna for black-market sale. Around the sides of the square are some of Vienna's greatest patrician residences, including the **Ferstel, Harrach, and Kinsky palaces.**

Found on the Freyung square and designed by Joseph Kornhäusel in a very different style from his Fleischmarkt tower, the **Schottenhof** is a shaded courtyard. The facade typifies the change that came over Viennese architecture during the Biedermeier era (1815–48). The Viennese, according to the traditional view, were at the time so relieved to be rid of the upheavals of the Napoleonic Wars that they accepted without protest the iron-handed repression of Prince Metternich, chancellor of Austria, and retreated into a cozy and complacent domesticity. Restraint also ruled in architecture, with Baroque license rejected in favor of a new and historically "correct" style that was far more controlled and reserved. Kornhäusel led the way in establishing this trend in Vienna; his Schottenhof facade is all sober organization and frank repetition. But in its marriage of strong and delicate forces it still pulls off the great Viennese-waltz trick of successfully merging seemingly antithetical characteristics. ⊠ *At Am Hof and Herrengasse, 1st District* Ⓤ *U3/Herrengasse.*

need a break? In summer, **Wienerwald** restaurant, in the delightful tree-shaded courtyard of the Schottenhof at Freyung 6, is ideal for relaxing over lunch or dinner with a glass of wine or frosty beer. The specialty here is chicken, and you can get it just about every possible way. Especially good is the spit-roasted *Knoblauch* (garlic) chicken. It's open daily.

🄔 Judenplatz Museum. In what was once the old Jewish ghetto, construction workers discovered the remains of a 13th-century synagogue while digging for a parking garage. Simon Wiesenthal (a Vienna resident) helped to turn it into a museum dedicated to the Austrian Jews who died in World War II. Marking the outside is a rectangular concrete cube resembling library shelves, signifying Jewish love of learning, designed by famed contemporary British sculptor Rachel Whitehead. Downstairs are three exhibition rooms on medieval Jewish life and the synagogue excavations. Also in Judenplatz is a statue of the 18th-century playwright Gotthold Ephraim Lessing, erected after World War II. ⊠ *Judenplatz 8, 1st District* ☎ *01/535–0431* ⊕ *www.jmw.at* 🎫 *€3; combination ticket with Jewish Museum €7* ☉ *Sun.–Fri. 10–6, Thurs. 10–8 PM* Ⓤ *U1 or U4/Schwedenplatz.*

🄘 Kirche Am Hof. On the east side of the Am Hof square, the Kirche Am Hof, or the Church of the Nine Choirs of Angels, is identified by its sprawling Baroque facade, designed by Carlo Carlone in 1662. The somber interior lacks appeal, but the checkerboard marble floor may remind you of Dutch churches. ⊠ *Am Hof 1, 1st District* Ⓤ *U3/Herrengasse.*

Kunstforum. The huge gold ball atop the doorway on the Freyung at the corner of Renngasse marks the entrance to the Kunstforum, an extensive art gallery run by Bank Austria and featuring outstanding temporary exhibitions. ⊠ *Freyung 8, 1st District* ☎ *01/537–3326* ⊕ *www. kunstforumwien.at* 🎫 *€9* ☉ *Daily 10–7, Fri. 10–9 PM except July and Aug.* Ⓤ *U3/Herrengasse.*

🄒 Minoritenkirche (Church of the Minorite Order). The Minoritenplatz is named after its centerpiece, the Minoritenkirche, a Gothic affair with a strange stump of a tower, built mostly in the 14th century. The front is brutally ugly, but the back is a wonderful, if predominantly 19th-century, surprise. The interior contains the city's most imposing piece of kitsch: a large mosaic reproduction of Leonardo da Vinci's *Last Supper,* commissioned by Napoléon in 1806 and later purchased by Emperor Francis I. ⊠ *Minoritenplatz 2A, 1st District* ☎ *01/533–4162* Ⓤ *U3/Herrengasse.*

🄔 Palais Ferstel. At Freyung 2 stands the Palais Ferstel, which is not a palace at all but a commercial shop-and-office complex designed in 1856 and named for its architect, Heinrich Ferstel. The facade is Italianate in style, harking back, in its 19th-century way, to the Florentine palazzi of the early Renaissance. The interior is unashamedly eclectic: vaguely Romanesque in feel and Gothic in decoration, with here and there a bit of Renaissance or Baroque sculpted detail thrown in for good measure. Such eclecticism is sometimes dismissed as mindlessly derivative, but here the architectural details are so respectfully and inventively combined that the interior becomes a pleasure to explore. The 19th-century stock-exchange rooms upstairs are now gloriously restored and used for conferences and concerts. ⊠ *Freyung 2, 1st District* Ⓤ *U3/Herrengasse.*

🄔 Palais Harrach. Dominating the Freyung square, the Palais Harrach was once the repository of one of the world's most famous collections of Old Master paintings, the result of centuries of purchases by the

Counts von Harrach, who garnered fame as Austrian ambassadors (a remnant is on view at the family's Schloss Rohrau in Lower Austria). In 1689 Count Ferdinand Bonaventura von Harrach commissioned Domenico Martinelli to build this bulky town palais. Next door to the Palais Ferstel, it has been an adjunct gallery for the Kunsthistorisches Museum since 1994 and now includes a small but worthwhile gallery of paintings and art objects. Mozart and his sister, Nannerl, performed here when children for Count Ferdinand during their first visit to Vienna in 1762. The palace looks much different from Mozart's day, however, since it was altered after 1845 and severely damaged by World War II. Many of the state rooms have lost their historical lustre but the Marble Room, set with gold boiseries, and the Red Galley, topped with a spectacular ceiling painting, still offer grand settings for receptions, readings, and exhibitions. ⊠ *Freyung 3, 1st District* ☎ *01/523–1753* ⊕ *www.khm.at/* ▱ *€7* ☉ *During special exhibits, daily 10–6* Ⓤ *U3/Herrengasse.*

★ ㉒ **Palais Daun-Kinsky.** Just one of the architectural treasures that comprise the urban set piece of the Freyung, the Palais Daun-Kinsky is the square's best-known palace, and is one of the most sophisticated pieces of Baroque architecture in the whole city. It was built between 1713 and 1716 by Johann Lukas von Hildebrandt for the Prince von Daun, and its only real competition comes a few yards farther on: the Greek-temple facade of the Schottenhof, which is at right angles to the Schottenkirche, up the street from the Kinsky Palace. Due to the cramped footage on the square itself, Hildebrandt opted for trading in the usual six-bay-across facade for a six-story-high design, and covered the facade with a particularly rich array of sculpted goodies, including writhing atlantes, nymphs, and pedimental figures, along with tapering pilasters that conjure up the design for a banqueting table. The facade has recently been rather floridly painted in bright yellow and white by its owners, the Wiener Kunst Auktionen, a public auction business offering artworks and antiques. If there is an auction viewing, try to see the palace's spectacular 18th-century staircase, all marble goddesses and crowned with a trompe-l'oeil ceiling painted by Marcantonio Chiarini. ⊠ *Freyung 4, 1st District* ☎ *01/532–4200* ⊕ *www.palais-kinsky.com/* 🖷 *01/532–42009* ☉ *Weekdays 10–6* Ⓤ *U3/Herrengasse.*

㉕ **Pasqualatihaus.** This was one of the 30-odd addresses Beethoven lived in during his years in Vienna. Here, in an apartment building paid for by Pasqualati, the court physician of Empress Maria Theresa, Beethoven composed his only opera, *Fidelio,* as well as his Seventh Symphony and Fourth Piano Concerto. Today his apartment houses a small commemorative museum, but it has nothing left from the 18th century. Instead of the composer's domestic disarray, there are modern glass vitrines and pastel walls. Some exhibits are fascinating: note particularly the prints that show what the window view out over the Mölker bastion was like when Beethoven lived here and the piano that dates from his era—one that was beefed-up to take the banging Beethoven made fashionable. After navigating the narrow and twisting stairway, you might well ask how he maintained the jubilant spirit of the works he wrote there. This house is around the corner from the "Third Man" Portal. ⊠ *8 Mölker Bastei, 1st District* ☎ *01/535–8905* ⊕ *www.wienmuseum.at/* 🎫 *€2* 🕐 *Tues.–Sun. 9–12:15 and 1–4:30* Ⓤ *U2/Schottentor.*

☾ ⓰ **Puppen und Spielzeugmuseum** (Doll and Toy Museum). As appealing as the clockworks of the Uhrenmuseum next door is this doll and toy museum, with its collections of dolls, dollhouses, teddy bears, and trains. ⊠ *Schulhof 4, 1st District* ☎ *01/535–6860* 🎫 *€4.70* 🕐 *Tues.–Sun. 10–6* Ⓤ *U1 or U3/Stephansplatz.*

㉓ **Schottenkirche.** From 1758 to 1761, the noted Italian *vedutiste* (scene-painter), Bernardo Bellotto, did paintings of the Freyung square looking north toward the Schottenkirche; the pictures hang in the Kunsthistorisches Museum, and the similarity to the view you see about 240 years later is arresting. In fact a church has stood on the site of the Schottenkirche since 1177; the present edifice dates from the mid-1600s, when it replaced its predecessor, which had collapsed after the architects of the time had built on weakened foundations. The interior, with its ornate ceiling and a decided surplus of cherubs and angels' faces, is in stark contrast to the plain exterior. The adjacent small **Museum im Schottenstift** includes the best of the monastery's artworks, including the celebrated late-Gothic high altar, dating from about 1470. The winged altar is fascinating for its portrayal of the Holy Family in flight into Egypt—with the city of Vienna clearly identifiable in the background. ⊠ *Freyung 6, 1st District* ☎ *01/534–98–600* ⊕ *www.schottenstift.at* 🎫 *Church free, museum €4* 🕐 *Museum Mon.–Sat. 10–5* Ⓤ *U2/Schottentor.*

㉔ **"Third Man" Portal.** The doorway at Schreyvogelgasse 8 (up the incline) was made famous in 1949 by the classic film *The Third Man* (see the Close-up box, *below*); it was here that Orson Welles, as the malevolently knowing Harry Lime, stood hiding in the dark, only to have his smiling face illuminated by a sudden light from the upper-story windows of the house across the alley. The film enjoys a renaissance each summer in the Burg Kino and is fascinating for its portrayal of a postwar Vienna still in ruins. To get here from the nearby and noted Schottenkirche, follow Teinfaltstrasse one block west to Schreyvogelgasse on the right. ⊠ *1st District* Ⓤ *U2/Schottentor.*

★ ⓯ **Uhrenmuseum** (Clock Museum). Kurrentgasse leads south from the east end of Judenplatz; the beautifully restored 18th-century houses on its east side make this one of the most unpretentiously appealing streets in the city. And at the far end of the street is one of Vienna's most appealing museums: the Uhrenmuseum, or Clock Museum (enter to the right on the Schulhof side of the building). The museum's three floors of blankly modern rooms display a splendid parade of clocks and watches—more than 3,000 timepieces—dating from the 15th century to the present. The ruckus of bells and chimes pealing forth on any hour is impressive, but for the full cacophony try to be here at noon. Right next door is the Puppen und Spielzeugmuseum. ⊠ *Schulhof 2, 1st District* ☎ *01/533–2265* 🎫 *€4, Sun. free* 🕐 *Tues.–Sun. 9–4:30* Ⓤ *U1 or U3/Stephansplatz.*

CloseUp

TRACKING DOWN THE THIRD MAN

PROBABLY NOTHING HAS DONE more to create the myth of postwar Vienna than Carol Reed's classic 1949 film The Third Man. The bombed-out ruins of this proud, imperial city created an indelible image of devastation and corruption in the war's aftermath.

Vienna was then divided into four sectors, each commanded by one of the victorious American, Russian, French, and British armies. But their attempts at rigid control could not prevent a thriving black market. Reed's film version of the great Graham Greene thriller features Vienna as a leading player, from the top of its Ferris wheel in the Prater to the depth of its lowest sewers—"which run right into the Blue Danube"—thrillingly used for the famous chase scene. It is only fitting to note that this was the first British film to be shot entirely on location.

In the film, Joseph Cotten plays Holly Martins, a pulp-fiction writer who comes to Vienna in search of his friend Harry Lime (Orson Welles). He makes the mistake of delving too deeply into Lime's affairs, even falling in love with his girlfriend, Anna Schmidt (Alida Valli), with fatal consequences.

Many of the sites where the film was shot still remain and are easily visited. Harry Lime appears for the first time nearly one hour into the film in the doorway of Anna's apartment building at No. 8 Schreyvogelgasse, around the corner from the Mölker-Bastei (a remnant of the old city wall). He then runs to Am Hof, a lovely square lined with Baroque town houses and churches, which appears much closer to Anna's neighborhood than it actually is.

The famous scene between Lime and Martins on the Ferris wheel was filmed on the Riesenrad at the Prater, the huge amusement park across the Danube canal. While the two friends talk in the enclosed compartment, the wheel slowly makes a revolution, with all Vienna spread out below them.

In the memorable chase at the end of the movie, Lime is seen running through the damp, sinister sewers of Vienna, hotly pursued by the authorities. In reality, he would not have been able to use the sewer system as an escape route because the tunnels were too low and didn't connect between the different centers of the city.

But a movie creates its own reality. In fact, a more feasible, if less cinematic, possibility of escape was offered by the labyrinth of cellars that still connect many buildings in the city.

Lime's funeral is held at the Zentralfriedhof (Central Cemetery), reachable by the 71 streetcar. This is the final scene of the movie, where Anna Schmidt walks down the stark, wide avenue (dividing sections 69 and 70), refusing to acknowledge the wistful presence of Holly Martins.

After touring sewers and cemeteries, a pick-me-up might be in order. You couldn't do better than to treat yourself to a stop at the Hotel Sacher, used for a scene in the beginning of the movie when Holly Martins is using the telephone in the lobby. The bar in the Sacher was a favorite hangout of director Carol Reed, and when filming finally wrapped, he left a signed note to the bartender, saying: "To the creator of the best Bloody Marys in the whole world."

— Bonnie Dodson

VIENNA'S SHOP WINDOW:
FROM MICHAELERPLATZ TO THE GRABEN

The compact area bounded roughly by the back side of the Hofburg palace complex, the Kohlmarkt, the Graben, and Kärntnerstrasse belongs to the oldest core of the city. Remains of the Roman city are just below the present-day surface. This was and still is the commercial heart of the city, dense with shops and markets for various commodities; today, the Kohlmarkt and Graben in particular offer the choicest luxury shops, overflowing into the Graben end of Kärnterstrasse. The area is marvelous for its visual treats, ranging from the squares and varied architecture to shop windows. The evening view down Kohlmarkt from the Graben is an inspiring classic, with the night-lit gilded dome of Michael's Gate to the palace complex as the glittering backdrop. Sights in this area range from the sacred—the Baroque church of Peterskirche—to the more profane pleasures of Demel's, Vienna's beloved pastry shop and the modernist masterwork of the Looshaus.

a good walk

Start your walk through this fascinating quarter at **Michaelerplatz** ㉘ ⌐, one of Vienna's most evocative squares, where the feel of the imperial city remains very strong; the buildings around the perimeter present a synopsis of the city's entire architectural history: medieval church spire, Renaissance church facade, Baroque palace facade, 19th-century apartment house, and 20th-century bank. Look in the Michaelerkirche (St. Michael's Church). Opposite the church is the once-controversial **Looshaus** ㉙, considered a breakthrough in modern architecture (visitors are welcome to view the restored lobby) when it was designed by Adolf Loos in 1911. From Michaelerplatz, take the small passageway to the right of the church; in it on your right is a relief dating from 1480 of Christ on the Mount of Olives. Follow the Stallburggasse through to Dorotheergasse, and turn right to discover the **Dorotheum**, the government-run auction house and Viennese equivalent of Christie's or Sotheby's. On your right in the Dorotheergasse (toward the Graben) is the enlarged **Jewish Museum** ㉚, which includes a bookstore and café. On the left is the famous Café Hawelka, haunt to the contemporary art and literature crowd. Turn right in the Graben to come to **Stock-im-Eisen** ㉛; the famous nail-studded tree trunk is encased in the corner of the building with the Bank Austria offices. Opposite and impossible to overlook is the aggressive **Neues Haas-Haus** ㉜, an upmarket restaurant and shopping complex. Wander back through the **Graben** ㉝ for the full effect of this harmonious street and look up to see the ornamentation on the buildings. Pass the 17th-century memorial of the Pestsäule, or Plague Column, which shoots up from the middle of the Graben like a geyser of whipped cream. Just off to the north side is the **Peterskirche** ㉞, St. Peter's Church, a Baroque gem almost hidden by its surroundings. At the end of the Graben, turn left into the **Kohlmarkt** ㉟ for the classic view of the domed arch leading to the Hofburg, the imperial palace complex. Even if your feet aren't calling a sit-down strike, finish up at **Demel** ㊱, at Kohlmarkt 14, for some of the best *Gebäck* (pastries) in the world.

TIMING Inveterate shoppers, window or otherwise, will want to take time to pause before or in many of the elegant shops during this walk, which then could easily take most of a day or even longer. If you're content with facades and general impressions, the exercise could be done in a bit over an hour, but it would be a shame to bypass the narrow side streets. In any case, look into St. Michael's and consider the fascinating Dorotheum, itself easily worth an hour or more.

HOW TO GET THERE The U3 stop at Herrengasse drops you nearly at the door to the Kohlmarkt and Graben and all their attractions. A more stately entrance would be to take Tram 1 or 2 to Heldenplatz, walking through the Imperial gates and the Hofburg to the Kohlmarkt.

What to See

③⑥ **Demel.** Just across from the Hofburg palace, the lavish pastry shop of **Fodor'sChoice** Demel's was founded in 1848 by the court confectioner. It was an in- **★** stant success with those privileged to dine with the emperor, for not only was Franz Josef a notoriously stodgy and paltry eater, but when he stopped eating, protocol dictated that all others stop, too. Dessert at Demel's, just across the Kohlmarkt plaza, soon became a must for hungry higher-ups. It is well known that Anna Demel, after the end of World War I and the destruction of the Austrian monarchy, refused to give up the "K.u.K." seal—*kaiserlich und königlich*—that adorned her candy boxes. Today, the waitresses—as in a princely household—still address you in the third person. Demel's also now flaunts a flawless midday buffet offering venison en croûte, chicken in pastry shells, beef Wellington, and meat tarts (with frequent warnings to "leave room for the desserts"). They have a dizzying selection of pastries, so if you have a sweet tooth, a visit will be worth every euro and, in a city famous for its tortes, their Senegaltorte takes the cake. Of course, chocolate lovers will want to participate in the famous Viennese Sachertorte debate by sampling Demel's version and then comparing it with its rival at the **Café Sacher,** which is in the Hotel Sacher—but everybody knows that the Viennese themselves prefer the one here. Also coveted are the spectacular ice-cream creations and the connoisseur chocolates and candies (and those treasure boxes they can be packaged in). High-cavity, too, is the rich Habsburgian decor designed in the 19th century by Portois and Fix—dig the gilt-leaf chandeliers and wood paneling. Don't forget to press your nose against the shop windows, whose displays are among the most mouth-watering and inventive in Austria. And during the hours of 10:30 to 4 PM, Thursday and Friday, you can visit the Demel museum in the basement. ⊠ *Kohlmarkt 14, 1st District* ☎ *01/535–1717–0* ⊕ *www.demel. at/* Ⓤ *U1 or U3/Stephansplatz.*

Dorotheum. The narrow passageway just to the right of St. Michael's, with its large 15th-century relief depicting Christ on the Mount of Olives, leads into the Stallburggasse. The area is dotted with antiques stores, attracted by the presence of the Dorotheum, the famous Viennese auction house that began as a state-controlled pawnshop in 1707 (affectionately known as "Aunt Dorothy" to its patrons). Merchandise coming up for auction is on display at Dorotheergasse 17. The showrooms—packed with everything from carpets and pianos to cameras and jewelry and postage stamps—are well worth a visit. Some wares are not for auction but for immediate sale. ⊠ *Dorotheergasse 17, 1st District* ☎ *01/515–60–200* ⊕ *www.dorotheum.com/* ⊗ *Weekdays 10–6, Sat. 9–5* Ⓤ *U1 or U3/Stephansplatz.*

㉝ **The Graben.** One of Vienna's major crossroads, the Graben, leading west from Stock-im-Eisen-Platz, is a street whose unusual width gives it the presence and weight of a city square. Its shape is due to the Romans, who dug the city's southwestern moat here (Graben literally means "moat" or "ditch") adjacent to the original city walls. The Graben's centerpiece is the effulgently Baroque **Pestsäule.** Erected by Emperor Leopold I between 1687 and 1693 as thanks to God for delivering the city from a particularly virulent plague, today the representation looks more like a congealed fountain of whipped cream, studded with cherubs and angelic figures. Staunch Protestants may be shocked to learn that the foul figure of the Pest stands also for the heretic plunging away from the "True Faith" into the depth of hell—but they will have to get used to the fact that the Catholic Church has triumphed over Protestantism in Austria and frequently recalls the fact in stone and on canvas. No matter: By the 18th-century, the square had become a favored rendezvous for prostitutes. These weren't what drew the notoriously randy Mozart here to rent a fourth floor room at No. 17 in the summer of 1782; he lived here for almost a year because his wife Constanze's family, the Webers, lived around the corner. It was here that he finished *The Abduction from the Seraglio* and wrote the Wind Serenade, K. 375. To his delight, six musicians performed this very piece under his window late on Halloween night, 1781, just as he was getting undressed for bed. ⊠ *At Kärntnerstrasse and Kohlmarkt, 1st District* Ⓤ *U1 or U3/Stephansplatz.*

㉚ **Jewish Museum.** The former Eskeles Palace, once an elegant private residence, now houses the city's Jüdisches Museum der Stadt Wien. Permanent exhibitions tell of the momentous role that Vienna-born Jews played in realms from music to medicine, art to philosophy, both in Vienna—until abruptly halted in 1938—and in the world at large. Changing exhibits add contemporary touches. The museum complex includes a café and bookstore. ⊠ *Dorotheergasse 11, 1st District* ☎ *01/535–0431* ⊕ *www.jmw.at* 🎫 *€5* ⊗ *Sun.–Fri. 10–6, Thurs. 10–8* Ⓤ *U1 or U3/ Stephansplatz.*

㉟ **Kohlmarkt.** The Kohlmarkt, aside from its classic view of the domed entryway to the imperial palace complex of the Hofburg, is best known as Vienna's most elegant shopping street—here you can buy Demel's chocolate goodies and purchase Thonet's ever-stylish bentwood chairs. The shops, not the buildings, are remarkable, although there is an entertaining odd-couple pairing: No. 11 (early 18th century) and No. 9 (early 20th century). The mixture of architectural styles is similar to that of the Graben, but the general atmosphere is low-key, as if the street were consciously deferring to the showstopper dome at the west end. At No. 7 is the building where Mozart and his wife, Constanze, lived temporarily in an apartment. Despite its proximity to the grandeur of the Hofburg Palace, the Mozarts found their lodgings miserable, and soon moved to another establishment on the Judenplatz. The composers Haydn and Chopin also lived in houses on the street. ⊠ *At Hofburg Palace and Kohlmarkt, 1st District* Ⓤ *U3/Herrengasse.*

★ ㉙ **Looshaus.** In 1911 Adolf Loos, one of the founding fathers of 20th-century modern architecture, built the Looshaus on august Michaelerplatz, facing the Imperial Palace entrance. It was considered nothing less than an architectural declaration of war. After 200 years of Baroque and neo-Baroque exuberance and whipped-cream ornamentation, the first generation of 20th-century architects had had enough. Loos led the revolt against architectural tradition; *Ornament and Crime* was the title of his famous manifesto, in which he inveighed against the conventional architectural wisdom of the 19th century. Instead he advocated buildings that were plain, honest, and functional, and this building began the trend to 20th-century modernism. When he built the Looshaus for Goldman and Salatsch (men's clothiers) in 1911, the city was scandalized. Archduke Franz Ferdinand, heir to the throne, was so offended that he vowed never again to use the Michaelerplatz entrance to the Imperial Palace and Emperor Franz Josef had all his curtains overlooking the Michalerplatz forever drawn. Today the Looshaus has lost its power to shock, and the facade seems quite innocuous; argument now focuses on the postmodern Neues Haas-Haus opposite St. Stephan's Cathedral. The interior of the Looshaus remains a breathtaking surprise; the building now houses a bank, and you can go inside to see the stylish chambers and staircase. To get up close and personal with Loos, head to the splendor of his Loos American Bar, five blocks or so to the east at No. 10 Kärntnerdurchgang. ⊠ *Michaelerplatz 3, 1st District* Ⓤ *U3/Herrengasse.*

❷❽ **Michaelerplatz.** One of Vienna's most historic squares, this small plaza is now the site of an excavation revealing Roman plus 18th- and 19th-century layers of the past. The excavations are a latter-day distraction from the Michaelerplatz's most noted claim to fame—the eloquent entryway to the palace complex of the Hofburg. Two of Mozart's six children were baptized in the Michaelerkirche (they died in infancy) and in the adjacent house, the 12-year-old Mozart underwent a "test" by Pietro Metastasio, the famous librettist, to prove that he, not his father, was the author of his compositions.

In 1945 American soldiers forced open the doors of the crypt in the **Michaelerkirche** for the first time in 150 years and made a singular discovery. Found lying undisturbed, obviously for centuries, were the mummified remains of former wealthy parishioners of the church—even the finery and buckled shoes worn at their burial had been preserved by the perfect temperatures contained within the crypt. Fascinatingly ghoulish tours are offered from Easter to the end of November (at 11, 1, and 3, weekdays; on Saturday and other times of the year, check the posted announcement at the church, or phone 0699/104–74–828). The cost is €4. The tour is given first in German and then in English. Visitors are led down into the shadowy gloom and through a labyrinth of passageways, pausing at several tombs (many of which are open in order to view the remains), with a brief explanation of the cause of death given at each site. ⊠ *At Hofburg Palace and Kohlmarkt, 1st District* Ⓤ *U3/Herrengasse.*

㉜ Neues Haas-Haus. Stock-im-Eisen-Platz is home to central Vienna's most controversial (for the moment, at least) piece of architecture: the Neues Haas-Haus designed by Hans Hollein, one of Austria's best-known living architects. Detractors consider its aggressively contemporary style out of place opposite St. Stephan's, seeing the cathedral's style parodied by being stood on its head; advocates consider the contrast enlivening. Whatever the ultimate verdict, the restaurant and shopping complex has not proved to be the anticipated commercial success; its restaurants may be thriving, but its boutiques are not. ⌗ *Stephansplatz 12, 1st District* ☉ *Shops weekdays 9–6, Sat. 9–noon* Ⓤ *U1 or U3/Stephansplatz.*

★ **㉞ Peterskirche** (St. Peter's Church). Considered the best example of church Baroque in Vienna—certainly the most theatrical—the Peterskirche was constructed between 1702 and 1708 by Lucas von Hildebrandt. According to legend, the original church on this site was founded in 792 by Charlemagne, a tale immortalized by the relief plaque on the right side of the church. The facade has angled towers, graceful turrets (said to have been inspired by the tents of the Turks during the siege of 1683), and an unusually fine entrance portal. Inside the church the Baroque decoration is elaborate, with some fine touches (particularly the glass-crowned galleries high on the walls to either side of the altar and the amazing tableau of the martyrdom of St. John Nepomuk), but the lack of light and the years of accumulated dirt create a prevailing gloom, and the much-praised ceiling frescoes by J. M. Rottmayr are impossible to make out. Just before Christmastime each year, the basement crypt is filled with a display of nativity scenes. The church is shoehorned into tiny Petersplatz, just off the Graben. Mozart's fourth child, Theresa, was baptized here. ⌗ *Petersplatz, 1st District* Ⓤ *U1 or U3/Stephansplatz.*

㉛ Stock-im-Eisen. In the southwest corner of Stock-im-Eisen-Platz, set into the building on the west side of Kärntnerstrasse, is one of the city's odder relics: the Stock-im-Eisen, or the "nail-studded stump." Chronicles first mention the Stock-im-Eisen in 1533, but it is probably far older, and for hundreds of years any apprentice metalsmith who came to Vienna to learn his trade hammered a nail into the tree trunk for good luck. During World War II, when there was talk of moving the relic to a museum in Munich, it mysteriously disappeared; it reappeared, perfectly preserved, after the threat of removal had passed. ⌗ *At Graben and Singerstrasse, 1st District* Ⓤ *U1 or U3/Stephansplatz.*

AN IMPERIAL CITY: THE HOFBURG

A walk through the Imperial Palace, known as the Hofburg, brings you back to the days when Vienna was the capital of a mighty empire. You can still find in Vienna shops vintage postcards and prints that show the revered and bewhiskered Emperor Franz Josef leaving his Hofburg palace for a drive in his carriage. Today, at the palace—which faces Kohlmarkt on the opposite side of Michaelerplatz—you can walk in his very footsteps, gaze at the old tin bath the emperor kept under his simple iron bedstead, marvel at his bejeweled christening robe, and, along the way, feast your eyes on great works of art, impressive armor, and some of the finest Baroque interiors in Europe.

Until 1918 the Hofburg was the home of the Habsburgs, rulers of the Austro-Hungarian Empire. As a current tourist lure, it has become a vast smorgasbord of sightseeing attractions: the Imperial Apartments, two Imperial treasuries, six museums, the National Library, and the famous Winter Riding School all vie for attention. The newest Hofburg attraction is a museum (opened April 2004) devoted to "Sisi," the beloved Empress Elisabeth, wife of Franz Josef, whose beauty was the talk of Europe and whose tragic death was mourned by all. The entire complex takes a minimum of a full day to explore in detail; if your time is limited (or if you want to save most of the interior sightseeing for a rainy day), you should omit the Imperial Apartments and all the museums mentioned below except the museum of court silver and tableware, the Silberkammer, and probably the Schatzkammer. An excellent multilingual, full-color booklet describing the palace in detail is for sale at most ticket counters within the complex; it gives a complete list of attractions and maps out the palace's complicated ground plan and building history wing by wing.

Vienna took its imperial role seriously, as evidenced by the sprawling Hofburg complex, which is still today, as then, the seat of government. But this is generally understated power, while the buildings cover a considerable area, the treasures lie within, not to be flamboyantly flaunted. Certainly under Franz Josef II the reign was beneficent—witness the broad Ringstrasse he ordained and the panoply of museums and public buildings it hosts. With few exceptions (Vienna City Hall and the Votive Church), rooflines are kept to an even level, creating an ensemble effect that helps integrate the palace complex and its parks into the urban landscape without making a domineering statement. Diplomats still bustle in and out of high-level international meetings along the elegant halls. Horse-drawn carriages still traverse the Ring and the roadway that cuts through the complex. Ignore the cars and tour buses and you can easily imagine yourself in a Vienna of a hundred or more years ago.

Architecturally, the Hofburg—like St. Stephan's—is far from refined. It grew up over a period of 700 years (its earliest mention in court documents is from 1279, at the very beginning of Habsburg rule), and its spasmodic, haphazard growth kept it from attaining any sort of unified identity. But many of the bits and pieces are fine, and one interior—the National Library—is a tour de force.

Numbers in the text correspond to numbers in the margin and on the Hofburg map.

a good
walk

When you begin to explore the Hofburg you realize that the palace complex is like a nest of boxes, courtyards opening off courtyards and wings (*Trakte*) spreading far and wide. First tackle **Josefsplatz** ㊲ ▶, the remarkable square that interrupts Augustinerstrasse, ornamented by the equestrian statue of Josef II—many consider this Vienna's loveliest square. Indeed the beautifully restored imperial decor adorning the roof of the buildings forming Josefsplatz is one of the few visual demonstrations of Austria's onetime widespread power and influence. On your right to the north is the **Spanische Reitschule** ㊳, the Spanish Riding School—one emblem of Vienna known throughout the world—where the famous white horses reign. Across Reitschulgasse under the arches are the **Lipizzaner Museum** ❸ and the Imperial Stables. To the south stands the **Augustinerkirche** ❹, St. Augustine's Church, where the Habsburg rulers' hearts are preserved in urns. The grand main hall (Prunksaal) of the **Hofbibliothek** ❹, the National Library, is one of the great Baroque treasures of Europe, a site not to be missed (enter from the southwest corner of Josefsplatz).

Under the Michaelerplatz dome is the entrance to the **Kaiserappartements** ❹, with the sort of perfunctory elegance you would normally associate with royalty, although Franz Josef II, the residing emperor from 1848 to 1916, added some "homey" touches. A new focus of these state rooms comprises a "Sisi" museum, devoted to his wife, Empress Elisabeth. For more splendor, go through into the **In der Burg** ❹ courtyard and look in at the elegant **Silberkammer** ❹ museum of court silver and tableware. Go through the **Schweizertor** ❹, the Swiss gate, to the south off In der Burg, to reach the small **Schweizer Hof** ❹ courtyard with stairs leading to the **Hofburgkapelle** ❹, the Imperial Chapel where the Vienna Boys Choir makes its regular Sunday appearances. In a back corner of the courtyard is the entrance to the **Schatzkammer** ❹, the Imperial Treasury, overflowing with jewels, robes, and royal trappings. From In der Burg, the roadway leads under the **Leopold Wing** ❹ of the complex into the vast park known as **Heldenplatz** ❺, or Hero's Square. The immediately obvious heroes are the equestrian statues of Archduke Karl and Prince Eugene of Savoy. The Hofburg wing to the south with its concave facade is the **Neue Burg** ❺, the "new" section of the complex, now housing four specialized museums. Depending on your interests, consider the **Ephesus Museum** ❺, with Roman antiquities; the **Musical Instruments Collection** ❺, where you also hear what you see; the impressive **Weapons Collection** ❺, with tons of steel armor; or the ethnological collections of the **Museum für Völkerkunde** ❺, including Montezuma's headdress. Ahead, the **Burgtor** ❺ gate separates the Hofburg complex from the Ringstrasse. The quiet oasis in back of the Neue Burg is the **Burggarten** ❺, home to the magical Schmetterlinghaus (Butterfly House). Catch your breath and marvel that you've seen only a small part of the Hofburg—a large part of it still houses the offices of the Austrian government and is not open to the public.

TIMING   You could spend a day in the Hofburg complex. For most of the smaller museums, figure on anything from an hour upward.

HOW TO   You can enter the Hofburg arena and all the sights within by taking Tram
GET THERE 1 or 2 to Heldenplatz, entering on foot through the Imperial gates. Another option is to take the U3 to Herrengasse.

What to See

★ ❹ **Augustinerkirche** (Augustinian Church). Across Josefsplatz from the Riding School is the entrance to the Augustinerkirche, built during the 14th century and presenting the most unified Gothic interior in the city. But the church is something of a fraud; the interior, it turns out, dates from the late 18th century, not the early 14th. A historical fraud the church may be, but a spiritual fraud it is not. The view from the entrance doorway is stunning: a soaring harmony of vertical piers, ribbed vaults, and

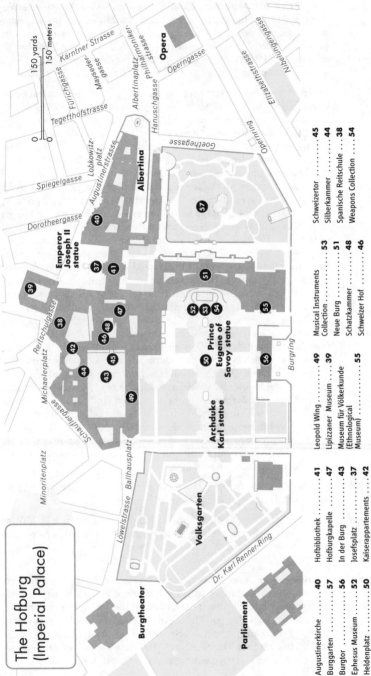

The Hofburg (Imperial Palace)

Augustinerkirche **40**
Burggarten **57**
Burgtor **56**
Ephesus Museum **52**
Heldenplatz **50**

Hofbibliothek **41**
Hofburgkapelle **47**
In der Burg **43**
Josefsplatz **37**
Kaiserappartements **42**

Leopold Wing **49**
Lipizzaner Museum . . . **39**
Museum für Völkerkunde
(Ethnological
Museum) **55**

Musical Instruments
Collection **53**
Neue Burg **51**
Schatzkammer **48**
Schweizer Hof **46**

Schweizertor **45**
Silberkammer **44**
Spanische Reitschule . . . **38**
Weapons Collection **54**

150 yards
150 meters

Opera

hanging chandeliers that makes Vienna's other Gothic interiors look earth-bound by comparison. The imposing Baroque organ sounds as heavenly as it looks, and the Sunday morning high mass sung here—frequently by Mozart or Haydn—can be the highlight of a trip; traditionally, an orchestra plays, a homage to the many years Anton Bruckner was church musician here. Note the magnificent **Tomb of the Archduchess Maria-Christina,** sculpted by the great Antonio Canova in 1805, with mournful figures of her and her family (her husband founded the Albertina) trooping into a temple. To the right of the main altar in the small Loreto Chapel stand silver urns containing the hearts of Habsburg rulers. This rather morbid sight is viewable after early mass on Sunday, Monday, or by appointment. ⊠ *Josefsplatz, 1st District* ☎ *01/533–7099–0* Ⓤ *U3/Herrengasse.*

★ ❺❼ **Burggarten.** The intimate Burggarten in back of the Neue Burg is a quiet oasis that includes a statue of a contemplative Kaiser Franz Josef and an elegant statue of Mozart, moved here from the Albertinaplatz after the war, when the city's charred ruins were being rebuilt. This park emerged after city walls were destroyed by the fleeing French army in the early 19th century. Emperor Franz I made the area into the gardens of the Hofburg and they proved a popular retreat for the royal family—Franz II even became known as the "Blumenkaiser" since he loved to tend his flowers in the glass conservatories. Today the park is one of the most favored time-out spots for the Viennese; the alluring backdrop is formed by the striking former greenhouses that are now the gorgeous Palmenhaus restaurant and the **Schmetterlinghaus.** Total enchantment awaits you here at Vienna's unique Butterfly House. Once located in Schönbrunn Palace, it was relocated to one of the magisterial greenhouses of the Burggarten in 1998. Inside are towering tropical trees, waterfalls, a butterfly nursery, and more than 150 species on display (usually 400 winged jewels are in residence). Elsewhere are orchids and other floral dislays. Don't miss! ⊠ *Access from Opernring and Hanuschgasse/Goethegasse, 1st District* ☎ *01/533–8570* ⊕ *www.schmetterlinghaus.at* ⊠ *€4.70* ☉ *Butterfly House: Apr.–Oct., weekdays 10–4:45, weekends 10–6:15; Nov.–Mar., daily 10–3:45* Ⓤ *U2/MuseumsQuartier; Tram: 1, 2, and D/Burgring.*

❺❻ **Burgtor.** The failure to complete the **Hofburg** building program left the old main palace gate stranded in the middle of the Heldenplatz.

❺❷ **Ephesus Museum.** One of the museums in the Neue Burg, the Ephesus Museum contains exceptional Roman antiquities unearthed by Austrian archaeologists in Turkey at the turn of the century. ⊠ *Hofburg, 1st District* ⊕ *www.hofburg-wien.at* ⊠ *Combined ticket with Musical Instrument Collection and Weapons Collection €8, more for special exhibits* ☉ *Wed.–Mon. 10–6* Ⓤ *Tram: 1, 2, and D/Burgring.*

❺⓿ **Heldenplatz.** The long wing with the concave bay on the south side of the square is the youngest section of the palace, called the Neue Burg. Although the Neue Burg building plans were not completed and the Heldenplatz was left without a discernible shape, the space is nevertheless punctuated by two superb equestrian statues depicting Archduke Karl and Prince Eugene of Savoy. The older section on the north includes the offices of the federal president. ⊠ *Hofburg, 1st District* Ⓤ *Tram: 1, 2, and D/Burgring.*

㊶ Hofbibliothek (formerly Court, now National Library). This is one of the

grandest Baroque libraries in the world, in every sense a cathedral of
★ books. Its centerpiece is the spectacular **Prunksaal**—the Grand Hall of
the National Library—which probably contains more book treasures
than any comparable collection outside the Vatican. The main entrance
to the ornate reading room is in the left corner of Josefsplatz. Designed
by Fischer von Erlach the Elder just before his death in 1723 and completed by his son, the Grand Hall is full-blown High Baroque, with trompe-
l'oeil ceiling frescoes by Daniel Gran. This floridly Baroque library may
not be to everyone's taste, but in the end it is the books themselves that
come to the rescue. They are as lovingly displayed as the gilding and
the frescoes, and they give the hall a warmth that the rest of the palace
decidedly lacks. On the third floor is an intriguing museum of carto-
graphic globes that should not be overlooked. Beginning in 1782 Mozart
performed regularly at the Sunday matinees of Baron Gottfried van Swieten, who lived in a suite of rooms in this grand, palacelike library. Four
years later, the baron founded the Society of Associated Cavaliers, which
set up oratorio performances with Mozart acting as conductor. Across
the street at Palais Palffy, Mozart reportedly first performed *The Marriage of Figaro* before a select, private audience to see if it would pass
the court censor. ⊠ *Josefsplatz 1, 1st District* ☎ *01/534–100* ⊕ *www.
hofburg-wien.at* ☜ *€5* ⊗ *May–Oct., daily 10–4, Thurs. 10–7; Nov.–Apr.,
Mon.–Sat. 10–2* Ⓤ *U3/Herrengasse.*

㊸ Hofburgkapelle (Chapel of the Imperial Palace). Fittingly, this is the main
venue for the beloved Vienna Boys' Choir (Wiener Sängerknaben), since
they actually have their earliest roots in the Hofmusikkapelle choir
founded by Emperor Maximilian I four centuries ago (Haydn and Schubert as young boys were both participants). Today the troop sings mass
here at 9:15 on Sunday from mid-September to June (and, yes, even though
this is a mass, tickets are sold to hear the choir, ranging from €5 to €30).
Alas, the arrangement is such that you *hear* the choirboys but don't see
them; their soprano and alto voices peal forth from a gallery behind the
seating area. But the choir can be seen in all their apple-cheek splendor
at other places around town, notably the Musikverein and Schönbrunn
Palace; see their Web site for their concert schedule. For ticket information, *see* Nightlife & the Arts, *below*. ⊠ *Hofburg, Schweizer Hof,
1st District* ☎ *01/533–9927* 📠 *01/533–9927–75* ⊕ *www.wsk.at; www.
bmbwk.gv.at/kultur/musik.xml* Ⓤ *U3/Herrengasse.*

㊸ In der Burg. This prominent courtyard of the Hofburg complex is cen-
tered around a statue of Francis II and the noted **Schweizertor** gateway.
Note the **clock** on the far upper wall at the north end of the courtyard:
It tells time by the sundial, also gives the time mechanically, and even,
above the clock face, indicates the phase of the moon. ⊠ *Hofburg, 1st
District* Ⓤ *U3/Herrengasse.*

㊲ Josefsplatz. Josefsplatz is the most imposing of the Hofburg courtyards,
with an equestrian **statue of Emperor Joseph II** (1807) in the center. ⊠ *Herrengasse, 1st District* Ⓤ *U3/Herrengasse.*

★ ㊷ **Kaiserappartements** (Imperial Apartments). Entering the spectacular portal gate of the Michaelertor—you can't miss the four gigantic statues of Hercules and his Labors—you enter and climb the marble Kaiserstiege (Emperor's Staircase) to begin a tour of a long, repetitive suite of 18 conventionally luxurious state rooms. The red-and-gold decoration (19th-century imitation of 18th-century Rococo) tries to look regal, but much like the empire itself in its latter days it is only going through the motions and ends up looking merely official. Still, these are the rooms where the ruling family of the Habsburg empire ate, slept, and dealt with family tragedy—in the emperor's study on January 30, 1889, Franz Josef was told about the tragic death of his only son, Crown Prince Rudolf, who had shot himself and the 17-year-old Baroness Vetsera at the hunting lodge at Mayerling. Among the few signs of genuine life are Emperor Franz Josef's spartan, iron field bed, on which he slept every night, and his Empress Elisabeth's wooden gymnastics equipment (obsessed with her looks, "Sisi" suffered from anorexia and was fanatically devoted to exercise).

To commemorate the 150th wedding anniversary of this mismatched pair in 2004, a Sisi Museum was inaugurated, which is actually part of the regular tour. Five rooms are given over to the myths and realities of this Princess Diana of the 19th century; exhibits are displayed in high-style fashion, with colored spotlights, painted murals, and many of her treasured items, including her jewels, the gown she wore the night before her marriage, her dressing gown, the reconstructed, opulent Court Salon railroad car she used, and her death mask, made after her assasination by an Italian anarchist in Geneva in 1898 (when she was leaving the home of the Baroness Rothschild). Famed for her five foot fall of hair, fabled as a fashionplate extraordinare, notorious for her hatred of court protocol (and even her husband), "the lonely empress" has been the subject of many books, films (most notably, the 1968 *Mayerling,* where she was stunningly portrayed by Ava Gardner), and even a long-running Broadwayesque musical, *Elisabeth,* which has been running in Vienna for years. ⊠ *Hofburg, Schweizer Hof, 1st District* ⊕ *www.hofburg-wien.at* ☏ *01/533–7570* 💶 *€7.50, with guided tour €9.40* ⊙ *9–5; July and Aug., daily 9–5:30* Ⓤ *U3/Herrengasse.*

㊾ **Leopold Wing.** A long tract of offices known as the Leopold Wing separates In der Burg courtyard from the vast Heldenplatz. It was here that Mozart met and performed for Empress Maria Theresa in 1773 with the hope of landing a court sinecure (only granted to him 10 years later). ⊠ *Hofburg, 1st District* Ⓤ *U3/Herrengasse.*

㊴ **Lipizzaner Museum.** If you're interested in learning more about the Lipizzaners, visit this museum, in what used to be the old imperial pharmacy. Exhibitions document the history of the Lipizzans, including paintings, photographs, and videos giving an overview from the 16th century to the present. A highlight is a visit to the stables, where you can see the horses up close, through a glass window. ⊠ *Reitschulgasse 2, 1st District* ☏ *01/533–7811* ⊕ *www.lipizzaner.at* 💶 *€5; combined ticket with morning training session €14.50* ⊙ *Daily 9–6* Ⓤ *U3/Herrengasse.*

⑤⑤ Museum für Völkerkunde (Ethnological Museum). This anthropology museum is entered at the west end pavilion in the Neue Burg. Montezuma's feathered headdress is a highlight of its collections. The museum is closed for renovation until 2006. ⊠ *Hofburg, 1st District.* Ⓤ *U2/MuseumsQuartier.*

⑤③ Musical Instruments Collection. This Neue Burg museum houses pianos that belonged to all the greats—Brahms, Schumann, Mahler, and Beethoven (one reader wrote, "On our last visit, we had the delight of hearing Beethoven's piano being tuned, and its clear bell-like notes followed us around the galleries like Papageno's magic chimes"). But the instruments here come in all shapes and sizes: a harp in the form of a harpooned fish, a table clavier with drawers and inkwells, a piano with a curved keyboard, another with the black-and-white notes reversed. Yes, there are a lot of pianos—when Mozart called Vienna "Piano Land," he wasn't exaggerating. An acoustic guided tour allows you actually to hear the various instruments on headphones as you move from room to room. ⊠ *Hofburg, 1st District* 🎫 *Combined ticket with Ephesus Museum and Weapons Collection €8, more for special exhibits* ⊙ *Wed.–Mon. 10–6* Ⓤ *U2/MuseumsQuartier.*

⑤① Neue Burg. The Neue Burg stands today as a symbol of architectural overconfidence. Designed for Emperor Franz Josef in 1869, this "new château" was part of a much larger scheme that was meant to make the Hofburg rival the Louvre, if not Versailles. The German architect Gottfried Semper planned a twin of the present Neue Burg on the opposite side of the Heldenplatz, with arches connecting the Neue Burg and its twin with the other pair of twins on the Ringstrasse, the Kunsthistorisches Museum (Museum of Art History), and the Naturhistorisches Museum (Museum of Natural History). But World War I intervened, and with the empire's collapse the Neue Burg became merely the last in a long series of failed attempts to bring architectural order to the Hofburg. (From its main balcony, in April 1938, Adolf Hitler, telling a huge cheering crowd below of his plan for the new German empire, declared that Vienna "is a pearl! I am going to put it into a setting of which it is worthy!") Today crowds flock to the Neue Burg because it houses no fewer than four specialty museums: the **Ephesus Museum, Musical Instruments Collection, Ethnological Museum,** and **Weapons Collection.** For details on these museums, see separate listings. ⊠ *Heldenplatz, 1st District* 📞 *01/525240* Ⓤ *U2/MuseumsQuartier.*

④⑧ Schatzkammer (Imperial Treasury). The entrance to the Schatzkammer, with its 1,000 years of treasures, is tucked away at ground level behind the staircase to the Hofburgkapelle. The elegant display is a welcome antidote to the monotony of the Imperial Apartments, for the entire Treasury was completely renovated in 1983–87, and the crowns and relics and vestments fairly glow in their surroundings. Here you'll find such marvels as the Holy Lance—reputedly the lance that pierced Jesus's side—the Imperial Crown (a sacred symbol of sovereignty once stolen on Hitler's orders), and the Saber of Charlemagne. Don't miss the Burgundian Treasure, connected with that most romantic of medieval orders of chivalry, the Order of the Golden Fleece. ⊠ *Schweizer Hof, 1st District* ☎ *01/525240* 🎫 *€8* ⊙ *Wed.–Mon. 10–6* Ⓤ *U3/Herrengasse.*

46 **Schweizer Hof.** This courtyard was named after the Swiss guards who were once stationed here. In the southeast corner (at the top of the steps) is the entrance to the Hofburgkapelle. ⊠ *Hofburg, 1st District* Ⓤ *U3/ Herrengasse.*

45 **Schweizertor** (Swiss Gate). Dating from 1552 and decorated with some of the earliest classical motifs in the city, the Schweizertor leads from In der Burg through to the oldest section of the palace, a small courtyard known as the Schweizer Hof. The gateway is painted maroon, black, and gold; it gives a fine Renaissance flourish to its building facade. ⊠ *Hofburg, Schweizertor, 1st District* Ⓤ *U3/Herrengasse.*

44 **Silberkammer** (Museum of Court Silver and Tableware). The large courtyard on the far side of the Michaelertor rotunda is known as In der Burg; here on the west side is the entrance to the sparkling Silberkammer. There's far more than forks and finger bowls here; stunning decorative pieces vie with glittering silver and gold for attention. Highlights include Franz Josef's vermeil banqueting service, the jardinière given to Empress Elisabeth by Queen Victoria, and gifts from Marie-Antoinette to her brother Josef II. The presentation of full table settings gives an idea of court life both as lived daily and on festive occasions. ⊠ *Hofburg, Michaelertrakt, 1st District* ☎ *01/533-7570* ⊕ *www.hofburg-wien.at* 🎫 *€7.50, including Kaiserappartements* ⊙ *Daily 9–5; July and Aug., daily 9–5:30* Ⓤ *U3/Herrengasse.*

★ **38** **Spanische Reitschule** (Spanish Riding School). Between Augustinerstrasse and the Josefsplatz is the world-famous Spanish Riding School, a favorite for centuries, and no wonder: who can resist the sight of the stark-white Lipizzan horses going through their masterful paces? For the last 300 years they have been perfecting their *haute école* riding demonstrations to the sound of Baroque music in a ballroom that seems to be a crystal-chandeliered stable. The breed was started in 1580, and the horses proved themselves in battle as well as in the complicated "dances" for which they are famous. The interior of the riding school, the 1735 work of Fischer von Erlach the Younger, is itself an attraction—surely Europe's most elegant sports arena—and if the prancing horses begin to pall, move up to the top balcony and examine the ceiling.

The school's popularity is hardly surprising, and tickets to some performances must be ordered in writing many weeks in advance, or through their Web site. Information offices have a brochure with the detailed schedule (performances are usually March–December, with the school on vacation in July and August). Generally the full, 80-minute show takes place Sunday at 11 AM plus selected Fridays at 6 PM—the evening performance is the best because the vast hall is ablaze with chandeliered light. There are two yearly classical dressage final rehearsals with music, at the end of August and the end of December. Check the Web site for details.

Morning training sessions with music are held Tuesday–Saturday 10–noon. Tickets are available at the visitor center, Michaelerplatz 1, from Tuesday to Saturday (except holidays) 9–5, and at Josefsplatz, Gate 2 on the day of the morning exercise 9–12:30. It's best to get there early to get a place in line. Note that if you purchase your tickets through a ticket agency for an actual performance, they can legally add a commission of 22%–25% to the face price of the ticket. For performance ticket orders, write to **Spanische Reitschule** (⊠ Hofburg, A–1010 Vienna). Pick up reserved tickets at the office under the Michaelerplatz rotunda dome. ⊠ *Michaelerplatz 1, Hofburg, A–1010, 1st District* ☎ *01/533–9031–0* 🖷 *01/535–0186* ⊕ *www.srs.at* 🎫 *€40–€160; standing room €24–€28, morning training sessions €11.50; Sat. classical dressage final rehearsal, €20* ⊗ *Mar.–June and late Aug.–mid-Dec.* ⊗ *Closed tour wks* Ⓤ *U3/Herrengasse.*

❺❹ **Weapons Collection.** Rivaling the armory in Graz as one of the most extensive arms and armor collections in the world is this Neue Burg museum. Enter at the triumphal arch set into the middle of the curved portion of the facade. ⊠ *Heldenplatz, 1st District* 🎫 *Combined ticket with Ephesus Museum and Musical Instrument Collection €8, more for special exhibits* ⊗ *Wed.–Mon. 10–6* Ⓤ *U2/MuseumsQuartier.*

THE RINGSTRASSE: GEMS OF THE "RING"

Along with the Hofburg, the **Ringstrasse** comprises Vienna's major urban set piece. This grand series of thoroughfares circles the heart of Vienna, the Innere Stadt (Inner City), or 1st District. It follows the lines of what were, until an imperial decree ordered them leveled in 1857, the city's defenses. In that year Emperor Franz Josef issued a decree announcing the most ambitious piece of urban redevelopment Vienna had ever seen. The inner city's centuries-old walls were to be torn down, and the *glacis*—the wide expanse of open field that acted as a protective buffer between inner city and outer suburbs—was to be filled in. In their place was to rise a wide, tree-lined boulevard, upon which would stand an imposing collection of new buildings that would reflect Vienna's special status as the political, economic, and cultural heart of the Austro-Hungarian Empire. During the 50 years of building that followed, many factors combined to produce the Ringstrasse as it now stands, but the most important was the gradual rise of liberalism after the failed Revolution of 1848. By the latter half of the Ringstrasse era, support for constitutional government, democracy, and equality—all the concepts that liberalism traditionally equates with progress—was steadily increasing. As the Ringstrasse went up, it became the definitive symbol of this liberal progress; as Carl E. Schorske put it in his *Fin-de-Siècle Vienna*, it celebrated "the triumph of constitutional *Recht* (right) over imperial *Macht* (might), of secular culture over religious faith. Not palaces, garrisons, and churches, but centers of constitutional government and higher culture dominated the Ring."

The highest concentration of public building is found in the area around the Volksgarten, where are clustered (moving from south to north, from

Burgring to Schottenring) the **Kunsthistorisches Museum,** the **Naturhis-torisches Museum,** the **Justizpalast** (Central Law Courts), the **Parliament,** the **Rathaus** (City Hall), the **Burgtheater** (National Theater), the **Univer-sität** (University of Vienna), the **Votivkirche** (Votive Church), and slightly farther along, the **Börse** (Stock Exchange) on Schottenring (for all of these sights, see either *above* or *below*). As an ensemble, the collection is astonishing in its architectural presumption: it is nothing less than an at-tempt to assimilate and summarize the entire architectural history of Eu-rope. As critics were quick to notice, however, the complex suffers from a serious organizational flaw: most of the buildings lack effective context. Rather than being the focal points of an organized overall plan, they are plunked haphazardly down on an avenue that is itself too wide to present a unified, visually comprehensible character. To some the monumental-ity of the Ringstrasse is overbearing; others find the architectural panorama exhilarating, and growth of the trees over 100 years has served to put the buildings into a different perspective. There is no question but that the tree-lined boulevard with its broad sidewalks gives the city a unique rib-bon of green and certainly the distinction that the emperor sought.

In and around the Ring ribbon, you'll find an array of other unmiss-able gems: the quaint-now-trendy Spittelberg Quarter, Freud's apartment, and Vienna's new/old dazzler, the Liechtenstein garden palais, now home to princely Old Masters, including a fabled collection of paint-ings by Peter Paul Rubens.

Numbers in the text correspond to numbers in the margin and on the Eastern Ringstrasse & MuseumsQuartier map.

a good walk

Is there a best way to explore the Ring? You can walk it from one end to the other—from where it begins at the Danube Canal to where it re-turns to the canal after its curving flight. Or, you can explore it when-ever you happen to cross it on other missions. Although it is a pleasant sequence of boulevards, seeing its succession of rather pompous build-ings all in one walk can be overpowering. Or you can obtain the best of both options by following this suggested itinerary, which leavens the bombast of the Ring with some of Vienna's most fascinating sights.

Immediately across the Ringstrasse from the Hofburg are twin buildings, both museums. To the west is the **Naturhistorisches Museum** 58 ☞; to the east, the **Kunsthistorisches Museum** 59, the art museum packed with world-famous treasures. Allow ample time for exploration here. Not far away is the new, headline-making **MuseumsQuartier** 60, a museum complex that includes several highly important modern art collections, including the Leopold Collection of Austrian Art and the Museum Moderner Kunst. Farther west of the museum square is the compact and hip **Spit-telberg Quarter** 61 of tiny streets between Burggasse and Sibensterngasse, often the site of handicraft and seasonal fairs. For more, and superspec-tacular, evidence of handicraft of an earlier era, detour south to Mari-ahilferstrasse and the **Kaiserliches Hofmobiliendepot,** the repository of much of the sumptuous furnishings of the old Habsburg palaces.

Heading back to the Ring, the **Volksgarten** 62 on the inside of the Ringstrasse to the north of the museum square includes a café and rose garden among its attractions; look also for the small memorial to Franz Josef's wife, Empress Elisabeth, in the rear corner. Tackle the Ringstrasse buildings by starting with the **Justizpalast** ⓖ (Central Law Courts), moving along to **Parlament** ⓖ, the **Rathaus** ⓖ (City Hall), the **Burgtheater** ⓖ opposite on the inside of the Ring, then the **Universität** ⓖ (the main building of Vienna's university) beyond, again on the outside of the Ring. Next to the university stands the neo-Gothic **Votivkirche** ⓖ. The outside end of Hohenstaufengasse leads into Liechtensteinstrasse, which will bring you to Berggasse. Turn right to reach No. 19, the **Freud Haus** ⓖ, now a museum and research facility. Not far from Freud's Apartment and just off the Liechtensteinstrasse on Fürstengasse, is the **Liechtenstein Museum** ⓖ, home of the Prince of Liechtenstein's fabulous private art collection, housed in the family's summer palace.

TIMING   If you can, plan to visit Vienna's Louvre—the Kunsthistorisches Museum—early in the day before the crowds arrive, although the size of crowds depends greatly on whatever special shows the museum may be exhibiting. As for the main sights off the Ringstrasse, you could easily lump together visits to the Freud Apartment and the Museum of Modern Art, figuring on about a half day for the two combined.

HOW TO   The easiest way to quickly reach the attractions around the Ring is to
GET THERE   hop on and off Trams 1, 2, and D (though keep in mind Tram D veers off the Ring at Schwarzenbergplatz). For the Kunsthistorisches Museum, MuseumsQuartier, and the Spittelberg quarter, you can also take the U2 to Volkstheater or MuseumsQuartier. The U2 is expanding, so sections may be closed off in 2005. Palais Liechtenstein can be reached from Bus 40A, picked up at the Plaza Hilton on the Ring, just across from the Börse.

What to See

ⓖ **Burgtheater** (National Theater). One of the most important theaters in the German-speaking world, the Burgtheater was built between 1874 and 1888 in the Italian Renaissance style, replacing the old court theater at Michaelerplatz. Emperor Franz Josef's mistress, Katherina Schratt, was once a star performer here, and famous Austrian and German actors still stride across this stage. The opulent interior, with its 60-foot relief *Worshippers of Bacchus* by Rudolf Wyer, foyer ceiling frescoes by Ernst and Gustav Klimt (the *Antique Theater at Taormina,* above the main staircase), and one of Vienna's grandest marble staircases make it well worth a visit. Tours in English are given only upon request. For information about performances here, *see* Theater *in* Nightlife and the Arts, *below.* ⊠ *Dr. Karl-Lueger-Ring 2, 1st District* ☎ *01/514–4441–40* ⊕ *www.burgtheater.at* Ⓤ *Tram: 1, 2, and D/Burgtheater, Rathausstrasse.*

ⓖ **Freud Haus.** Not far from the historic Hofburg district, beyond the Votivkirche at the Schottenring along the Ringstrasse, you can skip over several centuries and visit that outstanding symbol of 20th-century Vienna: Sigmund Freud's apartment at Berggasse 19 (Apartment 6, one flight up; ring the bell and push the door simultaneously); this was his residence from 1891 to 1938. The five-room collection of memorabilia is mostly a photographic record of Freud's life, with some documents, publications, and a portion of his collection of antiquities also on dis-

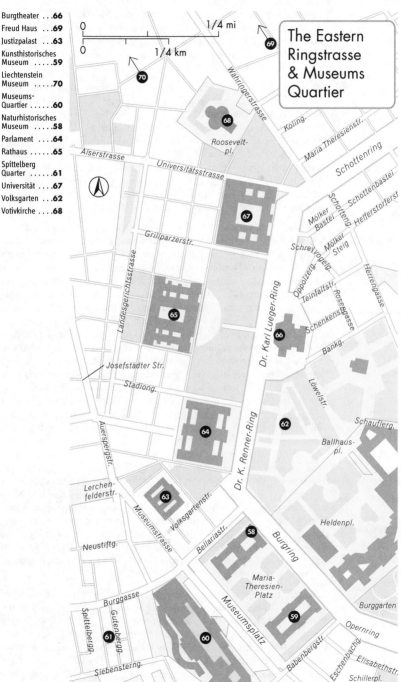

The Eastern
Ringstrasse
& Museums
Quartier

play. The waiting-room furniture is authentic, but the consulting room and study furniture (including the famous couch) can be seen only in photographs. ⊠ *Berggasse 19, 9th District/Alsergrund* ☎ *01/319–1596* ⊕ *www.freud-museum.at* ⊠ *€5* ☉ *Jan.–June and Oct.–Dec., daily 9–5; July–Sept., daily 9–6* Ⓤ *U2/Schottentor.*

㉦ Justizpalast (Central Law Courts). Alexander Wielemans designed this monumental building in the Italian Renaissance style. It was built between 1875 and 1881. The main hall is nearly 70 feet high and is topped by a glass ceiling. At the end of World War II this area was the center of the Austrian resistance movement, known as the "O5." The "O" stands for Österreich, or Austria, and the "5" is for the fifth letter of the alphabet, which translates into Ö, or OE, the abbreviation for Österreich. Between 1945 and 1955 it served as the headquarters for the Allied military leadership. The Justizpalast is closed for renovation until 2010. ⊠ *Schmerlingplatz 10–11, 1st District* Ⓤ *Tram: 1, 2, or D/Stadiongasse, Parliament.*

㊾ Kunsthistorisches Museum (Museum of Fine Art). Pieter Brueghel's *Hunters in the Snow . . .* Vermeer's *Artist in His Studio . . .* Giorgione's *Three Philosophers:* You get the picture. Ranked right up there with Paris's Louvre, London's National Gallery, and Florence's Uffizi, this is one of the greatest art collections in the world. While home to some of the most beloved paintings of all time, it is no dry-as-dust museum merely illustrating the history of art (as its name implies). Rather its collections of Old Master paintings reveal the royal taste and style of many members of the mighty House of Habsburg, who during the 16th and 17th centuries ruled over the greater part of the Western world. Today you can enjoy what this great ruling house assiduously (and in most cases, selectively) brought together through the centuries. The showstopper here is the largest collection of paintings under one roof by the Netherlandish 16th-century master Pieter Brueghel the Elder—just seeing his sublime *Hunters in the Snow* is worth a trip to Vienna, many art historians will tell you. Brueghel's depictions of throngs of peasants, often set in magnificent landscapes, distill the poetry and magic of the 16th century as few other paintings do. Room RX is the Brueghel shrine—on its walls, in addition to *Hunters in the Snow,* hang *Children's Games,* the *Tower of Babel,* the *Peasant Wedding,* the *Nest-Robber,* and eight other priceless canvases. But there are also hundreds of other celebrated Old Master paintings here, most assembled by the Habsburgs over many centuries. Even a cursory description would run on for pages, but a brief selection of the museum's most important works will give you an idea of the riches to be enjoyed. The large-scale works concentrated in the main galleries shouldn't distract you from the equal share of masterworks in the more intimate side wings.

In respect to some schools of painting, it is hard to think of any gallery in the world that is equally richly endowed. Look, for instance, at the 15th-century Netherlandish collection of works by Jan van Eyck, Roger van der Weyden, Hans Memling, and Geertgen von Sint Jans; or at the German 16th-century masterpieces by Dürer, Holbein, Cranach, and Altdorfer. The Flemish wing includes Rogier van der Weyden's *Triptych Crucifixion,* Holbein's *Portrait of Jane Seymour, Queen of England,* a fine

FodorśChoice
★

series of Rembrandt portraits, and Vermeer's peerless *Artist in His Studio (Allegory of the Art of Painting)*. The grand style of the 17th century is represented by Rubens's towering altarpieces and his *Nude of Hélène Fourment*. In the Italian wing are works by Titian, including his *Portrait of Isabella d'Este*, whose fiercely intelligent eyes make you realize why she was the first lady of the Renaissance, and Giorgione's *The Three Philosophers*, an enigmatic composition in uniquely radiant Venetian coloring.

A short list of other highlights include Raphael's *Madonna in the Meadow*, Correggio's *Jupiter Embracing Io*, Parmigianino's *Cupid Cutting a Bow*, Guercino's *Return of the Prodigal Son*, and Caravaggio's *Madonna of the Rosary*. One level down is the remarkable, less-visited *Kunstkammer*, displaying priceless objects created for the Habsburg emperors. These include curiosities made of gold, silver, and crystal, and more exotic materials, such as ivory, horn, and gemstones. Sadly, Benevenuto Cellini's legendary salt cellar, valued at €50 million, was stolen in 2003. In addition there are rooms devoted to Egyptian antiquities, Greek and Roman art, sculpture (ranging from masterworks by Tilmann Riemenschneider to Italian Mannerist bronzes, which the Habsburgs collected by the roomful) and the decorative arts, and numerous other collections. When your feet are ready to call a sit-down strike, repair to the wonderful café on the museum's second floor. Set under a grand dome, adorned with paintings, sculpture, and framed by gilt-tipped black marble columns. As this spot is run by Gerstner, the famed pastry-shop, you'll know the fruit tortes will ensure a refined time-out. ⌧ *Maria-Theresien-Platz, 7th District/Neubau* ☎ *01/525240* ⊕ *www.khm.at* 🎟 *€10* ☉ *Tues.–Sun. 10–6; extended hrs for picture galleries, Thurs. until 9 PM* Ⓤ *U2/MuseumsQuartier, U2, or U3/Volkstheater.*

⑳ Liechtenstein Museum. For the first time since 1938, Palais Liechtenstein
Fodor'sChoice is again home to the Prince of Liechtenstein's fabulous private art col-
★ lection, an accumulation so vast only a tenth of it is on display (little wonder: Prince Karl I of Liechtenstein began collecting art back in the 17th century, and each of his descendents have since added to the family treasure trove, including the current prince). The palace itself is a splendid work of art. While this was built up on the then-outskirts of the city, Prince Johann Adam Andreas I felt that a mere "summer palace" (his gigantic winter palace was in the city center on Bankgasse) would not be grand enough. He forthwith commissioned a full-blown Baroque town palace from plans drawn up by Domenicio Martinelli. A Marble Hall, grand staircases, impressive stucco work by Santino Bussi (who was paid with 40 buckets of wine in addition to a tidy sum), and sumptuous ceiling frescoes by Marcantonio Franceschini and Andrea Pozzo made this a residence fitting for one of the J. Paul Gettys of his day. Surrounding the palace was a great swampland soon dubbed "Liechtenthal" when it was transformed into a magnificent italianate garden; today, it has been restored along the lines of an English landscape park with Baroque statues and topiaries.

Visitors enter through the grand Sala Terrena, whose centerpiece is the golden carriage that looks like it just rolled out of a fairy tale. Once you enter the museum, there is an attempt to make visitors look at each painting rather than make a beeline for those by famous artists. Each work is identified by a number and a pamphlet guide is provided to match the number with the artist, along with a short description of the work. Paintings are well-lit, but arranged in two levels, which makes looking at the upper section rather difficult.

The pride of the museum is the Peter Paul Rubens Room, showcasing the tremendous Decius Mus cycle, which illustrates episodes from the life of the heroic ancient Roman consul who waged a war against the Latins. The grandest picture of the eight-painting cycle illustrates the death of the consul and it is high drama, indeed: Decius Mus gazes up to heaven as he falls off his massive grey steed as a lance pierces his throat in the middle of a pitched battle. All these paintings were made as models for a tapestry series, which is why Rubens' panels are so enormous. There are other Rubens gems here, including one of his best children's portraits, that of his daughter, *Clara Serena Rubens*. Marie Antoinette's favorite court painter, Elisabeth Vignée-Lebrun is represented with portraits of *Princess Karoline of Liechtenstein* and *Princess Hermenegilde of Liechtenstein*, along with a glimpse of the French queen's ill-fated friend, the Princesse de Lamballe, fetchingly rendered by Anton Hickel. Other paintings to look for are Angelika Kaufmann's portrait of *King Ferdinand IV of Sicily* with his family, Bernardino Luini's *Mary with Baby Jesus*, Raphael's *Portrait of a Man*, Bernardino Zaganelli da Cotignola's charming *Portrait of a Lady in Red Dress* from 1500, Lucas Cranach's *Portrait of Friedrich III*, Jean Valentin de Boulogne's *Cheerful Company with Fortune Teller*, and Paris Bordone's outstanding *Portrait of Nikolaus Körbler*. Before leaving, don't miss out on the magnificent library designed in the Neoclassical fashion by Joseph Hardtmuth (1758–1816) in the Gentlemen's Apartment side wing.

It's easy to spend the greater part of a day here. Behind the palace is the exquisite landscaped park—after wandering through the museum, stroll through the prince's shaded gardens. Even better, try to book a table at Rubens' Palais, the important new restaurant masterminded by top chef Ruben Brunhart, or its slightly cheaper counterpart, Ruben's Brasserie, whose umbrella-shaded outdoor bar is the perfect place to seek refreshment and savor the esthetic feast you have just enjoyed. ⊠ *Fürstengasse 1, 9th District/Alsergrund* ☎ *01/319–5767–0* ⊕ *www. liechtensteinmuseum.at* ⊠ *€10* ☉ *Wed.–Mon., 9–8 PM* Ⓤ *Bus: 40A/ Bauernfeldplatz, Tram: D/Bauernfeldplatz.*

★ ℭ ⑥⓪ **MuseumsQuartier.** (Museum Quarter). New and old, past and present, Baroque and Modernism dazzlingly collide in this headline-making vast culture center, opened in 2001. Claiming to be the largest of its kind in the world, the MuseumsQuartier—or **MQ** as many now call it—is housed in what was once the Imperial Court Stables, the 250-year-old Baroque complex designed by Fischer von Erlach and ideally situated in the heart of the city, near the Hofburg and set, appropriately, between the great Old Master treasures of the Kunsthistorisches Museum and the Spittelberg neighborhood, today one of Vienna's hippest enclaves. Where once 900 Lipizzaner horses were housed, now thousands of artistic masterworks of the 20th century and beyond are exhibited, all in a complex that is architecturally an expert and subtle blending of historic and cutting-edge—the original structure (fetchingly adorned with pastry-white stuccoed ceilings and Rococo flourishes) was retained, while ultra-modern wings were added to house five museums, most of which showcase modern art at its best. Once ensconced in the Palais Liechtenstein, the **Leopold Museum** comprises the holdings amassed by Rudolf and Elizabeth Leopold and famously contains one of the greatest collections of Egon Schiele in the world, as well as impressive works by Gustav Klimt and Oskar Kokoschka. Other artists worth noting are Josef Dobrowsky, Anton Faistauer, and Richard Gerstl. Emil Jakob Schindler's landscapes are well-represented, as are those by Biedermeier artist Ferdinand Georg Waldmüller. Center stage is held by Schiele (1890–1918), who died young, along with his wife and young baby, in one of Vienna's worst Spanish flu epidemics. His colorful, appealing landscapes are here, but all eyes are invariably drawn to the artist's tortured and racked depictions of nude mistresses, orgiastic self-portraits, and provocatively sexual couples, all elbows and organs.

Adjacent, in a broodingly modernistic, dark stone edifice, is the **Museum moderner Kunst Stiftung Ludwig (MUMOK)**, or Modern of Modern Art, which houses the national collection of 20th-century art on eight floors, mainly a bequest of Herr Ludwig, a billionaire industrialist who collected the cream of 20th-century art. Top works here are of the American Pop Art school, but all the trends of the last century—Nouveau Réalisme, Radical Realism, and Hyperrealism of the 1960s and '70s, Fluxus, Viennese Actionism, Conceptual Art and Minimal Art, Land Art and Arte Povera, as well as installation art vie for your attention. Names run from René Magritte and Max Ernst to Andy Warhol, Jackson Pollock, Cy Twombly, Nam June Paik, and the very latest superstars of contemporary art, such as Chris Burden (whose installation was of $1 million worth of gold ingots) and Kara Walker's daringly revisionist silhouettes. Kids will make a beeline for Claes Oldenburg's walk-in sculpture in the shape of Mickey Mouse.

Nearby, the **Kunsthalle** is used for temporary exhibitions—gigantic halls used for the installation of avant-avant-garde art. The emphasis is on the ethos of "temporariness," so these halls are used to show off myriad works of contemporary art in an ever-changing schedule of installations and happenings—one recent exposition was called "Scandal and Myth," so you can take it from there. A definite change of pace is offered by the **ZOOM Kinder Museum,** which caters to children. In the ZOOM lab, kids age 7 and up can experience the fine line between the real and virtual world, making their imagined screenplays come to life by becoming directors, sound technicians, authors, and actors. For the little ones there's the ZOOM Ozean (ocean), where with their parents they can enter a play area inhabited by magical creatures from the underwater world, featuring a ship with a captain's quarters and lighthouse. It's probably a good idea to reserve tickets in advance for this museum. The **Architekturzentrum** (Architecture Center) displays new architecture models, with computers showing the latest techniques used in restoring old buildings.

In the huge Fischer von Erlach wing facing the Museumsplatz, the **Quartier21** showcases up-and-coming artists and musicians. Artists have their own studios, open to the public for free. At the end of two years their output are judged—*Survivor*-fashion?—by a panel of visiting museum curators who decide if they should be invited to remain another two years. In addition to all this, the annual Wiener Festwochen (theater-arts festival) and the International Tanzwochen (dance festival) are held every year in the former Winter Riding Hall, and a theater for the annual Viennale Film Festival is planned. All in all, modern-art lovers will find it very easy to spend the entire day at MuseumsQuartier (even that may not be enough), and with several cafés, restaurants, gift shops, and bookstores, they won't need to venture outside. ⊠ *Museumsplatz 1–5, 7th District/Neubau* ☎ *01/523–5881, 01/524–7908 ZOOM Kinder Museum* ⊕ *www.mqw.at; www.kindermuseum.at* ⊠ *Leopold Museum €9; Kunst Stiftung Ludwig €8; Kunsthalle €6.50; Architekturzentrum €5; ZOOM Kindermuseum €5; ZOOM Ozean €4, including 1 companion for this only; combination ticket to all museums €25* ⊙ *Open daily 10–7* Ⓤ *U2/MuseumsQuartier or U3/Volkstheater.*

🏛️ **Naturhistorisches Museum** (Natural History Museum). The palatial, archetypally "Ringstrasse" 19th-century museum complex just outside the Ring has two elements—to the east is the celebrated Kunsthistorisches Museum, to the west is the Naturhistorisches Museum. This is the home of, among other artifacts, the famous Venus of Willendorf, a tiny statuette (actually, replica—the original is in a vault) thought to be some 20,000 years old; this symbol of the Stone Age was originally unearthed in the Wachau Valley, not far from Melk. The reconstructed dinosaur skeletons understandably draw the greatest attention. ⊠ *Maria-Theresien-Platz, 7th District/Neubau* ☎ *01/521–77-0* ⊕ *www.nhm-wien.ac.at* ⊠ *€8* ⊙ *Wed. 9–9, Thurs.–Mon. 9–6:30* Ⓤ *U2 or U3/Volkstheater.*

🏛️ **Parlament** (Parliament). This sprawling building reminiscent of an ancient Greek temple is the seat of Austria's elected representative assembly. An embracing, heroic ramp on either side of the main structure is lined with carved marble figures of ancient Greek and Roman historians. Its centerpiece is the **Pallas-Athene-Brunnen** (fountain), designed by Theophil Hansen, which is crowned by the goddess of wisdom and surrounded by water nymphs symbolizing the executive and legislative powers governing the country. ⊠ *Dr. Karl-Renner-Ring 1, 1st District* ☎ *01/401–110–2570* ⊕ *www.parlament.gv.at* ⊠ *€3* ⊙ *Tours mid-Sept.–June, Mon., Wed. 10 and 11, Tues., Thurs. 2 and 3, Fri. 11, 1, 2, and 3, except on days when Parliament is in session; July–mid-Sept., weekdays 9, 10, 11, 1, 2, and 3* Ⓤ *Tram: 1, 2, or D/Stadiongasse, Parliament.*

🏛️ **Rathaus** (City Hall). Designed by Friedrich Schmidt and resembling a Gothic fantasy castle with its many spires and turrets, the Rathaus was actually built between 1872 and 1883. The facade holds a lavish display of standard-bearers brandishing the coats of arms of the city of Vienna and the monarchy. Guided tours include the banqueting hall and various committee rooms. A regally landscaped park graces the front of the building and it is usually brimming with activity. In winter it is the scene of the *Christkindlmarkt*, the most famous Christmas market in Vienna; in summer, concerts are performed here. ⊠ *Rathausplatz 1, 1st District* ☎ *01/5255–0* ⊕ *www.wien.gv.at* ⊠ *Free* ⊙ *Guided tours Mon., Wed., Fri., at 1. 5-person minimum* Ⓤ *Tram: 1, 2 or D/Rathaus.*

⑥ **Spittelberg Quarter.** Where artists go, crowds follow. Thanks to a decade-
Fodor'sChoice long program of renovation (some say gentrification), this cobblestoned,
★ increasingly chic quarter welcomed a slew of artist ateliers and now teems with art galleries, restaurants, and plenty of promenaders. People have always liked to come to the Spittelberg because it's a slice of Old Vienna, a perfectly preserved little enclave that allows you to experience the 18th century by strolling along pedestrian streets lined with pretty Baroque town houses. As such, the quarter—situated one block northwest of Maria-Theresien-Platz off the Burggasse and just a few blocks behind the MuseumsQuartier—offers a fair visual idea of the Vienna that existed outside of the city walls a century ago. Most buildings have been replaced, but the engaging 18th-century survivors at Burggasse 11 and 13 are adorned with religious and secular decorative sculpture, the latter with a niche statue of St. Joseph, the former with cherubic work-and-play bas-reliefs. For several blocks around—walk down Gutenberggasse and back up Spittelberggasse—the 18th-century houses have been beautifully restored. The sequence from Spittelberggasse 5 to 19 is an especially fine array of Viennese plain and fancy.

Around holiday times, particularly Easter and Christmas, the Spittelberg quarter, known for arts and handicrafts, hosts seasonal markets offering unusual and interesting wares; the Christmas market is held throughout December. The new arts center of the quarter is a great place to head: **Amerlinghaus** is housed in a lovely 18th-century house that was the birthplace of the painter Friedrich von Amerling (1803–87). Rooms here are filled with art and community activities but check out the table-set inner courtyard, which, completely shaded by grand trees and bordered by a balcony, wouldn't look out of place in a Biedermeier canvas. A Spittelberg community association Web site with details about the district's sights, restaurants, and hotels can be found at ⊕ www.spittelberg.at. ⊠ *Stiffgasse 8, 7th District/Spittelberg* ☎ *01/523–6475* ⊕ *www.amerlinghaus.at* Ⓤ *U2 or U3/Volkstheater.*

off the
beaten
path

KAISERLICHES HOFMOBILIENDEPOT (Imperial Furniture Museum) –
– In the days of the Habsburg empire, palaces remained practically empty if the ruling family was not in residence. Cavalcades laden with enough furniture to fill a palace would set out in anticipation of a change of scene, while another caravan accompanied the royal party, carrying everything from traveling thrones to velvet-lined portable toilets. Much of this furniture is now on display here, allowing you a fascinating glimpse into everyday court life. The upper floors contain re-created rooms from the Biedermeier to the Jugendstil periods, and document the tradition of furniture-making in Vienna. Explanations are in German and English. ⊠ *Mariahilferstrasse 88/entrance on Andreasgasse, 7th District/ Neubau* ☎ *01/524–3357–0* ⊠ *€7* ⊙ *Tues.–Sun., 10–6* Ⓤ *U3 Zieglergasse/follow signs to Otto-Bauer-Gasse/exit Andreasgasse.*

⑥⑦ Universität (University of Vienna). After the one in Prague, Vienna's is the oldest university in the German-speaking world. It was founded in 1365 by Duke Rudolf IV and reorganized during the reign of Maria Theresa. The main section of the university is a massive block in Italian Renaissance style designed by Heinrich Ferstel and built between 1873 and 1884. Thirty-eight statues representing important men of letters decorate the front of the building, although the rear, which encompasses the library (with nearly 2 million volumes), is adorned with *sgraffito*. In the courtyard is the *Kastaliabrunnen*, the fountain for the guardians of spring, designed by Edmund Hellmer in 1904. ⊠ *Dr.-Karl-Lueger-Ring/Universitätstrasse, 1st District* Ⓤ *U2/Schottentor.*

⑥② Volksgarten. Just opposite the Hofburg is a green oasis with a beautifully planted rose garden, a 19th-century Greek temple, and a rather wistful white marble monument to Empress Elisabeth—Franz Josef's Bavarian wife, who died of a dagger wound inflicted by an Italian anarchist in Geneva in 1898. If not overrun with latter-day hippies, these can offer appropriate spots to sit for a few minutes while contemplating Vienna's most ambitious piece of 19th-century city planning: the famous Ringstrasse. ⊠ *Volksgarten, 1st District* Ⓤ *Tram: 1, 2 or D/ Rathausplatz, Burgtheater.*

⑥⑧ Votivkirche (Votive Church). When Emperor Franz Josef was a young man, he was strolling along the Mölker Bastei, now one of the few remaining portions of the old wall that once surrounded the city, when he was taken unawares and stabbed in the neck by an Italian tailor. The assassination attempt was unsuccessful, and in gratitude for his survival Franz Josef ordered that a church be built exactly at the spot he was gazing at when he was struck down. The neo-Gothic church was built of gray limestone with two openwork turrets between 1856 and 1879. ⊠ *Rooseveltplatz, 9th District/Alsergrund* ☎ *01/406–1192* ⊙ *Tours by prior arrangement* Ⓤ *U2/Schottentor.*

MONARCHS & MOZART: FROM ST. STEPHAN'S TO THE OPERA HOUSE

The cramped, ancient quarter behind St. Stephan's Cathedral offers a fascinating contrast to the luxurious expanses of the Ringstrasse and more recent parts of Vienna. This was—and still is—concentrated residential territory in the heart of the city. Mozart lived here; later, Prince Eugene and others built elegant town palaces as the smaller buildings were replaced. Streets—now mostly reserved for pedestrians—are narrow, and tiny alleyways abound. Facades open into courtyards that once housed carriages and horses. The magnificent Staatsoper (State Opera) shares with St. Stephan's the honor of being one of the city's most familiar and beloved landmarks.

The sector contains both the most neon-lit of Vienna streets—Kärntnerstrasse—and some of its most time-stained. The maze of tiny streets including Ballgasse, Rauhensteingasse, and Himmelpfortgasse (literally, "Gates of Heaven Street") masterfully conjures up the Vienna of the 19th century. The most impressive house on Himmelpfortgasse is the Ministry of Finance. At No. 7, Mozart conducted his arrangement of the Pastorale from Handel's *Acis and Galatea* in 1788 for Baron van Swieten. It was also here in this building that Mozart performed publicly for the last time, three years later, playing the Piano Concerto in B flat, K. 595. After his death, Baron van Swieten directed Mozart's *Requiem* on January 2, 1793 to benefit Mozart's widow, Constanze. Café Frauenhuber now occupies the No. 6 spot and still has a facade that Wolfie himself might recognize. The back side of the Steffl department store on Rauhensteingasse now marks the site of the house in which Mozart died in 1791. There's a commemorative plaque that once identified the streetside site together with a small memorial corner devoted to Mozart memorabilia that can be found on the fifth floor of the store.

In contrast are the beckoning big lights of Kärntnerstrasse, Vienna's leading central shopping street. These days Kärntnerstrasse is much maligned. Too commercial, too crowded, too many tasteless signs, too much gaudy neon—the complaints go on and on. Nevertheless, when the daytime tourist crowds dissolve, the Viennese arrive regularly for their evening promenade, and it is easy to see why. Vulgar the street may be, but it is also alive and vital, with an energy that the more tasteful Graben and the impeccable Kohlmarkt lack. For the sightseer beginning to suffer from an excess of art history, classic buildings, and museums, a Kärntnerstrasse window-shopping respite will be welcome.

a good walk

To pass through these streets is to take a short journey through history and art. In the process—as you visit former haunts of Mozart, kings, and emperors—you can be easily impressed with a clear sense of how Vienna's glittering Habsburg centuries unfolded. Start from St. Stephan's Cathedral by walking down Singerstrasse to Blutgasse and turn left into the **Blutgasse District** ㉑ ▶—a neighborhood redolent of the 18th century. At the north end, in Domgasse, is the so-called **Figarohaus** ㉒, now a memorial museum, the house in which Wolfgang Amadeus Mozart lived when he wrote the opera *The Marriage of Figaro*. Follow Domgasse east to Grünangergasse, which will bring you to Franziskanerplatz and the Gothic-Renaissance Franziskanerkirche (Franciscan Church). Follow the ancient Ballgasse to Rauhensteingasse, turning left onto Himmelpfortgasse—Gates of Heaven Street. Prince Eugene of Savoy had his town palace here at No. 8, now the **Finanzministerium** ㉓, living here when he wasn't enjoying his other residence, the Belvedere Palace. Continue down Himmelpfortgasse to Seilerstätte to visit a museum devoted to the wonders of music, the **Haus der Musik** ㉔. Then turn into Annagasse with its beautiful houses, which brings you back to the main shopping street, Kärnterstrasse, where you can find everything from Austrian jade to the latest Jill Sander fashion turnouts. Turn left, walk north two blocks, and take the short Donnergasse to reach **Neuer Markt** square and the Providence Fountain. At the southwest corner of the square is the **Kaisergruft** ㉕ in the Kapuzinerkirche (Capuchin Church), the burial vault for rows of Habsburgs. Tegetthofstrasse south will bring you to Albertinaplatz, the square noted for the obvious war memorial and even more for the **Albertina Museum** ㉖, one of the world's great collections of Old Master

MOZART, MOZART, MOZART!

FOR THE MUSICAL TOURIST who is excited at the prospect of treading in the footprints of Wolfgang Amadeus Mozart (1756–91), seeing where his masterpieces were committed to paper, or standing where a long-loved work was either praised or damned at its first appearance, Vienna is saturated with Mozartiana. The great composer crammed a prodigious number of compositions into his Vienna years (the last ten of his life—he moved to Vienna in March 1781), along with the arrival of his six children and his constantly changing Viennese addresses. Certainly, it's easy to find the places he lived in or visited, all carefully marked by memorial plaques. For it was in Vienna that many of his peaks were achieved, both personal and artistic. He wed his beloved Constanze Weber at St. Stephan's Cathedral in August, 1782, and led the premieres of several of his greatest operas, including The Abduction from the Seraglio (July 16, 1782, at the city's Burgtheater), Così Fan Tutte (January 16, 1790, at the same theater), and The Magic Flute (September 30, 1791, at the Freihaus Theater). But a knowledge of his troubled relations with his home city of Salzburg makes his Vienna soujourn an even more poignant one.

From the beginning of Wolfgang's precocious career, his father, frustrated in his own musical ambitions at the archbishopric in Salzburg, looked beyond the boundaries of the Austro-Hungarian empire to promote the boy's fame. At the age of six, his son was presented to the royal courts of Europe and caused a sensation with his skills as an instrumentalist and impromptu composer. As he grew up, however, his virtuosity lost its power to amaze and he was forced to make his way as an "ordinary" musician, which then meant finding a position at court. In this he was not much more successful than his father had been. In Salzburg he was never able to rise beyond the level of organist (allowing him, as he noted with sarcastic pride, to sit above the cooks at table), and, in disgust, he relocated to Vienna, where despite the popularity of his operas he was able to obtain only an unpaid appointment as assistant Kapellmeister at St. Stephan's mere months before his death. By then, patronage subscriptions had been taken up in Hungary and the Netherlands that would have paid him handsomely. But it was too late. Whatever the truth about the theories still swirling around his untimely death, the fact remains that not only was he not given the state funeral he deserved, but he was buried in an unmarked grave (although most Viennese at that time were) after a hasty, sparsely attended funeral.

Only a hard-boiled cynic can fail to be moved. Only the flint-hearted can stand in Vienna's Währingerstrasse and look at the windows behind which Mozart wrote those last three symphonies in the incredible short time of six weeks in the summer of 1788 and not be touched. For this was the time when the Mozart fortunes had slumped to their lowest. "If you, my best of friends, forsake me, I am unhappily and innocently lost with my poor sick wife and my child," he wrote. And if one is inclined to accuse Mozart's fellow countrymen of neglect, they would seem to have made up for it with a vengeance. The visitor to Vienna and Salzburg can hardly ignore the barrage of Mozart candies, wine, beer, coffee mugs, T-shirts, baseball caps—not to mention the gilt statues that make do for a nonexistent monumental tomb or the 24/7 festivities scheduled for 2006, the 250th anniversary of his birth. Mozart, always one to appreciate a joke, would surely see the irony in the belated veneration.

— Gary Dodson

drawings and prints. The southeast side of the square is bounded by the famous **Staatsoper** 🔞, the State Opera House; check for tour possibilities or, better, book tickets for a great *Rosenkavalier*. Enjoy a delicious finale at the **Café Sacher** 🔞.

TIMING A simple walk of this route could take you a full half day, assuming you stop occasionally to survey the scene and take it all in. The restyled Figarohaus is worth a visit, and the Kaisergruft in the Kapuzinerkirche is impressive for its shadows of past glories, but there are crowds, and you may have to wait to get in; the best times are early morning and around lunchtime. Tours of the State Opera House take place in the afternoons; check the schedule posted outside one of the doors on the arcaded Kärntnerstrasse side. Figure about an hour each for the various visits and tours.

HOW TO The U1 and U3 subway will deposit you at Stephansplatz and Karlsplatz,
GET THERE both in the heart of the city. The U1, U2, and U4 will also bring you to Karlsplatz.

What to See

🔞 **Albertina Museum.** Home to some of the greatest Old Master drawings
Fodor'sChoice in Vienna—including Dürer's iconic *Praying Hands* and beloved *Alpine
★ Hare*—this unassuming building contains the world's largest collection of drawings, sketches, engravings, and etchings. Partly built into Augustinerbastei—part of the original old city walls—and occupying the 17th-century Sylva-Tarouca palace, which is famed for its gilded Neoclassical rooms, the museum reopened in 2003 after a major renovation and new extension. In a seamless marvel of Baroque and modern styles, the Albertina now has an attached four-floor contemporary building designed by Austrian architects Steinmayer and Mascher, which also provides room for a study center and temporary exhibition hall, and more than ever makes the best of the Albertina's ideal location between the opera and the Hofburg.

The 18th-century Duke Albert of Saxon Teschen, probably better known as the husband of Marie Antoinette's sister, Marie Christine, was responsible for much of the art collection, which eventually passed into the hands of the Austrian republic after the collapse of the Habsburg monarchy. And what a collection it is—65,000 drawings and almost a million prints ranging from late Gothic to modern, and that's just for starters. The Old Masters are represented by Leonardo da Vinci, Michelangelo, Raphael, Rembrandt, Rubens, Correggio, and those great Albrecht Dürers. There are also mystical landscapes by Claude Lorrain, as well as works by Delacroix, Manet, and Cézanne. Moving on to the 20th century, the museum has many works by Gustav Klimt, the controversial Egon Schiele, and Picasso. It also houses the largest collection in the world of Oskar Kokoschka's drawings and watercolors. Needless to say, the museum's entire holdings are so vast that only a limited number can be displayed at one time (many are now stored in a high-tech warehouse underground, and some drawings are so delicate that they can be shown only in facsimile. The mansion's glorious early-19th-century salons—all giltboiserie and mirrors—provide a jewelbox setting. An excellent in-house

restaurant with an immense patio long enough for an empress's promenade offers splendid vistas of the historical center and the Burggarten—
the perfect place to take a break for a meal. ⊠ *Augustinerstrasse 1, 1st
District* ☎ *01/534–830* 🖷 *01/533–7697* ⊕ *www.albertina.at* 🖃 *€9*
⊙ *Daily 10–6, Wed. 10–9* Ⓤ *U3/Herrengasse.*

㊑ Blutgasse District. The small block bounded by Singerstrasse, Grünangergasse, and Blutgasse is known as the Blutgasse District. Nobody
knows for certain how the gruesome name—*Blut* is German for "blood"—
originated, although one legend has it that Knights Templar were slaughtered here when their order was abolished in 1312. Today the block is a
splendid example of city renovation and restoration, with cafés, small
shops, and galleries tucked into the corners. You can look inside the courtyards to see the open galleries that connect various apartments on the
upper floors, the finest example being at Blutgasse 3. At the corner of
Singerstrasse sits the 18th-century **Neupauer-Breuner Palace,** with its monumental entranceway and inventively delicate windows. ⊠ *1st District*
Ⓤ *U1 or U3/Stephansplatz.*

㊗ Café Sacher. Popular with prominent Viennese and tourists alike since the
Sacher Hotel opened in 1876, the Sacher Café is steeped in tradition, and
though it's elegant and dignified, you don't need to wear a suit and tie
to be admitted. Choose a table in either the formal café with its sparkling
chandeliers and plush wine-red banquettes, the more modern Wintergarten,
or the small outdoor café with its glimpse of the Opera and try to decide among an abundance of tempting pastries—though here, and only
here, can you sample the original Sachertorte. There is live piano music
every day from 4:30 to 7 PM. ⊠ *Philharmonikerstrasse 4, 1st District*
☎ *514–5666–1* ☰ *AE, DC, MC* ⊙ *Open daily, 8 AM–11:30 PM* Ⓤ *U1,
U2, or U4/Karlsplatz.*

★ ㊐ Figarohaus (Mozart Haus Vienna). The only one of Mozart's 11 rented
Viennese residences still extant—and probably the composer's most "lavish" abode—the Figarohaus fronts the tiny alley behind St. Stephan's (although the facade on Schulerstrasse is far more imposing). During the nearly
three years Mozart lived in this house (September 1784–April 1787)—then
known as the Camesina Haus—he wrote dozens of piano concertos, as
well as *The Marriage of Figaro,* and the six quartets dedicated to Joseph
Haydn (who once called on Mozart here, saying to Leopold, Mozart's father,
"your son is the greatest composer that I know in person or by name").
For two weeks in April 1787 Mozart taught a pupil who would become
famous in his own right, the 16-year-old Beethoven. Set on the second floor,
the apartment he occupied had four principal rooms and a rather steep
rent for the time: 450 Gulden per annum. Unfortunately, you'll have to
use your imagination to picture how Mozart lived and worked here—no
decor of the Mozarts remains (although the house does have a lovely pink
faux-marbre room) but they would have done it up in the sober style of
the Josephian era, more Neoclassical than florid Rococo. For the Mozart
2006 Year, five other floors are being renovated: a basement event center,
a ground-floor café and gift shop, a third-floor exhibit on the "Genius of
Mozart," and a fourth-floor gallery on "Mozart and his Times." Special
guided tours can be booked, complete with a mini piano recital. ⊠ *Dom-*

gasse 5, 1st District ☎ *01/513–6294* ⊕ *www.mozarthausvienna.at* ▨ €9
⊙ *Daily, 10–8* Ⓤ *U1 or U3/Stephansplatz*

73 **Finanzministerium** (Ministry of Finance). The architectural jewel of Himmelpfortgasse, this imposing abode—designed by Fischer von Erlach in
1697 and later expanded by Hildebrandt—was originally the town
palace of Prince Eugene of Savoy. As you study the Finanzministerium,
you'll realize its Baroque details are among the most inventively conceived and beautifully executed in the city; all the decorative motifs are
so softly carved that they appear to have been freshly squeezed from a
pastry tube. The Viennese are lovers of the Baroque in both their architecture and their pastry, and here the two passions seem visibly merged.
Such Baroque elegance may seem inappropriate for a finance ministry,
but the contrast between place and purpose could hardly be more Viennese. ⊠ *Himmelpfortgasse 8, 1st District* Ⓤ *U1 or U3/Stephansplatz.*

★ ⓒ **74** **Haus der Musik** (House of Music). It would be easy to spend an entire day
at this ultra-high-tech museum housed on several floors of an early-19th-
century palace near Schwarzenbergplatz. Pride of place goes to the special rooms dedicated to each of the great Viennese composers—Haydn,
Mozart, Beethoven, Strauss, and Mahler—complete with music samples
and manuscripts. For the 2006 Mozart Year, Wolfgang takes center stage,
with a police identitkit to help reconstruct what he looked like, a manuscript
of the immortal *Requiem,* and the chance to use a "virtual conductor"
and lead the Vienna Philharmonic as it plays "A Little Night Music." You
can also mix *The Magic Flute* with your own sound additions and take
it home with you on your own personal CD. Other exhibits trace the evolution of sound (from primitive noises to the music of the masters) and
illustrate the mechanics of the human ear (measure your own frequency
threshold). There are also dozens of interactive computer games. On the
first floor is a handy coffeehouse, while the top floor has the luxe and excellent Cantina restaurant. ⊠ *Seilerstätte 30, 1st District* ☎ *01/51648*
⊕ *www.hdm.at* ▨ *€10* ⊙ *Daily 10–10* ♿ *Restaurant, café* Ⓤ *U1, U2
or U4/Karlsplatz, then Tram D/Schwarzenbergplatz.*

**need a
break?** Take a break at a landmark café in one of the most charming squares
in Vienna, between Himmelpfortgasse and Singerstrasse. The **Kleines
Cafe** (⊠ Franziskanerplatz 3, 1st District), open daily, is more for
coffee, cocktails, and light snacks than for pastries, and few places are
more delightful to sit in and relax on a warm afternoon or evening. In
summer, tables are set outside on the intimate cobblestone square
where the only sounds are the tinkling fountain and the occasional
chiming of bells from the ancient Franciscan monastery next door.

75 **Kaisergruft** (Imperial Burial Vault). In the basement of the Kapuzinerkirche, or Capuchin Church (on the southwest corner of the Neuer
Markt), is one of the more intriguing sights in Vienna: the Kaisergruft,
or Imperial Burial Vault. The crypts contain the partial remains of some
140 Habsburgs (the hearts are in the Augustinerkirche and the entrails
in St. Stephan's) plus one non-Habsburg governess ("She was always
with us in life," said Maria Theresa, "why not in death?"). Perhaps starting with their tombs is the wrong way to approach the Habsburgs in

WAS AMADEUS MURDERED?

AS ONE OF THE MORE FAMOUS *Cold Case* files of the 18th century, the death of Wolfgang Amadeus Mozart continues to haunt historians. The great composer died at 1:05 PM on December 5, 1791, just shy of his 36th birthday, but was his death due to natural causes or something much more nefarious? Let's look at the CSI findings. The scene: his second-floor apartment at 8 Rauhensteingasse (now the Steffl store), a few blocks south of the cathedral of St. Stephan. During his final three weeks, Mozart's hands and feet were greatly swollen and he became partly paralyzed; After death, his entire body swelled up, giving rise to the suspicion that he had been poisoned, especially as his body did not achieve rigor mortis but maintained a soft and elastic form, a state consistent with poisoning. Mozart himself started the rumor: "Someone has given me acqua toffana (a compound of arsenic, antimony, and lead) and has calculated the precise time of my death—for which they have ordered a Requiem, one that I am now writing for myself," he confided to Costanze, his wife. Mozart was referring to the arrival, earlier that fall—at the very time he was presiding over the premieres of two of his greatest operas, The Magic Flute and The Clemency of Tito—of a "masked messenger" bearing a commission for a Mass for the Dead. Historical records indicate that the mysterious messenger was sent by Count van Wallseg, a Viennese nobleman who wanted the Requiem to honor his recently deceased wife and who insisted on anonymity because—the count was notorious for doing this—he wanted to pass off the composition as his own. In other words, Mozart found himself reduced to "ghosting" a musical composition for a hack court-dilettante. Is it any wonder the composer—who often suffered bouts of depression—descended into severe, brooding melancholy? Overwork, a mountain of pressing debt, and a lethal return of Mozart's childhood rheumatic fever further hastened the artist's end.

However, in Anthony Schaffer's 1984 Oscar-winning Amadeus, this masked man is the noted composer Antonio Salieri, one of Mozart's fiercest rivals and the person who had helped popularize Italian opera (not the German form preferred by Mozart) in Vienna. Since it was well known that the Italianists and the Germanists working in Vienna were often at each other throats, the rumor that Salieri had despatched his brilliant rival quickly gained ground. The film depicts a Salieri so resentful of the musical gifts that had been providentially bestowed upon such an undisciplined, giggling, upstart fop that he decides to tip Mozart over the edge by posing as "the divine messenger."

Diehard conspiracy theorists point to yet another suspect: the brotherhood of Freemasons. Having recently become a member of this supersecret sect, Mozart was commissioned to write a pro-Masonic opera: The Magic Flute, which was to present a symbolic enactment of the struggle between Free-Thinkers and Christianity. Mozart, however, subverted much of the Masonic philosophy in the opera and, so the story goes, was poisoned as punishment for his betrayal. In the end, his interment was not that of a lowly pauper or a dog, as legend has it; rather, Mozart was laid out in a simple cloth sack and buried in a common grave, in keeping with the wishes of Austria's Emperor Joseph II, who had decreed—as an adherent of the Enlightenment—simplified burials as a stand against superstition. Mozart would have agreed entirely, as would his family, which is why no one accompanied the casket on its final four-mile journey to the cemetery—no one, that is, but Mozart's faithful dog.

Vienna, but it does give you a chance to get their names in sequence as they lie in rows, their coffins ranging from the simplest explosions of funerary conceit—with decorations of skulls and other morbid symbols—to the lovely and distinguished tomb of Maria Theresa and her husband. Designed while the couple still lived, their monument shows the empress in bed with her husband—awaking to the Last Judgment as if it were just another weekday morning, while the remains of her son (the ascetic Josef II) lie in a simple casket at the foot of the bed as if he were the family dog. ⊠ *Neuer Markt/Tegetthoffstrasse 2, 1st District* ☎ *01/ 512–6853–12* 🎫 *€4* 🕙 *Daily 9:30–4* Ⓤ *U1, U3/Stephansplatz or U1, U4/Karlsplatz.*

77 Staatsoper (State Opera House). The famous Vienna Staatsoper on the Ring vies with the cathedral for the honor of marking the emotional heart of the city—it is a focus for Viennese life and one of the chief symbols of resurgence after the cataclysm of World War II. Its directorship is one of the top jobs in Austria, almost as important as that of president, and one that comes in for even more public attention. Everyone thinks he or she could do it just as well, and since the huge salary comes out of taxes, they feel they have every right to criticize, often and loudly. The first of the Ringstrasse projects to be completed (in 1869), the opera house suffered disastrous bomb damage in the last days of World War II (only the outer walls, the front facade, and the main staircase area behind it survived). The auditorium is plain when compared to the red-and-gold eruptions of London's Covent Garden or some of the Italian opera houses, but it has an elegant individuality that shows to best advantage when the stage and auditorium are turned into a ballroom for the great Opera Ball.

The construction of the Opera House is the stuff of legend. When the foundation was laid, the plans for the Opernring were not yet complete, and in the end the avenue turned out to be several feet higher than originally planned. As a result, the Opera House lacked the commanding prospect that its architects, Eduard van der Nüll and August Sicard von Sicardsburg, had intended, and even Emperor Franz Josef pronounced the building a bit low to the ground. For the sensitive van der Nüll (and here the story becomes a bit suspect), failing his beloved emperor was the last straw. In disgrace and despair, he committed suicide. Sicardsburg died of grief shortly thereafter. And the emperor, horrified at the deaths his innocuous remark had caused, limited all his future artistic pronouncements to a single immutable formula: *"Es war sehr schön, es hat mich sehr gefreut"* ("It was very nice, it pleased me very much").

Renovation could not avoid a postwar look, for the cost of fully restoring the 19th-century interior was prohibitive. The original basic design was followed in the 1945–55 reconstruction, meaning that sight lines from some of the front boxes are poor at best. These disappointments hardly detract from the fact that this is one of the world's half-dozen greatest opera houses, and experiencing a performance here can be the highlight of a trip to Vienna. Tours of the Opera House are given regularly, but starting times vary according to opera rehearsals; the current schedule is posted at the east-side entrance under the arcade on the

Kärntnerstrasse marked GUIDED TOURS, where the tours begin. Alongside under the arcade is an information office that also sells tickets to the main opera and the Volksoper. ✉ *Opernring 2, 1st District* ☎ *01/ 514–44–2606* ⊕ *www.wiener-staatsoper.at* ✆ *€4.50* ☉ *Tours year- round when there are no rehearsals, but call for times* Ⓤ *U1, U2, or U4 Karlsplatz.*

POMP & CIRCUMSTANCE: SOUTH OF THE RING TO THE BELVEDERE

City planning in the late 1800s and early 1900s clearly was essential to manage the growth of the burgeoning imperial capital. The elegant Ringstrasse alone was not a sufficient showcase, and anyway it focused on public rather than private buildings. The city fathers as well as private individuals commissioned the architect Otto Wagner to plan and undertake a series of projects. The area around Karlsplatz and the fascinating open food market remain a classic example of unified design. Not all of Wagner's concepts for Karlsplatz were realized, but enough remains to be convincing and to convey the impression of what might have been. The unity concept predates Wagner's time in the former garden of Belvedere Palace, one of Europe's greatest architectural triumphs.

Karlsplatz is bookended by two of Vienna's greatest buildings, the spectacular Baroque-era church of the Karlskirche and that icon of modern architecture, Josef Olbrich's Secession Pavilion. When the latter's "gilded cabbage" dome was set in place, Vienna was outraged—never mind the fact that the government had donated the land to this group of artists for their exhibition hall. For decades so drab it went unnoticed, the building is now beloved by all fans of Jugendstil architecture, its cabbage regilded, its facade restored to its pristine white, gold, and green, and inside, a fitting repository for Gustav Klimt's eye-knocking *Beethoven Frieze.* But this is just one memorable treasure among many in this area: Other treats include the Hieronymus Bosch altarpiece on view in the paintings collection at the Akademie der bildenen Künste, Jugendstil residences designed by Otto Wagner, the sumptuous Palais Schwarzenberg hotel, and the famous Belvedere Palace, where many of the greatest 19th- and early-20th-century Austrian paintings, such as Gustav Klimt's *The Kiss,* remain on view in splendorous surroundings.

a good walk

The often overlooked **Akademie der bildenen Künste** ⑦⑨ ▶, or Academy of Fine Arts, is an appropriate starting point for this walk, as it puts into perspective the artistic arguments taking place around the turn of the century. While the Academy represented the conservative viewpoint, a group of modernist revolutionaries broke away and founded the Secessionist movement, with its culmination in the gold-crowned **Secession Building** ㉚. Now housing changing exhibits and Gustav Klimt's provocative *Beethoven Frieze,* the museum stands appropriately close to the Academy; from the Academy, take Makartgasse south one block. The famous **Naschmarkt** ㉛ open food market starts diagonally south from the Secession; follow the rows of stalls southwest. Pay attention to the northwest side of the Linke Wienzeile, to the Theater an der Wien at the intersection with Millöckergasse (Mozart and Beethoven personally premiered some of their finest works at this opera house–theater) and to the **Otto Wagner Houses** ㉒. For a saunter through hippest Vienna, head east down Faulmanngasse or Schleifmühlgasse to the **Freihaus** sector, whose streets are lined with hot-cool shops and art galleries. Then turn back north via Wiedner Hauptstrasse to the park complex that forms Karlsplatz, creating a frame for the classic **Karlskirche** ㉝. Around **Karlsplatz** ㉞ note the Technical University on the south side, and the Otto Wagner subway station buildings on the north. Across Lothringer Strasse on the north side are the Künstlerhaus art exhibit hall and the Musikverein. The out-of-place and rather undistinguished modern building to the left of Karlskirche houses the worthwhile **Wien Museum Karlsplatz** ㉟. Cut through Symphonikerstrasse (a passageway through the modern complex) and take Brucknerstrasse to **Schwarzenbergplatz** ㊱ The Jugendstil edifice on your left is the French Embassy; ahead is the Russian War Memorial. On a rise behind the memorial sits Palais Schwarzenberg, a jewel of a onetime summer palace, studded with palatial reception rooms and now a luxury hotel (why not plan a visit by way of drinks in one of its salons or a luncheon or dinner at its spiffy terrace restaurant?). Follow Prinz Eugen-Strasse up to the entrance of the **Belvedere Palace** ㊲ complex on your left. Besides the palace itself are other structures and, off to the east side, a remarkable botanical garden. After viewing the palace and the grounds, you can exit the complex from the lower building, Untere Belvedere, into Rennweg, which will steer you back to Schwarzenbergplatz.

TIMING   The first part of this walk, taking in the Academy of Fine Arts and the Secession, plus the Naschmarkt and Karlsplatz, can be accomplished in an easy half day. The Museum of the City of Vienna is good for a couple of hours, more if you understand some German. Give the Belvedere Palace and grounds as much time as you can. Organized tours breeze in and out—without so much as a glance at the outstanding modern art museum—in a half hour or so, not even scratching the surface of this fascinating complex. If you can, budget up to a half day here, but plan to arrive fairly early in the morning or afternoon before the busloads descend. Bus tourists aren't taken to the Lower Belvedere, so you'll have that and the formal gardens to yourself.

HOW TO   Take Tram D from the Ring to Schwarzenbergplatz, the Haus der Musik
GET THERE   (which is right behind), and Belvedere Palace, where you will be dropped off virtually at the portal. For all other sights, take the U1, U2, or U4 subway to Karlsplatz.

What to See

㉙ **Akademie der bildenen Künste** (Academy of Fine Arts). An outsize statue of the German author Schiller announces the Academy of Fine Arts on Schillerplatz. (Turn around and note his more famous contemporary, Goethe, pompously seated in an overstuffed chair, facing him from across the Ring.) The Academy was founded in 1692, but the present Renaissance Revival building dates from the late 19th century. The idea was conservatism and traditional values, even in the face of a growing movement that scorned formal rules. It was here in 1907 and 1908 that aspiring artist Adolf Hitler was refused acceptance on grounds of insufficient talent. He found this rejection devastating (his submitted Vienna cityscapes were done in a highly realistic manner but the people depicted in them resembled stick figures) and never again attempted to attain his dream of becoming a painter—one has to ponder how history would have different if he had been accepted as a student here. The Academy includes a museum focusing on Old Masters. The collection is mainly of interest to specialists, but Hieronymus Bosch's famous *Last Judgment* triptych hangs here—an imaginative, if gruesome, speculation on the hereafter. ✉ *Schillerplatz 3, 1st District* ☎ *01/588–16–225* ⊕ *www.akademiegalerie.at* 🎟 *€5* ⊙ *Tues.–Sun. 10–6* Ⓤ *U1, U2, or U4 Karlsplatz.*

87 **Belvedere Palace** (including Österreichische Galerie). One of the most
Fodor's Choice splendid pieces of Baroque architecture anywhere, the Belvedere Palace—
★ actually two imposing palaces separated by a 17th-century French-style garden parterre—is one of the masterpieces of architect Lucas von Hildebrandt. Wedged between Rennweg (entry at No. 6A) and Prinz Eugen-Strasse (entry at No. 27), it was built outside the city fortifications between 1714 and 1722 as the summer home of the immensely wealthy and refined Prince Eugene of Savoy; much later it became the home of Archduke Franz Ferdinand, whose assassination in 1914 precipitated World War I. Today the complex is home to three impressive museums, known as the Österreichische Galerie, and including the fabled Galerie des 19 und 20. Jahrhunders, home to many of the greatest paintings by such Austrian artists as Klimt and Schiele. But even without the museums, these palaces would constitute a must-see if you are interested in state splendor and Viennese opulence.

Though the lower palace is impressive in its own right, the upper palace is the cynosure of all eyes, due to its immense size and position atop the Rennweg hill. The usual tourist entrance for the Upper Belvedere is the gate on Prinz-Eugen-Strasse; for the Lower Belvedere, use the Rennweg gate—but for the most impressive view of the upper palace, approach it from the south garden closest to the South Rail Station. The upper palace displays a remarkable wealth of architectural invention in its facade, avoiding the main design problem common to all palaces because of their excessive size: monotony on the one hand and pomposity on the other. Hildebrandt's decorative manner here approaches the Rococo, that final style of the Baroque era when traditional classical motifs all but disappeared in a whirlwind of seductive asymmetric fancy. The main interiors of the palace go even farther: columns are transformed into muscle-bound giants, pilasters grow torsos, capitals sprout great piles of symbolic imperial paraphernalia, and the ceilings are set aswirl with ornately molded stucco. The result is the finest Rococo interior in the city. On the garden level, you are greeted by the celebrated Sala Terrena whose massive Atlas figures shoulder the marble vaults of the ceiling and, it seems, the entire palace above. The next floor is centered around a gigantic Marble Hall, covered with trompe l'oeil frescoes, while down in the Lower Belvedere palace, there are more 17th-century salons, including the Grotesque Room painted by Jonas Drentwett and another Marble Hall (which really lives up to its name).

Today both the upper and lower palaces of the Belvedere are noted museums devoted to Austrian painting. The **Österreichisches Barockmuseum** (Austrian Museum of Baroque Art) in the lower palace at Rennweg 6a displays Austrian art of the 18th century (including the original figures from Georg Raphael Donner's Providence Fountain in the Neuer Markt)—and what better building to house it? Next to the Baroque Museum (outside the west end) is the converted Orangerie, devoted to works of the medieval period.

The main attraction in the upper palace's **Galerie des 19 und 20. Jahrhunders** (Gallery of 19th and 20th Centuries) is the legendary collection of 19th- and 20th-century Austrian paintings, centering on the work of Vienna's three preeminent early-20th-century artists: Gustav Klimt, Egon Schiele, and Oskar Kokoschka. Klimt was the oldest, and by the time he helped found the Secession movement he had forged a highly idiosyncratic painting style that combined realistic and decorative elements in a way that was completely revolutionary. *The Kiss*—his greatest painting and one of the icons of modern art (although it is greatly inspired by the golden Byzantine mosaics of Ravenna and Venice)—is here on display. Schiele and Kokoschka went even further, rejecting the decorative appeal of Klimt's glittering abstract designs and producing works that completely ignored conventional ideas of beauty. Today they are considered the fathers of modern art in Vienna. Modern music, too, has roots in the Belvedere complex: the composer Anton Bruckner lived and died here in 1896 in a small garden house now marked by a commemorative plaque. ✉ *Prinz-Eugen-Strasse 27, 3rd District/ Landstrasse* ☎ *01/79557–0 or 01/79557–134* ⊕ *www.belvedere.at/* 🎫 *€7.50* ☉ *Tues.–Sun. 10–6* Ⓤ *U1, U2, or U4 Karlsplatz, then Tram D/Belvederegasse.*

83 **Karlskirche.** Dominating the Karlsplatz is one of Vienna's greatest buildings, the Karlskirche, dedicated to St. Charles Borromeo. At first glance, the church seems like a fantastic vision—one blink and you half expect the building to vanish. For before you is a giant Baroque church framed by enormous freestanding columns, mates to Rome's famous Trajan's Column. These columns may be out of keeping with the building as a whole, but were conceived with at least two functions in mind: one was to portray scenes from the life of the patron saint, carved in imitation of Trajan's triumphs, and thus help to emphasize the imperial nature of the building; and the other was to symbolize the Pillars of Hercules, suggesting the right of the Habsburgs to their Spanish dominions, which the emperor had been forced to renounce. Whatever the reason, the end result is an architectural tour de force.

Fodor'sChoice ★

The Karlskirche was built in the early 18th century on what was then the bank of the River Wien and is now the southeast corner of the park complex. The church had its beginnings in a disaster. In 1713 Vienna was hit by a brutal plague outbreak, and Emperor Charles VI made a vow: if the plague abated, he would build a church dedicated to his namesake, St. Charles Borromeo, the 16th-century Italian bishop who was famous for his ministrations to Milanese plague victims. In 1715 construction began, using an ambitious design by Johann Bernhard Fischer von Erlach that combined architectural elements from ancient Greece (the columned entrance porch), ancient Rome (the Trajanesque columns), contemporary Rome (the Baroque dome), and contemporary Vienna (the Baroque towers at either end). When it was finished, the church received a decidedly mixed press. History, incidentally, delivered a negative verdict: in its day the Karlskirche spawned no imitations, and it went on to become one of European architecture's most famous curiosities. Notwithstanding, seen lit at night, the building is magical in its setting.

The main interior of the church utilizes only the area under the dome and is surprisingly conventional given the unorthodox facade. The space and architectural detailing are typical High Baroque; the fine vault frescoes, by J. M. Rottmayr, depict St. Charles Borromeo imploring the Holy Trinity to end the plague. ⊠ *Karlsplatz, 4th District/Wieden* ☎ *01/504–61–87* ⊘ *Daily 8–6* Ⓤ *U1, U2, or U4 Karlsplatz.*

84 **Karlsplatz.** Like the space now occupied by the Naschmarkt, Karlsplatz was formed when the River Wien was covered over at the turn of the century. At the time, Wagner expressed his frustration with the result— too large a space for a formal square and too small a space for an informal park—and the awkwardness is felt to this day. The buildings surrounding the Karlsplatz, however, are quite sure of themselves: the area is dominated by the classic **Karlskirche,** made less dramatic by the unfortunate reflecting pool with its Henry Moore sculpture, wholly out of place, in front. On the south side of the Resselpark, that part of Karlsplatz named for the inventor of the screw propeller for ships, stands the **Technical University** (1816–18). In a house that occupied the space closest to the church, Italian composer Antonio Vivaldi died in 1741; a plaque marks the spot. On the north side, across the heavily traveled roadway, are the **Künstlerhaus** (the exhibition hall in which the Secessionists refused to exhibit, built in 1881 and still in use) and the famed **Musikverein.** The latter, finished in 1869, is now home to the Vienna Philharmonic. The downstairs lobby and the two halls upstairs have been gloriously restored and glow with fresh gilding. The main hall has what may be the world's finest acoustics; this is the site of the annual, globally televised New Year's Day concert.

Some of Otto Wagner's finest Secessionist work can be seen two blocks east on the northern edge of Karlsplatz—the **Otto Wagner Stadtbahn Pavilions,** at No. 1 Karlsplatz. In 1893 Wagner was appointed architectural supervisor of the new Vienna City Railway, and the matched pair of small pavilions he designed for the Karlsplatz train station in 1898 are among the city's most ingratiating buildings. Their structural framework is frankly exposed (in keeping with Wagner's belief in architectural honesty), but they are also lovingly decorated (in keeping with the Viennese fondness for architectural finery). The result is Jugendstil at its very best, melding plain and fancy with grace and insouciance. The pavilion to the southwest is utilized as a small, specialized museum. In the course of redesigning Karlsplatz, it was Wagner, incidentally, who proposed moving the fruit and vegetable market to what is now the Naschmarkt. ⊠ *4th District/Wieden* Ⓤ *U1, U2, or U4/Karlsplatz.*

⑧ Naschmarkt. Two blocks southeast of the Karlsplatz square, the area between Linke and Rechte Wienzeile has for 80 years been address to the Naschmarkt. This is Vienna's main outdoor produce market, certainly one of Europe's—if not the world's—great open-air markets, where packed rows of polished and stacked fruits and vegetables compete for visual appeal with braces of fresh pheasant in season; the nostrils, meanwhile, are accosted by spice fragrances redolent of Asia or the Middle East. It's open Monday to Saturday 6:30–6:30 (many stalls close two hours earlier in winter months). When making a purchase, be sure you get the correct change. ⊠ *Between the Linke and Rechte Wienzeile, 4th District/Wieden* Ⓤ *U1, U2, or U4 Karlsplatz, follow signs to Secession.*

need a break? Who can explore the Naschmarkt without picking up a snack? A host of Turkish stands offer tantalizing *Döner* sandwiches (thinly sliced lamb with onions and a yogurt sauce in a freshly baked roll). If you're in the mood for Italian *tramezzini* (crustless sandwiches filled with tuna and olives or buffalo mozzarella and tomato), there are a couple of huts to choose from on the Linke Wienzeile side about midway through the market. You can also have sushi and other fish snacks at the glass-enclosed seafood huts at the Karlsplatz end.

⑧ Otto Wagner Houses. The Ringstrasse-style apartment houses that line the Wienzeile are an attractive, if generally somewhat standard, lot, but two stand out: **Linke Wienzeile 38 and 40**—the latter better known as the "Majolica House"—designed (1898–99) by the grand old man of Viennese fin-de-siècle architecture, Otto Wagner, during his Secessionist period. A good example of what Wagner was rebelling against can be seen next door, at **Linke Wienzeile 42,** where decorative enthusiasm has blossomed into Baroque Revival hysteria. Wagner had come to believe that this sort of display was nothing but empty pretense and sham; modern apartment houses, he wrote in his pioneering text *Modern Architecture,* are entirely different from 18th-century town palaces, and architects should not pretend otherwise. Accordingly he banished classical decoration and introduced a new architectural simplicity, with flat exterior walls and plain, regular window treatments meant to reflect the orderly layout of the apartments behind them. There the simplicity ended. For exterior decoration, he turned to his younger Secessionist cohorts Joseph Olbrich and Koloman Moser, who designed the ornate Jugendstil patterns of red majolica-tile roses (No. 40) and gold stucco medallions (No. 38) that gloriously brighten the facades of the adjacent houses—so much so that their Baroque-period neighbor is ignored. The houses are privately owned. ⊠ *4th District/Wieden* Ⓤ *U1, U2, or U4/Karlsplatz.*

⑧ Schwarzenbergplatz. A remarkable urban ensemble, the Schwarzenbergplatz comprises some notable sights. The center of the lower square off the Ring is marked by an oversize equestrian sculpture of Prince Schwarzenberg—he was a 19th-century field marshal for the imperial forces. Admire the overall effect of the square and see if you can guess which building is the newest; it's the one on the northeast corner (No. 3) at Lothringer Strasse, an exacting reproduction of a building destroyed by war damage in 1945 and dating only from the 1980s. The military monument occupying the south end of the square behind the fountain is the **Russian War Memorial,** set up at the end of World War II by the Soviets; the Viennese, remembering the Soviet occupation, call its unknown soldier the "unknown plunderer." South of the memorial is the stately **Schwarzenberg Palace,** designed as a summer residence by Johann Lukas von Hildebrandt in 1697, completed by Fischer von Erlach father and son, and now (in part) a luxury hotel. The delightful formal gardens wedged between Prinz Eugen-Strasse and the Belvedere gardens can be enjoyed from the hotel restaurant's veranda. ⊠ *Schwarzenbergplatz, 3rd District/Landstrasse* Ⓤ *Tram: Schwarzenbergplatz.*

❽
Fodor'sChoice
★

Secession Building. If the Academy of Fine Arts represents the conservative attitude toward the arts in the late 1800s, then its antithesis can be found in the building immediately behind it to the southeast: the Secession Pavilion. Restored in the mid-1980s after years of neglect, the Secession building is one of Vienna's preeminent symbols of artistic rebellion. Rather than looking to the architecture of the past, like the revivalist Ringstrasse, it looked to a new antihistoricist future. It was, in its day, a riveting trumpet-blast of a building and is today considered by many to be Europe's first example of full-blown 20th-century architecture.

The Secession began in 1897, when 20 dissatisfied Viennese artists, headed by Gustav Klimt, "seceded" from the Künstlerhausgenossenschaft, the conservative artists' society associated with the Academy of Fine Arts. The movement promoted the radically new kind of art known as Jugendstil, which found its inspiration in both the organic, fluid designs of Art Nouveau and the related but more geometric designs of the English Arts and Crafts movement. (The Secessionists founded an Arts and Crafts workshop of their own, the famous Wiener Werkstätte, in an effort to embrace the applied arts.) The Secession building, designed by the architect Joseph Olbrich and completed in 1898, was the movement's exhibition hall. Interestingly, it was initially planned for a site on the Ringstrasse but public uproar made the city find a site on the Karlsplatz and was only to stand as a temporary gallery for 10 years. The lower story, crowned by the entrance motto *Der Zeit Ihre Kunst, Der Kunst Ihre Freiheit* ("To Every Age Its Art, To Art Its Freedom"), is classic Jugendstil: the restrained but assured decoration (by Koloman Moser) beautifully complements the facade's pristine flat expanses of cream-color wall. Above the entrance motto sits the building's most famous feature, the gilded openwork dome that the Viennese were quick to christen "the golden cabbage" (Olbrich wanted it to be seen as a dome of laurel, a subtle classical reference meant to celebrate the triumph of art). The gorgons and the owl that adorn the facade decoration are meant to allude to Pallas Athene, the goddess of wisdom, victory, and the crafts. As it turns out, the famous square pavilion that greets the viewer (for the most part, a 1960s reconstruction, as the original had been destroyed by Hitler's bombs) is actually only the "head" to the "body"—a vast art hall behind the pavilion that is plain, white, "shining and chaste," in Olbrich's words. It was also revolutionary in that it had movable walls, allowing the galleries to be reshaped and redesigned for every show. One early show, in 1902, was an exhibition devoted to art celebrating the genius of Beethoven; Gustav Klimt's *Beethoven Frieze,* painted for the occasion, has now been restored and is permanently installed in the building's basement. On view in the art hall are temporary exhibitions of contemporary cutting-edge art. ⊠ *Friedrichstrasse 12, 4th District/ Wieden* ☎ *01/587–5307* ⊕ *www.secession.at/* ⊠ *€4 exhibition, €5.50 exhibition with Beethoven Frieze, €1.50 guided tour* ☉ *Tues.–Sun. 10–6, Thurs. 10–8, guided tours Sat. at 3 and Sun. at 11* Ⓤ *U1, U2, or U4 Karlsplatz.*

㉟ **Wien Museum Karlsplatz** (Museum of Viennese History). Housed in an incongruously modern building at the east end of the regal Karlsplatz, this museum possesses a dazzlement of Viennese historical artifacts and treasures: models, maps, documents, photographs, antiquities, stained glass, paintings, sculpture, crafts, and reconstructed rooms. Everything from 16th-century armor to great paintings by Schiele and Klimt (notably his portrait of Emilie Flöge) and the preserved facade of Otto Wagner's *Die Zeit* offices; note the life-size portrait of the composer Alban Berg painted by his contemporary Arnold Schönberg. Display information and designations in the museum are in German and English. ⊠ *Karlsplatz, 4th District/Wieden* ☎ *01/505–8747–0* ⊕ *www.wienmuseum. at/94.htm* ⊠ *€4* ☉ *Tues.–Sun. 9–6* Ⓤ *U1, U2, or U4 Karlsplatz.*

off the beaten path

ZENTRALFRIEDHOF – Taking a streetcar out of Schwarzenbergplatz, music lovers will want to make a pilgrimage to the **Zentralfriedhof** (Central Cemetery), which contains the graves of most of Vienna's great composers: Ludwig van Beethoven, Franz Schubert, Johannes Brahms, the Johann Strausses (father and son), and Arnold Schönberg, among others. The monument to Wolfgang Amadeus Mozart is a memorial only; the approximate location of his unmarked grave can be seen at the now deconsecrated St. Marx-Friedhof at Leberstrasse 6–8. ⊠ *Simmeringer Hauptstrasse, 11th District/Simmering* Ⓤ *Tram: 71 to St. Marxer Friedhof, or on to Zentralfriedhof Haupttor/2.*

SPLENDORS OF THE HABSBURGS: A VISIT TO SCHÖNBRUNN PALACE

The glories of imperial Austria are nowhere brought together more convincingly than in the Schönbrunn Palace (Schloss Schönbrunn) complex. Brilliant "Maria Theresa yellow"—she, in fact, caused Schönbrunn to be built—is everywhere in evidence. An impression of imperial elegance, interrupted only by tourist traffic, flows unbroken throughout the grounds. This is one of Austria's primary tourist sites, although sadly, few stay long enough to discover the real Schönbrunn (including the little maiden with the water jar, after whom the complex is named). While the assorted outbuildings might seem eclectic, they served as centers of entertainment when the court moved to Schönbrunn in the summer, accounting for the zoo, the priceless theater, the fake Roman ruins, the greenhouses, and the walkways. In Schönbrunn you step back 300 years into the heart of a powerful and growing empire and follow it through to defeat and demise in 1917.

a good walk

The usual start for exploring the Schönbrunn complex is the main palace. There's nothing wrong with that approach, but as a variation, consider first climbing to the **Gloriette** 88 ⌐ on the hill overlooking the site, for a bird's-eye view to put the rest in perspective (take the stairs to the Gloriette roof for the ultimate experience). While at the Gloriette, take a few steps west to discover the **Tiroler House** 89 and follow the zigzag path downhill to the palace; note the picture-book views of the main building through the woods. Try to take the full tour of **Schönbrunn Palace** 90 rather than the shorter, truncated version. Check whether the ground-floor back rooms (*Berglzimmer*) are open to viewing. After the palace guided tour, take your own walk around the grounds. The Schöner Brunnen, the namesake fountain, is hidden in the woods to the southeast; continue along to discover the convincing (but fake) Roman ruins. At the other side of the complex to the west are the excellent **Tiergarten** 91 (zoo), and the **Palmenhaus** 92 (tropical greenhouse). Closer to the main entrance, both the **Wagenburg** 93 (carriage museum) and Schlosstheater (palace theater) are frequently overlooked treasures. Before heading back to the city center, visit the **Hofpavillon** 94, the private subway station built for Emperor Franz Josef, located to the west across Schönbrunner Schlossstrasse.

TIMING   If you're really pressed for time, the shorter guided tour will give you a fleeting impression of the palace itself, but try to allot at least half a day to take the full tour and include the extra rooms and grounds as well. The 20-minute hike up to the Gloriette is a bit strenuous but worthwhile, and there's now a café as reward at the top. The zoo is worth as much time as you can spare, and figure on at least a half hour to an hour each for the other museums. Tour buses begin to unload for the main building about mid-morning; start early or utilize the noon lull to avoid the worst crowds. The other museums and buildings in the complex are far less crowded.

HOW TO   The easiest, most direct way to Schönbrunn is the U4 subway. Get off
GET THERE at the Schönbrunn stop, or the Hietzing stop, if you plan to walk through the park and gardens first.

What to See

88   **Gloriette.** At the crest of the hill, topping off the Schönbrunn Schloss-
FodorsChoice park, sits a Baroque masterstroke: Johann Ferdinand von Hohenberg's
★   incomparable Gloriette, now restored to its original splendor. Perfectly scaled, the Gloriette—a palatial pavilion that once offered royal guests a place to rest and relax on their tours of the palace grounds and that now houses an equally welcome café—holds the whole vast garden composition together and at the same time crowns the ensemble with a brilliant architectural tiara. This was a favorite spot of Maria Theresa's, though in later years she grew so obese it took six men to carry her in her palanquin to the summit. Today, it has been completely restored and its white, whipped-cream elegance enchants as it did in the 18th century. ⊠ *13th District* ⊕ *www.gartenhotel.com* Ⓤ *U4Schönbrunn.*

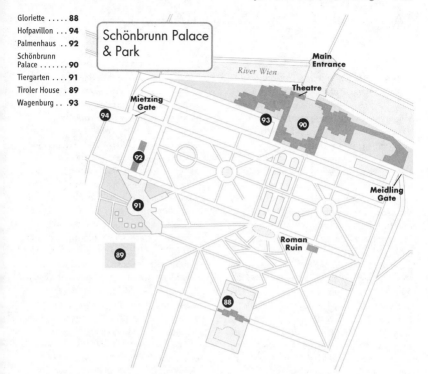

Schönbrunn Palace & Park

94 **Hofpavillon.** The most unusual interior of the Schöbrunn Palace complex, the restored imperial subway station known as the Hofpavillon is just outside the palace grounds (at the northwest corner, a few yards east of the Hietzing subway station). Designed by Otto Wagner in conjunction with Joseph Olbrich and Leopold Bauer, the Hofpavillon was built in 1899 for the exclusive use of Emperor Franz Josef and his entourage. Exclusive it was: the emperor used the station only once. The exterior, with its proud architectural crown, is Wagner at his best, and the lustrous interior is one of the finest examples of Jugendstil decoration in the city. ⊠ *Schönbrunner Schloss-Strasse, next to Hietzing subway station, 13th District/Hietzing* ☎ *01/505–8747–84013* ⊒ *€2* ⊙ *Sun. 11–12:30* Ⓤ *U4 Hietzing.*

92 **Palmenhaus.** On the grounds to the west of Schönbrunn Palace is a huge greenhouse filled with exotic trees and plants. ⊠ *Nearest entrance Hietzing, 13th District/Hietzing* ☎ *01/877–5087* ⊒ *€3.50* ⊙ *May–Sept., daily 9:30–6; Oct.–Apr., daily 9:30–5.*

★ **90** **Schönbrunn Palace.** Designed by Johann Bernhard Fischer von Erlach in 1696, Schönbrunn Palace, the huge Habsburg summer residence, lies well within the city limits, just a few subway stops west of Karlsplatz on line U4. The vast and elegantly planted gardens are open daily from dawn

TALES OF THE VIENNA WOODS

THOSE LUCKY VIENNESE. *When these urbane folk need to chill-out they can enjoy one of Europe's most urbane stretches of woodland, the* Wienerwald. *Immortalized in Johann Strauss's smaltzy waltz and muse to Schubert's greatest Lieder songs and Beethoven's Pastoral Symphony, the Vienna Woods stretches 50 miles south of the city. Droves of stressed-out residents strap their bicycles to the roof racks of their Mercedeses on weekends, so, for true peace, travel on a weekday and use the great tram and train system to make the short hop from Vienna. Explore the four relentlessly picturesque Wienerwald towns below, then tramp out into the woods, which are crisscrossed by country roads and hiking/biking paths (numbered and color-coded—tourist offices have guidebooks with all the details). Just over Vienna's city line lies* **Perchtoldsdorf,** *a charming market town with many wine taverns, a 13th-century Gothic parish church and a compact town square lined with Renaissance houses. Without a car, you can reach Perchtoldsdorf by taking the S-Bahn, or train, from Vienna's Westbahnhof, to Liesing, and then a short cab ride to the town. Ten miles to the southeast is* **Mödling,** *a beautiful Biedermeier-era village where Beethoven probably put the finishing touches to his "Ode to Joy." Tour its delightful Altstadt, the domineering St. Othmar Gothic Pfarrkirche, the Renaissance-style town hall, and the Art Nouveau–tinged streets. If you want your Vienna Woods garnished with statues and three castles right out of Grimm's fairy tales, head a couple of miles outside town to* **Schloss Laxenburg.** *Overnight in Mödling at the historic Hotel Höldrichsmühle; legend holds that the linden tree and the well found here inspired Schubert to compose one of his better-known pieces.*

Follow the scenic Weinstrasse (an unnumbered road to the west of the rail line) through lush vineyard country five miles south to the village of **Gumpoldskirchen,** *whose white wines enjoy a fame that is widespread. At one stage, there was more Gumpoldskirchner on the world markets than the village could ever have produced—a situation reminiscent of the medieval glut of fragments of the True Cross. Vintners' houses line the main street, many of them with the typical large wooden gates that lead to vine-covered courtyards where the Heuriger (wine of the latest vintage) is served up—the one with the most scenic vista of Vienna is Veigl Hütte (Beethoven-Wanderweg 40). Seven miles south, the Weinstrasse brings you to the serenely elegant spa town of* **Baden.** *Beethoven wrote large sections of his Ninth Symphony and Missa Solemnis when he lived at Rathausgasse 10, now the small Beethoven Haus museum (just one of several addresses Beethoven called his own hereabouts—the great man was always on the run from his creditors); both Johann Strausses—father and son—composed and directed many of their waltzes and operettas here, all still performed in Baden's regal Kurpark concert arena. You can reach Baden directly from Vienna by bus or, far more fun, by interurban streetcar, in about 50 minutes—the bus departs from the Ring directly opposite the Opera; the blue streetcar departs from the Ring across from the Bristol Hotel. By car from Vienna, travel south on Route A2, turning west at the junction of Route 305. It is possible to go on via bus to haunted* **Mayerling,** *where Crown Prince Rudolf and his amour, Baroness Maria Vetsera, died by their own hands (or did they?) on January 29, 1889. However, a convent now replaces the hunting lodge, so there is little left there but ghosts.*

until dusk, and multilingual guided tours of the palace interior are offered daily. A visit inside the palace is not included in most general city sightseeing tours, which offer either a mercilessly tempting drive past or else an impossibly short half hour or so to explore. The four-hour commercial sightseeing-bus tours of Schönbrunn offered by tour operators cost several times what you'd pay if you tackled the easy excursion yourself; their advantage is that they get you there and back with less effort. Go on your own if you want time to wander through the magnificent grounds.

The most impressive approach to the palace and its gardens is through the front gate, set on Schönbrunner Schloss-Strasse halfway between the Schönbrunn and Hietzing subway stations. The vast main courtyard is ruled by a formal design of impeccable order and rigorous symmetry: wing nods at wing, facade mirrors facade, and every part stylistically complements every other. The courtyard, however, turns out to be a mere appetizer; the feast lies beyond. The breathtaking view that unfolds on the other side of the palace is one of the finest set pieces in all Europe and one of the supreme achievements of Baroque planning. Formal *allées* (garden promenades) shoot off diagonally, the one on the right toward the zoo, the one on the left toward a rock-mounted obelisk and a fine false Roman ruin. But these, and the woods beyond, are merely a frame for the astonishing composition in the center: the sculpted fountain; the carefully planted screen of trees behind; the sudden, almost vertical rise of the grass-covered hill beyond, with the **Gloriette** a fitting crown.

Within the palace, the magisterial state salons are quite up to the splendor of the gardens, but note the contrast between these chambers and the far more modest rooms in which the rulers—particularly Franz Josef—lived and spent most of their time. Of the 1,400 rooms, 40 are open to the public on the regular tour, of which two are of special note. The first is the Hall of Mirrors, where the six-year-old Mozart performed for Empress Maria Theresa in 1762. Afterward, according to Leopold Mozart, the composer's father, "Wolferl leapt onto Her Majesty's lap, threw his arms around her neck, and planted kisses on her face." He also met the Empress's six-year-old daughter, Archduchess Marie Antoinette, the same day. Nothing of great moment must have occurred as the only note historians make is that while the little archduchess was showing her guest around the royal apartments, Mozart slipped on the gleaming floors and "Toni" hurried to help him up. The second room of special note is the Grand Gallery—one of the largest and most glittering Rococo halls in Europe—where the Congress of Vienna (1815) danced at night after carving up Napoléon's collapsed empire during the day. Ask about viewing the ground-floor living quarters (*Berglzimmer*), where the walls are fascinatingly painted with palm trees, exotic animals, and tropical views. As you go through the palace, glance occasionally out the windows; you'll be rewarded by a better impression of the beautiful patterns of the formal gardens, punctuated by hedgerows and fountains. These window vistas were enjoyed by rulers from Maria Theresa and Napoléon to Franz Josef. You'll find that many of the palace salons have the sort of pro forma splendor—the dull and official kind that drove Empress Elisabeth, the wife of Franz Josef, to flee the palace as often as possible—but a few of them—notably, the Walnut Study and the Vieux-Lacque Salon—are regally beautiful. ⊠ *Schönbrunner Schloss-Strasse, 13th District/Hietzing* ☎ *01/81113–239* ⊕ *www.schoenbrunn. at* 🖳 *Guided grand tour of palace interior (40 rooms) €13, self-guided tour €10.50* ☉ *Apr.–June and Sept. and Oct., daily 8:30–5; July and Aug. daily 8:30–6; Nov.–Mar., daily 8:30–4:30* Ⓤ *U4/Schönbrunn.*

Schönbrunn Schlosspark (Palace Park). The palace grounds entice with a bevy of splendid divertissements, including a grand zoo (the Tiergarten) and a carriage museum (the Wagenburg). Climb to the Gloriette for a panoramic view out over the city as well as of the palace complex. If you're exploring on your own, seek out the intriguing Roman ruin, now used as a backdrop for outdoor summer opera. The marble *schöner Brunnen* ("beautiful fountain"), with the young girl pouring water from an urn, is nearby. The fountain gave its name to the palace complex. ⊠ *Schönbrunner Schlosspark, 13th District/Hietzing* ⊕ *www. schoenbrunn.at* ☉ *Apr.–Oct., daily 6 AM–dusk; Nov.–Mar., daily 6:30 AM–dusk* Ⓤ *U4/Schönbrunn.*

Ⓒ ❾❶ **Tiergarten.** Claimed to be the world's oldest, the Tiergarten zoo has retained its original Baroque decor and today has acquired world-class recognition under director Helmut Pechlaner. Settings have been created for both animals and public; in one case, the public looks out into a natural display area from one of the Baroque former animal houses. The zoo is constantly adding new attractions and undergoing renovations, so there's plenty to see. ⊠ *Schönbrunner Schlosspark, 13th District/ Hietzing* ☎ *01/877-9294-0* ⊕ *www.zoovienna.at* 🖳 *€12; combination ticket with Palmenhaus €16* ☉ *Nov.–Jan., daily 9–4:30; Feb., daily 9–5; Mar. and Oct., daily 9–5:30; Apr.–Sept., daily 9–6:30* Ⓤ *U4/ Schönbrunn.*

❽❾ **Tiroler House.** This charming "Tyrolian-style" building to the west of the Gloriette was a favorite retreat of Empress Elisabeth; it now includes a small restaurant (open according to season and weather). ⊠ *Schönbrunner Schlosspark, 13th District/Hietzing* Ⓤ *U4/Schönbrunn.*

Ⓒ ❾❸ **Wagenburg** (Carriage Museum). Most of the carriages are still roadworthy and, indeed, Schönbrunn dusted off the gilt-and-black royal funeral carriage that you see here for the burial ceremony of Empress Zita in 1989. ⊠ *Schönbrunner Schlosspark, 13th District/Hietzing* ☎ *01/877-3244* ⊕ *www.schoenbrunn.at* 🖳 *€4.50* ☉ *Apr.–Oct., daily 9–6; Nov.–Mar., daily 10–4* Ⓤ *U4 Schönbrunn.*

VIENNA:
WHERE TO EAT

DINE LIKE A STAATSOPER DIVA
in the baronial salons of Korso ⇨*p.94*

TAP YOUR FEET TO A ZITHER BEAT
at the centuries-old Griechenbeisl ⇨*p.80*

SOAK UP AMBIENCE-*MIT-SCHLAG*
at the kaffeehaus of Café Central ⇨*p.113*

PREEN UNDER THE SOARING TREES
of the spectacular Palmenhaus ⇨*p.85*

CELEBRATE A STAR CHEF'S TAKE
on Styrian beef at Steirereck ⇨*p.90*

DINE ON THE KINGLY TERRACE
OF THE LICHTENSTEIN MUSEUM
at Ruben's Palais ⇨*p.105*

SAVOR SIPS OF "NEW" WINE
at the heurigen taverns of Grinzing ⇨*p.108*

ENJOY THE SWEETEST TORTE OF ALL
at the beloved Café Sacher ⇨*p.118*

By Diane
Naar-Elphee

TO APPRECIATE HOW FAR the restaurant scene in Vienna has come in recent years, it helps to recall past history. Up until five years ago, Austria was still dining in the 19th century. Most dinners were a *mittel-europisch* sloshfest of *Schweinsbraten, Knoedel,* and *Kraut* (pork, cabbage, and dumplings). Bouillon soups were lacking in everything but the soup-cube taste. Starchy sauces seemed to come straight from *Hunger*-y. And strudel desserts proved as heavy as a main course. Clearly, Austrian cuisine dated back to the *wurst* traditions of the imperial past. No one denies that such courtly delights as *Tafelspitz*—the blush-pink boiled beef famed as Emperor Franz Josef's favorite dish—are delicious, but most traditional carb-loaded, nap-inducing meals left you stuck to your seat like a suction pad. If you consumed a plate-filling Schnitzel and were able to eat anything after it, you were looked upon as a phenomenon—or an Austrian. A lighter, more nouvelle take on cuisine had difficulty making incursions because many meals were centered around *Rehrücken* (venison), served up in wine-cellar recipes of considerable—nay, medieval—antiquity.

Today Austrian cuisine is far from Middle-Aged and is now hip-hopping to a brand new beat. No longer tucked away in anonymous kitchens, top chefs now create signature dishes that rocket them to fame; they earn fan clubs, host television shows, write magazine articles, and tempt you with cookery club brochures. The Austrian chef has become a star, *even* in the U.S. Jaded New Yorkers can't seem to get enough at David Bouley's *Schutzkrapfen* (Austrian cheese ravioli) at his luxurious Danube restaurant, while the rich and famous of Hollywood continue to revel in the Spago creations of Wolfgang Puck. Back in Vienna, chefs want to delight an audience hungry for *Neu Wiener Küche* (New Vienna Cuisine). Schmaltzy schnitzels have been replaced by Styrian beef, while soggy *Nockerl* (small dumplings) are traded in for seasonal delights like Carinthian asparagus, Styrian wild garlic, or the common alpine-garden stinging nettle. Thanks to their nouvelle touch, the new chefs have taken the starch—in both senses—out of Vienna's dining scene and diners are clicking their heels for daring dishes. Tirolian eagle with three caviars, anyone?

Even those traditional standbys, the famous *Beisln,* Vienna's answer to Paris's bistros and London's gastro-pubs, now offer a great variety of tongue-tingling menus, thanks to chefs who incorporate accents from the far reaches of the former Habsburg Empire. Why shouldn't a restaurant within sight of the Hungarian-Czech borders use more real and figurative paprika in their menus, more Balkan spice on their dishes, and more Asian influences (after all, Austria long served as the bridge between east and west). You don't need to be a linguist to guess where the term Wiener Schnitzel comes from, but if you said Vienna you'd be wrong—it was created in Milan when that city was under Habsburg rule. In the course of centuries, Italians, Slavs, Turks, Magyars, Herzegovians, and Germans, as well as Jews ("Beisl" is Yiddish for "little house"), all flourished within the immediate homeland of the Habsburgs and influenced Vienna's cuisine.

But the primary inspiration behind the sweeping changes and new sophistication in food comes from whence it has always come—the time-

2

Dining Hours

Many restaurants are closed one or two days a week (sometimes weekends), and most serve meals only 11:30–2:30 PM and 7–11 PM. The custom of most Viennese restaurants is to remain closed on Sunday—although there has been talk about changing this custom, the church and powerful unions plan to stick to the old rules.

Dress

Although Vienna has become much more of a casual city in the last few years, and there are only a couple of restaurants still insisting on "jacket and tie" at dinner, the Viennese will still don more elegant attire when fitting. Be assured if you want to go out and dine "Vienna-style," you won't stand out.

Reservations

Most restaurants in Vienna prefer reservations, especially the centrally located ones, more so for dining out on Friday and weekends. During the week only the very popular restaurants will need prior bookings, both for lunch and dinner. You don't have to speak any German to reserve as spoken English will usually suffice.

Smoking

In Austria a general "no-smoking in public" law seems impossible (a huge number of Austrian politicians from all factions smoke). Happily, there are no-smoking sections in many restaurants, even some cafés.

Tipping

Although a service charge is automatically included on the menu prices, this has nothing to do with the tip the waiter will expect from you (providing the service warrants this). Generally speaking, the tip should be roughly 15% of the total sum on the bill, which is most happily received if you leave cash (if not, add the sum to the credit-card chit before you sign).

Prices

By and large, Vienna is still a "low-cost" sanctuary for dining out. While prices have gone up a bit since the introduction of the euro, there has been no major price increase like those of Paris and London. Those very "in" places will still prove costly—but not quite as costly as elsewhere. On average one can expect to pay about €14 for a simple dinner and €6–€12 for a simple lunch. Be aware that the basket of bread put on your table is not free. Most of the older-style Viennese restaurants charge €0.80–€1.50 for each roll that is eaten, but more and more establishments are beginning to charge a per-person cover charge—anywhere from €1.50 to €4—which includes all the bread you want, plus usually an herb spread and butter.

WHAT IT COSTS in euros				
$$$$	$$$	$$	$	¢
AT DINNER over €28	€23–€28	€17–€22	€10–€16	under €10

Prices are per person for a main course at dinner.

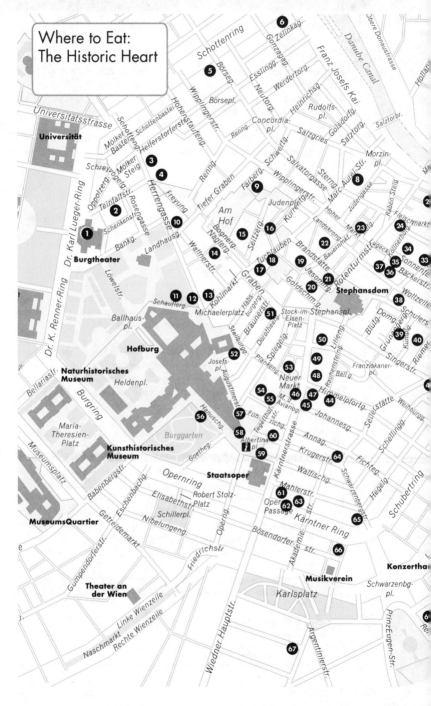

Where to Eat:
The Historic Heart

Restaurants ▼	
Alt Wien	**35**
Anna Sacher	**59**
Artner	**67**
Barbaro	**55**
Beim Czaak	**32**
Brezl Gwölb	**9**
Cantinetta Antinori	**20**
Cantino	**64**
Coburg	**43**
Culinarium Öuesterreich	**46**
DO & CO Albertina	**58**
DO & CO Stephansplatz	**21**
Dubrovnik	**71**
Fabios	**18**
Figlmüller	**37**
Gasthaus Puerstner	**40**
Gmoa Keller	**70**
Gösser Bierklinik	**16**
Griechenbeisl	**24**
Hansen	**5**
Imperial	**66**
Julius Meinl am Graben	**17**
Korso	**61**
La Ninfea	**11**
Lale	**25**
Lebenbauer	**2**
Livingstone	**6**
Lusthaus	**27**
Mörard im Ambassador	**45**
Ostaria Venexiana da Pablo	**69**
Palmenhaus	**56**
Plachutta	**41**
Reinthaler	**54**
Schweizerhaus	**28**
Steirereck	**72**
Strandcafé	**26**
Terrassenrestaurant Palais Schwarzenberg	**68**
Urania	**30**
Vestibül	**1**
Vincent	**26**
Walter Bauer	**33**
Weibels Wirthaus	**39**
Wild	**29**
Wrenkh	**22**
Zu den Drei Husaren	**50**
Zum Finsteren Stern	**8**
Zum Kuckuck	**44**

Munch-on-the-Run ▼	
Billa Corso	**63**
Karlsplatz Mall	**62**
Meinl am Graben	**17**
Radatz	**3**
Würstelstand	**23**
Zum schwarzen Kameel	**15**

Wine Taverns ▼	
Augustinerkeller	**57**
Esterházykeller	**14**
Melker Stiftskeller	**4**
Zwölf Apostel-Keller	**34**

Cafés ▼	
Café Bräunerhof	**52**
Café Central	**10**
Café Diglas	**38**
Café Englaender	**31**
Café Frauenhuber	**47**
Café Griensteidl	**12**
Café Hawelka	**51**
Café Korb	**19**
Café Mozart	**60**
Café Prueckel	**42**
Café Sacher	**59**
Café Schwarzenberg	**65**

Pastry Shops ▼	
Demel	**13**
Gerstner	**49**
Heiner	**36, 48**
Oberlaa	**53**

KEY

i Tourist Information

0 ———— 1/4 mi
0 ———— 1/4 km

honored standards of Wiener Küche. Take Tafelspitz (*beinfleisch*—or boiled beef). This is actually made from two different cuts of beef, both prepared in the same way: boiled in a beef bouillon (never in plain water) just to the point where the beef is tender but still retains a rosy pinkness indicative of not having surrendered all of its beef flavor to the soup. The trouble with this is that the tafelspitz should be eaten within a short time of having reached that exact point. And eaten surrounded by succulent fresh-grated horseradish mixed with apple juice (for those who like it mild) or wine vinegar (if you can take a bite on the tongue). But beef comes in a poor third on most menus: Pork and veal are far ahead of all other meats in Austrian taste, with schnitzel usually in the lead. This breaded veal cutlet is hand-pounded to a thin tenderness, covered with a batter of bread crumbs, fried to a puffy, succulent brownness, then usually served with potato salad lavished with the mayonnaise beloved of Austrian palates.

So while we acknowledge that the gastronomic revolution has taken place, Vienna's unhealthy but indisputably scrumptious culinary sins are still here to tempt you. Not easily translatable though definitely edible (and maybe you don't really want to know what *Blunzengeroestl, Hirn mit Ei* or an *Eitrige* are), the old Austrian reliables will still entice, put meat on your bones, and a smile on your face. And if you want to go whole hog, the city's classic Würstelstands are as popular as ever. Head to the big sausage stands on Seilergasse (off Stephansplatz) and Kupferschmiedgasse (off Kärntnerstrasse) to load up on frankfurters or bratwurst, served on a roll with mustard. As you sink into a heavenly *Käerkrainer* (a wurst studded with cheese bits), just remember that frankfurters were named after a Viennese butcher and are called Wieners almost everywhere else—*except* in Vienna.

RESTAURANTS BY NEIGHBORHOOD

1st District: The City Center

Encircled by the famous Ringstrasse avenues, Vienna's *Innere Stadt,* or 1st District, is studded with magnificent sights and some of the city's best restaurants.

AUSTRIAN ✕ **Anna Sacher.** Sacher is a name that almost has as many reverberations
$$$$ as Strauss's: The legendary Sachertorte cake, the family saga that began with Franz Sacher, Prince von Metternich's pastry chef, and the famed 19th-century hotel that was opened by Franz's son and his wife, the redoubtable Anna, Vienna's "hostess with the mostess." Near this entrance to the dining room, note the famous table cloth on show, embroidered with the names of the most illustrious guests by this very lady, then pay your respects to her oil portrait nearby—it reveals her formidable character and her weakness for cigars and bull dogs (shades of Churchill). The decor still exudes a monarchical magic: wainscotted oak walls, beige silk fabrics, gilt-framed oil paintings, and sparking chandeliers create a suitably aristo ambience. Adjacent is the Rote Bar, which may fulfill your fantasy of red baroque velvet and crystal luxury—a truly fitting spot

for a pre- or post-theater dinner (the state opera house is a skip and jump away). The menu showcases one of the city's best Tafelspitz (boiled beef), garnished with cream spinach and hash brown potatoes, with chive cream sauce and apple horse-radish adding extra flavor to this favorite dish of Emperor Franz Josef. Having quite a reputation to live up to, a jacket and tie is pro forma. If you're not into that stiff discipline of regimental restaurant rules, then choose the more informal Sacher Café for your slice of the world's most famous chocolate sponge cake, the Sachertorte with whipped cream (even if you're calorie counting, you'll still want that dollop of *Schlag Obers* to enhance the chocolate and apricot jam). But did you also know about the *Sacher Wuerstl*? These succulent sausages—served with a generous helping of creamy mustard, freshly grated horse radish, and aromatic brown bread—are delicious enough to convert even vegetarians. ⊠ *Philharmonikerstrasse 4, 1st District* ☎ *01/ 5145–6840* ⊕ *www.sacher.com* ✍ *Reservations essential* 🏛 *Jacket and tie* ▭ *AE, DC, MC, V* ⊙ *No lunch in Restaurant Anna Sacher* Ⓤ *U1, U2, or U4/Karlsplatz/Opera.*

★ **$$$$** ✕ **Mörwald im Ambassador.** The sleek renovation of the century-old Ambassador Hotel unveiled this restaurant, now acclaimed as one of Vienna's very best. Overlooking the famous Neuer Markt, one half of the restaurant is set in an elegant glassed-in "Wintergarten" (completely opened in fine weather) and flaunts a lovely view of the square's Donnerbrunnen, the Baroque-era fountain. On the other side of the restaurant is the Schau Kueche (open kitchen), set with dark wood floors, blue-green curtains, and inquisitive dinners who can watch the cooks at work behind glass. You can't blame them because chef Christian Domschitz, under the stewardship of Toni Moerwald (crowned Chef of the Year in 2004 and usually at his restaurant in Feuresbrunn in Lower Austria), is now one of the best "new Austrian" chefs. His signature dishes (literally—look for those dishes on the menu with his initials next to them) include his famous Szegediner lobster and cabbage dish or his breast of pigeon with beans and olives. Whatever your choice, don't miss the spring onion and wild garlic soup. After dinner you can repair to a comfortable lounge-bar area to enjoy drinks and cigars. There is no menu in English but you won't need one—the staff is that helpful and informative. ⊠ *Kärntnerstrasse 22, 1st District* ☎ *01/96161161* ✍ *Reservations essential* 🏛 *Jacket and tie* ▭ *AE, DC, MC, V* Ⓤ *U1, U2, or U4/Karlsplatz/Opera.*

$$$–$$$$ ✕ **Zu den Drei Husaren.** *Ou est les néiges d'antan?* Here, in the snowy linen table-topped time-warp of Vienna's oldest luxury restaurant. The interior has the elegance of a mansion, the warmth of refined hospitality, and the cuisine blends the many nostalgic flavors of the Habsburg Empire. The clientele is something of an old-fashioned imperial mix, too. The "Three Hussars" was created by Lord Paul Pálffy and two other soldierly noblemen who served together in World War I, decided to open a restaurant in 1933, and then made it the place for Viennese society. Restored to its prestigious perch after World War II under the ownership of Baron Egon von Fodermayer, Drei Husaren has changed little over the decades and, for many diners, that will be praise enough. The maître d' stands at attention at the end of a long, decorous corridor made for showy entrances, ready to lead you to your table through a series of sedate rooms accented in Biedermeier yellows and dark greens. Having been renovated one too many times, the salons are too shiny for some, but some of the old time-burnished charm remains in the Library room, adorned with sculpted busts and leather-bound volumes. Wiener Schnitzel and *Tafelspitz* (boiled beef) are cooked the old-fashioned way, but they are iconic in presentation. There are also some gorgeous game selections, such as the roast saddle of deer in puff pastry with red cabbage on quince-juniper sauce, Brussels sprouts, and glazed chestnuts and other exotica like the pork-stew Serbian style, "Baron Fodermayer." Even if dessert is not your thing, you shouldn't pass up such treats as *Husarenpfannkuchen,* the house crepes stuffed with walnuts, chocolate, strawberry-sauce, and whipped cream. And there is always that live piano music to relax the senses in an atmosphere of bygone days. ⊠ *Weihburggasse 4, 1st District* ☎ *01/512–1092–0* 🖷 *01/512–1092–18* ⊕ *www.drei-husaren.at/* ⌕ *Reservations essential* 🏛 *Jacket and tie* ▤ *AE, DC, MC, V* Ⓤ *U1 or U3/Stephansplatz.*

$$$–$$$$ ╳ **Zum schwarzen Kameel.** The Ladies Who Lunch love to shop and dine at "the Black Camel," which was already a foodie landmark back when Beethoven used to send his man-servant here to buy wine and ham. In timeless Viennese fashion, this provisioner split into both a *delikatessen* and a restaurant. You can use the former if you're in a hurry—the fabulously fresh sandwiches are served at the counter. But if you want to dine in elegance and intimacy then choose the glossy and gleaming glass-and-brass fin-de-siècle dining area just to the right of the entrance. Let the head waiter do his number—he's the one with the Emperor Franz Josef beard—who, in almost perfect English, will rattle off the specials of the day. But you'll never go wrong if you order the brown-bread sandwich of smoked ham with freshly grated horseradish. Depending on the time of the year, the menu changes accordingly, offering excellent beef dishes, fish, and venison, and cast an eye on the sensational wine selection. And don't overlook the best cup of Illy coffee in the city. ⊠ *Bognergasse 5, 1st District* ☎ *01/533–8125* ⌕ *Reservations essential* ▤ *AE, DC, MC, V* ⊘ *Closed Sun.* Ⓤ *U3/Herrengasse.*

★ $$–$$$ ╳ **Griechenbeisl.** Beethoven, Mozart, Schubert, and Gina Lollabrigida all dined here—so how can you resist? Neatly tucked away in an adorably quaint area of Alt Wien, this ancient inn goes back half a millenium. You can hear its age in the creaking floor boards when you walk through some of the small dark-wood-paneled rooms. Before you enter look out for the cannon ball stuck in the wall—a relic from the Turkish invasion. Then (perhaps after your meal?), take a glance into the cellar to see the mannequined figure of Augustine, the drunkard bagpipe player, who, according to legend, fell in a pit full of plague corpses, passed the night comfy and warm, and returned home the next day fit as a fiddle. An inn has been on this site since 1457, next to the glittering gold Greek Orthodox church, and its name refers to the many Levantine merchants who used to hang out here back when. Yes, it's historic and touristy yet the food, including all the classic hearty dishes like the goulash soup, Wiener Schnitzel, and *Apfelstrudel,* is as good as in many other beisln. Locals frequent the place just as much as tourists do to enjoy the

Styrian wrought-iron chandeliers, the zither music (showcased in the Zitherstüberl room), and the time-stained ambience, most impressively on show in the high-vaulted Karlsbader room, adorned with relics from the Bohemia spa of Carlsbad. The Mark Twain Room has the famous walls and ceiling covered with signatures of the famed who have chowed down here (get the waiter to point out the most famous). Since you are in one of the prettiest areas in the city and the building itself is a historical charmer, with its steep saddle roof and walls green with ivy, you may wish to choose a table outside in the summer months. Here, on this quaint town square, time happily stands still. ⊠ *Fleischmarkt 11, 1st District* ☎ *01/533–1941* ⊕ *www.griechenbeisl.at* ⊟ *AE, DC, MC, V* Ⓤ *U1 or U4/Schwedenplatz.*

★ $$–$$$ ✕ **Plachutta.** Wiener Schnitzel may honor the city in its name but is (surprise) an import from Habsburg Italy—the real McCoy is Tafelspitz. Beef has always been a Viennese favorite, and ox and calf have grazed on the green slopes of Styria and Lower Austria for centuries. Travelers used to rave—"In the pots of Vienna, boiled beef becomes juicy, tender, delicate, heavenly, unbeatable, deliciously beloved" (as one noted quote put it)—and it's still much the same today. Even better, there's no slimming diet that won't allow this meal. So it is little wonder that so many members of the Viennese upper-middle class come here to feast on Tafelspitz in all its "original" glory. In the city center, everyone heads to Plachutta's flagship on the Wollzeile. On either menu, there are veals and porks but you should come here for the classic dish. Did you know you can get more than 20 different cuts of beef, each one having its own particular taste, texture, and tenderness (get the waiter to show you a picture of the different parts and help you choose)? Elegant, but not swanky, the warm yellow-and-green decor has a homey feel, with dark-wood floors and 19th-century light fittings. Outside, a lovely garden area overlooks the partly reconstructed former bastion wall—a coveted spot for the many businesspeople who like to lunch here. Plachutta has a cozy Hietzing outpost located at Auhofstrasse 1. ⊠ *Wollzeile 38, 1st District* ☎ *01/512–1577* ⊕ *www.plachutta.at* ⌂ *Reservations essential* 🏛 *Jacket and tie* ⊟ *AE, DC, MC, V* Ⓤ *U3/Schottenring.*

$$–$$$ ✕ **Zum Kuckuck.** If you want to leave the modern world behind and escape to Old Vienna, head for this cocoon-cum-sanctorum. The warm wooden interior gets high marks for *Gemütlickeit* (coziness) thanks to its vaulted ceilings, tiled ceramic stoves, and walls covered with old prints from Emperor Franz Josef's time. Small and old-fashioned, yes, but foodwise the kitchen is quite innovative. Take a seat at a table set with pink linen, pewter candlestick, and fresh flowers to sip a glass of *Sekt* (sparkling wine) with blood-orange juice and peruse the surprisingly extensive menu. Freshwater catfish oven-cooked with dried tomatoes and artichoke? Wild boar sausages served up on elderberry cabbage? Roast Barbarie-duckbreast with honey-pepper sauce and almond fritters? If you still have room for dessert, dive into the sweet cottage-cheese dumplings with stewed plums. ⊠*Himmelpfortgasse 15, 1st District* ☎*01/512–8470* 🖷 *01/774–1855* ⊟ *AE, DC, MC, V* ☉ *Closed Sun.*

$$ ✕ **Culinarium Öesterreich.** Vienna's version of Fauchon, this is a sort of pan-Austrian foodie emporium and that's just what this place delivers

(literally—the take-out business is big here). Bringing together dishes, wines, and produce from every corner of the country—be it the Styrian rosé Schilcher or the Bregenzer Bergkaese, the friendly pumpkin-seed oil ("Styrian Viagra") or the hand-stirred apricot jams from the Wachau— chances are you'll find it here. Offering a menu with a definite Austrian stamp to it, the upstairs dining room is no-frills bright and airy, while downstairs an outside garden tempts many. Changing seasons mean changing dishes but there will always be the delicious cabbage meat and dumplings. In the vaulted brick cellar, the Winery has more than 400 different Austrian wines, which can be sampled with delicious whole-meal breads and an astonishingly delectable array of cheeses. Many enjoy stopping by for a snack while learning more about the incredible diversity of Austrian foods and farming. ⊠ *Neuer Markt 10, 1st District* ☎ *01/ 5138281* ⊕ *www.culinarium.at* ⊟ *AE, DC, MC, V* Ⓜ *U1 or U2 or U4/ Karlsplatz/Opera.*

$–$$ ✕ **Figlmüller.** *The* Wiener Schnitzel institution. Known for its gargantuan breaded veal and pork cutlets, which is so large it overflows the plate, Figlmüller is always packed. The cutlet is so large because it has been hammered into a two-fisted portion (you can hear the kitchen's pounding mallets from a block away). They wind up wafer-thin but delicious because the quality, as well as the size, is unrivaled (a quarter kilo of quality meat for each schnitzel). At first sight, it seems there is no room for anything else on the plate, but if you just dive into the middle of the cut your side order of salad, potato, or vegetable (everything is à la carte) will fit nicely. As the Viennese are fond of saying, "A Schnitzel should swim," so don't forget the lemon juice. Guests share the benches, long tables, and the experience. You can enter from either Baeckerstrasse or Wollzeile but try to get a table in the small, enclosed "greenhouse" in the entry passageway. ⊠ *Wollzeile 5, 1st District* ☎ *01/512–6177* ⊟ *AE, DC, MC, V* ⊘ *Closed 1st 2 wks Aug.* Ⓤ *U1 or U3/Stephansplatz.*

★ $–$$ ✕ **Zum Finsteren Stern.** Paging all Mozart maniacs! This is the old Gothic cellar of the one and only Palais Collalto, the site where six-year-old Amadeus made his first public appearance ever. Being the playful chappy he was, he was probably scampering along these ancient walls and right out into the street (where the cobblestones are the same) when he "played the palace" with his father. Not much has changed in the *Keller* since 1762—the vaulted ceiling, cool white walls, and dark wooden-planked floor are just as they have always been. Enter the green glass door—the one modern note—and you'll find only four tables on the ground floor, nine more in the cellar (so reserve if you are come by late). As for food and zeitgeist, the easy-going Mozart would have loved "To The Dark Star." It takes courage in Vienna to only offer a choice of two three-course menus but the success of Ella de Silva's establishment proves her right. For the indecisive or less ravenous, however, there is also a minimenu of six small shared courses. If available, go for the rabbit with sweet and sour lentils or the lamb steak with polenta tomato, zucchini cakes. and red-wine shallot sauce. Because the proprietors also run an excellent wine business expect both incredible variety and excellent quality on offer (the dark red Blaufraenkisch and the ruby Zweigelt are perfect for the dishes mentioned above). Opening hours are 5 PM until 1 AM and on a warm summer's evening there is a lovely seating area outside in the quietest of corners underneath an old blue-bell tree. ✉ *Schulhof 8, at Parisergasse, 1st District* ☎ *01/535–2100* 🖃 *MC, V* ⊙ *Closed Sun.* Ⓤ *U3/Herrengasse.*

$ ✕ **Gasthaus Puerstner.** Ever fancy sitting in an enormous wine barrel for dinner? Turned on its side and cut almost in half, this one seats four and, after a while, the bouquet of its former contents reaches the ole-factory organ and mingles oh-so-pleasantly with the aromas of Austrian cooking. That's what dining at Puerstner's is all about. This is one of those places proud to offer classic Austrian fare—no surprises or cre-ativity, please. Although a large establishment, separate seating areas lend a pleasant, intimate air. Even better, there's lots of dark wood and rustic Tirolean carpentry work; the alpine atmosphere is enhanced by the folklore vests the waiters wear. You can't go wrong with the carpac-cio of Styrian beef with Parmesan cheese or the veal goulash with potato gnocci. Lots of young people come here because it is such good value). Open daily until midnight, this is one of those places to remember as Sunday closures can still pose a problem in Vienna. The place does fill up for dinner—but the waiters will always try to find room for you. ✉ *Riemergasse 10, 1st District* ☎ *01/512–6357* ⊕ *www.puerstner. com/* 🖃 *MC, V* Ⓜ *U3/Schottenring.*

★ ¢–$ ✕ **Alt Wien.** Gulasch and a glass of beer, that's all you need for lunch, no? Ageing Vienna Pop-idols Danzer and Ambros sang that refrain in 1975 and for many Viennese, nearly 30 years later, that line is truer than ever. To date, there are at least 500 spots where, from about 11 AM on, you can get a small Gulasch, but how do you figure out where to go first? One of the best, most succulent goulashes is served up in defini-tive Viennese style here at Old Vienna (the small portion is €4.75, the large, €6.90). The gravy is, of course, the most important part of the dish—for dunking (don't worry about table manners) use the crispy sem-mel or, even better, a couple of the slices of dark bread. Is there any-thing in the world that tastes better? Oh, and don't forget the glass of beer—ask for a Seidl herbes Gösser, which harmonizes just perfectly with the dish. The cultured and chic clientele (writers, journalists, artists, poets) and the interior—replete with huge vaulted ceilings and walls covered with artsy posters—give the place a quintessentially Vienna feel. One small snag: the place can get a bit smoky in the evenings. ✉ *Bäcker-strasse 9, 1st District* ☎ *01/512–5222* 🖃 *No credit cards* Ⓤ *10–2 Uhr.*

¢–$ ✕ **Beim Czaak.** Pronounced "bime chalk," this homey spot with friendly service is a favorite with locals. It's long and narrow, with forest-green wainscoting, framed caricatures of a few well-known Viennese on the walls, and a small outside seating area. Choose a glass of excellent Aus-trian wine to go along with Waldviertler pork stuffed with bacon, onions, and mushrooms, spinach dumplings drizzled with Parmesan and browned butter, or a big Wiener Schnitzel. ✉ *Postgasse 15, corner of Fleischmarkt, 1st District* ☎ *01/513–7215* 🖃 *No credit cards* ⊙ *Closed Sun.* Ⓤ *U1 or U2 or U4/Karlsplatz/Oper.*

¢–$ ✕ **Brezl Gwölb.** A real medieval cellar, which looks like a stage set from *Phantom of the Opera*, tiny wooden nooks and crannies, and no fancy frills, make this a great choice for chilling out after all those extravagant luxury eateries. Indeed, this snuggery fills up fast at night. Tucked away just off Am Hof down a cobbled alley, this tavern is housed in a former 15th-century pretzel factory. The comfort level is great, the wine selection impressive, and the food scrumptious: *Tyroler G'röstl* (home-fried potatoes, ham, onions, and cheese served in a blackened skillet) or the *Kasnockerl* (spätzle in a pungent cheese sauce) are two best bets. Try to get a table downstairs in the most historic part and then try not to remember the story about Haydn's head being found in a jar in this very same cellar. ⊠ *Ledererhof 9, near Am Hof, 1st District* ☎ *01/533–8811* ▭ *AE, DC, MC, V* Ⓤ *U3/Herrengasse.*

¢–$ ✕ **Gösser Bierklinik.** In the very heart of Vienna, where the cobblestone streets remain a hazard to high-heel wearers, you come across this engaging Old World house, which dates back four centuries. Ambience freaks will love its dark-wood trim and gothic stained-glass windows. One of the top addresses for beer connoisseurs in Austria, this serves up brews, both draught and bottled, *dunkeles* (dark) and *helles* (light) from the Gösser brewery in Styria. Of the four dining areas (including a no-smoking room), many diners opt for the covered courtyard, where your beer will taste better no matter the weather. Besides the obligatory (but first-class) Wiener Schnitzel there are substantial, dark whole wheat sandwiches stuffed with ham, cheese, and different vegetables, served up either cold or toasted, along with *kas'nocken,* (little pasta dumplings topped with melted Tyrolean mountain cheese and crispy fried onions) and the bountiful *Bauernsalat* (farmer's salad) with sheep's cheese. Note that the English menu lists only about half of what's offered on the German one. Up the sandstone stairway you'll find a sister establishment, the Steindlzimmer restaurant, which has an evocative courtyard view. ⊠ *Steindlgasse 4, 1st District* ☎ *01/533–7598* ▭ *DC, MC, V* ☺ *Closed Sun.* Ⓤ *U3/Herrengasse.*

★ ¢–$ ✕ **Reinthaler.** Not many "tourists" meander down this lane with the idea of finding one of the best home-cooked Viennese lunches, but tucked away in this hidden corner, not far from the resting place of a hundred Hapsburgs (the Kaisergruft), is the vintage-1950s Reinthaler Gasthaus. Because this place is so popular with the locals it's packed at lunchtime so don't hesitate to sit down at one of the big communal tables. If you see there are a few diners eating alone at a table that would easily seat at least another four, ask if you could join them with a *"Ist hier frei bitte?"*. Chances are if you sit down at one of these brown wooden tables, set with clean, crisp yellow-and-white chequered cloths, you'll make some new friends. First, see what the others are tucking into, or consult the daily specials for pot-luck. Or, if you prefer to be on the safe side, choose the classic *Griess knockerl* (bouillon with small fluffy semolina dumplings) followed by *Krautrouladen* (juicy meat-filled cabbage rolls) or *Kraut Fleisch,* a tasty cabbage-meat dish. The lady of the house has been cooking up a storm for decades, so this is the place to try that great Viennese dessert, *Topfen Marillen Knoedel,* a sweet, tangy, tender and mouthwatering curd dumpling filled with ripe apricots, covered in golden brown butter-roasted breadcrumbs, and dusted (while still hot) with a snowy coating of icing sugar (the serving is big enough for two so ask for a second spoon and fork). The wines are local, fresh, and fruity.

Clearly, this spot is one of the best places in town to get real value for money. ⊠ *Gluckgasse 5, 1st District* ☎ *01/512–3366* ▭ *No credit cards* ⊗ *Closed weekends* Ⓤ *U1, U2, or U4/Karlsplatz/Oper.*

CONTEMPORARY ✕ **Julius Meinl am Graben.** You might think you're in the wrong place
$$$$ when you arrive at Meinl, one of Vienna's best restaurants. Who goes
Fodor'sChoice to a *delikatessen* when dining out? This is no ordinary eatery, of course:
★ Just a few doors down from the Hofburg Palace, Meinl opened as a caterer to the Habsburgs in 1862, and has remained Vienna's poshest grocery store ever since. But if you go straight down the aisle through the fruit and pastry sections, head upstairs past the cheese bar, and then turn the corner, you'll find a cozy salon, all deep orange banquettes and dark wood. Try to reserve one of the window tables—*"Ich moechte ein Fenster-tisch fuer zwei personen reservieren, bitte"*—as they have stunning views over the pedestrian crossroads of Graben/Kohlmarkt. Happily, window aerie or not, there is also drama to be had on your table, as the maestro in command is Joachim Gradwohl, one of the chefs Viennese foodies love to praise. Why not start with lobster terrine and its side of lobster bisque (adorably served in an espresso cup), go on to grilled *Rochenflügel* (skate) with gnocchi and wild mushrooms, or sizzling duck, carved tableside and served with roasted chestnuts and apple-studded *Rotkraut* (red cabbage). Other winners include Gradwohl's saffron soup with crispy fried zucchini blossoms, or his stuffed kohlrabi with asparagus tips and red beets, or the pan-fried Zander with baked figs in phyllo jackets. If you don't like the plushy environment, you can opt for a perch in the sleeker seating area and if you totally lose out on a table reservation, full meals are served at the bar. ⊠ *Graben 19, entrance after 7* PM *from outdoor elevator on Naglergasse, 1st District* ☎ *01/532–3334–99* ⌖ *Reservations essential* ▭ *AE, DC, MC, V* ⊗ *Closed Sun.* Ⓤ *U3/Herrengasse.*

$$–$$$ ✕ **Livingstone.** If you're suffering from jet-lag, insomnia, or are just plain hungry at some unearthly hour, help is at hand. Right up to 4 AM you can get some good grub in this warm tropical-colonial setting. The ambience takes you back to the Hemmingway 1940s, although the food is as casual and today as it comes. Try the excellent T-bone steak or a great Austrian beef hamburger in a homemade bun—served with crisp fries and a creditable slaw, this is a great protein booster. If you want something more exotic, opt for the serving of scallops in a lime-and-lemongrass sauce or enjoy a great wok dish of tender chicken in coconut milk. Because the cook's on expensive overtime, drinks tend to be a bit steep, price-wise. ⊠ *Zelinkagasse 4, 1st District* ☎ *01/5333–39312* ▭ *AE, DC, V* ⊗ *No lunch* Ⓜ *U1 or U4/Schwedenplatz.*

$–$$$ ✕ **Palmenhaus.** Vienna has rarely looked better than from a table at Pal-
Fodor'sChoice menhaus. A soaring glass-and-marble conservatory—created in 1904 by
★ Friedrich Ohlmann, whose *Jugendstil* designs pleased even the fussy Habsburgs—it once harbored the orchids grown for Emperor Franz Josef's dinner table. Renovated in 1998 to become a bar-restaurant, it is now one of the city's most popular scene-arenas, where Viennese love to preen and parade. It's hard to beat the view from the terrace that looks across the idyllic Burggarten to the grandiose facade of the Hofburg palace, and in good weather, you'll want to wait for a table outside. Fortunately, there

ON THE MENU

ONCE YOU TASTE the entire gamut of Austrian cooking—from soups to Sachertorte—you'll see nearly all of it is truly deli-schoss-ious. The trick with this cooking is to remember that even Emperor Franz Josef liked his meals to be Gutbürgerlich—good home cooking. Consequently, the specialties of even the most rarefied restaurants originated from meals cooked on farms for hard-working hands who needed both sustenance and bulk in their diets. Little wonder many dishes tend to be both hearty and rich (and why the Viennese prefer a schnapps afterward to help the digestion). The best place to find traditional Austrian food is at one of Vienna's noted Beisln—traditional "inns" that are somewhat akin to France's bistros and London's gastro-pubs. Although there is a nouvelle version—the newly chic "neo-Beisln" teeming with trendsetters—the traditional ones are where you'll find honest, no-frills cooking (and often at a price you can't even match cooking at home). You know you're in a Beisln if Beuschel (small pieces of offal—mainly heart and lung—served in a spicy sauce) is on the menu. But have no fear, you can get most of the main standards. Wiener Schnitzel is the most famous, but note that, although the original recipe is made from veal, many prefer the pork variation because it is juicier. Look for the words Kalb (veal) or Schwein (pork). The best of these Schnitzels have a light puff to the breading. A popular main course is Grammelknoedel (dumplings with bacon bits inside), usually accompanied by warm cabbage salad. Tafelspitz is the dish beloved by Franz Josef: thick slices of tender, succulent boiled beef, cooked in a beef bouillon, traditionally served with hash browns (Röstkartoffeln) and spinach and side dishes of apple horseradish and cream with chive sauce. Then there is Gulasch, or, to use the Hungarian,

Gulyas: Viennese really start dreaming of their spicy goulashes, served with dumplings (or just a roll), when the weather gets cold in autumn. As for chicken, everyone loves Backhuhn or Backhendl (young, medium-size chicken breaded and fried in deep fat until a golden brown); and Steirisches Brathuhn (roast chicken turned on a spit). Having no seacoast, Austria is naturally not fish country, yet you can enjoy pike and fogosch from the Danube or Hungarian lakes, krebs (crawfish)—usually served cold and dipped in mayonnaise—or great brook and rainbow trout, either "blue" or Müllerin (sautéed in butter to a crisp brown). In summer everyone looks for the special dishes made with Spargel (asparagus). And last, but certainly not least, desserts. Distant relatives of the French crepe, Palatschinken, are sweet pancakes filled with Marillenmarmelade (apricot jam) or chocolate sauce. Kaiserschmarren, meaning "Imperial fluff," is a dessert made of shredded pancakes, sprinkled with sultanas and sugar and served with stewed plums. Powiderltascherln are small potato pastry shells filled with hot stewed plums and covered in sweet butter-fried breadcrumbs. Buchterln are another typical dessert served in a Beisl, made from yeast pastry, shaped like a dumpling, and filled with jam and best served with vanilla sauce. Ask where to go for a good coffee and some of that mouth-watering Viennese pastry and you'll hear the word Konditorei—this means patisserie, or pastry shop, although some think it just means Nirvana.

is plenty of space inside and the garden atmosphere is just as impressive: Twenty-foot-high palm trees soar up to the glass-paned vault while one side of the hall abuts the historic Schmetterlinghaus, allowing you to study butterflies as you munch on pumpkin gnocchi. As the evening wears on, the bar crowd—artists, writers, and clubsters—takes center stage and things tend to become a bit boisterous (and smoky). But for lunch or dinner—or even just a quick coffee and bitter-chocolate mousse—don't miss this extraordinary setting. Chef Andreas Böhm is a great fan of fine wines, so check out the excellent selection of vintages found on the menu, including some rare Austrian top reds from 1997. A blackboard menu lists daily fish specials, like the grilled wild salmon with anchovies, capers and lentils, or scallops in whiskey with tomato salsa, while other treats range from vegetarian selections to the signature wild rabbit in cognac-plum sauce. Many diners don't make it past the dazzling desserts on view in the display case just inside the entrance, but wait for the dessert menu proffered at the end of the meal, for it has far more choice. ⊠ *Burggarten, entrance through Goethegasse gate after 8* PM, *1st District* ☎01/533–1033 ⌸ *Reservations essential* ▤ *DC, MC, V* ☉ *Closed Mon. and Tues. during Nov.–Mar.* Ⓤ *U1, U2, or U4/Karlsplatz/Oper.*

CONTINENTAL ✕ **Walter Bauer.** The track record here is impressive: two former chefs,
★ **$$$** Christian Domschitz and Herbert Malek, have gone off and established their own highly touted Viennese culinary kingdoms. They were probably sad to leave as Herr Bauer is one of the finest hosts in Vienna. He creates such an alluring sanctorum that his clientele, who may be inclined to stray, always return to the fold. And how could those city power brokers and high-ranking politicians do otherwise? Who wouldn't be seduced by this elegantly intimate room, all soft pastel-peach painted walls and white stuccoed ceilings? Or succumb to such creative delights as the breast of Quail bedded on puree of leek and morel or the Pigeon Saltimbocca? Today, Bauer's best man is Guenther Maier whose wooden spoon is being wielded wondrously, as you'll know with one bite of the octopus risotto. ⊠ *Sonnenfelsgasse 17, 1st District* ☎ *01/512–9871* ⌸ *Reservations essential* 🎩 *Jacket and tie* ▤ *AE, DC, MC, V* ☉ *Closed weekends* Ⓜ *U1 orU4/Schwedenplatz.*

ECLECTIC ✕ **DÖ & CO Stephansplatz.** For front-row seats for the medieval splendor
★ **$$–$$$** of St. Stephan's Cathedral, the best perch in town is a window seat at this restaurant, set across the square atop the semi-circular glass-fronted Haas House. You have to head up to the seventh floor in this Hans Hollein–designed landmark but the reward is a gorgeously relaxing setting—all dark-blue furniture, deep-blue carpets, and those large windows featuring That View. Some couldn't care less about dining "on" Gothic and take a table instead bordering the open kitchen. Don't laugh—the food is very spiffy here. Cooks hurry about preparing everything from stir-fry wok dishes to carpaccio parmigiana to tafelspitz. The Mediterranean-meets-Asian-meets-Austrian menu is masterminded by Attila Dogudan, one of Vienna's gourmet giants. The locals know a good thing and continue to cram this place and overtip the pretty waitresses in their short black miniskirts. ⊠ *Stephansplatz 12, 1st District* ☎ *01/535–3969* ⊕ *www.doco.com* ⌸ *Reservations essential* ▤ *V* Ⓜ *U1 or U3/Stephansplatz.*

ITALIAN ✕ **Cantinetta Antinori.** How can you resist a restaurant that posts this no-
$$$–$$$$ tice on occasion: *Tartuffo, Ancora Tartuffo, Solo Tartuffo*—"Truffles,
More Truffles, Only Truffles." Thanks to the Antinori wine barons, Vi-
enna now enjoys a truly authentic taste of Tuscany, and only steps from
the main entrance of St. Stephan's Cathedral (follow the tiny street di-
rectly across from the main entrance). The first Cantinetta opened its
doors 30 years ago in the Palazzo Antinori in Florence, continuing the
Florentine aristocracy's custom of offering visitors wine and other prod-
ucts from their country estates. The Antinori family maintains this cus-
tom here, having brought their wines and their cuisine to Vienna. For
years now this has been the one of the best places for antipasti literally
swimming in olive oil, to be eaten with the obligatory olive bread,
washed down with the expertly chilled Torralta Spumante–Prosecco di
Conegliano, and followed by *linguine al gamberoni* or the *calamari alla
livornese*. Highly popular and often overcrowded, this cantinetta is sit-
uated in a century-old building; one room has a lovely wintergarden decor.
⊠ *Jasomirgottstrasse 3–5, 1st District* ☎ *01/533–7722* ▤ *AE, DC, MC,
V* Ⓜ *U1 or U3/Stephansplatz.*

$$ ✕ **Barbaro.** With a cool and chic chill-out zone cellar for tired professionals,
a ground floor lounge for gourmands, and a roomy second-floor Italian
Bar (with DJ and live music), this Neuermarkt address offers something
for nearly everyone. Luigi Barbaro (who hails from Naples) has successfully
expanded his empire with this flagship that offers everything from a glass
of wine to a seven-course feast. Chef Harald Riedl cooks nouvelle Cucina
Italiana and serves up the best antipasti and pizzas in the area. The overall contemporary design was delivered by star architect Manfred Wehdorn.
If you want this sunnyside-up, grab a table in the comfortable outdoor
seating area. Barbaro is open every day from 8 AM until 4 AM. ⊠ *Neuer
Markt 8, 1st District* ☎ *01/955–2525* ⊕ *www.barbaro.at* ▤ *AE, DC,
MC, V* Ⓜ *U1 or U2 or U4/Karlsplatz/Oper.*

MEDITERRANEAN ✕ **Cantino.** After a visit to the Haus der Musik—Vienna's inspiring mu-
$$$$ seum devoted to music—just take its glass elevator to the roof, climb the
Fodor'sChoice few stairs to the attic, and discover a wonderful new restaurant with a
★ view overlooking the towers, roofs, and steeples of the city. The space is
intimate enough to let you think you're in a modern production of "La
Boheme." Mimi and Rodolfo would certainly cotton to the Mediterranean
aromas wafting out of the kitchen. Chef Richard Rainer's lemon risotto
is unbeatable, while his *Bonito del Norte* (White Spanish Tuna) on rocket
salad with lemon-olive oil dressing is a delight. Another winner is the
pasta shells stuffed with essence of chanterelle. You can wind your way
to Spain with the excellent selection of tapas. There's a different choice
every month. Wines are mainly home-grown Austrian, but there is also
a fine array of Italian vintages. When you've tired of the view out of the
enormous windows, study the historic prints and photos decorating the
slanting ceiling to see if you can recognize any of the celebrated conductors
and composers. If it is just a coffee and cake you are looking for, the comfortable bar set on a mezzanine level offers a great selection of pastries—
the museum courtyard also has a snack-bar but aim for the heights here.
⊠ *Seilerstätte 30, 1st District* ☎ *01/512–54–46* ▤ *AE, DC, MC, V*
🕙 *Closed Sun. evening* Ⓤ *U1 or U3/Stephansplatz.*

$$$-$$$$ ✕ **Fabios.** The easiest way Viennese visit sleek, suave, power-dining New York—short of paying $800 for a round-trip ticket, that is—is to book a table at this cool-hot spot. If they can, that is. Exceedingly popular and wait-listed weeks in advance, this modernist extravaganza has brought a touch of big-city glamour to Alt Wien, and foodies to fashionistas love it. With soaring mirrored walls, towering black-leather banquettes, a levitating pine ceiling, and acres of wood floor so polished women can check their make-up in it, Fabios has a decor that is high drama. As for color, just look at all the Escada-clad execs and cigar-toting TV moguls. Also colorful is the wonderfully sophisticated Mediterranean cuisine. Fabio Ciacobello's connections are tops (he previously worked at Antinori and Novelli), so you find the best ingredients on hand, with fish and fowl flown in from destinations around the world for innovative chef Christoph Brunnhuber. The winner's circle includes the octopus carpaccio with paprika, crispy pork with orange pesto on fennel, or duckling breast on kumquat-Cassis-sauce with potato-olive puree. If you drop in just for a drink at the bar, don't be surprised to see faces you saw in last month's edition of German *Vogue*. ⊠ *Tuchlauben 6, 1st District* ☎ *01/532-2222* ⊕ *www.fabios.at* ⌲ *Reservations essential* ⊟ *AE, DC, MC, V* ⊘ *Closed Sun.*

$$ ✕ **Hansen.** One foot past the entrance of the beautiful Lederleitner garden store and you're enjoying a walk through paradise in spring (or fall, winter, and summer, for that matter). This fashionable establishment, housed in the basement of the 19th-century Vienna Stock Exchange, is home to countless flowers and plants, and, as it turns out, an elegant restaurant. As you walk to your table passing all those scented shrubs, it is hard to say what's better: the sweet perfume of the tuberoses or the tantalizing whiff of the truffle. The restaurant is at one end of the flower shop, so diners can see shoppers browsing for everything from a single rose to a $2,000 lemon tree. Although this eatery is named after Theophil Hansen—the ornament-crazy architect of the Börse—its decor is sleek and modern. Tables set a bit too close together are compensated by the fantastic food. An Austrian-Mediterranean mix on the menu includes delicious spaghettini with oven-dried tomatoes in a black-olive cream sauce, risotto of asparagus, or grilled zander fillet with kolhrabi, eggplant, and honey. Lunch is the main event here, though you can also come for breakfast or a pretheater dinner. ⊠ *Wipplingerstrasse 34, 1st District* ☎ *01/ 532-0542* ⌲ *Reservations essential* ⊟ *AE, DC, MC, V* ⊘ *Closed Sun. and after 9 PM weekdays. No dinner Sat.* Ⓤ *U2/Schottenring.*

$-$$ ✕ **Weibels Wirtshaus.** Down old cobbled lanes between Singerstrasse and Schulerstrasse and just a stone's throw from St. Stephan's Cathedral, you'll find this to be one of the coziest places to have a lazy lunch or a delightful dinner. Try to reserve a table upstairs in the area called the Galerie, which is almost like a tiny attic with room for just a few tables and guests, and feel immediately at home in the peaceful pine-wood setting. Warm light from the low-hanging dark-glass lamp-shades just above the tables make this a great place for an intimate and romantic evening out. The friendly waiter helps you make your decisions and if he gets too busy, the witty and wiry "Wirt"—Mr. Weibel, the host— will be charmingly helpful. The menu runs from Viennese classics to

Mediterranean mixes and goes hand-in-hand with the very best of Austrian wines and Schnapps. The menu changes with the seasons but, when available, the asparagus ravioli is a true winner. Don't dare miss out on the honey ice cream served on a juicy bed of tangy sweet rhubarb-rice pudding. And now for the really good news: This place is open seven days a week, with hot dishes available until nearly midnight. ⊠ *Kumpfgasse 2, 1st District* ☎ *01/512–3986* ⌲ *Reservations essential* ⊟ *AE, MC, V* Ⓤ *U1 or U3/Stephansplatz.*

VEGETARIAN
¢–$$

✕ **Wrenkh.** Once Vienna's vegetarian pioneer extraordinaire, Christian Wrenkh now prefers a mixed cuisine in his house (over in the 15th District his ex-wife keeps up with the healthy kitchen). Happily, those delightful dishes like the wild-rice risotto with mushrooms, or the Greek fried rice with vegetables, sheep's cheese, and olives, or the tofu and tomato and basil-pesto tarts still carry his signature. Now, however, you can also be tempted by steak, fish, and fowl. The minimalist-style café section offers inexpensive lunch specials, while the more elegant adjacent dining room is perfect for a nice, relaxed lunch or dinner. ⊠ *Bauernmarkt 10, 1st District* ☎ *01/533–1526* ⊕ *www.wrenkh.at* ⊟ *AE, DC, MC, V* Ⓤ *U1 or U3/Stephansplatz.*

The Ringstrasse, Stadtpark & Beyond

The Ringstrasse is Vienna's 5th Avenue and Rue de la Paix, aglitter with great museums, glamorous hotels, and some top restaurants.

AUSTRIAN
$$$$

✕ **Imperial.** By the time of the 1873 Universal Exposition, the Prince of Württenberg's home had been transformed into the Hotel Imperial, one of Vienna's most magnificent and monarchial, so you'll need to pass inspection under the Winterhalter portraits of Franz Josef and his empress. Once you do, you can settle into a meal that oozes with ostentatious elegance. The main salon, glamorously paneled in woods (a little too shiny for some tastes), is vast so you may wish to opt for one of the cozy alcoves. Candlelight and piano music do add to the enjoyment of your lobster bisque (with a dash of Armagnac), the unusual baby lamb lettuce soup, the deliciously rich Styrian beef in Barolo with spinach gnocchi and spring vegetables, or the glazed chicken with green and white lasagna, asparagus tips, and balsamic shallots. If your wallet isn't chubby enough to dine here, enjoy a sandwich or a slice of the famed Imperial Torte in the adjacent Café Imperial or savor a cocktail in the hotel's stunningly opulent Marmorsaal hall—Ringstrasse splendor in all its glory. ⊠ *Kärntner Ring 16, 1st District* ☎ *01/5011–0356* ⊟ *AE, DC, MC, V* ☺ *Closed 3 wks in July or Aug. No lunch* Ⓤ *U1, U2, or U4/Karlsplatz/Oper.*

$$$$

★

✕ **Steirereck.** The best restaurant in Austria, Steirereck completed its 2004 move to a location worthy of its status as a culinary temple: the former Milkhauspavilion, a grand Jugendstil-vintage "drinking hall" overlooking the Wienfluss (Vienna River) promenade in the centrally located Stadtpark, the main city park on the Ringstrasse. You are first greeted by a huge, 20-foot-long rococo banqueting table, above which a video screen allows a preview peek into the famed kitchen. The dining room itself is *eine Fantasie,* with uniquely structured floors and ceilings styled to form the leaves from indigenous Styrian trees, oak, linden, birch, and sycamore; if you want the real thing, opt for a table on the two terraces so you can enjoy the lushest of the Stadtpark's green landscapes. The main rooms are suitably impressive stages for longtime chef Helmut Öster-reicher, who has been voted Austria's chef of the year twice. His out-standing and trailblazing fusion of different flavors never fails to amaze. Warm artichoke cocktail will be accompanied by caviar and artichoke cream, while crayfish is garnéed with basil bread and sweet organic cherry tomatoes. Styrian venison soars with sauteed *Eierschwammerl* (chanterelle) mushrooms. Other winners include delicate smoked catfish, turbot in an avocado crust, or char with mashed potatoes on a bed of white gar-lic sauce. Extra touches include a bread trolley overflowing with freshly baked breads and, at the end of the meal, an outstanding selection of cheeses from Steirereck's own cheese cellar. Steirereck offers the best spe-cial coffees in Austria, and you can be advised which one to choose to accompany your palette of homemade ice cream or brandy by a "cof-fee sommelier." If you don't want the gala Steirereck experience, opt for a bite in the first-floor restaurant—a "milk hall" now given a 21st-century spin. This eaterie showcases the delights of dairy—from cheeses to curds and beyond—in a striking decor: The floor, hand-painted, re-sembles a huge slab of Roquefort, the arty furniture is in shades of milky white, while the milk bar shimmers with a milky-glass wall. For a restaurant that is fully booked every night, the wait staff handles itself with a Benedictine calm, and service is friendly and even playful, adding the final touch to the spectacular meal. ⊠ *Im Stadtpark, 3rd District/ Landstrasse* ☎ *01/713–3168* ⊕ *www.steirereck.at* ⌂ *Reservations es-sential* ⊟ *AE, DC, MC, V* Ⓤ *U4/Stadtpark.*

$$–$$$ ✕ **Vestibül.** Even if you're not attending a play at the extravagantly sumptuous Burgtheater, it's fun to dine in this thoroughly theatrical set-ting, in what was once the carriage vestibule of the emperor's court the-ater. In the Marmorsaal room, Corinthian marble columns, coiffured arcades, and lots of candlelight add romance to the scene. Don't expect high drama: as an example of Ringstrasse architecture, the Burgtheater offers up splendor at its most staid. In fact, you might opt instead for a lighter meal in the adjoining bar salon, which has gigantic glassed-in doors overlooking the grand boulevard, sculpted 19th-century putti, mod-ernist lighting, and a sense of fun. The menu changes frequently, and may include such Viennese classics as veal goulash and Wiener Schnitzel as well as some classical *Beuschel* (a hash made of heart and lung, Vi-ennese-style), plus a full array of nouvelle novelties, including some great grilled fish. Service is impeccable. It's open late to accommodate the-atergoers. In warm weather you can also choose a table on the Ringstrasse garden terrace. ⊠ *Burgtheater/Dr.-Karl-Lueger-Ring 2* ☎ *01/532–4999* ⌂ *01/532–4999–10* ⊕ *www.vestibul.at* ⊟ *AE, DC, MC, V* ⊙ *Closed Sun. No lunch Sat.* Ⓤ *Tram: 1 or 2.*

CONTEMPORARY ✕ **Coburg.** Just off the Ringstrasse, the massive Neoclassical Palais
★ **$$$–$$$$** Coburg stands proud—or, rather, prouder than ever. Recently reno-vated to become the sleek and airy Hotel Coburg, this masterpiece of 19th-century architecture—which the Viennese deprecatingly nicknamed "Spargelburg" (Asparagus Castle, because of the row of slender tapered columns adorning the front facade)—has also become home to one of

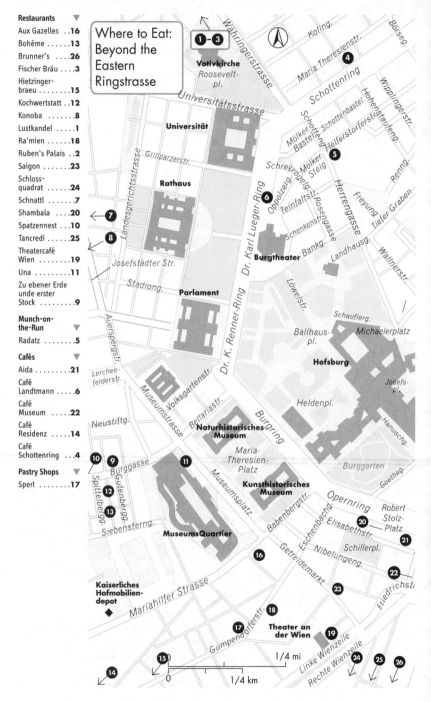

Where to Eat:
Beyond the
Eastern
Ringstrasse

Restaurants ▼
Aux Gazelles ..**16**
Bohème **13**
Brunner's **26**
Fischer Bräu ...**3**
Hietzinger-
braeu **15**
Kochwertstatt ..**12**
Konoba **8**
Lustkandel **1**
Ra'mien **18**
Ruben's Palais ..**2**
Saigon **23**
Schloss-
quadrat **24**
Schnattl **7**
Shambala **20**
Spatzennest ...**10**
Tancredi **25**
Theatercafé
Wien **19**
Una **11**
Zu ebener Erde
unde erster
Stock **9**

**Munch-on-
the-Run** ▼
Radatz **5**

Cafés ▼
Aida **21**
Café
Landtmann **6**
Café
Museum **22**
Café
Residenz **14**
Café
Schottenring ...**4**

Pastry Shops ▼
Sperl **17**

the most exceptional dining spots for gourmands and wine aficionados. Headed by the team of chef de cuisine Christian Petz and Karl Seiser (wines and service), the hotel offers three dining venues: the 70-seat, dinner-only Restaurant Coburg; the Gartenpavilion (Garden Pavilion), which is open for lunch; and the redwood and elm Basteibar (Bastion Bar), which is adjacent to the 16th-century fortifications that were retained by the palace. Petz was Austria's Chef of the Year 2002, trained at Meinl am Graben, and has earned three Gault-Millau crowns. At dinner, you can savor his obsession with pure flavor and carefully chosen ingredients. Roasted breast of duck with artichoke puree, salmon trout tartare on savoy cabbage with almonds, goose liver on quince cabbage, or pheasant with roast apple, goose liver, and poppyseed polenta are just some of the extravaganzas you can treat your palate to. And you'll have grape expectations when you see the wine list, for the Palais Coburg wine cellar consists of a 25,000-bottle wine collection. ⊠ *Coburgbastei 4, 1st District* ☎ *1/5181–8800* ⊕ *http://members.magnet.at/coburg.fv/en/html/gourmet_restaurant.html* ⚑ *Reservations essential* ▤ *AE, DC, MC, V* Ⓤ *U3/Stubentor.*

★ **$$–$$$$** ✕ **Shambala.** Named after a legendary Himalayan kingdom, Shambala has plenty of magic. Conceived by Michel Rostang, one of the high priests of the Parisian dining scene, this hypermodern restaurant has cool subtle colored lighting that changes hues from time to time, an electronic soundtrack to stimulate the imagination, and—needless to say—transcendentally trendy food. Rostang is aided by the young, creative Christian Brandstaetter, and together they give Vienna a sublime taste of "Cuisine Mondiale." The menu just doesn't hop from continent to continent but often combines three countries in one dish. Start with gingered shrimp, move on to West African lemon chicken–okra soup, then ease into the crayfish with poached quail eggs served with truffled salad. The decor is understated to let the food shine through, but there are enough eye-knocking details, including some of the weirdest green hologram lamps, which, from a certain angle, seem to contain a blue-bottle fly. Don't ask us why—just go and plug in. ⊠ *Le Meridien Vienna, Opernring 13, 1st District* ☎ *01/588900* ▤ *AE, DC, MC, V* Ⓤ *U1, U2, or U4/Karlsplatz/Oper.*

★ **$$** ✕ **DÖ & CO Albertina.** When you're ready to drop from taking in all the art treasures at the fabulous Albertina, then just drop into the museum's new Do & Co café. Not only will the five huge painted copies of some of Egon Schiele's most famous works prolong the art experience, you'll be dining on one of the liveliest menus in town and be allured by a Vienna Moderne room, all glass, red marble, high-backed, camel-colored leather seating, and windowsills with large vases filled with flowers. This is but the latest—and definitely the most luxe—of the Do & Co fleet, a chain of eateries that has gained an enormous following of faithful customers. With the menu being in English and the staff more than efficient, you'll relax while you wait for your order. Go for the Albertina BLT-Burger, a grand-size fist of the finest Styrian beef, complete with crispy bacon, tomatoes, and coleslaw (or a side of the classic potato goulash if you want something more local). If you fancy just a snack, sit at the bar and enjoy the Baguette Albertina, stuffed with fresh farmer's ham, cheese, tomatoes, egg and crème fraîche mustard, or the one with juicy smoked salmon, cream cheese, arugula, and sun-dried tomatoes. Last but not least, this place is open all day, every day, 10 AM to midnight (and is handy to the opera house). On summery days, you can also sit outside on the terrace overlooking the Burggarten. ⊠ *Albertinaplatz 1, 1st District* ☎ *01/532–9669* ⊕ *www.doco.com* ⌧ *Reservations essential* ▭ *V* Ⓤ *U1, U2, or U4/Karlsplatz/Oper.*

CONTINENTAL   ✕ **Korso.** Set in the Bristol Hotel, just across from the Staatsoper (don't
★ $$$–$$$$ be surprised if you see Domingo or a leading diva at the next table), the Korso bei Der Oper has long been regarded as the darling of the rich and famous. Chef Reinhard Gerer is known throughout Austria for his creative touch—and the salons for such gastronomic excellence are appropriately delicious, with gleaming wood-panel walls, beveled glass, tables set with fine linen, sparkling Riedel crystal, fresh flowers, and a massively baronial fireplace, complete with period columns. Fish is Gerer's specialty, and he prepares it in ways like no other chef in Vienna. Delicately fried *Rotbarsch* (rosefish) is paired with tiny, crispy fried parsley and the smoothest of pureed polenta, Salzkammergut lake trout is grilled and drizzled with a sensational shallot sauce, and *Saibling* (char) caviar is enhanced by organic olive oil. The taste sensations continue with such delights as *Felchen,* a delicate white fish served with glass noodles, while fresh lobster comes with white beans, arugula, and polenta. Meat and game dishes are also available, and be sure to save room for the fresh out-of-the-oven rhubarb strudel. ⊠ *Mahlerstrasse 2, 1st District* ☎ *01/515–16–546* 📠 *01/ 515–16–550* ⌧ *Reservations essential* ⌂ *Jacket and tie* ▭ *AE, DC, MC, V* ⊙ *Closed 3 wks in Aug. No lunch Sat.* Ⓤ *U4/Karlsplatz.*

ITALIAN   ✕ **La Ninfea.** At lunchtime you might find much of Austria's government
$$$ adorning the tan-color upholstered seats here. Just down the road from the office of the chancellor of Vienna, this Italian hotspot is *buonissimo bellissimo*. Many a politico breaks bread here and it wouldn't be too much of a surprise to find the prime minister and his team feasting on some of Luigi Barbaro's delicious *Zuppa di pesce* (heavenly fish soup, with leek, zucchini and fennel) or the *Quadratini Astice* (pasta squares filled with lobster). The interior is exquisitely designed, with a blue glass-domed ceiling, dark oak floor, and natural white walls hung with eye-knocking modern art. ⊠ *Schauflergasse 6, 1st District* ☎ *01/329126* ▭ *AE, DC, MC* Ⓤ *U3/Herrengasse.*

Donaustadt

At the northern border of the 1st District, the neighborhood fronted by the Danube Canal is one of the most happening areas of Vienna, headlined by a strong nightlife scene and lots of restaurants. The gateway to the area is the bustling square of Schwedenplatz. To escape the crowds, head over the Danube Canal to find a pleasant area threaded by other rivers, such as the Alte Donau.

AUSTRIAN   ✕ **Strandcafé.** When the going gets hot in the center of town, the over-
$–$$ heated get going (via the U1 subway) to the lake area known as the Alte Donau (or Old Danube). Since the construction of the Danube Canal—

and, in consequence, the diverting of the Danube waters in the 1870s—this lake has been cut off from the river's water supply and had become a highly popular recreation area for city dwellers. Sitting on the Strand-café's wooden pier directly over the water and watching swans glide beneath the weeping willows and paddle-boats paddle by is a great way to spend a relaxing afternoon. That, in itself, would be reason enough to come but there is an even stronger appeal: the spare ribs. These beautifully barbecued pork ribs come in huge meaty portions and are served with scrumptious roast potatoes. Have a glass of house wine or a cold beer to wash them down and enjoy this Edenic setting just a stone's skip from the bustling city. ⊠ *Florian-Berndl-Gasse 20, 22nd District/ Donaustadt* ☎ *01/203–6747* ⌂ *Reservations essential* ▤ *No credit cards* Ⓤ *U1/Alte Donau.*

CONTEMPORARY ★ $$–$$$
✕ **Urania.** The year 1910 saw the inauguration of the Urania under the auspices of Franz Josef. Nearly a hundred years later this Jugendstil building, which then served as an observatory, cinema, school, and puppet theater, has been beautifully restored and serves the same purposes with the additional boon of a gourmet temple. Wolfgang Reichl is the charming cosmopolitan chap who is responsible for making this one of Vienna's trendiest locations. The interior design, conceived entirely by him, matches his persona—cool, modern, and urban. His chef, young Norbert Fiedler, is ditto and doesn't like the use of the word fusion to describe his cooking. Best bets include the creamy cauliflower soup with Thai asparagus, the fillet of trout on chanterelle risotto, and tender duck served with ginger ravioli. Don't worry about the calories—all these dishes can be served as small portions, which the chic clientele here appreciates. You can sit inside to take in the crowd and some of the handsomest waiters in town (rumor has it they are mostly models). Or sit outside on the upper or lower terrace overlooking the Danube Canal: on the lower, note the lights of the Prater's ferris wheel in the distance, although on the upper, you can study the stars while you tuck into some nouvelle barbecue. Friendly opening times run from 9 AM until 2 AM, but the big hour on Sunday is brunch. ⊠ *Uraniastrasse 1, 1st District* ☎ *01/7133066* ⌂ *Reservations essential* ▤ *AE, DC, MC, V* Ⓤ *U1 or U4/Schwedenplatz.*

TURKISH $
✕ **Lale.** Vienna has a substantial Turkish population, and this modern, inviting restaurant in the heart of the Schwedenplatz area serves some of the best Turkish cuisine in the city. Specialties include *Huhnerspiess* (chunks of grilled chicken breast on a skewer) and *Iskender kebab* (slivers of tender lamb served with yogurt and tomato sauce). Don't miss the tasty selection of *meze* (appetizers) temptingly arrayed in the front counter. A perfect choice for a take-out lunch is the vegetarian sandwich—a mouthwatering combination of grilled eggplant, feta, spinach, and hummus in a soft, freshly baked bun. ⊠ *Franz Josef-Kai 29, 1st District* ☎ *01/535–2736* ▤ *No credit cards* Ⓤ *U1/Schwendenplatz.*

2nd District (Leopoldstadt)

The 2nd District of Leopoldstadt is landmarked by the famous Prater amusement park. Set across the Danube Canal, it is just a quick ride on the U1 subway line to the center city.

AUSTRIAN
$$–$$$

✕ **Lusthaus.** When the sun is shining and the romance of Old Vienna beckons, why not splurge on a Fiaker carriage and take a trip back to the 19th century? Head to the Prater park, where, along the grand and imperial Hauptallee, you'll find a pleasure pavilion designed for Emperor Josef II by Isidore Canevale. Often the center of imperial festivities in the past, it is now one of Vienna's most romantic restaurants (as such, telephone to make sure the place is open, since it often hosts weddings). As you alight in princely fashion from your horse-drawn cab you'll climb the steps and enter a Baroque world of yesteryear. Octagonal in shape, with a fanciful roof, and elegant garden windows, the Lusthaus sparkles with crystal chandeliers, white-stuccoed ceilings, fine white damask, silver cutlery, and candles. Recalling the 19th century (when the Habsburgs ruled Italy), the menu has one foot in Austria, the other in the Mediterranean. Wonderfully light is the truffle gnocchi on a bed of morel sauce and field salad. Chicken livers roasted in red wine and onion with a side of polenta is delicately different, while the pumpkin-zucchini risotto is a delight. You can also head here in the afternoon for a high tea, replete with whipped-cream cakes and a mouthwateringly sweet chestnut puree with sherry-soaked pear and whipped cream. Champagne, anyone? ✉ *Freudenau 254, on the Prater Hauptallee, 2nd District/Leopoldstadt* ☎ *01/728–9565* ⊕ *www.lusthaus-wien.at/* ⌂ *Reservations essential* ▭ *DC, MC, V* ☾ *Closed Wed.* Ⓤ *U3, 77/Lusthaus.*

$–$$

✕ **Schweizerhaus.** This is one of the best places to come when the going gets hot in the city. Or if you decide to go for a ride on the Prater's Big Wheel, choose this for a lunch spot underneath the ancient shade-giving spreading horse-chestnut trees. It's a typical, and very busy, beer-garden venue offering the best Beck's in town, and the very best pork knuckles, grilled to crispy perfection without and sweet juicy perfection within, with fresh grated horseradish and coleslaw salad. If you're still peckish later, then try the typical sweet poppy-seed noodles with a dusting of icing sugar. Relax and listen to the chatter of the Viennese, or watch those serving scurry from kitchen to client, laden with platters full of steamy cabbage, dumplings, and Cevapcici (spicy sausages). It has been said many times that here you'll find the strongest and the fastest waiters worldwide. After you've eaten you might want to enjoy a pleasant walk through the Prater fun-fair, seeing the attractions and getting rid of some of those calories climbing on the colorful Helter-Skelter. ✉ *Prater 116, 2nd District/Leopoldstadt* ☎ *01/728–0152* ▭ *No credit cards* ☾ *Closed Nov. 1–Mar. 14* Ⓤ *U1/Praterstern.*

ECLECTIC
★ $$$$

✕ **Vincent.** You almost need to coin a new adjective—"Vincentine"—to describe the allures of this places. Or the tastes: the "Lobster Kiss" with zucchini blossoms, the deer doused in madeira. Or the setting: just a stone's throw from the Augarten, one of Vienna's loveliest parks, this includes a winter-garden that resonates with positive vibes (thanks to a Feng Shui expert), as black furniture and cool black-marble floors tiles contrast beautifully with white walls, linens, and pine woodwork. And let's not forget one of the few Vienna air-conditioning systems that works. But then everything works about this place, thanks to proprietor Frank Gruber. His gifted chef, Gerold Kulterer, serves up highly acclaimed menus, from the light four-course "So good for me" dinner to a 10-course feast. Doors open at 5 PM when the chill-out crowd arrives for the so-called "Kleine Karte" snacks and sparkling wine by the glass. With so much on tap here, expect expert advice on choosing both menu and wines. The younger-generation gourmet will home in on the four-course "surprise" menu, priced at only €19.50, which, considering the top quality, is quite a deal. ⊠ *Grosse Pfarrgasse 7 2nd District/Leopoldstadt* ☎ *01/214–1516* ⊕ *www.restvincent.at* ⌕ *Reservations essential* ⊟ *AE, DC, MC, V* ⊙ *Closed Sun.* Ⓜ *Tram: 21 to Grosse Pfarrgasse.*

3rd District (Landstrasse)

Framed by the sylvan Stadpark on one side and the grandeur of the Belvedere Palace on the other, this remains one of Vienna's most "imperial" districts and, fittingly, is home to many of the city's embassies and consulates.

AUSTRIAN

★ $$$–$$$$

✕ **Terrassenrestaurant Palais Schwarzenberg.** It's not every day that you know "mein host" is Prince Karl Johannes von Schwarzenberg but when you sit down here, you're dining in his home—the last privately owned palais in Vienna and now one of Austria's best hotels. Well, you're not exactly dining *in* his home. This luxe restaurant is, in fact, set on the hotel's lovely glassed-in terrace. Your "appetizer" proves to be a pretty and panoramic view of the green lawns, rose hedges, and Baroque marble statues of the palace's private park. As for gilt-and-chandelier Habsburgian splendor, you'd have to attend one of the many functions and parties that are held in the palace's rented-out 18th-century state rooms. The terrace restaurant decor relies on a sense of cool chic year-round, with superb table linens, pretty wicker chairs, and waiters who bear themselves like courtly retainers. The cooking is Austrian with a Mediterranean flair and the results are usually as delicious as they are stylish. Who can resist starters like fried goose liver glazed in honey and served with papaya risotto, or vanilla-perfumed spit-roasted prawns on lime noodles, followed by such entrées as fillet of beef with a mango-pecan nut crust, or desserts like orange-grapefruit aspic with iced-tea sauce and Campari sherbert? If you simply want to enjoy a luxe Viennese tea with all the trimmings, book a spot in the palace's Kamminzimmer salon, a noble but fairly plain salon adjacent to the ruby-red Palais Bar, which is the perfect spot for that final glass of Mumm's. ⊠ *Schwarzenbergplatz 9, 3rd District/Landstrasse* ☎ *01/798–45–15–600* ⌕ *Reservations essential* ⊟ *AE, DC, MC, V* Ⓤ *U1, U2, or U4/Karlsplatz.*

★ ¢–$

✕ **Gmoa Keller.** One of the friendliest places in Vienna, this wonderful old vaulted spot—just across the street from the Konzert Haus (Vienna's second most revered concert hall, home to the Vienna Symphony)—offers some of the most *gutbürgerlich* (hearty) home cooking in town. Come here to enjoy dishes that hail from Carinthia, one of the best being the *Kasnudeln* (potatoes and spinach pasta filled with cheese and onion), served best with green leaf salad. Or you can opt for the fried feta cheese in bacon on lettuce or the *Blunzen-Groestl* (black pudding with cabbage salad and horseradish), two unusual but absolutely delicious options. Needless to say, a real favorite here is the *Tafelspitzsulz mit Kernoel und Zwiebeln* (cold cut of beef in aspic served with onions and lashings of dark green pumpkin seed oil)—like everyone else, you'll wind up using the *Semmel* (the white bread roll) to sop up that last drop of wonderful oil. Once you're got your second wind, dive into one of the pancake desserts. The classic is the one filled with apricot jam (with a squeeze of lemon juice to give it that touch of tartness), though to make decisions more difficult the lush chocolate- and nut-filled, whipped cream one is delectable, while the cranberry number is a true bit of scrumptiousness. ⊠ *Am Heumarkt 25, 3rd District/Landstrasse* ☎ *01/712–5310* 🖃 *AE, DC, MC, V* ⊘ *Closed Sun.* Ⓤ *U4/Stadtpark.*

¢–$ ✕ **Wild.** Touring the eye-crossing Friedensreich Hundertwasser Haus may leave you peckish and looking for something more sane than the zany architecture you've just seen. Well, a few minutes walk down to the end of Loewengasse you'll find the most down-to-earth Gasthaus you could wish for. It's a sensibly revitalized, great-value-for-the-money Beisl and now one of the most comfortable options in this most Viennese of districts. A former wine tavern, there is a touch of melancholy about the place, perhaps due to the lasting aura of all those emptied bottles of yore. The interior is suitably mellow, with soft yellow walls and a warming red counter. The menu changes regularly but almost always features the heavily protein-packed offal dishes the locals love. But the more sensitive of palates have plenty of other choices, including the juicy leg of lamb served with steamy red cabbage and dumplings, or the *Schinkenfleckerl* (the hyperdelicious pasta squares stuffed with ham and cabbage). If you choose the lamb, have a glass of Zweigelt, a delicious dark fruity red of the very best flavor. ⊠ *Radetzkyplatz 1, 3rd District/Landstrasse* ☎ *01/920–9477* 🖃 *V* ⊘ *Closed Mon.* Ⓤ *Tram: N and O/Radetzkyplatz.*

CROATIAN ✕ **Dubrovnik.** Opposite Vienna's central Stadtpark and just down the road
$–$$ from Austria's national mint, Dubrovnik is one of Vienna's oldest yet most highly regarded Croatian restaurants. Recently renovated without removing too much of the 40-year-old patina, it retains a pleasant and manorhouselike atmosphere, replete with spacious seating, vaulted ceilings, leather alcoves, and elegant wooden chair seating. In the kitchen, tradition gets a heaping spoonful of the modern. The regional stars are fish specialties—the best are grilled with lashings of garlic—but you can also order *Cevapcici* and *Sarma* (stuffed cabbage and sour cream), a nice letscho (spicy) schnitzel, and yummy pork fillet with onion stuffing and potato salad. ⊠ *Am Heumarkt 5, 3rd District/Landstrasse* ☎ *01/7137–10213* 🖃 *AE, DC, MC, V* Ⓤ *U4/Stadtpark.*

ITALIAN ✕ **Ostaria Venexiana da Pablo.** If you're planning a visit to the Belvedere
$$ Palace to see the great Klimt paintings on view in its Österreichische Galerie, this is an excellent choice. Set between the palace—former home of Prince Eugene of Savoy, whose regal roots were Italian—and the city's Italian Embassy (housed in the glamorous Palais Metternich), this casual Italian spot revels in charm and coziness. On offer: delicious San Danieli smoked ham (hanging from the rafters, no less), numerous antipasti dishes, and daily specials listed on the blackboard at the door. The best bet, if available, is the steamy truffle risotto or the juicy *Branzino* (sea bass) on a bed of lentils, eggplant, and sundried tomatoes. A good assorted Italian wine cellar brings forth some delicious light whites from the Friuli region, and why not start with some refreshing Prosecco with peach nectar as an aperitif? ⊠ *Rennwegasse 11, 3rd Dis-*

REFUEL AROUND TOWN

IF YOU DON'T HAVE TIME *for a leisurely lunch, or you'd rather save your money for a splurge at dinner, here's a sampling of the best places in the city center to grab a quick, inexpensive, and tasty bite to eat.*

In the lower level of the Ringstrasse Galerie shopping mall, the gourmet supermarket **Billa Corso** *(⊠ Kärntner Ring 9–13, 1st District ☎ 01/512–6625 ⊗ Closed Sun.) has a good salad bar, and will prepare the sandwich of your choice at the deli counter. (The Ringstrasse Galerie is in two similar buildings, so make sure you're in the one on the Kärntner Ring.)*

Next to the produce section on the ground floor of Vienna's premier gourmet grocery store, **Meinl am Graben** *(⊠ Graben 19, 1st District ☎ 01/532–3334 ⊗ Closed Sun.) is a smart, stand-up café where you can choose from a*

selection of soups, sandwiches, or antipasti (don't confuse it with the full-service restaurant upstairs). Near the Freyung, the epicurean deli **Radatz** *(⊠ Schottengasse 3a, 1st District ☎ 01/ 533–8163 ⊗ Closed Sun.) offers made-to-order sandwiches from a vast selection of mouthwatering meats and cheeses.*

Around the corner from Am Hof, **Zum Schwarzen Kameel** *(⊠ Bognergasse 5, 1st District ☎ 01/533–8967 ⊗ Closed Sun.) serves elegant little open-face sandwiches and baby quiches in their stand-up section.*

Directly beneath the Vienna State Opera House, discover the **"Karlsplatz" underground mall** *(⊠ Opern Passage, 1st District), where you'll find a huge choice of quick-food alternatives within the space of a hundred yards. Take the escalator at the corner of the Opera across from Hotel Bristol and descend to the subway station "Karlsplatz" mall.*

---

trict/Landstrasse ☎ *01/714–6003* ⚑ *Reservations essential* ▭ *DC, MC, V* ⊗ *Closed Sun. No lunch Sat.* Ⓤ *Tram: 71/Unteres Belvedere.*

4th District (Wieden)

South of the Opernring, the fashionable 4th District, or Wieden, is studded with some dazzling sights, such as the Karlskirche, set on the main square of the area, the Karlsplatz.

AUSTRIAN   ✕ **Artner.** Markus Artner has his star securely fixed in Vienna's gastro-
★ **$$–$$$**   nomic heaven for having the taste to source his own ingredients, and that includes a 350-year-old winery in the Carnuntum region east of Vienna. He decided to wrap grilled goats cheese in bacon, and that dish is now served just about everywhere. His signature Artner sandwich—crusty grilled bread stuffed with melted goat cheese and grilled steak strips—has entered the winner's circle with diners far and wide. So has his restaurant, a chic-and-sleek modern establishment with discreet lighting. Recommended main courses are the crispy pike perch with black olive risotto or the wild boar schnitzel with a potato-and-greens salad. Lamb and veal dishes are also tempting. Artner is around the corner from Taubstummengasse, one subway stop from Karlsplatz on the U1. ⊠ *Flor-*

agasse 6, entrance on Neumanngasse, 4th District/Wieden ☎ *01/503–5033* 🖷 *01/503–5034* ⊕ *www.artner.co.at* 🖃 *AE, DC, MC, V* ☉ *No lunch weekends.*

★ **$$** ✕ **Tancredi.** Ever since this upscale Beisl with a Sicilian name opened, it's been the talk of the town because of the kitchen's fresh approach to Austrian cooking. *Beisln* (a cross between a pub and a café) are traditionally known for their solid, old-fashioned renditions of Austrian standards like Wiener Schnitzel and *Tafelspitz*, but Tancredi has set out to revamp the Beisl image. No plain, dark-wood tables, lace curtains, and smoke-stained walls here—instead the decor is elegantly light and modern, dominated by a huge bar along one wall and clean-lined tables fronting the window opposite. The menu changes seasonally and may include crispy fried chicken and chunky potato salad (using homemade mayonnaise), tender, succulent steak topped with matchstick fried onions and light, grilled dumplings, or *Wels G'röstl*, hunks of catfish, vegetables, potatoes and *Spätzle* cooked in a blackened skillet. ⊠ *Grosse Neugasse 5, 4th District/Wieden* ☎ *01/941–0048* ⌂ *Reservations essential* 🖃 *No credit cards* ☉ *Closed Sun. No lunch Sat.* Ⓤ *U1, U2, or U4/Karlsplatz, then Tram 62 or 65/Mayerhofgasse.*

5th District (Margareten)

A residential quarter once the haunts of Franz Schubert and Chrstoph Gluck, the 5th District is now filled with plenty of middle-class sprawl.

ECLECTIC ✕ **Schlossquadrat.** In an attempt to get the younger generation heading
$–$$ back to the less hip Margareten area, Stephan Gergelys has created a quadruplex eaterie, offering everything from tandoori to Tex-Mex to corral the spoiled *Schickimicki* (yuppie) crowd. He started in 1988, renovating a Jugendstil mansion into a restaurant called Schlossgasse 21. Two decades later, three adjoining dining establishments have opened and the entire complex has been baptized "Castle Quarter." The original eaterie has a menu that is multiculti—with all sort of pan-Asian food, steaks, and Viennese dishes—and a cavernous room that has become one of Vienna's favored places for book launches and art exhibitions. If you prefer something calmer, the Silberwirt is next door and offers an array of Schnitzerl and more down-to-earth Beisl food. Then there is the designer Café Cuadro, with a Bauhaus-style interior, a sleek counter, and a menu that offers four—get it?—salads, ditto burgers, soups, salads, and breakfasts (the latter served from 8 AM to 6 PM). Last but not least is the Hofstöckl, which offers a more elegant, intimate ambience. If all these fail to entice, you can always make a meal of the *Bauernsalat* (farmer's salad with field greens, Styrian sheep's cheese, and white beans in a pumpkin-seed oil dressing) in the lovely garden courtyard. ⊠ *Schlossgasse 21, 5th District/Margareten* ☎ *01/544–0767* ⊕ *www.schlossquadr.at* 🖃 *V* ☉ *No lunch* Ⓤ *U4/Pilgrimgasse.*

6th District (Mariahilf)

The combined neighborhoods of Mariahilf and Neubau (the 6th and 7th Districts, respectively) are near the major museums, including the Kunsthistorisches and the MuseumsQuartier. And not far away is that phenomenal shopping street, the Mariahilferstrasse. Also contained in this vibrant sector of the city is the famous food market on the Naschmarkt.

CONTEMPORARY ✕ **Theatercafe Wien.** Up until recently, it was practically a scandal there
★ $$–$$$ were few options for fine dining in the Mariahilf District. After all, it is home to not only Vienna's legendary Theater an der Wien but Olbrich's iconic Secession Pavilion, Otto Wagner's Majolikahaus, and Beethoven's residence (when he was supervising performances of his work at the der Wien). Historic ground, indeed. Now, not only is Beethoven's room being reconstructed, but eight new restaurants have opened up in the immediate area, including this spot, just next door to Vienna's finest theater. Although Ludwig might have wondered at the style of this place—a creation of Hermann Czech, it is polished and puristic, with light pine furniture, metal trim, and white walls—he would have adored the food. Saddle of lamb on zucchini mousse, the finely cut carpaccio with Venetian mustard sauce, and the curd dumplings with rhubarb and strawberry sauce are all creations of Martin Stein, only 26 but a student of Domschitz and Bauer, two of the very best chefs in Vienna. His style is Austrian with a soupçon of Asia and a pinch of Mediterranean spice. Before or after dinner, you can sit at the bar or enjoy a cigar in the luxe humidor and perhaps bump into one of the famous stars that appear next door—Michel Piccoli, Luc Bondy, and Pierre Boulez have all been spotted here. ✉ *Linke Wienzeile 6, 6th District/Mariahilf* ☎ *01/585–6262* ⊕ *www.theatercafe-wien.at/* ⌛ *Reservations essential* ▤ *AE, DC, MC, V* ⊘ *Closed Sun.* Ⓤ *U4/Karlsplatz.*

MOROCCAN ✕ **Aux Gazelles.** Take a heaping helping of Orientalism, mix in some high-
★ $$–$$$$ tech modernism (à la John Pawson), garnish with beaten-copper tables, tagine-hue walls, Berber ornament, and bursts of Arab decor. Result: a historical-futuristic homage to North African style. The quickest way to travel to Morocco from Vienna without an airplane, Aux Gazelles was transformed into a chunk of maghreb magic from an empty brick factory (located between Naschmarkt and the MuseumsQuartier) by Christine Ruckendorfer. Her idea was to create not just a place to eat and drink, but an exotic atmosphere comprised of a series of spaces that would conjure up—in minimalist fashion—the *palmeraie* landscapes, shady patios, and stuccoed courtyards of Marrakech. First, there's the Deli, done in light Swedish woods, offering hot-and-cold specials, a fine soup selection, an array of delicious cheeses, and pastries. For protein there's the Caviar & Oyster bar—just behind the Deli—offering caviar, fines claires, and some great champagnes. If that wasn't enough, there's the Brasserie, offering French–African fusion flavors, and set next to the lush inner courtyard (an oasis in the city). And then, a first in Vienna, the Hammam, a classic *Orientaliste* steam bath. After all that washing, brushing, massaging, and oiling, why not head to the Salon de Thé, where mint tea allows the seduced senses to return to normal. ✉ *Rahlgasse 5, 6th District/Mariahilf* ☎ *01/585–6645* ⊕ *www.auxgazelles.at* ▤ *AE, DC, MC, V* ⊘ *Closed Sun. and Mon.* Ⓤ *U2/MuseumsQuartier.*

PAN-ASIAN ✕ **Ra'mien.** Designer chic, Asian sleekness, cool glass, trendy in white
$ and red: this place is a great alternative if you've had enough of dumplings and pork and long for lighter fare and a no-pomp surround. Just a stone's

throw from the Akadamie der Bildenden Künste—home to Hieronymus Bosch's *Last Judgment* and other Old Master paintings—this remains Vienna's hippest noodle bar and one of the most interesting southeastern Asian kitchens in town. If you're on a museum tour and want a quick lunch, don't miss the great pad thai or papaya salad. For an evening meal try the green prawn curry served in a fresh coconut or the shrimp salad, atingle with water spinach, fresh ginger, chili, and nuts. Downstairs a club lounge remains open until 4 AM. ⊠ *Gumpendorferstrasse 9, 6th District/Mariahilf* ☎ *01/585–4798* ⌕ *Reservations essential* ▤ *AE, DC, MC, V* ⊙ *Closed Mon.* Ⓤ *U2/MuseumsQuartier.*

VIETNAMESE   ✕ **Saigon.** After a successful start in the 16th District, the Saigon crew
¢–$ opened up a second location nearer the heart of town and helped make the Nasch Markt neighborhood become one of the hot spots for Asian food. Easy to find, spacious and friendly, the second Saigon seems to be already just as popular as the first. Despite the Asian competition (Ra'mien, Eat, Fusan, and sushi stalls galore), Saigon offers just that little taste-telling difference: an unbeatable authenticity of the spices and condiments. Traditional Vietnamese cuisine has a lot in common with nouvelle-contemporary: light and fresh, no heavy sauces nor hot surprises, yet intensive and exciting. Many diners here swear by the incredibly juicy fried pork rolls, the jelly fish, and the green spinach salad and noodles—and you may, too. ⊠ *Getreidemarkt 7, 6th District/Mariahilf* ☎ *01/585–6395* ▤ *AE, DC, MC, V* ⊙ *Closed Mon. in July and Aug.* Ⓤ *U1 or U4/Karlsplatz.*

7th District (Neubau & Spittelberg)

Shoulder to shoulder with the spectacular MuseumsQuartier, the 7th, or Neubau, district also allures with its quaint and relentlessly charming Biedermeier quarter, the Spittelberg.

AUSTRIAN   ✕ **Bohème.** If Rodolfo, Mini, and all the other bohemians of Puccini's
$–$$ *La Boheme* lived in Vienna instead of Paris, there is a good chance this
Fodor'sChoice   would have been their neighborhood hangout. As charming and casual
★   as Café Momus must have been, Bohème occupies a former 18th-century bakery and is on a boutique-lined passageway in the heart of Vienna's luxe-bohemian, cobblestoned quarter of Spittelberg. A low-vaulted ceiling, cherrywood walls, a menu divided into "overtures," "preludes," and "first and second acts," and Bellini on the soundtrack make for a setting frequently favored by stars appearing across town at the Staatsoper (as you'll see from the autographed pictures of some of the opera-loving owner's more famous patrons on the walls). Chef Robert Rauch believes in cuisine that's down to earth but not lacking in fantasy. The cream of pumpkin soup is a fine start, perhaps accompanied by a tasty salad of field greens and fried zucchini in a yogurt dressing; two favorite entrées are the pork medallions with potato cakes in a mushroom cream sauce and the more traditional roast duck with dumplings and *Rotkraut* (red cabbage). One of the true, bona-fide Viennese desserts is showcased—the *Kaiserschmarren with Zwetschkenröster* (a kind of bread and butter pudding with plum preserve). By the way, there is a wine cellar one can actually look into. The menu is conveniently printed in English. ⊠*Spit-

telberggasse 19, 7th District/Neubau ☎ *01/523–3173* ⊟ *AE, DC, MC, V* ⊘ *Closed Sun. No lunch* Ⓤ *U2, U3/Volkstheater.*

¢–$ ✕ **Spatzennest.** This is simple, hearty Viennese cooking at its best, located on a quaint, cobblestone pedestrian street straight out of a 1930s Hollywood movie set in Old Vienna. Tasty dishes include Wiener Schnitzel, roast chicken, and pillowy fried spätzle with slivers of ham and melted cheese. It's especially delightful in summer when tables are set outside. It can be smoky indoors. ⊠ *Ulrichsplatz 1, 7th District/Neubau* ☎ *01/526–1659* ⊟ *MC, V* ⊘ *Closed Fri. and Sat.* Ⓤ *U2, U3/Volkstheater.*

CONTEMPORARY ✕ **Kochwerkstatt.** On one of the prettiest Baroque streets in Vienna, in $$$ the Spittelberg district near the MuseumsQuartier, Kochwerkstatt has created a buzz about town because of its young creative chef. The room is intimate, with close-set tables, plum walls, and slender granite columns. The changing menu may offer jumbo shrimp and tuna with mango or *Lachsforellen* (salmon trout) with sticky red rice. Be sure to end your meal with the warm chocolate-mousse pudding. The limited wine list is good, but priced at the high end. The place gets a bit smoky in winter. ⊠ *Spittelberggasse 8, 7th District/Neubau* ☎☎ *01/523–3291* ✍ *Reservations essential* ⊟ *No credit cards* ⊘ *No lunch* Ⓤ *U2, U3/Volkstheater.*

★ $–$$$ ✕ **Zu ebener Erde und erster Stock.** This mint-green historic cottage near the Volkstheater was named after a play by Nestroy and means "the ground level and first floor." Upstairs is the cozy Biedermeier room with crocheted pillows and old family photos on the walls, and downstairs is an informal room that appeals to diners who want a light, pretheater meal. Every month a new seasonal menu is offered, and choices may include mouthwatering chestnut soup, crispy goose breast with a polenta terrine, or delicate truffle cheese in a puff pastry. For dessert try the light *Topfenknödel* with plums. ⊠ *Burggasse 13, 7th District/Neubau* ☎ *01/ 523–6254* ✍ *Reservations essential* ⊟ *AE, V* ⊘ *Closed Sat. lunch, Sun. and Mon., and 1st 3 wks of Aug.* Ⓤ *U2, U3/Volkstheater.*

¢–$ ✕ **Una.** Set in one of the former imperial stables that were renovated to become part of Vienna's mammoth MuseumsQuartier, this spot has drawn crowds attracted by its unpretentious air, knowing menu, and spectacular decor. Or, to be precise, its vaulted tiled ceiling that has now become an extravaganza with a vaguely Turkish/Indian look. Under this white-and-turquoise fantasia of arabesques, camels, and Bosporus blues, an arty crowd ponders a menu that is varied, reasonably priced, and comes with plenty of vegetarian dishes. Try the couscous and herb salad with a sprinkling of mint or the tangy prawn and watercress sandwich. Adjacent to the unpretentious main room is a comfortable loungelike seating area with coffee tables set with magazines and newspapers. If you want a different degree of reading matter, go through to the directly adjoining AC (Architecture Center) where the well-equipped library offers plenty to browse and check up on what's new on Vienna's architectural front. Or just ask Una, the owner herself—she happens to be the daughter of Raimund Abraham, architect of New York's eye-popping Austrian Cultural Institute. ⊠ *Museumsplatz 1, MuseumsQuartier, 7th District/Neubau* ☎ *1/523–6566* ⊟ *No credit cards* Ⓤ *U2/MuseumsQuartier.*

8th District (Josefstadt)

Set behind the Rathaus city hall, Josefstadt, or the 8th District is one of the smallest and quaintest city districts, home to many council members (as well as Austria's new Federal President, who prefers to stay in his own apartment than move into the presidential Villa).

AUSTRIAN ✕ **Schnattl.** One of Vienna's "neo"-Beisln, Schnattl is a popular choice
$$ for lovers of traditional Austrian and Styrian fare who enjoy the more-than-occasional flair for the innovative. If you're not outdoors in the idyllic courtyard, the setting could be described as cool postmodern: the main room has now acquired a warmer patina but is relatively unadorned, letting you concentrate instead on the attractively set tables and excellent cuisine. Wilhelm Schnattl has set mouths talking, and salivating, by adding a light mustard sauce to roast pork, rosemary to saddle of lamb, and marinated almonds to medallions of mountain ram or deer. All of these dishes goes down splendidly with one of Schnattl's great Styrian wines, especially the famous Schilcher, a rosé blend with a slightly acidic aftertaste. No matter what you order, don't forget to also have one of the Kürbiskernöl (pumpkin-seed) oil–drenched salads. You'll find many of the local politicos lunching here (the city hall is around the corner) do just that. The big bargain here is the daily €6 lunch special. ⊠ *Langegasse 40, 8th District/Josefstadt* ☎ *01/405–3400* ▤ *AE, DC* ☉ *Closed weekends, 2 wks around Easter, and last 2 wks of Aug.* Ⓤ *U2/Rathaus.*

CROATIAN ✕ **Konoba.** Tired of sushi and fed up with flounder? Try the unpreten-
$$ tious and uncomplicated delights of authentic Dalmatian Coast cooking on show here. "Konoba" is what fish restaurants are called in Croatia and this place showcases the freshest of Adriatic aquatic creatures. They arrive twice a week to ensure the freshest tastes. White walls, floor boards, and massive wood tables and ventilation ceiling pipe recall the days this spot was a flower market. Nowadays, however, there is an open kitchen at the center of it all. Seated at the table you can see, hear, and almost taste the fish sizzling on the grill or frying in the pans. The no-frills fish soup (don't expect salmon or lobster in this one) is highly recommended. Try the national dish, "Buzara"—scampi shrimp (or some other seafood) cooked in a wine-garlic-olive-oil-parsley sauce with lots of onions (be sure to mop up the heavenly sauce with bread). Branzino comes with parsley potatoes, fresh spinach, and loads of garlic in a grilled crispy coat. The wine that goes down perfectly well with the fish is the mild, fruity Zlahtina or, if you prefer a heavier drop, try the Dingac. ⊠ *Lerchenfelderstrasse 66–68, 8th District/Josefstadt* ☎ *01/ 929–4111* ▤ *MC, V* Ⓤ *Tram: 46/Strozzigasse.*

VEGETARIAN ✕ **Lebenbauer.** Here in the heart of ministerial Vienna, you cannot only
¢–$ have lunch rubbing elbows with city councillors but get that bothersome cholesterol level sliding down. Vegetarian is the main mode here, and you'll be surprised how often your taste buds will be thanking you when you enjoy such specialties as *Hirsegröstl,* a millet hash with pumpkin seeds in an oyster mushroom sauce, or the gluten-free pasta with smoked salmon and shrimp in a dill cream sauce. There are also several free-

range chicken and fish entrées. Clean white-and-yellow colors, plenty of green plants around, and a no-smoking restriction all add up to a great value-for-money vegetarian venue. If you're in need of still more energy, try one of the refreshing freshly pressed fruit juices. ✉ *Teinfaltstrasse 3, 8th District/Josefstadt* ☎ *01/5335–5560* 🚫 *AE, DC, MC, V* 𝄐 *Closed weekends and 3 wks in July and Aug.* Ⓤ *U3/Herrengasse.*

9th District (Alsergrund)

The 9th District is centered around Vienna's university, so this academic quarter is filled with the serious and the mod. The big attraction used to be the Freud Haus but now the crowds are heading here to dine in its smart restaurants and to see the new and *palais*-tial Lichtenstein Museum.

FRENCH ✕ **Ruben's Palais.** Once your aesthetic liver is crying for mercy after view-
$$–$$$$ ing the incomparable Old Master paintings on view at the newly reopened
Fodor'sChoice Palais Liechtenstein, wouldn't it be wonderful to enjoy a feast for the
★ taste buds along with this feast for the eyes? Well, the Princes of Liecht-
enstein aim to please and have now opened this restaurant in their im-
maculately restored family palace. Having just seen the Decius Mus cycle
upstairs, you might think that the place's name refers to the great Peter
Paul Rubens canvases on view. But that honor goes to manager and chef
de cuisine Ruben A. Brunhart, who himself looks like he stepped out of
a 17th-century portrait, with his amazingly long red beard (twisted into
two long thin threads). Brunhart's inspiration comes from the creations
of the great cook Escoffier, but he takes "classic" and "exclusive" into
new realms, as you can see with one taste of his dandelion omelette. For
starters the grilled duck liver with rhubarb-coconut ragout is a sensa-
tion, as is the terrine of green asparagus, mozzarella cheese, and smoked
ham. Top main courses include the scallops with mustard and white beet
or the smoked deer with grapes and pink pepper. In the elegantly de-
signed cellar, the finest matching wines, from Burgundy, Bordeaux,
Piemont, and Tuscany, wait to be served. The restaurant setting is
exquisite—nut-wood floors, dark walls, and beautifully upholstered
furniture—and makes a fitting contrast to the kitchen, reputedly the most
high-tech in all Austria. For a slightly cheaper take on Brunhart's cre-
ations, repair to the museum's Ruben's Brasserie, which is set around
a chic bar. Both restaurants also feature wonderful alfresco dining on
the palace's Baroque Ehrenhof terrace. ✉ *Fürstengasse 1, at Palais
Liechtenstein, 9th District/Alsergrund* ☎ *01/3123–9613* ⊕ *www.rubens.
at* ⟨⟩ *Reservations essential* 🚫 *AE, DC, MC, V* 𝄐 *Closed Mon. and
Tues.* Ⓜ *U4/Friedensbruecke.*

ITALIAN ✕ **Lustkandel.** No matter if Lehar, Strauss, or Kalman are being performed
★ $–$$ tonight at the Volksoper (a must for every visitor to Vienna), why not
enjoy a pre- or post-theater dinner a two-minute walk away in the Ital-
ianate warmth of Lustkandel. Red velvet drapes and Biedermeier up-
holstered chairs add Vienna charm to the otherwise mildly Mediterranean
decor, but any winter chill in the air is forgotten thanks to the terra-
cotta-tile floors, the wood-burning fireplace, and the beautiful orange
trees that adorn the dining room. Ingeborg Treiber's classic Italian cuisine is prepared using time-honored recipes (no pizza), best accompa-

WITH CHILDREN?

VIENNA BEING VIENNA it has to be different. It has often been said that dogs are treated with more kindness in restaurants in Vienna than juveniles (just watch—a dog in a restaurant or coffeehouse will receive a bowl of water before anyone else gets a drop to drink). And older ladies, suitably attired in lace gloves, accompanied by their dachshunds, will lay out their canine's cushion on a seat for the dog to lay its weary legs. So what about children? Fortunately, there are plenty of places to feed the infants. One of the best spots to head for is the MQ (MuseumsQuartier), not only for fun and games—there is always something going on outside the museums themselves to entertain the brood—but for food and goodies, as there are many eateries open throughout the day, every day. Just outside the MQ begins the longest shopping street in Vienna, the Mariahilferstrasse, which caters to youngsters formidably. Check out Bortolotti, one of Vienna's best ice-cream parlors, right next door to McDonald's and opposite a branch of Starbucks. Most coffeehouses will serve smaller portions if asked, and the long-time favorite for sweet-toothed tots is the Palatschinken platter (crepes), which comes with many different fillings. All Italian restaurants will show offspring favor, offering smaller pizza and spaghetti portions if desired. Definitely one of the most recommended places for children has to be the Rosenberger restaurant (just behind the Sacher Hotel). Not only can kids choose their own small-size-plates-available meal at this fantastic self-service cafeteria, but the freshly made waffles are just unbeatable. And there's a small gift waiting at the check-out for every youngster that goes through.

nied by fine wines. She uses only homegrown spices, home-made bread and pasta, and seafood from the best suppliers. Pre-operetta, opt for the grilled octopus on green-leaf salad starter, followed by a chanterelle risotto. If you come after the show, try the somewhat more substantial plate of grilled giant prawns with garlic and rocket salad, or the juicy tuna with lemon-cream sauce. If you snag a table in the lovely garden, you'll be surrounded by lemon trees, cascading roses, and blossoming oleander. Who needs to be in Italy? ⊠ *Säulengasse 27, at Lustkandlgasse, 9th District/Alsergrund* ☎ *01/317–3581* ⌚ *Reservations essential* ⊟ *AE, DC, MC, V* ☉ *Closed Sun.* Ⓜ *U6/Volksoper.*

10th District (Favoriten)

The 10th District of Favoriten is the city's largest in population and size. Adjacent to the splendor of the Belvedere Palace estate, the district is famous for its Czech roots, perhaps most apparent in its quaint Böhmscher Prater fairway grounds.

ECLECTIC
$$$$

✕ **Brunner's.** Take a trip high above the roofs of Vienna to this restaurant in the clouds. On the 22nd floor of the Immofinanz Tower in the Vienna Business Park (yes, skyscrapers are now dotting the city skyline), this spot offers not only a great meal but throws in a spectacular view into the bargain. In fact, that wraparound view represents the cosmopolitan, all-inclusive philosophy here. Chef Harald Brunner waves his wooden spoon and conjures up the whole world onto your plate, whether Thai bouillabaisse, Wiener Schnitzel, or sashimi of tuna fish and salmon. At his finest, Brunner succeeds in combining the echo of the sea with an alpine glow. At the center of the restaurant—alluring decorated with walls of "floating bottles"—is the Wine Bar, where you can sip everything from fine wines to champagnes to barrique-matured Rioja served with tempting little delicacies. All in all, architects Adele Geitzinger and Christian Heiss have created a minimalist design for a plain and elegant yet pleasant atmosphere, allowing the view and the food to take center stage. ✉ *Wienerbergstrasse 7, 10th District/Favoriten* ☎ *01/607–6500* ⚖ *Reservations essential* ▤ *AE, DC, MC, V* ☉ *Closed Sun.*

13th District (Hietzing)

In the shadows of the majestic Schönbrunn Palace, the elegant 13th District has always been an address of choice, no where more so than the district's famous Gloriettegasse, where villas and houses by Josef Hoffmann, Friedrich Ohmann, and Adolf Loos sit side by side.

AUSTRIAN
★ $$$

✕ **Hietzingerbraeu.** If you are going to test-eat the most famous of all original Austrian fare, start here at the city's Tafelspitz temple, where Eva and Ewald Plachutta celebrate this unpretentious art seven days a week. Did Franz Josef really eat this dish of boiled beef every single day? Legend says it is so—after all, how did he manage to live to 86 otherwise? In those good old days, it was considered necessary to identify at least 12 different cuts of boiled beef (*Schulterscherzel,* or shoulder; *Beinfleisch,* or shank, etc.) or you weren't part of the in-crowd. Here at "Hietzing's Brewery," in time-honored fashion, the beef is presented in its vegetable soup. Only once you've slurped up the broth will the waiter help you dish up your succulent, tender beef onto a plate (have you ever tried eating meat from a soup bowl?). Side dishes are creamed spinach, carrots, and hash browns and the blissful garnishes: white chive cream and apple with freshly grated horseradish. The restaurant is Vienna elegant, as the famed green and yellow colors of the neighboring Schönbrunn Palace dominate the decor. Those high Austrian virtues of constancy and reliability are always on show here, so there are no disappointments to be had (and that goes for the wines and the service). ✉ *Auhofstrasse 1, 13th District/Hietzing* ☎ *01/8777–0870* ⚖ *Reservations essential* ▤ *AE, DC, MC, V* Ⓤ *U4/Hietzing.*

19th District (Döbling)

Sometimes compared to London's Hampstead, the residential 19th District rubs shoulders with the very posh Grinzing area. Some streets are still redolent of the Biedermeier era. Set quite to the north of the city center, the neighborhood enjoys a handy U-Bahn connection to downtown.

AUSTRIAN
★ ¢

✕ **Fischer Bräu.** This is known as Vienna's number one brewery restaurant, and though it's located in the 19th District, it's worth the effort to get here. Several varieties of their own fresh beer are featured, and the menu, though extensive, is nothing fancy. You can choose from stuffed baked potatoes, salads, or Wiener Schnitzel—huge and served with a side order of potato salad. Especially scrumptious is the golden-fried *Hühnerschnitzel* (chicken breast). The beer garden with its twinkling lights strung through the trees is packed on summer evenings, so come early to get a table. Every Sunday there is a popular jazz brunch, with live music. ⊠ *Billrothstrasse 17, 19th District/Döbling* ☎ *01/369–5949* ✍ *Reservations essential* ▭ *No credit cards* ⊙ *No lunch, except Sun. brunch* Ⓤ *U2/Schottentor; Tram: 37 or 38/Döblinger Hauptstrasse.*

WINE TAVERNS & HEURIGE

Why has Vienna always been the capital of classical music? One theory is that it was the *wine,* as what other metropolis spawned so many vineyards and so many musical geniuses at the same time? Could Beethoven have composed the *Moonlight Sonata* without his favorite nightcap? Or Strauss put the final note to his *Blue Danube* without commiserating with the fellows at the corner tavern? Or Haydn done without his Esterházykeller? Vienna's tart-tasting "new wine"—the *Heurige,* harvested every September and October in hills around the city—was probably the elixir they needed not only to help them compose, but probably also proved to be the evening's answer to the problems of the day. No wonder the Viennese like to say that "although one might occasionally drink one too many, one can never drink enough." The city's light and slightly fizzy wines were served up in taverns around the city and, in the suburbs, in the spots known as "Heuriger," which were taverns named after the "last year's wine" they served. These remain some of Vienna's most charmingly rustic spots and the suburban ones sometimes radiate a 19th-century time-warp feel. In the city center, wine taverns are better known as *Weinkeller.* Hundreds of years ago, Vienna's vintners started taking advantage of the cavernous spaces found below ancient monasteries and old houses and converted them into underground wine cellars. The fact that these subterranean "Kellers" were some of the coolest spots in summertime Vienna also proved a big drawing card.

Today, most Heurigen open up in the evening and are intended primarily for the enjoyment of wine. When you sit down, order the classic *Ein Viertel*—a quarter liter of wine—to get you going, then check out the buffet. In the old days, the *Salamutschi* (sausage seller) would trot his wares from one tavern to another. Today, increasingly, full dinners are available, although most food is hypercalorific tourist-fodder. If you go to a Heurige in fall, be sure to order a glass of Sturm, a cloudy drink halfway between grape juice and wine, with a delicious yeasty fizz.

While the city cellars fulfill the authenticity quota, the true Heurige experience is found in the rollicking rustic taverns set in the picturesque wine villages that dot Vienna's outskirts (wine-growing here dates back to the ancient Roman era): Stammersdorf, Grinzing, Sievering, Nussdorf, Neustift, and a corner of Ottakring, and sometimes in the vineyards themselves (tram lines to take from the city center are listed under the reviews below). Grinzing is a particularly enchanting destination:

WINE·WIEN·WEIN·VIENNA

T MAKES FOR A MEMORABLE EXPERIENCE to sit at the edge of a vineyard on the Kahlenberg with a tankard of young white wine and listen to the Schrammel quartet playing sentimental Viennese songs. The wine taverns, called Heurige (the singular is Heuriger) for the new wine that they serve, sprang up in 1784 when Joseph II decreed that owners of vineyards could establish their own private wine taverns; soon the Viennese discovered it was cheaper to go out to the wine than to bring it inside the city walls, where taxes were levied. The Heuriger owner is supposed to be licensed to serve only the produce of his own vineyard, a rule more honored in the breach than the observance. These taverns in the wine-growing districts on the outskirts of the city vary from the simple front room of a vintner's house to ornate settings. The true Heuriger is open for only a few weeks a year to allow the vintner to sell a certain quantity of his production, tax-free, when consumed on his own premises. The choice is usually between a "new" and an "old" white (or red) wine, but you can also ask for a milder or sharper wine according to your taste. Most Heurige are happy to let you sample the wines before you order. You can also order a Gespritzter, half wine and half soda water. The waitress brings the wine, usually in a ¼-liter mug or liter carafe, but you serve yourself from the food buffet. The wine tastes as mild as lemonade, but it packs a punch. If it isn't of good quality, you will know by a raging headache the next day.

Although colonized by faux-heurige and tour buses, Grinzing has enough winding streets, antique lanterns, stained-glass windows, hanging balconies, and oh-so-cozy taverns that you may feel you're wandering through a stage set for an operetta (don't forget to look for the town organ-grinder). The best times to visit the Heurige are in summer and fall, when many of these places famously hang a pine branch over their doorway to show they are open, though often the more elegant and expensive establishments, called *Noble-Heurige,* stay open year-round. If you are visiting off-season, be sure to call to make sure a particular tavern is open.

$$–$$$ ✕ **Kronprinz Rudolfshof.** Named after the crown prince who died a tragic death at Mayerling, this Heuriger has always been one of Grinzing's most famous. Sigmund Freud, C.G. Jung, and Albert Einstein sipped glasses of Viennese wine here. Although it might be hard to channel their spirits—a new Hundertwasser modern pavilion has been added here—you might enjoy the kitschy blast of Alt Wien on tap here: the "1st Grinzinger Heurigen Show," which features a troupe of costumed singers and musicians warbling the heart out of "Wiener Blut" and "Ob blond, ob braun, ich liebe alle Frauen," along with other goodies favored by *Heurigensänger.* The price is €40 a ticket. If not, if you're lucky, you might catch a *Natursänger* roaming the village streets. ⊠ *Cobenzlgasse 8, 19th District/Grinzing* ☎ *01/524–7478* ⊕ *www.heuriger.com/* ⊟ *AE, DC, MC, V* Ⓤ *U2/Schottentor; Tram: 38/Grinzing.*

★ $$–$$$ ✕ **Mayer am Pfarrplatz.** Heiligenstadt is home to this legendary Heuriger in one of Beethoven's former abodes. Ludwig van Beethoven lived in this house on Pfarrplatz in the summer of 1817. At that time there was a spa in Heiligenstadt, which Beethoven visited, hoping to find a cure to his deafness. He had fond memories of this village, since he had previously stayed here when he composed his 6th Symphony (Pastoral), and while staying in this house, had also created parts of his famous 9th Symphony (Ode to Joy). The atmosphere in the collection of rooms is genuine, with vaulted rooms filled with Tirolian iron chandeliers, antique engravings, and mounted antlers. The à la carte offerings and buffet are more than abundant and the house wines among the most excellent of all heurigen nectars. You'll find lots of Viennese among the tourists here. ⊠ *Heiligenstädter Pfarrplatz 2, 19th District/Nussdorf* ☎ *01/370–1287* ⊕ *www.mayer.pfarrplatz.at/* ⊟ *DC, MC, V* ⊗ No *lunch weekdays or Sat.* Ⓤ *Tram: D/Nussdorf from the Ring.*

$$–$$$ ✕ **Weingut Reinprecht.** The grandest Heurigen in Grinzing (the town has
FodorśChoice more than 30 of them), Reinprecht is gemütlichkeit-heaven: Tirolian
★ wood beams, 19th-century oil paintings, Austrian-eagle banners, portraits of army generals, globe lanterns, marble busts, trellised tables, and the greatest collection of corkscrews in Austria. The building—a former monastery—is impressive, as is the garden, which can hold up to 700 people (to give you an idea of how popular this place is). If you want to ignore the crowds, get a cozy corner table, and focus on the archetypal *atmosphäre*, you might have a great time. ⊠ *Cobenzlgasse 20, 19th District/Grinzing* ☎ *01/320–1389* ⊕ *http://heuriger-reinprecht.at/* ⊟ *AE, DC, MC, V* ⊗ *Closed Dec.–Feb.* Ⓤ *U2/Schottentor; Tram: 38/Grinzing.*

★ $–$$ ✕ **Augustinerkeller.** Built into the old brick vaults of the 16th-century historic fortifications surrounding the old city, this is one of the last monastic wine-cellars in central Vienna. The atmosphere is very gemutlichkeit— vaulted brick ceiling, wooden "cow-stall" booths, street lanterns, Austrian bric-a-brac, and a lovely troupe of roaming musicians (dig that accordian!) in the evenings. The spit-roasted chicken is excellent, as is the filling *Stelze* (roast knuckle of pork). For dessert, try the *Apfelstrudel,* moist and warm from the oven. Daily brunches including three mains, three sides, salads, fruits, and bread for a best-deal €10. You can enjoy an evening buffet with beer, wine, and soft drinks included for €24.50, or the "gourmands" buffet, which even covers coffee, tea, strudels, and cheese for €29.50. ⊠ *Augustinerstrasse 1, Albertinaplatz, 1st District* ☎ *01/533–1026* ⊕ *http://members.aon.at/augustinerkeller/eframe.htm* ⊟ *DC, MC, V* Ⓤ *U3/Herrengasse.*

$–$$ ✕ **Esterházykeller.** The roots here go way back to 1683 when this opened as one of the official "Stadtheuriger" (city wine taverns). Below the Esterházy palace, the atmosphere is like a cozy subterranean cave, with low-hanging vaults and alpine wooden booths. The maze of rooms offers some of the best Keller wines in town plus a typical Vienna menu noontime and evenings, as well as a hot-and-cold buffet. Note this cellar may be too smoky for some although proposed no-smoking city laws may be introduced soon. ✉ *Haarhof 1, 1st District* ☎ *01/533–3482* ⊕ *www.esterhazykeller.at/* ⊘ *Closed weekends in summer. No lunch weekends* Ⓤ *U1 or U4/Stephansplatz.*

★ $ ✕ **Melker Stiftskeller.** Down and down you go, into one of the friendliest Keller in town, where Stelze is a popular feature, along with outstanding wines by the glass or, rather, mug. Part of the fabled Melkerhof complex—dating from 1438 but rebuilt in the 18th century—this originally was the storage house for wines from the great Melk Abbey in the Danube Valley. This is a complex of six cavernous rooms, with the most atmospheric having low-hanging vaults right out of a castle dungeon. ✉ *Schottengasse 3, 1st District* ☎ *01/533–5530* ⊕ *http://members.aon.at/melkerstiftskeller/* ▤ *AE, DC, MC, V* ⊘ *Closed Sun. and Mon. No lunch* Ⓤ *U2/Schottentor.*

★ $ ✕ **Schreiberhaus.** In Neustift am Walde, the Schreiberhaus heuriger has one of the prettiest terraced gardens in the city, with picnic tables stretching straight up into the vineyards. The buffet offers delicious treats such as spit-roasted chicken, salmon pasta, and a huge selection of tempting grilled vegetables and salads. The golden Traminer wine is excellent. ✉ *Rathstrasse 54, 19th District/Neustift am Walde* ☎ *01/440–3844* ▤ *AE, DC, MC, V* Ⓤ *U4, U6/Spittelau; Bus 35A/Neustift am Walde.*

$ ✕ **Schübel-Auer.** In Nussdorf seek out the Schübel-Auer Heuriger for its series of atmospheric rooms and good wines. Known for its home-style cooking, it also offers vegetarian dishes and has several varieties of Austrian cheese. ✉ *Kahlenbergerstrasse 22, 19th District/Nussdorf* ☎ *01/370–2222* ▤ *No credit cards* ⊘ *Closed Sun. and Mon. No lunch* Ⓤ *Tram: D/Nussdorf from the Ring.*

¢–$ ✕ **Passauerhof.** If you want live folk music (offered nightly) to accompany your meal, this is the place to go. But you may have to share the experience with the tour groups that descend on Grinzing. The food from the heurigen menu, such as roast chicken and Wiener Schnitzel, is tasty, while the buffet offers a limited selection. It's a pleasant five-minute walk up the hill from the town center. ✉ *Cobenzlgasse 9, 19th District/Grinzing* ☎ *01/320–6345* ▤ *AE, DC, MC, V* ⊘ *Closed Jan.and Feb. No lunch* Ⓤ *U2/Schottentor; Tram: 38/Grinzing.*

★ ¢–$ ✕ **Wieninger.** Heurigen wine and food are both top-notch here, and the charming, tree-shaded inner courtyard and series of typical vintner's rooms are perfect for whiling away an evening. Wieninger's bottled wines are ranked among the country's best. It's located across the Danube in Stammersdorf, one of Vienna's oldest Heurige areas. ✉ *Stammersdorferstrasse 78, 21st District/Floridsdorf* ☎ *01/292–4106* ▤ *V* ⊘ *Closed late-Dec.–Feb. No lunch except Sun.* Ⓤ *U2, U4/Schottenring; Tram: 31/Stammersdorf.*

¢–$ ✕ **Zimmermann.** East of the Grinzing village center, the Zimmermann Heuriger has excellent wines, an enchanting tree-shaded garden, and an endless series of small paneled rooms and vaulted cellars. You can order from the menu or choose from the tempting buffet. This well-known Heuriger attracts the occasional celebrity, including fashion model Claudia Schiffer when she's in town. ✉ *Armbrustergasse 5/Grinzingerstrasse, 19th District/Grinzing* ☎ *01/370–2211* ▤ *AE, DC, MC, V* ⊘ *No lunch* Ⓤ *U2/Schottentor; Tram: 38/Grinzing.*

¢–$ ✕ **Zwölf-Apostelkeller.** You pass a huge wood statue of St. Peter on the way downstairs to the two underground floors in this deep-down cellar in the oldest part of Vienna. The atmosphere is rather crammed; the Apostelstüberl has some rather cheesy folk reliefs of the 12 apostles. The young crowd comes for the good wines and the atmosphere, and there's buffet food as well. ⊠ *Sonnenfelsgasse 3, 1st District* ☎ *01/512–6777* ⊕ *www.zwoelf-apostelkeller.at/* 🖃 *AE, DC, MC, V* ⊗ *No lunch* Ⓤ *U1, U2/Stephansplatz.*

TO BEAN OR NOT TO BEAN?
COFFEEHOUSES & CAFÉS

Is it the coffee they come for, or the coffeehouse? This question is one of the hot topics in town as Vienna's café scene has become increasingly overpopulated with Starbucks branches and Italian outlets. The ruckus over whether the quality of the coffee or the *atmosphäre* is more important is not new, but is becoming fiercer as competition from all sides increases.

The result is that the legendary landmark Wiener Kaffeehäuser—the famous cafés known for a century as the "Viennese Parlors," where everyone from Mozart and Beethoven to Lenin and Andy Warhol were likely to hang out—are smarting from the new guys on the block. On the plus side, their ageless charms remain mostly intact: the sumptuous red-velvety padded booths, the marble-topped tables, the rickety yet indestructible Thonet bentwood chairs, the waiter—still the *Herr Ober* dressed in a Sunday-best outfit—pastries, cakes, strudels, and rich tortes, newspapers, magazines, and journals, and, last but not least, a sense that here, time stands still. The interiors of these grand sites are palatial and therefore—and here's the rub—costly to maintain. The customer who goes to his or her "local" will consume fairly little, perhaps a coffee, a wine, or a small snack. It becomes a losing battle to make a profit from an order of *Kaffee mit Schlag* that is nursed all afternoon. Needless to say, the traditional coffeehouse owners are increasingly worried about meeting their overheads (albeit as Viennese, who are always worried about everything). The fact remains that it is sometimes whispered that the quality of the coffee in many of the most famous houses has been compared to that of *gschluder*—dishwater. Is this, in fact, yet another way these Viennese institutions are attempting to reduce costs and stay alive?

So when you're in Vienna and trying to decide which of these institutions to patronize, extend your connoisseurship beyond the glories of coffee to their tempting treats, the seductive vibes, and, most of all, the priceless time-patinated ambience. Although nowadays the quintessential Viennese coffeehouse is club, pub, and bistro rolled into one, their evolution into a social institution—which took place over the greater part of the 20th century—was a product of the warm but noncommittal atmosphere they offered the middle class for convenient, gracious entertaining outside the home.

To savor the traditional coffeehouse experience, set aside a morning or an afternoon, or at least a couple of hours. Read a while or catch up on your letter writing or plan tomorrow's itinerary: there is no need to worry about overstaying one's welcome, even over a single small cup of coffee, though don't expect refills.

And remember that in Austria coffee is never merely coffee. It comes in countless forms and under many names. Ask for *ein Kaffee* from a waiter and you'll get a vacant stare. If you want a black coffee, you must ask for a *kleiner* or *grosser Schwarzer* (small or large black coffee, with small being the size of a demitasse cup). If you want it strong, add the word *gekürst* (shortened); if you want it weaker, *verlängert* (stretched). If you want your coffee with cream, ask for a *Brauner* (again *gross* or *klein*); say *Kaffee Creme* if you wish to add the cream yourself. Others opt for a *Melange,* a mild roast with steamed milk (which you can even get *mit Haut,* with skin, or *Verkehrter,* with more milk than coffee). The usual after-dinner drink is espresso. Most delightful are the coffee-and-whipped-cream concoctions, universally cherished as *Kaffee mit Schlag,* a taste that is easily acquired and a menace to all but the very thin. A customer who wants more whipped cream than coffee asks for a *Doppelschlag.* Hot black coffee in a glass with one knob of whipped cream is an *Einspänner* (literally, "one-horse coach"—as coachmen needed one hand free to hold the reins). Then you can go to town on a *Mazagran,* black coffee with ice and a tot of rum, or *Eiskaffee,* cold coffee with ice cream, whipped cream, and cookies. Or you can simply order a *Portion Kaffee* and have an honest pot of coffee and jug of hot milk. And watch out: if you naively request a Menu, you'll wind up with a Schwarzer with a double shot of pear liqueur.

As for the actual *Spieisekarte* (menu), most places offer hot food, starting with breakfast, from early morning until around 11 AM, lunch menus in some, and many offer a great variety of meals until about an hour before closing time. Whichever one, or more, of Vienna's coffeehouses you visit, do so with the intention of spending enough time to observe what might still be called *savoir vivre,* undeniably so very scarce in this day and age. Who cares what the coffee tastes like when you are privileged to drink in history?

✕ **Café Bräunerhof.** A spirit you can channel here is that of the noted Austrian writer, Thomas Bernhard, an enfant terrible of 1960s literary fame, who came here to hide from public life. Little has changed within these four walls, which exude a distant uncanny feel that must have appealed to Bernhard (who had the most unfortunate love/hate relationship with his own country). The interior is original, the upholstery and the posters on the yellow walls, too. Breakfasts and small snacks are best and attract the customers who come here every day. The waiters are haughty but not unfriendly and they serve an excellent cup of coffee. On weekends there is an additional treat—live music performed by a string trio that plays in the afternoons for about three hours. ✉ *Stallburggasse 2* ☎ *01/512–3893* Ⓤ *U3/Herrengasse.*

FodorsChoice ★ ✕ **Café Central.** *The* coffeehouse supreme. Made famous by its illustrious guests, the Café Central is probably the world's most famous coffeehouse—outside of Florian's in Venice. Although recently somewhat over-restored (by its Donald Trump–like new owner), its old vibes remain attached to it as though by suction-pad. Don't expect a cozy-hole-in-the-wall kaffeehaus: With soaring ceiling and gigantic columns giving it the look of an apse strayed from St. Stephan's cathedral, it provided a rather sumptuous home-away-from-home for Leon Trotsky, who mapped out the Russian Revolution here under the portraits of the imperial family. Set just across from the Spanish Riding School—and once the legendary writers' café—it still has seated in the doorway the mannequin of early-20th-century Viennese muse and essayist Peter Altenberg (the scrounging author who was forever borrowing money from his friends, yet died a millionaire). Piano music fills the marble pillared hall in the afternoons and although it will never again be all that it used to be it, Central should be on the "must see" list. ⊠ *Herrengasse 14, at Strauchgasse, 1st District* ☎ *01/5333–76424* ⊕ *www.palaisevents.at/* Ⓤ *U3/Herrengasse.*

✕ **Café Diglas.** When the going gets hot, the kitchen can get backed up here, so why not just stick to the sweets? Freshly made every day, the puddings and pastries lay waiting in their trays as you walk through the door. Fluffy filo filled with fresh fruit and topped with golden meringue; vanilla cream slices juicy with red currants; massive portions of cream cheese strudel with vanilla sauce; or apfelstrudel with whipped cream are the best and safest alternatives to a meal. Shoppers and shop keepers frequent the Diglas—so do lovers, as it has a couple of very shady intimate booths. On a Wednesday afternoon there is a pianist at the piano for a few hours. ⊠ *Wollzeile 10, 1st District* ☎ *01/512–5765* ⊕ *www.diglas.at/* Ⓤ *U1 or U3/Stephansplatz.*

✕ **Café Englaender.** One of the most pleasant cafés in Vienna has both a quiet corner for the pensive and a busy bar with the TV monitor for the plugged-in. Overall, the warm red-and-cool beige combination exudes a casual yet classic Vienna style. Fine sketches and attractive posters adorn the walls and a large oil painting of the former proprietress, Salomea Englaender, proudly showing off her timeless beauty—she hosted many art salons and was a leading figure in the history of modern art during the 1930s in Central Europe. As far as coffeehouse menus go, the Englaender has to be among the most innovative. International and local wines, assorted teas, and imaginative meals help round out this option, an off-the-beaten-track favorite for the Viennese. ⊠ *Postgasse 2, 1st District* ☎ *01/966–8665* Ⓤ *U3/Stubentor.*

✕ **Café Frauenhuber.** Repair here to find some peace and quiet away from the Himmelpfortgasse's busy shoppers. A visual treat is the original turn-of-the-20th-century interior with the obligatory red-velvet seating and somewhat tired upholstery (if you don't suffer from back problems you'll be fine). The breakfasts served here are legendary, having never lost that original "egg-in-a-glass" touch. You'll find fewer tourists here than in other typical Viennese cafés, so head here for real patina, which it has earned as this establishment first opened its doors in 1824. ⊠ *Himmelpfortgasse 6, 1st District* ☎ *01/512–4323* Ⓤ *U1 or U3/Stephansplatz.*

✕ **Café Griensteidl.** Once the site of one of Vienna's oldest coffeehouses and named after the pharmacist Heinrich Griensteidl—the original dated back to 1847 but was demolished in 1897—this café was resurrected in 1990. Here, Karl Kraus, the sardonic critic, spent many hours writing his feared articles and here, Hugo von Hofmannsthal took time-outs from writing libretti for Richard Strauss. Although this establishment is still looking for the patina needed to give it back its real flair, locals are pleased by the attempt to re-create the former atmosphere that exuded history. The daily, reasonably priced midday menu is a winner. Numerous newspapers and magazines hang on the rack (with a goodly number in English). This is one of the coffeehouses that does not usually fill up with cigarette smoke—if it does, head for the café's no-smoking section. Even better, there is an outside so-called "Schanigarten"—the kind of garden Viennese have considered an urban oasis for centuries—where you can sit and watch the horse-and-carriage trade rattle over the cobbles of the Michaelerplatz. ✉ *Michaelerplatz 2 , 1st District* ☎ *01/533–2692* Ⓤ *U3/Herrengasse.*

Fodor'sChoice ✕ **Café Hawelka.** Practically a shrine, nearly a museum, the beloved Hawelka has been presided over for more than 70 years by Josefine and Leopold Hawelka, in person, day in, day out. Josefine, sometimes working 14 hours a day, rules the empire (except on Tuesday) with circumspect, incredible energy and an iron glove—she is the one who decides which of her "beloved guests" sits where. Will this institution live on forever? This troubles many of the regulars. Well, if the Hawelka becomes a museum, it will be ready. This was the hang-out of most of Vienna's modern artists and the café has acquired quite an admirable art collection over the years. As you enter the rather dark interior, wait to be seated—unusual in Vienna—and then speak up and ask to have a look at the guest book, in itself a work of art, with entries including some very illustrious names (Elias Canetti, Andy Warhol, Tony Blair). Back in the 1960s, the young John Irving enjoyed the atmosphere here, too, as you can see when reading *The Hotel New Hampshire.* If you want to try what the Hawelka is most famous for, then ask for Buchteln, a baked bun with a sweet filling that goes down well with a Melange. ✉ *Dorotheergasse 6, 1st District* ☎ *01/512–8230* Ⓤ *U1 or U3/Stephansplatz.*

✕ **Café Korb.** If you're feeling philosophical, every second Saturday there's an afternoon meeting of some of Vienna's university professors of philosophy here—open discussion is desired. If that's a bit too heavy, head downstairs when you can find the strangest bowling lane in Vienna. It dates from the '60s and there's music downstairs, too. There is also a chill-out lounge with art works on view from names like Guenter Brus, Peter Kogler, and Manfred Plotteg. Coffee and good no-frills food are available in the café. The space is small so it can feel squeezed, but Korb has a most undeniable 1960s feel to it and that, in itself, is worth the visit. ✉ *Brandstaette 9, 1st District* ☎ *01/533–7215* Ⓤ *U1 or U3/ Stephansplatz.*

★ ✕ **Café Landtmann.** A recent $500,000 government-sponsored renovation has brought new lustre to the chandeliers of Landtmann, a century-old favorite of politicians, theater stars (the Burg is next door), and celeb-watchers. Sigmund Freud, Burt Lancaster, Hillary Rodham Clinton, and Sir Paul McCartney are just a few of the famous folk who have patronized this vaguely Secession-ish looking café, whose glass-and-brass doors have been open since 1873. If you want a great meal, at almost any time of the day, there are few places that can beat this one. If you just want coffee and cake, then choose the right-hand-side seating area (just beyond the door). But if it is bustle and star-sightings, head for the elongated salon that runs parallel with the Ring avenue, just opposite the main University building. At night lots of theatergoers turn up after the Burg has turned out. ⊠ *Dr.-Karl-Lueger-Ring 4, 1st District* ☎ *01/ 532–0621* Ⓤ *U2/Schottenring.*

★ ✕ **Café Mozart.** Graham Greene, staying in the Hotel Sacher next door, loved having his coffee here while working on the script for *The Third Man* (in fact, Greene had the café featured in the film and Anton Karas, the zither player who did the famous Harry Lime theme, wrote a waltz for the place). The café was named after the monument to Mozart (now in the Burggarten) that once stood outside the building; reputedly, Wolfie came here to enjoy his coffee, but the decor is entirely changed from his era. Although overrun with sightseers, the waiters are charming as all get out and manage to remain calm even when customers run them ragged. Crystal chandeliers, a brass-and-oak interior, comfortable seating, and delicious food—the excellent Tafelspitz here has to be mentioned— add to its popularity. No matter that it appears full most of the time—a waiter will always help you to find a seat. If it turns out you want more room, head to the outdoor Schanigarten terrace—but not until you've peeked inside the door to see the array of mouth-watering cakes and pastries in the glass case. With the state opera house just behind the café, this is a fine place for an after-performance snack. Be on the lookout for opera divas doing just the same. ⊠ *Albertinaplatz 2 1st District* ☎ *01/ 2410–0210* ⊕ *www.cafe-wien.at/* Ⓤ *U1, U2, or U4/Karlsplatz/Oper.*

$$ ✕ **Café Museum.** The controversial architect Adolf Loos (famed for his pronouncement: "Ornament is a sin") laid the foundation stone for this "puristically" styled coffeehouse in 1899. Throughout the past century, this was a top rendezvous spot for Wien Secession artists, along with actors, students, and professors due to the proximity of the Secession Pavilion, the Academy of Fine Arts, the Theater an der Wien, and Vienna's Technical University. Gustav Klimt, Egon Schiele, and Josef Hoffmann all enjoyed sipping their Melange here. Today, after years of intensive and painstaking restoration (following Loos's detailed documents discovered in the Albertina), it once again lives up to its former glory. Although some patrons complain about the loss of patina and charm, gone are the threadbare upholstery and the drab, yellowing interior, and in today's new light and airy atmosphere, you can while away the hours daily from 8 AM (Sunday from 10 AM) until midnight perusing an array of national and international newspapers and magazines. Excellent food, fine wines, and a wide range of pastries, cakes, and good coffee can also be enjoyed. ⊠ *Friedrichstrasse 6, 1st District* ☎ *01/586– 5202* Ⓤ *U1, U2, or U4/Karlsplatz/Oper.*

✕ **Café Prueckel.** Although this is a great favorite with young hip students at the nearby Academy of Applied Arts, the Prueckel has a smoky atmosphere that can get to be too much. Recent renovation has given a shine to its 1950s-era style. It has to be said that the food is good and lunch menus are excellent value for money. What saves the Prueckel is the fact that you can sit outside in the large Schanigarten enjoying the afternoon sun just across the street. If you don't mind the smoke, there's

VIENNA'S SWEETEST VICE

MANY THINK THAT THE CHIEF contribution of the people who created the Viennese waltz and the operetta naturally comes with the dessert course, in the appropriate form of rich and luscious pastries, and in the beloved and universal Schlagobers (whipped cream). Most people would agree that the finest pastry shops and confectioners are found in Vienna. There is even one place where you can stand and watch the confectioner at work. Watch the cakes being iced, marzipan figures shaped to form flower petals, strudels being rolled, or chocolate being poured over the dark sponge. Mmmmmmmmmm . . . Spend an afternoon at one of these places and you'll understand why the Viennese consider whipped cream to be one of the four main food groups.

First stop for sweet lovers, pastry fans, and marzipan maniacs has to be **Demel** (⊠ Kohlmarkt 14, 1st District ☎ 01/535-1717-0), a 200-year-old confectioner famous for its sweetmeats that make every heart beat faster (and eventually slower). The display cases are filled to the brim; all you have to do is point at what you want and then go and sit where you want. But don't forget to watch the pastry chef at work in the glassed-over, glassed-in courtyard. If you belong to those who like to see freak shows, then peep into the cellar and see the Marzipan Museum with a strange display of famous heads— among others Bill Clinton, Barbara Cartland, and Kofi Annan—in colored marzipan.

Beyond the shop proper are stairs that lead to dining salons where the decor is almost as sweet as the chocolates, marzipan, and sugar-coated almonds on sale. **Gerstner** (⊠ Kärntnerstrasse 13–15 ☎ 01/5124963) is in the heart of the bustling Kärntnerstrasse and is one of the best places for the dark, moist, mouthwatering poppy-seed cake (Mohntorte), carrot cake, and chocolate-dipped strawberries. Its decor is modern but the place has been here since the mid-18th century. **Heiner** (⊠ Kärntnerstrasse 21–23 ☎ 01/512–6863 ⊠ Wollzeile 9 ☎ 01/512–2343) is dazzling for its crystal chandeliers as well as for its pastries. The great favorite here has to be the almond-orange torte. **Oberlaa** (⊠ Neuer Markt 16 ☎ 01/513–2936 ⊠ Babenbergerstrasse 7, opposite Kunsthistoriches Museum ☎ 01/5867–2820 ⊠ Landstrasser Hauptstrasse 1 ☎ 01/7152–7400) has irresistible confections such as the "Oberlaa Kurbad Cake," Truffle Cake, and Chocolate Mousse Cake. Highly popular with the locals and great value for money, there are now six Oberlaa branches to choose from. **Sperl** (⊠ Gumpendorferstrasse 11, 6th District/Mariahilf ☎ 01/586–4158), founded in 1880, has an all-around Old Viennese ambience.

It doesn't really matter which of the many branches of **Aida** (⊠ Neuer Markt 16 ☎ 01/513–2936 ⊠ Opernring 7 ☎ 01/533–1933 ⊠ Bognergasse 3 ☎ 01/533–9442 ⊠ Stock-im-Eisen-Platz 2 ☎ 01/512–2977 ⊠ Wollzeile 28 ☎ 01/512–3724 ⊠ Praterstrasse 78 ☎ 01/216–2137 ⊠ Rotenturmstrasse 24 ☎ 01/58–2585) you go to as they are all quite similar. Aida is most famous for the cheapest cup of (excellent) coffee in town, but the incredibly inexpensive pastries are just fantastic. Since 1971 200 million "Topfengolatschen" (cream-cheese pastries) have been counted and consumed.

piano music on Monday, Wednesday, and Friday evenings from 7 until 10 PM. ⊠ *Stubenring 24, 1st District* ☎ *01/512–6115* Ⓤ *U1 or U3/ Stephansplatz.*

✕ **Café Residenz.** After a visit to Schönbrunn Palace (Austria's most popular tourist site), this on-site café should definitely be on the agenda. If you want to know how to make an Apfelstrudel before you devour one, then go into the historic vaulted kitchen downstairs first, and watch (and possibly help) the cooks at the job. The demonstration takes about 15 to 20 minutes and starts on the hour every hour from 10 until 5 PM. The Schönbrunner apfelstrudeljause includes the demonstration and coffee, tea, or chocolate served with the freshly baked strudel for €7. Upstairs in the wonderfully palatial surroundings of the Residenz there's room to relax and enjoy the most courteous of customs. The waiters and waitresses are congenial and kind, helpful, and humorous. Some say the cuisine matches any of the best restaurants in town and the coffee is very good indeed. ⊠ *Kavalierstrakt 52, Schloss Schönbrunn, 13th District/Hietzing* ☎ *01/817–5715* Ⓤ *U4/Hietzing.*

✕ **Café Sacher.** You'll see people wandering out of this legendary café in a whipped-cream stupor. Yes, you can famously enjoy life at its sweetest here. This legend began life as a *delikatessen* opened by Sacher, court confectioner to Prince von Metternich, the most powerful prime minister in early-19th-century Europe and fervent chocoholic (*see also* this café in "Monarchs & Mozart: From St. Stephan's to the Opera House" *in* Exploring Vienna). Back then, cookbooks of the day devoted more space to desserts than to main courses and Sacher's creations were practically ranked on the order of painting and sculpture. When the populace at large was allowed to enjoy the prime minister's favorite chocolate cake—a sublime mixture of flour, eggs, butter, chocolate, and apricot preserves—the fashion for Sachertorte was created. War-weary Metternich must have been amused to see a battle break out between Sacher and Demel's—a competing confectioner—as to who served the real Sachertorte, but the jury has now awarded the prize to Sacher, after a much-publicized trial, which came to a decision worthy of Solomon, that the original article should be spelled as one word, those others using the similar recipe must use two words. The difference between the Demel version? Sacher puts its apricot jam in the cake middle, while Demel's puts it just below the icing? Which do you prefer (gossip has it that a true Viennese likes Demel's version best)? Red flocks the drapes, walls, and floors here, mirrors and chandeliers add glitter, and there is live piano music every day from 4:30 until 7 PM. ⊠ *Philharmonikerstrasse 4, 1st District* ☎ *01/514560* Ⓤ *U1, U2, or U4/Karlsplatz/Oper.*

✕ **Café Schottenring.** If you're looking for peace and quiet, try this place (wouldn't you know, just across from the Stock Exchange). Restful, relaxing, and quite uneventful, the clientele love the steady way of life in here, and it's been that way for 125 years. Plenty of civil servants come for breakfast, lunch, and anything in between; by mid-afternoon the housewives have moved in. The fare is good and inexpensive, not fancy. ⊠ *Schottenring 19, 1st District* ☎ *01/315–3343* Ⓤ *U2/Schottentor.*

✕ **Café Schwarzenberg.** A bright yellow facade and a large terrace welcomes all to this café. Wall-to-wall mirrors reflect the elegant clientele

THE BEST OF THE WÜRSTS

A sure way to spike a lively discussion among the Viennese is to ask which Würstelstand serves the most delicious grilled sausages. Here are three that are generally acknowledged to be the best.

Ehrenreich's (⊠ Naschmarkt, on the Linke Wienzeile side across from Piccini, under the clock, 1st District ⊘ Closed Sun.) serves scrumptious Käsekrainer (beef sausages oozing with melted cheese), alongside a Semmel (soft roll) and mild, sweet mustard.

Behind the Opera House, Oper (⊠ Corner of Philharmonikerstrasse/Hanuschgasse, 1st District) entices passersby with its plump, sizzling Bratwurst.

Würstelstand am Hoher Markt (⊠ Hoher Markt, corner of Marc-Aurel-Strasse, 1st District) serves American-style hot dogs and is open daily from 7 AM to 5 AM.

perched on green leather seats. Across from the Hotel Imperial, this location is perfect if you want a snack after a concert at the Musikverein or the Konzerthaus, both just a couple of minutes away. Open until midnight, this has a good choice of food and pastries and, even though the waiters can be a little condescending, the overall atmosphere is still nice enough to encourage longer stays. Piano music can be heard until late on Wednesday and Friday, and from 5 until 7 PM on weekends. ⊠ *Kärntner Ring 17, 1st District* ☎ *01/512–8998* Ⓤ *U2/Schottentor.*

Of course, when tourists think of Viennese cafés, Demel and Café Sacher leap to mind, but they are hardly typical. When you want a quick (but excellent) coffee and dessert, look for an **Aida** café; they are scattered throughout the city—see our listings in the Close-Up box, "Vienna's Sweetest Vice."

VIENNA:
WHERE TO STAY

3

By Bonnie
Dodson

RIDING HIGH IN THE COCOON of your horse-drawn *fiaker*—nerves soothed by the clip-clop of hooves on cobblestones—you rest your head against the soft Moroccan leather, the better to observe the grandiose Habsburg-era monuments that stream by. With a sudden shift, the carriage enters a narrow lane behind St. Stephan's cathedral. Much of this neighborhood—still in parts an 18th-century diorama—remains unchanged since Mozart's time and, in fact, he wrote his immortal *Marriage of Figaro* while living at No. 5 Domgasse. As it happens, your carriage pulls up just next door before the König von Ungarn, a hotel that opened in 1815. Inside, a beaming concierge comes from behind his polished mahogany desk to greet you, and while getting you settled confides that Empress "Sisi" used to be a visitor (her Hungarian aristo friends used to rent suites here). Your room, a small attic chamber with the feel of a private apartment, has enough old-fashioned touches to remind you of a grandmother's hoopskirt, right down to the rosewood armoire and featherbed duvet.

If you want Viennese grand instead of Viennese cozy, you'll opt instead to stay at one of those grand Ringstrasse palais that seem to be stage-sets for a production of *Der Rosenkavalier.* Their red velvet–gilt mirror–and–crystal chandelier opulence still stands supreme even in today's world of lavish hospitality, and these establishments pride themselves on staff that appear to anticipate your every desire. Of course, such grand service and profound luxuries come with a heady price, but for those with more modest requirements, and purses, ample rooms are available in less costly but entirely adequate hotels. No matter if the high-flown elegance is sparse and the layers of charm a bit thin, most of our lower-price options offer the best in location, value, and, in many instances, a quaint echo of Alt Wien (Old Vienna) atmosphere.

Other than the palace hotels around the Ringstrasse, where are the most delightful neighborhoods to rest your head? The "Biedermeier" quarter of Spittelberg has cobblestone streets, lots of 19th-century houses, and a wonderful array of art galleries and restaurants and, increasingly, hotel options. To the east is the fabulous MuseumsQuartier, where you'll also discover some nice hotel finds. Schwedenplatz is the area fronted by the Danube Canal—a neighborhood that is one of the most happening in the city. Other sweet hotel options are set in the Josefstadt area—a district noted for antique shops, good local restaurants, bars, and theater. Shop-till-you-droppers will want to stay near the designer shops of the 1st District, as well as the posh Ringstrasse Galerie shopping mall, or along the Mariahilferstrasse, the Champs-Elysées of Vienna.

Our hotel categories correspond more or less to the official Austrian rating system, with five stars the equivalent of our very expensive ($$$$) category. Air-conditioning is customary in the top category only (and sometimes in the $$$ and $$–$$$ categories), but since Vienna has very few extremely hot days, with temperatures cooling off at night, it's usually not necessary. Assume that all guest rooms have air-conditioning, room phones, and room TVs unless noted otherwise. Pets are welcomed in most hotels, but you must pay a small surcharge, usually between €8 and €15 per night; inquire when booking. Note that neighborhoods are *only* listed for those hotels and pensions that are outside the central 1st District.

The Lanes of St. Stephan's

Clustered around the medieval Stephansdom cathedral in the heart of Vienna are little cobblestone lanes with charming hotels, some of them hundreds of years old, and none that will make you open the wallet too far.

$$$ ▦ **Kaiserin Elisabeth.** Named after the unhappy 19th-century wife of Emperor Franz Josef, Elisabeth, this unassuming hotel offers a splendid domed drawing room that wouldn't be out of place in the Hofburg palace, though alas, the rooms don't live up to the grandeur of its imperial namesake. More reminiscent of the 1970s than Biedermeier Vienna, they contain nice Oriental rugs, but a few display rather sad, worn bedspreads and frosted windows (making it impossible to look out on the quaint street below). Baths are without character and a trifle small. Still, you're in a superb location around the corner from St. Stephan's (and across the street from the Drei Husaren), and the staff is eager to please. ⊠ *Weihburggasse 3, A–1010* ☎ *01/51526* 🖷 *01/515–267* ⊕ *www. kaiserinelisabeth.at* ⇥ *63 rooms* ☖ *Minibars, bar, Internet; no a/c in some rooms* ▭ *AE, DC, MC, V* ¶◎¶ *BP* Ⓤ *U1 or U4/Stephansplatz.*

$$$ ▦ **König von Ungarn.** In a dormered, 16th-century house in the shadow
Fodor'sChoice of St. Stephan's Cathedral, this hotel began catering to court nobility
★ in 1815—many Hungarian aristos rented rooms here back when. Famously, the complex is joined to the Figarohaus—an adjacent house where, as it turns out, Mozart lived when he wrote *The Marriage of Figaro.* Wolfie would undoubtedly cotton to this hostelry, now outfitted with the glowing "Mozartstuberl" restaurant, which is beautifully aglow in "Schönbrunn yellow"; a courtyard-atrium (so gigantic a tree sprouts in the middle of it); and guest rooms that radiate charm: some with Styrian wood-paneled walls are furnished with country antiques and have walk-in closets and double sinks in the sparkling bathrooms. The eight suites are two-storied, and two have balconies with rooftop views of Old Vienna. The inviting atrium bar, bedecked with marble columns, ferns, and hunting trophies, beckons you in to sit and have a drink. Needless to say, this is a highly popular option, so insist on written confirmation of bookings. ⊠ *Schulerstrasse 10, A–1010* ☎ *01/515–840* 🖷 *01/515–848* ⊕ *www.kvu.at* ⇥ *33 rooms* ☖ *Restaurant, minibars, bar, Internet* ▭ *DC, MC, V* ¶◎¶ *BP* Ⓤ *U1 or U4/Stephansplatz.*

$$ ▦ **Royal.** Around the corner from St. Stephan's and Kärntnerstrasse, this standard-issue modern hotel is on the site of a former pilgrim hostel from the early 16th century. It was destroyed in World War II and rebuilt in dreary 1960s fashion. However, all the guest rooms are piquantly decorated, in "Art Nouveau" and "Biedermeier" styles; despite the prime location, none have a great view. The hotel's Italian restaurant, Firenze Enoteca, is favored by opera singers, including Pavarotti (note that Richard Wagner's piano is on display in the lobby). In summer the restaurant also operates Settimo Cielo (Seventh Heaven), set on the rooftop terrace, complete with glass-roof and a spectacular view of the Graben and St. Stephan's. ⊠ *Singerstrasse 3, A–1010* ☎ *01/51568–0* 🖷 *01/513–9698* ⊕ *www.kremslehnerhotels.at* ⇥ *81 rooms* ☖ *2 restaurants, minibars; no a/c* ▭ *AE, DC, MC, V* ¶◎¶ *BP.*

Prices

According to recent surveys, Vienna is the third most expensive city in Europe for travelers, after London and Paris. Though Vienna has never been known as a bargain travel destination, it's still possible to stay in reasonably priced and even cheap hotels or pensions in the city center that are clean, pleasant, and often captivating. Mid-level hotels are the most varying in price, with no apparent reason for some of them costing over €200 a night while others charge less and offer more. If you're driving into town, many hotels have garage parking, either in the building or at a protected facility within a couple of blocks, though you'll pay an average of €25 a night for the privilege. You can count on breakfast (Frühstück) being included in the room price except at the top luxury five-star hotels; most, but not all, seasonal hotels and youth hostels include breakfast. Even in the most humble pension, breakfast usually includes coffee or tea and a buffet of rolls, butter, and marmalade, along with a selection of cheese and cold cuts. Sometimes yogurt, fresh fruit, muesli, and dry cereals are available as well. And at some of the better hotels you may be offered a boiled egg, or there will be a chafing dish of scrambled eggs and bacon. Juice is often of the packaged variety. At the finest hotels, breakfast is almost always extra, but expect fresh-squeezed orange juice and a buffet fit for an emperor for your money. Price categories are assigned based on the range between the least and most expensive standard double rooms in non-holiday high season and prices listed include all taxes.

WHAT IT COSTS In euros				
$$$$	$$$	$$	$	¢
HOTELS Over €270	€170–€270	€120–€170	€80–€120	Under €80

Prices are for two people in a standard double room in high season, including taxes and service charge.

Reservations

The busiest months for Vienna hotels are April, May, September, and October. Travelers arrive en masse at peak points during the year. These begin with springtime, when Vienna is at its prettiest, with its burst of chestnut blossoms and flowers, but autumn is also alluring, with mild temperatures and leaves changing color along the Ringstrasse. Because of the famous Christmas markets, the weeks leading up to the holidays are also a popular time, as well as the week around New Year's (Silvester), with all the orchestral concerts. Expect to pay accordingly, and, at the very top hotels, a lot (around €300–€550 a night). Reservations should be made well in advance. Surprisingly, summer months are not as busy, perhaps because the opera is not in season. You'll find good bargains at this time of year, especially in August. Vienna summers are usually full of warm, sunny days, and it hardly ever gets uncomfortably hot. But no matter how high the temperature soars during the day, it always cools off in the evenings. Note that the Vienna tourist office can assist in getting hotel rooms, even at the last minute.

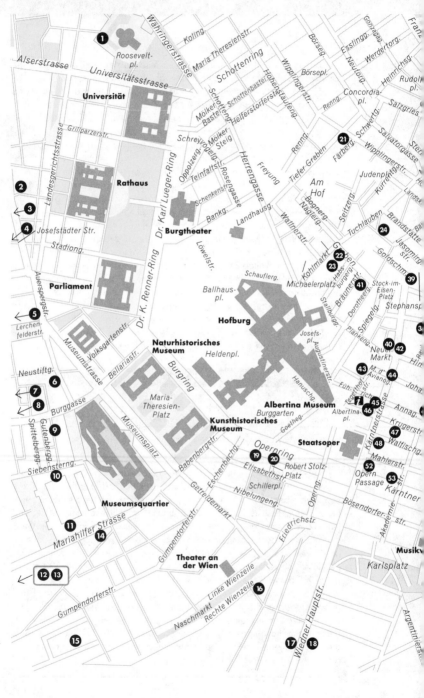

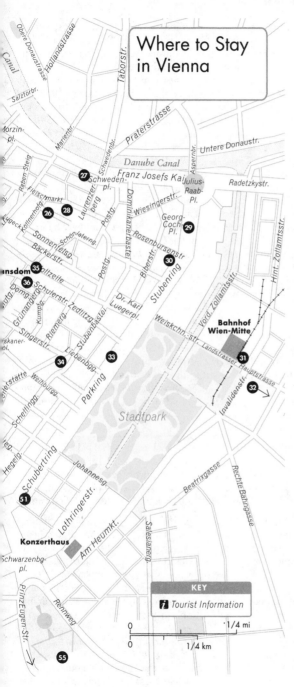

Where to Stay in Vienna

Altstadt **7**
Ambassador **44**
Am Stephansplatz **39**
Arenberg **30**
Astoria **45**
Austria **28**
Biedermeier im Sünnhof **32**
Bristol **52**
Das Triest **18**
Drei Kronen **16**
Erzherzog Rainer **17**
Europa **42**
Fürstenhof **13**
Graben **41**
Graf-Stadion **4**
Grand Hotel Wien **53**
Hilton Stadtpark **31**
Imperial **54**
K&K Maria Theresia **8**
Kaiserin Elisabeth **38**
Kärntnerhof **26**
König von Ungarn **35**
Kugel **10**
Kummer **11**
Le Méredien **19**
Mailberger Hof **49**
Museum **6**
Neuer Markt **40**
Opernring **20**
Palais Coburg **34**
Palais Schwarzenberg **55**
Pension Aviano **43**
Pension Christina **27**
Pension City **25**
Pension Domizil **36**
Pension Nossek **22**
Pension Pertschy **23**
Pension Reimer **12**
Pension Riedl **29**
Pension Suzanne **48**
Pension Wild **5**
Pension Zipser **2**
Radisson **33**
Rathaus Wine & Design **3**
Regina **1**
Römischer Kaiser **50**
Royal **37**
Sacher **45**
Schubertring **51**
Tigra **21**
Tulbingerkogel **15**
Tyrol **14**
ViennArt **9**
Wandl **24**
Zur Wiener Staatsoper **47**

$$ ▦ **Am Stephansplatz.** You can't get a better location than this, directly across from the magnificent front entrance of St. Stephan's Cathedral. Despite this modern hotel's gray, lackluster facade, it offers surprisingly nice, spacious rooms furnished with Turkish carpets, lovely prints and paintings, and elegant furniture. Some rooms are a bit over the top with red wallpaper, but others have more subtle shades of pale yellow and beige. If the bells from the cathedral pose a problem, ask for a room facing the inner courtyard. ⊠ *Stephansplatz 9, A–1010* ☎ *01/53405–0* 🖷 *01/53405–710* ⊕ *www.nethotels.com/am_stephansplatz* 🛏 *57 rooms* ₺ *Café, minibars, Internet; no a/c* ⊟ *AE, DC, MC, V* ⏐◯⏐ *BP* Ⓤ *U1 or U4/Stephansplatz.*

$$ ▦ **Pension Domizil.** Around the corner from the house where Mozart wrote *The Marriage of Figaro,* the Domizil offers quiet, well-equipped rooms furnished with rather bland contemporary furniture. Breakfast is a notch above the average, with both hot and cold selections. Another nice thing about staying here is free access to the Internet in the lobby. The staff is pleasant, and you're right in the middle of a series of charming Old World cobblestone streets near St. Stephan's. ⊠ *Schulerstrasse 14* ☎ *01/513–3199–0* 🖷 *01/512–3484* ⊕ *www.hoteldomizil.at* 🛏 *40 rooms* ₺ *Internet; no a/c* ⊟ *AE, DC, MC, V* ⏐◯⏐ *BP* Ⓤ *U1 or U4/Stephansplatz.*

$ ▦ **Pension City.** You'll be on historic ground here: in 1791 the noted Austrian playwright and critic Franz Grillparzer was born in the house that then stood here; a bust and plaques in the entryway commemorate him. On the second floor of the present 100-year-old house, about three minutes away from St. Stephan's Cathedral, the rooms are outfitted in a successful mix of modern and 19th-century antique furniture against white walls. The baths are small but complete. ⊠ *Bauernmarkt 10, A–1010* ☎ *01/533–9521* 🖷 *01/535–5216* ⊕ *www.inthotels.com* 🛏 *19 rooms* ₺ *Minibars; no a/c* ⊟ *AE, DC, MC, V* ⏐◯⏐ *BP* Ⓤ *U1 or U4/Stephansplatz.*

From the Hofburg to the Graben

From the imposing grandeur of the Habsburg imperial palace to the ancient Graben (the former moat surrounding the palace) are streets—many of them pedestrian—lined with some of the poshest shops and cafés in the city. Tucked in between, or sometimes above a shop, are some wonderful hostelry finds, very reasonably priced, considering their location.

$$–$$$ ▦ **Wandl.** The restored facade identifies a 300-year-old house that has been in family hands as a hotel since 1854. You couldn't find a better location, tucked behind St. Peter's Church, just off the Graben. The hallways are punctuated by cheerful, bright openings along the glassed-in inner court. The rooms are modern, but some are a bit plain and charmless, despite parquet flooring and red accents. If you can, ask for one of the rooms done in period furniture, with decorated ceilings and gilt mirrors; they're rather palatial, with plush Victorian chairs, carved wood trim, and velvet throws. ⊠ *Petersplatz 9, A–1010* ☎ *01/534–55–0* 🖷 *01/534–55–77* ⊕ *www.hotel-wandl.com* 🛏 *138 rooms* ₺ *Bar, Internet; no a/c* ⊟ *AE, DC, MC, V* ⏐◯⏐ *BP* Ⓤ *U1 or U4/Stephansplatz.*

$$ ▦ **Tigra.** Part of the Best Western group, the Tigra is on a quiet, hidden-away street, midway between St. Stephan's Cathedral and the Ringstrasse.

Two historic buildings, the Gottlieb Fischer House and Johannes Ditscher House, have been joined together to form this pleasant establishment, where the public salons are pure white, cheerfully decorated with colorful drapes and modern sofas and art prints. Mozart lived with his father in each house, first in 1762 when he was ill with scarlet fever, then in 1773, when he composed six string quartets and several choruses of *Thamos, König in Ägypten*. Guest rooms are basic modern, but some are quite large, with sitting areas. Make sure you're not booked into the annex, which means having to go outside and into the main hotel for breakfast. Also, ask for a room away from the elevators because they can be noisy. ⊠ *Tiefer Graben 14–20, A–1010* ☎ *01/533–9641* ᵬ *01/533–9645* ⊕ *www.bestwestern.com/* ↪ *57 rooms* ௸ *Minibars, Internet; no a/c* ⊟ *AE, DC, MC, V* ⑂ *BP* Ⓤ *Herrengasse/U3.*

$$ 🏨 **Graben.** A small, family-run hotel in the heart of the city, the Graben has been in business since the late 18th century. Its tavern was a once popular literati hangout, and Franz Grillprazer, Franz Kafka, and Peter Altenberg made it into a mini-Bohemia—today, they would simply head to the famous and beloved Café Hawelka, across the street. Guest rooms offer an assortment of high ceilings, chandeliers, and antique paintings mixed with durable carpets and modern, unexciting furniture, but several of them have a graceful "Biedermeier" stylistic echo. Some rooms are crying out for refurbishment, but are still comfortable. The best part of staying here is that you can walk virtually everywhere. Insist on a written confirmation of your booking. ⊠ *Dorotheergasse 3, A–1010* ☎ *01/512–1531–0* ᵬ *01/512–1531–20* ⊕ *www.kremslehner.at* ↪ *41 rooms* ௸ *Restaurant, bar, minibars, Internet; no a/c* ⊟ *AE, DC, MC, V* ⑂ *BP* Ⓤ *U1, U2, or U4/Karlsplatz.*

★ **$$** 🏨 **Pension Pertschy.** Housed in the former Palais Cavriani just off the Graben, this pension is as central as you can get—behind the Hofburg and down the street from the Spanish Riding School. One of those typical Viennese mansion-turned-apartment-houses, the structure is still graced with a massive arched portal and yellow-stone courtyard, around which the 18th-century edifice was built. Private apartments occupy some of the building but the Pertschy has taken over most of the town house. A few guest rooms contain lovely old ceramic stoves (just for show). Most rooms are spacious, and each one is comfortable. Some rooms are sweet, with bed canopies and chandeliers, although others are decorated with "repro"—antique furniture that verges on the kitsch. Baths are satisfactory. As for noise, the street outside gets many fiaker carriages (and street sweepers at night!), so opt for a courtyard room if you need complete peace and quiet. Use the elevator, but don't miss the palatial grand staircase. ⊠ *Habsburgergasse 5, A–1010* ☎ *01/534–49–0* ᵬ *01/534–49–49* ⊕ *www.pertschy.com* ↪ *43 rooms* ௸ *Minibars; no a/c* ⊟ *AE, DC, MC, V* ⑂ *BP* Ⓤ *U1 or U4/Stephansplatz.*

★ **$–$$** 🏨 **Pension Nossek.** What a past: Mozart worked on *The Abduction from the Seraglio* while he lived here in the early 1780s. A family-run establishment on the upper floors of a 19th-century office and apartment building, the Nossek lies at the heart of the pedestrian and shopping area. The rooms have high ceilings and are eclectically but comfortably furnished; those on the front have a magnificent view of the Graben. Do as the many regular guests do: book early. ⊠ *Graben 17, A–1010* ☎ *01/533–7041–0* 🖷 *01/535–3646* ⊕ *www.pension-nossek.at* ↷ *27 rooms, 25 with bath* ♿ *Internet; no a/c* ▭ *No credit cards* ⍾ *BP* Ⓤ *U1 or U4/Stephansplatz.*

Along the Kärntnerstrasse

It can be noisy along the city's busiest shopping street, but sometimes it pays to be centrally located.

$$$–$$$$ 🏨 **Ambassador.** Franz Lehár, Marlene Dietrich, the Infanta Isabel of Spain, and Mick Jagger are just a few of the celebrities who have stayed at this old dowager (from 1866), given a face-lift overhaul in 2001. The lobby is small but grand, and the high-ceilinged guest rooms, differing only in size, are uniformly decorated with pale yellow-striped wallpaper, deep blue carpets, and faux Empire furniture. Unless you want the excitement of a direct view onto the lively pedestrian Kärntnerstrasse, ask for one of the quieter rooms on the Neuer Markt side. Don't expect warmth from the staff—the trade-off is the central location. The Ambassador also houses the top-flight restaurant Mörwald, which offers stunning views of the square. ⊠ *Kärntnerstrasse 22/Neuer Markt 5, A–1010* ☎ *01/961610* 🖷 *01/5132–999* ⊕ *www.ambassador.at* ↷ *86 rooms* ♿ *Restaurant, minibars, bar, Internet* ▭ *AE, DC, MC, V* ⍾ *EP* Ⓤ *U1 or U4/Stephansplatz.*

$$$ 🏨 **Astoria.** Built in 1912 and still retaining the outward charm of that era, the Astoria is one of the grand old Viennese hotels and in a superb location on the Kärnterstrasse between the Opera and St. Stephan's. You are greeted by a wood-panel lobby that is an essay in Wiener Werkstätte style. Two of the floors have been renovated and have a lovely, soft contemporary style with pretty fabrics in beige tones, polished dark wood, and Oriental rugs. The other floors retain their old-fashioned appeal, though some are a little worn around the edges. Whatever their style, is there anything nicer than sinking into a downy feather bed after being on your feet all day? Some rooms even have a fireplace and small balcony. Sometimes special prices are offered, which are a tremendous value. ⊠ *Kärntnerstrasse 32–34, A–1010* ☎ *01/51577* 🖷 *01/515–7782* ⊕ *www.austria-trend.at/asw* ↷ *118 rooms* ♿ *Bar, minibars, Internet; no a/c* ▭ *AE, DC, MC, V* ⍾ *BP* Ⓤ *U1 or U4/Stephansplatz.*

$$ 🏨 **Europa.** Renovated from top to bottom, this 1957-vintage hotel greets you with a bright, airy, "International Style" (the sofas are Mies van der Rohe knockoffs) lobby. Upstairs, the minimalist, modern touch continues so guest rooms are, thus, rather charmless. Still, they have all the amenities and their comfortable size means you won't be cramped. The selling point here is the great location directly on the pedestrian Kärntnerstrasse, about halfway between the Opera and St. Stephan's. A nice plus is the substantial breakfast served in the house café with windows overlooking all the bustling activity on the street. The back side of the hotel faces the Neuer Markt, a quiet, pretty square whose focal point is the Kaisergruft, the final resting place of several Habsburg rulers. Rooms on this side are quieter than those on Kärntnerstrasse. ⊠ *Neuer Markt 3, A–1010* ☎ *01/515–94–0* 🖷 *01/515–9438* ⊕ *www.austria-trend.at*

🛏 *113 rooms* ♦ *Restaurant, café, minibars, bar, Internet* ▭ *AE, DC, MC, V* ⥥ *BP* Ⓤ *U1 or U4/Stephansplatz.*

In the Shadow of the Staatsoper

You don't have to be a music lover to stay in this prime location comprising the Ringstrasse area around the State Opera House (Staatsoper) and the small, quiet 18th-century streets leading off the Kärntnerstrasse. But staying in this grand area does have its price, and the closer you are to the Opera, the higher it is.

$$$$ 🏨 **Bristol.** A Bösendorfer grand of a hotel, this venerable landmark, dating from 1892, has one of the finest locations in the city, on the Ring next to the state opera house. The accent here is on tradition—a note struck by the lobby, which is fairly and disappointingly standard-issue when it comes to luxe: the usual oval salons, domed ceilings, traditional overstuffed chairs, modern wood paneling, and potted palms. There are enough chandeliers, surely—too bad there are so many ugly recessed ceiling lights. For real grandeur, you have to book one of the top penthouses and suites, gloriously furnished in Biedermeier style with decorative fireplaces, thick carpets, wing-back chairs, crystal chandeliers, and lace curtains. Penthouse rooms have terraces with staggering views of the Opera. Other rooms miss out on this Ringstrasse splendor but are most comfortable and stylish nevertheless. Sometimes the hotel offers special rates at great value. The Bristol also houses the acclaimed Korso restaurant, the convivial Café Sirk, and a music salon complete with a pianist lulling the after-theater crowd with tunes on a time-burnished—yes—Bösendorfer. ✉ *Kärntner Ring 1, A–1010* ☎ *01/515–16–0* 📠 *01/515–16–550* ⊕ *www.westin.com/bristol* 🛏 *141 rooms* ♦ *2 restaurants, minibars, health club, bar, Internet, business services* ▭ *AE, DC, MC, V* ⥥ *EP* Ⓤ *U1, U2, or U4/Karlsplatz.*

★ $$$$ 🏨 **Le Méridien.** One of Le Méridien's super-cool "art and tech" ventures, their Vienna outpost occupies three former 19th-century Ringstrasse palaces but you'd never know it after one step inside the front door. Sleek as a *Wallpaper* magazine layout, adorned with Mies van der Rohe–style sofas and ottomans, acres of nouvelle fluorescent light panels (which change hue from day to night), and contemporary art renditions of Austrian actors Oskar Werner and Romy Schneider in the spare, minimalist lobby, you know you're in a different kind of Viennese five-star at first glance. Ideally located two minutes from the state opera house, the hotel is also home to Shambala, the luxe restaurant masterminded by Michel Rostang, the Parisian chef-guru—so you can enjoy the latest in Austrian/Asian fusion cuisine (and more than 50 Austrian wines by the glass). Adjacent is a bar that hops with a DJ and some of the hippest people in town. Guest rooms are strikingly decorated with glass headboards, contempo vases, and other cutting-edge items. A survey showed that guests' top three priorities are a great bed, TV, and shower, and they have outdone themselves in providing cloudlike mattresses and soft Turkish bed-linen, flat-screen TVs, and roomy "tower of power" showers with three massaging jets (all baths also include deep clawfoot tubs and heated mirrors to prevent fogging). Outside, visual excitements continue, as the tranquil, soundproofed rooms offer views of the Hofburg, Burggarten, and Ring. Add to this a complimentary minibar and Internet service, and you have the makings for a truly pampered stay, which you can enjoy from the get-go: the stupendous buffet breakfast is arguably the best in the country. ⊠ *Opernring 13, A–1010* ☎ *01/588–900* 🖷 *01/588–9090–90* ⊕ *www.lemeridien.com/austria/vienna/hotel at1806.shtml* ⤳ *294 rooms* ⌂ *Restaurant, café, minibars, bar, Internet, fitness center, indoor pool, no-smoking rooms* ⊟ *AE, DC, MC, V* ⦿ *EP* Ⓤ *U1, U2, or U4/Karlsplatz.*

★ $$$$ 🏨 **Sacher.** One of Europe's legends, originally founded by Eduard Sacher, chef to Prince Metternich—for whom the famous chocolate cake was invented—the Sacher dates from 1876. It has retained its sense of history over the years while providing luxurious, modern-day comfort. The staff is helpful and gracious, in great contrast to decades gone by when most guests got the chilly monocle treatment. Sacher's widow, Anna, turned the hotel into the phenomenon that it still is. In an age when every moment had to be lived in public, her *separé* dining rooms offered privacy and comfort to archdukes and their mistresses, to dancers and their hussars. It was an empire that she watched over, supreme and always with a cigar in her mouth. Today, the corridors serve as a veritable art gallery, and the exquisitely furnished bedrooms also contain original artwork. The location directly behind the Opera House could hardly be more central, and the ratio of staff to guests is more than two to one. Meals in the Red Room are first-rate, with both a continental and Viennese menu. The Café Sacher, of course, is legendary. British director Carol Reed filmed some of his classic 1949 film *The Third Man* in the reception area. During 2004, the hotel carried out a renovation program, which is now complete except for the third floor and the Restaurant Anna Sacher, both of which will reopen sometime in 2005. ⊠ *Philharmonikerstrasse 4, A–1010* ☎ *01/514–56–0* 🖷 *01/514–56–810* ⊕ *www.sacher.com* ⤳ *113 rooms* ⌂ *2 restaurants, café, minibars, bar, Internet, no-smoking rooms* ⊟ *AE, DC, MC, V* ⦿ *EP* Ⓤ *U1, U2, or U3/Karlsplatz.*

$$$ 🏨 **Opernring.** With an ideal location on the Ringstrasse and catercorner from the state opera house, the Opernring has rooms that are nicer than you would imagine considering the rather unprepossessing entrance and lobby. Guest rooms are spacious with good carpets, cheerful and soigne furniture done up in Swedish woods, and sitting areas, and about half have small terraces. Discounts can be arranged for longer stays. ⊠ *Opernring 11, A–1010* ☎ *01/587–5518* 🖷 *01/587–5518–29* ⊕ *www.opernring.at* ⤳ *35 rooms* ⌂ *Minibars, Internet; no a/c* ⊟ *AE, DC, MC, V* ⦿ *BP* Ⓤ *U1, U2, or U4/Karlsplatz.*

★ $$–$$$ 🏨 **Mailberger Hof.** The Knights of Malta—those famous "Hospitallers"—knew something about hospitality and their former Vienna palace continues to offer travelers a comforting welcome mat. You arrive at this Baroque mansion to find an atmospheric carriage entrance and a cobblestoned and captivating courtyard, set in a wonderful location just off the Kärntnerstrasse. A recent renovation has given some of its formerly rather dour rooms some charm, with lovely golden and crimson bedspreads, reproduction furniture, and soft carpets, but most remain traditional in the extreme (that's a compliment for many). The rooms on the first floor are the most attractive; try to get one facing the pretty Baroque street. In summer the inner courtyard is set with tables for dining; at other times, you'll dine on Vienna specialties and "Naturküche" under regal vaulted arches. ⊠ *Annagasse 7, A–1010* ☎ *01/512–0641* 🖷 *01/512–0641–10* ⊕ *www.mailbergerhof.at* ➳ *40 rooms, 5 apartments with kitchenettes, available by the month* 🖏 *Restaurant, minibars, Internet; no a/c in some rooms* ☰ *AE, DC, MC, V* ⊺⊙⊺ *BP* Ⓤ *U1, U2, or U4/Karlsplatz.*

★ **$$–$$$** 🏨 **Römischer Kaiser.** A pastel pink confection of a hotel (with whipped-cream white stone trim), housed in a late-17th-century former town palace between the Opera and St. Stephan's, the Roman Emperor has been host to an impressive musical clientele over the years—Mozart, Liszt, Wagner, Bruckner, and Grieg, to name a few. Happily, a sense of history still pervades throughout, and the elegant guest rooms have real charm, with lots of burnished wood trim and armoires, crystal chandeliers, pale pink or yellow wallpaper, expensive fabrics, and in some of the larger doubles, dramatic tie-back curtains separating the sleeping area. The style of most is staidly, wonderfully "Viennese." A few of the baths—called Versace-style (trumped up with the historicizing motifs of the famous fashion house—are fit for an empress, with pink, white, and gold accents. Breakfast is served in a adorable Louis XVI nook. Pretty, *ja?* ⊠ *Annagasse 16, A–1010* ☎ *01/512–7751–0* 🖷 *01/512–7751–13* ⊕ *www.bestwestern-ce.com/roemischerkaiser* ➳ *24 rooms* 🖏 *Minibars, Internet* ☰ *AE, DC, MC, V* ⊺⊙⊺ *BP* Ⓤ *U1, U2, or U4/Karlsplatz.*

$$ 🏨 **Pension Aviano.** Tucked away in a corner of the Neuer Markt, this small pension is part of the group that owns the well-known Pension Pertschy. Like its sister, this one is set in a 19th-century apartment house, now mostly given over to private apartments, offices, and stores. On the upper stories you'll find the Aviano, whose guest rooms are cheerful and quiet. Some are rather regal, with flocked wallpapers, tiny chandeliers, bed canopies, and other Biedermeier grace notes. The two junior suites have a charming turret where you can sit and gaze out over the rooftops of Vienna. Music lovers favor this option since it is close to the Opera House. In summer, breakfast tables are set outside on the balcony overlooking the inner courtyard. ⊠ *Marco d'Avianogasse 1, A–1010* ☎ *01/512–8330* 🖷 *01/512–8330–6* ⊕ *www.pertschy.com* ➳ *17 rooms* 🖏 *Minibars, Internet; no a/c* ☰ *DC, MC, V* ⊺⊙⊺ *BP* Ⓤ *U1 or U4/Stephansplatz.*

$–$$ 🏨 **Zur Wiener Staatsoper.** A great deal of loving care has gone into this family-owned hotel near the State Opera, reputed to be one of the Viennese settings in John Irving's *The Hotel New Hampshire*. The florid facade, with oversize torsos supporting its upper bays, is pure 19th-century Ringstrasse style. Rooms are small but have high ceilings and are charmingly decorated with pretty fabrics and wallpaper. ⊠ *Krugerstrasse 11, A–1010* ☎ *01/513–1274–0* 🖷 *01/513–1274–15* ⊕ *www.zurwienerstaatsoper.at* ➳ *22 rooms* 🖏 *No a/c* ☰ *AE, MC, V* ⊺⊙⊺ *BP* Ⓤ *U1, U2, or U4/Karlsplatz.*

$ 🏨 **Neuer Markt.** At the head of the famous and beautiful Neuer Markt square, steps away from the lively Kärntnerstrasse, St. Stephan's, and the Opera, you'll find this rather grand building. Constructed in the early years of the 20th century and adorned with mansard roof and scalloped marble trim, the third and fourth floors of this attractive pastel-yellow structure contain this pension. Its guest rooms are modern, comfortable, and pleasant, though a few, unfortunately, have astro turf carpeting and dated plywood paneling. The main drawback here are the thin walls, which means you'll hear hallway noise or possibly your neighbors in the next room. The staff tries its best to make you feel at home by their friendliness (and willingness to make phone calls for you). If street noise bothers you, ask for a room overlooking the courtyard or Seilergasse. ⊠ *Seilergasse 9, A–1010* ☎ *01/512–2316* 🖷 *01/513–9105* ⊕ *www. hotelpension.at/neuermarkt* 🛏 *37 rooms* ♿ *No a/c* ☰ *AE, DC, MC, V* ⦿ *BP* Ⓤ *U1 or U4/Stephansplatz.*

$ 🖼 **Pension Suzanne.** The Opera House is a stone's throw from this 1950s building on a small side street off the Ring. Don't be deceived by the nondescript exterior; once you step inside the doors of the pension you'll be enveloped in Viennese warmth and coziness. Most rooms are not spacious, but all are charmingly and comfortably furnished in 19th-century Biedermeier style. Baths are modern, although short on shelf space. Breakfast is on the skimpy side, but that leaves room for sampling some of the delectable pastries from nearby cafés. You'll be able to walk to nearly all major sights from this location. ⊠ *Walfischgasse 4, A–1010* ☎ *01/513–2507–0* 🖷 *01/513–2500* ⊕ *www.pension-suzanne.at* 🛏 *26 rooms* ♿ *Internet; no a/c* ☰ *AE, MC, V* ⦿ *BP* Ⓤ *U1, U2, or U4/Karlsplatz.*

South of the Ring to the Belvedere

Palaces, palaces, and more palaces! If you want to live like an emperor and empress, direct the driver of your carriage to take you along the Ringstrasse to the area around the Schwarzenbergplatz, where you'll have your pick of regal hotel-palaces to choose from.

$$$$ 🖼 **Imperial.** One of the great landmarks of the Ringstrasse, this hotel
FodorśChoice has exemplified the grandeur of imperial Vienna ever since Emperor Franz
★ Josef formerly opened its doors in 1873. Adjacent to the famed Musikverein concert hall and two blocks from the Staatsoper, the emphasis here is on Old Vienna elegance and privacy, which accounts for a guest book littered with names like Elizabeth Taylor, Plácido Domingo, and Bruce Springsteen. Originally the home of Duke Philipp von Württemberg, this monstrously large "Ringstrasse Palais" was a monument of 19th-century style whose architectural model derived from Baroque Roman palaces. Today the lobby and state rooms remain a symphony of potted-palm luxe. Don't overlook, as if you could, the grand marble staircase, a wonder in colored marbles modeled on the one in Munich's court library. The main lobby—a two-story yellow-marble affair with towering pilasters and coiffured ceiling—looks as opulent as a Hofburg ballroom. On the ground floor is the true showpiece: the Marmorsaal, or Marble Hall, where you can now dine amid Corinthian columns and gold-leafed "groteschi" designs or enjoy drinks. Upstairs, the reception floor is filled with rooms done in whipped cream neo-Rococo. As for the beautiful guest rooms, they are furnished with sparkling chandeliers,

gorgeously swagged fabrics, and original 19th-century paintings. The larger suites are found on the lower floor; as you ascend, guest rooms get smaller, but those on the top floor are done in an enchanting Biedermeier style, and several have small terraces offering amazing views of the city. Suites come with your own personal butler. The hotel also houses the Imperial restaurant and the Imperial Café, which headlines the famed, handmade Imperial torte. ⊠ *Kärntner Ring 16, A–1010* ☎ *01/501–10–0* 🖷 *01/501–10–410* ⊕ *www.luxurycollection.com/ imperial* ↪ *138 rooms* △ *Restaurant, café, minibars, gym, piano bar, Internet, no-smoking rooms* ⊟ *AE, DC, MC, V* ⫶❍⫶ *EP* Ⓤ *U1, U2, or U4/Karlsplatz.*

★ $$$$ 🏨 **Palais Coburg.** Across from the Stadtpark and discreetly set behind the original Wasserkunst *bastei* wall that once enclosed the city is the 19th-century white palace once known throughout the city as "Fort Aspargus," due to the slender marble columns that adorn the garden facade. Built as the home for the princes of Saxe-Coburg-Kohary), the last of that line died out in 1978 and the palace was used for offices until a private buyer invested millions in this new resurrection. The family carriage used to sweep through what is now the lobby, now all ablaze with modern white stone and plate glass. Duke Ferdinand, however, would find comfort in the fact that up the grand staircase his Blue Salon and Chinese Salon remain the same, as does the hyperopulent pink-and-yellow marble ballroom where Johann Strauss conducted his orchestra as dancers waltzed across the parquet floor. There are no double rooms here, only deluxe modern or imperial-style suites, all named after Coburg titles. Many of them are spectacular two-storied showpieces, the best done in a gilded-yellow 19th-century Biedermeier or Empire style. All offer fresh flowers, fully equipped kitchenettes with a complimentary stock of champagne, wine, beer, and soft drinks (replenished daily), espresso makers, laptops with free Internet, and two bathrooms, some with gigantic whirlpool baths and saunas, along with separate showers with gold faucets. Some of the suites have a large terrace with lordly views of the Stadtpark or St. Stephan's spire (others look out on unprepossessing modern hotels). Popular in its own right is the house restaurant, manned by one of the most famous chefs in the country, Christian Petz. All in all, the Coburg succeeds as an eye-knocking marriage of 19th-century luxe and 21st-century comfort. ⊠ *Coburgbastei 4, A–1010* ☎ *01/51818–0* 🖷 *01/51818–1* ⊕ *www.palaiscoburg.at* ↪ *33 suites* △ *Restaurant, bar, minibars, Internet, indoor pool, fitness room* ⊟ *AE, DC, MC, V* ⫶❍⫶ *EP* Ⓤ *U1, U2, or U4/Karlsplatz.*

★ $$$$ 🏨 **Palais Schwarzenberg.** It's not every day you get to call a palace designed by Lukas von Hildebrandt (architect of the nearby Belvedere Palace) and Fischer von Erlach (whose Karlskirche crowns the nearby skyline) your home-away-from-home. But this enchanting residence allows you to feel like a prince—Prince Adam Franz zu Schwarzenberg, to be exact, who completed the mansion in 1716—or his princess. Complete with five historic salons, including the Marmorsaal, one of Vienna's most glittering ballrooms, this hotel has everything, including a 16-acre private park. Though it's just a few minutes' walk from the heart of the city, the hotel feels like a country estate—the loudest sounds you'll often hear are the thwack of croquet balls on the lawn. Guest rooms are individually and luxuriously appointed, with the family's original artwork adorning the walls; only those with ultramodern tastes will want to book the suites by Italian designer Paolo Piva, in a separate wing in the park. All bathrooms are sleekly done, with heated towel racks and long, deep bathtubs. Happily, you don't have to be a guest here to come for a drink, coffee, or light lunch, served outside on the terrace in summer—overlooking the formal gardens studded with marble statues, this is one of Vienna's most gorgeous settings—or beside a roaring fireplace in the palace's Kamminzimmer salon in winter. ⊠ *Schwarzenbergplatz 9, 3rd District/Landstrasse* ☎ *01/798–4515* 🖷 *01/798–4714* ⊕ *www.palais-schwarzenberg.com* ⟋ *44 rooms* ⟋ *Restaurant, minibars, tennis court, bar, Internet, free parking* ▭ *AE, DC, MC, V* ⏐◯⏐ *EP* Ⓤ *U1, U2, or U4/Karlsplatz.*

$ 🔲 **Pension Riedl.** Not far from Schwedenplatz, and across the square from the Postsparkasse, the 19th-century postal savings bank designed by Otto Wagner, this small establishment set back from the Ring offers modern, pleasant rooms with cable TV. One pretty room has a small balcony filled with flower pots. As an added touch, breakfast is delivered to your room. Cheerful owner Maria Felser is happy to arrange concert tickets and tours. The Stubentor tram and U-Bahn stop is just steps away. ⊠ *Georg-Coch-Platz 3/4/10, A–1010* ☎ *01/512–7919* 🖷 *01/512–79198* ⊕ *www.pensionriedl.at* ⟋ *8 rooms* ⟋ *No a/c* ▭ *DC, MC, V* ☾ *Closed first 2 wks of Feb.* ⏐◯⏐ *BP* Ⓤ *Stubentor/U3 or Schwedenplatz/U1 or U4.*

The Ringstrasse, Stadtpark & Beyond

The Ringstrasse circles the old city just as the ancient wall did before it—while still the main artery of the city, not all of it is lined with grand buildings and exclusive shopping. A few hotels face the greenery of the Stadtpark, which is perfect for a morning jog or afternoon stroll.

$$$$ 🔲 **Grand Hotel Wien.** Vienna's first luxury hotel, dating from 1870, the Grand is still a favored option for those who want Ringstrasse luxury. However, this hotel has been so highly renovated that the time-burnished ambience is hard to find. Instead, faux-Fragonard murals, acres of blindingly white marble floors, a Trumpily gilded staircase, and spotlights galore lend a bit of a Las Vegas air to it all. Its location remains tops, right next to the city's premier shopping mall. Where the Grand still comes through loud and clear are its guest rooms, which are all done in great taste. The top of the line are truly sumptuous, with chandeliers, tasseled drapes, brocade wallpaper, and elegant antique-style furniture, yet they are also high-tech. A simple touch of a button will do everything from closing your drapes to lighting the DO NOT DISTURB sign outside your door. Baths are Italian marble, and Frette terry robes are provided for lounging. Each of the eight suites is fit for a king, but even the smaller rooms are graceful and alluring. The hotel also houses the excellent Le Ciel restaurant on the top floor, with an innovative Continental menu, and Vienna's only authentic Japanese restaurant, Unkai, along with two cafés and bars. ⊠ *Kärntner Ring 9, A–1010* ☎ *01/515–800* 🖷 *01/515–*

1313 ⊕ www.grandhotelwien.com ☞ 197 rooms, 8 suites ⚴ 2 restaurants, 2 cafés, kitchenettes, minibars, gym, 2 bars, Internet, meeting rooms ⊟ AE, DC, MC, V ⏍ EP Ⓤ U1, U2, or U4/Karlsplatz.

$$–$$$$ 🏨 **Hilton Stadtpark.** Famous Austrian architect Hans Hollein added his modernist flair to this Hilton 1960s-highrise by creating a series of glass "waves" that wrap around the lower level of the building to reflect the trees in the city park across the street. Inside, the stylish lobby displays artworks by prominent Austrian artists. All rooms are the same size, rather smallish though not cramped, but the stupendous views of the Stadtpark and Vienna skyline more than make up for any lack of space. It's always apparent when a hotel pays attention to little details, and the Hilton abounds in this. The rooms manage to be cheerful and calming, and baths have state-of-the-art faucets and pretty green grouting between the sparkling white tiles. The house restaurant, S'parks (so-named because it's practically in the Stadtpark) is excellent, serving Austrian nouvelle cuisine, while on the basement level, the jazz club, Birdland, is masterminded by jazz great Joe Zawinul. Breakfast, which is extra, is a buffet feast that can keep you going all day. *⊠ Am Stadtpark 3, A–1030 ☎ 01/71700–0 ☒ 01/713–0691 ⊕ www.hilton.com ☞ 527 rooms ⚴ Restaurant, bar, minibars, Internet, fitness room ⊟ AE, DC, MC, V ⏍ EP Ⓤ U4/Stadtpark.*

★ $$$ 🏨 **Biedermeier im Sünnhof.** On a cobblestoned passageway, this jewel of a hotel is tucked into a renovated 1820s house that even with all modern facilities still conveys a feeling of Old Vienna. The rooms are compact but efficient, the public areas tastefully done in the Biedermeier style, and the service is friendly. The courtyard passageway around which the hotel is built has attracted a number of interesting boutiques and handicrafts shops, but at times there is an excess of coming and going as tour groups are accommodated. It's about a 20-minute walk or a six-minute subway ride from the center of the city. *⊠ Landstrasser Hauptstrasse 28, 3rd District/Landstrasse ☎ 01/716–71–0 ☒ 01/716–71–503 ⊕ www.dorint.de ☞ 203 rooms ⚴ Restaurant, minibars, bar, Internet, parking (fee) ⊟ AE, DC, MC, V ⏍ BP Ⓤ Between 2 stops, Landstrasse/U3 or U4 or Rochusgasse/U3.*

★ $$$ 🏨 **Radisson.** One of the handsomest of all Ringstrassen palaces comprises the core of Radisson's Vienna outpost. Along with the fin-de-siècle Palais Leitenberger, the Palais Henckel von Donnersmarck, built in 1872, was occupied by an exceedingly patrician family, and their taste shows in the superbly designed facade, articulated with window pediments and caryatids. Inside, a grand staircase leads you up to a gallery of ancestral portraits, spotlighted in a sober marble hall. The location is also princely—directly across from the Stadtpark, Vienna's main city park. Inside, the rooms are done in an understated, traditional, and soigné manner. Quiet and comfortable, some have pretty floral drapes and matching bedspreads, others allure with a more masculine Biedermeier look. The staff is ready to help with anything and Le Siecle restaurant offers food as stylish as its decor. *⊠ Parkring 16, A–1010 ☎ 01/515170 ☒ 01/512–2216 ⊕ www.radissonsas.com ☞ 246 rooms ⚴ 2 restaurants, café, minibars, gym, bar, Internet ⊟ AE, DC, MC, V ⏍ EP Ⓤ U4/Stadtpark.*

$$ 🏨 **Schubertring.** The fantastic location on the Ringstrasse—with the Opera House down the street and the Musikverein and Konzerthaus a few steps away—make this small hotel a popular choice for music lovers. The lobby and breakfast room are on the generic side but most guest rooms are cozily furnished with a very fetching mix of modern pieces and reproduction antiques. Windows are on the small side since all rooms are on the top floor of the building, but this also ensures the utmost quiet. A nice plus at this price: all rooms have air-conditioning. ⊠ *Schubertring 11, A–1010* ☎ *01/717020* 🖷 *01/713–9366* ⊕ *www. schubertring.at* 🛏 *35 rooms* ♨ *Some kitchenettes, minibars, bar, Internet* ⊟ *AE, DC, MC, V* ⦿| *BP* Ⓤ *U1, U2, or U4/Karlsplatz.*

Schwedenplatz

The neighborhood fronted by the Danube Canal is one of the most happening areas of Vienna, headlined by a strong nightlife scene and lots of ethnic restaurants. But, on the other side of the coin, you'll also find one of the oldest enclaves in the city, with cobblestoned lanes nestled around St. Ruprecht's church, founded in the 11th century.

$$ 🏨 **Arenberg.** Near Schwedenplatz and the Danube Canal, the Arenberg is an old-fashioned pension with lots of character. Despite its corner location on the Ringstrasse, serenity reigns, because the pension is on the upper floors of the building. Rooms have a charming, old-fashioned appearance, with plump beds, overstuffed chairs, and patterned carpets. The No. 1 streetcar is virtually outside the front door, allowing easy access to the city center, or you can walk about 10 minutes up the Ring. ⊠ *Stubenring 2, A–1010* ☎ *01/512–5291* 🖷 *01/513–9356* ⊕ *www. arenberg.at* 🛏 *22 rooms* ♨ *Internet; no a/c* ⊟ *AE, DC, MC, V* ⦿| *BP* Ⓤ *U1 or U4/Schwedenplatz.*

$–$$ 🏨 **Austria.** This older house, tucked away on a tiny cul-de-sac, offers the ultimate in quiet and is only five minutes' walk from the heart of the city. The high-ceiling rooms are pleasing in their combination of dark wood and lighter walls; the decor is mixed, with Oriental carpets on many floors. Rooms without full bath are a bit cheaper. There is a nice courtyard terrace that is perfect for sipping coffee after a day of sightseeing. You'll feel at home here, and the staff will help you find your way around town. ⊠ *Wolfengasse 3, Fleischmarkt, A–1010* ☎ *01/ 515–23–0* 🖷 *01/515–23–506* ⊕ *www.hotelaustria-wien.at* 🛏 *46 rooms, 42 with bath* ♨ *Minibars, Internet; no a/c* ⊟ *AE, DC, MC, V* ⦿| *BP* Ⓤ *U1 or U4/Schwedenplatz.*

$–$$ 🏨 **Kärntnerhof.** Behind the "Maria Theresa yellow" facade of this 100-year-old building, on a quiet corner, lies one of the friendliest small hotels in the center of the city. Take the restored Biedermeier elevator to the guest rooms upstairs, which are standard-issue, with antique repros and modern baths. The staff is willing to try to land theater and concert tickets for "sold-out" performances and will happily put together special outing programs for guests. ⊠ *Grashofgasse 4, A–1010* ☎ *01/ 512–1923–0* 🖷 *01/513–1923–39* ⊕ *www.karntnerhof.com* 🛏 *43 rooms* ♨ *Internet, some pets allowed; no a/c* ⊟ *AE, DC, MC, V* ⦿| *BP* Ⓤ *U1 or U4/Schwedenplatz.*

$ 🛏 **Pension Christina.** Steps from Schwedenplatz and the Danube Canal, this quiet pension offers mainly smallish modern rooms, warmly decorated with attractive dark-wood furniture set off against beige walls. The location is extremely convenient, near the U-Bahn and tram lines, or just a short, pleasant walk through ancient streets to the heart of the Altstadt. For night owls, the Bermuda Triangle, a late-night hot spot of bars and cafés clustered around the Rupertskirche, is close by. ⊠ *Hafnersteig 7, A–1010* ☎ *01/533–2961-0* 🖷 *01/533–2961–11* ⊕ *www. pertschy.com* ⤻ *33 rooms* ⚏ *Minibars; no a/c* ☰ *MC, V* ⏐◯⏐ *BP* ⓤ *U1 or U4/Schwedenplatz.*

Wieden

The neighborhood of Wieden (4th District) is the most up and coming in the whole city. Fascinating shops, fragrant espresso bars, and intimate restaurants are opening up all the time. The city's largest open-air market, the Naschmarkt, is also here. You're not smack in the city center, but you can walk there in 10 minutes.

★ $$$ 🛏 **Das Triest.** A single yellow tulip perched—toothbrush-fashion—against a white closet. Beige-on-beige fabrics offset by glowing pine headboards the size of walls. A staircase suave as a Bauhaus image. Yes, this is Sir Terrence Conran country, the Vienna outpost of the man who has, since the 1970s, colonized every hip neighborhood in the world with his signature flair. The first in a growing Viennese trend of spare, chic hotels, Das Triest gives you the feeling of being on board an ultrasleek ocean liner—a bit surprising, considering this was once the stable of the old Vienna-Trieste mail-route posthouse. All of this has attracted the requisite celebrities, including Britney Spears and Johnny Depp. They would certainly appreciate the extra (and plentiful) little touches in the rooms; even the doorknobs feel nice to the touch. Decor is delightful—linen-fresh, with accents of blue carpeting and honey-hue woods, and high-style as only a Conran hotel can be. The hotel also allures with an excellent Austro-Italian restaurant, Collio. Das Triest may be a little off the beaten track but is still within easy walking distance of the city center. And the prices are quite gentle considering the pedigree. ⊠ *Wiedner Hauptstrasse 12, A–1040, 4th District/Wieden* ☎ *01/589–180* 🖷 *01/589–1818* ⊕ *www.dastriest.at.* ⤻ *73 rooms* ⚏ *Restaurant, café, minibars, health club, bar, Internet; no a/c in some rooms* ☰ *AE, DC, MC, V* ⏐◯⏐ *BP* ⓤ *U1, U2, or U4/Karlsplatz.*

$$ 🛏 **Erzherzog Rainer.** On a fountained square in a good location near the Naschmarkt and within walking distance of Karlsplatz and the city center, the lovely pale green Archduke Rainer opened in 1913 as a grand hotel, with its restaurant a meeting place for prominent Viennese society. Guest rooms are extremely pleasant, with a mixture of modern and antique reproduction furniture providing a regal touch, and baths are well designed. Breakfast is ample. ⊠ *Wiedner Hauptstrasse 27–29, 4th District/Wieden* ☎ *01/501110* 🖷 *01/50111–350* ⊕ *www.schick-hotels. com* ⤻ *84 rooms* ⚏ *Restaurant, minibars, Internet; no a/c* ☰ *AE, DC, MC, V* ⏐◯⏐ *BP* ⓤ *U1, U2, or U4/Karlsplatz.*

$ 🛏 **Drei Kronen.** If the hotel is pastel, no matter—right outside the door is the exceedingly colorful Naschmarkt, Vienna's largest and most famous outdoor market. That means that things can get a bit noisy, but, happily, the food stalls shut down in the early evening (and the market is shuttered on Sunday). Inside, guest rooms are modern and a bit dull, but perfectly adequate, and have cable TV. A hop, skip, and a jump away is the Schleifmühlgasse, one of Vienna's great, rejuvenated neighborhood streets, lined with espresso bars, cozy restaurants, and art galleries. You'll be within walking distance of the city center, or you can catch the U-Bahn at Kettenbrückengasse or Karlsplatz, both about a five-minute walk left or right from the hotel. ⊠ *Schleifmühlgasse 25, 4th District/Wieden* ☎ *01/587-3289* 🖷 *01/587-3289–11* ⊕ *www.hotel3kronen.at* ➫ *41 rooms* ⌂ *Internet; no a/c* 🖃 *AE, DC, MC, V* ⎥○⎢ *BP* Ⓤ *U1, U2, or U4/Karlsplatz.*

Museum Row

The combined neighborhoods of Mariahilf and Neubau (the 6th and 7th Districts, respectively) are near the major museums, including the Kunsthistorisches and the MuseumsQuartier. And not far away is that phenomenal shopping street, the Mariahilferstrasse.

$$$ 🖭 **K&K Maria Theresia.** If you want to be where the museums are, this is certainly a convenient, if uninspiring, option. The Maria Theresia is walking distance from the Kunsthistorisches and MuseumsQuartier, with the artsy Spittelberg quarter and its artisans shops and restaurants just steps away. Though the hotel is just 20 years old or so, it was designed to blend in with the historic buildings around it—although it hardly succeeds, due to its mass and, inside, an overly colorful decor, with harsh yellows, reds, and pinks thrown about. The token "K&K" refers to *Kaiserlich und Königlich,* or "by appointment to the Emperor of Austria and King of Hungary"—but is simply a hotel chain nomenclature. Rooms are sleekly furnished, and some have unique round windows. The staff can be negligent about relaying messages. ⊠ *Tiefer Graben 14–20, A–1010* ☎ *01/52123* 🖷 *01/521–2370* ⊕ *www.kkhotels.com* ➫ *123 rooms* ⌂ *Restaurant, minibars, bar, Internet; no a/c* 🖃 *AE, DC, MC, V* ⎥○⎢ *BP* Ⓤ *U2 or U3/Volkstheater.*

★ **$$$** 🖭 **Kummer.** With a lobby that is as old-world Viennese as they come, this 19th-century landmark has a distinguished history dating back to 1872 (the Strauss family once resided in a hotel on the site; Friedrich Schlögl, one of the founding fathers of the Viennese literature tradition, began a literary and art salon in this hotel's reception rooms). You enter and are caught up in a waltz of beveled glass, gilded globe-lanterns, colored marble trim, and painted boiserie, all surrounding a grand staircase atrium. Upstairs, each comfortably furnished room is different, and the ones facing the busy Mariahilferstrasse have soundproof windows. Some rooms have an alcove sitting area; single rooms are very much on the bijou side. Yes, you are in the very heart of the shopping district, which means crowds and neon signs—but the hotel is close to the Westbahnhof, major museums, and you may feel you've wandered onto a set for *Die Fledermaus* when you see that lobby. ⊠ *Mariahilferstrasse 71/a, 6th District/Mariahilf* ☎ *01/58895* 🖷 *01/587–8133* ⊕ *www. hotelkummer.at* ➫ *100 rooms* ⌂ *Restaurant, minibars, bar, Internet, parking (fee); no a/c* 🖃 *AE, DC, MC, V* ⎥○⎢ *BP* Ⓤ *U3/Neubaugasse.*

★ **$$–$$$** ▦ **Tyrol.** On a busy corner of Mariahilferstrasse, this small, luxurious hotel is a good choice for those who want to be close to the MuseumsQuartier and some fun shopping, too. Rooms are exceptionally pleasing, with fabrics and tony furniture from posh Viennese stores like Backhausen, Thonet, and Wittmann. There are many nice touches, from the exquisite bedcovers, stylish high-back chairs and fashionable, elongated lamps to the elegant, subtle drapes that dress the long windows. Baths are sparkling white with glossy black accents. It's in a neighborhood that has everything, including a host of good restaurants to choose from. ✉ *Mariahilferstrasse 15, A–1060* ☎ *01/587–5415* 🖶 *01/ 587–5415–9* ⊕ *www.das-tyrol.at* ⤳ *30 rooms* ⅄ *Bar, minibars, Internet* ☰ *AE, DC, MC, V* ⟨◎⟩ *BP* Ⓤ *U2 or U3/Volkstheater.*

$$–$$$ ▦ **ViennArt.** A member of the Austrotels group, the ViennArt is in a truly prime location just behind the MuseumsQuartier and near the quaint Spittelberg area and Mariahilferstrasse shopping street. The exterior combines a lower section in sleek plate glass, with upper stories in conventional yellow brick. As you can judge by the name, the ViennArt emphasizes contemporary art, and Viennese artist Hans Mlenek's "Wall of Initiation" dominates the glass-roof atrium lobby. Rooms are modern and really nothing special, with mustard accent walls, bold striped curtains and busy carpets. Some baths have shower and tub combinations. ✉ *Breitegasse 9, A–1070* ☎ *01/523–1345–0* 🖶 *01/523–1345–111* ⊕ *www.austrotel.at* ⤳ *56 rooms* ⅄ *Bar, minibars, Internet* ☰ *AE, DC, MC, V* ⟨◎⟩ *BP* Ⓤ *U3/Volkstheater.*

$$ ▦ **Altstadt.** A cognoscenti favorite, this small hotel was once a patrician
Fodor'sChoice home and is set in one of Vienna's most pampered neighborhoods—and
★ we mean neighborhood: a plus here is being able to really interact with real Viennese, their stores (hey, supermarkets!), and residential streets. In fact, you are lucky enough to be in the chic and quaint Spittelberg quarter. The Altstadt is blessed with a personable and helpful management. Palm trees, a Secession-style, wrought-iron staircase, modernist fabrics, and halogen lighting make for a very design-y interior. Guest rooms are large with all the modern comforts, though they retain an antique feel. The English-style lounge has a fireplace and plump floral sofas. Upper rooms have lovely views out over the city roofline. Last but not least, you are one streetcar stop or a pleasant walk from the main museums. ✉ *Kirchengasse 41, 7th District/Neubau* ☎ *01/526–3399–0* 🖶 *01/523–4901* ⊕ *www.altstadt.at* ⤳ *25 rooms* ⅄ *Minibars, bar; no a/c* ☰ *AE, DC, MC, V* ⟨◎⟩ *BP* Ⓤ *U3/Volkstheater.*

$ ▦ **Museum.** In a beautiful Belle Epoque mansion a five-minute walk from the Kunsthistorisches Museum, Naturhistorisches Museum, and the MuseumsQuartier, this elegant pension offers good-size rooms mixed in with few that are a bit squeezy. Baths are modern, but again, can vary in size, with shelf space as an afterthought in some cases. Considering this is an old-style pension, the need for renovation can be excused, especially since the price is reasonable for such a great location. There is also a pretty, sunny sitting room with deep, overstuffed (albeit worn) sofas and wingback chairs, perfect for curling up with a good book. This is a popular place for European travelers, so book ahead. ✉ *Museumstrasse 3, 7th District/Neubau* ☎ *01/523–44–260* 🖶 *01/523–*

44–2630 ♺ 15 rooms ⚿ No a/c ▤ AE, DC, MC, V |◎| BP Ⓤ U2 or U3/Volkstheater.

$ 🏨 **Fürstenhof.** This 1912 building directly across from the Westbahnhof describes its large rooms as "old-fashioned comfortable," and you reach them via a marvelous hydraulic elevator. Furnishings are a mixed bag, but all rooms are scrupulously clean and agreeable. The side rooms are quieter than those in front, and the best deals are for three to four people. Rooms without bath are in the $ category. A very nice breakfast is included in the price. ⊠ *Neubaugürtel 4, A–1070, 7th District/Neubau* ☎ *01/523–3267* 🖷 *01/523–3267–26* ⊕ *www.hotel-fuerstenhof.com* ♺ *58 rooms, 28 with bath* ⚿ *Minibars, Internet; no a/c* ▤ *AE, DC, MC, V* |◎| *BP* Ⓤ *U3 or U6/Westbahnhof.*

$ 🏨 **Kugel.** The Kugel has been a hotel since the late 19th century and from the grand exterior you can tell it was once one of the best places to stay in the city. Some rooms are really a nice surprise, with bright-yellow-and-white color schemes, modern canopied beds, nice throw rugs, and lots of grandly scaled windows adorned with elegant yellow curtains. Other rooms, however, are rather plain and modern with little charm. Since the prices are so gentle here, why not simply opt for the top of the price scale and wind up with a room that seems to be a real bargain. Siebensterngasse is a hopping street, with fun shops, restaurants, and a brew pub. The MuseumsQuartier and Kunsthistorisches are easily reachable by subway, tram, or five-minute walk. ⊠ *Siebensterngasse 43, A–1070, 7th District/Neubau* ☎ *01/523–3355* 🖷 *01/523–3355–5* ⊕ *www.hotelkugel.at* ♺ *37 rooms* ⚿ *Minibars in some rooms; no a/c* ▤ *No credit cards* |◎| *BP* Ⓤ *U2/Volkstheater.*

¢   🏨 **Pension Reimer.** Friendly and comfortable, this hotel is in a prime location just off Mariahilferstrasse. The modern rooms have high ceilings and large windows, and the atmosphere throughout is cheerful, though plain. Note, however, this place is located on the fourth floor and access is via an elevator that can only be operated with a key, leaving you and your arriving luggage at a bit of a loss. But not to worry—if you're willing to leap up the stairs first, the elevator key is happily handed over. ⊠ *Kirchengasse 18, A–1070, 7th District/Neubau* ☎ *01/523–6162* 🖷 *01/524–3782* ♺ *14 rooms* ⚿ *No a/c, no room phones, no room TVs* ▤ *MC, V* |◎| *BP* Ⓤ *U2/Volkstheater.*

The Rathaus & Josefstadt

At night, the Rathaus (Town Hall) resembles a lit-up castle at Disneyland, and during the day you can almost always find a market set up in front. In winter you can go ice skating here, and it's also the sight of Vienna's main outdoor Christmas market. In summer, opera movies are shown at night on a big screen. And if you like hunting for antiques, Josefstadt—one of Vienna's quaintest residential neighborhoods—is the place to go.

$$ 🏨 **Rathaus Wine & Design.** As if Josef Hoffman, Otto Wagner, and other
Fodor'sChoice   great designers of the Wiener Werkstatte and Secession movements de-
★   signed a hotel for the 21st century, this new option on the Vienna lodging scene conjures up that soigné past with moderne color schemes, striking

Werkstatte light fixtures, and the kind of Bauhaus-y chairs that Marlene Dietrich would have liked to perch on. But that is just the half of it. The brainchild of entrepreneurs Petra und Klaus Fleischhaker of Salzburg, this exclusive boutique hotel also pays homage to the winemakers of Austria. With the acclaim Austrian wine is getting lately, it's a winning idea. Completely overhauled, the spacious, high-ceiling, ultramodern rooms have polished wooden floors and accent wood walls, with warm orange, yellow, ocher, and cream accents. On each door is the name of a different winemaker, with a bottle of the vintner's wine inside (sorry, it's not included in the room price). Some of the greatest Austrian winemaker's are represented, such as Bründelmayer, Gesellmann, Sattlerhof, and Markowitsch. Guests can take a grape escape in the chic, minimalist lounge, where vintages and snacks are served (dinners can also be arranged, if advance notice is given). ⊠ *Langegasse 13, A–1080* ☎ *01/400–1122* 🖷 *01/400–1122–88* ⊕ *www.hotel-rathaus-wien.at* ⤶ *33 rooms* ⚲ *Wine bar, minibars, Internet* 🖃 *AE, DC, MC, V* 🍽 *EP* Ⓤ *U2/Rathaus.*

$$ 🏨 **Regina.** Sitting regally on the edge of the Altstadt, this is a quintessen-
Fodor'sChoice tially Viennese hotel: The building is "grand" in the Ringstrasse style,
★ with French mansard roof, Italianate pilasters, the works. Inside, the decor is dignified grande dame—nothing showy, slightly matronly, but with solid good taste and refinement, with thick velvet drapes, vaulted hallways, baroque-style chandeliers, and an air that everything function *exactly* as it should, in a very proper Austrian manner. Little wonder that Freud, who lived nearby, used to eat breakfast in the hotel café every morning—this hotel's "correctness" must have given him much needed balance and ballast. Today, fittingly, the hotel commands a view of Sigmund Freud Park. Beyond the grand reception rooms, the high-ceiling guest rooms are quiet, spacious, and decorated in a subdued, staid, nearly Germanic manner; many come with charming sitting areas. The Regina is near the imposing Votivkirche and about a 10-minute walk from the city center. ⊠ *Rooseveltplatz 15, 9th District/Alsergrund* ☎ *01/404–460* 🖷 *01/408–8392* ⊕ *www.hotelregina.at* ⤶ *125 rooms* ⚲ *Restaurant, minibars, Internet; no a/c* 🖃 *AE, DC, MC, V* 🍽 *BP* Ⓤ *U2 or U4/Schottenring.*

$ 🏨 **Graf-Stadion.** "Small is beautiful"—so declares this hotel's Web site in touting its charming Josefstadt neighborhood, which is fitted out with coffeehouses, little squares, hidden courtyards, and city palais. Set just behind the towering Rathaus, the Graf-Stadion is appropriately named after the famous 19th-century foreign minister, Count Stadion. Within easy walking distance of the Ring, it retains a bit of Biedermeier charm. The reception area and breakfast room have vaulted ceilings, while the pleasant, spacious rooms have floral tie-back curtains and somewhat busy bedspreads. Most of the furniture, however, is rather modern and featureless. The hotel sometimes offers last minute deals that are a good value. ⊠ *Buchfeldgasse 5, A–1080, 8th District/Josefstadt* ☎ *01/405–5284* 🖷 *01/405–0111* ⊕ *www.graf-stadion.com* ⤶ *40 rooms* ⚲ *Internet; no a/c* 🖃 *AE, DC, MC, V* 🍽 *BP* Ⓤ *U2/Rathaus.*

¢–$ 🏨 **Pension Zipser.** With an ornate facade and gilt-trimmed coat of arms, this 1904 house is one of the city's better values. It's in the picturesque Josefstadt neighborhood of small cafés, shops, bars, and good restaurants, yet within steps of the J streetcar line to the city center. The rooms are in browns and beiges, with modern furniture and well-equipped baths. The balconies of some of the back rooms overlook tree-filled neighborhood courtyards. The accommodating staff will help get theater and concert tickets. ⊠ *Langegasse 49, A–1080, 8th District/Josefstadt* ☎ *01/404–540* 🖷 *01/404–5413* ⊕ *www.zipser.at* 📞 *47 rooms* ⚭ *Bar, Internet; no a/c* ⊟ *AE, DC, MC, V* ⎥⊙⎢ *BP* Ⓤ *Rathaus/U2.*

★ ¢ 🏨 **Pension Wild.** This friendly, family-run pension on several floors of an older apartment house draws a relaxed, younger crowd to one of the best values in town. Rooms are simple, modern and welcoming, with light-wood furniture. An ample breakfast is included in the room rate. The close proximity to the major museums makes this a top choice. This is a gay-friendly pension. ⊠ *Langegasse 1, A–1080, 8th District/Josefstadt* ☎ *01/406–5174* 🖷 *01/402–2168* ⊕ *www.pension-wild.com* 📞 *19 rooms* ⚭ *Kitchenette, minibars; no a/c* ⊟ *AE, DC, MC, V* ⎥⊙⎢ *BP* Ⓤ *U2/Lerchenfelder Strasse.*

Vienna Woods

Just outside of Vienna proper are the "lungs" of the city, a place where Strauss and Beethoven used to walk for inspiration.

★ $$–$$$ 🏨 **Tulbingerkogel.** What could be more relaxing after a day of sightseeing than to stay in the tranquillity of the Vienna Woods? The Bläel family (pronounced Bloy-el) owns this charming, terraced establishment 8 km (5 mi) from the outskirts of the city (a driver will even meet your plane at the airport). Set atop the famous hill called Tulbingerkogel—immortalized in the 19th century by Adalbert Stifter, the noted Austrian poet—this large hotel complex was built in the 1930s, then expanded with a modern wing. Over the decades it attracted the rich and famous. It's easy to see why. The centerpiece of each stylish room—decorated in sleek, rejuvenating contemporary style—is an enormous window, offering panoramic views of lush greenery and rolling hills, and the owner's own vineyard. Some rooms have bathrooms with glass walls, with those views. The outdoor pool, heated year-round, goes right to the edge of the woods. In winter you can actually swim inside to a cozy room, then lie back on heated cushions before a crackling fire. Herr Bläel, who is fluent in English, is passionate about wine and has 20,000 bottles in his wine cellar, so let him recommend the perfect accompaniment to dinner in the hotel's acclaimed restaurant. The hotel rents cars for those wishing to drive to the Danube Valley for the day. Guests can also be dropped off at the Hütteldorf stop on the U4 subway, which offers easy access to the city center. ⊠ *Mauerbach bei Wien, A–3001* ☎ *02273/7391* 🖷 *02273/7391–73* ⊕ *www.tulbingerkogel.at* 📞 *35 rooms* ⚭ *Restaurant, minibars, Internet* ⊟ *AE, DC, MC, V* ⎥⊙⎢ *BP.*

VIENNA: NIGHTLIFE & THE ARTS

KEEP A RESOLUTION
to hear the New Year's Day concert
at the gilded Musikverein ⇨*p.154*

SET YOUR PULSE TO MATCH
the three-quarters beat of a waltz ⇨*p.154*

CATCH ONTO THE LATEST TRENDS
in the hot-hot Freihaus-Quartier ⇨*p.153*

MAKE MERRY WITH THE WIDOWS
at a Volksoper operetta ⇨*p.160*

DECLARE YOUR LOVE FOR MOZART
in a gilded 18th-century music salon ⇨*p.157*

GO-GO 'TIL MORNING
at a Secession-style disco ⇨*p.148*

GET YOU TO THE CHURCH ON TIME
to hear the fabled Vienna Boys' Choir ⇨*p.158*

BEG, BORROW, OR BUY A TICKET
to an opera at the Wiener Staatsoper ⇨*p.159*

By Diane
Naar-Elphee

EVER SINCE JOHANN STRAUSS composed his immortal waltzes for a plea-sure-crazed, wealthy, self-indulgent, sensuous Vienna, the city has been celebrated for its nighttime extravagance and gaiety. The Congress of Vienna—*elle danse, mais elle ne marche pas* ("it dances, but never gets anything done")—established the city's reputation as the dancing cap-ital back in 1814. *Fasching,* the season of Prince Carnival, kept the ball rolling with its fantastic Court balls, Opera balls, masked balls, and a hundred other glittering gatherings. By the late 19th century, Vienna had become a city of dazzling evenings filled with beauties in magnificent gowns, gold-braided uniforms, towering headdresses, feathered fans, flir-tations, *chambres séparees,* powder, perfume, "Wine, Women, and Song," champagne, *Die Fledermaus,* and plenty of hand-kissing. Fast forward to the 21st century and you'll discover a Vienna that is as party-hearty as ever. Of course, instead of doing a step-step-close to "The Beau-tiful Blue Danube," many of today's scene-heads are grooving to a disco beat at a modish danceteria. Happily, you'll find that between these two realms—the chandeliered, waltzing whirl of Imperial Austria and the electroclash buzz of the city's latest dance clubs—Vienna offers a vibrant kaleidoscope of nighttime and arts options.

Enjoying Vienna at night means being confronted with a tantalizing myr-iad of choices, so only by combining Admiral Byrd-ish foresight with a movie editor's ruthless selectivity can you hope to ride herd on it all. What shall it be? Do you want to time-warp back to the 18th century at Mozart concerts featuring bewigged musicians in the opulent surrounds of the tiny jewelbox Sala Terrena (which has seats for no more than 50 and shimmers with Venetian-style frescoes)? Or do you want to catch a Broadway-musical extravaganza devoted to the life of the tragic em-press Elisabeth at the Theater an der Wien (where Beethoven's *Fidelio* premiered in 1805)? Or bravo! the divas at the grandest of grand opera at the Staatoper? Or dive into the Franz-Josef splendor of an evening concert of Strauss waltzes? Or catch a recital of the greatest *Altemusik* (Old Music) ensemble, Nikolaus Harnoncourt's Concentus Musicus? Or enjoy a trombone troupe at a "jazzkeller"? Or take in an operetta at the beloved Volksoper (whose 2004–05 season included its first-ever staged version of Rodgers and Hammerstein's *The Sound of Music,* 40 years after the film's premiere and 100 years after the birth of Maria von Trapp)? Most famously, as the city that churned out the likes of Beethoven, Bruckner, and Mahler, Vienna is still the preeminent place to savor great music, whether it be small *Schubertiaden* concerts or grand performances by two of the finest symphony orchestras in the world—heard around the globe thanks to the New Year's Day concert televised annually from the spectacular Musikverein.

New and innovative music halls and stages are spreading to heretofore unlikely venues in the city. The newly blossoming Gürtel, the big, city ring road, often viewed as a traffic-troubled and crime-connected area, has begun to attract the hip hoards. The rave crowd meets in stylish clubs installed under some of the brick arches of Otto Wagner's urban train line, which runs above the Gürtel. The Gasometer—a former power sta-tion with four gigantic brick-built 19th-century gas-storage structures—has made room for a huge stage for live performances. Vienna's biggest festival (the largest in central Europe), however, is the Danube Island Festival, the Donauinselfest: during the last weekend in June, hundreds of bands and cabaret artists and singers from around the world draw millions of visitors to the Danube Island—and there's no admission charge! But the biggest party kicks off January 27, 2006, when all of Austria launches a yearlong gala commemorating the 250th anniversary of the birth of native son Mozart. As the city where "Wolfie" spent the last (and most productive) 10 years of his life, Vienna will be pulling out all the stops and giving even the city of Salzburg (his birthplace) a run for its euros, with major performances and special events scheduled in all the major concert and theater halls.

NIGHTLIFE

Where once night-owls had to head to Vienna's *Bermuda Dreieck* "Bermuda Triangle," around St. Ruprecht's church on the Ruprecht-splatz, two blocks south of the Danube Canal, today's nightclub scene has blossomed with a profusion of delightful and sophisticated bars, clubs, and lounges. Many of the trendoisie like to head to the clubs around the Naschmarkt area, then move on to nearby Mariahilferstrasse to shake their groove thing. For the current listings, see the "Party Time" section in *Der Falter* or *City* newspapers (weekly publications, they cost, respectively, €4.50 and €3). A Web site that features a wide array of nightlife activities is ⊕ www.hauptstadt.at.

Bars, Lounges & Nightclubs

The ultimate don't-miss Viennese bar extravaganza is the **Loos American Bar** (⊠ Kärntner Durchang 10, 1st District ☎ 01/512–3283 Ⓤ U1 or U3/Stephansplatz). Designed by the famed Adolph Loos in 1908, this gleaming black marble and onyx showplace delivers a mise-en-scène right out of a Fritz Lang movie. The ambience is truly memorable, so don't complain about the high drink tabs.

A sort of spaceship has landed smack between the Hofburg palace and the Kunsthistorisches Museum—actually in the underground passage designed as a pedestrian-friendly underpass, which connects the two. Just look for the glowing orange kiosk at the intersection of the Ring and Mariahilferstrasse and head downstairs to find **Babenberger Passage** (⊠ Passage-corner of Ringstrasse at Babenbergerstrasse, 1st District ☎ 01/961–8800 ⊕ www.sunshine.at/ Ⓤ U2/Museumsquartier), one of the hippest places in Vienna these days. State-of-the-art lighting systems, futuristic decor, and adaptable design elements come together in a blush-hue bar and a sizzling-blue dance room. What the kings of Babenberg—the 10th-century dynasty that helped found Austria—would have thought of Club Passage we can only guess.

Modish Marcello Mastroianni's by the dozen can be found at the fashionable **Bar Italia Lounge** (⊠ Mariahilfer Strasse 19, 6th District/Mariahilf ☎ 01/585–2838 ⊕ www.baritalia.net Ⓤ U3/Neubaugasse), a "little Italy," which occupies the coolest of downstairs locations just below the

CloseUp

GET THE BALL ROLLING

BACK IN THE DAYS of Emperor Franz Josef, white-gloved women and men in white tie would glide over marble floors waltzing to Johann Strauss's heavenly melodies. They still do, for Vienna's old three-quarter-time rhythm strikes up anew each year during Carnival, from New Year's Eve until Mardi Gras. During January and February, as many as 40 balls may be held in a single evening, but the ball season actually extends from November 11 to June. Many events are organized by a professional group, including the Kaffeesiederball (Coffee Brewers' Ball), the Zuckerbaeckerball (Confectioners' Ball), or the Opernball (Opera's Ball). The latter is the most famous—some say too famous. This event transforms the Vienna Opera House into the world's most beautiful ballroom (and transfixes all of Austria when shown live on national television). The invitation reads "Frack

mit Dekorationen," which means that ball-gowns and tails are required for most events (you can always get your tux from a rental agency) and women must not wear white (reserved for debutantes). But there's something for everyone these days, including the "Ball of Bad Taste" or "Wallflower Ball." Other noted venues are the imperial Hofburg palace and the famous Musikverein concert hall. Prices usually run from about €75 to €450 and up per person. For a calendar of the main balls see www.top.wien.at/ballkalender, or ask your discerning hotel concierge for tips and pointers. If you go, remember that you must dance the Linkswalzer—the counterclockwise, left-turning waltz that is the only correct way to dance in Vienna. Dance the night away and then greet the morning with a Kater Frühstuck—a hangover breakfast—of goulash soup.

exceedingly popular Bar Italia restaurant. The Yupps come here for their after-work "Vienna Sling" cocktails and small snacks, to chill out to DJ music (including just about everything except mainstream), then head off to the Babenberger Passage to spend the rest of the night.

With so many hipster spots opening up around town, you might overlook **Barfly's** (⊠ Esterházygasse 33, 6th District/Mariahilf ☎ 01/586–0825 Ⓤ U3/Neubaugasse) but if you want a classic, dark, mahogany-wood bar (set near the Mariahilferstrasse) with a real old-fashioned air—you can almost imagine Bogart or Hemingway strolling in—head here. One of the most dazzling settings for a Viennese club is in one of the city's cavernous subway stations and **Café Carina** (⊠ Josefstädter Strasse 84/Stadtbahnbogen, 8th District/Josefstadt ☎ 01/406–4322 Ⓤ U6/Josefstädter Strasse) has one of the best—an actual Otto Wagner original. Vienna's new "subway-station clubs" are proof positive that nightlife is no longer centered in and around the old city center. Carina is very off-beat, artistic, and action-packed—anything can happen here, from an airguitar competition to an evening with 1980s hits.

Das Möbel (⊠ Burggasse 10, 7th District/Neubau ☎ 01/524–9497 ⊕ www.dasmobel.at Ⓤ U3/Volkstheater) means "the furniture" and that's what you get here—most of the decor has been designed by Austria's modern designers and if you like the chair you're sitting on, chances are you can buy it. This is also a great place to lounge in, with snacks, long drinks, and cool chill-out corners. The best mixture of Galerie, art club, and bar that Vienna has to offer, **Futuregarden** (⊠ Schadekgasse 6, 6th District/ Mariahilf ☎ 01/585–2613 Ⓤ U3/Neubaugasse) is reminiscent of a construction site with colorful lamps and a minimalistic ambience, all the better to showcase the always changing exhibitions of art works on view here. The crowd is creative and the visiting DJs offer pulsing sounds.

Another chicly recycled urban landmark, the brick-built "Stadtbahn-bogen" (municipal rail arches) that dot the big ring road called the Gürtel have been renovated and this one sports the **Halbestadt** (⊠ Währinger Guërtel/Stadtbahnbogen 155, 9th District/Alsergrund ☎ 01/319–4735 Ⓜ Ⓤ U6/Währinger Gürtel), a nifty new club. Its name means "halved city," which is what the Gürtel—the busy thoroughfare that cuts Vienna into inner and outer districts). To match the Otto Wagner-designed pedigree, Halbestadt is small, elegant, and cosmopolitan, with some of the best bar staff in town. Owners Robert Hayes and Erich Wassicek (who has won many international awards in cocktail-mix competitions) are often on the premises to greet and meet. Near the Naschmarkt, **Kalei-doskop** (⊠ Schleifmühlgasse 13, 4th District/Wieden ☎ 01/920–3343 Ⓤ U4/Kettenbrueckengasse) sits shoulder to shoulder with a number of top art galleries, so the hip and happening art crowd tends to come here. Contempo art on view pleasures the eye as the vibes—the DJs lay everything from '70s disco to Viennese electronica on the crowd—sizzle the ear.

While **Ra'mien** (⊠ Gumpendorfer Strasse 9, 6th District/Mariahilf ☎ 01/ 585–4798 ⊕ www.ramien.at Ⓤ U2/MuseumsQuartier) is the hippest of Vienna's *nudel* (Asian noodle) hotspots, it's the cellar that is the eye-knocker: a bona fide Hong Kong nightclub joint, replete with gold-tassled red Chinese lanterns, carved opium-bed walls, and enough *chinoiserie* to please any chop-socky fan. The venue of lots of parties (the kind that get written up in the columns), the cellar hosts live DJs every night for a crowd that grooves to the latest sounds. Chic, chic, and once again chic, the designer café-bar **Shultz** (⊠ Siebensterngasse 31. 7th District/ Neubau ☎ 01/ 522–9120 ⊕ www.schultz.at? Ⓤ U4/Kettenbruecken-gasse) seduces fashionable folk with its long drinks, retro cocktails, and its Vienna Moderne setting. The café has one of the tastiest breakfasts in town. Back in 1870, Viennese used to come to the **Volksgarten** (⊠ Bur-gring 2, 1st District ☎ 01/532–0907 ⊕ www.volksgarten.at Ⓤ U2/3 Mu-seumsQuartier) to waltz, share champagne, and enjoy the night in candlelit garden. Today, they come to the same site to *diskothek* the night away under pink strobes, enjoy some boogie-woogie or tango dancing in the Tanzcafe (Dance Cafe), and sip a beer against the greenery. A best bet when you don't know where else to head, this one-in-all club complex is within a lush garden and has a pretty, vaguely Jugendstil dining salon, with a vast curved wall of windows overlooking a terrace set with tables. Beyond lies the Pavilion, a 1950s jewel that looks airlifted from California, which serves brews and nibbles.

As for slightly more low-key, less trendy surrounds, there are always the old standbys. In the "Bermuda Triangle" area you'll find the **First Floor** ⊠ *At Seitenstettengasse/Rabensteig* ☎ 01/533–7866. (⊠ At Seitenstettengasse/Rabensteig ☎ 01/533–7866), which is actually up one floor from ground level. The **Kruger Bar** (⊠ Krugerstrasse 5 ☎ 01/512–2455), off Kärntnerstrasse near the Opera, has an English gentlemen's club atmosphere in a former 1950s cinema. Near the Börse (Vienna Stock Exchange) is the **Planter's Club** (⊠ Zelinkagasse 4 ☎ 01/533–3393–16), offering a nice selection of rums in an exotic, tropical colonial setting. Let the outdoor glass elevator at the Steffl department store whisk you up to the **Skybar** (⊠ Kärntnerstrasse 19 ☎ 01/513–1712) for soft piano music to go along with the stunning view. The best place to sample wines from all over Austria is the intimate **Eulennest Vinothek** (⊠ Himmelpfortgasse 13 ☎ 01/513–5311), off Kärntnerstrasse. The "Owl's Nest" also has cheese, olives, and other snacks to have with your wine. The owners speak English.

Dance Clubs & Discos

In the quaint old days—-a decade ago—visitors who wanted to shake their groove thing would usually make a beeline to the "queen of the discos," Queen Anne. That is still the place if you want to boogie to "Evergreens," but the revved-up dance-club scene these days makes it harder for the in-crowd to choose a venue. For those seeking the electronic music scene, however, the best has to be the Flex.

Occupying one of the former stables of the Habsburgs in the MuseumsQuartier, **Café Leopold** (⊠ Museumsplatz 1, MuseumsQuartier, 1st District ☎ 01/523–6732 ⊕ www.cafe-leopold.at/ Ⓤ U2 or 3/ MuseumsQuartier) is in the big modern white cube that is the Leopold Museum, one of the leading components of the MQ. Fun and games here go on until very late at this coffeehouse-restaurant-disco, with food being served after midnight. After frugging to the house and electro music, you can escape to a table outdoors in the plaza.

The first club to take up residence in one of the vaulted arches under Vienna's Stadtbahn, the elevated city railroad system designed by the great Jugendstil architect, Otto Wagner, **Chelsea** (⊠ Stadtbahnbogen 29–32, Lerchenfelder Gürtel, 8th District/Josefstadt ☎ 01/ 407–9309 ⊕ www.chelsea.co.at Ⓤ U6/Thaliastrasse) soon triggered a host of restaurants and bars to also open up in these historic sites. Still packed most evenings, Chelsea is primarily a music club and but it also has a mean following with fans of English soccer—on Sunday at 4 PM there's a Happy Hour with a jumbo-screen televised game.

★ "U" stands for underground and **Club U im Otto-Wagner-Café** (⊠ Karlsplatz/Kuenstlerhauspassage, 4th District/Wieden ☎ 01/505–9904 ⊕ www.club-u.at Ⓤ U1, U2, or U4/Karlsplatz) is located just underneath one of the two celebrated Jugendstil pavilions that Otto Wagner built on the Karlsplatz square when designing Vienna's subway, the Stadtbahn. Which means this disco is easy to find. One of the best dance halls for alternative music, it is open on Sunday, has outdoor seating, live music, a great atmosphere and excellent DJs, who turn this place into a real Soul City most nights. In the middle of one of Vienna's latest hipster districts, the Freihaus-Quarter, **Club Schikaneder** (✉ Margaretenstrasse 22–24, 4th District/Wieden ☎ 01/585–2867 ⊕ www.schikaneder.at Ⓤ U1, U2, or U4/Karlsplatz),a former cinema, has become a multimedia art-and-dance center. There are three to five films screened every day, exhibitions, and first-class DJ–lines to groove to. The Freihaus-Quarter sizzles with cafés and shops. Some of Vienna's trendiest fashion designers have their studios here. For all the scoop, log on to ⊕ www.freihausviertel.at.

★ **Flex** (✉ Donaukanal/Augartenbrücke, 1st District ☎ 01/533–7525 ⊕ www.flex.at Ⓤ U1, U2, or U4/Karlsplatz) has the grooviest grunge— quite literally, as this is set in a dark, dungeonlike cave—with an internationally famed sound system, considered by some to be the best in the world. From drum n' bass to noise to jungle and hardcore, the varied programs are hosted by DJs so cool they are looked on as local heroes. Amazing acoustics and free sparkling water to boot, but watch out if you have the wine—it has been known to leave you with a headache (or was it the music?). Practically an institution, the disco **Queen Anne** (✉ Johannesgasse 12, 1st District ☎ 01/512–0203 Ⓤ U4/Stadtpark) offers a retro trip, complete with a marble dance floor (paging John Travolta) and a bar where the tunes date from the '50s. Just a few steps from the Chelsea, set behind a glass facade, is the **Rhiz** (✉ Stadtbahnbogen 37/38, Lerchenfelder Gürtel, 8th District/Josefstadt ☎ 01/ 409–2505 ⊕ www.rhiz.org Ⓤ U6/Lerchenfelder Gürtel), which is noted for its role in crafting uniquely Viennese house music. One of the most comfortable hang-outs for scenesters, Rhiz has some great command-your-soul DJs in charge.

★ Movers and shakers like to head to **Tanzcafé Jenseits** (✉ Nelkengasse 3, 6th District/Mariahilf ☎ 01/587–1233) as much for the period decor and sexy ambience—rumor has it that this was a former brothel—as for the sing-along-and-leave-your-cares-behind tunes from the '70s and '80s (a house specialty). This place is simply chic, cool, and usually jammed. A mainstay for party-hearty Viennese for more than two decades, **U–4** (✉ Schönbrunnerstrasse 222, 12th District/Meidling ☎01/ 815–8307 ⊕ www.u4club.com/ Ⓤ U4/Meidling) might be said to be living on its history of glory and galas ("the night Prince"). It still draws a crowd, especially on Thursday—Gay Night—for sounds that range from New Wave to Gothic, '80s to Electronic. For the best Soul in the city on Sunday, head to the Soul Sugar club in the **WUK** (✉ Waehringer Strasse 59, 9th District/Alsergrund ☎ 01/401–210 ⊕ www.wuk.at Ⓤ U6/Währingerstrasse). There are all sorts of reasons to head to the Werk und Kultur center, for that matter, as this complex has workshops, galleries, and studios. But the club draws the biggest crowds. On other nights, groove to house, hip hop, and electro.

Gay & Lesbian Bars

Vienna has become more liberal over the past few years and today has quite a sizeable gay and lesbian crowd that, nowadays openly, adds spark and color to the city. From bathhouses to danceclubs, lesbian restaurants to queer cafés there are many options. The Vienna Tourist Board publishes an excellent "Queer Guide." The highlights of the year, for the queer crowd, are the Life Ball, Rainbow Parade, Rose Ball, and the *Wien ist andersrum*("Vienna is the other way around") art festival lasting three weeks in June, which will celebrate its 10th anniversary in 2005.

Near the Vienna University, just up from Freud's former home, **Café Berg** (⊠ Berggasse 8, 9th District/Alsergrund ☎ 01/ 319–5720) is the only gay and lesbian daytime café in town. This rather chic spot is near the gay bookshop Loewenherz (Lionheart), so you can purchase the latest editions of Edmund White, then savor it over a coffee here (open from 10 AM). In the crazy patchwork-Jugendstil style of Friedensreich Hundertwasser, **Café im KunstHausWien** (⊠ Weissgerber Laende 14, 3rd District/Landstrasse ☎ 01/712–0497) is a draw for an eclectic mix of gay, lesbian, and straights. Good food is complemented by the top art shows on tap—Keith Haring, Pierre and Gilles, you know. Just around the corner from the Naschmarkt, the cute **Chamaeleon Bar** (⊠ Stiegengasse 8, 6th District/Mariahilf ☎ 01/585–1180) caters to a middle-aged crowd until 4 AM Friday and Saturday. Prices are very reasonable and the patrons particularly pleasant.

For those wishing to be inspired by the bold and the beautiful, **Motto** (⊠Schönbrunner Strasse 30, enter from Ruedigergasse, 5th District ☎01/ 587–0672) is a must. Hey, Helmut Lang was a waiter here before he found fame and fortune. The clientele is pansexual and draws celebrities at times, the drink selection is enormous, and an excellent wine menu accompanies the meals. **Nightshift** (⊠ Corneliusgasse 8, 6th District/Mariahilf ☎ 01/586–2337) is a popular option that stays open until the early hours and attracts a smart young crowd of gays. Known as a fine place to make friends, it's open until 5 AM weekends, otherwise until 4 AM. If it's a dance floor you're looking for, **Why Not?** (⊠ Tiefer Graben 22, 1st District ☎ 01/925–3024) is a hotspot that throbs on weekends.

The name ("Women's Café") means women *only* at the cozy **Frauencafé** (⊠ Langegasse 11, 8th District/Josefstadt ☎ 01/406–3754) and the owner means business. Many party nights and events are held at **Frauenzentrum Bar** (⊠ Waehringerstrasse 59, entrance on Prechtlgasse, 9th District/Alsergrund ☎ 01/402–8754) and there's a lively bar scene and a Saturday night disco. **Orlando** (⊠Mollardgasse 3, 6th District/Mariahilf ☎ 01/941–9988) is a restaurant named, of course, after the leading character of Virginia Woolf's famous novel. People of all persuasions come here—the food is that good.

Jazz Clubs

If you think Vienna is only about Mozart, Strauss, and Alban Berg, think again. You are definitely going to be surprised to hear that the jazz scene here is one of the hottest in Europe. The biggest splash has recently been made by **Birdland** (⊠ Am Stadtpark 3 (enter Landstrasser Hauptstrasse 2) 3rd District ☎ 01/2196–39315 ⊕ www.birdland.at) opened in the newly renovated Hilton Hotel in 2004. This club has been a dream come true for the great jazz legend Joe Zawinul who named it after one of his most renowned compositions and New York City's legendary temple of jazz. After a long stint in the States, where he became famous playing with Cannonball Adderley and Miles Davis, then set up the jazz-rock Weather Report, Zawinul came back to his home town to encourage young Austrian talent. He has initiated new musical projects as well as inviting great names to perform live, which he himself does regularly. The Birdland Club and restaurant opens on most nights at 7 PM, closed on Monday.

Set in a cellar under St. Ruprecht's church and the grandaddy of Vienna's jazz clubs, **Jazzland** (✉ Franz-Josefs-Kai 29, 1st District ☎ 01/533–2575 ⊕ www.jazzland.at) opened more than 30 years ago when there was just a small local jazz scene. But thanks to the pioneering work of the club's founder, Axel Melhardt, Austrian jazz musicians have vibed with the best American stars, including Big Joe Williams, Little Brother Montgomery, Bud Freeman, Max Kaminsky, Teddy Wilson, Clark Terry, Benny Carter, Art Farmer, Ray Brown, Herb Ellis, and Lee Konitz. The club also serves excellent and authentic Viennese cuisine.

In the course of a few years, **Porgy & Bess** (✉ Riemergasse 11, 1st District ☎ 01/512–8811 ⊕ www.porgy.at) has become a fixed point in the native and international jazz scene. Founded by the incredibly versatile and friendly Swiss musician Mathias Rueegg in 1993, it moved in 2001 to a new and attractive home in a former cinema. There's a wide and dazzling array of choices here, with sessions, workshops, "Jazz for Kids," and the presentation of troupes from far-off lands—a recent night starred a group from Siberia. Recent stints have included Pharoah Sanders, Teofilovic Twins, Larry Coryell, and the Moscow Art Trio. The programming is adventuresome and cool and even the food on offer is excellent.

THE ARTS

Beethoven! Strauss! *Die Rosenkavalier!* Mozart! The Vienna Boys' Choir! Lehár! Bruckner! *The Merry Widow!* Vienna packs a giant cultural wallop through its numerous venues: from the Vienna Staatsoper (one of the world's five top opera houses) to the Volksoper (fabled shrine of Viennese operetta) to the acoustical supremacy of the Musikverein concert hall. Although healthy government subsidies play a role, it is more the interest of a culturally inclined people that supports a milieu whose spectrum ranges from the austerely classical to the outrageously avant-garde. So book that ticket fast. Vienna's theater and music season begins in September and runs through June, when the Wiener Festwochen (Vienna Festival) is held. For weekly updates on all the happenings, check the listings in the *Der Falter* or *City* newspapers and also consult the monthly calendar brochure, the *Wien-Programm,* published by the Vienna Tourist Board.

TICKETS With a city as music mad and opera crazy as Vienna, it is not surprising to learn that the bulk of major performances are sold out in advance (often by subscription). But with thousands of seats to be filled every night, you may luck out with a bit of planning and the State Theatre Booking Office, or **Österreichischer Bundestheaterkassen** (✉ Theaterkassen, back of Opera, Hanuschgasse 3, in courtyard ☎ 01/513–1513 ⊕ www.bundestheater.at). They sell tickets for the Akademietheater, Schauspielhaus, Staatsoper, Volksoper, and Burgtheater. Call the (frequently busy) phone line weekdays, 8 AM to 5 PM. To purchase tickets at the box office, the above address also operates as a central clearing house, open weekdays, 8 AM to 6 PM, weekends from 9 AM to noon. Tickets for the Staatsoper and Volksoper go on sale one month before the date of performance; credit-card reservations are taken up to six days before the performance. You can also purchase tickets using the Web site; tickets to opera performances can be purchased online— (⊕ www.culturall.at)— and when sales have not yet begun you are allowed to put in a "reservation" to hold tickets. In addition, these state theaters will now accept reservations by telephone against a credit card; you pick up your ticket at the box office with no surcharge. The same applies to concert tickets. However, other ticket agencies—the most trusted is **Liener Brünn** (☎ 01/533–0961 ⊕ www.ims.at/lienerbruenn)—charge a minimum 22% markup and generally deal in the more expensive seats. Expect to pay (or tip) a hotel porter or concierge at least as much as a ticket-agency markup for their help in obtaining hard-to-get tickets.

Tickets to musicals and some events including the Vienna Festival are available at the **"Salettl" gazebo** kiosk alongside the Opera House on Kärntnerstrasse, open daily 10 AM to 7 PM. Tickets to that night's musicals are reduced by half after 2 PM. You can write ahead for tickets for many performances in the city as well. The nearest **Austrian National Tourist Office** can give you a schedule of performances and a ticket order form. Send the form (no payment is required) to the **ticket office** (✉ Kartenvorverkauf Bundestheaterverband, Goethegasse 1, A–1010 Vienna), which will mail you a reservation card; when you get to Vienna, take the card to the main box office to pick up and pay for your tickets.

Film

The film schedule in the daily newspapers *Der Standard* and *Die Presse* lists foreign-language films (*Fremdsprachige Filme*) separately. In film listings, *OmU* means original language with German subtitles. Vienna has a thriving film culture, with viewers seeking original rather than German-dubbed versions. There are several theaters offering English-language films.

Just around the corner from Tuchlauben street, the **Artis** (✉ Corner of Shultergasse/Jordangasse, 1st District ☎ 01/535–6570) has six screens altogether, showing the latest blockbusters three to four times a day. The **Burg Kino** (✉ Opernring 19, 1st District ☎ 01/587–8406) features Carol Reed's Vienna-based classic *The Third Man,* with Orson Welles and Joseph Cotton, every Friday and Sunday. Otherwise all the new releases are usually shown in the original English version. The **Haydn** (✉ Mariahilferstrasse 57, 6th District/Mariahilf ☎ 01/587–2262) is a multiplex theater. Most English films are shown with German subtitles.

In the famous Albertina museum, the **Filmmuseum,** (✉ Augustinerstrasse 1, 1st District ☎ 01/533–7054 ⊕ www.filmmuseum.at) has one of the most ambitious and sophisticated schedules around, with original-version classics and a heavy focus on English-language films. The monthly calendar (posted outside) usually features retrospectives of the work of important and cutting-edge artists, directors, and producers. Membership costs €12 a year. Tickets are €5 each (if you aren't a member, you'll have to purchase a guest membership at €4 per day). The theater is closed July, August, and September. The arty **Votiv-Kino** (⊠ Währinger Strasse 12, 9th District/Alsergrund ☎ 01/317–3571) usually features less mainstream, more alternative fare, with most films being shown in their original version with German subtitles. In winter the Votiv Kino offers a leisurely Sunday-brunch/feature-film package. Like the Votiv Kino, **Film Casino** (⊠ Margaretenstrasse 78, 5th District/Margareten ☎ 01/58–9062) specializes in art films in their original version, with German subtitles. Documentaries and the occasional first-run film blown up to humongous size draw the crowds to the **Imax** (⊠ Mariahilfer Strasse 212, 14th District/Penzing ☎ 01/8940101); Trams nos. 52 and 58 (starting at Westbahnhof) drop you off at Penzingerstrasse, just opposite the theater.

Galleries

With new and hip contemporary art museums springing up across Austria like a rampant spread of edelweiss (notably the Kunsthaus in Graz and the Museum der Moderne in Salzburg), art in Vienna needs to remain cutting-edge, and that it has succeeded in doing thanks to notable galleries that have opened up in two quarters of the city. The first is behind the MQ (MuseumsQuartier) complex, while the second is in the 4th District—the Freihaus-Quartier, where some of the most exciting contemporary galleries in town have set up shop, appropriately within range of the famed Secession Pavilion. Until the pioneer gallery of Georg Kargl put down roots there a few years ago the area was deemed derelict—shop windows were boarded up and streets were uninviting. Today, Freihaus has become one of the hottest areas in Vienna for everything that's trendy, fashionable, and fun. The more traditional art galleries are still grouped around the now privatized Dorotheum auction house (see the chapter on shopping) in the city center.

The leading address for contemporary galleries in the Freihaus-Quartier is Schleifmuehlgasse. Here is where you'll find, in a former printing shop, **Gallery Georg Kargl** (⊠ Schleifmuehlgasse 5, 4th District/Wieden ☎ 01/585–4199), which shows art that sidesteps categorization and is a must for serious art collectors. Another of the "Schleifmuehlgasse" galleries is **Gallery Christine Koenig** (⊠ Schleifmuehlgasse 1a, 4th District/Wieden ☎ 01/585–7474), which focuses on introducing new artists, particularly those whose work emphasizes painters' propensities, such as Pierre Klossowski and Karin Kneffel. Installations are usually tailor-made for the gallery.

Over near the MQ, **Gallery Hubert Winter** (⊠ Breite Gasse 17, 7th District/Neubau ☎ 01/524–0976) is one of Vienna's pioneer contemporary galleries and has now moved to a great location just behind the MuseumsQuartier. It represents mainly first-class American avant-garde names and is one of the best places to start a walk through one of the quieter areas in town. **IG Bildende Kunst** (✉ Gumpendorfer Strasse 10–12, 7th District/Neubau ☎ 01/524–0909) concentrates on showing the work of as-yet unknown talent. Works from artists completing master classes at the Academy of Art are frequently exhibited here for the first time, allowing the open-minded spectator to get a taste of what's to come. A presence at cutting-edge art fairs around the world, **Krinzinger Gallery** (✉ Schottenfeldgasse 45, 7th District ☎ 01/513–30 06) has been going strong since the 1970s, when it pushed Vienna Actionism. Its Krinzinger Projects are among the most important blips on the contemporary Austrian art radar screen, and it is close to the MQ (MuseumsQuartier), a very appropriate backdrop.

One of the most traditional art galleries, **Gallery Dr. Sternat** (✉ Lobkowitzplatz 1, 1st District ☎ 01/512 20 63) has a focus on fine Austrian paintings, Viennese bronzes, Thonet furniture, and beautiful Biedermeier pieces. It is around the corner from the Opera House. Wonderful works by Josef Hoffmann, Max Fabiani, Dagobert Peche, Vally Wieselthier, and Fritz Dietl entice onlookers to spend more than just time at **Bel Etage** (✉ Mahlerstrasse 15, 1st District ☎ 01/512–2379). The assortment of Art Nouveau art and furniture is amazing and well worth a visit. Close to the MAK Museum of Applied Art, **KlausEngelhorn20** (✉ Stubenring 20, 1st District ☎ 01/5127–94020) offers contemporary art, installations, and experiments. During Vienna's film festival "Viennale" there is a complementary exhibition held here, which attracts the occasional illustrious visitor, such as Yoko Ono. Art and design merge here in some important trends. **Gallery Julius Hummel** (✉ Bäckerstrasse 14, 1st District ☎ 01/512–1296) concentrates mainly on themes concerning the human body in art. It's in an old Gothic building in one of the most charming spots in Vienna, nestled between the likes of such venerable institutions as Café Alt-Wien and Oswald & Kalb. Franz West is one of the artists shown here.

Music

Vienna is without question one of the main music centers of the world. Contemporary music gets its due, but it's the hometown standards— the works of Beethoven, Brahms, Haydn, Mozart, and Schubert—that draw the Viennese public and make tickets to the Wiener Philharmoniker the hottest of commodities. A monthly printed program, the *Wien-Programm,* put out by the city tourist board and available at any travel agency or hotel, gives a general overview of what's going on in the worlds of opera, concerts, jazz, theater, and galleries, and similar information is posted on billboards and fat advertising columns around the city. Vienna is home to four full symphony orchestras: the great Wiener Philharmoniker (Vienna Philharmonic), the outstanding Wiener Symphoniker (Vienna Symphony), the broadcasting service's ORF Symphony Orchestra, and the Niederösterreichische Tonkünstler. There are also hundreds of smaller groups, from world-renowned trios to chamber orchestras.

Among the many fine concert halls in town there is still only one
★ **Musikverein** (✉ Dumbastrasse 3; ticket office at Karlsplatz 6, 1st Dis-

trict ☎ 01/505 8190 🖷 01/505 8190-94 ⊕ www.musikverein.at). Actually, there are six auditoria in this magnificent theater but the one that everyone knows is the venue for the annually televised New Year's Day Concert—the "Goldene Saal," the Golden Room, officially called the Grosser Musikvereinssaal. Possibly the most beautiful in the world, this Parthenon of a music hall devoted to the classic Western symphonic repertory is designed in suitably "classical" fashion. The architecture of Theophil Hansen, the Danish 19th-century architect, was clearly inspired by ancient Greece. For his 1869 design of the hall, he arrayed an army of gilded caryatids in the main concert hall, planted Ionic columns in the 660-seat Brahmssaal, and placed the figure of Orpheus in the building pediment. But the surprise is that the smaller Brahmssal is even more sumptuous—a veritable Greek temple with more caryatids and lots of gilding and green malachite marble. What Hansen would have made of the four newly constructed (2004) subsidiary halls, set below the main theater, must remain a mystery, but the avant-garde Glass, Metal, Wooden and Stone Halls (Gläserne, Hölzerne, Metallene, Steinerne Saal) make fitting showcases for contemporary music concerts. But the Musikverein will always be known as *the* place to hear Beethoven, Brahms, Bruckner and their ilk because it is home to such outstanding troupes as the Wiener Philharmoniker (everyone from Berlioz to Bernstein have considered this the greatest orchestra in the world although, with only one female member, it may also rank as the most male-dominated) and the Wiener Symphoniker, along with many of the world's finest orchestra conductors. The Wiener Philharmoniker presents only 15 or so concerts a year (they tour relentlessly) so tickets are as rare as hens' teeth. Happily, you can purchase standing room tickets for these performances at the box office up to three weeks in advance. As for orchestra seats in the Grosser Musikvereinssaal, the best are—surprise—at the very back, since only the back five rows rise up to give a satisfying view of the entire room. Another vantage point to covet are seats in the balcony boxes.

★ A three-minute walk from the Musikverein, crossing Schwarzenbergplatz, is the **Konzerthaus** (✉ Lothringerstrasse 20, 1st District ☎ 01/242002 🖷 01/242–0011–0 ⊕ www.konzerthaus.at), home to three auditoria—the Grosser Konzerthaussaal, Mozartsaal, and Schubertsaal halls. The first is a room of magnificent size, with red velvet and gold accents. The calendar of Grosser Konzerthaussaal is packed with goodies, including the fabulous early-music group, Concentus Musicus Wien, headed by Nicolaus Harnoncourt, and concerts of the Wiener Philharmoniker and the Wiener Symphoniker. Several smaller halls here, like the Alban Berg Saal, feature recitals.

★ If the white-gloved, whirling waltzes of Strauss are your thing, you'll want to head to the "Johann Strauss Konzerte im Wiener Kursalon" concerts at the **Wiener Kursalon** (✉ Johannesgasse 33, 1st District ☎ 01/513–2477 🖷 01/512–5791 ⊕ www.strauss-konzerte.at/), a majestic palace-like structure set in Vienna's sylvan Stadtpartk, which was built in the Italian Renaissance Revival style in 1865. Here, in (somewhat distressingly overrenovated) gold-and-white salons, the Salonorchester "Alt

CloseUp
JUST LIKE TAKING CANDY FROM MOZART

A FITTING TITLE FOR A SPECIAL FESTIVAL offered by the Vienna Kammeroper to honor the 250th birthday year of Mozart. Just the maraschino cherry atop of a multi-layered cake of events scheduled for 2006—hundreds of concerts, operas, and recitals years in the planning—it is only appropriate that this chamber-opera troupe (⊕ www.wienerkammeroper.at) present the baby composer's earliest works in their Fleischmarkt theater. Considering the wunderkind started composing at age 8, he would probably delight in the Marionettentheater Schloss Schönbrunn's production of The Magic Flute (⊕ www. marionettentheater.at) or its "Greatest Hits" Mozart show, mounted at Empress Maria Theresa's palace. But these are only two of the sweetest birthday offerings. The grandest? Perhaps the concert-spectacular on Rathausplatz on May 12 to kick off the annual Vienna Festival (⊕ www.festwochen. at); another open-air concert will be held on Josefsplatz on July 9. One of the most moving events will be the Easter Night concert on April 16 at St. Stephan's Cathedral, scene of Mozart's marriage and burial service. The Mozart Year will reach its crescendo on December 5th—the day of the composer's death—when the Wiener Philharmoniker will perform his last work, the Requiem, under Christian Thielemann at the Staatsoper, while Nikolaus Harnoncourt's Concentus Musicus will mount Mozart's Mass in C Minor at the Musikverein (⊕ www.musikverein.at).

This legendary concert hall has a 2006 calendar packed with Mozart. Under the auspices of the Osterklang Wien festival (⊕ www.osterklang.at), the Wiener Philharmoniker will perform the last three symphonies on April 7 and 8; during May and June, Rudolf Buchbinder will play the piano concertos; in October, German star violinist Anne Sophie Mutter will grace Mozart's violin sonatas, while "Mozart and More" will showcase the Vienna Boys' Choir

(⊕ www.mondial.at). Over at one of the world's premier opera houses, the Vienna Staatsoper (⊕ www.wiener-staatsoper.at), Mozart will be bravi-ed with January 2006 performances of The Magic Flute, Don Giovanni, The Marriage of Figaro and Così fan tutte, with May bringing The Abduction from the Seraglio. More opera will be on tap over at the Vienna Volksoper (⊕ www. volksoper.at): The Magic Flute (date of premiere, 12/17/05); The Marriage of Figaro (2/26/06); La Clemenza di Tito (4/28/06); Don Giovanni (9/16/06) and Così fan Tutte (9/29/06). Perhaps the best house in the world to hear a Mozart opera, the Theater an der Wien (opened 1801), has some special treats (⊕ www. klangbogen.at): Neil Shicoff in Idomeneo (late January, early Feb., late June); the rare Lucio Silla (March); Patrice Chereau's provocative Così fan tutte (early June, late Nov.); and Sir Simon Rattle conducting the Wiener Philharmoniker in the last three symphonies (early Dec). Other events include free open-air showing of Mozart films, like Amadeus and Ingmar Bergman's Magic Flute on Rathausplatz, every dusk July 1 to September 3 (⊕ www.wien-event.at); a series of Mozart Galas at the Palais Auersperg (⊕ www.wro.at); and the "New Crowned Hope" fall festival (⊕ www. festwochen.at) directed by the noted Peter Sellars. Museum shows? Mozart's most notable Viennese residence, the Figarohaus—now rechristened the Mozart Haus Vienna (⊕ www.mozarthausvienna. at)—has a new exhibition gallery. Over at the Haus der Musik (⊕ www.hdm.at), you'll be able to "conduct" some Mozart ditties, make your own custom-tailored Magic Flute, and marvel at the autograph Requiem. Finally, the regal Albertina museum (⊕ www. albertina.at) will host an extensive exhibition of Mozartiana mid-March through August. For the complete rundown of concerts and special events, log on to http://b2b.wien. info/data/mozart-sales-wien-e.pdf.

Wien" performs concerts, accompanied at times by dancers, of the works of "Waltz King" Johann Strauss and his contemporaries, with waltzes, polkas, parade themes, operetta melodies, traditional "Schrammeln," and *Salonmusik* at the fore. In addition, the Wiener Johann Strauss Capelle, dressed in period costume, also presents concerts of the Strauss era in "Original Viennese Waltz Show" evenings, replete with singers, dancers, and your very own glass of champagne (no dancing by the audience allowed). Both these adorably romantic evenings are presented throughout the year. Also of note are the Strauss concerts offered at the Festsaal in the Hofburg palace at the Orangerie in the Schönbrunn Palace.

★ Happily, there is a plethora of period-era, chocolate-box, jeweled concert salons in Vienna. Perhaps the most opulent is the **Schlosstheater Schönbrunn** (✉ Schönbrunner Schloss-strasse, 13th District/Hietzing ☎ 01/71155–158 ⊕ www.mdw.ac.at), built for Empress Maria Theresa in the Valerie Wing of the palace, with glittering chandeliers and a gigantic mural painted on the ceiling. Students of the Universität für Musik und Darstellende Kunstand and other troupes give concerts here during the fall to spring season. Built in 1754, the **Orangerie Schönbrunn** (✉ Schönbrunner Schloss-strasse, 13th District/Hietzing ☎ 01/8125004 ⊕ www.imagevienna.com) offers Mozart and Strauss concerts in the Orangerie "greenhouse" of the palace. Here, legend has it, Mozart and Salieri once battled it out in their only head-to-head musical competition. On special occasions the orchestra moves into the palace's Great Gallery. For a grand evening of Strauss and Mozart in imperial surroundings, head to the Wiener Hofburgorchester concerts given in the Hofburg palace auditoria of the Red-

★ outensaal (enter this one, once destroyed by bombs, now rebuilt, using the Josefsplatz) and the mammoth 19th-century **Festsaal** (✉ Heldenplatz, 1st District ☎ 01/587–2552 🖷 01/587–4397 ⊕ www.hofburgorchester.at/). The concerts are offered Tuesday, Thursday, and Saturday, May until October. The 18th-century Palais Pálffy presents concerts in its small **Figarosaal** (✉ Josefsplatz 6, 1st District ☎ 01/512–5681–0 ⊕ www.palaispálffy.at/), where the young Mozart gave a recital in October 1762. Unfortunately, the gold-and-red decor has been rather too blatantly renovated. The most enchanting place to hear Mozart in Vienna (or anywhere,

★ for that matter?) is the exquisite 18th-century Sala Terrena of the **Deutschordenskloster** (✉ Singerstrasse 7, 1st District ☎ 01/911–9077 ⊕ www.mozarthaus.at). Here, in a tiny room—seating for no more than 50 people—a bewigged chamber group offers Mozart concerts in a jewel box overrun with Rococo frescoes in the Venetian style. The concerts are scheduled by the nearby Mozarthaus. Said to be the oldest concert "hall" in Vienna, the Sala Terrena is part of the German Monastery, where, in 1781, Mozart worked for his despised employer, Archbishop Colloredo of Salzburg. Concerts are usually scheduled for Thursdays and Sundays at 7:30 PM and Saturday at 5 PM.

Radio Kulturhaus (✉ Argentinierstrasse 30A, 4th District/Wieden ☎ 01/501–70–377) is a major concert venue, comprising three halls, with the Vienna Radio Orchestra taking center ring. A hallowed Valhalla for piano lovers, the **Bösendorfersaal** (✉ Graf-Starhemberg-Gasse 14, 4th District/Wieden ☎ 01/504–6651 🖷 01/504–6651) offers a venue adjacent to the museum devoted to the legendary Bösendorfer piano, which has been prized by kings, emperors, and composers for centuries. Students of the **Universität für Musik und Darstellende Kunst** (University of Music and Performing Arts; ✉ Seilerstätte 26 and Johannesgasse 8 ☎01/711550) regularly give class recitals in the school's concert halls during the academic year; look for announcements posted outside for dates and times.

Although the well-known summer-season Vienna Festival, the **Wiener Festwochen** (☎ 01/589–22–11), held mid-May to mid-June, wraps up the primary season, the rest of the summer musical scene, from mid-July to mid-August, nowadays brims with activities. One top event is the **Festival KlangBogen** (✉ Stadiongasse 9, 1st District ☎ 01/42717 ⊕ www.klangbogen.at), which features rare and contemporary operas starring some famous singers and performers. Recently they performed Smetana's *Dalibor* and Gian Carlo Menotti's *Goya,* featuring Placido Domingo. Outdoor symphony concerts are performed weekly in the vast arcaded courtyard of the Rathaus (entrance on Friedrich Schmidt-Platz). You can also catch musical events in the Volksgarten. **Church music,** the mass sung in Latin, can be heard Sunday mornings during the main season at St. Stephan's; in the Franciscan church, St. Michael's; the Universitätskirche; and, above all, in the Augustinerkirche. The Friday and Saturday newspapers carry details. St. Stephan's also has organ concerts most Wednesday evenings from early May to late November.

The beloved Vienna Boys' Choir, the **Wiener Sängerknaben** (✉ Hofburg, Schweizer Hof, 1st District ☎01/533–9927 ⊠01/533–9927–75 ⊕www.wsk.at) are far from just being living "dolls" out of a Walt Disney film (remember the 1962 movie, *Almost Angels*?). Their pedigree is royal, and their professionalism such that they regularly appear with the best orchestras around the world. The troupe originated as a choir founded by Emperor Maximilian I in 1498, but with the demise of the Habsburg empire in 1918, they were on their own and became a private outfit, subsidizing themselves by giving public performances starting in the 1920s. These became so popular, the troupe grew to 100 boys, splitting off into four different minichoirs, which now offer about 300 concerts every year. While they are aged only 10 to 14, the boys are sophisticated musicians, testimony to a five-century-old tradition fostered by such legends as Haydn (who sang with them), Salieri (who taught them), Schubert (who wrote for them), and Bruckner (who rewarded them with cake if they sang well). While they shine with Mozart and Bach, their repertory also includes modern works, such as Mahler's *Das klagende Lied* and Bernstein's *Chichester Psalms*. And why do they wear sailor suits? When the troupe lost its imperial patronage, they traded in their court costume for these charming costumes, then the height of fashion (a look even sported by Donald Duck, who was also born in that era).

From mid-September to late-June, the apple-cheeked lads sing mass at 9:15 AM Sunday in the Hofburgkapelle. Written requests for seats should be made at least eight weeks in advance (✍ Verwaltung der Hofmusikkapelle, Hofburg, A–1010 Vienna). You will be sent a reservation card, which you exchange at the box office (in the Hofburg courtyard) for your tickets. Tickets are also sold at ticket agencies and at the box office (open Friday, 11 AM–1 PM and 3–5 PM; any remaining seats may be available Sunday morning, 8:15 to 8:45). General seating costs €5, prime seats in the front of the church nave €29. It's important to note that only the 10 side balcony seats allow a view of the actual choir; those who purchase floor seats, standing room, or center balcony will not have a view of the boys. On Sunday at 8:45 AM any unclaimed, preordered tickets are sold. You can also opt for standing room, which is free. If you miss hearing choir at a Sunday mass, you may be able to catch them in a more popular program in the Musikverein or Konzerthaus or, in August, at the Schönbrunn Palace.

Opera & Operetta

Fodor'sChoice

★

The house built, in a manner of speaking, by Richard Strauss, Gustav Mahler, and Herbert von Karajan, the **Wiener Staatsoper** (Vienna State Opera House) (✉ Opernring 2, 1st District ☎ 01/514–440 ⊕ www.wiener-staatsoper.at) is one of the world's top five opera houses. It has been the scene of countless musical triumphs and a center of unending controversies over how it should be run and by whom; when Lorin Maazel was unceremoniously dumped as head of the Opera not many years ago, he pointed out that the house had done the same thing to Mahler half a century earlier. Happily, Seiji Ozawa has been Music Director since the 2002 season and has overseen a number of brilliant performances and premieres. Other guest conductors include Runnicles, Young, Bychkov, and Jones, to name just a few. All operas are performed in their original language but each seat now has a miniscreen offering subtitles (in German or English).

Unlike some of the other great opera houses in Europe (which perform their operas in weeklong runs), the Vienna state opera has a revolving repertory (and a big government subsidy to facilitate this) throughout the season, which means you might manage to see five different operas within a week. An opera or ballet is performed virtually every night from September 1 to June 30. Recent triumphs include productions of Richard Strauss's *Daphne, Elektra,* and *Salome,* while the highlight of the 2004 season was the new Wagner *Parsifal,* starring the great Thomas Quasthoff as Amfortas (the role of his life). There are nearly 25 operas presented every year, ranging from such rarities as Korngold's *Die Tote Stadt* and Nina Rota's *Aladdin* to *Aida.* Several productions are mounted in a lavish and lush crowd-pleasing manner, such as *La Traviata, Die Rosenkavalier, La Boheme, L'Italiana in Algieri,* etc. Others, such as the Wagner Ring cycle, are presented in minimalist fashion (a bit hard to justify when ticket prices are *so* expensive—they range from €9 to €179).

Guided tours of the Opera House are held year-round (subject to change due to rehearsals and auditions). Although the opera scene in Vienna has always been one where an elegant audience is expected, nowadays an anything-goes-attire attitude is appearing. For the complete scoop on ordering tickets, see the Tickets section above. Tickets are available online one month before the showing, although the best seats are usually snapped up within an hour of being posted, with the exception of the most expensive seats, usually still available within the last week before the performance, not including premieres. Standing-room tickets are available only from the *Stehplätze* box office, which opens 80 minutes before the performance begins.

For a century the Staatsoper and **Volksoper** (✉ Währingerstrasse 78 ☎ 01/514–440 ⊕ www.volksoper.at) have been the fiercest of rivals and today, Volksoper director Rudolf Berger is continuing to rattle his sabers. In fact, although considered by some to be home to second-class opera and operetta, this has become one of Vienna's biggest surprises and most fashionable venues. By introducing new productions of Lehár's *The Merry Widow,* in a 100th anniversary production, and a range of premiered rarities, including the late-Romantic masterpiece, Franz Schreker's *Irrelohe* or Emmerich Kálmán's rediscovered operetta, *The Duchess from Chicago,* let alone the first-ever production of Rodgers and Hammerstein's *The Sound of Music* (ever the delicate production, in view of the story's political undertones), this has become the theater that opera lovers most talk up. Berger continues to show brilliance and foresight with new productions of Smetana's *The Bartered Bride,* Walter Braunfels's *Die Vögel,* and Alexander Zemlinsky's *King Candaules.* For some, however, this theater is most beloved for its operetta performances (more than 100 a year). In fact, to open and close the theater's season, the Volksoper presents "Operetta Weeks," usually scheduled for the last week in June, the first two weeks of September, and the final two weeks of June. The Volksoper's own ballet ensemble has impressed its audience with new and successful productions of *Nudo* (with dancers in the nude) and *Der Nussknacker* (yes, "The Nutcracker," to compete with the one on view at the Staatsoper). The Volksopera is outside the city center at Währingerstrasse and Währinger Gürtel (third stop on Streetcar 41, 42, or 43, all of which run from "downstairs" at Schottentor, U2, on the Ring).

You'll also find musicals and operetta at several theaters. The **Raimundtheater** (✉ Wallgasse 18 ☎ 01/599–77–0 ⊕ www.musicalvienna.at) mostly offers musicals by local composers. For cabaret and traveling music groups, try the **Ronacher** (✉ Seilerstätte/Himmelpfortgasse ☎ 01/514–
★ 110 ⊕ www.musicalvienna.at). Built in 1801, the **Theater an der Wien** (✉ Linke Wienzeile 6 ☎ 01/588–30–0 ⊕ www.musicalvienna.at) is one of Vienna's most legendary theaters. Here were premiered such masterworks as Beethoven's *Fidelio* (1805) and Johann Strauss's *Die Fledermaus* (1874). Today, it offers glitzy musicals, such as *Mozart!* and *Jekyll and Hyde.* During the 2006 Mozart Year, however, the Staatsoper will take over and host smaller operas of the great composer. During summers, the Festwochen and Klangbogen festivals offer a calendar of concerts and operettas here. Opera and operetta are performed on an irregular schedule at the **Kammeroper** (✉ Fleischmarkt 24 ☎ 01/512–01–000 ⊕ www.wienerkammeroper.at), which is known for its adventuresome repertory.

Dance

Both modern dance and classical ballet have been given a boost, due to new choreographers, new venues, and new blood appearing on the Vienna stage. A small revolution has been brewing on the modern dance front, thanks to **Tanzquartier Wien** (⊠ Museumsplatz 1, 7th District/ Neubau ☎01/581–35 91 ⊕ www.tqw.at). DanceQuarter Vienna is now Austria's foremost center for contemporary dance and performances. The Tanzquartier season lasts from October through April. In May and June, it is followed by the so-called "Factory Season," when the center concentrates solely on the projects presented in its dance studios. The TQW complex also includes a public information center with a library. The **ballet evenings** (☎01/514–44–0) on the Staatsoper and Volksoper seasonal schedule measure up to international standards and are seeing far more contemporary pieces performed. Vienna also has **Szene Wien** (⊠ Hauffgasse 26, 11th District/Simmering ☎01/749–3341 🖷01/749–2206), a theater offering contemporary dance with some of Austria's up-and-coming choreographers on show. **Dietheater Wien** (⊠ Karlsplatz 5, 1st District ☎01/587–0504–0 🖷01/587–8774–31) is a popular venue for cutting-edge dance arts.

Theater

Vienna's **Burgtheater** (⊠ Dr.-Karl-Lueger-Ring 2, 1st District, Vienna) is one of the leading German-language theaters of the world. The repertoire covers all the German classics mixing them with with more modern and controversial pieces. The Burg's smaller house, the **Akademietheater** (⊠ Lisztstrasse 1), draws on much the same group of actors for classical and modern plays. Both houses are closed during July and August. *See* Tickets, *above,* for details.

The **Kammerspiele** (⊠ Rotenturmstrasse 20 ☎01/42700–304) does modern plays. The **Theater in der Josefstadt** (⊠ Josefstädterstrasse 26, 8th District/Josefstadt ☎01/42700–306) stages classical and modern works year-round in the house once run by the great producer and teacher Max Reinhardt. The **Volkstheater** (⊠ Neustiftgasse 1, 7th District/ Neubau ☎01/523–3501–0) presents dramas, comedies, and folk plays.

For theater in English head for **Vienna's English Theater** (⊠ Josefsgasse 12, 8th District/Josefstadt ☎01/402–1260). Another option is the equally good **International Theater** (⊠ Porzellangasse 8, 9th District/ Alsergrund ☎01/319–6272).

SHOPPING

5

By Diane
Naar-Elphee

VIENNA'S KÄRNTNERSTRASSE COULD BOAST that it once created its exquisite jewelry, fine leather goods, or petit-point handbags (as Viennese as St. Stephan's Cathedral) for the imperial Habsburgs. The court vanished long ago, but some of the *Hoflieferanten* (court suppliers) still proffer their wares in the city's famous "golden triangle": Kärntnerstrasse, Graben, and Kohlmarkt, flaunting their imperial pedigree with signs that announce they are "K & K"—*Kaiserlich und Königlich,* "By appointment to the Imperial and Royal Household." Some of these emporia still maintain their name, with, at times, the old-fashioned grace, slightly fawning touch, and lots of *Gnä Frau* and *der Herr* thrown in for good measure.

But if the archduchesses of yore came back today to make more posh purchases, they would find that fashion houses like Zara or H&M, the cheap yet chic clothes chain, have taken over where legendary names once reigned supreme. Nowadays, Vienna's grand shopping boulevards have lost many of the good old institutionalized shops. The most recent shock for locals was the closure of Braun and Co. on the Graben, which for more than 100 years had supplied distinguished patrons with elegant attire and everything that went with it (private shopping was available for royals and aristos). Some see these closings as a second fall of the Empire.

The recent arrival of trendy outfitters signals that Vienna's shopping scene is undergoing a (perhaps) much needed rejuvenation. To the delight of fashionistas, Gucci and Chanel have now colonized the Kohlmarkt—still the most up-market shopping street. Nowadays the "triangle" offers a real eclectic mix of buys, with some of the best "Made in Austria" shops for exclusive designer goods found on the side streets branching off from the main pedestrian precincts. Speaking of which, anyone looking for the trendiest hot-spot should trot along to the Freihaus-Quartier, around the corner from Vienna's Naschmarkt (Wienzeile, 4th District). The Freihaus has just the right blend of suburban flair and hipsterious bars and cafés—glam girls like to saunter along the Schleif-muehlgasse to take in as many art galleries as fashion boutiques.

For a mix of old and new, nothing tops the biggest flea market in Vienna—the Flohmarkt—held on Saturday at the Kettenbrückengasse tube station, just a few steps from the Freihaus. Be sure to get there early as the best buys are soon gone. If you're out for more creative handicrafts, try the shops in the Spittelberg—the "Biedermeier" quarter—in the 7th District. Elsewhere, hand-knitted woollies, homemade candles, ornaments, and eccentric jewelry are all found in profusion on the Mariahilferstrasse. This, Vienna's longest shopping avenue, has been given a face lift and offers some trendy boutiques, book and music stores, a number of department stores, and plenty of places for regaining strength in-between.

Antique lovers will be best off sticking to the center of town—they will make a bee-line for the Dorotheum auction house and the surrounding area along Spiegelgasse, Braeunerstrasse, and Habsburgergasse. The famous Chrismas holiday markets, or *Christkindlmärkte,* can be found at Freyung, Am Hof, and on Karlsplatz (in front of the church). At Christmas time, the biggest market is the tinselly Christkindlmarkt on Rathausplatz in front of City Hall; in protest over its mass-commercialization, smaller markets specializing in handicrafts have sprung up on such tra-

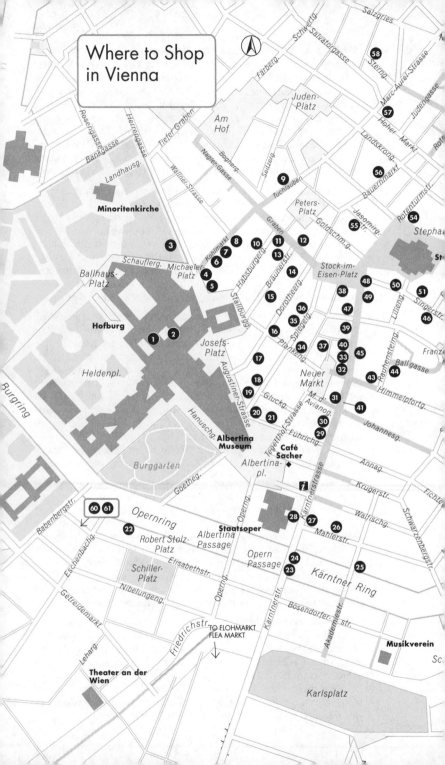

Where to Shop in Vienna

ditional spots as Am Hof and the Freyung, also the venue for other seasonal markets. Last but not least, don't forget the 20% VAT, included in the purchase price on every item (except books)—this tax can help make that authentic Vienna Secession chandelier a real bargain.

Shopping Districts & Streets

The Kärntnerstrasse, Graben, and Kohlmarkt pedestrian areas in the 1st District, **Inner City,** claim to have the best shops in Vienna, and for some items, such as jewelry, some of the best anywhere, although you must expect high prices. The side streets within this area have developed their own character, with shops offering antiques, art, clocks, jewelry, and period furniture. **Ringstrasse Galerie,** the indoor shopping plaza at Kärntner Ring 5–7, brings a number of shops together in a modern complex, although many of these stores have other, larger outlets elsewhere in the city. Outside the center, concentrations of stores are on **Mariahilferstrasse,** straddling the 6th and 7th districts; **Landstrasser Hauptstrasse** in the 3rd District; and, still farther out, **Favoritenstrasse** in the 10th District.

A collection of attractive small boutiques can be found in the **Palais Ferstel** passage at Freyung 2 in the 1st District. A modest group of smaller shops has sprung up in the **Sonnhof** passage between Landstrasser Hauptstrasse 28 and Ungargasse 13 in the 3rd District. The **Spittelberg** market, on the Spittelberggasse between Burggasse and Siebensterngasse in the 7th District, has drawn small galleries and handicrafts shops and is particularly popular in the weeks before Christmas and Easter.

Note: If no neighborhood is listed under the address of the stores listed below, that means the store is in the center-city 1st District.

Department Stores

Kaufhaus Steffl (⊠ Kärntnerstrasse 19 ☎ 01/514310 ⊕ www.kaufhaussteffl.at) is moderately upscale without being overly expensive. The larger department stores are concentrated in Mariahilferstrasse. By far the best is **Peek & Cloppenburg** (⊠ Mariahilferstrasse 26–30, 6th District ☎01/805-211-900 ⊕www.peekundcloppenburg.at). Farther up the street you will find slightly cheaper goods at **Gerngross** (⊠ Mariahilferstrasse and Kirchengasse, 6th District).

Markets

★ In the 6th District (U-Bahn: Karlsplatz), Vienna's **Naschmarkt** can be found between Linke and Rechte Wienzeile, starting at Getreidemarkt. Its many food stalls comprise one of Europe's last and most colorful food and produce markets, a great holdover from the days when all foodstuffs were sold in open-air markets. Today, of course, we have supermarkets, but the Naschmarkt is such an institution—and such a spectacle—many Viennese (some of the top city chefs among them) prefer to do their food shopping here. The variety is amazing, the noshing can be fun, the salesfolk manning the stalls snappish and ill-mannered. Stalls open at 5 or 6 AM, and the pace is lively until 5 or 6 PM. Saturday is the big day, when farmers come into the city to sell at the back end of the market, but shops close around 3 PM. Also Saturday there's a huge flea market at Kettenbrückengasse end. It is closed Sunday.

★ Every Saturday (except holidays), rain or shine, from about 7:30 AM to 4 or 5, the **Flohmarkt** in back of the Naschmarkt, stretching along the Linke Wienzeile from the Kettenbrückengasse U4 subway station, offers a staggering collection of stuff ranging from serious antiques to plain junk. Haggle over prices. On Thursday and Friday from late spring to mid-fall, an outdoor combination arts-and-crafts, collectibles, and flea market takes place on **Am Hof.** On weekends in summer from about 10 to 6, an outdoor **art and antiques market** springs up along the Danube Canal, stretching from the Schwedenbrücke to beyond the Salztorbrücke. Lots of books are sold, some in English, plus generally better goods and collectibles than at the Saturday flea market. Bargain over prices.

Specialty Stores

Antiques

You will find the best antiques shops in the 1st District, many clustered close to the Dorotheum auction house, in the Dorotheergasse, Stallburggasse, Plankengasse, and Spiegelgasse. You'll also find interesting shops in the Josefstadt (8th) district, where prices are considerably lower than those in the center of town. Wander up Florianigasse and back down Josefstädterstrasse, being sure not to overlook the narrow side streets.

★ Just around the corner from the Opera House, **Gallery Dr. Sternat** (✉ Lobkowitzplatz 1, ☎ 01/512–2063) is one of the most traditional art galleries, with a focus on fine Austrian paintings, Viennese bronzes, Thonet furniture, and beautiful Biedermeier pieces. **Bel Etage** (✉ Mahlerstrasse 15 ☎ 01/512–2379) has wonderful works by Josef Hoffmann, Dagobert Peche, and other Wiener Werkstätte masters, all of which entice onlookers to spend more than just time here. **D & S Antiquitäten** (✉ Dorotheergasse 13 ☎ 01/512–1011) specializes in old Viennese clocks.

★ For military memorabilia, including uniforms, medals, and weapons from the Austrian monarchy through World War I, go to **Doppeladler** (✉ Opernring 9 ☎ 01/581–6232). Look in at **Glasgalerie Kovacek** (✉ Spiegelgasse 12 ☎ 01/512–9954) to see a remarkable collection of glass paperweights and other glass objects. Auctions are also held at the grand and regal **Palais Kinsky** (✉ Freyung 4 ☎ 01/532–42009) for paintings and antiques.

Books

If you are planning a hiking holiday in Austria then stock up on the necessary maps at **Freytag & Berndt** (✉ Kohlmarkt 9 ☎ 01/533–8685 ⊕ www.freytagberndt.at), the best place for maps and travel books in Vienna. The biggest book store in Vienna, **Morawa** (✉ Wollzeile 11 ☎ 01/513–7513 ⊕ www.morawa.at), has titles on everything under the sun. Thankfully, help is always at hand if you can't find that one book. The magazine and newspaper section is vast and don't pass over some of the cute printed gifts, such as a calendar made out of paper shopping bags (put the bags to good use when the year has passed). The biggest Harry Potter launch in Austria took place at the **British Bookshop** (✉ Weihburggasse 24 ☎ 01/512–1945 ⊕ www.britishbookshop.at), always well stocked with

CloseUp

THE MOST SUMPTUOUS "STORE" IN VIENNA

F YOU ARE LOOKING *for that something truly special—an 18th-century oil portrait or a fake fur, a Rococo mirror or a fine silk fan, modern or retro jewelry, a china figurine or solid silver spoon, an old map of the Austrian Empire or even a stuffed parrot—the one place that may have the answer is the* **Dorotheum** *(⌗ Dorotheergasse 17 ☎ 01/515–60–0 ⊕ www.dorotheum.at), Vienna's fabled auction house. Have you ever wanted to see how the Austrian aristocracy once lived, how their sumptuous homes were furnished? Well, don't bother with a museum—you can inspect their antique furnishings, displayed as if in use, for free, and without the eagle eyes of sales personnel following your every move, in peace and quiet in the gilded salons here. This was the first imperial auction house (oops, pawn-shop), established in 1707 by Emperor Joseph I.*

Occupying the former site of the Dorothy Convent (hence the name), the Dorotheum has built up a grand reputation since it was privatized in the early 1990s. The neo-Baroque building was completed in 1901 and deserves a walk-through (you can enter from Spiegelgasse and exit Dorotheergasse) just to have a look, even if it is only to admire the gorgeous stuccoed walls and palatial interiors, or to take a peek into the glass-roofed patio stocked with early-20th-century glass, furniture, and art. With more than 600 auctions a year, this has become one of the busiest auction houses in Europe. There are auctions held daily except Sunday. And if you don't fancy bidding for something, there are large cash-sale areas in the ground and second floors where loads of stuff (that didn't sell at auction) can simply be bought off the floor.

all the latest editions and best sellers. The friendly staff encourage browsing, which gives the place a very pleasant feel. **Herder** (⌗ Wollzeile 33 ☎ 01/5121413) is a very noted bookshop, with three floors packed with the very best on religion, philosophy, self-help, and many other empowering subjects. When you've worked out your path in between the piles of new arrivals, stacked thigh-high on the floor, then you can start to discover the charm of the tucked-away **Shakespeare & Company** (⌗ Sterngasse 2 ☎ 01/5355053). This treasure trove is in the very heart of town and has an excellent assortment of English books, with special emphasis on design, cultural studies, and politics. If you're an art book lover, **Wolfrum** (⌗ Augustinerstrasse 10 ☎ 01/512–5398) will be your home-away-from-home. If you have money to burn, you can also spring for a Schiele print or special art edition to take home.

Ceramics & Porcelain

The best porcelain in town can be found at **Augarten** (⌗ Graben/Stock-im-Eisen-Platz 3 ☎ 01/512–1494–0 ⊕ www.augarten.at), and it comes with a lifelong guarantee to restock, should breakage occur. The Lipizzaner stallion balancing on two hind hoofs is an expensive piece but an eye-catcher. Smaller hand-painted gifts like the tiny vases or candleholders are affordable and such little, pretty pieces are *so* typically Vienna. The

manufactory in the 2nd District in Vienna offers tours of the palais Augarten is housed in, and you can study the steps involved in making these precious pieces. Is it a "Maria-Theresia," ornately cut diamanté chandelier with a 30%–34% lead content, you're looking for? If it is, head and
★ hunt here at **Lobmeyr** (✉ Kärntnerstrasse 26 ☎ 01/512–0508–0 ⊕ www.lobmeyr.at), one of the world's finest addresses for the best in glass and crystal. Even if you're not buying, go upstairs and have a look at the museum on the second floor. Once you follow the development of the Secession movement in the display of objects in the museum vitrines, you can then go buy a piece of Viennese Arts & Crafts for yourself—there is the set of tumblers designed in 1931 by Adolf Loos with a brilliant cut pattern on the base still being produced today and suitable both for the festive dinner table and for the house bar. Before leaving, have a look at the central crystal chandelier. Yes, it's a smaller version of the giant one hanging in the lobby of New York's Metropolitan Opera House, which was crafted here as a gift from the Austrian government.

If you want to enter an old-fashioned interior that makes time stand still and is little changed from the time when Empress Elisabeth shopped here, **Albin Denk** (✉ Graben 13 ☎ 01/512–4439 ⊕ www.albindenk.at) is the place to head. The shop entrance itself is a vitrine, as it is lined with glass cases and filled with a wonderful-if-kitschy army of welcoming porcelain figurines. Inside the shop, founded in 1702, are three salons chock full of porcelain and china treasures, ranging from lovely baroque-style pieces from various porcelain manufactories like Meissen and Dresden to full china services bearing names like Wedgwood, Spode, Villeroy, and Royal Copenhagen. A longtime favorite for bridal couples' wedding gift registries,
★ **Rasper & Söhne** (✉ Graben 15 ☎ 01/534–33–0) must have a lot of satisfied customers if all the photos of smiling brides and bridegrooms in the windows mean anything. For fun kitchen items, **Rasper's Loft** (✉ Habsburgergasse 10 ☎ 01/534–33–39) is a top resource.

Pottery from **Berger** (✉ Weihburggasse 17 ☎ 01/512–1434) may be just the great gift you're looking for—how about a pretty decorative wall plate blooming with a hand-painted flowering gentian. Gmunden ceramics have been the housewife's favorite for centuries. The typical green-and-white design with the tiny painted buttercups or the irregular bands of color are present in nearly every Austrian country home. But these quaint pieces can add that rustic touch to any dinner table, so stock up at **Pawlata** (✉ Kärntnerstrasse 14 ☎ 01/512–1764). More country-style ceramics can be found downstairs at **Plessgott** (✉ Kärntner Durchgang ☎ 01/512–5824). Some pieces are slightly less pricey than in other shops. Although primarily a Rosenthal porcelain shop you'll find some great Wedgwood pieces at **Rosenthal** (✉ Kärntnerstrasse 16 ☎ 01/512–3994), which is also well stocked with glass and household ornaments.

Christkindlmärte

Vienna keeps the Christmas olympic flame burning perhaps more brightly than any other metropolis in the world. Here, during the holiday season, no less than five major *Christkindmärte* (Christmas Markets) proffer their wares, with stands selling enough woodcarved Austrian toys, crêche figures, and Tannenbaum ornaments to tickle anybody's mistletoes. Many of the markets offers food vendors selling dee-scrumptious *Glühwein* mead and *Kartoffelpuffer* potato patties. Here are the best of the markets. **Altwiener Christkindlmarkt** (⊠ The Freynung ☏ 01/5121296) is held on one of Vienna's biggest squares. **Karlsplatz** (⊠ Karlsplatz) has some of the more refined stands in town.The biggest holiday market is the famous **Rathausplatz** (⊠ Rathausplatz) held in front of the magnificently Gothic fantasy that is Vienna's Rathaus city hall. All the glitter and gilt of the season frames the market held at the Habsburgs' splendid **Schönbrunn** (⊠ Schönbrunn Palace) The cognoscenti love the arty market held in the enchanting Biedermeier quarter of **Spittelberg** (⊠ Burggasse and Siebensterngasse) Merry, merry!

Gifts That Say "Vienna"

Are you looking for an old postcard, a hand-carved walking stick, an old record or ball gift, or even an old photograph of the Opera House
★ from before the war? Head to **Alt-Österreich** (⊠ Himmelpfortgasse 7 ☏ 01/5121296)—its name translates as "Old Austria" and this treasure trove has just about everything dealing with that time-burnished subject. Trachten for the toddlers, dirndl for the dames, and cute hand-embroidered cardigans for the kids are all found at **Giesswein** (⊠ Kärntnerstrasse 5–7 ☏ 01/512–4597), famed for some of the best traditional clothing in town.

Michaela Frey is the name of a well-known brand of Viennese decorative art jewelry and you'll find her creations at **M. Frey-Wille** (⊠ Lobkowitzplatz 1 ☏ 01/5122217 ⊕ www.m-frey.com). Her designs have become a typical memento of Austria and are made of enamel copper with exquisite art-historically inspired designs; particularly popular are the pieces inspired by the Art Nouveau and Secession movements. Bracelets, rings, brooches, and pins make a great gift at a fair price. Austria's one and only cooperative for art and crafts, **Österreichische Werkstätten** (⊠ Kärntnerstrasse 6 ☏ 01/512–2418) stocks Austrian handicrafts of the finest quality. The range covers home accessories, from brass or pewter candlesticks to linen tablecloths, to quality souvenirs, ranging from enamel jewelry to embroidered brooches—all goods that make for exceedingly decorative gifts to take back home. One of those Austrian products that never changes, yet never ceases to please, is the needlework called *petit point*. For some it may be a little old-fashioned and matronly, but it is still an honest work of art. Among the items on sale at **Petit Point Kovalcec** (⊠ Kärntnerstrasse 16 ☏ 01/512–4886) are small elegant handbags, cute pill boxes, pretty purses, fancy brooches, and tiny rings. Fancy a composer's portrait–bust collection? Schubert, Mozart, Beethoven, Haydn, and the rest of the gang can be had at
★ **Souvenir in der Hofburg** (⊠ Hofburgpassage 1 and 7 ☏ 01/533–5053). While you're at it, you might want to go for a ceramic figure of a Lipizzaner stallion, too (it may not be an Augarten porcelain original but it is certainly more affordable). Postcards, vintage booklets on Vienna, imperial memorabilia, small busts of former Habsburg rulers, and petite gifts for the folks back home will tempt one and all connoisseurs at **Stransky** (⊠ Hofburgpassage 2 ☏ 01/533–6098). Ireland has its Waterford, France
★ its Baccarat, and Austria has **Swarovski** (⊠ Kärntnerstrasse 8 ☏ 01/5129032 ⊕ www.swarovski.com), purveyors of some of the finest cut crystal in the world and, thanks to the newer generation of Swarovskis, trin-

SWEETS FOR DER SCHWARZENEGGER

*If Proust had been Austrian, not French, he would have gone "in search of past time" nibbling on Manners, not madeleines. Sold the world over, the ubiquitous nougat wafer fingers now have a shop all their own: **Manner** (⊠ Stephansplatz 7 ☎ 01/488220), which, appropriately enough, faces Vienna's famous cathedral. Its pink packaging bears the St. Stephan's Cathedral silhouette as a logo; Manner is the only brand that may use a picture of the venerable cathedral on its packaging (in return for the advertising, the company covered the cost of its stonemason restoration work for some 20 years now). The shop, ultracontemporary in design, stocks a wide range of gifts for Manner fans, ranging from T-shirts and rucksacks to umbrellas and cycling tops. Besides the classic wafers (now a cult classic—Arnold Schwarzenegger was seen eating some in Terminator 3), there are other famous goodies such as Mozartkugel chocolates and nougat cubes by Ildefonso. Expatriates and lovers of sweets have long savored these wafers, but now they have a proper Viennese home.*

kets increasingly fashionable in style and outlook. There are your typical collector items and gifts here, but also high-style fashion accessories (Paris couturiers now festoon their gowns with Swarovski crystals the way they used to with ostrich feathers), crystal figurines, jewelry, and home accessories. This flagship store opened recently is one heck of a cave of coruscating crystals that gleam and glitter. Assorted souvenirs, including all sorts of bric-a-brac and jewelry, can be found at **Wiener Geschenke** (⊠ Reitschulgasse 4/Michaelerplatz ☎ 01/533–7078)—everything from silver spoons to key-rings, but also pretty woven and hand-embroidered textiles for household use.

Jewelry

The finest selection of watches in Vienna can be found at **Haban** (⊠ Kärntnerstrasse 2 ☎ 01/512–6730–0), but the gold-and-diamond jewelry selection is top-notch, too. In the city of Freud, father of psychoanalysis, what else can you expect but jewelry designed to go with the "archetypes of your dreams." Here, at the **Golden Genius** (⊠ Kohlmarkt 3 ☎ 01/470–94–82), dream symbols are individually cast in different shades of gold as a surround for colorful precious stones. These playful masterworks, designed by Willy C. F. Kunze, are manufactured by outstanding goldsmiths. One of Vienna's fabled K & K (*Kaiserlich and Königlich*—Imperial and Royal) suppliers, **A. E. Köchert** (⊠ Neuer Markt 15 ☎ 01/512–5828–0), has been Vienna's jeweler of choice for nearly two centuries. Almost 150 years ago Empress Elisabeth ordered some diamond studded stars here to adorn her legendary auburn hair (so long she could sit on it). Guess what? Those diamond stars are more fashionable than ever since Köchert has started reissuing them. And if you're ever in need of a crown, Köchert will even craft your very own. With an eye-knocking portal designed by Hollein, **Schullin** (⊠ Kohlmarkt 7 ☎ 01/533–9007–0) stands out from the pack. Inside, small vitrines hold just a handful of the most exquisite pieces of jewelry but each will make some woman's heart beat faster. Modern design and creative cutting of gems make Schullin a top spot for precious treasures. Discover interesting pieces of Austrian jade at **Burgenland** (✉ Opernpassage ☎ 01/587–6266).

Men's Clothing
Although his shops now span the globe, Vienna-born **Helmut Lang** (✉ Seilergasse 6 ☎01/5132588 ⊕ www.helmutlang.com) rightly has an outlet in his old home town. His choice colors are black and white, with just a touch of beige and his minimalist designs represent the peak of understatement in fashion. **Peek & Cloppenburg** (✉Mariahilferstrasse 26–30, 6th District) is the right place for those who hate having to go to various shops to find what they are looking for. It's all here—suits, shirts, ties, socks, jumpers, underwear in every shape, size, and color—with brand names, designer labels, and excellent value for money. Austrians love their hats and **Collins Hüte** (✉Opernpassage ☎01/587–1305) is one of the best sources in town—not only for hats but also for accessories, such as scarves, gloves, and the stray sombrero (for that glaring summer sun on the slopes at Lech). If you want to look like Captain von Trapp, head for **Loden-Plankl** (✉Michaelerplatz 6 ☎01/533–8032) where you can get the best, and priciest, men's *Trachten,* or typical Austrian clothing, including lederhosen.

Music
You just might bump into Placido, Jose, or even Dame Joan Sutherland—and if you do, you know where to buy that picture postcard and then ★ run and have it autographed—at Vienna's noted **Arcadia** (✉ Staatsoper Opera House, Opernring 2 ☎ 01/513–9568-0), which is stocked with not only a grand selection of latest CD releases from the operatic world, but quite a few classic rarities, too. Also here is a book department with loads of literature on music and musicians and choice items of opera memorabilia. Helpful sales assistants are at the ready if you're looking for any special titles at **EMI** (✉ Kärntnerstrasse 30 ☎ 01/512–3675)—one of the big mainstays for classical music (find it upstairs) plus the whole gamut from ethno to pop. All connoisseurs of classic will want to head to **Havlicek** (✉ Herrengasse 5 ☎01/533–1964). If there is one particular recording that's missing in your collection, you are most likely going to find it here. The owner is not only particularly knowledgeable but also incredibly helpful and friendly.

Shoes & Leather Goods
The embossed leather at **R. Horn** (✉ Braünerstrasse 7 ☎ 01/513–8294) is used to make the most precious and perfectly hand-crafted handbags, leather purses, briefcases, and small accessories in designs that are simply timeless. One of the biggest chains for inexpensive foot-wear, **Humanic** (✉ Kärntnerstrasse 51 ☎01/512–5892 ✉ Singerstrasse 2 ☎01/512–9101) is present on nearly every main shopping street. Good bargains and helpful shop assistants make shoe shopping fun. Fashionable and trendy but also comfortable and classic-styled shoes are here in abundance. You can rarely walk right by **Popp and Kretschmer** (✉ Kärntnerstrasse 51 ☎01/512–6421-0) since the window dresser usually does such an eye-catching display. This is one of the leading stores for elegant footwear and handbags, though the ladies wear has its extravagant allure, too. **Zak** (✉ Kärntnerstrasse 36 ☎01/512–7257) has a great selection of leather boots, handbags, and belts.

Toys

Emperor Franz Josef in his horse-drawn carriage, the K & K Infantry cheering him on, and the Prussian emperor to meet him at the battle-

★ field—here at **Kober** (✉ Graben 14–15 ☎ 01/533–6018) you can find all of the historic tin soldiers you'll ever need to relive those eventful last years of the empire. If you prefer something a little less military-like, go for the full Johann Strauss Orchestra, it's a scream. If this toy shop had existed when Mozart lived just across from here, he'd have loved **Spielzeugschachtel** (✉ Rauensteingasse 5 ☎ 01/512–3994). Fun-lovers of all ages, not just kids, can find everything they'll ever want to play with. Emphasis is often put on the educational value of the toys. Of special charm are the wooden toys that need assembly. All items can be tested before purchase—it might not be a surprise present anymore but at least there are no disappointed faces.

Women's Clothing

Bright colors, trendy but absolutely wearable, especially tailored for the businesswoman of today—that's **Doris Ainedter** (✉ Jasomirgottstrasse 5 ☎ 01/5320369 ⊕ www.doris-ainedter.com). Fashion designer Doris is very often in her own shop so she can help you with decision mak-

★ ing. Vienna-born **Helmut Lang** (✉ Seilergasse 6 ☎ 01/5132588 ⊕ www. helmutlang.com) has become one of the fashion Masters of the Universe, so those who want the chicest in modern, minimalist clothes head here to pay homage. **Wiener Blut** (✉ Spiegelgasse 19 ☎ 01/5132015) has lots of temptations. Monika Bacher's zippy knitwear, striking pieces by Berlin designers, zany shoes from Canada, and the finest crafted hand-bags from Italy. Fashionistas make a beeline for the studio of Austrian designer **Schella Kann** (✉ Singerstrasse 14/2 ☎ 01/513–2287)—extrav-agant and trendy, these are clothes you never want to take off. Ever fan-tasize about wearing clothes that adopt your every shape without seams ripping? If so, head to **Mila Style** (✉ Bauernmarkt 1 ☎ 01/513–2287). The small shop is like a den draped in what you might think is just dec-orative fabric. Wrong, this stretch cloth decor is actually covered in Mila's unique fabrics. Top designer fashions can be found at **Donna** (✉ Tuch-lauben 7a ☎ 01/535–6050).

Giesswein (✉ Kärntnerstrasse 5–7 ☎ 01/512–4597) is one of the most noted places to shop for a selection of dirndls and women's *Trachten*, the typical Austrian costume with white blouse, print skirt, and apron. There are some children's clothes available. Another outpost of tradi-tional Austrian garb, **Lanz** (✉ Kärntnerstrasse 10 ☎ 01/512–2456) is known for its great selection of Geiger jackets. Otherwise, plenty of tra-ditional Tirolean attire for all shapes, sizes, and ages. Perhaps the best

★ place for that extra special piece of folklore wear, **Loden-Plankl** (✉ Michael-erplatz 6 ☎ 01/533–8032) stocks some really gorgeous hand-embroi-dered jackets, not to mention the "Leder Hosen" leather breeches for kids (famed for being just about indestructible). The building, opposite the Hofburg, is a centuries-old treasure. **Resi Hammerer** (✉ Kärntner-strasse 29–31 ☎ 01/512–6952) offers Folklore fashion with a touch of the trendy. The color and fabric mix has that certain casual, sportive touch but still is conservative enough to suit most fraus.

THE DANUBE VALLEY
TO THE
SALZKAMMERGUT

6

CLIMB FROM TOWER TO TURRET
of the fantastic Burg Kreuzenstein ⇨*p.178*

COUNT THE MANY BRANCHES
of Mozart's family tree in St. Gilgen ⇨*p.195*

HUM STRAUSS'S LILTING WALTZ
while cruising the Blue Danube River ⇨*p.182*

GO FOR BAROQUE
at the abbey masterpiece at Melk ⇨*p.184*

UNWIND IN A DRIFTING PADDLEBOAT
to St. Wolfgang of operetta fame ⇨*p.193*

CELEBRATE EMPEROR FRANZ JOSEF
at his Kaiservilla in Bad Ischl ⇨*p.190*

GET BECALMED AND CHARMED
in the riverside town of Dürnstein ⇨*p.183*

By Bonnie
Dodson and
Horst Ernst
Reischenböck

IF AUSTRIA WERE RATED ON A BEAUTY-MEASURING GAUGE, the needle would fly off the scale in the regions that stretch east-to-west and
lie directly between Vienna and Salzburg. Here, conveniently linking
these two great Austrian metropoli, are two areas that have been ex-
traordinarily blessed by nature. Ready your camera, dust off your supply of *wunderschöns,* and prepare for enchantment just 5 miles
northwest of Vienna's city borders, where the Danube Valley starts to
unfold like a picture book. Roman ruins (some dating to Emperor
Claudius), medieval castles-in-air, and Baroque monasteries with "candle-snuffer" cupolas perching precariously above the river, stimulate
the imagination with their historic legends and myths. This is where
Isa—cousin of the Lorelei—lured sailors onto the shoals; where Richard
the Lion-Hearted was locked in a dungeon for a spell; and where the
Nibelungs—later immortalized by Wagner—caroused operatically in
battlemented forts. Here is where Roman sailors threw coins into the
perilous whirlpools near Grein, in hopes of placating Danubius, the
river's tutelary god. The route that brought the ancient Romans to
the area and contributed to its development remains one of Europe's
most important waterways. As the saying went, "Whoever controls
the Danube controls all Europe."

From the greatest sight of the Danube Valley, Melk Abbey, we head south-
ward down to the Salzkammergut (literally, "salt estates"), which presents the traveler with soaring mountains and needlelike peaks, forested
valleys that are populated with the *Rehe* (roe deer) immortalized by Felix
Salten in *Bambi,* and a glittering necklace of turquoise lakes. The Wolfgangsee, the Mondsee, and the Attersee (*See* is German for "lake") are
the best known of the region's 76 lakes. The entire region remains idyllic and largely unspoiled because of its salt mines, which date back to
the Celtic era; with salt so common and cheap nowadays, many forget
it was once a luxury item mined under strict government monopoly. The
Salzkammergut was closed to the casually curious for centuries, opening up only after Emperor Franz Josef I made it his official summer residence in 1854 and turned it into the "drawing room" of the Lake District.
Today, thanks to those famous scenes in *The Sound of Music,* the
Salzkammergut's castles fronting on water, mountains hidden by whipped-
cream clouds, and flower-strewn valleys crisped with cool blue lakes represent Austria in all its Hollywoodian splendor.

Exploring the Danube Valley & the Salzkammergut

Although much of the river is tightly wedged between steep hills rising
from a narrow valley, the north and south banks of the Danube present
differing vistas. The hills to the north are terraced to allow its famous
vineyards to catch the full sun; to the south, the orchards, occasional
meadows, and shaded hills have just as much visual appeal, if a less dramatic sight. Upstream from the Wachau region the valley broadens, giving way to farmlands and, straddling the river, the bustling city of Linz,
which we pass, eyes averted (there are more than enough cosmopolitan
pleasures to enjoy in Vienna and Salzburg). As for the Salzkammergut,
our journey passes through the land of operetta: the 19th-century re-

sort towns of Bad Ischl and St. Wolfgang, before heading westward to St. Gilgen, birthplace of Mozart's mother, and Fuschl, on the very doorstep of Salzburg itself.

About the Restaurants & Hotels

Wherever possible, restaurants along the Danube Valley make the most of the river view, and alfresco dining overlooking the Danube is one of the region's unsurpassed delights. Simple *Gasthäuser* are everywhere, but better dining is more often found in country inns. The cuisine usually runs along traditional lines, but the desserts are often brilliant inventions, including the celebrated Linzertorte and Linzer Augen, jam-filled cookies with three "eyes" planted in the top layer. Wine is very much the thing on the north bank of the Danube in the Wachau region. Here you'll find many of Austria's best white wines, slightly dry with a hint of fruitiness. In some of the smaller villages, you can sample the vintner's successes right on the spot in his cellars. Restaurants, whether sophisticated and stylish or plain and homey, are often rated by their wine offerings as much as by their chef's creations.

In the Salzkammergut, fresh, local lake fish is on nearly every menu in the area, so take advantage of the bounty. The lakes and streams are home to several types of fish, notably trout, carp, and perch. They are prepared in numerous ways, from plain breaded (*gebacken*), to smoked and served with *Kren* (horseradish), to fried in butter (*gebraten*). Look for *Reinanke,* a mild whitefish straight from the Hallstättersee. Sometimes at country fairs you will find someone charcoaling fresh trout wrapped in aluminum foil with herbs and butter: it's worth every euro. *Knödel*—bread or potato dumplings usually filled with either meat or jam—are a tasty specialty. Desserts are doughy as well, though *Salzburger Nockerl* consist mainly of air, sugar, and beaten egg whites. And finally, keep an eye out for seasonal specialties: in summer, restaurants often serve chanterelle mushrooms (*Eierschwammerl*) with pasta, and in October it's time for delicious venison and game during the *Wildwochen* (game weeks).

As for accommodations, your choices range from castle-hotels, where you'll be treated like royalty, to the often family-managed, quiet and elegant country inn. There are also luxurious lakeside resorts, small country rivertown inns, even guest houses without private baths; in some places, the *Herr Wirt,* his smiling wife, and his grown-up children will do everything to make you feel comfortable. Some hotels offer half-board, with dinner included in addition to buffet breakfast (although most $$$$ hotels charge extra for breakfast). The half-board room rate is usually an extra €15–€30 per person. Occasionally, quoted room rates for hotels already include half-board, though a "discounted" rate may be available if you prefer not to take the evening meal. Inquire about any pension food plans when booking. Assume all rooms have TV, telephones, and private bath, unless otherwise noted; air-conditioning, in rare instances, is noted. Happily, these hotels do not put their breathtakingly beautiful natural surroundings on the bill.

The Wachau section of the Danube Valley is a favorite outing for Viennese seeking a pleasant Sunday drive and a glass or two of good wine, but for foreign sojourners to treat the region this casually would cause them to miss some of Austria's greatest castles and abbeys, along with the valley's many vine-covered wine gardens. Beyond to the west lies the Salzkammergut, that Austrian Shangri-la, where picturesque villages beg to be explored and prove nearly irresistible.

If you have 3 days

Start out early from Vienna, planning for a stop to explore the medieval center of **Krems ❷**. The Weinstadt Museum Krems will give you a good idea of the regions's best wines. Along the northern, Krems side of the Danube, you can opt to spend a night in a former cloister, now an elegant hotel, in 🏠 **Dürnstein ❸**, probably the most famous, if not prettiest, town of the Danube Valley. Here you'll find the ruined castle where Richard the Lion-Hearted was imprisoned—an early-morning climb up to the ruin will reward you with great views. Take time to explore enchanting Dürnstein before heading west along the Danube crossing over to 🏠**Melk ❹**, rated one of the greatest abbeys in Europe. This is high Baroque at its most glorious. Then for your third day, head to regal 🏠 **Bad Ischl ❾**, a town proud of its links with Emperor Franz Josef and filled with villas that seems right out of an operetta set (not surprisingly, the composer Léhar often vacationed here).

If you have 8 days

A more leisurely schedule would follow the same basic route but permit some magical detours, including a stop at the fairytale castle of Burg Kreuzenstein, near **Korneuburg ❶**, before continuing on to attractive **Krems ❷** to tour its wine museum, the Weinstadt Museum Krems. Overnight in gorgeous 🏠 **Dürnstein ❸**. Spend the morning exploring Dürnstein, including the colorfully restored Baroque Stiftskirche. On Day 3, take in the grandest abbey of all, 🏠 **Melk ❹**. On Day 4, continue east to another magnficent abbey, **St. Florian ❺** (where composer Anton Bruckner spent a good deal of time), then head south to the enchanting medieval town of 🏠 **Steyr ❻**. On Day 5, head southeast to the Salzkammergut, with a stopover at the abbey in **Kremsmünster ❼**, before enjoying an idyllic overnight in the gateway town to the Lake District, 🏠 **Gmunden ❽**, beloved of Brahms. On Day 6, make a beeline for the heart of the region, the elegant 19th-century spa town of 🏠 **Bad Ischl ❾**, Emperor Franz Josef's old stomping ground. On Day 7, head for 🏠 **St. Wolfgang ❿**, which harbors one of Austria's great art treasures, the altarpiece by the late-Gothic wood-carver Michael Pacher, in the parish church. However, it was the inn near the dock—now Hotel Weisses Rössl (White Horse)—that spread the little Alpine town's fame (and made its fortune): It became the subject of a very popular operetta, *Im Weissen Rössl*. On Day 8, head north to **St. Gilgen ⓫**. The town gets very crowded in summer, especially along the shore, which is lined with ice-cream parlors and souvenir shops. But the little house near the dock on Ischler Strasse where Mozart's mother was born and his sister later lived should be starred on your itinerary, as no more fitting overture can be sounded for your grand entry into Mozart's own home town, Salzburg, a few miles to the west.

	WHAT IT COSTS In euros				
	$$$$	$$$	$$	$	¢
RESTAURANTS	over €22	€18–€22	€13–€17	€7–€12	under €7
HOTELS	over €175	€135–€175	€100–€135	€70–€100	under €70

Restaurant prices are per person for a main course at dinner. Hotel prices are for a standard double room in high season, including taxes and service. Assume that hotels operate on the European Plan (EP, with no meal provided) unless we note that they use the Breakfast Plan (BP), Modified American Plan (MAP, with breakfast and dinner daily, known as "halb pension"), or Full American Plan (FAP, or "voll pension," with three meals a day). Higher prices (inquire when booking) prevail for any meal plans.

Timing

The Wachau—both north and south Danube banks—is packed wall-to-wall with crowds in late April to early May, but of course there's a reason: apricot and apple trees are in glorious blossom, and bright orange poppies blanket the fields. Others prefer the chilly early- to mid-autumn days, when a blue haze curtains the vineyards. Throughout the region, winter is drab. Year-round, vacationers flock to the Salzkammergut Lake District; however, late fall is the worst time to visit the region, for it is rainy and cold, and many sights are closed or operate on a restricted schedule. By far the best months are July and September. August, of course, sees the countryside overrun with families on school holidays and music lovers from the nearby Salzburg Music Festival.

THE WACHAU: JEWEL OF THE DANUBE VALLEY

Unquestionably the loveliest stretches of the Danube's Austrian course run from the outskirts of Vienna, through the narrow defiles of the Wachau to the Nibelungengau—the region where the mystical race of dwarfs, the Nibelungs, are supposed to have settled, at least for a while. The Danube river itself is a marvel—on a summer day it can take on the authentic shade of Johann Strauss blue. Continuing south toward Salzburg, explore the Gothic and Baroque sights found in the towns of St. Florian, Kremsmünster, and Steyr, the latter a gorgeously Gothic-flavored town once home to the great composer Anton Bruckner that certainly merits an overnight stay. Along the way you'll be dazzled by two masterworks of the Austrian Baroque, the great abbeys of St. Florian and Stift Kremsmünster.

Korneuburg

❶ *18 km (11¼ mi) northwest of Vienna.*

Castle lovers, prepare yourselves. Seemingly lifted from the pages of a Germanic fairy tale, **Burg Kreuzenstein**, bristling with storybook turrets and towers, might have made Albrecht Dürer drop his sketch pad in a second. Sitting atop a hillside 3 km (2 mi) beyond Korneuburg along Route 3, "Castle Cross-stone," in fact, is a 19th-century architectural fantasy built to conjure up "the last of the knights"—Emperor Maximilian I himself. Occupying the site of a previously destroyed fort, the

FodorsChoice
★

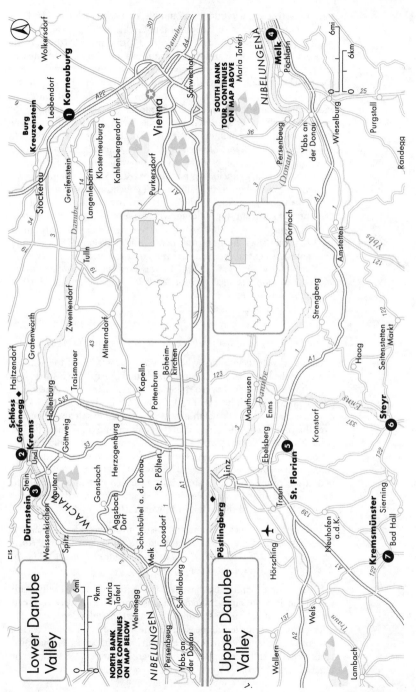

Lower Danube Valley

0 6mi
0 9km

Maria
Taferl

NORTH BANK TOUR CONTINUES ON MAP BELOW

Persenbeug
Ybbs an
der Donau

NIBELUNGEN

Weitenegg
Schallaburg

Melk
Loosdorf
Schönbühel a. d. Donau

WACHAU

Aggsbach
Dorf
Gansbach
Herzogenburg
St. Pölten

Spitz
Weissenkirchen
Mautern
Stein

3 **Dürnstein**
Und

2 **Schloss**
Grafenegg ◆
Krems

Göttweig
Hollenburg
Traismauer
Haitzendorf
Grafenwörth
Grafenwörth

Zwentendorf
Mittendorf
Böheim-
kirchen
Kapelln
Pottenbrun

Tulln

Langenlebarn
Greifenstein
Stockerau

Burg
Kreuzenstein
◆

1 **Korneuburg**
Leobendorf

Wolkersdorf

Klosterneuburg
Kahlenbergerdorf

Purkersdorf

Vienna

Schwechat

Danube

Upper Danube Valley

Pöstlingberg ◆

Linz
Traun
Hörsching

Wels
Lambach
Wallern

Ebelsberg
Enns

Mauthausen

5 **St. Florian**
Kronstorf

Neuhofen
a.d.K.

7 **Kremsmünster**
Sierning
Bad Hall

6 **Steyr**
Enns
Ybbs

Seitenstetten
Markt
Haag

Strengberg

Amstetten

Dornach

Persenbeug

Ybbs an
der Donau
Wieselburg
Purgstall
Randegg

Maria Taferl

SOUTH BANK TOUR CONTINUES ON MAP ABOVE

4 **Melk**
Pöchlarn

NIBELUNGEN

0 6mi
0 6km
0 25

Danube

enormous structure was built by Count Nepomuk Wilczek between 1879 and 1908 to house his collection of late-Gothic art objects and armor, including the "Brixner Cabinet" dating from 15th-century Salzburg. Using old elements and Gothic and Romanesque bits and pieces, the castle was carefully laid out according to the rules of yore, complete with a towering Burgtor, "Kennel" corridor (where attackers would have been cornered), Gothic arcades, and tracery parapet walls. The Burghof courtyard, with its half-timbered facade and Baltic loggia, could be a stand-in for a stage-set for Wagner's *Tannhäuser*. Inside, the medieval thrills continue with rooms full of armaments, a festival and banquet hall, a library, a stained-glass chapel, vassal kitchens, and the Narwalzahn, a room devoted to hunting trophies (if you've ever wanted to see a "unicorn horn," here's your chance). It is possible to reach Kreuzenstein from Vienna via the suburban train (S-Bahn) to Leobendorf, followed by a ¾-hour hike up to the castle. Until recently, the town of Korneuburg was the center of Austrian shipbuilding, where river passenger ships, barges, and transfer cranes were built to order for Russia, among other customers. Stop for a look at the imposing neo-Gothic city hall (1864), which dominates the central square and towers over the town. ⊠ *Leobendorf bei Korneuburg* ☎ *01/283–0308* ⊕ *www.kreuzenstein.com and www. werbeka.com/wien/kreuzend.htm* 🎫 *€8* ⊙ *Apr.–Oct., daily 10–4, guided tour on the hr.*

Krems

② *63 km (45 mi) west of Korneuburg, 80 km (50 mi) northwest of Vienna.*

Krems marks the beginning (when traveling upstream) of the Wachau section of the Danube. The town is closely tied to Austrian history; here the ruling Babenbergs set up a dukedom in 1120, and the earliest Austrian coin was struck here in 1130. In the Middle Ages, Krems looked after the iron trade while neighboring Stein traded in salt and wine, and over the years Krems became a center of culture and art. Today the area is the heart of a thriving wine production, while Krems is most famed for the cobbled streets of its Altstadt (Old Town), which is virtually unchanged since the 18th century. The lower Old Town is an attractive pedestrian zone, while up a steep hill (a car can be handy) you'll find the upper Old Town, with its Renaissance Rathaus town hall and a parish church that is one of the oldest in Lower Austria.

A 14th-century former Dominican cloister now serves as the **Weinstadt Museum Krems,** a wine museum that holds occasional tastings. ⊠ *Körnermarkt 14* ☎ *02732/801–567* ⊕ *www.weinstadtmuseum.at* 🎫 *€3.60* ⊙ *Mar.–Nov., Tues.–Sun. 10–6.*

A frozen-in-time hamlet that has, over the years, become virtually a suburb of the adjacent city of Krems, **Stein** is dotted with lovely 16th-century houses, many on the town's main street, Steinlanderstrasse. The 14th-century Minoritenkirche, just off the main street, now serves as a museum with changing exhibits. Nearby, an imposing square Gothic tower landmarks the 15th-century St. Nicholas parish church, whose altar painting and ceiling frescoes were done by Kremser Schmidt.

Where to Stay & Eat

$$$ ✕ **Jell.** In the heart of Krems' medieval Altstadt, this storybook stone cottage run by Ulli Amon-Jell (pronounced "Yell") is a cluster of cozy rooms with lace curtains, dark-wood banquettes, candlelight and Biedermeier knickknacks on the walls, making it seem like you've stepped into an early-20th-century grandmother's house. Your meal begins with tantalizing breads and dips, fine starters such as cream of asparagus soup, then delicious main courses like the pheasant breast wrapped in their own home-cured bacon. ✉ *Hoher Markt 8–9* ☎ *02732/82345* 🖷 *02732/ 82345–4* ✍ *Reservations essential* ☰ *AE, DC, MC, V* ⊙ *Closed Mon. No dinner weekends.*

★ **$$$** ✕ **M. Kunst. Genuss.** Another popular, hip restaurant belonging to star chef and entrepreneur Toni Mörwald, this strikingly minimalistic, cathedral-roofed, glass-sided structure is situated at the Karikaturmuseum and has a name that signifies "Mörwald, Art, and Pleasure." Look for the big salad of field greens topped with a generous herb-marinated skirt steak, or the perfectly cooked wild salmon filet with basmati rice and a profusion of colorful grilled vegetables. Service is without fault. This is one of the few restaurants in the area open for lunch all day. ✉ *Franz-Zeller-Platz 3* ☎ *02732/908–0102–1* 🖷 *02732/908011* ☰ *AE, DC, MC, V.*

★ **$$$** ✕🖭 **Am Förthof.** An inn has existed on the riverside site of this small, multiwindowed hotel for hundreds of years. Comfortably set back from the busy main road, it gives a sense of seclusion because of the large front garden shaded by 200-year-old chestnut trees and a multitude of flowers. The charming rooms are done in pale yellow, blue, or pink, and have antique pieces and soft carpets. Those in front have views of the Danube and Göttweig Abbey across the river while the back rooms overlook a swimming pool. At dinnertime there's no need to leave the premises as the kitchen is more touted than the hotel. Partake of the optional five-course Degustation menu, with a different local wine to accompany each course. Breakfast is a sumptuous feast of organic products and fresh-baked *Wachauer Semmel*, as well as silver tureens of sweet strawberries, red currants, and apricots picked from the *Marillen* trees of the neighboring medieval village of Stein. For those settling in to do a bit of wine tasting in the Wachau, friendly owner Frau Figl will gladly arrange wine tours. ✉ *Förthofer Donaulände 8, A–3500* ☎ *02732/83345* 🖷 *02732/83345–40* ⊕ *www.tiscover.at/feinschmecker.foerthof* ⬡ *16 rooms* ♨ *Restaurant, minibars, pool, sauna, Internet, some no-smoking rooms, free parking* ☰ *AE, DC, MC, V* ⊙ *Closed Jan. and Feb.*

★ **$** ✕🖭 **Alte Post.** The oldest inn in Krems, for centuries the mail-route posthouse for the region, this hostelry is centered around an adorable Renaissance-style courtyard, which is topped with a flower-bedecked arcaded balcony and storybook mansard roof. If you're a guest here, you'll be able to drive into the pedestrian zone of the Old Town and pull up next to the Steinener Tor (Stone Gate) to find this inn. The rooms are in comfortable yet elegant country style (full baths are scarce), but the real draw here is dining on regional specialties or sipping a glass of the local wine in the courtyard. ✉ *Obere Landstrasse 32, A–3500 Krems* ☎ *02732/ 82276–0* 🖷 *02732/84396* ⊕ *www.altepost-krems.at* ⬡ *23 rooms, 4 with bath* ♨ *Restaurant* ☰ *No credit cards* ⊙ *Closed Dec.–Mar.*

AND THE DANUBE WALTZES ON

THE WHOLE WORLD SIGHS *when it hears the opening strains of the Blue Danube waltz. Who, then, can resist a cruise upon the river immortalized by Johann Strauss II's unforgettable melody? Below, you'll find information about these popular day-trip cruises, which originate from Vienna's piers along the city's Danube Canal. As it turns out, when Strauss composed this piece, he was living on Vienna's Praterstrasse, a river's breath away from the Donaukanal, and enamored of a poem by Karl Beck whose refrain "By the Danube, beautiful blue Danube" he couldn't get out of his mind. It comes as a surprise to learn that the "waltz king" was, in fact, a terrible dancer and never took to the floor. But if you listen to the first motif of "'An der schonen blauen Donau" (Strauss's title)—developing from the D major triad D–F# sharp–A—it seems the composer must have been a wonderful swimmer. Sublimely, the melody suggests flowing waters—to be exact, the interplay of main current and subsidiary little whirlpools you often find on the Danube as you cruise its banks. When Strauss composed this dittie for a war memorial concert given by the Men's Choral Association at Vienna's Imperial Winter Riding School in 1867, it was politely applauded, then forgotten the next week. Austria had been trounced by Prussia the year before and was licking its wounds, so hopes were high for the premiere, when the piece was accompanied by a chorus singing lyrics by poet Josef Weyl— "Vienna, be gay!" But once the chorus was banished (the words were fighting the waltzing rhythm), and it was taken up at the great World Exposition given that year in Paris, "The Blue Danube" exploded around the world.*

Now, as in Strauss's time, a cruise up the Danube to the Wachau valley is a tonic in

any season. The main company that offers these cruises is the Blue Danube Schifffahrt/DDSG (Donau-Dampfschifffahrts-Gesellschaft's "Blue Danube") for contact information; see Boat Travel in this chapter's Danube Valley A to Z section. Their boats leave from the company's piers at Handelskai 265 every Sunday between May 11 and September 28 at 8:45 AM. Departing from the Reichsbrücke (Vienna Piers) on the city's Danube Canal, they arrive in Krems at 1:55 PM, Dürnstein at 2:30 PM, returning from Dürnstein at 4:30 PM, Krems at 4:50 PM, and get back to Vienna by 8:45 PM. One-way is €17.50—the ticket office is at the Vienna piers (take the U-Bahn line U1 to Vorgartenstrasse).

Another way to cruise the Danube is to leapfrog ahead by train from Vienna to Krems, where a short walk will lead you to the Schiffstation Krems piers, where river cruises run by Brandner Schifffahrt depart (10:15 AM; 1 PM; 3:45 PM; for contact information, see Boat Travel in this chapter's A to Z section) for a ride to glorious Melk Abbey and Dürnstein. Tickets for one-way are €16.50, but their Web site offers an enticing array of extra goodies—"ump-pah" band concerts, wine cruises, and the like—for extra prices. If you opt for either cruise, remember that it takes longer to travel north: the trip up the canal to Krems, Dürnstein, and Melk will be shorter than the return back to Vienna, which is why many travelers opt to return to the city by train, not boat.

Dürnstein

★ ❸ *9 km (5 mi) west of Dürnstein, 90 km (56 mi) northwest of Vienna.*

If a beauty contest were held among the towns along the Wachau Danube, chances are Dürnstein would be the winner, hands down—as you'll see when you arrive along with droves of tourists. The town is small; leave the car at one end and walk the narrow streets. The main street, Hauptstrasse, is lined with picturesque 16th-century residences. The trick is to overnight here—when the daytrippers depart, the storybook spell of the town returns. The top night to be here is the Summer Solstice, when hundreds of boats bearing torches and candles sail down the river here at twilight to honor the longest day of the year, a breathtaking sight best enjoyed from the town and hotel terraces over the Danube. In October or November, the grape harvest from the surrounding hills is gathered by volunteers from villages throughout the valley. Locals garnish their front doors with straw wreaths if they can offer tastes of the new wine, as members of the local wine cooperative, the Winzergenossenschaft Wachau.

Set among terraced vineyards, the town is landmarked by its gloriously Baroque **Stiftskirche**, dating from the early 1700s, which sits on a cliff overlooking the river—this cloister church's combination of luminous blue facade and stylish Baroque tower is considered the most beautiful of its kind in Austria. After taking in the Stiftskirche, head up the hill, climbing 500 feet above the town, to the famous **Richard the Lion-Hearted Castle** where Leopold V held Richard the Lion-Hearted of England, captured on his way back home from the Crusades. Leopold had been insulted, so the story goes, by Richard while they were in the Holy Land and when the English lord was shipwrecked and had to head back home through Austria, word got out—even though Richard was disguised as a peasant—and Leopold pounced. In the tower of this castle, the Lionheart was imprisoned (1192–93) until he was located by Blondel, the faithful minnesinger. It's said that Blondel was able to locate his imprisoned king when he heard his master's voice completing the verse of a song Blondel was singing aloud—a bit famously recycled in Sir Walter Scott's *Ivanhoe* (and the Robert Taylor MGM film). Leopold turned his prisoner over to the emperor, Henry VI, who held him for months longer until the ransom was paid by Richard's mother, Eleanor of Aquitaine. The rather steep 30-minute climb to the ruins will earn you a breathtaking view up and down the Danube Valley and over the hills to the south.

Where to Stay & Eat

★ $$$–$$$$ ✕ **Loibnerhof.** It's hard to imagine a more idyllic frame for a memorable meal, especially if the weather is fine and tables are set out in the invitingly fragrant apple orchard. The house is famous for its *Butterschnitzel,* an exquisite variation on the theme of ground meat (this one's panfried veal with a touch of pork). To reach Loibnerhof, look for the Unterloiben exit a mile east of Dürnstein. ⊠ *Unterloiben 7* ☎ *02732/82890–0* 🖶 *02732/82890–3* ⌲ *Reservations essential* ▤ *MC, V* ⊗ *Closed Mon. and Tues. and early Jan.–mid-Feb.*

★ **$$$$** ✕⛉ **Schloss Dürnstein.** Once the preserve of the princes of Starhemberg, this 17th-century early-Baroque castle, on a rocky terrace with exquisite views over the Danube, is one of the most famous hotels in Austria. Its classic elegance and comfort have been enjoyed by the ilk of King Juan Carlos of Spain, Prince Hirohito of Japan, Rudolf Nureyev, and a bevy of other celebs. The best guest rooms look onto the river, but all are elegantly decorated, some in grand Baroque or French Empire style. Biedermeier armoires, ceramic stoves, and country antiques grace public rooms. The restaurant is cozily nestled under coved ceilings—half-board is standard and a good value, but not required. The kitchen matches the quality of the excellent wines from the area, and the tables set outside on the large stone balcony overlooking the river make dining here a memorable experience, with pike perch from the Danube, Waldviertler beef, or roast pheasant stuffed with apricots among the menu's delights. Even if you don't stay at the hotel, it's worth a stop for lunch or a leisurely afternoon Wachauer torte and coffee. ⊠ *A–3601* ☎ *02711/ 212* 🖷 *02711/351* ⊕ *www.schloss.at* 🖙 *37 rooms* ♨ *Restaurant, mini-bars, indoor-outdoor pools, gym, sauna, bar, Internet* ▭ *AE, DC, MC, V* ⊘ *Closed Nov.–Mar.*

★ **$$$–$$$$** ✕⛉ **Richard Löwenherz.** Built up around the former church of a vast 700-year-old convent, this noted inn occupies a fine point overlooking the Danube. If you can tear yourself away from its bowered terrace and balcony walkways, you'll enter the hotel and discover impressive, vaulted reception rooms beautifully furnished with antiques and bowls of fresh roses. The balconied guest rooms in the newer part of the house have more modern furnishings. Wander through the grounds among the roses, oleanders, and fig trees, all set against the dramatic backdrop of 600-year-old stone walls. The outstanding restaurant—with an impressively Danubian decor—is known for its local wines and regional specialties, such as crispy duck with dumplings and red cabbage. ⊠ *A–3601* ☎ *02711/222* 🖷 *02711/222–18* ⊕ *www.richardloewenherz. at* 🖙 *38 rooms* ♨ *Restaurant, minibars, pool, bar* ▭ *AE, DC, MC, V* ⊘ *Closed Nov.–Easter or mid–Apr.*

$ ⛉ **Sänger Blondel.** Nearly under the shadow of the exquisitely Baroque spire of Dürnstein's parish church, this *gasthof-pension* welcomes you with a lovely, sunny-yellow, flower-bedecked facade. Owned by the same family since 1729, the inn—named after the minstrel famous for tracking Richard the Lion-Hearted—has a large garden, quite the treat to enjoy in the heart of town. The simply furnished, country-style rooms are of medium size and have attractive paneling and antique decorations. The hotel's restaurant serves hearty Austrian food, and offers zither music on Thursday evenings. ⊠ *No. 64, A–3601* ☎ *02711/253–0* 🖷 *02711/ 253–7* ⊕ *www.saengerblondel.at* 🖙 *16 rooms* ♨ *Restaurant* ▭ *V* ⊘ *Closed mid-Nov.–mid-Mar.*

Melk

❹ *33 km (20¾ mi) southwest of Krems, 88 km (55 mi) west of Vienna.*

At Melk, cross over to the southern bank of the Danube. Unquestionably one of the most impressive sights in all Austria, the abbey of Melk is best approached in mid- to late afternoon, when the setting sun sets the abbey's ornate Baroque yellow facade aglow. As you head eastward paralleling the Danube, the abbey, shining on its promontory above the river, comes into view. It easily overshadows the town—located along Route 1—but remember that the riverside village of Melk itself is worth exploring. A self-guided tour (in English, from the tourist office) will head you toward the highlights and the best spots from which to photograph the abbey. Melk is easily accessible from Vienna. By car, use Autobahn A1 or the Danube-side Route 3; trains connect you, with a one-hour trip, to Vienna's Westhahnhof; or take one of the river boats run by DDSG Blue Danube Steamships which depart from Vienna

FodorsChoice
★

By any standard, **Stift Melk** (Melk Abbey) is a Baroque-era masterpiece. Part palace, part monastery, part opera-set, Melk is a magnificent vision thanks greatly to the upward-reaching twin towers, capped with Baroque helmets and cradling a 208-foot-high dome, and a roof bristling with Baroque statuary. Symmetry here beyond the towers and dome would be misplaced, and much of the abbey's charm is due to the way the early architects were forced to fit the building to the rocky outcrop that forms its base. Locale for part of Umberto Eco's *Name of the Rose*, once Napoléon's Upper Austria redoubt, erected on the site of an ancient Roman fort, and still a working monastery, the Benedictine abbey has a history that extends back to the 11th century, as it was established in 1089. The glorious building you see today is architect Jakob Prandtauer's reconstruction, completed in 1736, in which some earlier elements are incorporated; two years later a great fire nearly totally destroyed the abbey and it had to be rebuilt. A tour of the building includes the main public rooms: a magnificent library, with more than 90,000 books, nearly 2,000 manuscripts, and a superb ceiling fresco by the master Paul Troger; the **Marmorsaal,** whose windows on three sides enhance the ceiling frescoes; the glorious spiral staircase; and the **Stiftskirche** (abbey church) of Saints Peter and Paul, an exquisite example of the Baroque style. Call to find out if tours in English will be offered on a specific day. The **Stiftsrestaurant** (closed November–April) offers standard fare, but the abbey's excellent wines elevate a simple meal to a lofty experience—particularly on a sunny day on the terrace. ⊠ *Abt Berthold Dietmayr-Strasse 1* ☎ *02752/555–225* 🖷 *02752/ 555–226* ⊕ *www.stiftmelk.at* 🖰 *€7; with tour €8.60* ☯ *End of Mar., Apr., and Oct., daily 9–5, ticket office closes at 4; May–Sept., daily 9–6, ticket office closes at 5.*

Where to Stay & Eat

★ **$-$$$** ✕🏠 **Tom's.** The Wallner family has given son Tom full creative control of the kitchen in this Melk landmark, and to show their approval, they even changed the name from Stadt Melk to Tom's. Nestled below the golden abbey in the center of the village square, the high standards of this elegant outpost (whose guest roster includes the Duke and Duchess of Windsor) have been upheld, and the decidedly Biedermeier atmosphere unchanged. The seasonal menu may include zucchini Parmesan lasagne with truffles or fresh grilled crayfish dribbled with butter and lemon. The fried chicken is excellent. Desserts are irresistible, such as chocolate pudding with a Grand Marnier parfait or cheese curd soufflé with homemade pistachio ice cream. After an evening feast here, you may wish to avail yourself of one of the 16 (rather plain) bedrooms in the $ category upstairs. In any event, everyone should plan to overnight in magical Melk. ⊠ *Hauptplatz 1, A–3390* ☎ *02752/52475* 🖷 *02752/52475–19* 🍽 *16 rooms* ▤ *AE, DC, MC, V* ⊙ *Closed Wed. and variable wks in winter.*

$ 🏨 **Hotel zur Post.** Here in the center of town you're in a typical village hotel with the traditional friendliness of family management. The rooms are nothing fancy, though comfortable, and the restaurant offers solid, standard fare. ⊠ *Linzerstrasse 1, A–3390* ☎ *02752/52345* 🖷 *02752/52345–50* 🍽 *27 rooms* ♨ *Restaurant* ▤ *DC, MC, V* ⊙ *Closed Jan. and Feb.*

St. Florian

❺ *81 km (46 mi) west of Melk.*

St. Florian is best known for the great Augustinian abbey, considered among the finest Baroque buildings in Austria. Composer Anton Bruckner (1824–96) was organist here for 10 years and is buried in the abbey. Built to honor the spot on the river Enns where St. Florian was drowned by pagans in 304 (he is still considered the protector against fire and flood by many Austrians), the **Stift St. Florian** (St. Florian Abbey) over the centuries came to comprise one of the most spectacular Baroque showpieces in Austria, landmarked by three gigantic "candle-snuffer" cupolas. In 1686 the Augustinian abbey was built by the Italian architect Carolo Carlone, then finished by Jakob Prandtauer. More of a palace than anything else, it is centered around a mammoth marble **Marmorsaal**—covered with frescoes honoring Prince Eugene of Savoy's defeat of the Turks—and a sumptuous library filled with 140,000 volumes. In this setting of gilt and marble, topped with ceiling frescoes by Bartolomeo Altomonte, an entire school of Austrian historiographers was born in the 19th century. Guided tours of the abbey begin with the magnificent figural gateway which rises up three stories and is covered with symbolic statues. The "Stiegenhaus," or Grand Staircase, leads to the upper floors, which include the **Kaiserzimmer,** a suite of 13 opulent salons (where you can see the "terrifying bed" of Prince Eugene, fantastically adorned with wood-carved figures of captives). The tour includes one of the great masterworks of the Austrian Baroque, Jakob Prandtauer's **Eagle Fountain courtyard,** with its richly sculpted figures. In the over-the-top **abbey church,** where the ornate surroundings are somewhat in contrast to Bruckner's music, the Krismann organ (1770–74) is one of the largest and best of its period and Bruckner used it to become a master organist and composer. Another highlight is the **Altdorfer Gallery,** which contains several masterworks by Albrecht Altdorfer, the leading master of the 16th-century Danube School and ranked with Dürer and Grunewald as one of the greatest northern painters. ⊠ *Stiftstrasse 1* ☎ *07224/8902–0* 🖷 *07224/8902–31* ⊕ *www.stift-st-florian.at* 🎫 *€5.30* ⊙ *70-min tour Easter–Oct., daily at 10, 11, 2, 3, and 4.*

Fodor'sChoice ★

Nightlife & the Arts

Summer concerts are held weekends in June and July at the Kremsmünster and St. Florian abbeys; for tickets, contact **Oberösterreichische Stiftskonzerte** (✉ Domgasse 12 ☎ 0732/776127 ⊕ www.stiftskonzerte. at). A series of **concerts** (☎ 0732/221022 🖷 0732/727–7701 ⊕ www. florianer.at) on the Bruckner organ are given in the church of St. Florian during varying summer months.

Steyr

★ ⑥ *24 km (11 mi) southeast of St. Florian.*

Steyr is one of Austria's best-kept secrets, a stunning Gothic market town that watches over the confluence of the Steyr and Enns rivers. Today the main square is lined with Baroque facades, many with Rococo trim, all complemented by the castle that sits above. The Bummerlhaus at Number 32, in its present form dating from 1497, has a late-Gothic look. On the Enns side, steps and narrow passageways lead down to the river. Across the River Steyr, St. Michael's church, with its Bohemian cupolas and gable fresco, presides over the postcard-perfect scene. In the center of town is the Stadtplatz, lined with arcaded houses, along with a Rococo-era town hall and a Late Gothic "Burger" house. Elsewhere in town is a bevy of lovely Gothic, Baroque, and Rococo churches. In Steyr you are close to the heart of Bruckner country. He composed his Sixth Symphony in the parish house here, and there is a Bruckner room in the Meserhaus, where he composed his "sonorous music to confound celestial spheres." Schubert also lived here for a time. So many of the houses are worthy of attention that you will need to take your time and explore.

Where to Stay & Eat

★ **$$$–$$$$** ✕ **Rahofer.** You'll have to search for this popular restaurant, which is hidden away at the end of one of the passageways off the main square. Inside it's warm and cozy with dark-wood accents and candlelight. The focus here is Italian, from the Tuscan bread and olives that are brought to your table on your arrival to the selection of fresh pastas and lightly prepared meat and fish dishes. Individual pizzas are baked to perfection. ✉ *Stadtplatz 9* ☎ *07252/54606* ▤ *MC, V* ☉ *Closed Sun. and Mon.*

$$–$$$ ✕▥ **Minichmayr.** From this traditional hotel the view alone—out over the confluence of the Enns and Steyr rivers, up and across to the Schloss Lamberg and the Baroque cupolas of St. Michael's church—will make your stay memorable. And what could be more wonderful than falling asleep while listening to the river outside your window? Some of the bedrooms have been renovated with modern-style Biedermeier furnishings, complementing the Old World charm of the building's exterior and public rooms, while others have traditional cherrywood furniture. Try to get a room on the river side. The restaurant, with a Secession-style inspired bar, offers classic Austrian cuisine, specializing in fresh fish. ✉ *Haratzmüllerstrasse 1–3, A–4400* ☎ *07252/53410–0* 🖷 *07252/ 48202* ⊕ *www.hotel-minichmayr.at* ⇝ *47 rooms* ⚹ *Restaurant, bar, Internet* ▤ *AE, DC, MC, V.*

Kremsmünster

7 *32 km (14 mi) west of Steyr.*

The vast Benedictine **Stift Kremsmünster** was established in 777 and remains one of the most important abbeys in Austria. Most travelers arrive here by taking Route 139 (or the train) heading southwest from Linz. Inside the church is the Gothic memorial tomb of Gunther, killed by a wild boar, whose father, Tassilo, duke of Bavaria (and nemesis of Charlemagne), vowed to build the abbey on the site. Centuries later, the initial structures were replaced in the grand Baroque manner, including the extraordinary tower. Magnificent rooms include the Kaisersaal and the frescoed library with more than 100,000 volumes, many of them manuscripts. On one side of the Prälatenhof courtyard are Jakob Prandtauer's elegant fish basins, complete with sculpted saints holding squirming denizens of the deep, and opposite is the Abteitrakt, whose art collection includes the Tassilo Chalice, from about 765. The seven-story observatory (*Sternwarte*) houses an early museum of science. ☎ 07583/5275–151 ⊕ *www.kremsmuenster.at* ✉ *Rooms and art gallery €4, observatory and tour €4.50* ☉ *Rooms and art gallery tour (minimum 5 people) Easter–Oct., daily at 10, 11, 2, 3, and 4; Nov.–Easter, Tues.–Sun. at 11 and 2. Observatory tour (minimum 5 people) May–Oct., daily at 10 and 2.*

SALZKAMMERGUT: THE LAKE DISTRICT

Remember the exquisite opening scenes of *The Sound of Music*? Castles reflected in water, mountains veiled by a scattering of downy clouds, flower-strewn valleys dotted with cool blue lakes: a view of Austria as dreamed up by a team of Hollywood's special-effects geniuses—so we thought. But, no, those scenes were filmed right here, not far from where the Trapp children "Do-Re-Mi"-ed. Here, we feature just a few jewels from this scenic treasure-box, including the delightfully picturesque towns of Gmunden, St. Wolfgang, St. Gilgen, and Bad Ischl, which seems to be on sabbatical from an operetta set.

Gmunden

8 *35 km (22 mi) southwest of Kremsmünster.*

Gmunden, at the top of the Traunsee, is an attractive town to stroll about in. The tree-lined promenade along the lake is reminiscent of past days of the idle aristocracy and artistic greats—the composers Franz Schubert, Johannes Brahms, Karl Goldmark, Béla Bartók, Arnold Schoenberg, and Erich Wolfgang Korngold were just some of the notables who strolled under the chestnut trees. The gloriously ornate, arcaded yellow-and-white **town hall**, with its corner towers topped by onion domes, can't be overlooked; it houses a famous carillon, with bells fashioned not from the local clay but from fabled Meissen porcelain (which gives a better sound) decorated in the Gmunden style. Head to the upper town and take in the parish church on Pfarrhofgasse. It has a beautiful high altar dedicated to the Three Holy Kings.Music lovers will enjoy the Brahms

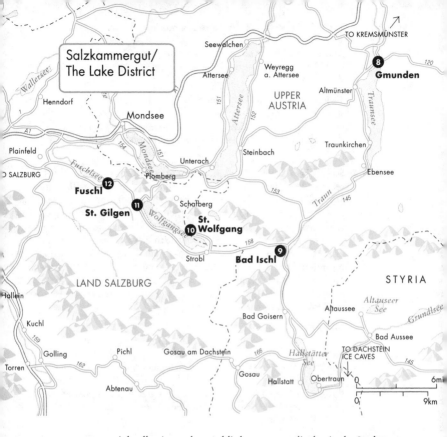

memorial collection—the world's largest—on display in the **Stadtmuseum** (City Museum) at the town Kammerhof. Other exhibitions are devoted to the town's history and the region's salt and mineral resources. ⊠ *Kammerhofgasse 8* ☎☎ *07612/794420* 🎫 *€4* ⏰ *May–Oct., Dec. and Jan. Mon.–Sat. 10–noon and 2–5, Sun. 10–noon.*

Take time to look at, or visit, the "lake" castle, **Schloss Orth,** on a peninsula known as Toskana, was originally built in the 15th century. It was once owned by Archduke Johann, who gave up his title after marrying an actress and thereafter called himself Orth. He disappeared with the casket supposedly holding the secret of the Mayerling tragedy after the death of Emperor Franz Josef's son Rudolf.

★ From Gmunden, take a lake trip on the *Gisela,* built in 1872, the oldest coal-fired steam side-wheeler running anywhere. It carried Emperor Franz Josef in the last century and is now restored. For departure times, check with **Traunseeschiffahrt Eder** (☎ *07612/66700* ⊕ *www. traunseeschiffahrt.at/*). The boat route crisscrosses the whole 12-km (7-mi) length of the lake.

From beyond the railroad station, a 12-minute cable-car ride brings you to the top of the **Grünberg.** From here you will have a superb view over the Traunsee, with the Dachstein glacier forming the backdrop in the south. In winter there are good ski runs here. ✉ *Freygasse 4* ☎ *07612/64977–0* 🕮 *Round-trip €10, one-way €7* ⊙ *Apr.–June and Sept., daily 9–5; July and Aug., daily 9–6; Oct., daily 9–4:30.*

To get to Bad Ischl from Gmunden, take Route 145 along the western shore of the Traunsee—note the Traunstein, Hochkogel, and Erlakogel peaks on the eastern side, the latter nicknamed *die schlafende Griechin* ("the slumbering Greek girl")—and then along the Traun River.

Where to Stay

$$$ Schloss Freisitz Hotel Roith. Crowning the eastern shores of the Traunsee, this landmark "schloss" draws all eyes, thanks to its flapping flag atop its white turret, its *mittel-europisch* Baroque pediments, and expansive "hunting-lodge" facade. Gracing a castle site from 1550, it was renovated in 1887 by Gustav Faber. In 1964 the mansion became a hotel and now anyone can experience the 19th-century luxe that the famous German pencil maker once enjoyed—Oriental carpets, Art Nouveau furniture, and those breathtaking vistas down to the lake. The breakfast buffet is almost as beautiful. ✉ *Traunsteinstrasse 87, A–4810* ☎ *07612/64905* 🖷 *07612/649–0517* ⊕ *www.schlosshotel.at* ⛵ *14 rooms* ♨ *Restaurant, sauna, steam-bath, gym* ☰ *AE, DC, MC, V.*

Shopping

Among the many souvenirs and handicrafts you'll find in Salzkammergut shops, the most famous are the handcrafted ceramics of Gmunden. The green-trimmed, white country ceramics are decorated with blue, yellow, green, and white patterns, including the celebrated 16th-century *Grüngeflammte* design, solid horizontal green stripes on a white background. You'll find them at **Gmundner Keramik** (✉ Keramikstrasse 24 ☎ 07612/786–0).

Bad Ischl

❾ *35 km (15 mi) southwest of Gmunden, 56 km (35 mi) east of Salzburg, 16 km (10 mi) southeast of St. Wolfgang.*

Many travelers used to think of Bad Ischl primarily as the town where Zauner's pastry shop is located, to which connoisseurs drove miles for the sake of a cup of coffee and a slice of *Guglhupf,* a lemon sponge cake studded with raisins and nuts. Pastry continues to be the best-known drawing card of a community that symbolizes, more than any other place except Vienna itself, the Old Austria of resplendent uniforms and balls and waltzes and operettas. The town is charmingly laid out on a peninsula between the Rivers Traun and Ischl, whose amazing waters still run crystal clear. Bad Ischl was the place where Emperor Franz Josef chose to establish his summer court: when he died in 1916 at an age of 85, he had spent 82 summers in Ischl (the story goes that his mother, Sophie, had stayed at the spa in 1829 at the time of his conception, thereby earning the ruler his nickname, the "saltprince"). And it was also here that Franz Josef met and fell in love with his future empress, the troubled Sisi, though his mother had intended him for Sisi's elder sister. Today, you can enjoy the same sort of pastries *mit Schlag* (whipped cream) that the emperor loved. Afterward, you can hasten off to the town's modern spa, one of the best-known in Austria. The town initially grew up around the curative mineral springs. One of the town's main landmarks is the classic 19th-century *Kurhaus* (spa building), which is now a theater for operetta festivals (note the monuments to Lehár and Kálman in the adjoining park). Nearby are buildings from the 1860s, which still offer spa treatments. You'll want to stroll along the shaded **Esplanade,** where the pampered and privileged of the 19th century loved to take their constitutionals, usually after a quick stop at the spa pavilion of the **Trinkhalle** in the style of the 19th century, still in the middle of town on Ferdinand-Auböck-Platz.

★ In Bad Ischl the quickest way to travel back in time to the gilded 1880s is to head for the **Kaiservilla,** the imperial-yellow (signifying wealth and power) residence, which looks rather like a miniature Schönbrunn: its ground plan forms an E to honor the empress Elisabeth. Markus von Habsburg, great-grandson of Franz Josef I, still lives here, but you can tour parts of the building to see the ornate reception rooms and the surprisingly modest residential quarters (through which sometimes even the archduke guides guests with what can only be described as a very courtly kind of humor). It was at this villa that the emperor signed the declaration of war against Serbia, which officially marked the start of World War I. ⊠ *Kaiserpark* ☎ *06132/23241* 🖭 *Grounds €3.50; combined ticket, including tour of villa, €9.50* ⊘ *Easter, Apr. weekends, and May–mid-Oct., daily 9:30–4:45.*

Fascinating is the only word to describe the **Museum der Stadt Ischl,** which occupies the circa 1880 Hotel Austria—the favored summer address for archduke Franz Karl and his wife Sophie (from 1834 on). More momentously, the young Franz Josef got engaged to his beloved Elisabeth here in 1853. After taking in the gardens (with their Brahms monument), explore the various exhibits, which deal with the region's salt, royal, and folk histories. From December until the beginning of February, the museum shows off its famous *Kalss Krippe,* an enormous mechanical Christmas créche. Dating from 1838, it has about 300 figures. The townsfolk of Ischl, in fact, are famous for their Christmas "cribs" and you can see many of them in tours of private houses opened for visits after Christmas until January 6th. ⊠ *Esplanade 10* ☎ *06132/30114* 🖭 *€4.20* ⊘ *Jan.–Mar., Fri.–Sun. 1–4; Apr.–Oct. and Dec., Thurs.–Tues. 10–5, Wed. 2–7.*

A steady stream of composers followed the aristocracy and the court to Bad Ischl. Anton Bruckner, Johannes Brahms (who composed his famous *Lullaby* here as well as many of his late works), Johann Strauss the Younger, Carl Michael Ziehrer, Oscar Straus, and Anton Webern all spent summers here, but it was the Hungarian born Franz Lehár, composer of *The Merry Widow,* who left the most lasting musical impression. With the royalties he received from his operettas, he was able to afford his own house from 1912 on. Previously, he rented the **Rosenvilla,** set between the trees to the left of the Kongresshaus, and some sumptuous period interiors remain. Today, Bad Ischl's summer operetta festival (*see Music in* Nightlife & the Arts, *below*) always includes one Lehár work. ⊠ *Lehárkai 8* ☎ *06132/26992* 🖭 *€4.50* ⊘ *May–Sept., daily 9–noon and 2–5.*

Bad Ischl is accessed easily via various routes. From St. Wolfgang, back-track south to Strobl and head eastward on Route 158. To get to the town directly from Salzburg, take the A1 to Mondsee, then Routes 151 and 158 along the Wolfgangsee and the Mondsee. There are many buses that depart hourly from Salzburg's main railway station; you can also travel by train via the junction of Attnang-Puchheim or Stainach-Irdning (several transfers are required)—a longer journey than the bus ride, which is usually 90 minutes.

Where to Stay & Eat

★ $–$$ ✕ **Weinhaus Attwenger.** This inviting restaurant is set in a turn-of-the-20th-century gingerbread villa in a shady garden overlooking the river. The house was formerly the summer residence of composer Anton Bruckner, who journeyed here to be the emperor's organist in the town parish church. The tranquil garden is ideal for summer dining, and in-side the villa the cozy, wood-panel rooms are decorated with antique country knickknacks. Order the crispy duck in a honey-ginger sauce or the basket of country-fried chicken, or ask for seasonal recommendations; the fish and game dishes are particularly good. ⊠ *Lehárkai 12* ☎ *06132/23327* ▭ *No credit cards* ✆ *Closed Wed., Thurs., and 2 wks in Mar.*

¢–$ ✕ **Café Zauner.** If you haven't been to Zauner, you've missed a true high-light of Bad Ischl. There are two locations, one on the Esplanade over-looking the River Traun (open only in summer) and the other a few blocks away on Pfarrgasse. The desserts—particularly the house creation, *Zaunerstollen,* a chocolate-covered confection of sugar, hazelnuts, and nougat (and worth taking one home with you, too)—have made this one of Austria's best-known pastry shops. Emperor Franz Josef used to visit every day for a Guglhupf, a lemon sponge cake. ⊠ *Pfarrgasse 7* ☎ *06132/23522* ▭ *MC* ✆ *Closed Tues.*

★ $$–$$$$ ✕▥ **Villa Schratt.** About a mile outside of Bad Ischl on the road to Salzburg is the enchanting, secluded villa, fabled retreat of the actress Katharina Schratt. "Kati"—star of Vienna's k.k. Hofburgtheater (the Imperial and Royal court theater)—was Emperor Franz Josef's mistress in his later years and almost every summer morning, the emperor would stroll over here for his breakfast. Over the course of their time together, most of European royalty dropped in for a visit. Nowadays the Villa Schratt is one of the best places to dine in the area. Choose between two dining rooms—one with a Jugendstil slant, the other, country-style with chintz curtains, a ceramic stove, and a hutch displaying homemade jams. Try the *Zanderfilet* (pike perch) on a bed of delicate beets soaked in port wine, or beef tenderloin strips with oyster mushrooms in a cream sauce. For dessert, order the traditional Guglhupf sponge cake, Franz Josef's favorite—it even comes warm out of the oven. Upstairs are four lovely, antiques-filled bedrooms for overnighters. ⊠ *Steinbruch 43, A–4820* ☎ *06132/27647 restaurant, 06132/23535 rooms* 🖷 *06132/27647–4* ⊕ *www.tiscover.com/villa.schratt* ⌦ *Reservations essential* ☞ *2 rooms* ▭ *AE, MC* ✆ *Closed Tues., Wed., early to mid-Nov., and varying wks in spring.*

$ ▥ **Goldener Ochs.** The "Golden Ox" is in a superb location in the town center, with the sparkling River Traun a few steps away. Rooms are modern with blond-wood furniture; some have balconies, and there are a few large rooms designed for families. The kitchen prides itself on its health-oriented cooking. ✉ *Grazerstrasse 4, A–4820* ☎ *06132/235290* 🖷 *06132/235293* 🌐 *www.tiscover.com/goldener-ochs* 🛏 *48 rooms* 🍴 *Restaurant, gym, sauna, Internet* 🚫 *AE, DC, MC, V.*

Nightlife & the Arts

The main musical events of the year in the Salzkammergut are the July and August operetta festivals held in Bad Ischl. In addition, performances of at least two operettas (*The Merry Widow* is a favorite standard) take place every season in the **Kongress and Theaterhaus** (☎ 06132/23420), where tickets are sold. For early booking, contact the **Operrettengemeinde** (✉ Kurhausstrasse 8, A–4820 Bad Ischl ☎ 06132/23839 🖷 06132/23839–39).

St. Wolfgang

★ **❿** *21 km (9 mi) northwest of Bad Ischl, 19 km (12 mi) east of St. Gilgen, 50 km (31 mi) east of Salzburg.*

A delightful way to enter the picture-book town of St. Wolfgang is to leave your car at Strobl, at the southern end of the Wolfgangsee, and take one of the steamers that ply the waters of the lake. Between St. Wolfgang and Strobl, the Wolfgangsee still retains its old name of "Abersee." One of the earliest paddleboats on the lake is still in service, a genuine 1873 steamer called the *Kaiser Franz Josef*. Service is regular from May to mid-October. Unless your hotel offers parking, you'll have to park on the fringes of town and walk a short distance, as the center is a pedestrian-only zone. The town has everything: swimming and hiking in summer, cross-country skiing in winter, and natural feasts for the eye at every turn. Here you will find yourself in the Austria of operetta. Indeed, St. Wolfgang became known around the world thanks to the inn called the **Weisses Rössl,** which was built right next to the landing stage in 1878. It featured prominently in a late 19th-century play that achieved fame as an operetta by Ralph Benatzky in 1930. Ironically, the two original playwrights, Gustav Kadelburg and Oskar Blumenthal, had another, now destroyed, Weisses Rössl (set along the road from Bad Ischl to Hallstatt) in mind! In the years following World War II both the composers Samuel Barber and Gian Carlo Menotti spent summer vacations here, too.

You shouldn't miss seeing Michael Pacher's great altarpiece in the 15th-century **Wallfahrtskirche** (pilgrimage church), one of the finest examples of late-Gothic wood carving to be found anywhere. This 36-foot masterpiece took 10 years (1471–81) to complete. As a winged altar, its paintings and carvings were used as *Armenbibel* (a bible for the poor)—illustrations for those who couldn't read or write. The coronation of the Virgin Mary is depicted in detail so exact that you can see the stitches in her garments. Pacher set his painted scenes in landscapes inspired by his homeland, South Tirol (now Italy). You're in luck if you're at the church on a sunny day, when sunlight off the nearby lake dances on the ceiling in brilliant reflections through the stained-glass windows. ⊘ *May–Sept., daily 9–5; Oct.–Apr., daily 10–4; altar closed to view during Lent.*

In St. Wolfgang, free brass band concerts are held on the Marktplatz every Saturday evening at 8:30 in May, and on both Wednesday and Saturday at 8:30 PM from June to September. Folk events are usually well publicized with posters (if you are lucky, even Benatzky's operetta *Im Weissen Rössl* might be on schedule). Not far from St. Wolfgang, the town of Strobl holds a Day of Popular Music and Tradition in early July—"popular" meaning brass band, and "tradition" being local costume. Check with the regional tourist office for details.

off the beaten path

SCHAFBERG – From May to mid-October the rack railway trip from St. Wolfgang to the 5,800-foot peak of the Schafberg offers a great chance to survey the surrounding countryside from what is acclaimed as the "belvedere of the Salzkammergut lakes." On a clear day you can almost see forever—at least as far as the Lattengebirge mountain range west of Salzburg. Figure in advance for crowds, so reserve in advance or start out early. The train—itself a curiosity dating from 1893—departs hourly early May to early July; from the second week in July until early September, daily from 8:25 AM to 7:55 PM; early September to late October, daily from 9:55 AM to 2:55 PM. The train does not run in bad weather. Allow at least a good half day for the outing, which costs €22 (☎ 06138/2232 🖷 06138/2232–12).

Where to Stay & Eat

★ **$$$–$$$$** ✕🖫 **Weisses Rössl.** The "White Horse" has been featured in films and theater over the years, thanks to the famous operetta set here. Much of the hotel was extensively renovated in the 1960s, but most guest rooms are still full of country charm, with pretty chintz fabrics and quaint furniture, and many have a balcony with a lake view. Baths are luxurious, complete with controls to set the exact water temperature you desire. The buffet breakfast is outstanding. An added attraction is the outdoor pool, situated directly on the lake and heated to a constant 86°F year-round. The dining terraces, built to float over the water, are enchanting, where you can enjoy the noted leek cream soup with scampi, *Forelle Müllerin* (trout "miller's daughter" simply fried in butter), or corn-fed chicken in a rosemary gravy. The hotel is world famous, so book well in advance, especially for the summer. ✉ *Markt 74, A–5360* ☎ *06138/2306–0* 🖷 *06138/2306–41* ⊕ *www.weissesroessl.at* ⬚ *72 rooms ⬚ 2 restaurants, minibars, tennis court, indoor and outdoor pool, lake, sauna, windsurfing, boating, bar, Internet* ▤ *AE, DC, MC, V* ☉ *Closed Nov.–mid-Dec.*

★ **$$–$$$** ✕🖫 **Cortisen am See.** A large chalet-style structure, with a glowing yellow facade, "At the Court" has become one of St. Wolfgang's most stylish and comfortable hotels. It has a lakeside perch, of course, replete with its own beach, rowing boats, terrace dining, and plenty of mountain bikes. Inside, all is gemütlichkeit nouvelle—chintz fabrics, tin-wrought lanterns, Swedish woods, sash windows, and exquisitely designed guest rooms make this a Lake District xanadu. The restaurant sparkles with a mix of 19th-century fabrics and gleaming white trim. The menu is mighty spiffy and owner Roland Ballner is proud to offer not only the largest wine selection in the area but also its most exotic cigar collection. ✉ *Markt 15, A–5360* ☎ *06138/2376–0* 🖷 *06138/236744* ⊕ *www.*

cortisen.at 🖘 *36 rooms* ⚒ *Restaurant, bar, Internet, sauna, steambath, gym* ☰ *AE, DC, MC, V.*

¢ 🖥 **Gasthof Zimmerbräu.** This pretty, pleasant budget Gasthof is four centuries old and was once a brewery, though for the last hundred years it has been an inn run by the Scharf family. Centrally located, the Zimmerbräu is not near the lake but does maintain its own bathing cabana by the water. The decor is appealingly rustic in some rooms, contemporary in others, but all rooms have balconies, and there is a lovely sitting room with Biedermeier furnishings on the first floor. ✉ *Im Stöck 85, A–5360* ☎ *06138/ 2204* 🖷 *06138/2204–45* ⊕ *www.zimmerbraeu.com* 🖘 *25 rooms* ⚒ *Restaurant, bar* ☰ *MC, V* ☺ *Closed Nov. and Dec. 26.*

St. Gilgen

★ ⓫ *15 km (6 mi) northwest of St. Wolfgang, 10 km (6 mi) south of Fuschl, 34 km (21 mi) east of Salzburg.*

Though its modest charms tend to be overshadowed by neighboring St. Wolfgang, St. Gilgen has a pretty main square and an impressive musical pedigree. A Mozart fountain in the pretty town square commemorates the fact that Mozart's mother was born here while his sister Nannerl later lived in a little house near the dock on Ischler Strasse. Nearby, the town museum is run by the International Foundation Mozarteum and contains a collection of items (duplicates, actually, from Salzburg's Mozart's birthplace museum). In the small Baroque parish church Mozart's grandparents and sister married and his mother was baptized. The town is adorned with a nice beach, the northernmost strand on the Wolfgangsee. Get out on the water by enjoying a ride on one of the sidewheel steamships that ply the lake.

Where to Stay & Eat

★ $$$$ ╳ **Timbale.** Cozy and cheerful, Timbale is one of the premier restaurants in the Salzkammergut, known far and wide for regional specialties done just so. The taste treats start with the corn, whole wheat, and French breads baked on the premises, and dazzle on to the *Stubenküken* (chicken breast) stuffed with a cheese soufflé and wild mushrooms, or the *Kalbsrücken* (veal) with risotto and grilled shallots. Your eyes, as well as your stomach, will be happy—the crocheted red flower petals on periwinkle-blue tablecloths make everyone smile. ✉ *Salzburgerstrasse 2, A–5340* ☎🖷 *06227/7587* ⚒ *Reservations essential* ☰ *No credit cards* ☺ *Closed all day Thurs., Fri. lunch, and Aug.*

★ $$ ╳🖥 **Hotel Gasthof zur Post.** An inn since 1415, the family-owned Post is one of the most attractive houses in town, a former domicile of Mozart's grandfather. A beautiful old sprucewood staircase leads to spacious rooms with contemporary furniture and stunning views of the village and the Wolfgangsee (most rooms have balconies). Owner Norbert Leitner is also a top chef—his seasonal menus might include a salad of wild greens with duck breast, spinach and garlic soup with slivers of smoked freshwater salmon, and *Tafelspitz* (boiled beef). On Friday evenings from September to mid-November, the restaurant offers live folk music. Be sure to have a glass of wine in the Vinothek, with its original 12th-century entrance. And get to know the secret behind the old hunting-scene fresco in the main parlor (with hidden motifs symbolizing "hunted" Lutherans). ✉ *Mozartplatz 8, A–5340* ☎ *06227/2157* 🖷 *06227/2157–600* ⊕ *www.gasthofzurpost.at* 🛏 *18 rooms* ⟋ *Restaurant, sauna* 🚬 *AE, DC, MC, V* ⊙ *Closed 1 mo (variable) in winter. Restaurant closed Wed. and Thurs., Nov.–Apr.*

Fuschl

⓬ *8 km (6 mi) northwest of St. Gilgen, 30½ km (19 mi) east of Salzburg.*

Fuschl is so close to Salzburg that many attendees of the Salzburger Festspiele choose to stay in a hotel here, enjoying urban comforts while getting to savor rural pleasures at the same time. Located on Route 158, the town is on the Fuschlsee—a gem of a very clear small (only 2 mi long) deep lake, whose bluish-green water is ideal for swimming and wind-surfing—surrounded by a nature preserve. There's not much to do in Fuschl, the beaches being very limited in number, though those willing to hike can reach an extremely narrow strip on the northern shore that is especially popular with nudists. The town is noted for its many good places to eat and spend the night, including Schloss Fuschl, one of the finest establishments in the Salzkammergut.

Where to Stay & Eat

★ **$$$$** ✕🖭 **Schloss Fuschl.** Just 16 km (10 mi) from Salzburg, this dramatic 15th-century towerlike castle, which became a hotel in the 1950s, was originally built as a hunting lodge for the Salzburg prince-archbishops. Ringed by mountains and on three sides by the pristine Fuschlsee, it has one of the most magical settings in Austria. Suites and superior rooms are regally splendid, and though the standard rooms are more modern, most have spectacular views of the lake. In fine weather, dining is outdoors on the beautiful stone terrace. Opt for the trout caught in the Fuschlsee (which is unpolluted by motorboats) and then delicately smoked in the smokehouse on the premises. The adjoining **Arabella Sheraton Hotel Jagdhof,** built in 2003, now offers rooms in more modern, though no less classy, surrounds. It took an 18th-century manor house and grew exponentionally over a scenic hillside. It offers Sheraton posh yet retains a good number of regional accents. ✉ *A–5322 Hof bei Salzburg* ☎ *06229/2253–0* 🖷 *06229/2253–531* ⊕ *www.schlossfuschl. com* 🛏 *Castle 84 rooms, hotel 143 rooms* ⟋ *Restaurant, minibars, pool, Internet* 🚬 *AE, DC, MC, V.*

DANUBE VALLEY/SALZKAMMERGUT A TO Z

To research prices, get advice from other travelers, and book travel arrangements, visit www.fodors.com

AIR TRAVEL

The air hub of the Danube Valley is the big city of Linz, whose airport is served mainly by Austrian Airlines, Lufthansa, Swissair, and Tyrolean. Regular flights connect with Vienna, Amsterdam, Berlin, Düsseldorf, Frankfurt, Paris, Stuttgart, and Zürich. The Salzburg airport is about 53 km (33 mi) from Bad Ischl.

AIRPORTS   The Linz airport is in Hörsching, about 12 km (7½ mi) southwest of
the city. Buses run between the airport and the main train station according to flight schedules.

🚹 Airport Information **Linz airport** ☎ 07221/600-0.

BIKE TRAVEL

For details on the scenic Danube river route, ask for the folder "Danube
Cycle Track" (in English, from Tourist Office of Lower Austria). The
brochure "Radfahren" is in German but lists contact numbers for cycle
rentals throughout Austria. At train stations along the Danube Valley,
you can rent bikes from various concessioners. The best option is to rent
from Pedal Power in Vienna. They have a great guidebook in English,
"The Danube Bike Trail" for €13 (€20 if mailed to the U.S.). As for
taking the bikes on trains—many trains, especially Vienna's Inner City
trains, limit the amount of bikes they'll haul, and in summer it's really
hard to get a space for your bike. Regional trains are then the best bet,
and they'll also stop in Melk and Krems, for instance. Much of the
Salzkammergut is rather hilly if you are just a casual cyclist, but you'll
find reasonably good cycling country around the lakes, including the
Wolfgangsee (though Route 158 can become quite noisy and fume-
filled). Sports shops throughout the areas rent bikes; local tourist offices can point you to the right places. You can cycle the 14 km (9 mi)
from St. Wolfgang to Bad Ischl on back roads.

🚹 Bike Maps **Tourist Office of Lower Austria** ☎ 01/53610-6200 🖷 01/53610-6060.
🚹 Rentals **Pedal Power** ✉ Ausstellungsstrasse 3, A-1020 Vienna ☎ 01/729-7234
🖷 01/729-7235 ⊕ www.pedalpower.at.

BOAT & FERRY TRAVEL

For full information on cruises offered by the Blue Danube Schifffahrt/
DDSG (Vienna to Dürnstein) and the Brandner Schifffahrt (Krems to
Melk), *see* this chapter's Close-Up box, "And the Danube Waltzes On."

🚹 Boat & Ferry Information **Blue Danube Schifffahrt/DDSG** ✉ Friedrichstrasse 7,
A-1043 Vienna ☎ 01/588-800 🖷 01/58880-440 ⊕ www.ddsg-blue-danube.at. **Brandner Schifffahrt** ✉ Ufer 50, A-3313 Wallsee ☎ 07433/2590-21 ⊕ www.brandner.at.

BUS TRAVEL

If you link them together, bus routes will get you to the main points in
the Danube Valley and even to the hilltop castles and monasteries, assuming you have the time. The main bus routes through the Salzkammergut are: Bad Aussee, to Gründlsee; Bad Ischl, to Gosau, Hallstatt,
Salzburg, and St. Wolfgang; Mondsee, to St. Gilgen and Salzburg; St.
Gilgen, to Mondsee; Salzburg, to Bad Ischl, Mondsee, St. Gilgen, and
Strobl. If you coordinate your schedule to arrive at a point by train or
boat, you can usually make reasonable bus connections to outlying destinations. You can book bus tours in Vienna or Linz by calling central
bus information, listed below.

🚹 Bus Information **Central bus information** ☎ 01/71101.

CAR TRAVEL

A car is certainly the most comfortable way to see this region, as it conveniently enables you to pursue the byways. The trickiest part may be getting out of Vienna. Follow signs to Prague to get across the Danube, but once across, avoid the right-hand exit marked Prague—which leads to the autobahn—and continue ahead, following signs for Pragerstrasse and turning left at the traffic light. Pragersttrasse (Route 3) heads toward Langenzersdorf and Korneuburg. The main route along the north bank of the Danube is Route 3; along the south bank, there's a choice between the autobahn Route A1 and a collection of lesser but good roads. Roads are good and well marked, and you can switch over to the A1 autobahn, which parallels the general east–west course of the Danube Valley route.

Driving is by far the easiest and most convenient way to reach the Lake District; traffic is excessive only on weekends (although it can be slow on some narrow lakeside stretches). From Salzburg you can take Route 158 east to Fuschl, St. Gilgen, and Bad Ischl or the A1 autobahn to Mondsee. Coming from Vienna or Linz, the A1 passes through the northern part of the Salzkammergut; get off at the Steyrermühl exit or the Regau exit and head south on Route 144/145 to Gmunden, Bad Ischl, Bad Goisern, and Bad Aussee. From the Seewalchen exit, take Route 152 down the east side of the Attersee, instead of the far less scenic Route 151 down the west side.

EMERGENCIES

If you need a doctor and speak no German, ask your hotel how best to obtain assistance.

🔢 Emergency services **Ambulance** ☎ 144. **Fire** ☎ 122. **Police** ☎ 133.

TOURS

Tours out of Vienna take you to Melk and back by bus and boat. For example, see the tour offered by www.viennasightseeingtours.com/efirst. htm (click on Danube Valley and then full day tours). These tours usually run about eight hours, with a stop at Dürnstein. Bus tours operate year-round except as noted, but the boat runs only April–October.

Day-long tours of the Salzkammergut, offered by Dr. Richard /Albus/ Salzburg Sightseeing Tours and Salzburg Panorama Tours, whisk you all too quickly from Salzburg to St. Gilgen, St. Wolfgang, and Mondsee. Full-day tours to Salzburg from Vienna pass through Gmunden and the Traunsee, Bad Ischl, the Wolfgangsee, St. Gilgen, and Fuschlsee, but you can't see much from a bus window.

🔢 Fees & Schedules **Cityrama Sightseeing** ✉ Börsegasse 1 ☎ 01/534–130 🖷 01/534–1328. **Dr. Richard/Albus/Salzburg Sightseeing Tours** ✉ Mirabellplatz 2, A–5020 Salzburg ☎ 0662/881616 🖷 0662/878776. **Salzburg Panorama Tours** ✉ Schrannengasse 2/2, A–5020 Salzburg ☎ 0662/883211 🖷 0662/871628. **Vienna Sightseeing Tours** ✉ Stelzhammergasse 4/11, A–1031 Vienna ☎ 01/712–4683–0 🖷 01/714–1141.

TRAIN TRAVEL

Rail lines parallel the north and south banks of the Danube. Fast services from Vienna run as far as Stockerau; beyond that, service is less frequent. The main east–west line from Vienna to Linz closely follows the south bank for much of its route. Fast trains connect German cities via Passau with Linz.

All the larger towns and cities in the region can be reached by train, but the train misses the Wachau Valley along the Danube's south bank. The rail line on the north side of the river clings to the bank in places; service is infrequent. You can combine rail and boat transportation along this route, taking the train upstream and crisscrossing your way back on the river.

Trains leave Vienna's Westbahnhof several times a day for Melk; from Vienna's Franz-Josefs Bahnhof, you can catch a train to Krems, which can then link up with Dürnstein.

The geography of the Salkammergut means that rail lines run mainly north–south. Trains run from Vöcklabruck to Seewalchen at the top end of the Attersee and from Attnang-Puchheim to Gmunden, Bad Ischl, Hallstatt, Bad Aussee, and beyond. Both starting points are on the main east–west line between Salzburg and Linz. There is a major train connection between Bad Ischl and Salzburg.

🚆 Train Information **LILO** ☎ 0732/600703 or 0732/707-0145-0. **ÖBB–Österreichisches Bundesbahn** ☎ 05/1717 ⊕ www.oebb.at.

VISITOR INFORMATION
Most towns in these areas have their own *Fremdenverkehrsamt* (tourist office), which are listed below by town name.

ℹ Tourist Information **Bad Ischl** ✉ Bahnhofstrasse 6, A-4820 ☎ 06132/277570 🖨 06132/27757-77 ⊕ www.badischl.at. **Dürnstein** ✉ Rathaus, A-3601 ☎ 02711/200. **Gmunden** ✉ Am Graben 2, A-4810 ☎ 07612/64305 🖨 07612/71410 ⊕ www.oberoesterreich.at/gmunden. **Klosterneuburg** ✉ Rathausplatz 1, A-3400 ☎ 02243/34396 ⊕ www.klosterneuburg.net/tourismus. **Krems/Stein** ✉ Undstrasse 6, A-3500 ☎ 02732/82676 🖨 02732/70011 ⊕ www.krems.at. **Melk** ✉ Babenbergerstrasse 1, A-3390 ☎ 02752/52307-410 🖨 02752/52307-490. **Steyr** ✉ Stadtplatz 27, A-4400 ☎ 07252/53229-0 🖨 07252/53229-15. **St. Gilgen** ✉ Mozartplatz 1, A-5340 ☎ 06227/2348 🖨 06227/7267-9 ⊕ www.wolfgangsee.at. **St. Wolfgang** ✉ Au 140, A-5360 ☎ 06138/8003 🖨 06138/8003-81 ⊕ www.wolfgangsee.at. **Salzkammergut/Salzburger Land** ✉ Wirerstrasse 10, A-4820 Bad Ischl ☎ 06132/26909-0 🖨 06132/26909-14 ⊕ www.salzkammergut.at. **Wachau** ✉ Schlossgasse 3, A-3620 Spitz an der Donau ☎ 02713/300-6015 🖨 02713/300-6030 ⊕ www.wachau.at.

SALZBURG

7

By Horst Erwin
Reischenböck

"ALL SALZBURG IS A STAGE," Count Ferdinand Czernin once wrote. "Its beauty, its tradition, its history enshrined in the grey stone of which its buildings are made, its round of music, its crowd of fancy-dressed people, all combine to lift you out of everyday life, to make you forget that somewhere far off, life hides another, drearier, harder, and more unpleasant reality." Shortly after the count's book, *This Salzburg,* was published in 1937, the unpleasant reality arrived; but having survived the Nazis, Salzburg once again became one of Austria's top drawing cards. Art lovers call it the Golden City of High Baroque; historians refer to it as the Florence of the North or the German Rome; and, of course, music lovers know it as the birthplace of one of the world's most beloved composers, Wolfgang Amadeus Mozart (1756–91). If the young Mozart was the boy wonder of 18th-century Europe and Salzburg did him no particular honor in his lifetime, it is making up for it now. Since 1920 the world-famous Salzburger Festspiele (Salzburg Festival), the third oldest on the continent, has honored "Wolferl" with performances of his works by the world's greatest musicians. To see and hear them, celeb-heavy crowds pack the city from the last week in July until the end of August. Whether performed in the festival halls—the Grosses Festspielhaus, the "House for Mozart," and the Felsenreitschule, to name the big three—or outdoors with opulent Baroque volutes and pillasters of Salzburg's architecture as background, Mozart's music serves as the heartbeat of the city. No more so than during the 2006 Mozart Year, when the city will celebrate the 250th birthday of its most famous home boy with a nearly 24/7 yearlong party, which kicks off on the big B-day itself, January 27.

Ironically many who come to this golden city of High Baroque may first hear the instantly recognizable strains of music from the film that made Salzburg a household name: from the Mönchsberg to Nonnberg Convent, it's hard to go exploring without hearing someone humming "How Do You Solve a Problem Like Maria?" A popular tourist exercise is to make the town's acquaintance by visiting all the sights featured in that beloved Hollywood extravaganza, *The Sound of Music,* filmed here in 1964. Julie Andrews may wish it wasn't so, but one can hardly imagine taking in the Mirabell Gardens, the Pferdeschwemme fountain, Nonnberg Convent, the Residenzplatz, and all the other filmed locations without imagining Maria and the von Trapp children trilling their hearts out. Oddly enough, just like Mozart, the Trapp family—who escaped the Third Reich by fleeing their beloved country—were little appreciated at home; Austria was the only place on the planet where the film failed, closing after a single week's showing in Vienna and Salzburg. It is said that the Austrian populace at large didn't cotton to a prominent family up-and-running in the face of the Nazis; Whispers persist, however, that if the Austrians made a show of disdaining the anti-Nazi von Trapps, well, that proves. . . . Even now, locals are amazed by *The Sound of Music*'s popularity around the world, but slowly, more and more Austrians are warming up to the film. In fact, it was just in 2005 that Vienna's Volksoper premiered the first Austrian stage production of the Broadway musical, so it may just be a matter of time before the Panorama Sightseeing bus tours of Salzburg's *SoM* sites may be crammed with as many Austrians as Americans.

But whether it is the arias of Mozart or the ditties of Rodgers and Hammerstein, no one can deny music is the element that shapes the life of the city. It is heard everywhere: in churches, castles, palaces, town house courtyards, and, of course, concert halls. During the five weeks of the Salzburger Festspiele, there are as many as 10 concerts a day to select from (months in advance, of course—many events are presold out). If the Salzburg Music Festival remains one of the world's most stirring musical events, this is also due to its perfect setting. Salzburg lies on both banks of the Salzach River, at the point where it is pinched between two mountains, the Kapuzinerberg on one side, the Mönchsberg on the other. In broader view are many beautiful Alpine peaks. To these many gifts of Mother Nature, man's contribution is a trove of buildings worthy of such surroundings. Salzburg's rulers pursued construction on a grand scale ever since Wolf-Dietrich von Raitenau—the "Medici prince-archbishop who preached in stone"—began his regime in the latter part of the 16th century. Astonishingly, they all seem to have shared the same artistic bent, with the result that Salzburg's many fine buildings blend into a harmonious whole. Perhaps nowhere else in the world is there so cohesive a flowering of Baroque architecture. That is because Wolf-Dietrich employed nothing but Italian architects. At the age of only 28, he envisioned "his" Salzburg to be the Rome of the Alps, with a town cathedral grander than St. Peter's, a Residenz as splendid as a Roman palace, and his private Mirabell Gardens flaunting the most fashionable styles of Italianate horticulture. This amazing man did not deny himself passion simply because he was a bishop: he honored his mistress with 12 children and a palace of her very own. After he was deposed by the rulers of Bavaria—he was imprisoned (very elegantly, thank you) in the Hohensalzburg fortress—other cultured prince-archbishops took over. Markus Sittikus and Paris Lodron dismissed the Italian artists and commanded the masters of Viennese Baroque, Fischer von Erlach and Lukas von Hildebrandt, to complete Wolf-Dietrich's vision. Today, thanks to these patrons and architects, Salzburg remains a visual pageant of Baroque motifs.

But times change and the Salzburgians with them. Despite its seeming emphasis on past glory, the stop-press news is that this dowager of Old Europe is ready to straighten up and once again lead the vanguard. Museums of contemporary art are springing up as fast as edelweiss across Austria, so it is not surprising to learn that Salzburg is now home to one of its most striking: the Museum der Moderner Salzburg. As if to announce that this Baroque city is virtually leapfrogging from yesterday to tomorrow, the avant-garde showcase opened in 2004 on the very spot where Julie Andrews "do-re-mi"-d with the von Trapp brood: where once the fusty Café Winkler stood atop the Mönchsberg mount, and commanding one of the grandest views of the city, a moderne, cubical structure now glitters as a museum devoted to the latest in cutting-edge art. Celebrating both this new museum and Mozart's 250th birthday, Salzburg is reveling in its passementeried past while it takes a Giant Step Forward.

Numbers in the text correspond to numbers in the margin and on the Salzburg map.

If you have
1 day

It is the tourist who comes to Salzburg outside of festival season who will have the most time to explore its many fascinating attractions. But even for festival-busy visitors, making the acquaintance of the town is not too difficult, for most of its sights are within a comparatively small area. Of course, if you are doing this spectacular city in just one day, there is a flip-book approach to Salzburg 101: take one of those escorted bus tours through the city. However, much of Salzburg's historic city center is for pedestrians only, and the bus doesn't get you close to some of the best sights, so some will prefer to take a walking tour run by city guides every day at 12:15 PM, setting out from the tourist information office, **Information Mozartplatz,** at Mozart square (closed on some Sundays during the off-season).

So if you are joining the army of bipeds exploring the town on foot, start at the **Mozartplatz** ❶, not just to make a pit stop at the main tourist information office, but to sweeten your tour with a few *Salzburger Mozartkugeln* from the nearby chocolate manufacturers Fürst (Brodgasse 13, at Alter Markt, on the square), the creators of these omnipresent candy balls of pistachio-flavor marzipan rolled in nougat cream and dipped in dark chocolate, which bear a mini-portrait of Mozart on the wrapper. Flower-bedecked cafés beckon, but this is no time for a coffee—one of the glories of Europe is just a few steps away: the palatial **Residenz** ❹, home to the great Prince-Archbishops and the veritable center of Baroque Salzburg. Nearby is the **Dom** ❺, Salzburg's grand 17th-century cathedral. Across the Domplatz is the Francescan church, the **Franziskanerkirche** ❽). A bit to the south is the Romanesque-turned-Rococo **Stiftskirche St. Peter** ❼, where, under the cliffs, you'll find the famous **Petersfriedhof** ❻—St. Peter's Cemetery, whose wrought-iron grills and Baroque vaults shelter the final resting place of Mozart's sister and much of Old Salzburg. This famed locale was re-created for the escape scene in *The Sound of Music*. After exploring St. Peter's Abbey, you're now ready to take the Festungsbahn cable car (it's just behind the cathedral) up to the **Fortress Hohensalzburg** ❿—the majestic castle atop the Mönchsberg peak that overlooks the city. Enjoy a rest at the Stadt Alm restaurant, or opt for enjoying some picnic provisions in a quiet corner. Descend back to the city via the Mönchsberg express elevators, which will deposit you at Gstättengasse 13. Head over to the **Pferdeschwemme** ⓭—the Baroque horse trough that is a somewhat bewildering tribute to the equine race—then over to the **Getreidegasse,** the Old City's main shopping street. Here, posh shops set in pastel-covered town houses announce their wares through the overhanging wrought-iron scroll signs, which one writer has compared to chandeliers (there is even one for the neighborhood McDonalds). Wander around this venerable merchant's quarter—some of the houses have hidden and enchanting courtyards set with timber-lined balconies—then head to the most famous address in town: No. 9 Getreidegasse—**Mozarts Geburtshaus** ⓱, the birthplace of Mozart. After paying your respects, head over to the nearby and charming **Alter Markt** square to welcome twilight with a *Kaffee mit Schlag* (coffee with whipped cream) at its famous Café Tomaselli. Choose from the more than 40 pastries and congratulate yourself: you may not have seen everything in Salzburg, but you've missed few of its top sights.

If you have
3 days

With three days, you can explore the **Old City** and the **Fortress Hohensalzburg and the New Town** as described in the two walking tours below. Try to catch an evening concert—perhaps of Mozart's music—at one of the many music halls in the city (before you arrive in Salzburg, do some advance telephone calls to determine the music schedule of the city for the time you will be there and, if need be, book reservations; if you'll be attending the summer Salzburg Festival, this is a must). For your third day, try one of four options: book a *Sound of Music tour,* then, in the afternoon, relax and take a ride up the **Untersberg**; or opt for a boat trip along the Salzach River south to the 17th-century **Hellbrunn Palace** (famous for its mischievous water fountains); or try to arrange an excursion to the picture-book towns of the **Salzkammergut** (*see* Chapter 6). Yet another idea is to walk for about two hours over the Mönchsberg, starting in the south at the **Nonnberg Convent** ㉚ and continuing on to the **Richterhöhe** to enjoy the southwestern area of the city. Above the Siegmundstor, the tunnel through the mountain, there is a nice belvedere to take in a city view. But the most fascinating view is from the terrace in front of the new **Museum der Moderne** ⑯, which you reach after passing the old fortifications from the 15th century. Then, you can either head back to the center of town by using the rock-face elevator or just continue on to the Bräustübl, the large beer cellar at the northern end of the hill for some of the best brews and conviviality in town.

EXPLORING SALZBURG

The Altstadt (Old City)—a very compact area between the jutting outcrop of the Mönchsberg and the Salzach River—is where most of the major sights are concentrated. The cathedral and interconnecting squares surrounding it form what used to be the religious center, around which the major churches and the old archbishops' residence are arranged. The rest of the Old City belonged to the wealthy burghers: the Getreidegasse, the Alter Markt (old market), the town hall, and the tall, plain burghers' houses (like Mozart's Birthplace). The Mönchsberg cliffs emerge unexpectedly behind the Old City, crowned to the east by the Hohensalzburg Fortress. Across the river, in the small area between the cliffs of the Kapuzinerberg and the riverbank, is Steingasse, a narrow medieval street where working people lived. Northwest of the Kapuzinerberg lie Mirabell Palace and its gardens, now an integral part of the city but formerly a country estate on the outskirts of Salzburg.

It's best to begin by exploring the architectural and cultural riches of the Old City, then go on to the fortress and after that cross the river to inspect the other bank. Ideally, you need two days to do it all. An alternative, if you enjoy exploring churches and castles, is to stop after visiting the Rupertinum and go directly up to the fortress, either on foot or by returning through the cemetery to the funicular railway.

About the Restaurants & Hotels

Salzburg has some of the best—and most expensive—restaurants in Austria, so if you happen to walk into one of the Altstadt posheries without a reservation, you may get a sneer worthy of Captain von Trapp. Happily, the city is plentifully supplied with pleasant eateries, offering not only good, solid Austrian food (not for anyone on a diet), but also exceptional Italian dishes and newer-than-now *neue Küche* (nouvelle cuisine) delights. There are certain dining experiences that are quintessentially Salzburgian, including restaurants perched on the town's peaks that offer "food with a view"—in some cases, it's too bad the food isn't up to the view—or rustic inns that offer "Alpine evenings" with entertainment. Favorite dishes are fresh fish caught from the nearby lakes of the Salzkammergut, usually *gebratene* (fried), and that ubiquitous Salzburgian dessert *Salzburger Nockerln*—a snowy meringue of sweetened whisked egg whites with a little bit of flour and sugar.

The Old City has a wide assortment of hotels and pensions, some in surprising locations and with considerable ambience, but everything has its price and there are few bargains. In high season, and particularly during the festival (July and August), some prices soar over their already high levels and rooms are very difficult to find, so try to reserve at least two months in advance. In fact, during the high season, rate differences may push a hotel into the next-higher price category.

WHAT IT COSTS In euros				
$$$$	**$$$**	**$$**	**$**	**¢**
RESTAURANTS over €22	€18–€22	€13–€17	€7–€12	under €7
HOTELS over €270	€170–€270	€120–€170	€80–€120	under €80

Restaurant prices are per person for a main course at dinner. Hotel prices are for a standard double room in high season, including taxes and service. Assume that hotels operate on the European Plan (EP, with no meal provided) unless we note that they use the Breakfast Plan (BP), Modified American Plan (MAP, with breakfast and dinner daily, known as "halb pension"), or Full American Plan (FAP, or "voll pension," with three meals a day). Higher prices (inquire when booking) prevail for any meal plans.

THE ALTSTADT: IN MOZART'S FOOTSTEPS

Intent on becoming a patron of the arts, the Prince-Bishop Wolf-Dietrich lavished much of his wealth on rebuilding Salzburg into a beautiful and Baroque city in the late 16th and early 17th centuries. In turn, his grand townscape came to inspire the young Joannes Chrysostomus Wolfgangus Amadeus Theophilus Mozart. It is no surprise that there is no better setting for his music than the town in which he was born. For, in point of fact, growing up in the center of the city and composing minuets already at five years of age, Mozart set lovely Salzburg itself to music. He was perhaps the most purely Austrian of all composers, a singer of the smiling Salzburgian countryside, of the city's gay Baroque and Rococo architecture. So even if you are not lucky enough to snag a ticket to a performance of *The Marriage of Figaro* or *Don Giovanni* in the Grosses

Festspielhaus, you can still enjoy his melodies just by strolling through his streets and, as critic Erich Kästner once put it, "seeing a symphony."

With the Mozart Year celebrations coming to a head, Salzburg symbolizes Mozart more than ever. Ever since the 1984 Best Film Oscar-winner *Amadeus* (remember Tom Hulse as "Wolfie"?), the composer has been the 18th-century equivalent of a rock star. Born in Salzburg on January 27, 1756, he crammed a prodigious number of compositions into the 35 short years of his life, many of which he spent in Salzburg (he moved to Vienna in 1781). Indeed, the Altstadt (or Old Town) revels in a bevy of important sights, ranging from his birthplace on the Getreidegasse to the abbey of St. Peter's, where the composer's "Mass in C Minor" was first performed. Beyond the Altstadt—the heart of the Baroque Salzburg familiar to the young prodigy—other Mozart-related sights are included in our second Salzburg tour. As you tour the composer's former haunts, why not listen to Papageno woo Papagena on your Walkman?

In Salzburg, as anywhere else, if you start from the right departure point you will have a good journey and ultimately arrive at the proper place. For this city, there is no more appropriate center-of-it-all than **Mozart-platz** ① ▶, the square named to honor Salzburg's native genius. Get in the mood by noticing, near the statue of Mozart, the strolling street violinists, who usually play a Mozart sonata or two. Walk past the Glockenspiel café into the next square, the Residenzplatz, centered by the 40-foot-high Court Fountain, which is often illuminated at night. Take in the famous **Glockenspiel** ② (chances are the tunes it plays will be by you-know-who), set atop the Neubau Palace, now the city's newly renovated **Salzburg Museum** ③—doors open in January 2006 just in time to kick off the Mozart Year with a major exhibition on the composer. Then cross the plaza to enter the **Residenz** ④, the opulent Baroque palace of Salzburg's prince-archbishops and Mozart's patrons. From the Residenzplatz, walk through the arches into Domplatz, the city's majestic cathedral square—in August, set out with seats for the annual presentation of Hofmannsthal's play *Jedermann*. The **Dom St. Rupert** ⑤ (Salzburg Cathedral) is among the finest Italian-style Baroque structures in Austria. Walk into the Kapitelplatz through the arches across the square and go through two wrought-iron gateways into **St. Peter's Cemetery** ⑥—one of the most historic and beautiful places in Salzburg. Enter the church of **St. Peter's Abbey** ⑦. Above the main entrance the Latin inscription reads: "I am the door—by me if any man enters here, he shall be saved." If it's nearing lunchtime, be sure to stop at the Stiftskeller St. Peter—so legendary a restaurant that the story has it Mephistopheles met Faust here.

As you leave St. Peter's, look up to the right to see the thin Gothic spire of the **Franziskanerkirche** (Franciscan Church) ⑧. Leave the courtyard in this direction, cross the road, and enter around the corner by the main entrance (the side one is closed). It will bring you into the Gothic apse crowned by the ornate red-marble altar designed by Fischer von Erlach. Return back up the Romanesque aisle an exit on Sigmund-Haffner-Gasse). Opposite is the rear entrance to one of Salzburg's galleries of contemporary art, the **Rupertinum** ⑨. Turn left around the corner into **Toscanini-hof** ⑩, the square cut into the dramatic Mönchsberg cliff. The wall

7

A Lot of Night Music

Music in Salzburg is not just *Eine Kleine Nacht-musik*, to mention one of Mozart's most famous compositions (which, incidentally, he composed in Vienna . . .). The city's nightlife is livelier than it is reputed to be. The "in" areas include the "Bermuda Triangle" (Steingasse, Imbergstrasse) and Rudolfskai; young people tend to populate the bars and discos around Gstättengasse. Of course, Salzburg is most renowned for its **Salzburger Festspiele** of music and theater (end of July–August), and most festival goers come during this season. Much of Salzburg's very special charm can, however, be best discovered and enjoyed off-season. For instance, real Mozart connoisseurs come to Salzburg for the **Mozart Week** (a 10-day festival held around Mozart's birthday, January 27). And in general, music lovers face an embarrassment of riches in this most musical of cities, ranging from chamber concerts, held in the Marmorsaal (Marble Hall) of the Mirabell Palace, the Goldene Stube (Golden Hall) of the Fortress, or the Gotischer Saal (Gothic Hall) at St. Blasius, to the numerous concerts organized by the International Mozarteum Foundation from October to June in the Grosser Saal (Great Hall) of the Mozarteum and those by the Salzburger Kulturvereinigung in the Grosses Festspielhaus (Large Festival House). Salzburg concerts by the Mozarteum Orchestra and the Camerata Academica are now just as much in demand as the subscription series by the Vienna Philharmonic in the Musikverein in Vienna. The **Landestheater** season runs from September to June and presents operas, operettas, plays, and ballet. No music lover should miss the chance to be enchanted and amazed by the skill and artistry of the world-famous **Salzburg Marionette Theater,** not only performing operas by Mozart, but also goodies by Rossini, Strauss the younger, Offenbach, Humperdinck, and Mendelssohn (who wrote the accompanying music for the troupe's delightful show devoted to William Shakespeare's "A Midsummer Night's Dream."

Bicycling

As most Salzburgers know, one of the best and most pleasurable ways of getting around the city and the surrounding countryside is by bicycle. Bikes can be rented (for rental places, *see* Salzburg A to Z, *below*), and local bookstores have maps of the extensive network of cycle paths. The most delightful ride in Salzburg? The **Hellbrunner Allee** from Freisaal to Hellbrunn Palace is a pleasurable run, taking you past Frohnburg Palace and a number of elegant mansions on either side of the tree-lined avenue. The more adventurous can go farther afield, taking the **Salzach cycle path** north to the village of Oberndorf, or south to Golling and Hallein.

Everybody Drink!

Salzburg loves beer and has some of the most picturesque Bierkellers in Austria. A top beer paradise is the **Stieglkeller** (✉ Festungsgasse ☎ 0662/842681 ⊕ www.imlauer.com ☉ May 1–Sept. 30), set by the funicular station of the Hohensalzburg tram. The noted local architect Ceconi devised this sprawing place around 1901. The Keller is set partly inside the Mönchsberg hill so its cellars guarantee the quality and right temperature of the drinks. The gardens here have chestnut trees and offer a marvelous view above the roofs of the old city—a lovely place to enjoy your *Bauernschmaus* (farmer's dish). The **Sternbräu** (✉ Griesegasse 23 ☎ 0662/842140) is a mammoth Bierkeller, set with eight rambling halls festooned with tile stoves, paintings, and wood beams. The chestnut-tree beer garden or the courtyard are divine on hot summer nights. Many travelers head here for the Sound of Music Dinner Shows, presented May through September daily, 7:30 to 10 PM. A three-course meal and show costs €40, or you can arrive at 8:15 PM to see the show and just have apfelstrudel and coffee for €25. On the first Sunday of the month, a *Fruhschoppen*—a traditional Salzburger music fest—is presented at 10:30 PM, or you can enjoy another musical evening, a *Happing*, staged from May to September every Thursday evening at 6.

---

bearing the harp-shape organ pipes is part of the famed **Festspielhaus ⑪**. The carved steps going up the Mönchsberg are named for Clemens Holzmeister, architect of the festival halls. If you climb them, you get an intimate view of the Salzburg churches at the level of their spires, and if you climb a little farther to the right, you can look down into the open-air festival hall, the Felsenreitschule, cut into the cliffs. From Hofstallgasse—the main promenade (sometimes floodlit and adorned with flags during the festival) connecting the main festival theaters—you can either walk directly up to Herbert-von-Karajan-Platz or, preferably, walk around by Universitätsplatz to take a look at one of Johann Bernhard Fischer von Erlach's Baroque masterpieces, the **Kollegienkirche ⑫**, or Collegiate Church. In Herbert-von-Karajan-Platz is another point at which building and cliff meet: the **Pferdeschwemme ⑬**, a horse trough decorated with splendid Baroque-era paintings. To the left is the Siegmundstor, the impressive road tunnel blasted through the Mönchsberg in 1764. The arcaded Renaissance court on your left houses the **Spielzeugmuseum ⑭**, a delightful toy museum.

Pass by the tiny church of St. Blasius, built in 1350, and follow the road on through the Gstättentor to the **Mönchsberg elevator ⑮** for a trip up the hill to a rocky terrace formerly known as the Winkler Terrace, Salzburg's most famous outlook, now the site of a large "white marble brick" (as critics carp), the **Museum der Moderne ⑯**, or Museum of Modern Art, which includes a restaurant, which opened in October 2004. After descending from the heights, turn left into the short street leading to Museumsplatz where you could explore the Haus der Natur, one of the Europe's finest museums of natural history. Walk back toward the Blasius church, which stands at the beginning of the Old City's major shopping street, **Getreidegasse,** hung with numerous signs depicting little wrought-iron cobblers and bakers (few people could actually read centuries ago). Amid the boutiques and Salzburg's own McDonald's (featuring its own elegant sign) is **Mozarts Geburtshaus ⑰**, the celebrated composer's birthplace. Continue down the street past the Rathaus (town hall), and enter the **Alter Markt ⑱**, the old marketplace, adorned with historic buildings, including the Café Tomaselli (1703) and the Baroque Hofapotheke (prince-archbishop's court apothecary, 1591), still kept as it was back then. Finish up with some "I Was Here" photographs at the marble St. Florian's Fountain, then enjoy a finale back on Mozartplatz.

TIMING The Old City—the left bank of the Salzach River—contains many of the city's top attractions. Other than exploring by horse-drawn cabs (*Fiakers*), available for rental at Residenzplatz, most of your exploring will be done on foot, since this historic section of town bans cars. The center city is compact and cozy, so you can easily cover it in one day. Note that many churches close at 6 PM, so unless you're catching a concert at one of them, be sure to visit them during the daylight hours.

What to See

⑱ Alter Markt (Old Market). Right in the heart of the Old City is the Alter Markt, the old marketplace and center of secular life in centuries past. The square is lined with 17th-century middle-class houses, colorfully hued in shades of pink, pale blue, and yellow ocher. Look in at the old royal pharmacy, the **Hofapotheke,** whose incredibly ornate black-and-gold Rococo interior was built in 1760. Inside, you'll sense a curious apothecarial smell, traced to the shelves lined with old pots and jars (labeled in Latin). These are not just for show: this pharmacy is still operating today. You can even have your blood pressure taken—but preferably not after drinking a *Doppelter Einspänner* (black coffee with whipped cream, served in a glass) in the famous Café Tomaselli just opposite. In warm weather, the café's terrace provides a wonderful spot for watching the world go by as you sip a *Mélange* (another coffee specialty, served with frothy milk), or, during the summer months, rest your feet under the shade of the chestnut trees in the Tomaselli garden at the top end of the square. Next to the coffeehouse, you'll find the **smallest house in Salzburg,** now a shop for the "*Salzburger Engerl,*" a little silver putto modelled after a pattern by the Baroque sculptor Meinrad Guggenbichler that has become a traditional souvenir of Salzburg; note the slanting roof decorated with a dragon gargoyle. In the center of the square, surrounded by flower stalls, is the marble **St. Florian's Fountain,** dedicated in 1734 to the patron saint of firefighters.

★ ⑤ Dom St. Rupert (St. Rupert's Cathedral). When you walk through the arches leading from Residenzplatz into **Domplatz,** it is easy to see why Max Reinhardt chose it in August of 1920 as the setting for what has become the annual summer production of Hugo von Hofmannsthal's *Jedermann* (*Everyman*). The plaza is a complete, aesthetic concept and one of Salzburg's most beautiful urban set pieces. In the center rises the Virgin's Column, and at one side is the cathedral, considered to be the first early Italian Baroque building north of the Alps, and one of the finest. Its facade is of marble, its towers reach 250 feet into the air, and it holds 10,000 people (standing . . .).

There has been a cathedral on this spot since the 8th century, but the present structure dates from the 17th century. The cathedral honors the patron saint of Salzburg, St. Rupert, whose relics lie buried beneath the altar; Rupert founded the town's St. Peter's Church and its Nonnberg Abbey around 700. Archbishop Wolf-Dietrich took advantage of (some say caused) the old Romanesque-Gothic cathedral's destruction by fire in 1598 to demolish the remains and make plans for a huge new structure facing onto the Residenzplatz to reaffirm Salzburg's commitment to the Catholic cause. His successor, Markus Sittikus, and the new court architect, Santino

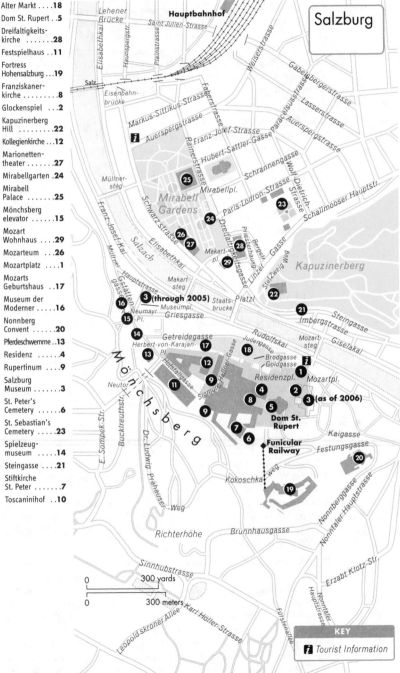

Solari, also ordered to build the city walls protecting Salzburg during the Thirty Years' War in the first half of the 17th century, started the present cathedral in 1614, which was consecrated with great ceremony in 1628. The church's simple sepia-and-white interior, a peaceful counterpoint to the usual Baroque splendor, dates from a later renovation.

Mozart's parents, Leopold and Anna-Maria, were married here on November 21, 1747. Mozart was christened, the day after he was born, at the 13th-century font inside this cathedral, where he later served as organist from 1779 to 1781. Some of his compositions, such as the *Coronation Mass,* were written for the cathedral, and many were performed here for the first time. On Sunday and all Catholic holidays, mass is sung here at 10 AM—the most glorious time to experience the cathedral's full splendor. This remains the only house of worship worldwide with no less than five independent fixed organs, which are sometimes played together during special church music concerts. Many of the church's treasures are in a special museum on the premises. ⊠ *Domplatz* ☎ *0662/844189* 🖷 *0662/840442* ⊕ *www.kirchen.net/dommuseum* 🖾 *Museum: €4.50* ☉ *Early-May–late Oct., Mon.–Sat. 10–5, Sun. and holidays 1–6.*

❶ Festspielhaus (Festival Hall Complex). With the world-famous Salzburg Festival as their objective, music lovers head for the Hofstallgasse, the street where the three main festival theaters are located. Arrow-straight and framing a grand view of the Fortress Hohensalzburg, the street takes its name from the court stables once located here. Now, in place of the prancing horses, festival goers promenade along Hofstallgasse during the intervals of summer performances, showing off their suntans and elegant attire.

The festival complex consists of three theaters. The first is the new **Haus für Mozart** (House for Mozart). This was the former Kleines Festspielhaus, or Small Festival Hall. It will now seat about 1,600 and will be specially used for productions of Mozart's operas. The center ring is occupied by the famous **Grosses Festspielhaus** (Great Festival Hall, 1956–60), leaning against the solid rock of the Mönchsberg and opened in 1960, with a maximum stage width of 104 feet and a seating capacity of more than 2,150. In recent times the Grosses Festspielhaus, nicknamed the Wagner Stage because of its width (not to mention its headline-making productions of the "Ring of the Nibelungs") has been the venue for spectacular productions of Modest Mussorgsky's *Boris Godunov* and Richard Strauss's *Der Rosenkavalier,* along with concerts by the world's most famous symphony orchestras. Stage directors are faced with the greatest challenge in the third theater, the **Felsenreitschule** (the Rocky Riding School), the former Summer Riding School, which—hewn out of the rock of the Mönchsberg during the 17th century by architect Fischer von Erlach—offers a setting that is itself more dramatic than anything presented on stage.

Here, in the days of the prince-archbishops, the famous Lipizzaner stallions were put through their paces (in winter, they were moved to Vienna). Max Reinhardt made the first attempt at using the Summer Riding School for Salzburg Festival performances in 1926. With its retractable roof it gives the impression of an open-air theater; the three tiers of arcades cut into the rock of the Mönchsberg linger in the mind of fans of *The Sound of Music* film, for the von Trapps were portrayed as singing "Edelweiss" here in their last Austrian concert (according to Hollywood—in fact, this 1950 Festival farewell by the Trapp Family Singers, conducted by Franz Wasner, actually was given in the Mozarteum and at the cathedral square). The theaters are linked by tunnels (partially in marble and with carpeted floors) to a spacious underground garage in the Mönchsberg. If you want to see the inside of the halls, it's best to go to a performance, but guided tours are given and group tours can be booked on request. ⊠ *Hofstallgasse 1* ☎ *0662/849097* 🖨 *0662/847835* ⊕ *www.salzburgfestival.at* ✉ *Guided tours: €5* ☉ *Group tour Jan.–May, Oct.–Dec. 20, daily at 2; June, Sept., daily at 2 and 3:30; July and Aug., daily at 9.30, 2, and 3:30.*

❽ Franziskanerkirche (Franciscan Church). The graceful, tall spire of the Franciscan Church stands out from all other towers in Salzburg; the church itself encompasses the greatest diversity of architectural styles. There was a church on this spot as early as the 8th century, but it was destroyed by fire. The Romanesque nave of its replacement is still visible, as are other Romanesque features, such as a stone lion set into the steps leading to the pulpit. In the 15th century the choir was rebuilt in Gothic style, then crowned in the 18th century by an ornate red-marble and gilt altar designed by Austria's most famous Baroque architect, Johann Bernhard Fischer von Erlach. Mass—frequently featuring one of Mozart's compositions—is celebrated here on Sunday at 9 AM. In summer, organ concerts are given. ⊠ *Franziskanergasse 5* ☎ *0662/843629–0* ✉ *Free* ☉ *Daily 6:30 AM–7 PM.*

★ Getreidegasse. As for centuries, this today is the main shopping street in the Old City center. According to historians, the historic name means "trade street"—not "grain street," as many people believe. Today it is the address of elegant fashion houses, international shoe chains, and a McDonald's (note its wrought-iron sign—one of many on the street—with classy bronze lettering: like all the other shops, it has conformed with Salzburg's strict Old City conservation laws). Other than coming to shop, crowds flock to this street because at No. 9 they'll find Mozart's birthplace, the **Mozarts Geburtshaus.** Needless to say, in summer the street is as densely packed with people as a corncob with kernels. You can always escape for a while through one of the many arcades—mostly flower-bedecked and opening into delightful little courtyards—that link the Getreidegasse to the river and the Universitätsplatz. At No. 37 you'll find one of the most glamorous hotels in the world, the Goldener Hirsch—just look for its filigree-iron sign showing a leaping stag with gilded antlers. Its interiors are marvels of Salzburgian gemütlichkeit so, if appropriately attired, you may wish to view the lobby and enjoy an aperitif in its gorgeous bar, *the* watering hole of chic Salzburg. The western end of Getriedegasse becomes Judengasse, part of the former Jewish ghetto area, which is also festooned with more of Salzburg's famous wrought-iron signs.

❷ Glockenspiel (Carillon). The famous carillon tower is perched on top of the **Residenz Neubau** (New Residence), Prince-Archbishop Wolf-Diet-

rich's government palace. The carillon is a later addition, brought from
the Netherlands in 1696 and finally put in working order in 1702. The
35 bells play classical tunes (usually by Mozart, Carl Maria von Weber,
and his teacher in Salzburg, Michael Haydn) at 7 AM, 11 AM, and 6 PM—
with charm and ingenuity often making up for the occasional musical
inaccuracy. From Easter to October, the bells are immediately followed
by a resounding retort from perhaps the oldest mechanical musical instrument in the world, the 200-pipe "Bull" organ housed in the Hohensalzburg Fortress across town. Details about the music selections are
listed on a notice board across the square on the corner of the Residenz
building. ⊠ *Mozartplatz 1.*

⓬ **Kollegienkirche** (Kollegienkirche, or Collegiate Church). Completed by Fischer von Erlach in 1707, and under restoration for its 300 anniversary,
this church, sometimes called the Universitätskirche, is one of the purest
examples of Baroque architecture in Austria. Unencumbered by Rococo
decorations, the modified Greek cross plan has a majestic dignity worthy of Palladio. ⊠ *Universitätsplatz* ☎ *0662/841–327–72* ⊙ *Mon.–Sat.,
9–7, Sun. 10–7, winter closing hrs approximately 3 hrs earlier.*

⓯ **Mönchsberg Elevator.** Just around the corner from the Pferdeschwemme
horse-fountain, at Neumayr Platz, you'll find the Mönchsberg elevator,
which carries you up through solid rock not only to the new **Museum
der Moderne** but to wooded paths that are great for walking and gasp-
ing—there are spectacular vistas of Salzburg. In summer this can be a
marvelous, and quick, way to escape the tiny crowded streets of the Old
City. At the top of the Mönchsberg, follow the signs and path south to
Stadt Alm, a popular café-restaurant open May–mid-October with a magnificent view of the churches and the fortress from its outdoor garden.
⊠ *Gstättengasse 13* ☎ *Round-trip €2.60, one-way €1.60* ⊙ *Open
Oct.–May, daily 9 AM–9 PM; June–Sept., daily 9 AM–11 PM.*

❶ **Mozartplatz** (Mozart Square). In the center of the square stands the statue
of Wolfgang Amadeus Mozart, a work by sculptor Ludwig Schwanthaler
unveiled in 1842 in the presence of the composer's two surviving sons.
It was the first sign of public recognition the great composer had received
from his hometown since his death in Vienna in 1791. The statue shows
a 19th-century stylized view of Mozart, draped in a mantle, holding a
page of music and a copybook. A more appropriate bust of the composer,
modeled by Viennese sculptor Edmund Heller, is found on the Kapuzinerberg. It contains the inscription *Jung gross, spät erkannt, nie er-
reicht*—"Great while young, belatedly appreciated, never equaled."

★ ⓱ **Mozarts Geburtshaus** (Mozart's Birthplace). As an adult the great composer
preferred Vienna to Salzburg, complaining that audiences in his native city
were no more responsive than tables and chairs. Still, home is home, and
this was Mozart's—when not on one of his frequent trips abroad—until
the age of 17. Mozart was born on the third (in American parlance, the
fourth) floor of this tall house, then owned by a family friend, one Johann Lorenz Hagenauer, on January 27, 1756, and the family lived on
this floor, when they were not on tour, from 1747 to 1773. As the child
prodigy composed many of his first compositions in these rooms, it is fitting and touching that Mozart's tiny first violin, his clavicord, and a copy

of his fortepiano (the original is on view in the Wohnhaus across the river) are on display. For the Mozart Year, special loan exhibitions will also be shown, including original portraits of the family, autograph letters, and manuscripts, all exhibited in cases illuminated by laser to make them easier to read. On the second floor, the day-to-day living and traveling circumstances of his day are the focus of the exhibits, while on the third floor a special annual exhibition is mounted, which normally opens the last week in January and runs until early October.

Most of rooms here are fitted out with modern museum vitrines and there is nothing extant from Mozart's time other than a cupboard on the landing of the fourth floor. Happily, a rear apartment facing Universitätsplatz has been refurbished to look like a "typical Salzburg commoner's apartment of Mozart's day." Like performing monkeys, the five- to seven-year-old Mozart, along with his slightly older sister, were trotted around by their father to entertain the crowned heads of Europe for months at a stretch. Returning from the gilded splendor of royal palaces—not to say the archbishop's residence just across town—to this very modest domicile must have only whetted the young Mozart's taste for grandeur and fine living, which he managed to indulge to the utmost whenever he could afford to do so (not very often—he was a spendthrift). Before leaving this hallowed place, be sure to pay your respects to Joseph Lange's famous unfinished portrait of Mozart, considered the most realistic depiction extant today. ⊠ *Getreidegasse 9* ☎ *0662/ 844313* ⊕ *www.mozarteum.at* ✉ *€6; combined ticket for Mozart residence and birthplace €9* ⊙ *Sept.–June, 9–5:30; July and Aug., 9–6:30.*

⑯ Museum der Moderne. Enjoying one of Salzburg's most famous scenic spots—the Café Winkler terrace (a setting immortalized in *The Sound of Music*—this is where Julie and the kids start warbling "Doe, a deer, a female deer . . . ")—Salzburg's dramatic new museum of modern and contemporary art, the Museum der Moderne, now reposes atop the sheer cliff face of the Mönchsberg. Clad in minimalist white marble, the museum (opened in October 2004) was designed by Friedrich Hoff Zwink of Munich. It has two exhibition levels, which bracket a restaurant with a large terrace—now, as always, *the* place to enjoy the most spectacular view over the city while sipping a coffee. The museum is mounting an impressive calendar of temporary exhibitions of cutting-edge contemporary art. However, its permanent collection features a fine array of paintings and sculptures from the 20th century, ranging from works by Gustav Klimt, Oskar Kokoschka, and Alfred Kubin to important movements like Informel, Fluxus, and Actionism. The contemporary collection is a veritable pantheon of important new Austrian and German artists, including Arnulf Rainer, Maria Lassnig, Hubert Schmalix, Siegfried Anzinger, Erwin Bohatsch, Valie Export, Elke Krystufek, Hermann Nitsch, Rudolf Schwarzkogler, Otto Muehl, and Günter Brus. ⊠ *Mönchsberg 32* ☎ *0662/842220* ⊕ *www.museumdermoderne.at* ✉ *€8* ⊙ *Tues.–Sun. 10–6, Wed. 10–9.*

⑬ Pferdeschwemme (Horse Pond). If Rome had fountains, so, too, would Wolf-Dietrich's Salzburg. The city is studded with them and none is so odd as this monument to the equine race. You'll find it if you head to the western end of the Hofstallgasse to find Herbert-von-Karajan-Platz (named after Salzburg's second-greatest musical son, maestro Herbert von Karajan, the legendary conductor and music director of the Salzburg Festival for many decades and also founder of its Easter Festival in 1967). On the Mönchsberg side of the square is the Pferdeschwemme—a royal trough where prize horses used to be cleaned and watered, constructed in 1695; as they underwent this ordeal they could delight in the frescoes of their pin-up fillies on the rear wall. The Baroque monument in the middle represents the antique legend of the taming of a horse, Bellerophon and his mount, Pegasus. ⊠ *Herbert-von-Karajan-Platz.*

❹ **Residenz.** At the very heart of Baroque Salzburg, the Residenz overlooks
FodorśChoice the spacious Residenzplatz and its famous fountain. The palace in the present
★ condition was built between 1600 and 1619 as the home of Wolf-Dietrich, the most powerful of Salzburg's prince-archbishops. The *Kaisersaal* (Imperial Hall) and the *Rittersaal* (Knight's Hall), one of the city's most regal concert halls, can be seen along with the rest of the magnificent **State Rooms** on a self-guided tour with headphones. Of particular note are the frescos by Johann Michael Rottmayr and Martino Altomonte depicting the history of Alexander the Great. Upstairs on the third floor is the **Residenzgalerie,** a princely art collection specializing in 17th-century Dutch and Flemish art and 19th-century paintings of Salzburg. On the state room floor, Mozart's opera, *La Finta Semplice,* was premiered in 1769 in the Guard Room. Mozart often did duty here, as, at age 14, he became the first violinist of the court orchestra (in those days, the leader, as there was no conductor). Today the reception rooms of the Residenz are often used for official functions, banquets, and concerts. The palace courtyard has been the lovely setting for Salzburg Festival opera productions since 1956—mostly the lesser-known treasures of Mozart. ⊠ *Residenzplatz 1* ☎ *0662/8042–2690, 0662/840451 art collection* ⊕ *www.residenzgalerie. at/* ⊠ *€7.30 for both museums; art collection only, €5* ۞ *Daily 10–5, closed 2 wks before Easter. Tours by arrangement. Art collection: daily 10–5, closed early Feb.–mid-Mar. and Wed., Oct.–Mar.*

❾ **Rupertinum.** If you are interested in 20th-century art, don't miss the chance to see the outstanding permanent collection of paintings and graphic art on display in this gallery, now part and parcel of Salzburg's new **Museum der Moderne Kunst** (which you can spot, shining in white marble atop the Mönchsberg hill, from the Rupertinum's main entrance. ⊠ *Wiener-Philharmoniker-Gasse 9* ☎ *0662/8042–2336* ⊕ *www. rupertinum.at* ⊠ *€9* ۞ *Sept.–mid-July, Tues., Thurs.–Sun. 10–5, Wed. 10–9; mid-July–Aug., Thurs.–Tues. 10–6, Wed. 10–9.*

❸ **Salzburg Museum** (Neugebäude). The biggest "gift" to Mozart will be opened
FodorśChoice one day shy of his 250th birthday, when, on January 26, 2006, Salzburg's
★ mammoth 17th-century **Residenz Neubau** (New Residence) will welcome visitors after a year-long renovation with the **"Viva! Mozart"** exhibition. The setting will be splendid, as this building was Prince-Archbishop Wolf-Dietrich's "overflow" palace (he couldn't fit his entire archiepiscopal court into the main Residenz across the plaza). As such, it features 10 state reception rooms that were among the first attempts at a classizing Renaissance style in the North. Under their sumptuous stucco-ceilings, the

Mozart homage will unfold in an interactive fashion: in the former dancing hall, visitors will be able to learn historic gavottes, in another, recipes of Mozart's time will be offered. Most of the display will be devoted to Mozart's music, with exhibitions on loan from around the world. All will be overseen by the guests of honor—Mozart's "virtual" family and friends (using state-of-the-art multimedia presentations). This "birthday party" will run through July 1, 2007. In other wings of the building, you can romp through Salzburg history thanks to the collections of the former **Carolino-Augusteum Museum.** Displays include Hallstatt Age relics, remains of the town's ancient Roman ruins, the famous Celtic bronze flagon found earlier this century on the Dürrnberg near Hallein (15 km, or 10 mi, south of Salzburg), and an outstanding collection of old musical instruments. Art lovers will see the Old Masters paintings, which range from Gothic altarpieces to wonderful "view" paintings of 18th- and 19th-century Salzburg. Pride of place will be given to the new installation of the spectacular **Sattler Panorama,** one of the few remaining 360-degree paintings in the world, which shows the city of Salzburg in the early 19th century. Also here is the original composition of "Silent Night," composed by Franz Gruber and Josef Mohr in nearby Oberndorf in 1818. A new exhibition space below the interior courtyard and restaurant will hold temporary shows. ⊠ *Museumsplatz 1, until end of 2005; Mozartplatz 1, 2006 on* ☎ *0662/620808–200* 🖷 *0662/620808–220* ⊕ *www.smca.at* 🖅 €7 ⊙ *Mon.–Wed., Fri.–Sun. 9–5, Thurs. 9–8.*

❼ Stiftkirche St. Peter (Collegiate Church of St. Peter). The most sumptuous church in Salzburg, St. Peter's is where Mozart's famed *Mass in C Minor* premiered in 1783, with his wife, Constanze, singing the lead soprano role. Wolfgang often directed orchestra and choir here, and also played its organ. During every season of the city's summer music festival in August the *Mass in C Minor* is performed here during a special church music concert. For a long time his *Requiem* was also played every year on the anniversary of his death (December& 5): now the annual performance has been moved into the Grosser Saal at the Mozarteum across the river. Originally a Romanesque basilica, St. Peter's front portal dates from 1245. Inside, the low-ceiling aisles are charmingly painted in Rococo candy-box style. The porch has beautiful Romanesque vaulted arches from the original structure built in the 12th century; the interior was decorated in the characteristically voluptuous late-Baroque style when additions were made in the 1770s. Note the side chapel by the entrance, with the unusual crèche portraying the Flight into Egypt and the Massacre of the Innocents. Behind the Rupert altar is the "Felsengrab," a rockface tomb where St. Rupert himself may be buried. To go from the sacred to the profane, head for the abbey's legendary Weinkeller restaurant, adjacent to the church. ⊠ *St. Peter Bezirk* ☎ *0662/844578–0* 🖅 *Free* ⊙ *Apr.–Sept., daily 6:30 AM–7 PM; Oct.–Mar., daily 6:30 AM–6 PM.*

❻ St. Peter's Cemetery. The eerie but intimate Petersfriedhof, or St. Peter's Cemetery, is the oldest Christian graveyard in Salzburg, in the present condition dating back to 1627. Enclosed on three sides by elegant wrought-iron grilles, Baroque arcades contain chapels belonging to Salzburg's old patrician families. The graveyard is far from mournful:

Fodor'sChoice
★

HAPPY 250TH BIRTHDAY, WOLFERL!

THE MOZART YEAR 2006 BIRTHDAY CELEBRATIONS in the composer's home town get a build-up to the big B-day, January 27, 2006, when the annual Salzburg Mozart Week (Mozartwoche) opens on January 20th—there are so many star-studded concerts scheduled it runs a full two weeks at the Grosses Festspielhaus and the Mozarteum theaters (🌐 www.mozarteum.at). On Wolfgang Amadeus Mozart's 250th birthday itself, the city becomes an immense concert stage, with the composer's music to flood out from regal squares and courtyards; on the same day, the city's Mozart instititions to unveil their birthday exhibitions, including the biggest, "Viva Mozart!", at the Salzburg Museum in the Neue Residenz on Mozartplatz (where a special Mozart Corner booth will be found all year long). Holy of holies, Mozart's Birthplace (🌐 www.mozarteum. at), will introduce special guided tours that even include a mini-piano recital. By summer, most of the civilized world will be heading to the famous Salzburger Festspiele (🌐 www.salzburgfestival.at), end-July to end-August, during which all of the composer's 22 operas will be presented in the three Festspielhäuser theaters. The Grosses Festspielhaus and the Mozarteum theaters will also be hosting special "Best of Mozart" concerts (🌐 www.salzburgticket.com) on thirty weekends from February 18 to November 18. All of Mozart's masses, including the Missa brevis and the Coronation mass, will be presented on Sunday mornings from January through December.

For pure birthday sparkle, book the Mozart Gala Banquets, held in the gilded Baroque staterooms of Salzburg's Residenz (where Mozart often conducted "dinner music"). Concert-banquets, these are mounted by the Konzerthüro Salzburg Special (offered February 10; May 6, 13, 20, 27; June 3, 10, 17, 24; July 1, 8, 15; August 5, 12; and September 2, 9, 16). Or repair to the Residenz for its series of mid-day recitals, the Mozart Matineès, running from late July to late August. Other historic surrounds where you can raise a glass of champagne in Wolfie's honor? At the Fortress Hohensalzburg, the Salzburger Festungkonzerte (🌐 www. mozartfestival.at) will host concerts, often offered in tandem with candlelit dinners, in its Prince's Chamber. Weekly Mozart dinner-concerts—replete with bewigged musicians—will be presented in the beautiful Baroque Hall of the Stiftskeller St. Peter (🌐 www.mozart-serenaden.com), while the Salzburger Schlosskonzerte will be presenting many Mozart concerts in the spectacular Marble Hall of the Mirabell palace (🌐 www.salzburger. schlosskonzerte.at).

If you want your Mozart to be kid-friendly, head over to the Salzburger Marionettentheater (🌐 www.marionetten. at) for its enchanting Mozart opera shows (nicely shortened) or its special Mozart Year one-hour "Best of" show (every Friday from May through September at 2 PM). During the autumn, catch the three-week-long festival of Mozartian sacred music, from October 22 to November 12, at the city's leading churches. To bring the gala year to a close, on December 3 and 4, a wide range of memorial concerts will be mounted, with the anniversary of his death on December 5 marked by a performance of his Requiem at the Mozarteum's Grosser Saal theater (🌐 www.mozarteum.at). For a complete rundown on all the hundreds of Salzburg events and concerts for the Mozart Year, log on to http://www.mozart2006.net/downloads/en/MSM_e_150904.pdf

dles, fir branches, and flowers—especially pansies (because their name means "thoughts"). In Crypt XXXI is the grave of Santino Solari, architect of the cathedral; in XXXIX that of Sigmund Haffner, a patron for whom Mozart composed a symphony and named a serenade. The final communal crypt LIV (by the so-called "catacombs") contains the body of Mozart's sister, Nannerl, and the torso of Joseph Haydn's younger brother, Michael (his head is in an urn stored in St. Peter's). The cemetery is in the shadow of the Mönchsberg mount; note the early Christian tombs carved in the rockface. ✉ *St. Peter Bezirk* ☎ *0662/ 844578–0* ☉ *Open daily dawn–dusk.*

☺ **⑭ Spielzeugmuseum** (Toy Museum). On a rainy day this is a delightful diversion for both young and old, with a collection of dolls, teddy bears, model railways, and wooden sailing ships. At 3 o'clock on Tuesday, Wednesday, and the first Friday of the month, special Punch and Judy–style puppet shows are presented. Performance days change in the summer, so call ahead. ✉ *Bürgerspitalplatz 2* ☎ *0662/620808–300* ⊕ *www.smca.at* 🎫 *€2.70* ☉ *Daily 9–5.*

⑩ Toscaninihof (Arturo Toscanini Courtyard). The famous Italian maestro Arturo Toscanini conducted some of the Salzburg Festival's most legendary performances during the 1930s. Throughout the summer months the courtyard of his former festival residence is a hive of activity, with sets for the stage of the "House for Mozart" being brought in through the massive iron folding gates.

ACROSS THE RIVER SALZACH: FROM THE FORTRESS TO THE NEW TOWN

According to a popular saying in Salzburg, "If you can see the fortress, it's just about to rain; if you can't see it, it's already raining." Fortunately there are plenty of days when spectacular views can be had of Salzburg and the surrounding countryside from the top of this castle. Looking across the River Salzach to the Neustadt (New Town) area of historic Salzburg, you can pick out the Mirabell Palace and Gardens, the Landestheater, the Mozart Residence and the Mozarteum, the Church of the Holy Trinity, and the Kapuzinerkloster perched atop the Kapuzinerberg. Ranging from the "acropolis" of the city—the medieval Fortress Hohensalzburg—to the celebrated Salzburg Marionette Theater, this part of Salzburg encapsulates the city's charm. If you want to see the most delightful Mozart landmark in this section of town, the Zauberflötenhäuschen—the mouthful used to describe the little summerhouse where he finished composing *The Magic Flute*—it can be viewed when events and concerts are scheduled in the adjacent Mozarteum.

a good walk

Start with Salzburg's number one sight—especially the case at night, when it is spectacularly spotlit—the famed **Fortress Hohensalzburg** ⑲ ▶, the 11th-century castle that dominates the town. Take the Mönchsberg elevator or the Festungsbahn cable car on Festungsgasse, behind the cathedral near St. Peter's Cemetery. If it's not running, you can walk up the zigzag path that begins a little farther up Festungsgasse; it's steep in parts but gives a better impression of the fortress's majestic nature. Once you've explored this, the largest medieval fortress in Central Europe, head back to the footpath, but instead of taking the steps back into town, turn right toward the **Nonnberg Convent** . Explore the church—the real Maria von Trapp almost found her calling here—then return along the path to the first set of steps, take them down them into Kaigasse, and continue on to Mozartplatz. From here you can cross the Salzach River over the oldest extant footbridge in the city, Mozartsteg. Cross the road and walk west a minute or two along Imbergstrasse until you see a bookstore on the corner. Here a little street runs into **Steingasse**—a picturesque medieval street, and the old Roman street coming into from the south. After exploring this "time machine," walk through the Steintor gate, past the chapel of St. Johann am Imberg to the Hettwer Bastion on the **Kapuzinerberg Hill** for another great vista of the city.

Continue up the path to the Kapuziner-Kloster. From here, follow the winding road down past the stations of the cross. Turn right at the bottom of the road into Linzergasse, the New Town's answer to the Getreidegasse. Continue up this street to St. Sebastian's Church on the left. An archway will lead you into the tranquil **St. Sebastian's Cemetery**—if it looks somewhat familiar that's because it inspired the scene at the end of *The Sound of Music,* where the von Trapps are nearly captured. When you leave the cemetery, walk north through a passageway until you reach Paris-Lodron-Strasse. To the left as you walk west down this street is the Loreto Church. At Mirabellplatz, cross the road to the **Mirabellgarten**—the Pegasus Fountain (remember "Do-Re-Mi"?) and the Dwarfs' Garden are highlights here.

Take in Prince-Archbishop Wolf-Dietrich's private Xanadu, the adjacent **Mirabell Palace** and its noted 18th-century Angel Staircase. Turn left out of the garden park onto busy Schwarzstrasse. Along this road you will find the famous center of Mozart studies, the **Mozarteum**, whose Great Hall is often the venue of chamber concerts (during which you can view the "Magic Flute" House in the nearby Bastionsgarten). Next door is the **Marionettentheater**—home to those marionettes known around the world. Turn left at the corner, around the Landestheater, and continue onto Makartplatz, dominated at the far end by Fischer von Erlach's **Dreifaltigkeitskirche**. Across from the Hotel Bristol is the second-most famous Mozart residence in the city, the **Mozart Wohnhaus**, where you can complete your homage to the city's hometown deity. Just to its right is the house where another famous Salzburger, the physicist Christian Doppler, was born in 1803.

TIMING   Allow half a day for the fortress, to explore it fully both inside and out. If you don't plan an intermission at one of the restaurants on the Mönchsberg, you can stock up on provisions at Nordsee (next door to Mozart's Birthplace) or Fasties (Pfeifergasse 3, near the Kajetanerplatz). Call the Mozarteum to see if there will be evening recitals in their two concert halls; hearing the *Haffner* or another of Mozart's symphonies could be a wonderfully fitting conclusion to your day.

Sights to See

Dreifaltigkeitskirche (Church of the Holy Trinity). The Makartplatz—named after Hans von Makart, the most famous Austrian painter of the

OH, THE HILLS ARE ALIVE . . .

FEW SALZBURGERS WOULD PUBLICLY ADMIT IT, *but* The Sound of Music, Hollywood's interpretation of the trials and joys of the local Trapp family, has become their city's most eminent emissary when it comes to international promotion. The year after the movie's release, international tourism to Salzburg jumped 20%, and soon The Sound of Music was a Salzburg attraction. The **Sternbräu Dinner Theater** (✉ Griesgasse 23 ☎ 0662/826617) offers a dinner show featuring those unforgettable songs from the movie, as well as traditional folksongs from Salzburg and a medley of Austrian operettas. The cost of the dinner show is €43; without dinner it's €31.

Perhaps the most important Sound spin-offs are the **tours** offered by several companies (for a number of them, see Guided Tours in Salzburg A to Z, below). Besides showing you some of the film's locations (usually very briefly), these four-hour rides have the advantage of giving a very concise tour of the city. The buses generally leave from Mirabellplatz; lumber by the "Do-Re-Mi" staircase at the edge of the beautifully manicured Mirabell Gardens; pass by the hardly visible Aigen train station, where in reality the Trapps caught the escape train; and then head south to Schloss Anif. This 16th-century water castle, which had a cameo appearance in the opening scenes of the film, is now in private hands and not open to the public.

First official stop for a leg-stretcher is at the gazebo in the manicured park of Schloss Hellbrunn at the southern end of the city. Originally built in the gardens of Leopoldskron Palace, it was brought out here to give the chance for taking pictures. This is where Liesl von Trapp sings "I Am Sixteen Going on Seventeen" and where Maria and the Baron woo and coo

"Something Good." The simple little structure is the most coveted prize of photographers. The bus then drives by another private palace with limited visiting rights, Schloss Leopoldskron. The estate's magical water-gate terrace, adorned with rearing horse sculptures and "site" of so many memorable scenes in the movie, was re-created elsewhere on the lake for the actual filming; its balcony, however, was really used for the scene where Maria and Baron von Trapp dance during the ball. The bus continues on to Nonnberg Convent at the foot of the daunting Hohensalzburg fortress, then leaves the city limits for the luscious landscape of the Salzkammergut. These are the hills "alive with music," where Julie Andrews prances about in the opening scenes. You get a chance for a meditative walk along the shore of the Wolfgangsee in St. Gilgen before the bus heads for the pretty town of Mondsee, where, in the movie, Maria and Georg von Trapp were married at the twin-turreted Michaelerkirche.

Tour guides are well trained and often have a sense of humor, with which they gently debunk myths about the movie. Did you know, for example, that Switzerland was "moved" 160 km (100 mi) eastward so the family could hike over the mountains to freedom (while singing "Climb Every Mountain")? It all goes to show that in Hollywood, as in Salzburg and its magical environs, almost anything is possible.

mid-19th century—is dominated at the top (east) end by Fischer von Erlach's first architectural work in Salzburg, built 1694–1702. It was modeled on a church by Borromini in Rome and prefigures von Erlach's Karlskirche in Vienna. Dominated by a lofty, oval-shape dome—which showcases a painting by Michael Rottmayr—this church was the result of the archbishop's concern that Salzburg's new town was developing in an overly haphazard manner. It is commonly thought that this church was erected to create a sense of order by introducing a spectacular monument of the Baroque—the signature style of the city—on the Makartplatz. But, in point of fact, up to the beginning of the 19th century, the church facade was hidden by the archbishop's pawnhouse. The church interior is small but perfectly proportioned, surmounted by its dome, whose trompe-l'oeil fresco seems to open up the church to the sky above. ⊠ *Dreifaltigkeitsgasse 14* ☎ *0662/877495* ⊘ *Mon.–Sat. 6:30–6:30, Sun. 8–6:30.*

Festungsbahn (funicular railway). This is the easy way up to Fortress Hohensalzburg; it's behind St. Peter's Cemetery. ⊠ *Festungsgasse 4* ☎ *0662/ 842682* ⊕ *www.festungsbahn.at* 🎟 *Round-trip including the entrance fee to the bastions of the fortress €8.50, one-way down €3.70* ⊘ *Every 10 min Oct.–Mar., daily 9–5; May–Sept., daily 9–9.*

⑲ **Fortress Hohensalzburg.** Founded in 1077, the Hohensalzburg is
Fodor'sChoice Salzburg's acropolis and the largest preserved medieval fortress in
★ Central Europe. Brooding over the city from atop the Festungsberg, it was originally founded by Salzburg's Archbishop Gebhard, who had supported the pope in the investiture controversy against the Holy Roman Emperor. Over the centuries, the archbishops gradually enlarged the castle, using it originally only sometimes as a residence, then as a siege-proof haven against invaders and their own rebellious subjects. The exterior may look grim, but inside there are lavish state rooms, such as the glittering **Golden Room,** the **Burgmuseum**—a collection of medieval art—and the **Rainer's Museum,** with its brutish arms and armor. Politics and Church are in full force here: there's a torture chamber not far from the exquisite late-Gothic **St. George's Chapel** (although, in fact, the implements on view came from another castle and were not used here). The 200-pipe organ from the beginning of the 16th-century, played during the warmer months daily after the carillon in the Neugebäude, is best listened to from a respectful distance, as it is not called the Bull without reason. Everyone will want to climb up the 100 tiny steps to the **Reckturm,** a grand lookout post with a sweeping view of Salzburg and the mountains. Remember that visitor lines to the fortress can be long, so try to come early. Children will love coming here, especially as some rooms of the castle are now given over to special exhibitions, the **Welt der Marionetten,** which offers a fascinating view into the world of marionettes—a great preview of the treats in store at the nearby Marionettentheater.

You can either take the funicular railway, the more than 110 years old **Festungsbahn,** up to the fortress (advisable with young children) or walk up the zigzag path that begins just beyond the Stieglkeller on Festungsgasse. Note that you don't need a ticket to walk down the footpath.

✉ *Mönchsberg 34* ☎ *0662/842430–11* ⊕ *www.salzburg-burgen.at*
🎫 *Fortress €3.60; apartments €3.60; marionette museum €3* ◷ *Mid-Mar.–mid-June, daily 9–6; mid-June–mid-Sept., daily 8:30–8; mid-Sept.–mid-Mar., daily 9–5; Marionette museum, Mar. 1–Dec. 31, daily 10–5.*

㉒ Kapuzinerberg Hill. Directly opposite the Mönchsberg on the other side of the river, Kapuzinerberg Hill is crowned by several interesting sights. By ascending a stone staircase near Steingasse 9 you can start your climb up the peak. At the top of the first flight of steps is a tiny chapel, **St. Johann am Imberg,** built in 1681. Farther on are a signpost and gate to the **Hettwer Bastion,** part of the old city walls that is one of the most spectacular viewpoints in Salzburg. At the summit is the gold-beige **Kapuzinerkloster** (Capuchin Monastery), originally a fortification built to protect the one bridge crossing the river, which dates from the time of Prince-Archbishop Wolf-Dietrich. It was restored for the 1988 visit by Pope John Paul II. The road downward—note the Stations of the Cross along the path—is called Stefan Zweig Weg, after the great Austrian writer who rented the **Paschingerschlössl** house (on the Kapuzinerberg to the left of the monastery) until 1935, when he left Austria after the Nazis had murdered chancellor Dollfuss. As one of Austria's leading critics and esthetes, his residence became one of the cultural centers of Europe in those days and visitors included James Joyce, Béla Bartók, Arturo Toscanini, and Richard Strauss (for whom he wrote some libretti).

★ ☾ **㉗ Marionettentheater** (Marionette Theater). This is both the world's greatest marionette theater and—surprise!—a sublime theatrical experience. Many critics have noted that viewers quickly forget the strings controlling the puppets, which assume lifelike dimensions and provide a very real dramatic experience. The theater itself is a Rococo concoction. The Marionettentheater is identified above all with Mozart's operas, which seem particularly suited to the skilled puppetry; a delightful production of *Così fan tutte* captures the humor of the work better than most stage versions. The company is famous for its world tours but is usually in Salzburg around Christmas, during the late-January Mozart Week, at Easter, and from May to September (schedule subject to change). ✉ *Schwarzstrasse 24* ☎ *0662/872406–0* 🖷 *0662/882141* ⊕ *www.marionetten.at* 🎫 *€18–€35* ◷ *Box office Mon.–Sat. 9–1 and 2 hrs before performance; Salzburg season May–Sept., Christmas, Mozart Week (Jan.), Easter.*

☾ **㉔ Mirabellgarten** (Mirabell Gardens). While there are at least four entrances to the Mirabell Gardens—from the Makartplatz (framed by the statues of the Roman gods), the Schwarzstrasse, and the Rainerstrasse—you'll want to enter from the Rainerstrasse and head for the Rosenhügel (Rosebush Hill): you'll arrive at the top of the steps where Julie Andrews and her seven charges showed off their singing ability in *The Sound of Music.* This is also an ideal vantage point from which to admire the formal gardens and one of the best views of Salzburg, as it shows how harmoniously architects of the Baroque period laid out the city. The center of the gardens—one of Europe's most beautiful parks, partly designed by Fischer von Erlach as the grand frame for the Mirabell Palace—is dominated by four large groups of statues representing the ancient ele-

FodorśChoice
★

ments of water, fire, air, and earth, and designed by Ottavio Mosto, who came to live in Salzburg from Padua. A bronze version of the horse Pegasus stands in front of the south facade of the palace in the center of a circular water basin.

The most famous part of the Mirabell Gardens is the **Zwerglgarten** (Dwarfs' Garden), which can be found opposite the Pegasus fountain. Here you'll find 12 statues of "Danubian" dwarves sculpted in marble—the real-life models for which were presented to the bishop by the landgrave of Göttweig. Prince-Archbishop Franz Anton von Harrach had the stone figures made for a kind of stone theater below. The **Heckentheater** (Hedge Theater), an enchanting natural stage setting that dates from 1700, will once again host chamber operas (like Mozart's *Bastien und Bastienne*) during the 2006 Mozart year. The Mirabell Gardens are open daily 7 AM–8 PM. Art lovers will make a bee-line for the **Barockmuseum** (⊠ Orangeriegarten ☎ 0662/877432), beside the Orangery of the Mirabell Gardens. It houses a collection of late-17th- and 18th-century paintings, sketches, and models illustrating the extravagant vision of life of the Baroque era—the signature style of Salzburg. Works by Giordano, Bernini, and Rottmayr are the collection's highlights. The museum is open Tuesday to Saturday, 9 to noon and 2 to 5, and Sunday and holidays 10 to 1; admission is €3.

㉕ Mirabell Palace The "Taj Mahal of Salzburg," Schloss Mirabell was built in 1606 by the immensely wealthy and powerful Prince-Archbishop Wolf-Dietrich for his mistress, Salomé Alt, and their 15 children: It was originally called Altenau in her honor. Such was the palace's beauty that it was taken over by succeeding prince-archbishops, including Markus Sittikus, Paris Lodron (who renamed the estate in honor of *his* mistress), and finally, Franz Anton von Harrach, who brought in Lukas von Hildebrandt to Baroque-ize the place in 1727. Unfortunately, a disastrous fire hit in 1818. Happily, three of the most spectacular set-pieces of the palace—the Chapel, the Marble Hall, and the Angel Staircase—survived. The Marble Hall is nowadays used for civil wedding ceremonies and is regarded as the most beautiful registry office in the world. Restored in 1999, its marble floor in strongly contrasting colors and walls of stucco and marble ornamented with elegant gilt scrollwork look more splendid than ever. The young Mozart and his sister gave concerts here, and he also composed *Tafelmusik* (Table Music) to accompany the prince's meals. It is only fitting that candlelit chamber concerts are now offered in this grand room.

Besides the chapel in the northeast corner, the only other part of the palace to survive the fire was the magnificent marble Angel Staircase, laid out by von Hildebrandt, with sculptures by Georg Rafael Donner. To welcome (and impress) guests, staircases were seen as monumentally important and they afforded many Baroque artists ideal showcases for ingenious and exuberant ornamentation—nowhere more so than here, as Donner produced a particularly charming example of this highly specialized art. The staircase is romantically draped with white marble putti, whose faces and gestures reflect a multitude of emotions, from questioning innocence to jeering mockery, leading the visitor upstairs to the reception rooms. The very first putti genuflects in an old Turkish greeting (a reminder of the Siege of Vienna in 1683). Outdoor concerts are held at the palace and gardens May though August, Sunday mornings at 10:30 and Wednesday evenings at 8:30. ⊠ *Off Makartplatz* ☎ *0662/889–87–330* 🖪 *Free* ☉ *Weekdays 8–6.*

Mozart Audio and Video Museum. In the same building as the Mozart Wohnhaus (Residence) is the Mozart Audio and Video Museum, an archive of thousands of Mozart recordings as well as films and video productions, all of which can be listened to or viewed on request. ⊠ *Makartplatz 8* ☎ *0662/883454* ⊕ *www.mozarteum.at/seiten/mtfset.htm* 🖪 *Free* ☉ *Mon., Tues., and Fri. 9–1, Wed. and Thurs. 1–5.*

☙ ㉙ **Mozart Wohnhaus** (Mozart Residence). The Mozart family moved from their cramped quarters in Getreidegasse to this house on the Hannibal Platz, as it was then known, in 1773. Wolfgang Amadeus Mozart lived here until 1780, his sister Nannerl stayed here until she married in 1784, and their father Leopold lived here until his death in 1787. The house is accordingly referred to as the Mozart Residence, signifying that it was not only Wolfgang who lived here. During the first Allied bomb attack on Salzburg in October 1944, the house was partially destroyed. Despite international protest at the time, a six-story office block was built in its place. In an exemplary building and sponsorship project the office block was demolished and the house reconstructed in 1996. Mozart composed the "Salzburg Symphonies" here, as well as all five violin concertos, church music and some sonatas, and parts of his early operatic masterpieces, including *Idomeneo*. Besides an interesting collection of musical instruments (for example, his own pianoforte), among the exhibits on display are books from Leopold Mozart's library. Autograph manuscripts and letters can be viewed, by prior arrangement only, in the cellar vaults. One room offers a multimedia show and wall-size map with more personal details about Mozart like his numerous travels across Europe (and he did travel—historians believe he may have spent up to a fourth of his life in carriages traveling from concert to concert). Another salon has been decorated in the domestic decor of Mozart's day. ⊠ *Makartplatz 8* ☎ *0662/874227–40* 🖨 *0662/872924* ⊕ *www.mozarteum.at* 🖪 *Mozart residence €6, combined ticket for Mozart residence and birthplace €9* ☉ *Sept.–June, daily 9–5:30; July and Aug., daily 9–6:30.*

㉖ **Mozarteum.** Two institutions share the address in this building finished just before World War I here—the International Mozarteum Foundation, set up in 1870, and the University of Music and Performing Arts, founded in 1880. Scholars come here to research in the **Bibliotheca Mozartiana**, the world's largest Mozart library. The Mozarteum also organizes the annual Mozart Week festival in January. Many important concerts are offered from October to June in its two recital halls, the Grosser Saal (Great Hall) and the Wiener Saal (Vienna Hall).

Other than attending concerts at the Mozarteum, the general public is not admitted to its facilities. However, if the concert is held in Mozarteum's Grosser Saal, a special treat is in store, for you can view the famous **Zauberflötenhäuschen**—the little summerhouse where Mozart finished composing *The Magic Flute* in Vienna, with the encouragement of his frantic librettist, Emanuel Schikaneder, who finally wound up locking the composer inside to force him to complete his work. Moved to a site adjacent to the concert hall and sheltered by the trees of the Bastiongarten, the house was donated to the Mozarteum by Prince Starhemberg. It is much restored: back in the 19th century, the faithful used to visit it and snatch shingles off its roof. ⊠ *Schwarzstrasse 26* ☎ *0662/88940–21* ⊕ *www.mozarteum.at* ◷ *Summerhouse: only during Grosser Saal concerts.*

⑱ Nonnberg Convent. Just below the south side of the Fortress Hohensalzburg—and best visited in tandem with it—the Stift Nonnberg was founded right after 700 by St. Rupert, and his niece St. Erentrudis was the first abbess (in the archway a late-Gothic statue of Erentrudis welcomes the visitor). Note, just below the steeple, some of the oldest frescos in Austria, painted in the Byzantine style during the 10th century). It is more famous these days as "Maria's convent"—both the one in *The Sound of Music* and that of the real Maria. She returned to marry her Captain von Trapp here in the Gothic church (as it turns out, no filming was done here—"Nonnberg" was recreated in the film studios of Salzburg-Parsch). Each evening in May at 7, the nuns sing a 15-minute service called Maiandacht in the old Gregorian chant (music historians tell us that, in fact, the oldest music found in the collections of the National Library in Vienna hails from Salzburg). Their beautiful voices can be heard also at the 11 PM mass on December 24. Parts of the private quarters for the nuns, which include some lovely, intricate woodcarving, can be seen by prior arrangement. ⊠ *Nonnberggasse 2* ☎ *0662/841607–0* ◷ *Fall–spring, daily 7–5; summer, daily 7–7.*

★ ㉓ St. Sebastian's Cemetery. Memorably recreated for the escape scene in *The Sound of Music* on a Hollywood soundstage, final resting place for many members of the Mozart family, and in the shadows of St. Sebastian's Church, the Friedhof St. Sebastian is one of the most peaceful spots in Salzburg. Prince-Archbishop Wolf-Dietrich commissioned the cemetery in 1600 to replace the old cathedral graveyard, which he planned to demolish. It was built in the style of an Italian *campo santo,* (sacred field) with arcades on four sides, and in the center of the square he had the Gabriel Chapel, an unusual, brightly tiled Mannerist mausoleum built for himself, in which he was interred in 1617 (now closed to visitors). Several famous people are buried in this cemetery, including the medical doctor and philosopher Theophrastus Paracelsus, who settled in Salzburg in the early 16th century (his grave is by the church door). Around the chapel are the graves of eight members of Mozart's family, including his wife, Constanze, his father, Leopold, and Genoveva Weber, the aunt of Constanze and the mother of Carl Maria von Weber (by the central path leading to the mausoleum). If the gate is closed, try going through the church, or enter through the back entrance around the corner in the courtyard. ⊠ *Linzergasse* ◷ *Daily 9 AM–6 PM.*

㉑ Steingasse. This narrow medieval street, walled in on one side by the bare cliffs of the Kapuzinerberg, was originally the ancient Roman entrance into the city from the south. The houses stood along the riverfront before the Salzach was regulated. Nowadays it's a fascinating mixture of artists' workshops, antiques shops, and trendy nightclubs, but with its tall houses the street still manages to convey an idea of how life used to be in the Middle Ages. Contrary to the commemorative plaques still shown **Steingasse 9** is not the birthplace of Josef Mohr, who wrote the words to the Christmas carol "Silent Night, Holy Night": according to new discoveries, he was born in the house at No. 21 in 1792. The **Steintor** marks the entrance to the oldest section of the street; here on summer afternoons the light can be particularly striking. House No. 23 on the right still has deep, slanted peep-windows for guarding the gate.

Short Side Trips from Salzburg

Gaisberg and Untersberg. Adventurous people might like to ascend two of Salzburg's "house mountains" (so-called because they are so close to the city settlements). You can take the bus to the summit of the Gaisberg, where you'll be rewarded with a spectacular panoramic view of the Alps and the Alpine foreland. In summer Dr. Richard/Albus bus (☎ 0662/424–000–0) leaves from Mirabellplatz at 10, 12, 2, and 5:15, and the journey takes about a half hour. The Untersberg is the mountain Captain von Trapp and Maria climbed as they escaped the Nazis in *The Sound of Music*. In the film they were supposedly fleeing to Switzerland; in reality, the climb up the Untersberg would have brought them almost to the doorstep of Hitler's retreat at the Eagle's Nest above Berchtesgaden (!). A cable car from St. Leonhard (about 13 km [8 mi] south of Salzburg) takes you up 6,020 feet right to the top of the Untersberg, giving you a breathtaking view. In winter you can ski down (you arrive in the village of Fürstenbrunn and taxis or buses take you back to St. Leonhard); in summer there are a number of hiking routes from the summit. ⊠ *Untersbergbahn* ☎ 06246/72477 ⊕ *www.untersberg. net* 🚠 *Round-trip* €17 ⊙ *Mid-Dec.–Feb., daily 10–4; Mar.–June and Oct., daily 9–5; July–Sept., daily 8:30–5:30.*

Oberndorf. This little village 21 km (13 mi) north of Salzburg has just one claim to fame: it was here on Christmas Eve, 1818, that the world famous Christmas carol "Silent Night, Holy Night," composed by the organist and schoolteacher Franz Gruber to a lyric by the local priest, Josef Mohr, was sung for the first time. The church was demolished and replaced in 1937 by a tiny commemorative chapel containing a copy of the original composition (the original is in the Museum Salzburg), stained-glass windows depicting Gruber and Mohr, and a Nativity scene. About a 10-minute walk from the village center along the riverbank, the local **Heimatmuseum** (⊠ Stille-Nacht-Platz 7 ☎ 06272/4422–0), opposite the chapel, documents the history of the carol. The museum is open daily 9–noon and 1–5; admission is €2.50. You can get to Oberndorf by the local train (opposite the main train station), by car along the B156 Lamprechtshausener Bundesstrasse, or by bicycle along the River Salzach.

Schloss Hellbrunn (Hellbrunn Palace). Just 6½ km (4 mi) south of Salzburg, the Lustschloss Hellbrunn was the prince-archbishops' pleasure palace. It was built early in the 17th century by Santino Solari for Markus Sit-

tikus, after the latter had imprisoned his uncle, Wolf-Dietrich, in the fortress. The castle has some fascinating rooms, including an octagonal music room and a banquet hall with a trompe-l'oeil ceiling. From the magnificent gardens and tree-lined avenues to the silent ponds, Hellbrunn Park is often described as a jewel of landscape architecture. It became famous far and wide because of its **Wasserspiele,** or trick fountains: in the formal gardens, a beautiful example of the Mannerism style including a later added outstanding mechanical theater, some of the exotic and humorous fountains spurt water from strange places at unexpected times—you will probably get doused (bring a raincoat). A visit to the gardens is highly recommended: nowhere else can you experience so completely the realm of fantasy that the grand Salzburg archbishops indulged in. You can get to Hellbrunn by Bus 25, by car on Route 159, or by bike or on foot along the beautiful Hellbrunner Allee past several 17th-century mansions. The restaurant in the castle courtyard serves good food. On the estate grounds is the little gazebo filmed in *The Sound of Music* ("You are 16 . . . ").
✉ *Fürstenweg 37, Hellbrunn* ☎ *0662/820372* ⊕ *www.hellbrunn.at*
🎫 *Tour of palace and water gardens €7.50* ⊙ *Apr. and Oct., daily 9–4:30; May–Sept., daily 9–5:30; evening tours July and Aug., daily on the hr 6–10.*

Schloss Leopoldskron (Leopold's Crown Palace). One of Salzburg's most glamorous pleasure palaces, this lakeside villa earned Hollywood immortality when it was used as the "back" of Baron von Trapp's house in *The Sound of Music.* The front was that of Schloss Frohnburg, across the lake. While the enchanting water terrace—framed by the winged horses (remember?)—was re-created elsewhere on the lake for many of the villa scenes, several shots did utilize this stepped lakeside garden, which, in fact, still exists in all its splendor. A gorgeous example of Austrian Rococo, the house itself dates back to the first half of the 18th century and was built for Archbishop Stuart. The house is now a conference center and is closed to the public. There is also no bus service through Leopoldskronstrasse, so you need to hike around the Nonnberg hill for some distance to get to the house. Happily, once you get to Leopoldskron, there is a pool set to the side of the palace where you can enjoy an appropriate vista of the house right out of *The Sound of Music.* With the Fortress Honhensalzburg looming in the distance, you'll want to have your Nikon handy. Note that the tree-lined road where Julie Andrews gets off the Albus bus to get to the von Trapp home can be found a short way from the Schloss.

WHERE TO EAT

Some of the most distinctive places in town are the fabled hotel restaurants, such as those of the Goldener Hirsch and the "Ratsherrenkeller" of the Hotel Elefant; see our hotel reviews for details. The newest spot in town, M32—the restaurant of the Museum der Moderer—was not open at this writing, but the decor will be formidably mod-minimalist (concrete walls and animal horns) and there are high hopes for an adventurous menu. Also in the news is the legendary Café Glockenspiel, the most popular café on Mozartplatz. It is now undergoing renovation and will reopen as a pricey restaurant in 2005. For fast food, Salzburgers love their broiled-sausages street-stands. Some say the most delicious are to be found at the Balkan Grill at Getreidegasse 33 (its recipe for spicy Bosna sausage has always been a secret).

★ $$$$ ✕ **Gasthof Hohlwegwirt.** It's worth a detour on the way to Hallein along the B159 Salzachtal-Bundesstrasse about 10 km (6 mi) south of Salzburg to dine at this inviting inn, run by the same family for more than 130 years. Visitors to the summer music festival may find a hard time landing a table since there are so many local regulars, all here to enjoy the suburban cooking, the wine cellar filled with more than 100 different vintages, and the unmistakable atmosphere of this *stil Salzburg* house with its four nicely decorated salons. Chef Ernst Kronreif uses recipes from his legendary mother, Ida: spring for the delicious *Butternockerlsuppe* (soup-broth with buttered dumplings), the *Kalbsbries* (calf's sweetbreads), or the *Salzburger Bierfleisch* (beef boiled in beer)—all Salzburgian classics and yet always so up-to-date. Upstairs are some delightfully gemütlich guest rooms. ⊠ *Salzachtal-Bundesstrasse Nord 62, A–5400 Hallein-Taxach* ☎ *06245/82415–0* 🖷 *06245/8241572* ⊕ *www.hallo-hallein.at/page/hohlwegwirt.html* ⌘ *Reservations essential* ⊗ *Closed Mon., except during Summer Festival* ▭ *MC, V.*

★ $$$$ ✕ **Pfefferschiff.** The "Pepper Ship" is one of the most acclaimed restaurants in Salzburg—or, actually, 3 km (2 mi) northeast of the center. It is set in a pretty, renovated rectory, dated 1640, adjacent to a pink-and-cream chapel. Klaus Fleishhaker, an award-winning chef, and his German wife Petra make your table feel pampered in the country-chic atmosphere, nicely adorned with polished wooden floors, antique hutches, and tabletops laden with fine bone china and Paloma Picasso silverware. The menu changes seasonally. A taxi is the least stressful way of getting here, but if you have your own car, drive along the north edge of the Kapuzinerberg toward Hallwang and then Söllheim. ⊠ *Söllheim 3, A–5300 Hallwang* ☎ *0662/661242* ⌘ *Reservations essential* ▭ *AE.*

★ $$$–$$$$ ✕ **Pan e Vin.** This tiny trattoria has only a handful of tables, and they're hard to obtain, since the Italian specialities on tap are top-flight. Burnt sienna walls are lined with wine bottles, colorful ceramic plates, and Italian dry stuffs, and the chef cooks in full view. The upstairs restaurant of the same name has a more extensive menu, but it's also much more expensive. ⊠ *Gstättengasse 1* ☎ *0662/844666* 🖷 *0662/844666–15* ▭ *AE, DC, MC, V* ⌘ *Reservations essential* ⊗ *Closed Sun. and Mon.*

$$–$$$$ ✕ **Stiftskeller St. Peter.** Legends swirl about the famous "St. Peter's Beer Cellar." Locals claim that Mephistopheles met Faust here, other say Charlemagne dined here, and some believe Columbus enjoyed a glass of its famous Salzburg Stiegl beer just before he set sail for America in 1492. But there is no debating the fact that this place—first mentioned in a document dating back to 803—is Austria's oldest restaurant, part of the famous abbey whose Benedictine monks were Christianity's first ambassadors in these formerly pagan parts. If this is Europe's oldest Gasthaus, it still remains one of the most dazzling dining experiences in Salzburg. Choose between the fairly elegant, dark-wood-paneled Prälatenzimmer (Prelates' Room) or one of several less formal banqueting rooms. On hot summer days, the dramatic gray-stone courtyard is a favorite for drinking a glass

Fodor's Choice ★

of wine or a glass of that noted beer, accompanied by fingerlickingly good morsels of fried Wiener Schnitzel. Along with other Austrian standards, you can dine on fish caught in local rivers and lakes, and, of course, Salzburger Nockerl. For the full St. Peter splendor and to get in on the Mozart festivities, attend a candlelit Mozart Dinner Concert (€45, plus drinks) in the abbey's beautiful Baroque Hall—a dazzling white-and-blue chandeliered wonder. Almost every evening during 2005 and 2006 at 8 PM, you'll be able to enjoy 18th-century delectables along with tunes by the Wolfgang played by musicians in historic costume. Dessert will be "Mozart's Secret Sweet." ⊠ *St. Peter Bezirk 4* ☎ *0662/841268–0, 0662/ 828695–0 Mozart dinner* ⊕ *www.stiftskellerstpeter.at; Mozart dinner: www.mozart–serenaden.com* ▤ *AE, DC, MC, V.*

$$$ ✕**Perkeo.** Small and modern with minimalist decor, close-set tables, and an open kitchen, this upscale establishment across the river from the Altstadt is one of the city's standard bearers for future-forward cuisine. Specialties of the house include crepes stuffed with braised oxtail and red-wine shallots or *Seeteufel* (monkfish) with thistle and spinach on a bed of buttery noodles. Wines by the glass are priced at the high end. The wine list by the bottle confusingly lists the cheaper "take-out" prices—make sure of the price before ordering. This place can, unfortunately, be somewhat smoky. ⊠ *Priesterhausgasse 20* ☎ *0662/870899* ⚑ *Reservations essential* ▤ *No credit cards* ◷ *Closed weekends.*

$$–$$$ ✕**Mundenhamer.** Set next to the Mirabell Palace, this old-fashioned restaurant is masterminded by chef Ernst Breitschopf. He knows the repertoire of good old Upper Austrian dishes inside out. So just come here and feast: an *Innviertler* raw ham with horseradish, dark bread, and butter; a garlic soup with bread croutons; a roast pork chop served in a pan with bread dumplings and warm bacon-cabbage salad; homemade spätzle with braised white cabbage and bacon; a *Salzburger Schnitzel* (scallop of veal filled with minced mushrooms and ham) with buttered finger dumplings. Dessert? Who can resist the *Mohr im Hemd* ("Moor-in-a-shirt"), the warm chocolate cake garnished with fruits, chocolate sauce, vanilla ice-cream, and whipped cream? Only problem? You may not be able to move after your last bite. ⊠ *Rainerstrasse 2* ☎ *0662/875693* ▤ *AE, DC, MC, V* ◷ *Closed Sun.*

$$–$$$ ✕**Zum Mohren.** Good food, a central location by the river, a friendly welcome, attentive service, and reasonable prices have made Zum Mohren very popular with both Salzburgers and tourists. The restaurant is in the cellar of a 15th-century house, with cozy lighting, polished copper pots adorning the walls, and a vaulted Gothic room. The menu is imaginative, featuring such dishes as *Zanderfilet* (pike perch) in an herb-cheese crust with potato leek ragout. There's also a good vegetarian selection. ⊠ *Judengasse 9/Rudolfskai 20* ☎ *0662/842387* ▤ *AE, MC, V.*

★ **$$–$$$** ✕**Zum Eulenspiegel.** What has Till Eulenspiegel, the 14th-century jester from Germany's Braunschweig, to do with Salzburg? Not much, but when Hans Grassl opened this restaurant in 1950 (set just across the way from Mozart's birthplace), he saw the surrounding medieval townscape—the old town wall, the "little gate," and its historic 1414 Griess rooms—and decided to go for it. This inn actually was first mentioned In 1713 and, today, spiffily restored, it allures with rustic wooden furniture, old folio volumes, antique weapons, and open firesides. Tables gleaming with white linen are set in wonderful nooks and crannies reached by odd staircases and charming salons, like the tiny "women's apartment," offer delightful views over the city and river. The unique setting is matched by the delicious food. Try the potato goulash with chunks of sausage and beef in a creamy paprika sauce, or the house specialty, fish stew Provençal. These are served at lunch, or all day in the bar downstairs. A final plus: the staff speaks English. ⊠ *Hagenauerplatz 2* ☎ *0662/843180–0* ♨ *Reservations essential* ☰ *AE, DC, MC, V* ☉ *Closed Sun., except during festival and Jan.–mid-Mar.*

$$–$$$ ✕ **Blaue Gans.** In a 500-year-old building with vaulted ceilings and windows looking out onto the bustling Getreidegasse, this formerly old-style restaurant in the Blaue Gans hotel has been revamped to showcase a more innovative style of Austrian cooking. There are always vegetarian choices, too. Service is top-notch, the *Wolfsbarsch* (perch) comes with a cilantro-chili cream sauce, and you can peer through a glass floor to study an old mystic cellar—this, as it turns out, was the site of the oldest inn in Salzburg. ⊠ *Getreidegasse 41–43* ☎ *0662/842491–0* ☰ *AE, DC, MC, V* ☉ *Closed Tues.*

$–$$$ ✕ **Café Sacher.** Red-velvet banquettes, sparkling chandeliers, and lots of gilt mark this famous gathering place, a favorite of well-heeled Salzburgers and an outpost of the celebrated Vienna landmark. It's a perfect choice for a leisurely afternoon pastry (especially the famous chocolate Sachertorte) and coffee—and of course the coffee is second to none. Full meals are also served and they offer a no-smoking room, too. (Pastries and coffee are in the $ category.) ⊠ *Schwarzstrasse 5–7* ☎ *0662/889770* ☰ *AE, DC, MC, V.*

$$ ✕ **Ährlich.** Just because this restaurant is all-organic doesn't mean it isn't fun. The dining room has a country casual ambience with cozy booths. ⊠ *Wolf-Dietrich-Strasse 7* ☎ *0662/871275* ☰ *AE, DC, MC, V* ☉ *Closed Sun. No lunch.*

$$ ✕ **Coco Lezzone.** You'll always find a lively crowd at this popular spot on the quay on the Altstadt side of the river. Spacious with a contemporary, informal dining room, it can be a bit noisy at night. The menu changes with the seasons. ⊠ *Franz-Josef-Kai 7* ☎ *0662/846735* ☰ *No credit cards* ☉ *Closed Sun. No lunch Sat.*

★ $$ ✕ **Daxlueg.** If you really want to enjoy "food-with-a-view," drive 3 km (2 mi) north along the B1 Linzer Bundesstrasse to Mayrwies and turn right up through the woods. Here, you can take in a Cineramic view of Salzburg from the mountainside perch of this former *Rupertialm* (St. Rupert's pasture), a famous scenic lookout even in Mozart's time. Owned by St. Peter's monastery and now nicely renovated, this restaurant allures with the romantic charm of an alpine chalet. Seasonal specialities of the region top the bill: not only venison and fried trout but heavenly garnishes—cress, elder blossoms, herbs from the meadows, raspberries, blueberries, *Schwammerl* (mushrooms) fresh out of the forest, cheese from goat and sheep. Ach, Salzburg! ⊠ *Daxluegstrasse 5, A–5300 Hallwang* ☎ *0662/665800* ☰ *AE, DC, MC, V.*

★ $$ ✕ **Die Weisse** This *Weissbierbrauerei* occupys one of Salzburg's most historic breweries and many locals consider it to be their ultimate private retreat (so much so that from Wednesday through Saturday, it's best to make a reservation). The beer garden really hits the spot on a hot summer day but, year long, you can delight in traditional Bavarian goodies (veal sausages with sweet mustard!) as well as the usual array of tempting Salzburg delights. ⊠ *Rupertgasse 10* ☏ *0662/8722460* ▤ *MC, V* ☉ *Closed Sun.*

$$ ✕ **Gablerbräu.** You like it quick and good? Many like to stop here for a fast bite, but you should ponder the historic vibes, too. In this old inn Richard Mayr—a famous star of Vienna's State Opera House (he was the first to record Baron Ochs in Strauss's *Der Rosenkavalier*)—was born. He later became one of the organizers of the famous Salzburg music festival. After studying the parlor of Mayr's parents—a dark-wood-carved, neo-Gothic interior of the end of the 19th century—head for a table and settle down to "hot breads and cold beer": a selection of beers from different provinces along with a large variety of sandwiches for any taste. There is also a self-service salad buffet. Other treats on the menu are Northern Italian (in former days, of course, Austrian), including the polenta croquets with ratatouille and Gorgonzola cream sauce or the homemade linguine with courgettes in tomato sauce—best paired with a glass of white or red wine from Guttmann's cellars. ⊠ *Linzergasse 9* ☏ *0662/88965* ▤ *AE, DC, MC, V.*

$$ ✕ **K&K am Waagplatz.** This old house was once the domicile of the Freysauff family, who once counted among their close friend Leopold Mozart, the composer's father. Its cellar, the downstairs section of the restaurant, is still called the Freysauff (but don't be misled—this translates into "free drinks"!). The restaurant is particularly pleasant, with white-linen tablecloths, candles, and flowers, and windows opening onto the street. Menu selections consist of locally caught fish, delicious chicken-breast medaillons, lentil salad with strips of goose breast, and traditional Austrian dishes and game in season. Service is friendly. ⊠ *Waagplatz 2* ☏ *0662/842156* ▤ *AE, DC, MC, V.*

★ **$$** ✕ **Kuglhof.** In Maxglan, a famous "farmer's village" of Austria, now part of the city tucked behind the Mönchsberg and next to the Stiegl brewery (best, therefore, reached by taxi), Alexander Hawranek perfects Old-Austrian specialties by giving them a nouvelle touch. The setting is your archetypal black-shuttered, yellow-hued, begonia-bedecked Salzburgian farmhouse, oh-so-cozily set with a tile oven, mounted antlers, embroidered curtains, and tons of yummy gemütlichkeit. The menu is seasonal, so you might not be able to enjoy the signature *Beuschl* (calf's lights) with dumplings. Best best for dessert is the *Äpfelschmarrn,* sliced pancake with apples. In the summer, opt for a table out in the shady garden. ⊠ *Kuglhofstrasse 13* ☏ *0662/832626* ⊕ *www.kuglhof.at* ▤ *AE, DC, MC, V.*

$–$$ ✕ **Café Tomaselli.** Not many years after the attacking Turks fled Vienna, FodorśChoice leaving behind tons of coffee beans, this inn opened its doors in 1705 ★ as an example of that new-fangled thing, a "Wiener Kaffeehaus" (Vienna coffeehouse). It was an immediate hit. Enjoying its more than 14 types of coffee was none other than Mozart's beloved, Konstanze, who often dropped in as her house was just next door. The Tomasellis set up shop here in 1753, became noted as "chocolatmachers," and are still

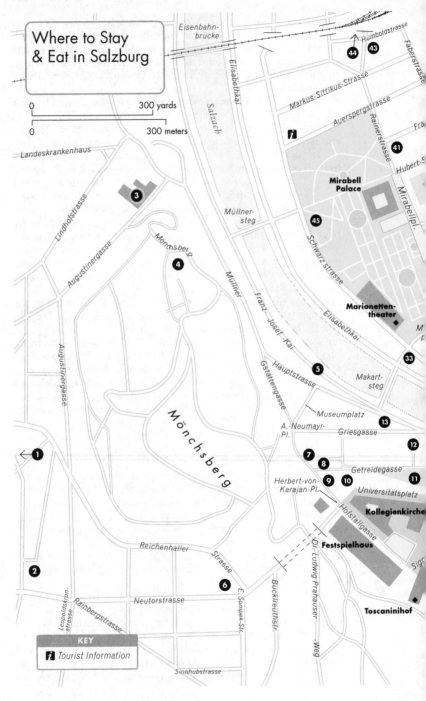

Where to Stay
& Eat in Salzburg

Eisenbahn-
brücke

0 ——————— 300 yards
0 ——————— 300 meters

Landeskrankenhaus

Humboldtstrasse

44 **43**

Markus-Sittikus-Strasse

Auerspergstrasse

Faberstrasse

ℹ

41

Hubert-s

Salzach

Elisabethkai

3

Lindhofstrasse

Augustinergasse

Mönchsberg

4

Müllner-
steg

Müllner

Franz-Josef-Kai

Mirabell
Palace

Mirabellpl.

45

Schwarz strasse

Marionetten-
theater

Elisabethkai

M

33

Augustinergasse

Mönchsberg

Gstättengasse

Hauptstrasse

5

Makart-
steg

Museumplatz

13

A.-Neumayr-
Pl.

Griesgasse

12

1 ←

7

8

Getreidegasse

11

Herbert-von-
Karajan-Pl.

9 **10**

Universitätsplatz

Kollegienkirche

Hofstallgasse

2

Reichenhaller

Strasse

Festspielhaus

E. Sompek-Str.

Bucklreuthstr.

Dr.-Ludwig-Prahauser-

Weg

Sig

Toscaninihof

Leopoldskron-
strasse

Rainbergstrasse

Neutorstrasse

6

Sinnhubstrasse

KEY
ℹ *Tourist Information*

Restaurants ▼

Ährlich **35**
Augustinerbräu **3**
Café Sacher **33**
Café Tomaselli **17**
Coco Lezzone **5**
Daxlueg **44**
Die Weisse **40**
Fabrizi Espresso **11**
Gablerbräu **27**
Gasthof Hohlwegwirt **25**
K&K am Waagplatz **20**
Krimpelstätter **4**
Kuglhof **2**
Mundenhamer **41**
Pan e Vin **8**
Perkeo **31**
Pfefferschiff **38**
Ristorante Pizzeria al Sole **7**
Stadtgasthof Blaue Gans **9**
Stiftskeller St. Peter **16**
Wilder Mann **13**
Zipfer Bierhaus **14**
Zum Eulenspiegel **12**
Zum Fidelen Affen **29**
Zum Mohren **19**

Hotels ▼

Altstadt Radisson SAS **18**
Am Dom **21**
Amadeus **34**
Auersperg **42**
Bristol **32**
Blaue Gans **9**
Cordial Theaterhotel **37**
Elefant **15**
Gersberg Alm **39**
Goldener Hirsch **10**
Haus Kernstock **1**
Kasererbräu **23**
Neutor **6**
NH Salzburg **36**
Pension Wolf **22**
Rosenvilla **26**
Sacher Salzburg **33**
Schloss Mönchstein **4**
Schwarzes Rössl **28**
Sheraton Salzburg **45**
Stadtkrug **30**
Stieglbräu/Imlauer **43**
Weisse Taube **24**
Wolf–Dietrich **35**

running the place. You'll want to feast on the famous "Tomaselliums Café" (mocca, Mozart liqueur, and whipped cream) and the large selection of excellent homemade cakes, tarts, and strudels. Inside, the decor is marble, wood, and walls of 18th-century portraits. In summer, however, the best seats are on the terrace and at the pretty "Tomsalli-Kiosk" on the square. ☒ *Alter Markt 9* ☎ *0662/844488–0* ⊕ *www.tomaselli. at* ☱ *No credit cards.*

$–$$ ✕ **Fabrizi Espresso.** Named after the former Italian owner of this historic house (note the beautiful small archway passage), this is a top spot for tasting *Marzemino,* the red wine Don Giovanni drinks in Mozart's opera. But there are plenty of other goodies here: some of the best Italian coffees in the city; outstanding Austrian *Apfel- oder Topfenstrudel* (apple or cheese pie—worth any money, but not expensive); excellent Prosecco Italian sparkling wine; various salads; and a fine Wiener Schnitzel. ☒ *Getreidegasse 21* ☎ *0662/845914* ☱ *No credit cards* ☉ *Closed Sun. Oct.–Easter.*

★ $ ✕ **Krimpelstätter.** About a 15-minute walk downriver from the Altstadt in the Müllner neighborhood, this is one of the top spots where the artists of the Summer Festival like to celebrate after their premieres. Everyone enjoys the traditional Salzburg cooking: seasonal and delicious *Bärlauch* (wild wood garlic) soup, or the potato goulash with chunks of country ham, or the homemade pork sausage with dumplings, or the *Zanderfilet* (pike perch). Happily, all this is served up in a delicious, centuries-old building, with fetching accents provided by vaulted ceilings, leaded-glass windows, and homespun tablecloths. Augustiner beer (from the monastery next door) is fresh on tap, and there's a big shady garden for dining in summer. ☒ *Müllner Hauptstrasse 31* ☎ *0662/432274* ⌂ *Reservations essential* ☱ *No credit cards* ☉ *Closed Sun. and Mon., Sept.–Apr.; Mon., May–Aug.*

$ ✕ **Wilder Mann.** "After a certain time all men become wild." So goes a famous Salzburg saying, perhaps coined after someone drank too much of the local "liquid bread"—Stiegl beer. In fact, when this inn opened its doors in 1884 it became one of the most important burgher houses in the Altstadt. Today, it offers a true time-stained ambience of an old Salzburg *Gasthaus,* right down to the wooden chairs that generations of locals have sat on and the enormous plates of *Bauernschmaus* (farmer's dish) overflowing with veal, pork, sausage, sour cabbage, and dumplings. ☒ *Getreidegasse 20* ☎ *0662/841787* ☱ *No credit cards* ☉ *Closed Sun.*

$ ✕ **Zipfer Bierhaus.** Arched ceilings, brick floors, flowered curtains, and wooden banquettes provide the right setting for good, standard local fare such as roast pork and dumplings. This is one of Salzburg's oldest Gasthäuser; look down the ancient cistern in the passageway connecting the two main rooms and try the different taste of the beer from Upper Austria. ☒ *Sigmund-Haffner-Gasse 12/Universitätsplatz 19* ☎ *0662/ 840745* ☱ *No credit cards* ☉ *Closed Sun.*

★ $ ✕ **Zum Fidelen Affen.** The name means "At the Faithful Ape," which explains the ape motifs in this popular Gasthaus dominated by a round copper-plated bar and stone pillars under a vaulted ceiling. Besides the beer on tap, the kitchen offers tasty Austrian dishes, such as

Schlutzkrapfen, cheese ravioli with a light topping of chopped fresh tomatoes, or a big salad with strips of fried chicken. It's always crowded, so be sure to arrive early or book ahead. ⊠ *Priesterhaus-gasse 8* ☎ *0662/877361* ⚞ *Reservations essential* ⊟ *DC, MC, V* ⊘ *Closed Sun. No lunch.*

★ ¢–$ ✕ **Augustinerbräu.** One of the largest beer cellars in Europe and Salzburg's homegrown version of a Munich beer house, the celebrated Augustinerbräu is at the north end of the Mönchsberg next to St. Augustine's church. You can even bring your own food—a relic of the old tradition that forbade breweries from serving meals in order to protect the status of restaurants. Pick up a stone jug of strong, frothy Augustiner beer and sit in the gardens or at a dark-wood table in one of the large refectory halls. Shops in the huge monastery complex sell a vast array of salads, breads, and pastries, as well as sausage and spit-roasted chicken. If you don't feel up to cold beer, there's an old copper beer warmer in the main hall. During Advent and Lent a special beer is offered, with the blessing of past popes, one of whom commented, "drinking does not interrupt fasting." ⊠ *Augustinergasse 4* ☎ *0662/431246* ⊟ *No credit cards* ⊘ *Weekdays 3–11, weekends 2:30–11.*

¢–$ ✕ **Ristorante Pizzeria al Sole.** Next to the Mönchsberg elevator you sit in this Italian restaurant upstairs in a pretty room lined with Venetian prints or in the more casual downstairs area. Choose from an impressive menu of scrumptious thin-crust pizzas. Pasta dishes are numerous and delicious, and may include tagliatelle with grilled shrimp or penne with tuna and capers. ⊠ *Gstättengasse 15* ☎ *0662/843284* ⊟ *AE, DC, MC, V.*

WHERE TO STAY

Note that many hotels in the Old City have to be accessed on foot, as cars are not permitted on many streets. If you have a car, of course, you may opt to do what many do—find a hotel or converted castle on the outskirts of the city. Needless to say, if you're planning to come at festival time you must book as early as possible. If you don't have a reservation, go to one of the tourist information offices or the accommodations service (*Zimmernachweis*) on the main platform of the railway station. Prices are highest during the festival weeks, and drop considerably in between.

★ $$$$ 🏨 **Altstadt Radisson SAS.** Venerable is the word to describe this current outpost of the Radisson group: after its founding in 1372 it was a brewery for centuries, then soon became one of the city's first inns, and has been a luxury hotel since 1992. The exterior is an Old City charmer, done up in buff pink, white trim, sash windows, and iron lanterns. Inside, much has been renovated to within an inch of its life, but historic stone arches and a super-tasteful assortment of antiques adorn many rooms, so the ambience allures. On one side, rooms overlook the river and the picturesque Capuchin cloister atop the hill opposite; on the other, upper rooms sneak a peek at the fortress. Despite smaller windows and original beamed ceilings, rooms are light and spacious and most are furnished with reproduction antiques and traditional accents. The Symphonie Restaurant is elegance personified, with royal-blue and gold hues ashimmer under Rococo chandeliers. Added bonuses are the central yet quiet location and generous buffet breakfast. ⊠ *Judengasse 15/Rudolfskai 28, A–5020* ☎ *0662/848571–0* 🖷 *0662/848–5716* ⊕ *www.austria-trend. at/ass* 🛏 *42 rooms, 20 suites* ᗌ *Restaurant, bar* ⊟ *AE, DC, MC, V* ⦿⊩ *BP.*

$$$$ 🖼 **Goldener Hirsch.** Picasso and Pavarotti, Rothschilds and Gettys, Tay-
Fodor'sChoice lor and Burton, Sayn-Wittgensteins and Queen Elizabeth—all have
★ made the "Golden Stag" their Salzburg home-away-from-home. You, too, will want to experience its unique champagne gemütlickeit, patrician pampering, and adorable decor, if not with a stay, then with a meal. The location is tops—just down the street from Mozart's Birthplace and steps from the Festspielhaus. This means crowds, but double-pane windows ensure you won't hear a thing once you enter the special, private world here. Inside it offers a delightfully rustic look with woodwork, peasant-luxe furniture, medieval statues, and some of the lowest ceilings in town; the stag motif is even on lamp shades, which were hand-painted by an Austrian countess. The hotel actually comprises four separate town houses, all connected in a welter of staircases and elevators. As a historic treasure expect some rooms to have snug (yet cozy) dimensions (in fact, some readers have written in alarm about some far-flung rooms tucked under the eaves—still, other "distant" chambers, such as those in the Kupferschmied Haus annex across the street, are prized since they are far from the fracas of this extremely popular place). There are two restaurants: the hotel's very regal dining room and its smaller bistro-brother, "s'Herzl." The latter is set on the pretty Sigmundsplatz, next to the hotel, and big stars and locals love its cozy, gemütlichkeit timbered look. To go beyond yum to yum-yum, be sure to get the house specialty, *Nürnberger Bratwürstl* (half a dozen little roasted Nürnberg sausages served with sauerkraut and served on pewter heart-shaped plates). During festival time, tables for aprés-performance dinners in the main restaurant are impossible to come by, having been booked eight months in advance, so why not try to rub elbows with *le tout Salzburg* in the hotel bar, probably the world's most beautifully decorated *Bauern-stil* room. Long run by Count Johannes Walderdorff, the hotel has now been taken over by a luxury chain, so some high-rollers are complaining that the hotel is not what it used to be (but what is?). The expensive breakfast is not included in the room price. ⊠ *Getreidegasse 37, A–5020* ☎ *0662/8084–0* 🖷 *0662/848511–845* ⊕ *www.goldenerhirsch. com* 🛏 *69 rooms* ᗌ *2 restaurants, minibars, bar, Internet, parking (fee)* ⊟ *AE, DC, MC, V* ⦿⊩ *EP.*

★ **$$$$** 🖼 **Sacher Salzburg.** Formerly famous as the Österreichischer Hof, this mammoth hotel on the bank of the Salzach River has attracted guests from the Beatles and the Rolling Stones to Hillary and Chelsea Clinton. A great fave of the Salzburg Festival crowd, it's owned by the Gürtler family, who also own the famous Hotel Sacher in Vienna. The staff has recently taken the monocle out of its eye, so even if you don't have a Vuitton steamer trunk, you'll probably feel welcome here. The main atrium is a symphony in marble, while the grand staircase still looks like the Empress Sissi could make a dazzling entrance amidst its ferns. Upstairs, guest rooms are so lovely there is a danger you won't want to leave to explore the city (especially if you get one with picture-perfect views of the Old City). Each is different, but all are exquisitely decorated. Room prices include a delicious buffet breakfast, including Sekt (Austrian sparkling wine). In nice weather tables are set outside on the terrace where you can enjoy a salad or hamburger (called a "Salzburger") for lunch while gazing across at the fortress. Restaurants include haute, tavern, and the Salzburg outpost of Vienna's fabled Café Sacher—enjoy your slice of Sachertorte at the latter. ⊠ *Schwarzstrasse 5–7, A–5020* ☎ *0662/ 88977* ☏ *0662/88977–14* ⊕ *www.sacher.com* ➔ *119 rooms* ♻ *5 restaurants, minibars, sauna, gym, bar, Internet, meeting rooms, parking (fee)* ⊟ *AE, DC, MC, V* ⏇ *BP.*

$$$$
FodorsChoice ★

Schloss Mönchstein. After extensive renovations in 2004, this fairy-tale and palatial mountain retreat has become even more magical. With gardens and hiking trails, yet just minutes from the city center, it's little wonder the 19th-century naturalist Alexander von Humboldt called this a "small piece of paradise." Catherine of Russia and the Duchess of Liechtenstein are just two of the notables who have stayed at this gable-roofed, tower-studded mansion. Inside, a series of lovely, luxurious rooms are hung with tapestries and adorned with painted chests and Old Master daubs; some salons have views of the woods and Salzburg in the distance. Service is pleasant and discreet, and the Paris Lodron restaurant is the epitome of Old World elegance (for hotel guests only)— a terrace is set with tables for great food-with-a-view under the ivy-covered walls. For those in love, the maximum treat might be a dinner in "the tiniest restaurant in the world"—a tower aerie set with banquettes and with windows offering fetching views (diner is €109—do book in advance). Suites are ravishing here. The castle has its own wedding chapel, which is particularly popular with American and Japanese couples. Getting in and out of town calls for a car or taxi, unless you are willing to negotiate steps or take the nearby Mönchsberg elevator, which is about an eight-minute walk away. ⊠ *Mönchsberg 26, A–5020* ☎ *0662/ 848555–0* ☏ *0662/848559* ⊕ *www.monchstein.com* ➔ *23 rooms* ♻ *Restaurant, café, minibars, tennis court, bar, free parking* ⊟ *AE, DC, MC, V* ⏇ *BP.*

$$$$

Sheraton Salzburg. With the lovely Mirabell park and gardens virtually at its back door, this beige, modern hotel tastefully blends in with the Belle Epoque buildings that surround it. Rooms are spacious and soothing in tone with contemporary furniture, and contain all the little extras and then some. Try to get a room facing the gardens. The buffet breakfast is outstanding—enough to keep you going all day. The house café, with attractive garden seating, bakes all its tempting pastries and strudels on the premises. It's about a 10-minute walk from the Altstadt across the river. ⊠ *Auerspergstrasse 4, A–5020* ☎ *0662/889990* ☏ *0662/ 881776* ⊕ *www.sheraton.at* ➔ *163 rooms* ♻ *2 restaurants, café, minibars, gym, sauna, bar, Internet, parking (fee), no-smoking floor* ⊟ *AE, DC, MC, V* ⏇ *BP.*

★ **$$$–$$$$**

Bristol. Just across the river from the Altstadt next to the Mirabell Gardens, this grand, pale yellow palace-hotel dating from 1892 as "electric hotel" (connected with the first power station in the city) has hosted, in turn, Franz Josef I, Freud, and the cast of *The Sound of Music.* The sunny lobby showcases a huge ancient tapestry along one wall and works by the Salzburg-born painter Hans von Makart, and the Piano-bar contains framed black-and-white photos of prominent guests (including Max, the Captain, and Liesl from the film cast). No two rooms are alike, but all have impressive fabrics, chandeliers, and marble baths (some have inner doors with their original etched glass). A few rooms are done in a whimsical Napoleonic-style with tented ceilings. The classy rooftop suite, known simply as "The View," has arguably the most stupendous views in the entire city. ☒ *Makartplatz 4, A–5020* ☎ *0662/873557* 🖷 *0662/873557–6* ⊕ *www.bristol-salzburg.at* ⟿ *60 rooms* ⚬ *Restaurant, minibars, bar, Internet, parking (fee)* ≡ *AE, DC, MC, V* ⊘ *Closed Feb. and Mar.* ℣ *BP.*

$$$ 🏨 **Blaue Gans.** "The Blue Goose" has always been a popular option—its location on the main shopping drag of Getriedegasse, within sight of the Festival theaters, Mozart's Birthplace, and the Pferdeschwemme fountain, is tops. Clearly, in light of its 400-year-old pedigree, it has one foot in Old World charm and still retains its ancient wood beams, winding corridors, and low archways. But in 2002, it took one giant step into the future when it was became the first "art hotel" in Salzburg, thanks to the efforts of such local artists Erich Shobesberger, Christian Ecker, and Waldemar Kufner, whose avant-garde works now adorn its walls. Upstairs, the guest rooms are spacious and have contemporary furnishings, whitewashed walls with cheeky framed posters and cheerful curtains; a few have skylights. The popular restaurant is a bright and festive place, with lively contemporary art on the walls and nouvelle Austrian delights on your dishes. Now that Salzburg's profile in the modern art world has expanded considerably with the opening of its new Museum der Moderne Salzburg, artists and curators will undoubtedly be touching down here, so be sure to make reservations well in advance. ☒ *Getreidegasse 43, A–5020* ☎☎ *0662/842491–0* ⊕ *www.blauegans.at* ⟿ *40 rooms* ⚬ *Restaurant, minibars, bar, Internet, parking (fee); no a/c in some rooms* ≡ *AE, DC, MC, V* ℣ *BP.*

$$$ 🏨 **Stieglbräu/Imlauer.** Midway between the train station and the Mirabell Gardens this interesting option is named after a noted Salzburg brewery. Modernized in 2004, it now features comfortably equipped rooms that come with individually adjustable air-conditioners and sound-proof windows. Just hop on the No. 1 bus to take you to the city center. The hotel has some leafy gardens and serves up the old fashioned treats the beer coachmen of yore liked, such as *Liptauer* (hot spiced cheese served with radish, bacon, cold pork, sausages, butter, and bread, along with a mug of the fresh beer on tap. ☒ *Rainerstrasse 12–14, A–5020* ☎ *0662/88992* 🖷 *0662/8899271* ⊕ *www.imlauer.com* ⟿ *99 rooms* ⚬ *Restaurant, free parking* ≡ *AE, DC, MC, V* ℣ *BP.*

$$–$$$ 🏨 **Auersperg.** Would you like to start your mornings with a stroll by a pool flowered with water lilies? You'll find this green oasis between the two buildings which comprise the Auersperg—the hotel, built in 1892 by the noted Italian architect Ceconi and its neighboring "villa." The lobby welcomes you with Biedermeier antiques, while upstairs, the guest rooms are decorated in a suave and soigne manner, with mostly modern pieces accented with classic ornaments. A rich breakfast buffet

and the use of the roof sauna and a steam-bath are included. Outside the door and it takes but five minutes to walk to the historic section. A big plus: just around the corner is that Salzburg treasure of a restaurant/beer garden, Die Weisse. ⊠ *Auerspergstrasse 61, A–5020* ☎ *0662/ 88944* 🖷 *0662/889–4455* ⊕ *www.auersperg.at* ⟿ *51 rooms* ⟲ *Sauna, steam bath, Internet, free parking; no a/c* ⊟ *AE, DC, MC, V* � *BP.*

$$–$$$ 🏨 **Elefant.** An old-time favorite, this hotel was once graced by the real Maria von Trapp (her personal check, written when she stayed here in 1981, is set under glass at the reception desk). But we mean really old: this 700-year-old house began life as an inn run by Salzburg citizen Hans Goldeisen, provisioner to Duke Ernst, and host to the likes of Maximilian II, who on his way from Spain to Vienna, took his new pet, an Indian elephant named Soliman. That's also the reason why guests are welcomed by the sight of an elephant sculpture in the lobby. Most of the decor is decidedly less exotic: A renovation finished in 2002 reduced the number of guest rooms in order to make each one more spacious and added air-conditioning to all of them. Some rooms are alluring, with pale yellow striped wallpaper, blue accents, and antique-style furniture, but others are much more generic. In fact, much of the local color has disappeared since the Elephant was rounded up by Best Western. For real history, repair to the hotel's "Ratsherrenkeller," one of Salzburg's most famous wine cellars in the 17th century. Today, it is the restaurant Bruno and offers alluring candlelit dinners. Cars can be parked in the Altstadt Garage. ⊠ *Sigmund-Haffner-Gasse 4, A–5020* ☎ *0662/843397* 🖷 *0662/840109–28* ⊕ *www.elefant.at* ⟿ *31 rooms* ⟲ *Restaurant, minibars, Internet, parking (fee)* ⊟ *AE, DC, MC, V* � *BP.*

$$–$$$ 🏨 **Rosenvilla.** A haven of peace and tranquillity, this upscale bed-and-breakfast is across the Salzach River from the Altstadt. Through an arbored garden gate, you enter the pretty suburban villa. Guest rooms, all designed with taste, are a seductive mixture of contemporary, French Empire, and Biedermeier accents, with pretty fabrics and lots of light. Some have balconies overlooking the soothing feng shui garden with its expanse of velvet green lawn, tiled pathways, and a little pond with ducks. A special three-day offer includes dinner at the owners' top-ranked restaurant, the important Pfefferschiff, which is a great value. The Rosenvilla is a 15-minute walk from the center, or you can take Bus 7, which normally runs every 10 minutes. ⊠ *Höfelgasse 4, A–5020* ☎ *0662/ 621765* 🖷 *0662/6252308* ⊕ *www.rosenvilla.sbg.at* ⟿ *14 rooms* ⟲ *Free parking; no a/c* ⊟ *AE, DC, MC, V* � *BP.*

$$ 🏨 **Amadeus.** There isn't much here to clue you into why the hotel has adopted Mozart's second name, but dig a bit. You'll learn that this 500-year-old, rather ramshackle-y yet charming house is not far from the St. Sebastian church and cemetery, where many members of his family are booked for an eternal stay. The hotel site was once home to one of Salzburg's communal baths. Back in Wolfgang's time, there was no running water in houses, so travelers—especially those arriving through the nearby Linz Gate—would immediately repair to this official bath after their long trip along dusty roads. Today, travelers still make a bee-line here. The guest rooms are each decorated differently, with several featuring charming wood armoires and beds, others in a calm and modern fashion. Downstairs, greet the day in one of the cutest breakfast nooks in Salzburg, festively done up in alpine red, white, and green (the large breakfast buffet is included in the room rate as well as afternoon coffee and tea). But if you have a problem with Salzburg's incessantly ringing church bells, beware—there is a church next door and its bell goes off every quarter hour. It stops at 11 PM but will prove a rather loud alarm clock at 5 AM. ☒ *Linzergasse 43–45, A–5020* ☏ *0662/871401* 🖷 *0662/876163–7* ⊕ *www.hotelamadeus.at* 🛏 *23 rooms* ♨ *No a/c* 🖃 *AE, DC, MC, V* ⦿ *BP.*

★ **$$** 🏨 **Gersberg Alm.** A picture-perfect Alpine chalet on the lofty perch of the Gersberg high above Salzburg, this Romantic Hotel is less than 15 minutes by car from the center of the city. Inside it has all the warmth and rustic coziness you would expect in a country house; indeed, it originally was a 19th-century farmhouse. Guest rooms are pleasantly decorated with contemporary furniture and have wooden balconies overlooking the mountain scenery. The house restaurant is excellent—top choices include ravioli stuffed with spinach in a tomato-butter sauce, or lightly fried pike perch in a tomato-olive crust with pesto spaghetti. Be sure to try the warm apricot fritters for dessert. The wine list has an outstanding selection of Austrian wines. ☒ *Gersberg 37, A–5020* ☏ *0662/641257* 🖷 *0662/ 644248* ⊕ *www.gersbergalm.at* 🛏 *43 rooms* ♨ *Restaurant, minibars, pool, sauna, free parking; no a/c* 🖃 *AE, DC, MC, V* ⦿ *BP.*

$$ 🏨 **Kasererbräu.** Standing on the site of an ancient Roman temple and just a few blocks from Salzburg's grand cathedral, this hotel offers a variety of tastes in design, resulting in a compatible mixture of folkloric kitsch and sleek elegance. The public rooms are decorated with antiques and Oriental carpets; some of the guest rooms have sleigh beds or pretty carved and handpainted headboards, although others are more plainly decorated. Apart from the friendly staff, the hotel has two big advantages: set in the Old City, it's close to everything and has pleasant sauna and steam-bath facilities included in the price. ☒ *Kaigasse 33, A–5020* ☏ *0662/842445–0* 🖷 *0662/84244551* ⊕ *www.kasererbraeu.at* 🛏 *43 rooms* ♨ *Sauna, Internet, parking (fee); no a/c* 🖃 *AE, DC, MC, V* ☾ *Closed early Feb.–mid-Mar.* ⦿ *BP.*

$$ 🏨 **NH Salzburg.** Although a modern construction, this is a very pretty building, with Art Nouveau awnings, Secession-style sash windows, and white stone trim. Inside all is sleek and comfy. The location is nice—you're only around the corner from the shopping street leading to the Salzach river or five minutes away from the beautiful Mirabell Gardens. There is a rich buffet-style breakfast and the restaurant has a garden terrace. ☒ *Franz-Josef-Strasse 26, A–5020* ☏ *0662/8820410* 🖷 *0662/ 874240* ⊕ *www.nh-hotels.com* 🛏 *140 rooms* ♨ *Restaurant, bar, garage, Internet; no a/c* 🖃 *AE, DC, MC, V* ⦿ *BP.*

$$ 🏨 **Neutor.** Only a two-minute walk from the Old City and next to the historic tunnel that plows through the Mönchsberg, this modern but classy option is divided between two buildings on opposite sides of the street. The decor is bright and shiny—a real blessing on a gray, rainy day—and all rooms are equipped with modern technology. Children ages six and under are free, from 7–12 they get a 50% reduction for the third bed in the parent's room. ☒ *Neutorstrasse 8, A–5020* ☏ *0662/844154–0*

🏨 *0662/84415416* ⊕ *www.schwaerzler-hotels.com* 🛏 *89 rooms* ♨ *Restaurant, bar, parking; no a/c* 🖻 *AE, DC, MC, V* 🍴 *BP.*

$$ 🏨 **Pension Wolf.** The embodiment of Austrian gemütlichkeit, just off Mozartplatz, the small, family-owned, in-the-center-of-everything Wolf offers spotlessly clean and cozy rooms in a rustic 1429 building. Rooms are idiosyncratically arranged on several upper floors, connected by narrow, winding stairs, and are decorated with a pleasing Salzburg mix of rag rugs and rural furniture. This is very popular so be sure to book far in advance. ⊠ *Kaigasse 7, A–5020* 🏨 *0662/843453–0* 🏨 *0662/842423–4* ⊕ *www.hotelwolf.com* 🛏 *12 rooms* ♨ *Sauna, parking (fee); no a/c* 🖻 *AE* ⊘ *Closed early Feb.–early Mar.* 🍴 *BP.*

$$ 🏨 **Stadtkrug.** Snuggled under the monument-studded Kapuzinerberg and a two-minute walk from the bridge leading to the center of the Altstadt, the Stadtkrug (dated 1353) hits an idyllic, romantic, and quiet vibe, thanks to its mountainside setting. A traditional-style wrought-iron sign greets you, the lobby tinkles with chandeliers, and the main floor restaurant is your archetypal, white, classic, vaulted Salzburg sanctorum. Upstairs, you can find a charming atmosphere, even if some of the rustic furnished rooms are tiny. Head up to the roof to enjoy a restaurant that is terraced into the mountainside and set with statues, potted begonias, echoes of Italy, and lovely views. ⊠ *Linzergasse 20, A–5020* 🏨 *0662/873545–0* 🏨 *0662/87353454* ⊕ *www.stadtkrug.at* 🛏 *34 rooms* ♨ *2 restaurants; no a/c* 🖻 *AE, DC, MC, V* 🍴 *BP.*

$$ 🏨 **Weisse Taube.** In the heart of the pedestrian-area of the Altstadt, the centuries-old "White Dove" is around the corner from Mozartplatz, the Residenz and a block from the cathedral. Comfortably renovated into a hotel—now family-run for four generations—this 14th-century Bürgerhaus (citizen's house) has been traditionally restored, but some time-burnished touches remains: uneven floors, ancient stone archways, and wood-beam ceilings. Guest rooms are simply furnished, with dark-wood accents. Several no-smoking rooms are available, and the main section of the breakfast room is also no-smoking. The staff is most friendly. ⊠ *Kaigasse 9, A–5020* 🏨 *0662/842404* 🏨 *0662/841783* ⊕ *www.weissetaube.at* 🛏 *33 rooms* ♨ *Bar, Internet, parking (fee), no-smoking rooms; no a/c* 🖻 *AE, DC, MC, V* ⊘ *Closed 2 wks in Jan.* 🍴 *BP.*

★ $$ 🏨 **Wolf-Dietrich.** Guest rooms in this small, family-owned hotel across the river from the Altstadt are elegantly decorated (some with Laura Ashley fabrics) and have extra amenities, such as VCRs (they stock *The Sound of Music*) and attractive sitting areas. Those in the back look out over the looming Gaisberg and the cemetery of St. Sebastian. The staff is warm and helpful. ⊠ *Wolf-Dietrich-Strasse 7, A–5020* 🏨 *0662/871275* 🏨 *0662/882320* ⊕ *www.salzburg-hotel.at* 🛏 *32 rooms* ♨ *Restaurant, indoor pool, Internet, parking (fee); no a/c* 🖻 *AE, DC, MC, V* 🍴 *BP.*

$ 🏨 **Cordial Theaterhotel.** Music lovers will enjoy studying the myriad production posters and photographs of famous artists that festoon the lobby here. Part of a classy chain, this is a modern option, with very comfy guest rooms. The location is about a 10-minute walk from the city center, as are the auditoriums on both sides of the Salzach River. The room rate includes the buffet-breakfast. ⊠ *Schallmooser Hauptstrasse 13, A–5020* 🏨 *0662/881681–0* 🏨 *0662/88168692* ⊕ *www.*

theaterhotel-salzburg.at ↘ *58 rooms with shower, 10 apartments with bath* ∆ *Bar, café, sauna, solarium; no a/c* ⊟ *AE, DC, MC, V* ⏀ *BP.*

¢–$ ▦ **Am Dom.** Tucked away on a tiny street near Residenzplatz, this small pension in a 14th-century building offers simply furnished, rustic-style rooms, some with oak-beamed ceilings. Note the beautiful hand-carved Renaissance reception desk. The selling point here is the great location in the heart of the Altstadt. ⊠ *Goldgasse 17, A–5020* ☏ *0662/842765* 🖶 *0662/842765–55* ⊕ *www.amdom.at* ↘ *15 rooms* ∆ *No a/c, no room TVs* ⊟ *AE, DC, MC, V* ⏀ *Closed 2 wks in Feb.* ⏀ *BP.*

¢   ▦ **Haus Kernstock.** This modest Alpine chalet near the airport is in a pretty spot at the end of a cul-de-sac. Rooms have a cheerful, homespun touch, and the ample breakfast headlines homemade jams. Frau Kernstock has two bikes that she lends for exploring the countryside, and she'll also meet you at the bus stop if you let her know in advance. From the city, take Bus 27, Kugelhof stop; from train station, Bus 2, Karolingerstrasse stop. ⊠ *Karolingerstrasse 29, A–5020* ☏ *0662/827469* 🖶 *0662/827469* ⊕ *www.salzburgerland.com/kernstock* ↘ *5 rooms* ∆ *Free parking; no a/c* ⊟ *MC, V* ⏀ *BP.*

¢   ▦ **Schwarzes Rössl.** Once a favorite with Salzburg regulars, this traditional Gasthof now serves as student quarters for most of the year but is well worth booking when available. Rooms are fresh and immaculate, if not charming, and the location is excellent—close to the nighttime action. ⊠ *Priesterhausgasse 6, A–5020* ☏ *0662/874426* 🖶 *01/401-76–20* ↘ *51 rooms, 4 with bath* ∆ *No a/c* ⊟ *AE, DC, MC, V* ⏀ *Closed Oct.–June* ⏀ *BP.*

NIGHTLIFE & THE ARTS

The Arts

The Salzburg Music Festival

Any office of the Salzburg Tourist Office and most hotel concierge desks can provide schedules for all the arts performances held year-round in Salzburg, and you can find listings in the daily newspaper, *Salzburger Nachrichten.* The biggest event on the calendar—as it has been since it was first organized by composer Richard Strauss, producer Max Reinhardt, and playwright Hugo von Hofmmansthal in 1920—is the world-famous **Salzburger Festspiele** (⊠ Hofstallgasse 1, A–5020 ☏ 0662/8045–500 for summer festival, 0662/8045–361 for Easter festival 🖶 0662/8045–555 for summer festival, 0662/8045–790 for Easter festival ⊕ www.salzburgfestival.at). This is usually scheduled for the last week of July through the end of August; the actual dates for 2005 are July 25 through August 31; the dates for 2006, the Mozart Year, should correspond approximately. In addition, the festival also presents two other major annual events: the Easter Festival (early April), and the Pentecost Baroque Festival (late May).

FodorsChoice
★

The most star-studded events—featuring the top opera stars and conductors such as Riccardo Muti, Claudio Abbado, and Nikolaus Harnoncourt—have tickets ranging from €22 to €340; for this glamorous events, first-nighters still pull out all the stops—summer furs, Dior dresses, and white ties stud the more expensive sections of the theaters. Other performances can run from €8 to €190, with still lesser prices on tap for events outside the main festival halls, the **Grosses Festspiel-haus** (Great Festival Hall) and the **Haus für Mozart** (House for Mozart, a new renovation of the former Small Festival Hall), located shoulder to shoulder on the grand promenade of Hofstallgasse. The whole city gets into the swing and their are glittering concerts and operas performed at many other theaters in the city. You can catch Mozart concertos in the 18th-century splendor of two magnificent state rooms the composer himself once conducted in: the Rittersaal of the Residenz and the Marble Hall of the Mirabell Palace. Delightful Mozart productions are offered by the Salzburger Marionetten Theater. In addition, many important concerts are offered in the two auditoria of the Mozarteum.

Note that you *must* order as early as possible; therefore, make your decisions as soon as the program comes out at the end of every year—many major performances are sold out two or three months in advance, as hordes descend on the city to enjoy staged opera spectacles, symphonic concerts by the Vienna Philharmonic and other great troupes, recitals, church oratorios, and special evenings at the Mozarteum year after year. Tickets can be purchased directly at the box office, at your hotel, or, most conveniently, at the festival Web site listed above. Next to the main tourist office is a box office where you can get tickets for Great Festival Hall concerts Monday through Friday, 8 AM to 6 PM: **Salzburger Kulturvereinigung** (⊠ Waagplatz 1A ☎ 0662/845346). The following agencies also sell tickets: **Salzburg Ticket Service** (⊠ Mozartplatz 5 ☎ 0662/840310 🖷 0662/842476). **Polzer** (⊠ Residenzplatz 3 ☎ 0662/846500 🖷 0662/840150). **American Express** (⊠ Mozartplatz 5 ☎ 0662/8080-0 🖷 0662/8080-9).

Music

There is no shortage of concerts in this most musical of cities. Customarily, the Salzburg Festival headlines the Vienna Philharmonic, but other orchestras can be expected to take leading roles as well. Year-round, there are also the Palace-Residenz Concerts, the Fortress Concerts, while in the summer, there are Mozart Serenades in the Gothic Room at St. Blase's Church. In addition, there are the Easter Festival, the Pentecost Baroque Festival, Mozart Week (late January), and the Salzburg Cultural Days (October). Mozart Week is always special; in recent seasons, Nikolaus Harnoncourt, Zubin Mehta, and Sir Charles Mackerras have conducted the Vienna Philharmonic, while Sir Neville Marriner, Daniel Harding, and Sir Roger Norrington were in charge with other orchestras.

Fodor'sChoice ★ The **Salzburger Schlosskonzerte** (⊠ Theatergasse 2 ☎ 0662/848586 ⊕ www.salzburger.schlosskonzerte.at 🖘 €26–€35) presents concerts in the palatial **Residenz** on Residenzplatz as well as at the Mirabell Palace. In the Residenz, recitals are performed in the magnficent Rittersaal and the Konferenzzimmer (Conference Room), where Mozart premiered some of his works. The grand courtyard sometimes hosts operas put on by the Summer Festival. Over at the **Mirabell Palace,** where Mozart also performed, recitals are presented in the legendary Marmorsaal (Marble Hall).

The **Salzburger Festungskonzerte** (⊠ Fortress Hohensalzburg ☎ 0662/
825858 ⊕ www.mozartfestival.at ⌖ €29–€36) are presented in the grand
Prince's Chamber at Festung Hohensalzburg. Concerts often include works
by Mozart (you can't hear *Eine kleine Nachtmusik* too often, can you?).

Organizer of the important Mozart Week held every January, the **Mozarteum** (⊠ Schwarzstrasse 26 ☎ 0662/88940–21 ⊕ www.mozarteum.at)
center is generally open to scholars only. However, thousands flock
here for its packed, year-around calendar of important concerts. The two
main concert rooms are in the main facility on Schwarzstrasse. Located
at Mirabellplatz 1, the Mozarteum's new building, in construction until
2006, will include the Great Studio and the Leopold-Mozart-Hall.

For live folk music and jazz, check out the **Salzburger Altstadt Keller**
(⊠ Rudolfskai 26 ☎ 0662/849688). The **Rockhaus** (⊠ Schallmooser
Hauptstrasse 46 ☎ 0662/884914) has live music for the younger gen-
eration on Monday nights in a 400-year-old cellar.

Opera

Fodor'sChoice
★ The great opera event of the year is, of course, the **Salzburger Festspiele**
(⊠ Hofstallgasse 1, A–5020 Salzburg ☎ 0662/8045–500 🖷 0662/
8045–555 ⊕ www.salzburgfestival.at). The Salzburg Festival annually
mounts a full calendar of operas (for example, just half of the schedule
for 2004 included Henry Purcell's *King Arthur,* Mozart's *Die Entführung
aus dem Serail (The Abduction from the Seraglio),* and *Così fan tutte,*
Richard Strauss's *Der Rosenkavalier,* Erich Wolfgang Korngold's *Die tote
Stadt (The Dead City),* and Vincenzo Bellini's *I Capuleti e i Montecchi*
(his version of Romeo and Juliet). These performances are held in the
Grosses Festspielhaus (Great Festival Hall), the Haus für Mozart (House
for Mozart), the Landestheater, the Felsenreitschule, the Mozarteum, and
numerous smaller venues, where lieder recitals and chamber works pre-
dominate. Prices range from €8 to €340.

The season at the **Landestheater** (⊠ Schwarzstrasse 22 ☎ 0662/871512–21
🖷 0662/871512–70 ⊕ www.theater.co.at) runs from September to June.
New productions in 2005 will include Verdi's *Falstaff,* Franz Lehár's *Die
lustige Witwe (The Merry Widow),* Andrew Lloyd Webber's *Jesus Christ
Superstar,* and Britten's *The Turn of the Screw.* You may place ticket orders by telephone Monday and Saturday 10–2, Tuesday–Friday 10–5.

Fodor'sChoice
★ The delightful, acclaimed **Salzburger Marionettentheater** (⊠ Schwarzstrasse
24 ☎ 0662/872406–0 🖷 0662/882141) is also devoted to opera, with a
particularly renowned production of *Così fan tutte* to its credit, and gives
performances during the first week of January, during Mozart Week (late
January), from May through September, and December 25 through January 6. Tickets usually range from €18 to €35. The box office is open
Monday through Saturday 9–1 and two hours before the performance.

Theater

The **Jedermann** ("Everyman") morality play, written by Hugo von Hofmannsthal, is famously performed annually (in German) in the forecourt
of the **city cathedral** (⌂ Salzburger Festspiele, Postfach 140 ☎ 0662/
8045–500 🖷 0662/8045–555 ⊕ www.salzburgfestival.at). This is a

spine-tingling presentation and few of the thousands packing the plaza are not moved at the moment at the height of the banquet when the voice of Death—"Jedermann—Jedermann—Jed-er-*mann*"—is heard from the Franziskanerkirche tower, then followed with echoes of voices from other steeples and from atop the Fortress Hohensalzburg. As the sun sets, the doors of the great cathedral hover open and the sounds of its organ announce the salvation of Everyman's soul. Unforgettable.

Nightlife

Bars/Nightclubs

Bazillus (⊠ Imbergstrasse 2a ☎ 0662/871631) is small, scruffy, and makeshift, but very cool; it's open daily 7 PM–4 AM. **Chez Roland** (⊠ Giselakai 15 ☎ 0662/874335) is the haunt of "loden-preppies," or the wealthy and stylish young, and is open Monday–Saturday 6 PM–2 AM. **Saitensprung** (⊠ Steingasse 11 ☎ 0662/881377), which means "having someone on the side," is an elegant cocktail bar with food, open daily 9 PM–4 AM. **Shamrock Irish Pub** (⊠ Rudolfskai 12 ☎ 0662/841610) attracts the young crowd and is always packed. Guinness is on tap. One of Salzburg's most popular bars is **Vis à Vis** (⊠ Judeng. 13 ☎ 0662/841290), which resembles a '60s nightclub with its cavelike atmosphere; it's open daily 7 PM–3 AM.

Casino

Salzburg's **Casino** (☎ 0662/854455 📠 0662/854455–16 ⊕ www.casino-salzburg.at) is a bit out of the center in the posh Schloss Klessheim. Admission is free. It's open daily from 3 PM to 3 AM (except November 1 and 2 and December 24). Men must wear a jacket and tie. Remember to take your passport. Have your hotel check with the casino about its free shuttle bus, which will take you to the casino and return you to town.

Discos

The local disco scene has become more volatile, so check with the tourist office or your hotel concierge for the current best attractions. **Jexx** (⊠ Gstättengasse 7 ☎ 0662/844181) is large, has a youngish crowd, and goes for the American market; it's open daily 9 PM–3 AM.

SHOPPING

For a small city, Salzburg has a wide spectrum of stores. The specialties are traditional clothing, like lederhosen and loden coats, jewelry, glassware, handicrafts, confectionery, dolls in native costume, Christmas decorations, sports equipment, and silk flowers. A *Gewürzsträussl* is a bundle of whole spices bunched and arranged to look like a bouquet of flowers (try the markets on Universitätsplatz). This old tradition goes back to the time when only a few rooms could be heated and, therefore, humans and their farm animals would often cohabitate on the coldest days. You can imagine how lovely the aromas must have been—so this spicy room-freshener was invented. At Christmas there is a special Advent market on the Domplatz offering regional decorations, held from the week before the first Advent-Sunday until

December 24, daily from 9 AM to 8 PM. Stores are generally open week-days 9–6 and Saturday 9–5. Many stores stay open until 5 on the first Saturday of the month and on Saturday during the festival and before Christmas. Some supermarkets stay open until 7:30 on Thursday or Friday. Only shops in the railway station, the airport, and near the general hospital are open on Sunday.

Shopping Streets

The most fashionable specialty stores and gift shops are to be found along Getreidegasse and Judengasse and around Residenzplatz. Linzergasse, across the river, is less crowded and good for more practical items. There are also interesting antiques shops and jewelry workshops in the medieval buildings along Steingasse and on Goldgasse.

Specialty Stores

Antiques

Ilse Guggenberger (⊠ Brodgasse 11 ☎ 0662/843184) is the place to browse for original Austrian country antiques. **Marianne Reuter** (⊠ Gstättengasse 9 ☎ 0662/842136) offers a fine selection of porcelain and 18th-century furniture. **Schöppl** (⊠ Gstättengasse 5 ☎ 0662/842154) has old desks, hutches, and some jewelry. For an amazing assortment of secondhand curiosities, try **Trödlerstube** (⊠ Linzergasse 50 ☎ 0662/871453).

Internationale Messe für Kunst und Antiquitäten (⊠ Residenzplatz 1 ☎ 0662/8042–2690) is the annual antiques fair that takes place from Palm Sunday to Easter Monday in the state rooms of Salzburg's Residenz.

Confectionery

If you're looking for the kind of *Mozartkugeln* (chocolate marzipan confections) you can't buy at home, try the store that claims to have invented in 1890 them: **Konditorei Fürst** (⊠ Brodgasse 13 ☎ 0662/843759–0); that's where they are still produced by hand after the original recipe this family never gave away. **Konditorei Schatz** (⊠ Getreidegasse 3, Schatz passageway ☎ 0662/842792) is a top mecca for Mozartkugeln and other delectable goodies.

Crafts

Fritz Kreis (⊠ Sigmund-Haffner-Gasse 14 ☎ 0662/841768) sells ceramics, wood carvings, handmade glass objects, and so on. **Salzburger Heimatwerk** (⊠ Residenzplatz 9 ☎ 0662/844110–0) has clothing, fabrics, ceramics, and local handicrafts at good prices. **Christmas in Salzburg** (⊠ Judengasse 10 ☎ 0662/846784) has rooms of gorgeous Christmas-tree decorations, some hand-painted and hand-carved. **Gehmacher** (⊠ Alter Markt 2 ☎ 0662/845506–0) offers whimsical home-decoration items.

Galleries

Salzburg is a good place to buy modern paintings, and there are several galleries on Sigmund-Haffner-Gasse. One of the best known, which also has an exhibition gallery plus a tiny coffee bar, is **Galerie Welz** (⊠ Sigmund-Haffner-Gasse 16 ☎ 0662/841771–0).

Jewelry

For exquisite costume jewelry and antique pieces, go to **Anton Koppenwallner** (✉ Klampferergasse 2 ☎ 0662/841298–0). Another choice for the same kind of items is **Paul Koppenwallner** (✉ Alter Markt 7 ☎ 0662/842617 ✉ Universitätsplatz 4 ☎ 0662/841449). **Franz Moltner** (✉ Getreidegasse 14 ☎ 0662/348116) offers lovely imitation Fabergé eggs that can be attached to a necklace. Explore the **Schmuckpassage** (Jeweler's Passageway), which joins buildings between Universitätsplatz and Getreidegasse. Behind the self-service restaurant in the gardens of the Sternbräu between Getreidegasse and Griesgasse is **Martin Steiner** (☎ 0662/840402), a top address for charms.

Men's Clothing

Adriano (✉ Schallmooser Hauptstrasse 8 ☎ 0662/841787) is a men's outfitter that remains a cut above the rest. **Resmann M Exclusiv** (✉ Getreidegasse 25 ☎ 0662/843214) allows the male peacock to strut his stuff.

Traditional Clothing

Dschulnigg (✉ Griesgasse 8, at Münzgasse ☎ 0662/842376–0) is a favorite among Salzburgers for lederhosen, dirndls, and *Trachten*, the typical Austrian costume with white blouse, print skirt, and apron. For a wide selection of leather goods, some made to order, try **Jahn-Markl** (✉ Residenzplatz 3 ☎ 0662/842610). **Lanz** (✉ Schwarzstrasse 4 ☎ 0662/874272) sells a good selection of long dirndls, silk costumes, and loden coats. **Madl am Grünmarkt** (✉ Universitätsplatz 12 ☎ 0662/845457) has more flair and elegance in its traditional designs.

Women's Clothing

If dirndls are not your style, try **Adriano** (✉ Schallmooser Hauptstrasse 8 ☎ 0662/871787). **Resmann Couture** (✉ Rudolfskai 6 ☎ 0662/841213–0) can whip up a gown for your special night at the opera.

SALZBURG A TO Z

To research prices, get advice from other travelers, and book travel arrangements, visit www.fodors.com.

AIR TRAVEL TO & FROM SALZBURG

There are direct flights from London and other European cities to Salzburg, but not from the United States. Americans can fly to Munich and take the 90-minute train ride to Salzburg.

AIRPORTS & TRANSFERS

Salzburg Airport, 4 km (2½ mi) west of the city center, is Austria's second-largest international airport.

🛈 Airport Information **Salzburg Airport** ✉ Innsbrucker Bundesstrasse 96 ☎ 0662/8580.

TRANSFERS   If you fly to Munich, you can take the 90-minute train ride to Salzburg. Alternatively, you can take a transfer bus from or to the Munich airport: contact Salzburger Mietwagenservice for details. Taxis are the easiest way to get downtown from the Salzburg airport; the ride costs around

€13–€14 and takes about 20 minutes. City Bus No. 2, which makes a stop by the airport every 15 minutes, runs down to Salzburg's train station (about 20 minutes), where you can change to Bus No. 3 or 5 for the city center.

🚕 Taxis & Shuttles **Salzburger Mietwagenservice** ✉ Ignaz-Harrer-Strasse 79a ☎ 0622/8161-0 🖷 0622/436324.

BIKE TRAVEL

Salzburg is fast developing a network of bike paths as part of its effort to reduce car traffic in the city. A detailed bicycle map with suggested tours (AS89) will help you get around. You can rent a bike by the day or the week from Shake & Snack. Also check Veloclub Salzburger Fahrradclub. It's best to call and reserve in advance; you will need to leave your passport or a deposit.

Just in time for the Mozart Year, a new **Mozart Radweg** (bicycle route) has been created by the Salzburg Land Tourist Office together with some travel agents so cyclists and music-lovers can follow his path around Salzburg and through the lake districts of Austria and Bavaria. All told, the itinerary can take 13 days and runs 410 km (255 mi), but shorter versions are custom-tailored by various outfitters in the region. For instance, there is an eight-day tour heading west to Bavaria, arranged by Austria Radreisen (✉ Joseph-Haydn-Strasse 8, A-4780 Schärding ☎ 07712/5511–0 ⊕ www.austria-radreisen.at). Heading east for five days is a planned itinerary mapped out by Oberösterreich Touristik (✉ Freistädter Strasse 49, A-4041 Linz ☎ 0732/663024–0 ⊕ www.touristik.at ⊕ www.mozartradweg.com).

🚲 Bike Rentals **Shake & Snack** ✉ Kajetanerplatz 3–4 ☎ 0662/848168. Next to the train station is **Top Bike** ✉ Rainerstrasse/Café Intertreff ☎ 06272/4656 or 0676/476-7259. **Veloclub Salzburger Fahrradclub** ✉ Franz-Josef-Strasse 23 ☎ 0662/882-7880.

BUS TRAVEL WITHIN SALZBURG

Single tickets bought from the driver cost €1.80. Special multiple-use tickets, available at tobacconists (*Tabak-Trafik*), ticket offices, and tourist offices, are much cheaper. You can buy five single tickets for €1.60 each (not available at tourist offices), a single 24-hour ticket for €3.40.

🚌 Bus Information **Salzburger Verkehrsverbund (Main ticket office)** ✉ Schrannengasse 4 ☎ 0662/44801500.

CAR TRAVEL

The fastest routes to Salzburg are the autobahns. From Vienna (320 km [198 mi]), take A1; from Munich (150 km [93 mi]), A8 (in Germany it's also E11); from Italy, A10.

RULES OF
THE ROAD The only advantage to having a car in Salzburg is that you can get out of the city for short excursions or for cheaper accommodations. The Old City on both sides of the river is a pedestrian zone (except for taxis), and the rest of the city, with its narrow, one-way streets, is a driver's nightmare. A park-and-ride system covering the major freeway exits is being developed, and there are several underground garages throughout the city.

CONSULATES

The U.K. consulate is open weekdays 9–11:30. The U.S. consulate is open Monday, Wednesday, and Friday 9–noon.

🔳 United Kingdom ⊠ Alter Markt 4 ☎ 0662/848133 🖷 0662/845563.

🔳 United States ⊠ Alter Markt 1/3 ☎ 0662/848776 🖷 0662/849777.

EMERGENCIES

If you need a doctor or dentist, call the Ärztekammer für Salzburg. For emergency service on weekends and holidays, call the Ärzte-Bereitschaftsdienst Salzburg-Stadt. The main hospital is the St. Johannsspital-Landeskrankenanstalten, located just past the Augustinian Monastery heading out of town. For medical emergencies or an ambulance, dial 144.

In general, pharmacies are open weekdays 8–12:30 and 2:30–6, Saturday 8–noon. When they're closed, the name and location of a pharmacy that's open are posted on the door.

🔳 Doctors & Dentists **Ärztekammer für Salzburg** ⊠ Bergstrasse 4 ☎ 0662/871327–0. **Ärzte-Bereitschaftsdienst Salzburg-Stadt** ⊠ Dr.-Karl-Renner-Strasse 7 ☎ 0662/141.

🔳 Emergency Services **Ambulance** ☎ 144. **Fire** ☎ 122. **Police** ☎ 133.

🔳 Hospitals **St. Johannsspital-Landeskrankenanstalten** ⊠ Müllner Hauptstrasse 48 ☎ 0662/44820.

ENGLISH-LANGUAGE MEDIA

BOOKS Höllrigl sells some paperbacks in English.

🔳 Bookstores **Höllrigl** ⊠ Sigmund-Haffner-Gasse 10 ☎ 0662/841146.

MONEY MATTERS

CURRENCY EXCHANGE Banks are open weekdays 8:30–12:30 and 2–4:30; American Express offices weekdays, 9–5:30, Saturday, 9 to noon. You can change money at the railway station daily 7:30 AM–8:30 PM.

TOURS

Because the Old City is largely a pedestrian zone, bus tours do little more than take you past the major sights. You would do better seeing the city on foot unless your time is really limited.

BOAT TOURS For a magically different vantage point, take a round-trip boat ride along the relentlessly scenic Salzach River, departing at the Makartsteg in the Altstadt, from April until October. The boat journeys as far south as Hellbrunn Palace (depending on the water level). In June, July, and August you can also take the cruise as you enjoy a Candlelight Dinner— the real dessert is a floodlit view of Salzburg!

🔳 Fees & Schedules **Salzburger Festungskonzerte GmbH** ⊠ Anton-Adlgasser-Wegasse 22 ☎ 0662/825769–12 🖷 0662/825859 ⊕ www.salzburgschifffahrt.at.

BUS TOURS American Express is one of several companies that offer day bus trips from Vienna to Salzburg. Vienna Sightseeing Tours runs one-day bus trips in winter on Tuesday and Saturday to Salzburg from Vienna, and in summer on Tuesday, Thursday, and weekends. The €100 fare includes a tour of the city, but not lunch. Cityrama Sightseeing offers a schedule similar to Vienna Sightseeing Tours.

Several local companies conduct 1½- to 2-hour city tours. The desk clerks at most hotels will book for you and arrange hotel pickup. Depending on the number of people, the tour will be in either a bus or a minibus; if it's the former, a short walking tour is included, since large buses can't enter the Old City. Tours briefly cover the major sights in Salzburg, including Mozart's Birthplace, the festival halls, the major squares, the churches, and the palaces at Hellbrunn and Leopoldskron. Bob's Special Tours is well known to American visitors—the company offers a 10% discount to Fodor's readers who book directly with them without help from their hotel. Salzburg Panorama Tours and Albus/Salzburg Sightseeing Tours offer similar tours.

🛈 Fees & Schedules **Albus/Salzburg Sightseeing Tours** ✉ Am Mirabellplatz 2, Salzburg ☎ 0662/881616 🖷 0662/878776 ⊕ www.welcome-salzburg.at. **American Express** ✉ Kärntnerstrasse 21–23, A-1010 Vienna ☎ 01/515-400 🖷 01/515-4070. **Bob's Special Tours** ✉ Rudolfskai 38, Salzburg ☎ 0662/849511-0 🖷 0662/849512. **Cityrama Sightseeing** ✉ Börsegasse 1, A-1010 Vienna ☎ 01/534-130 🖷 01/534-13-16. **Salzburg Panorama Tours** ✉ Schrannengasse 2/2, Salzburg ☎ 0662/883211-0 🖷 0662/871618 ⊕ www.panoramatours.com. **Vienna Sightseeing Tours** ✉ Stelzhammergasse 4/11, A-1030 Vienna ☎ 01/712-4683-0 🖷 01/714-1141.

SPECIAL-   The *Sound of Music* tour—for the complete scoop, see this chapter's
INTEREST TOURS   Close-Up box—has been a staple of visits to Salzburg for the past 20 years and is still a special experience. All tour operators conduct one. The bus company actually featured in the film, Albus/Salzburg Sightseeing Tours offers a four-hour bus tour departing daily, which includes such sights as Anif Castle, Mondsee Church, and the little summer house in the gardens of Hellbrunn. Some travelers say the most personal approach to Maria's Salzburg is found with Bob's Special Tours. One of the most popular is the tour offered by Salzburg Panorama (for contact information for this bus line, *see* Bus Tours, *above*).

WALKING TOURS   The tourist office's folder "Salzburg—The Art of Taking It All In at a Glance" describes a self-guided one-day walking tour that's marked on a map. Salzburg's official licensed guides offer a one-hour walking tour through the Old City every day at 12:15, which starts in front of the Information Mozartplatz (€8—owners of the Salzburg Card get a reduced fee).

TAXIS

There are taxi stands all over the city; for a radio cab, call the number listed below. Taxi fares start at €3, Sunday and holidays €3.50; a special offer is the bus-taxi running between 11:30 and 1:30 at night, which has routes through the city and into the neighboring villages—the fare is €3.70. Limousines can be hired for €200 to €245 per hour (three-hour minimum) from Salzburg Panorama Tours. They also offer a private "Sound of Music" limousine tour for €265.

🛈 Taxi Information **Radio Cab** ☎0662/8111. **Salzburg Panorama Tours** ☎0662/883211-0 🖷 0662/871628 ⊕ www.panoramatours.com.

TRAIN TRAVEL

You can get to Salzburg by rail from most European cities, arriving at Salzburg Hauptbahnhof, a 20-minute walk from the center of town in the direction of Mirabellplatz. A taxi to the center of town should take about 10 minutes and cost €9. Train information is available through the number listed below; don't be put off by the recorded message in German—eventually, you will be put through to a real person who should be able to speak English. You can buy tickets at any travel agency or at the station. The bus station and the suburban railroad station are at the square in front.

Train Information **Salzburg Hauptbahnhof** ⊠ Südtirolerplatz ☎ 05/1717.

TRANSPORTATION AROUND SALZBURG

The Old City, composed of several interconnecting squares and narrow streets, is best seen on foot. An excellent bus service covers the rest of the city. A tourist map (available from tourist offices in Mozartplatz and the train station) shows all bus routes and stops; there's also a color-coded graphic public-transport-network map, so you should have no problem getting around. Virtually all buses and trolleybuses (O-Bus) run via Mirabellplatz and/or Hanuschplatz.

One of the most delightful ways to tour Salzburg is by horse-drawn carriage. Most of Salzburg's fiakers are stationed in Residenzplatz, and cost €33 per fiaker (up to 4 people) for 20 minutes, €66 for 50 minutes. During the Christmas season, large, decorated horse-drawn carts take people around the Christmas markets.

Fiakers ☎ 0662/844772.

TRAVEL AGENCIES

American Express is next to the tourist office at Mozartplatz 5–7. Columbus is near the Mönchsberg in the Old City.

Local Agent Referrals **American Express** ☎ 0662/8080-0 🖷 0662/8080-9. **Columbus** ⊠ Griesgasse 2 ☎ 0662/842755-0 🖷 0662/842755-5.

VISITOR INFORMATION

The Salzburg City Tourist Office handles written and telephone requests for information. You can get maps, brochures, and information in person from Information Mozartplatz in the center of the Old City. The railway station also has a tourist office.

Don't forget to consider purchasing the **Salzburg Card.** SalzburgKarten are good for 24, 48, or 72 hours at €19–€34, respectively, and allow no-charge entry to most museums and sights, use of public transport, and special discount offers. Children under 15 pay half.

All the major highways into town have their own well-marked information centers. The Salzburg-Mitte center is open April–October, daily 9–7, and November–March, Monday–Saturday 11–5; the Salzburg-Süd, April–October, daily 9–7; and the Salzburg-Nord Kasern service facility is open June–mid-September, daily 9–7.

Tourist Information **Information Mozartplatz** ⊠ Mozartplatz 5. **Railway Station tourist office** ⊠ Platform 2A ☎ 0662/88987-330. **Salzburg City Tourist Office** ⊠ Auerspergstrasse 6, A–5024 Salzburg ☎ 0662/88987-0 🖷 0662/88987-435 ⊕ www.salzburginfo.at. **Salzburg-Süd** ⊠ Park & Ride-Parkplatz, Alpensiedlung-Süd, Alpenstrasse 67 ☎ 0662/88987-360.

UNDERSTANDING VIENNA & SALZBURG

DO I HEAR A WALTZ?

AN OFT-TOLD STORY CONCERNS an airline pilot whose prelanding announcement advised, "Ladies and gentlemen, we are on the final approach to Vienna Airport. Please make sure your seat belts are fastened, please refrain from smoking until you are outside the terminal, and please set your watches back one hundred years." Apocryphal or not, the pilot's observation suggests the allure of a country where visitors can sense something of what Europe was like before the pulse of the 20th century quickened to a beat that would have dizzied our great-grandmothers. Today's Austria—and in particular its capital, Vienna—reminds many of a formerly fat man who is now at least as gaunt as most people but still allows himself a lot of room and expects doors to open wide when he goes through them. After losing two world wars and surviving amputation, annexation, and occupation, a nation that once ruled Europe now endures as a somewhat balkanized republic but endures as one of the most popular tourist meccas in the world.

Julie Andrews may wish it wasn't so, but *The Sound of Music* hangs on as one of the most beloved films of all time and, in recent years, the annual New Year's Day Musikverein concerts televised from Vienna have attracted millions of equally devoted fans. Jaded New Yorkers are lining up for a taste of gemütlich-tinged elegance at superchef David Bouley's Danube restaurant and Ronald Lauder's Neue Galerie of Austrian art on upper 5th Avenue's Museum Mile. The year of 2003 saw the 100 anniversary of Wiener Werkstätte, whose decorative arts masterworks by Adolf Loos, Otto Wagner, Josef Hoffman, and Koloman Moser enchant collectors and connoisseurs everywhere. And with the 2006 Mozart Year, we will all be touched by the magic of the Mozart baton. These and other manifestations remind us of the large—and apparently growing—public still entranced by the champagne-splashed whirl of once-Imperial Austria. But despite the spell cast by Austria's never-never land, with its castles, turrets, swords, gold-braid, ravishing Secession School art, and clouds of whipped cream, the stop-press news is that this dowager of Old Europe is ready to straighten up and fly right, once again to lead the vanguard. Museums of contemporary art are opening across the country; Vienna's *Beisl*-bistros are getting trumped by the nouvelle novelties whipped up at Vienna hotspots (click your heels three times for Tirolian eagle garnished with three caviars); and cities everywhere are rumbling with architectural activity, from Vienna's massively renovated MuseumsQuartier to Salzburg's eye-knocking Museum fur Moderner Kunst, newly risen on the site of the fusty Café Winkler, where Julie "do-re-mi"-'d with the von Trapp brood. In many ways, it appears that Austria is taking a Giant Step Forward, virtually leapfrogging from yesterday to tomorrow.

In some sense, we should not be surprised, for Austria has always been "modern." In the purely geographic sense, the country only dates from 1918, the year in which the great and polyglot Austro-Hungarian Monarchy of the Habsburgs came to an end. Before that date, many of its millions had no consciousness of belonging to a race of "Austrians." They were simply the German-speaking peoples of the many-tongued Austro-Hungarian empire, which once reached from the black pine woods of Eastern Poland to the blue shores of the Adriatic. Those were the great times and many Austrians today just can't forget their exalted past. So, is it any wonder that History has given the Austrians a strong feeling for tradition?

Indeed, the most important clue to the Austrians is their love of the Baroque—not, of course, just its 18th-century architectural technicalities, but its spirit. When you understand this, you will not longer be a stranger in Austria. The *Barock* was the style taken up in painting, sculpture, and decoration to celebrate the Austrians' emergence from a century of tribulation—the woeful 17th-century, when the Viennese had battled invading Turks and the plague. Conquering both, the people embraced this new, flamboyant, bejeweled, and emotional import from Italy and went to town creating gilded saints and cherubs, gilt columns, painted heavens on ceilings, joyous patinated domes. From this theater, from this dream, the spirit of Austria has never really departed.

You can enter this dream at certain moments, such as those Sunday mornings from September to June when—if you've reserved months in advance—you can hear (but not see) those "voices from heaven," the Vienna Boys' Choir, sing mass in the marble-and-velvet royal chapel of the Hofburg. Lads of 8 to 13 in sailor suits, they peal out angelic notes from the topmost gallery, and you might catch a glimpse of them after mass as you cut across the Renaissance courtyard for the 10:45 performance of the Lipizzaner stallions in the Spanish Riding School around the corner. Beneath crystal chandeliers in a lofty white hall, expert riders in brown uniforms with gold buttons and black hats with gold braid put these aristocrats of the equine world through their classic paces to the minuets of Mozart and the waltzes of Strauss.

Music, like wine, takes its flavor from the soil and the season in which it grows, and the roots of Mozart's and Strauss's melodies were nourished by moments in history in which an aging civilization had reached peaks of mellowness. Nowhere but in Austria could they have composed their melodious messages, for they are Austria—her quiet lakes, her laughing streams and rushing rivers, her verdant forests, her sumptuous Baroque palaces. Somehow in Austria, everything seems to come back to music, and at nearly every bend in the road, you can see where masterpieces were committed to paper, whether it be Mozart's "Magic Flute" Cottage in Salzburg, Beethoven's Pasqualati House (where he wrote much of *Fidelio*), or the apartment of Johann Strauss the Younger on the Praterstrasse, in whose salon he composed his greatest waltzes, including "The Beautiful Blue Danube."

It is thanks to the Strausses, father and son, that the Viennese traditionally live in two countries. One is on the map. The other is the imaginary region where wine flows, love triumphs, and everything is silk-lined. This is the land of the waltz. This region of the Viennese mind is not just a shallow, sybaritic fantasy. Like Viennese music itself, it embodies a substantial premise. At its surprising best—in such creations as "Tales from the Vienna Woods" or the "Emperor's Waltz"—the waltz is perhaps the closest description of happiness ever attained in any art. Paradoxically, the music is not merry. A haze of wistfulness lies over the sunniest tunes, and their sweetness sometimes touches on melancholy. Though the dance is a swirling embrace, the music countermands sensual abandonment. It insists on grace; it remains pensive in the midst of pleasure.

In Vienna and Salzburg, there was a lot of pleasure to be had. For centuries, the Habsburg rulers maintained a tradition of fostering the arts. The implicit tenet was that beauty begets pleasure, and pleasure begets contentment. These two great imperial cities owe their splendor to the endering assumption that civic beauty is the key to civic tranquillity. Under these conditions, the whole of Austria came to be pervaded by a certain musicality—an innate, casual feeling for form and harmony. It was evident in the visual charm of the Austrian Baroque that left its mark on Austria's main cities. But a feeling for the Baroque and its later, lighter variants was by no means confined to the leading architects employed in the design of palaces. It filtered down to the humblest mason molding garlanded cherubs above the gate of an ordinary house. It guided the hand of the cabinetmaker who filled the house with the playful curves of Rococo and Biedermeier furniture. In such an ambience, the ear, too, became attuned to the refinements and delights of form, and therefore much of Austria became a natural breeding ground for musicians. A contemporary chronicler, Eduard Bauernfeld, observes that "every hole is full of musicians who play for the people. Nobody wants to eat his *Bratl* at the inn if he can't have table music to go with it." Mozart, in fact, began by composing "table music" to sooth the stomach of his first employer, Prince-Archbishop Hieronymus von Colloredo of Salzburg. No feast or celebration was complete without a special overture composed for the occasion. More than 60 piano factories flourished in 19th-century Vienna, which numbered a mere 250,000 inhabitants, and next to good looks and a dowry, musical talent was considered a girl's chief asset. Every Sunday, churches resounded with the musical settings of the Mass—"operas for the angels," as Mozart called them. Performed by choirs and orchestras of remarkable proficiency, these compositions often made divine services into public concerts.

Clearly no other city has ever been so suffused by an art as Vienna was by music. What other nations say with words, the Austrians say with music. In Paris or London, music was regarded as entertainment. Not so in Vienna. Here it was a personal necessity, an indispensable part of everyday life, shared alike by countesses as well as shopkeepers and janitors. In the crowds that thronged to hear performances of Beethoven symphonies, Haydn oratorios, or Mozart operas, burghers and artisans easily joined princes of the realm. Conversely, in the little rustic *Heurige* wine taverns tucked among the hillsides of the Vienna Woods, members of the nobility mixed quite casually with lesser folk to dance to the sweet and giddy folk tunes of the region. Music created an instant democracy of manners, and class barriers melted in the balmy atmosphere of relaxed hedonism. Is it any wonder that poets and musicians have always felt at home in Austria? The land pulses with the heartbeat of humanity. Mozart and Strauss were just two of the composers who felt that pulse and shaped it into special music that lifted Austria from its moorings on the map and fixed it to the souls of people everywhere.

BOOKS & MOVIES

Books

Gordon Brook-Shepherd's *The Austrians: A Thousand-Year Odyssey* traces the history of Austria through the postwar years. The 2,000-year history of Vienna is detailed in *The Viennese: Splendor, Twilight and Exile,* by Paul Hofmann. Alan Palmer's *Twilight of the Hapsburgs* covers the years of Emperor Franz Josef's life (1830–1916). For an intriguing portrait of Vienna in the months before and after the murder-suicide of Crown Prince Rudolf and his teenage mistress, read Frederic Morton's *A Nervous Splendor: Vienna 1888/1889. In the Shadow of Death: Living Outside the Gates of Mauthausen,* by Gordon J. Horwitz, explores what life was like for the townspeople living near Austria's largest concentration camp. *The World of Yesterday,* Stefan Zweig's haunting memoir, begins in what Zweig calls the "Golden Age of Security," the period that was shattered by the World War I. Zweig witnesses the rise of anti-Semitism, which causes him to flee Austria in the 1930s. Austria has produced many great composers. Recommended as background reading are Maynard Solomon's *Mozart: A Life* and Richard Rickett's *Music and Musicians in Vienna. Wittgenstein's Vienna,* by Allan Janik and Stephen Toulmin, tells the story of the brilliant young philosopher and his city in the waning days of the Austro-Hungarian Empire. In *Sigmund Freud,* Richard Wollheim provides a concise analysis of the man and his theories. Robert Musil's most famous work, the sprawling, unfinished, modernist novel *The Man Without Qualities,* is set in Vienna on the eve of World War I. John Irving's first novel, *Setting Free the Bears,* follows two university students as they conspire to liberate the animals at the Vienna Zoo. As for fiction, the leading figure these days is Elfriede Jelinek, whose novels include *The Piano Teacher, Lust, Women as Lovers,* and *Wonderful Times.* She explores the undercurrents of Viennese life in these startling works, including a heavy dose of sadomasochism (which was, in fact, "invented" in Vienna in Baron Leopold von Sacher-Masoch's 1870 novel, *Venus in Furs*).

Movies

Vienna and Austria have served as settings for a number of fine films. In *'38: Vienna Before the Fall* (1986), nominated for an Oscar for Best Foreign Language Film, a Gentile and a Jew fall in love just before the Nazi takeover. Postwar Vienna is the backdrop for Graham Greene's suspense classic *The Third Man* (1949), with direction by Carol Reed and zither music by Anton Karas. Ethan Hawke and Julie Delpy are strangers in Richard Linklater's *Before Sunrise* (1995); they meet on a train and impulsively decide to spend Hawke's last hours in Europe together by wandering through Vienna. *Brother of Sleep* (1995), about a musical genius who is unhappy in love, was filmed in Vorarlberg and was nominated for a Golden Globe for Best Foreign Language Film. The young Dr. Freud (Montgomery Clift) battles with the Viennese medical establishment for acceptance of his beliefs in John Huston's *Freud* (1962). In *The Seven Percent Solution* (1976), a cocaine-addicted Sherlock Holmes (Nicol Williamson) and his sidekick, Dr. Watson (Robert Duvall), team up with Sigmund Freud (Alan Arkin). Omar Sharif, Ava Gardner, James Mason and Catherine Deneuve star in *Mayerling* (1968), an account of the murder-suicide of Crown Prince Rudolf and his mistress Marie Vetsera. Rodgers and Hammerstein's *The Sound of Music* (1965) was filmed in Salzburg and the Lake District; it won Oscars for Best Director (Robert Wise) and Best Picture and is one of the most beloved films of all time.

WORDS AND PHRASES

Austrian German is not entirely the same as the German spoken in Germany. Several food names are different, as well as a few basic phrases.

Umlauts have no similar sound in English. An ä is pronounced as "eh." An äu or eu is pronounced as "oy". An ö is pronounced by making your lips like an "O" while trying to say "E" and a ü is pronounced by making your lips like a "U" and trying to say "E".

Consonants are pronounced as follows:

CH is like a hard H, almost like a soft clearing of the throat.

J is pronounced as Y.

Rs are rolled.

ß, which is written "ss" in this book, is pronouced as double S.

S is pronounced as Z.

V is pronounced as F.

W is pronounced as V.

Z is pronounced as TS.

An asterisk (*) denotes common usage in Austria.

English	German	Pronunciation
Basics		
Yes/no	Ja/nein	yah/nine
Please	Bitte	**bit**-uh
May I?	Darf ich?	darf isch?
Thank you (very much)	Danke (vielen Dank)	**dahn**-kuh (**fee**-len dahnk)
You're welcome	Bitte, gern geschehen	**bit**-uh, gairn ge**shay**-un
Excuse me	Entschuldigen Sie	ent-**shool**-di-gen zee
What? (What did you say?)	Wie, bitte?	vee, **bit**-uh?
Can you tell me?	Können Sie mir sagen?	kunnen zee meer **sah**-gen?
Do you know _____?	Wissen Sie _____?	**viss**-en zee
I'm sorry	Es tut mir leid.	es toot meer lite
Good day	Guten Tag	**goo**-ten tahk
Goodbye	Auf Wiedersehen	owf **vee**-der-zane
Good morning	Guten Morgen	**goo**-ten **mor**-gen
Good evening	Guten Abend	**goo**-ten **ah**-bend
Good night	Gute Nacht	**goo**-tuh nahkt
Mr./Mrs.	Herr/Frau	hair/frow

Miss	Fräulein	**froy**-line
Pleased to meet you	Sehr erfreut.	zair air-**froyt**
How are you?	Wie geht es Ihnen?	vee **gate** es **ee**-nen?
Very well, thanks.	Sehr gut, danke.	sair goot, **dahn**-kuh
And you?	Und Ihnen?	oont **ee**-nen?
Hi!	*Servus!	**sair**-voos

Days of the Week

Sunday	Sonntag	**zohn**-tahk
Monday	Montag	**moan**-tahk
Tuesday	Dienstag	**deens**-tahk
Wednesday	Mittwoch	**mitt**-voak
Thursday	Donnerstag	**doe**-ners-tahk
Friday	Freitag	**fry**-tahk
Saturday	Samstag	**zahm**-stahk

Useful Phrases

Do you speak English?	Sprechen Sie Englisch?	**shprek**-hun zee **eng**-glisch?
I don't speak German.	Ich spreche kein Deutsch.	isch **shprek**-uh kine doych
Please speak slowly.	Bitte sprechen Sie langsam.	**bit**-uh **shprek**-en zee **lahng**-zahm
I don't understand	Ich verstehe nicht	isch fair-**shtay**-uh nicht
I understand	Ich verstehe	isch fair-**shtay**-uh
I don't know	Ich weiss nicht	isch vice nicht
Excuse me/sorry	Entschuldigen Sie	ent-**shool**-di-gen zee
I am American/ British	Ich bin Ameri-kaner(in)/Eng-länder(in)	isch bin a-mer-i-**kahn**-er(in)/**eng**-len-der(in)
What is your name?	Wie heissen Sie?	vee **high**-sen zee
My name is . . .	ich heiße . . .	isch **high**-suh
What time is it?	Wieviel Uhr ist es? *Wie spät ist es?	**vee**-feel oor ist es **vee** shpate ist es
It is one, two, three . . . o'clock.	Es ist ein, zwei, drei . . . Uhr.	es ist ine, tsvy, dry . . . oor
Yes, please/	Ja, bitte/	yah **bi**-tuh/
No, thank you	Nein, danke	**nine** dahng-kuh
How?	Wie?	vee

When?	Wann? (as conjunction, als)	vahn (ahls)
This/next week	Diese/nächste Woche	**dee**-zuh/**nehks**-tuh **vo**-kuh
This/next year	Dieses/nächstes Jahr	**dee**-zuz/**nehks**-tuhs yahr
Yesterday/today/ tomorrow	Gestern/heute/ morgen	**geh**-stern/**hoy**-tuh/ **mor**-gen
This morning/ afternoon	Heute morgen/ nachmittag	**hoy**-tuh **mor**-gen/ **nahk**-mit-tahk
Tonight	Heute Nacht	**hoy**-tuh nahkt
What is it?	Was ist es?	**vahss** ist es
Why?	Warum?	vah-**rum**
Who/whom?	Wer/wen?	vair/vehn
Who is it?	Wer ist da?	vair ist dah
I'd like to have . . .	Ich hätte gerne . . .	isch **het**-uh gairn
a room	ein Zimmer	ine **tsim**-er
the key	den Schlüssel	den **shluh**-sul
a newspaper	eine Zeitung	i-nuh **tsy**-toong
a stamp	eine Briefmarke	i-nuh **breef**-mark-uh
a map	eine Karte	i-nuh **cart**-uh
I'd like to buy . . .	ich möchte . . . kaufen	isch **merhk**-tuh **cow**-fen
cigarettes	Zigaretten	tzig-ah-**ret**-ten
I'd like to exchange . . .	Ich möchte . . . wechseln	isch **merhk**-tuh . . . **vex**-eln/
dollars to	Dollars in	dohl-lars in
schillings	Schillinge	**shil**-ling-uh
pounds to	Pfunde in	pfoonde in
schillings	Schillinge	**shil**-ling-uh
How much is it?	Wieviel kostet das?	**vee**-feel **cost**-et dahss?
It's expensive/ cheap	Es ist teuer/billig	es ist **toy**-uh/**bill**-ig
A little/a lot	ein wenig/sehr	ine **vay**-nig/zair
More/less	mehr/weniger	mair/**vay**-nig-er
Enough/too much/ too little	genug/zuviel/ zu wenig	geh-**noog**/tsoo-**feel**/ tsoo **vay**-nig
I am ill/sick	Ich bin krank	isch bin krahnk
I need . . .	Ich brauche . . .	isch **brow**-khuh
a doctor	einen Arzt	I-nen artst
the police	die Polizei	dee po-lee-**tsai**
help	Hilfe	**hilf**-uh
Fire!	Feuer!	**foy**-er

Caution/Look out!	Achtung!/Vorsicht!	**ahk**-tung/**for**-zicht
Is this bus/train/ subway going to . . . ?	Fährt dieser Bus/ dieser Zug/ diese U-Bahn nach . . . ?	fayrt **deez**er buhs/ **deez**-er tsook/ **deez**-uh **oo**-bahn nahk . . .
Where is . . .	Wo ist . . .	**vo** ist
the train station?	der Bahnhof?	dare **bahn**-hof
the subway station?	die U-Bahn- Station?	dee **oo**-bahn- **staht**-sion
the bus stop?	die Bushaltestelle?	dee **booss**-hahlt-uh- **shtel**-uh
the airport?	der Flugplatz? *der Flughafen?	dare **floog**-plats dare **floog**-hafen
the hospital?	das Krankenhaus?	dahs **krahnk**-en-house
the elevator?	der Aufzug?	dare **owf**-tsoog
the telephone?	das Telefon?	dahs te-le-**fone**
the rest room?	die Toilette?	dee twah-**let**-uh
open/closed	offen/geschlossen	**off**-en/ge-**schloss**-en
left/right	links/rechts	links/recktz
straight ahead	geradeaus	geh-**rah**-day-owws
is it near/far?	ist es in der Nähe/ist es weit?	ist es in dare **nay**-uh? ist es vite?

INDEX